LOVE AND ITS CRITICS

Love and its Critics

From the Song of Songs to Shakespeare and Milton's Eden

Michael Bryson and Arpi Movsesian

https://www.openbookpublishers.com

© 2017 Michael Bryson and Arpi Movsesian

This work is licensed under a Creative Commons Attribution 4.0 International license (CC BY 4.0). This license allows you to share, copy, distribute and transmit the work; to adapt the work and to make commercial use of the work providing attribution is made to the authors (but not in any way that suggests that they endorse you or your use of the work). Attribution should include the following information:

Michael Bryson and Arpi Movsesian, *Love and its Critics: From the Song of Songs to Shakespeare and Milton's Eden*. Cambridge, UK: Open Book Publishers, 2017, https://doi.org/10.11647/OBP.0117

In order to access detailed and updated information on the license, please visit https://www.openbookpublishers.com/product/611#copyright

Further details about CC BY licenses are available at http://creativecommons.org/licenses/by/4.0/

All external links were active at the time of publication unless otherwise stated and have been archived via the Internet Archive Wayback Machine at https://archive.org/web

Digital material and resources associated with this volume are available at https://www.openbookpublishers.com/product/611#resources

Every effort has been made to identify and contact copyright holders and any omission or error will be corrected if notification is made to the publisher.

California State University Northridge has provided support for the publication of this volume.

ISBN Paperback: 978-1-78374-348-3
ISBN Hardback: 978-1-78374-349-0
ISBN Digital (PDF): 978-1-78374-350-6
ISBN Digital ebook (epub): 978-1-78374-351-3
ISBN Digital ebook (mobi): 978-1-78374-352-0
DOI: 10.11647/OBP.0117

Cover image: Ary Scheffer, *Dante and Virgil Encountering the Shades of Francesca da Rimini and Paolo in the Underworld* (1855), Wikimedia, https://commons.m.wikimedia.org/wiki/File:1855_Ary_Scheffer_-_The_Ghosts_of_Paolo_and_Francesca_Appear_to_Dante_and_Virgil.jpg

All paper used by Open Book Publishers is SFI (Sustainable Forestry Initiative), PEFC (Programme for the Endorsement of Forest Certification Schemes) and Forest Stewardship Council(r)(FSC(r) certified.

Printed in the United Kingdom, United States, and Australia
by Lightning Source for Open Book Publishers (Cambridge, UK)

I went to the Garden of Love,
And saw what I never had seen:
A Chapel was built in the midst,
Where I used to play on the green.
And the gates of this Chapel were shut,
And Thou shalt not, writ over the door;
So I turn'd to the Garden of Love,
That so many sweet flowers bore.
And I saw it was filled with graves,
And tomb-stones where flowers should be:
And Priests in black gowns, were walking their rounds,
And binding with briars, my joys & desires.
—William Blake, "The Garden of Love", *Songs of Experience*

Et si notre âme a valu quelque chose, c'est qu'elle a brûlé plus ardemment que quelques autres.
—André Gide, *Les Nourritures terrestres*

Die Wissenschaft unter der Optik des Künstlers zu sehn, die Kunst aber unter der des Lebens.
—Friedrich Nietzsche, *Die Geburt der Tragödie aus dem Geiste der Musik*

Contents

Acknowledgements	ix
A Note on Sources and Languages	x
1. Love and Authority: Love Poetry and its Critics	1
I. The Poetry of Love	1
II. Love's Nemesis: Demands for Obedience	3
III. Love's Critics: The Hermeneutics of Suspicion and the Authoritarian Approach to Criticism	10
IV. The Critics: Poetry Is About Poetry	23
V. The Critics: The Author Is Dead (or Merely Irrelevant)	29
2. Channeled, Reformulated, and Controlled: Love Poetry from the Song of Songs to Aeneas and Dido	37
I. Love Poetry and the Critics who Allegorize: The Song of Songs	37
II. Love Poetry and the Critics who Reduce: Ovid's *Amores* and *Ars Amatoria*	57
III. Love or Obedience in Virgil: Aeneas and Dido	77
IV. Love or Obedience in Ovid: Aeneas, Dido, and the Critics who Dismiss	89

3. Love and its Absences in Late Latin and Greek Poetry   97
   I. Love in the Poetry of Late Antiquity: Latin   97
   II. Love in the Poetry of Late Antiquity: Greek   113

4. The Troubadours and *Fin'amor*: Love, Choice, and the Individual   121
   I. Why "Courtly Love" Is Not Love   121
   II. The Troubadours and Their Critics   136
   III. The Troubadours and Love   165

5. *Fin'amor* Castrated: Abelard, Heloise, and the Critics who Deny   195

6. The Albigensian Crusade and the Death of *Fin'amor* in Medieval   215
   French and English Poetry
   I. The Death of *Fin'amor*: The Albigensian Crusade and its   215
      Aftermath
   II. Post-*Fin'amor* French Poetry: *The Roman de la Rose*   238
   III. Post-*Fin'amor* English Romance: Love of God and Country   275
        in *Havelok the Dane* and *King Horn*
   IV. Post-*Fin'amor* English Poetry: Mocking "Courtly Love"   280
       in Chaucer—the Knight and the Miller
   V. Post-*Fin'amor* English Poetry: Mocking "Auctoritee"   286
      in Chaucer—the Wife of Bath

7. The Ladder of Love in Italian Poetry and Prose, and the Reactions   295
   of the Sixteenth-Century Sonneteers
   I. The Platonic Ladder of Love   295
   II. Post-*Fin'amor* Italian Poetry: The Sicilian School to Dante   300
       and Petrarch
   III. Post-*Fin'amor* Italian Prose: *Il Libro del Cortegiano* (*The Book of* 330
        the Courtier)
   IV. The Sixteenth-Century: Post-*Fin'amor* Transitions in   336
       Petrarchan-Influenced Poetry

8. Shakespeare: The Return of *Fin'amor*	353
I. The Value of the Individual in the Sonnets	353
II. Shakespeare's Plays: Children as Property	367
III. Love as Resistance: Silvia and Hermia	378
IV. Love as Resistance: Juliet and the Critics who Disdain	393
9. Love and its Costs in Seventeenth-Century Literature	421
I. *Carpe Diem* in Life and Marriage: John Donne and the Critics who Distance	422
II. The Lyricist of *Carpe Diem*: Robert Herrick and the Critics who Distort	445
10. Paradise Lost: Love in Eden, and the Critics who Obey	467
Epilogue. Belonging to Poetry: A Reparative Reading	501
Bibliography	513
Index	553

Acknowledgements

This book emerges from multiple experiences and perspectives: teaching students at California State University and the University of California; leaving a religious tradition, and leaving a country and an entire way of life; extensive written and verbal conversations with people from all over the world—from the Middle East, Africa, Sri Lanka, Western Europe, the former Soviet Union, and the Asian Pacific Rim; and finally, an attempt to understand what has happened to the study of poetry, especially love poetry, in modern literary education. Our thanks go out to Alessandra Tosi, Lucy Barnes and Francesca Giovannetti at Open Book Publishers, who worked tirelessly with us on the manuscript to make this book possible. Thanks are due especially to Nazanin Keynejad, who read and commented upon the first draft of this book, and to Modje Taavon, who provided valuable insight into the similarities between the early modern European and contemporary Middle Eastern cultures. Special thanks are also due to Robert Bryson, Naomi Bryson, Heather Bryson, Alan Wolstrup, Steven Wolstrup, Yeprem Movsesian, Ruzan Petrosian, Haik Movsesian, and Edgar Movsesian, not only for their differing experiences and perspectives, but for personal encouragement and support.

A Note on Sources and Languages

This book works with material that spans two thousand years and multiple languages. Many, though by no means all, of the sources it works with are from older editions that are publicly available online. This is done deliberately in order to allow readers who may not be attached to insitutions with well-endowed libraries to access as much of the information that informs this work as possible, without encountering paywalls or other access restrictions. It was not possible to follow this procedure in all cases, but every effort has been made. Where the book works with texts in languages other than English, the original is provided along with an English translation. This is done in order to emphasize that the poetic and critical tradition spans both time and place, reflecting arguments that are conducted in multiple language traditions. This is also done, frankly, to make a point about language education in the English-speaking world, especially in the United States, where foreign-language requirements are increasingly being questioned and enrollment figures have declined over the last half-century—according to the 2015 MLA report, language enrollments per 100 American college students stands at 8.1 as of 2013, which is half of the ratio from 1960 (https://www.mla.org/content/download/31180/1452509/EMB_enrllmnts_nonEngl_2013.pdf, 37). Languages matter. Words matter. One of the arguments of this book is that the specific words and intentions of the poets *and* the critics matter; though English translation is necessary, it is not sufficient. Quoting the original words of the poets and the critics is a way of giving the authors their voice.

1. Love and Authority: Love Poetry and its Critics

I
The Poetry of Love

Love has always had its critics. They range far and wide throughout history, from Plato and the Neoplatonists, to the Rabbinic and Christian interpreters of the Song of Songs, from the clerics behind the savage Albigensian Crusade, to the seventeenth-century English Puritan author William Prynne, who never met a joy he failed to condemn. Love has never lacked for those who try to tame it for "higher" purposes, or those who would argue that "the worst evils have been committed in the name of love".[1] At the same time, love has always had its passionate defenders, though these have more often tended to be poets—the Ovids, Shakespeares, and Donnes—than critics of poetry. The relationship between the two—poets and critics—is one of the central concerns of this book.

The story this book tells follows two paths: it is a history of love, a story told through poetry and its often adversarial relationship to the laws and customs of its times and places. But it is also a history of the way love and poetry have been treated, not by our poets, but by those our culture has entrusted with the authority to perpetuate the understanding, and the memory, of poetry. This authority has been

---

1   Aharon Ben-Ze'ev and Ruhama Goussinsky. *In the Name of Love*: *Romantic Ideology and Its Victims* (Oxford: Oxford University Press, 2008), 63.

© 2017 Michael Bryson and Arpi Movsesian, CC BY 4.0   https://doi.org/10.11647/OBP.0117.01

abused by a tradition of critics and criticism over two thousand years old, a tradition dedicated to reducing poetry to allegory or ideology, insisting that the words of poems do not mean what they appear to mean to the average reader. And yet, love and its poetry fight back, not just against critics but against all the real and imagined tyrants of the world. As we will see in the work of Shakespeare, love stands against a system of arranged marriages in which individual desires are subordinated to the rule of the Father, property, and inherited wealth. Sometimes, as in Milton's *Paradise Lost*, love will even stand against God himself. As Dante demonstrates with his account of Paolo and Francesca, love lives the truth that Milton's Satan speaks: it is better to reign in hell than serve in heaven.

What is this love? And how is it treated in our poetry? Ranging from the ancients to the early moderns, from the Bible to medieval literature, from Shakespeare to the poetry of the seventeenth century and our own modern day, the love presented here is neither exclusively of the body, nor exclusively of the spirit. It is not merely sex—though some critics have been eager to dismiss it in just this way. Neither, however, is it only spiritual, intellectual, emotional, or what is popularly referred to as Platonic. The love this book considers, and that so much of our poetry celebrates, is a combination of the physical and the emotional, the sexual and the intellectual, the embodied and the ethereal. Above all, it is a matter of mutual choice between lovers who are each at once Lover and Beloved. Often marginalized by, and in opposition to church, state, and the institutions of marriage and law, this love is what the troubadour poets of the eleventh and twelfth centuries referred to as *fin'amor*.[2] It is anarchic and threatening to the established order, and a great deal of cultural energy has gone into taming it.

Fin'amor—passionate and mutually chosen love, desire, and regard—has been invented and reinvented over the centuries. It appears in Hellenistic Jerusalem as a glimpse back into the age of Solomon, then fades into the dim background of Rabbinical and Christian allegory. It

---

2   This working definition is at odds with much, though by no means all, of the specialized scholarship on troubadour poetry. One of the major contentions of this book is that too much of the work by specialists in many literary fields minimizes, reinterprets, or outright ignores the human elements of love and desire in poetry, a situation which scholars like Simon Gaunt and Sarah Kay admit has gone too far. See "Introduction". In Simon Gaunt and Sarah Kay, eds. *The Troubadours: An Introduction* (Cambridge: Cambridge University Press, 1999), 6.

is revived in France, in the eleventh and twelfth centuries, by poets and an unusual group of Rabbis, only to fade once again, betrayed by later poets writing under the twin spells of Neoplatonism and Christianizing allegory. These later poets radically reshape the ideas of love expressed in the poems of medieval Provençe and the ancient Levant, writing in what Dante calls the "sweet new style" (*dolce stil novo*) that changed love into worship, men into idolators, and women into idols. The influence of their verse is still observable in the English poetry of Philip Sidney two hundred years after the death of Petrarch, the *dolce stil novo*'s high priest. Subsequently, writers such as Shakespeare, Donne, Herrick, and Milton re-invent the love that had almost been lost, putting a new version of *fin'amor* on the stage and on the page, pulling it back into the light and out of the shadows of theology, philosophy, and law. For better, or for worse, *fin'amor* has been with us ever since.

II
Love's Nemesis: Demands for Obedience

Running parallel with the tradition of love poetry is a style of thought which argues that obedience, rather than passion, is the prime virtue of humankind. Examples of obedience demanded and given are abundant in our scriptures, such as the injunction in Genesis against eating from the Tree of Knowledge; in our poetry, such as the *Aeneid*'s portrayal of Aeneas rejecting Dido in obedience to the gods; and even in our philosophy, as in Aristotle's distinction between free men and slaves: "It is true, therefore, that there are by natural origin those who are truly free men, but also those who are visibly slavish, and for these slavery is both beneficial and just".[3] Such expectations of obedience often appear in the writing of those who argue that human law derives from divine law. Augustine argues that though God did not intend that Man should have dominion over Man, it now exists because of sin:

---

3   "ὅτι μὲν τοίνυν εἰσὶ φύσει τινὲς οἱ μὲν ἐλεύθεροι οἱ δὲ δοῦλοι, φανερόν, οἷς καὶ συμφέρει τὸ δουλεύειν καὶ δίκαιόν ἐστιν"(Aristotle. *Politics*, ed. by Harris Rackham [Cambridge, MA: Loeb Classical Library, Harvard University Press], 1932, 1255a, 22, 24). Unless otherwise noted, all translations are ours.

But by nature, as God first created us, no one was a slave either of man or of sin. In truth, our present servitude is penal, a penalty which is meant to preserve the natural order of law and forbids its disturbance; because, if nothing had been done contrary to that law, there would have been nothing to restrain by penal servitude.[4]

Nearly a millennium later, Thomas Aquinas argues from a similar perspective: "The order of justice requires that inferiors obey their superiors, for otherwise the stability of human affairs could not be maintained".[5] Even a famous rebel like Martin Luther directs ordinary citizens to obey the law God puts in place: "No man is by nature Christian or religious, but all are sinful and evil, wherefore God restrains them all through the law, so that they do not dare to practice their wickedness externally with works".[6] According to John Calvin, absolute obedience is due not only to benevolent rulers, but also to tyrants. Wicked rulers are a punishment from God:

> Truthfully, if we look at the Word of God, this will lead us further. We are not only to be subject to their authority, who are honest, and rule by what ought to be the gift of God's love to us, but also to the authority of all those who in any way have come into power, even if their rule is nothing less than that of the office of the princes of the blind. [...] at the same time he declares that, whatever they may be, they have their rule and authority from him.[7]

---

4   "Nullus autem natura, in qua prius Deus hominem condidit, seruus est hominis aut peccati. Verum et poenalis seruitus ea lege ordinatur, quae naturalem ordinem conseruari iubet, perturbari uetat; quia si contra eam legem non esset factum, nihil esset poenali seruitute coërcendum" (Augustine of Hippo. *De Civitate Dei* [Paris: 1586], Book 19, Chapter 15, 250, https://books.google.com/books?id=pshhAAAAcAAJ&pg=PA250).
5   "Ordo autem iustitiae requirit ut inferiores suis superioribus obediant, aliter enim non posset humanarum rerum status conservari" (Thomas Aquinas. *Summa Theologiae: Vol. 41, Virtues of Justice in the Human Community*, ed. by T. C. O'Brien [Cambridge: Cambridge University Press, 2006], 2a2ae. Q104, A6, 72).
6   "Nun aber kein Mensch von Natur Christ oder fromm ist, sondern sie allzumal Sünder und böse sind, wehret ihnen Gott allen durchs Gesetz, daß sie ihre Bosheit nicht äußerlich mit Werken nach ihrem Mutwillen zu üben wagen" (Martin Luther. *Von Weltlicher Obrigkeit* [Berlin: Tredition Classics, 2012], 10).
7   Verùm si in Dei verbum respicimus, longius nos deducet, ut non eorum modò principú imperio subditi simus, qui probè, & qua debét fide munere suo erga nos defungútur: sed omnium qui quoquo modo rerum potiuntur, etiamsi nihil minus praestét quàm quod ex officio principum. [...] simul tamen declarat, qualescunque sint, nonnisi à se habere imperium.

For these thinkers, obedience is the prime duty of humankind, because it is ultimately in service to the God who established all authority in the first place. To be obedient is therefore to be pleasing to God.

Such demands for obedience are ancient, and widespread, but resistance has its own long tradition. Étienne de La Boétie, the sixteenth-century author, judge, and friend to Michel Montaigne, argues that human beings have long become so used to servitude that they no longer know how to be free:

> It is incredible how a people, when it becomes subject, falls so suddenly and profoundly into forgetfulness of its freedom, so that it is not possible for them to win it back, serving so frankly and so happily that it seems, at a glance, that they have not lost their freedom but won their servitude.[8]

La Boétie maintains that obedience has become so engrained in most people, that they regard their subjection as normal and necessary:

> They will say they have always been subjects, and their fathers lived the same way; they will think they are obliged to endure the evil, and they demonstrate this to themselves by examples, and find themselves in the length of time to be the possessions of those who lord it over them; but in reality, the years never gave any the right to do them wrong, and this magnifies the injury.[9]

This "injury" leads La Boétie to reject the idea of natural obedience, proposing instead a model through which he accuses "the tyrants" ("les tyrans") of carefully inculcating the idea of submission into the populations they dominate:

Jean Calvin. *Institutio Christianae Religionis* (Geneva: Oliua Roberti Stephani, 1559), 559, https://books.google.com/books?id=6ysy-UX89f4C&dq=Oliua+Roberti+Stephani,+1559&pg=PA559

[8] "Il n'est pas croyable comme le peuple, dès lors qu'il est assujetti, tombe si soudain en un tel et si profond oubli de la franchise, qu'il n'est pas possible qu'il se réveille pour la ravoir, servant si franchement et tant volontiers qu'on dirait, à le voir, qu'il a non pas perdu sa liberté, mais gagné sa servitude" (Étienne de La Boétie. *Discours de la Servitude Volontaire* [1576] [Paris: Éditions Bossard, 1922], 67, https://fr.wikisource.org/wiki/Page:La_Boétie_-_Discours_de_la_servitude_volontaire.djvu/73).

[9] "Ils disent qu'ils ont été toujours sujets, que leurs pères ont ainsi vécu; ils pensent qu'ils sont tenus d'endurer le mal et se font accroire par exemple, et fondent eux-mêmes sous la longueur du temps la possession de ceux qui les tyrannisent; mais pour vrai, les ans ne donnent jamais droit de mal faire, ains agrandissent l'injure" (*ibid.*, 74–75, https://fr.wikisource.org/wiki/Page:La_Boétie_-_Discours_de_la_servitude_volontaire.djvu/80).

The first reason why men willingly serve, is that they are born serfs and are nurtured as such. From this comes another easy conclusion: people become cowardly and effeminate under tyrants.[10] [...] It has never been but that tyrants, for their own assurance, have made great efforts to accustom their people to them, [training them] not only in obedience and servitude, but also in devotion.[11]

Two centuries later, Jean-Jacques Rousseau raises his voice against the authority of "les tyrans", arguing that liberty is the very basis of humanity:

To renounce liberty is to renounce being a man, the rights of humanity, even its duties. [...] Such a renunciation is incompatible with the nature of man, and to remove all liberty from his will is to remove all morality from his actions. Finally, it is a vain and contradictory convention to stipulate on the one hand an absolute authority, and on the other an unlimited obedience.[12]

But what Rousseau calls a renunciation of liberty, framing it as a conscious act, La Boétie presents as something that is *done to* rather than *done by* average men and women: "they are born as serfs and nurtured as such". In the latter's view, it is those in authority who "nurture" (raise, nourish, even instruct) their populations into the necessary attitudes of what Rousseau will later call *une obéissance sans bornes*.

Such "nurture" performs a pedagogical function, teaching men and women to think their bondage is natural: for La Boétie, "it is certain that custom, which in all things has great power over us, has no greater

---

10 "[L]a première raison pourquoi les hommes servent volontiers, est pour ce qu'ils naissent serfs et sont nourris tels. De celle-ci en vient une autre, qu'aisément les gens deviennent, sous les tyrans, lâches et efféminés" (*ibid.*, 77–78, https://fr.wikisource.org/wiki/Page:La_Boétie_-_Discours_de_la_servitude_volontaire.djvu/83).

11 "il n'a jamais été que les tyrans, pour s'assurer, ne se soient efforcés d'accoutumer le peuple envers eux, non seulement à obéissance et servitude, mais encore à dévotion" (*ibid.*, 89, https://fr.wikisource.org/wiki/Page:La_Boétie_-_Discours_de_la_servitude_volontaire.djvu/95).

12 Renoncer à sa liberté, c'est renoncer à sa qualité d'homme, aux droits de l'humanité, même à ses devoirs. [...] Une telle renonciation est incompatible avec la nature de l'homme, et c'est ôter toute moralité à ses actions que d'ôter toute liberté à sa volonté. Enfin c'est une convention vaine et contradictoire de stipuler d'une part une autorité absolue et de l'autre une obéissance sans bornes.

Jean-Jacques Rousseau. *Contrat Social*. In *The Political Writings of Jean-Jacques Rosseau*, Vol. 2, ed. by C. E. Vaughan (Cambridge: Cambridge University Press, 1915), 28, https://books.google.com/books?id=IqhBAAAAYAAJ&pg=PA28

strength than this, to teach us how to serve".[13] Some seventy years later, the English revolutionary John Milton makes a similar argument, describing "custom" as part of the double tyranny that keeps mankind in subjection:

> If men within themselves would be govern'd by reason and not generally give up their understanding to a double tyrannie, of custome from without and blind affections within, they would discerne better what it is to favour and uphold the Tyrant of a Nation.[14]

Milton, in pamphlets that ridicule the pro-monarchical propaganda of his day, berates what he calls "the easy literature of custom and opinion",[15] the authoritative-sounding, but empty writing and speaking that teaches "the most Disciples" and is "silently receiv'd for the best instructer", despite the fact that it offers nothing but a "swoln visage of counterfeit knowledge and literature".[16] David Hume later notes "the easiness with which the many are governed by the few; and the implicit submission with which men resign their own sentiments and passions to those of their rulers". Hume explains this submission as a function of "opinion", or the "sense" that is inculcated into the many "of the general advantage" to be had by obeying "the particular government which is established".[17]

By the twentieth century, Martin Heidegger condemns "tradition" as a manipulative force that obscures both its agenda and its origins:

> The tradition that becomes dominant hereby makes what it "transmits" so inaccessible that at first, and for the most part, it obscures it instead. It hands over to the self-evident and obvious what has come down to us, and blocks access to the original "sources", from which the traditional

---

13 "Mais certes la coutume, qui a en toutes choses grand pouvoir sur nous, n'a en aucun endroit si grande vertu qu'en ceci, de nous enseigner à servir" (La Boétie, 68, https://fr.wikisource.org/wiki/Page:La_Boétie_-_Discours_de_la_servitude_volontaire.djvu/74).

14 John Milton. *The Tenure of Kings and Magistrates* (London, 1649), 1, Sig. A2r, http://quod.lib.umich.edu/e/eebo/A50955.0001.001/1:2?rgn=div1;view=fulltext;q1=Tenure+of+Kings+and+Magistrates and https://books.google.com/books?id=EIg-AQAAMAAJ&pg=PA1 (1650 edition).

15 John Milton. *Eikonoklastes* (London, 1650), 3, Sig. A3r, http://quod.lib.umich.edu/e/eebo/A50898.0001.001/1:2?rgn= div1;view=fulltext;rgn1=author;q1=Milton%2C+John

16 John Milton. *The Doctrine and Discipline of Divorce*. London, 1644, Sig. A2r, https://books.google.com/books?id=6oI-AQAAMAAJ&pg=PP9

17 David Hume. "Of the First Principles of Government". In *Essays, Literary, Moral, and Political* (London: Ward, Lock & Co., 1870), 23, https://babel.hathitrust.org/cgi/pt?id=uc2.ark:/13960/t1fj2db8p;view=1up;seq=27

categories and concepts in part were actually drawn. The tradition even makes us forget there ever was such an origin.[18]

In contrast, Edward Bernays—a member of the Creel Committee which influenced American public opinion in favor of entering WWI—regards such manipulation as necessary to ensure the obedience of the masses:

> The conscious and intelligent manipulation of the organized habits and opinions of the masses is an important element in democratic society. Those who manipulate this unseen mechanism of society constitute an invisible government which is the true ruling power of our country. We are governed, our minds are molded, our tastes formed, our ideas suggested, largely by men we have never heard of.[19]

Though Bernays thinks of such techniques as a good thing (foreshadowing developments elsewhere in the twentieth century),[20] for earlier thinkers like La Boétie, Milton, and Hume, it is crucial to keep a watchful eye on those who draw "the most Disciples" after them, for

---

18 "Die hierbei zur Herrschaft kommende Tradition macht zunächst und zumeist das, was sie 'übergibt', so wenig zugänglich, daß sie es vielmehr verdeckt. Sie überantwortet das Überkommene der Selbstverständlichkeit und verlegt den Zugang zu den ursprünglichen 'Quellen', daraus die überlieferten Kategorien und Begriffe z. T. in echter Weise geschöpft wurden. Die Tradition macht sogar eine solche Herkunft überhaupt vergessen" (*Sein und Zeit* [Tübingen: Max Niemeyer, 1967], 21).

19 Edward Bernays. *Propaganda* (New York: Horace Liveright, 1928), 9, https://archive.org/details/EdwardL.BernaysPropaganda#page/n3

20 It was, of course, the astounding success of propaganda during the war that opened the eyes of the intelligent few in all departments of life to the possibilities of regimenting the public mind. […] If we understand the mechanism and motives of the group mind, is it not possible to control and regiment the masses according to our will without them knowing it? (Bernays, 27, 47). Bernays' ideas are not far removed from those being promulgated on the other side of the Atlantic ocean by an aspiring literary critic and author whose Ph.D. in literature was obtained at the University of Heidelberg in 1921, and whose critical acumen was given a real-world application approximately a decade later:

> Propaganda is not an end in itself, but a means to an end. […] Whether or not it conforms adequately to aesthetic demands is meaningless. […] The end of our movement was to mobilize the people, to organize the people, and win them for the idea of national revolution.

> Denn Propaganda ist nicht Selbstzweck, sondern Mittel zum Zweck. […] ob es in jedem Falle nun scharfen ästhetischen Forderungen entspricht oder nicht, ist dabei gleichgültig. […] Der Zweck unserer Bewegung war, Menschen zu mobilisieren, Menschen zu organisieren und für die nationalrevolutionäre Idee zu gewinnen. [March 15, 1933].

In Joseph Goebbels, *Revolution der Deutschen: 14 Jahre Nationalsozialismus* (Oldenburg: Gerhard Stalling, 1933), 139.

what they are teaching may well be the lessons of obedience to what Aleksandr Pushkin calls "Custom, despot between the people".[21]

Alongside the long narrative of demands for obedience, stands a counter-narrative and counter-instruction in our poetry, framed in terms of forbidden love and desire. Love challenges obedience; it is one of the precious few forces with sufficient power to enable its adherents to transcend themselves, their fears, and their isolation to such a degree that it is possible to refuse the demands of power. Love does not always succeed. But for its more radical devotees—the Dido of Ovid's *Heroides*, the troubadour poets of the eleventh and twelfth centuries in Occitania, the famous lovers of Shakespeare, and Milton's Adam and Eve—love is revolutionary, an attempt to tear down the world and build it anew, not in the image of authority, but that of a love that is freely chosen, freely given, and freely received. Love rejects the claims of law, property, and custom. It opposes the claims of determinism—whether theological (Augustine, Luther, and Calvin, and the notions of original sin and predestination), philosophical (Foucault, and the idea that impersonal systems of power create "free subjects" in their image), or biological (as in Baron d'Holbach's 1770 work *Système de la Nature*, which maintains that all human thought and action results from material causes and effects).

These points of view can be found all too frequently, often dressed in the robes of what John Milton calls "pretended learning, mistaken among credulous men [...] filling each estate of life and profession, with abject and servil[e] principles".[22] But in the more radical examples of our poetry, love defies servile principles, and is unimpressed by pretended learning. Neither is love merely a Romantic construct, a product of "the long nineteenth century [that extends] well into the twenty-first",[23] nor a secular replacement for religious traditions. As Simon May points out, "[b]y imputing to human love features properly reserved for divine love, such as the unconditional and the eternal, we falsify the nature of this most conditional and time-bound and earthly emotion, and

---

21   "Обычай деспот меж людей". *Evgeny Onegin*, 1.25.4. In Aleksandr Sergeevich Pushkin. *Sobraniye Sochinenii*. 10 Vols., ed. by D. D. Blagoi, S. M. Bondi, V. V. Vinogradov and Yu. G. Oksman (Moscow: Khudozhestvennaia literatura, 1959), Vol. 4, 20, http://rvb.ru/pushkin/01text/04onegin/01onegin/0836.htm

22   John Milton. *The Doctrine and Discipline of Divorce*. London, 1644, Sig. A2r, https://books.google.com/books?id=6oI-AQAAMAAJ&pg=PP9

23   Simon May. *Love: A History* (New Haven: Yale University Press, 2011), xii.

force it to labor under intolerable expectations".[24] It is precisely "time-bound and earthly" love—a passion that always brings an awareness of time running out, and the concomitant urge to fight to extend that time even by the merest moments—that is the powerful counterweight to the "servil[e] principles" imposed on us by the individuals and institutions that demand our obedience. Too often, the poetry written about this love has been ill-served by its ancient and modern critics. Reading the theological and academic critics of poetry inspires the troubling realization that many such critics are part of the very system of authority and obedience which, La Boétie argues, accustoms people to tyrants, and against which the poetry itself protests.[25]

III
Love's Critics: The Hermeneutics of Suspicion and the Authoritarian Approach to Criticism

How does this alignment between literary criticism and repressive authority function? By denying poetry—particularly love poetry—the ability to serve as a challenge to the structures of authority in the societies in which it is written.[26] As we will see especially clearly

---

24 Ibid., 4–5.
25 Obedience is the soil in which universities first took root. In their beginnings, universities were training grounds for service in the church or at court (for those students who took degrees), and institutions that inculcated obedience in the wider population. The subversiveness of an Abelard or a Wycliffe—which in each case came at a far greater cost than any paid, or even contemplated by the academic critic today—is most clearly understood in that context. This is best illustrated by the Authentica Habita, the 1158 decree of the German Emperor Frederick I (Barbarossa) granting special privileges to teachers and students of the still-forming University of Bologna in order that "students, and divine teachers of the sacred law, [...] may come and live in security" ("scholaribus, et maxime divinarum atque sacrarum legum professoribus, [...] veniant, et in eis secure habitient"). This decree also outlined what Frederick believed to be the essential purpose of education: "knowledge of the world is to illuminate and inform the lives of our subjects, to obey God, and ourself, his minister" ("scientia mundus illuminatur ad obediendum deo et nobis, eius ministris, vita subjectorum informatur") (Paul Krueger, Theodor Mommsen, Rudolf Schoell, and Whilhelm Kroll, eds. *Corpus Iuris Civilis*, Vol. 2 [Berlin: Apud Weidmannos, 1892], 511, https://books.google.com/books?id=2hvTA AAAMAAJ&pg=PA511).
26 In the "human sciences", critics often "act as agents of the micro-physics of power" (Elisabeth Strowick. "Comparative Epistemology of Suspicion: Psychoanalysis, Literature, and the Human Sciences". *Science in Context*, 18.4 [2005], 654, https://doi.

when we consider the commentary that surrounds the poetry of John Milton, the thinking behind such work often displays "a high degree of submission to the authorities who are perceived to be established",[27] whether that authority is political, cultural, or intellectual. There is an endless body of criticism that serves not only to undermine poetry's potential for political, theological, and even aesthetic resistance, but to restrict the manner in which readers encounter and understand poetry. From the beginning, together with the tradition of love poetry, a tradition of criticism (expressed now from both "conservative" and "radical" points of view)[28] has grown that subordinates and dismisses human passion and desire, often arguing that what merely seems to be passionate love poetry is actually properly understood as something else (worship of God, subordination to Empire, entanglement within the structures of language itself). The pattern of such criticism—from the earliest readings of the Song of Songs to contemporary articles written about a *carpe diem* poem like Robert Herrick's "To the Virgins to Make Much of Time"—is to argue that the surface of a poem hides a "real" or "deeper" meaning that undermines the apparent one, and that the critic's job is to tear away the misleading surface in order to expose the "truth" that lies beneath it. Frederic Jameson exemplifies this technique in his argument that the true function of the critic is to analyze texts and culture through "a vast interpretive allegory in which a sequence of historical events or texts and artifacts is rewritten in terms of some deeper, underlying, and more 'fundamental' narrative".[29] Louis Althusser describes interpretation similarly, as "detecting the undetected in the very same text it reads, and relating it to another

---

org/10.1017/S0269889705000700). Noam Chomsky, when asked how "intellectuals [...] get away with their complicity [with] powerful interests", gives a telling response: "They are not getting away with anything. They are, in fact, performing a service that is expected of them by the institutions for which they work, and they willingly, perhaps unconsciously, fulfill the requirements of the doctrinal system" ("Beyond a Domesticating Education: A Dialogue". In Noam Chomsky, *Chomsky on Miseducation* [Lanham: Rowman & Littlefield, 2004], 17).

27 Bob Altermeyer. *The Authoritarian Specter* (Cambridge: Havard University Press, 1996), 6.
28 Along with the "right-wing" authoritarianism cited above, Altermeyer also defines a "left-wing" authoritarianism which displays "a high degree of submission to authorities who are dedicated to *overthrowing* the established authorities" (219).
29 Frederic Jameson. *The Political Unconscious: Narrative as a Socially Symbolic Act* (Ithaca: Cornell University Press, 1981), 13.

text, present as a necessary absence in the first".[30] We can trace similar thinking all the way back to the controversies over Homer and Hesiod in the sixth century BCE:[31]

> The Homeric representations of the gods roused a protest on the part of the founder of the Eleatics, Xenophanes of Colophon (fl. 540–500 B.C), who says that "Homer and Hesiod have imputed to the gods all that is blame and shame for men". [...] In reply to protests such as these, some of the defenders of Homer maintained that the superficial meaning of his myths was not the true one, and that there was a deeper sense lying below the surface. This deeper sense was, in the Athenian age, called the ὑπόνοια [hyponoia–suspicion], and the ὑπόνοια of this age assumed the name of "allegories" in the times of Plutarch. [...] Anaxagoras [...] found in the web of Penelope an emblem of the rules of dialectic, the warp being the premises, the woof the conclusion, and the flame of the torches, by which she executed her task, being none other than the light of reason. [...] But no apologetic interpretation of the Homeric mythology was of any avail to save Homer from being expelled with all the other poets from Plato's ideal Republic.[32]

Such readings originally tried to defend poetry against its critics,[33] though in a rather different sense than did Eratosthenes, the third-century BCE librarian of Alexandria, who held that "poets... in all

---

30 "décèle l'indécelé dans le texte même qu'elle lit, et le rapporte à un autre texte, présent d'une absence nécessaire dans le premier" (Louis Althusser. *Lire le Capital* [Paris: Presses Universitaires de France, 1996], 23).
31 BCE (Before Common Era) and CE (Common Era) are used here throughout (except in quotations, where usage may differ) in lieu of the theologically-inflected BC (Before Christ) and AD (*Anno Domini*).
32 Sir John Edwin Sandys. *A History of Classical Scholarship, Vol. I: From the Sixth Century B.C. to the End of the Middle Ages* (Cambridge: Cambridge University Press, 1903), 29–31, https://archive.org/stream/historyofclassic00sanduoft#page/29
33 Francois Rabelais, who finds a good reason to laugh at nearly everything, laughs also at this particular absurdity of literary history:

> Do you believe, in faith, that Homer, when he was writing the *Iliad* and *Odyssey*, thought of the allegories that Plutarch, Heraclides Ponticq, Eustalius, and Cornutus dressed him in, and which Politian took from them? If you believe that, you don't approach by foot or by hand anywhere near my opinion.

> Croyez vous en vostre foy qu'oncques Homere, escripvant Iliade et Odyssée, pensast es allegories lesquelles de lui ont calefreté Plutarque, Heraclides Ponticq, Eustatie, Phornute, et ce d'yceulx Politian ha desrobé? Si li croyez, vous n'aprochez ne de piedz, ne de mains a mon opinion.) (Francois Rabelais. "Prolog". *Gargantua et Pantagruel*. In *Œuvres de Rabelais*, Vol. 1 [Paris: Dalibon, 1823], 24–25, https://books.google.com/books?id=a6MGAAAAQAAJ&pg=PA24)

things aim to persuade and delight, not instruct",[34] or Philip Sidney, for whom "the Poet, he nothing affirmeth, and therefore never lieth".[35] But suspicion has long since been adopted by the critics as a method of attack, rather more in the spirit of Plato than in the spirit of Sidney or those early defenders of Homer and Hesiod.

Employing a method Paul Ricoeur calls the hermeneutics of suspicion (*les herméneutiques du soupçon*), the modern version of this reading strategy is a matter of cunning (falsification) encountering a greater cunning (suspicion), as the "false" appearances of a text are systematically exposed by the critic:

> Three masters, who appear exclusive from each other, are dominant: Marx, Nietzsche, and Freud. [...] The fundamental category of consciousness, for the three of them, is the relation between hidden-shown or, if one prefers, simulated-manifest. [...] What they have all three tried, by different routes, is to align their "conscious" methods of decryption with the "unconscious" work of encryption they attributed to the will to power, to social being, to the unconscious psyche. [...] What then distinguishes Marx, Freud and Nietzsche is the general hypothesis concerning both the process of "false" consciousness and the decryption method. The two go together, since the suspicious man reverses the falsifying work of the deceitful man.[36]

For Ricoeur, the hermeneutics of suspicion is not something that is simply borrowed from the "three masters"; rather, it is modern literature itself that teaches a reader to read suspiciously:

---

34 "Ποιητὴν [...] πάντα στοχάζεσθαι ψυχαγωγίας, οὐ διδασκαλίας". Strabo, *Geography*, 1.2.3. In *Strabo, Geography, Vol. I: Books 1–2*, ed. by Horace Leonard Jones. Cambridge, MA: Loeb Classical Library, Harvard University Press, 1917, 54.

35 Philip Sidney. *The Defence of Poesie*. In *The Complete Works of Sir Philip Sidney, Vol. III*, ed. by Albert Feuillerat (Cambridge: Cambridge University Press, 1923), 29, https://archive.org/stream/completeworks03sidnuoft#page/29

36 Troi maîtres en apperance exclusifs l'un de l'autre la dominent, Marx, Nietzsche et Freud. [...] La catégorie fondamentale de la conscience, pour eux trois, c'est le rapport caché-montré ou, si l'on préfére, simulé-manifesté. [...] Ce qu'ils ont tenté tous trois, sur des voies différentes, ce'st de faire coïncider leurs methods "conscientes" de déchiffrage avec le travail "inconscient" du chiffrage qu'ils attribuaient à la volonté de puissance, à l'être social, au psychisme inconscient. [...] Ce qui distingue alors Marx, Freud et Nietzsche, c'est l'hypothèse gènèrale concernant à la fois le processus de la conscience "fausse" et la méthode de déchiffrage. Les deux vont de pair, puisque l'homme du soupçon fait en sens inverse le travail de falsification de l'homme de la ruse. Paul Ricoeur. *De l'interprétation. Essai sur Freud* (Paris: Seuil, 1965), 32, 33–34.

> It may be the function of more corrosive literature to contribute to making a new type of reader appear, a suspicious reader, because the reading ceases to be a confident journey made in the company of a trustworthy narrator, but reading becomes a fight with the author involved, a struggle that brings the reader back to himself.[37]

Yet suspicion is more fundamental, more deeply rooted than can be explained by the lessons of reading. Not long after outlining his analysis of the "three masters", Ricoeur makes an even starker and more dramatic statement: "A new problem has emerged: that of the lie of consciousness, and of consciousness as a lie".[38] Here, if one desires it, is a warrant to regard all apparent meaning (indeed, all appearance of any kind) as a lie in need of being dismantled and exposed. Such ideas, and the reading strategies they have inspired, have done yeoman's work in literary and historical scholarship over the last several decades. But as with so many useful tools, this one can be, and has been overused.[39] Rita Felski pointedly questions why this approach has become "the default option" for many critics today:

> Why is it that critics are so quick off the mark to interrogate, unmask, expose, subvert, unravel, demystify, destabilize, take issue, and take umbrage? What sustains their assurance that a text is withholding something of vital importance, that their task is to ferret out what lies concealed in its recesses and margins?[40]

---

37 Ce peut être la fonction de la littérature la plus corrosive de contribuer à faire apparaître un lecteur d'un nouveau genre, un lecteur lui-même soupçonneux, parce que la lecture cesse d'être un voyage confiant fait en compagnie d'un narrateur digne de confiance, mais devient un combat avec l'auteur impliqué, un combat qui le reconduit à lui-même.

Paul Ricoeur. *Temps et Récit*, Vol. 3: *Le Temps Raconté* (Paris: Seuil, 1985), 238.

38 "Une problème nouveau est né: celui du mensonge de la conscience, de la conscience comme mensonge" (Paul Ricoeur. *Le Conflit des Interprétations: Essais D'Herméneutique* [Paris: Seuil, 1969], 101).

39 These readings demonstrate

> the thought pattern that's at the basis of literary studies, and of any self-enclosed hermetically sealed sub-world that seeks to assert theoretical hegemony over the rest of the world. […] The individual is not the measure of all things: I, the commentator, am the measure of all things. You always have to wait for me, the academic or theoretician, to explain it to you. For example, you're *really* doing A or B because you're a member of a certain class and accept its presuppositions. Or you're *really* doing C and D because of now-inaccessible events in your childhood. What you personally think about this doesn't matter.

Bruce Fleming. *What Literary Studies Could Be, And What It Is* (Lanham: University Press of America, 2008), 100.

40 Rita Felski. *The Limits of Critique* (Chicago: University of Chicago Press, 2015), 5.

Maintaining that "suspicious reading has settled into a mandatory method rather than one approach among others", Felski describes this method as "[i]ncreasingly prescriptive as well as excruciatingly predictable", portraying its influence as one that "can be stultifying, pushing thought down predetermined paths and closing our minds to the play of detail, nuance, quirkiness, contradiction, happenstance". Literary criticism that leans heavily on this method can lend itself to an authoritarian approach to reading, as "the critic conjures up ever more paralyzing scenarios of coercion and control",[41] while readers "have to appeal to the priestly class that alone can explain"[42] the text. Such criticism treats texts as "imaginary opponents to be bested"[43] in service of an accusatory, prosecutorial agenda, as "[s]omething, somewhere—a text, an author, a reader, a genre, a discourse, a discipline—is always already guilty of some crime".[44] The trials have become so zealous and overwhelmingly numerous that they have long since become formulaic,[45] products of a template-driven approach whose verdicts can be anticipated at the beginning of the essays and books that use this method.

But why? What is the appeal of this approach? Karl Popper suggests that it is because "[t]hese theories appear to be able to explain practically everything", while a devotion to this method has the effect "of an intellectual conversion or revelation, opening your eyes to a new truth hidden from those not yet initiated". Those who undergo this conversion behave in much the same way as new cult members, on the lookout for heresy,[46] dividing the world into believers and unbelievers: "Once your

---

41   Ibid., 34.
42   Fleming, 100.
43   Felski, *The Limits of Critique*, 111.
44   Ibid., 39.
45   As Felski notes:

> Anyone who attends academic talks has learned to expect the inevitable question: "But what about power?" Perhaps it is time to start asking different questions: "But what about love?" Or: "Where is your theory of attachment?" To ask such questions is not to abandon politics for aesthetics. It is, rather, to contend that both art and politics are also a matter of connecting, composing, creating, coproducing, inventing, imagining, making possible: that neither is reducible to the piercing but one-eyed gaze of critique.

> *The Limits of Critique*, 17–18.

46   Felski traces this attitude back to "the medieval heresy trial", noting that "[h]eresy presented a hermeneutic problem of the first order and the transcripts of religious inquisitions reveal an acute awareness on the part of inquisitors that truth is not self-evident, that language conceals, distorts, and contains traps for the unwary,

eyes [are] thus opened you [see] confirmed instances everywhere: the world [is] full of verifications of the theory [...] and unbelievers [are] clearly people who [do] not want to see the manifest truth; who refuse to see it".[47]

In addition to the influence of Ricoeur's "three masters", this approach also hinges on on a widely-diffused (mis)use of the work of Martin Heidegger, especially his engagement with the meaning of "truth" or *Wahrheit*. For Heidegger, "the essence of truth is always understood in terms of unconcealment",[48] a notion he derives from the Greek term ἀλήθεια (*aletheia*—discovered or uncovered truth) in the pre-Socratic philosophers Parmenides and Heraclitus. Heidegger divides the concept of truth into correctness (*Richtigkeit*) or accurate correspondence of ideas with things as they presently are in the world, and the unconcealedness or discoveredness (*Unverborgenheit* or *Entdecktheit*) of entities. The first is necessarily grounded in, and dependent upon the second, for there can be no truth about things in the world without *things in the world*. For Heidegger, truth as correctness "has its basis in the truth as unconcealedness",[49] while "the unconcealment of Being as such is the basis for the possibility of correctness".[50] Thus *Wahrheit* is both the surface truth of what exists and the deeper truth that existence itself exists.

But what has any of this to do with the reading of literature? Heidegger's thought proposes a two-level structure, much like that found in Parmenides, who argued that τὸ ἐόν—*to eon*, or What Is— should be understood in terms of an unchanging reality behind the changing appearances of the world.[51] It is also seen in the paradoxes

---

that words should be treated cautiously and with suspicion" ("Suspicious Minds". *Poetics Today*, 32: 2 [Summer 2011], 219, https://doi.org/10.1215/03335372-1261208).

47   Karl Popper. *Conjectures and Refutations: The Growth of Scientific Knowledge* (New York: Basic Books, 1963), 34.

48   Mark A. Wrathall. *Heidegger and Unconcealment: Truth, Language, and History* (Cambridge: Cambridge University Press, 2010), 12.

49   "hat ihren Grund in der Wahrheit als Unverborgenheit" (Martin Heidegger. *Grundfragen der Philosophie. Ausgewählte "Probleme" der "Logik". Gesamtausgabe.* II. *Abteilung: Vorlesungen 1923–1944.* Band 45 [Frankfurt am Main: Vittorio Klostermann Verlag, 1984], 97–98).

50   "Die Unverborgenheit des Seienden als solchen ist der Grund der Möglichkeit der Richtigkeit" (*ibid.*, 102).

51   In the extant fragments, Parmenides describes τὸ ἐόν as the kind of eternal, unchanging whole that later Christian theologians will use as a basis for their understandings of the divine:

of Zeno (designed, as in the example of Achilles and the Tortoise, to demonstrate the unreality of the world of motion and appearances[52]), and the dialogues of Plato (for whom the *eidos* or Idea is the ultimate reality that the world of appearances merely exemplifies or participates in—μέθεξις / *methexis*—in an incomplete and shadowy way[53]). Heidegger argues that to get at truth not merely in its surface, concrete, or *ontic* sense, but in its deeper, structural, ontological sense, the seeker must go through a process of unveiling, reaching a state he called disclosedness (*Erschslossenheit*), accompanied by a process of clearing (*Lichtung*), removing what is inessential and shining a light (*Licht*) on the core that remains.

The basic working method of much literary criticism in its modern European and American forms is indebted to Heidegger's recovery and

---

    ἔστιν ἄναρχον ἄπαυστον
    […]
    Ταὐτόν τ' ἐν ταὐτῷ τε μένον καθ' ἑαυτό τε κεῖται
    χοὔτως ἔμπεδον αὖθι μένει κρατερὴ γὰρ Ἀνάγκη
    πείρατος ἐν δεσμοῖσιν ἔχει, τό μιν ἀμφὶς ἐέργει,
    οὕνεκεν οὐκ ἀτελεύτητον τὸ ἐὸν θέμις εἶναι·

    It exists without beginning or ending
    […]
    Identical in its sameness, it remains itself and standing
    Thus firmly-set there, for strong and mighty necessity
    Limits it, holds it in chains, and shuts it in on both sides.
    Because of this, it is right *what is* should not be incomplete.

    Fragment 8, ll. 26, 29–32, *Die Fragmente der Vorsokratiker*, ed. by Hermann Diels (Berlin: Weidmannsche Buchhandlung, 1903), 124, https://archive.org/stream/diefragmenteder00krangoog#page/n140

52 According to Aristotle's summary,

    The second of these is called "Achilles". It is this in which the slowest runner is never overtaken by the fastest; because since the swifter runner in the chase is always, at any given moment, first forced to reach the point where the fleeing runner set into motion, of necessity the slowest runner, who had the headstart, will always be in the lead.

    Δεύτερος δ' ὁ καλούμενος Ἀχιλλεύς. ἔστι δ' οὗτος ὅτι τὸ βραδύτατον οὐδέποτε καταληφθήσεται θέον ὑπὸ τοῦ ταχίστου· ἔμπροσθεν γὰρ ἀναγκαῖον ἐλθεῖν τὸ διῶκον, ὅθεν ὥρμησε τὸ φεῦγον, ὥστ' ἀεί τι προέχειν ἀναγκαῖον τὸ βραδύτερον.

    Aristotle, *Physics, Vol. II, Books 5–8*, ed. by P. H. Wicksteed and F. M. Cornford (Loeb Classical Library, Cambridge, MA: Harvard University Press, 1934), 180, 182. This paradox is helpfully visualized in the following Open University video: https://www.youtube.com/watch?v=skM37PcZmWE

53 The Instance (or the Particular) shares in the nature of the *Eidos* (or form / idea), though imperfectly: "The term Methexis, Participation […] connote[s] a closer relation of the Instance to the Eidos […]: the Instance really has something of the Eidos in it, if not the Eidos in its full purity" (John Niemeyer Findlay. *Plato: The Written and Unwritten Doctrines* [New York: Routledge, 1974], 37).

reformulation of this pre-Socratic notion of truth as disguised, hidden away, and obscured by a layer of what one might call "lesser truth" or illusion. Heidegger's influence on French thinkers like Ricoeur and Jacques Derrida is profound,[54] and its traces work their way through American criticism like that of "Deconstructionists" such as Paul de Man,[55] and even the "New Historicist" work of Stephen Greenblatt (through Foucault[56]) and the innumerable scholars and critics who have followed in his wake in recent decades. Much of the criticism we encounter in this book operates on the assumption that a poem has a surface (the actual words and relationships between them) that must be cleared away in order to reveal the truth. The complexity of Heidegger's thought is often left behind by such a process,[57] but what remains is the

---

54 Walter A. Brogan refers to Derrida's concept of *différance* as "a radical and liberated affirmation of Heidegger's thought" ("The Original Difference". *Derrida and Différance*, ed. by David Wood and Robert Bernasconi [Evanston: Northwestern University Press, 1985], 32). As Andre Gingrich notes, "Heidegger's own phenomenological appreciation of literature influenced Ricouer's hermeneutic approach", and "[b]oth Ricouer and Derrida acknowledged Heidegger's strong influence upon major areas of their respective works" ("Conceptualising Identities: Anthropological Alternatives to Essentialising Difference and Moralizing about Othering". In Gerd Baumann and Andre Gingrich, eds. *Grammars of Identity / Alterity: A Structural Approach* [New York: Berghahn Books, 2004], 6–7). For a comprehensive account of Heidegger's influence on French intellectuals of the mid-twentieth century, see Dominique Janicaud's *Heidegger in France*, Indiana University Press, 2015.
55 "De Man's relation to Heidegger is especially contorted. De Man from the start contests Heidegger's signature notion of Being, but does so in an authentically deconstructive fashion, such that de Man's own counter-notion of 'language' cannot be grasped apart from an appreciation of Heidegger's project" (Joshua Kates. "Literary Criticism". In *The Routledge Companion to Phenomenology*, ed. by Sebastian Luft [New York: Routledge, 2012], 650–51).
56 In Foucault's account, "Heidegger has always, for me, been the essential philosopher" ("Heidegger a toujours été pour moi le philosophe essential"). In his "Le retour de la morale". In his *Dits et écrits, 1954–1988*. Vol. IV: *1980–1988* (Paris: Gallimard, 1994), 696–707 (703).
57 For Heidegger, *art itself* (and not its interpretation or interpreters) is that which reveals (or unconceals) the truth of Being: "The artwork opens the Being of beings in its own way. In the work this opening, this unconcealing, of the truth of beings happens. In art, the truth of beings has set itself in motion. Art is the truth setting itself-into-works" ("Das Kunstwerk eröffnet auf seine Weise das Sein des Seienden. Im Werk geschieht diese Eröffnung, d.h. das Entbergen, d.h. die Wahrheit des Seiended. Im Kunstwerk hat sich die Wahrheit des Seienden ins Werk gesetzt. Die Kunst ist das Sich-ins-Werk-Setzen der Wahrheit") ("Der Ursprung des Kunstwerkes". *Holzwege: Gesamtusgabe*, Vol. V [Frankfurt am Main: Vittorio Klostermann, 1977], 25).

basic notion that the truth of a poem is concealed by its words, and by its writer, and that the job of the critic is to pull back the curtains.

Some critics argue, however, that "truth" is a naïve concept, especially where the interpretation of poetry is concerned.[58] These critics argue that "to impute a hidden core of meaning [is] to subscribe to a metaphysics of presence, a retrograde desire for origins, a belief in an ultimate or foundational reality".[59] Richard Rorty addresses the split between the two camps that Felski calls "Digging Down" and "Standing Back"[60] by first emphasizing their similarity, arguing that "they both start from the pragmatist refusal to think of truth as correspondance to reality",[61] before outlining the crucial difference:

> The first kind of critic [...] thinks that there really is a secret code and that once it's discovered we shall have gotten the text right. He believes that criticism is discovery rather than creation. [The other kind of critic] doesn't care about the distinction between discovery and creation [...]

---

58   For Roland Barthes, the critical search for "truth" is quite useless, as there is no "truth", nor even any operant factor in a text, except language itself:

> Once the author is removed, the claim to "decipher" a text becomes quite useless. To give an Author to a text is to impose a knife's limit on the text, to provide it a final signification, to close the writing. This design is well suited to criticism, which then wants to give itself the important task of discovering the Author (or his hypostases: society, history, the psyche, liberty) beneath the work: the Author found, the text is "explained", the critic has conquered; so there is nothing surprising that, historically, the reign of the Author has also been that of the Critic, but also that criticism (even if it be new) should on this day be shaken off at the same time as the Author.

> L'Auteur une fois éloigné, la prétention de "déchiffrer" un texte devient tout à fait inutile. Donner un Auteur à un texte, c'est imposer à ce texte un cran d'arrêt, c'est le pourvoir d'un signifié dernier, c'est fermer l'écriture. Cette conception convient très bien à la critique, qui veut alors se donner pour tâche importante de découvrir l'Auteur (ou ses hypostases: la société, l'histoire, la psyché, la liberté) sous l'œuvre: l'Auteur trouvé, le texte est "expliqué", le critique a vaincu; il n'y a donc rien d'étonnant à ce que, historiquement, le règne de l'Auteur ait été aussi celui du Critique, mais aussi à ce que la critique (fût-elle nouvelle) soit aujourd'hui ébranlée en même temps que l'Auteur.

"La mort de l'auteur". In *Le Bruissement de la Langue. Essais Critiques IV*. Paris: Seuil, 1984, 65–66.

59   Felski, *The Limits of Critique*, 69.
60   "The first pivots on a division between manifest and latent, overt and covert, what is revealed and what is concealed. Reading is imagined as an act of digging down to arrive at a repressed or otherwise obscured reality", while the second works by "distancing rather than by digging, by the corrosive force of ironic detachment rather than intensive interpretation. The goal is now to 'denaturalize' the text, to expose its social construction by expounding on the conditions in which it is embedded" (*ibid.*, 53, 54).
61   Richard Rorty. *The Consequences of Pragmatism* (Minneapolis: University of Minnesota Press, 1982), 151.

He is in it for what he can get out of it, not for the satisfaction of getting something right.⁶²

Though Rorty might be accused of cynicism here, there is an identifiable split between the kinds of critics who apply a hermeneutics of suspicion in what might be called a "Freudian" sense—digging down through the layers and strata of a culture or text as a psychoanalyst would dig through the manifest content of a patient's dreams in search of a deeper, but hidden, content (or truth)—and those who apply a hermeneutics of suspicion in what might be called a "Nietzschean" sense, stripping away the pretenses and postures of a culture or text in order to demonstrate that it is pretenses and postures all the way down (that there is no truth but the provisional one we create, dismantle, modify, destroy, etc.).⁶³ But as Felski points out, "[in] spite of the theoretical and political disagreements between styles of criticism, there is a striking resemblance at the level of ethos—one that is nicely captured by François Cusset in his phrase 'suspicion without limits'".⁶⁴ Each kind of criticism is in the business of near-perpetual unveiling. Where they differ is that one school seeks to reveal what they believe lies behind the veils, while the other school seeks to reveal the "fact" that there are only veils with nothing behind them.⁶⁵

---

62 *Ibid.*, 152.
63 Such a "Nietzschean" reading can be seen in J. Hillis Miller's deconstructive reading of Percy Shelley's "The Triumph of Life", in which Miller claims that Shelley's poem, "like all texts, is 'unreadable', if by 'readable' one means open to a single, definitive, univocal interpretation" (J. Hillis Miller. "The Critic as Host". *Critical Inquiry*, 3: 3 [Spring, 1977], 447).
64 Felski, *The Limits of Critique*, 20.
65 New Historicism falls into the first camp. It is perpetually in a state of high alert for the operations of power, and constantly on the lookout for "complicity with structures of power in whose language [knowledge] would have no choice but to speak" (Vincent P. Pecora. "The Limits of Local Knowledge". In Harold Aram Veeser, ed. *The New Historicism* [New York: Routledge, 1989], 267). As Foucault—in many ways, the "godfather" of New Historicism—puts it: "there is no power relationship without a correlative constitution of a field of knowledge, nor any field of knowledge that does not presuppose and constitute power relations at the same time" ("qu'il n'y a pas de relation de pouvoir sans constitution corrélative d'un champ de savoir, ni de savoir qui ne suppose et ne constitue en même temps des relations de pouvoir") (*Surveiller et Punir: Naissance de la Prison* [Paris: Gallimard, 1975], 32). The New Historicist critic looks to unveil or reveal the operations (and cooperations) of power and knowledge, all the while risking being complicit with the very structures of power he or she seeks to unmask, since "every act of unmasking, critique, and opposition uses the tools it condemns and risks falling

Such skeptical criticism, whose two branches are more alike than different, "thinks of itself as battling orthodoxy yet it is now the reigning orthodoxy, no longer oppositional but obligatory".[66] This "obligatory" stance is frequently taken up in service of what its practitioners claim is an adversarial agenda, a way of reading texts that resists the ideologies and practices of power by revealing or unveiling them. It is in such criticism that we encounter terms like *interrogation*, with all of its none-too-subliminal suggestions of violence; a fire-against-fire use of violent analysis to uncover or reveal (or fabricate) a "violence" inherent in the text. As Kate McGowan puts it, "[t]he value of *unrelenting interrogation* is the value of *resistance*".[67] But it is often "far from evident" how interrogations of poems, plays, and novels "published in [...] undersubscribed academic journal[s]"[68] serve as effective resistance to anything except poetry itself. Such criticism and its "close ties to modes of professionalization and scholarly gatekeeping make it hard to sustain the claim that there is something intrinsically radical or resistant"[69]

---

prey to the practice it exposes" (Harold Aram Veeser. "Introduction". In his, ed. *The New Historicism*, xi). Deconstruction belongs to the second camp. For Paul de Man, literature obsessively points to "a nothingness", while "[p]oetic language names this void [...] and never tires of naming it again". For de Man, "[t]his persistant naming is what we call literature" (*Blindness and Insight, Essays in the Rhetoric of Contemporary Criticism* [New York: Oxford University Press, 1971], 18). For J. Hillis Miller, an author's works "are at once open to interpretation and ultimately indecipherable, unreadable. His texts lead the critic deeper and deeper into a labyrinth until he confronts a final aporia". The critic burrows further and further beneath the veil of surface appearances only to find unresolvability, an impasse, which leads us to understand that "personification" in literature "will always be divided against itself, folded, manifold, dialogical rather than monological". The final assertion (or unveiling) of the essay is that literature is best understood through "multiple contradictory readings in a perpetual fleeing away from any fixed sense" (J. Hillis Miller. "Walter Pater: A Partial Portrait". *Daedalus*, 105: 1, In Praise of Books [Winter, 1976], 112).

66 Felski, *The Limits of Critique*, 148. Bruce Fleming expresses a similar idea: "[t]he people in charge of contemporary classrooms see themselves as overthrowing prejudices, fiercely challenging the status quo. In fact, for the purposes of literary studies, they *are* the status quo" (27).
67 Kate McGowan. *Key Issues in Critical and Cultural Theory* (Buckingham: Open University Press, 2007), 26. Emphasis added.
68 Felski, *The Limits of Critique*, 143.
69 Ibid., 138.

about either its style or its substance.⁷⁰ Suspicion becomes its own point, perpetuating itself *for* itself, operating as a tribal *shibboleth*⁷¹ that allows members of an in-group to recognize one another. In Eve Sedgwick's view, readings that stem from this method battle with and obscure poetry, "blotting out any sense of the possibility of alternative ways of understanding or things to understand".⁷² As these alternative ways of understanding are blotted out, poetry, and its readers, can be reshaped into a desired ideological form. This reshaping presents itself in a number of ways, but two lines of argument have long been dominant: first, the idea that poetry, and language more generally, refers only to itself; and second, the idea that the author is "dead" and irrelevant—perhaps even an impediment—to the understanding of poetry.

---

70 In Noam Chomsky's view, such interrogations are *impediments* to meaningful resistance:

> In the United States, for example, it's mostly confined to Comparative Literature departments. If they talk to each other in incomprehensible rhetoric, nobody cares. The place where it's been really harmful is in the Third World, because Third World intellectuals are badly needed in the popular movements. They can make contributions, and a lot of them are just drawn away from this—anthropologists, sociologists, and others—they're drawn away into these arcane, and in my view mostly meaningless discourses, and are dissociated from popular struggles.

"Noam Chomsky on French Intellectual Culture & Post-Modernism [3/8]". Interview conducted at Leiden University (March 2011. Posted March 15, 2012), https://www.youtube.com/v/2cqTE_bPh7M&feature=youtu.be&start=409&end=451 [6:49–7:31].

71 This term, from Judges 12:5–6, comes out of a context of war and violence, in which one tribe needed a quick and easy way of identifying infiltrators from the enemy side:

וַיִּלְכֹּד גִּלְעָד אֶת־מַעְבְּרוֹת הַיַּרְדֵּן לְאֶפְרָיִם וְהָיָה כִּי יֹאמְרוּ פְּלִיטֵי אֶפְרַיִם אֶעֱבֹרָה וַיֹּאמְרוּ לוֹ אַנְשֵׁי־גִלְעָד הַאֶפְרָתִי אַתָּה וַיֹּאמֶר ׀ לֹא: וַיֹּאמְרוּ לוֹ אֱמָר־נָא שִׁבֹּלֶת וַיֹּאמֶר סִבֹּלֶת וְלֹא יָכִין לְדַבֵּר כֵּן וַיֹּאחֲזוּ אוֹתוֹ וַיִּשְׁחָטוּהוּ אֶל־מַעְבְּרוֹת הַיַּרְדֵּן וַיִּפֹּל בָּעֵת הַהִיא מֵאֶפְרַיִם אַרְבָּעִים וּשְׁנַיִם אָלֶף:

And the Gileadites captured the passages of the Jordan to Ephraim, and it happened that when the fugitive Ephraimites said "let me cross over", the men of Gilead said to them "are you an Ephraimite?" And if he said, "no", then they said, "say Shibboleth", and if he said "Sibboleth", because he could not pronounce it right, then they took him and slew him at the passages of the Jordan, and there fell at that time forty two thousand Ephraimites.

Unless otherwise noted, all Hebrew Biblical text is quoted from *Biblia Hebraica Stuttgartensia*, ed. by Karl Elliger and Willhelm Rudolph (Stuttgart: Deutsche Bibelgesellschaft, 1983). All Greek Biblical text is quoted from *The Greek New Testament*, ed. by Barbara Aland (Stuttgart: Deutsche Bibelgesellschaft, 2014).

72 Eve Kosofsky Sedgwick. *Touching Feeling: Affect, Pedagogy, Performativity* (Durham and London: Duke University Press, 2003), 131.

IV
The Critics: Poetry Is About Poetry

This notion can be traced to Maurice Blanchot, a right-wing journalist who became a left-wing philosopher and literary critic after the Second World War. Blanchot argues—in a sideswipe at Jean-Paul Sartre's 1948 work *What is Literature?*—that "it has been found, surprisingly, that the question 'What is literature?' has never received anything other than insignificant answers".[73] Sartre argues that the poet writes to escape the world, while the prose writer engages with it, "for one, art is a flight; for the other, a means of conquest".[74] The politically-committed prose writer works for the cause of liberty: "the writer, a free man addressing other free men, has only one subject: liberty",[75] and such work only has meaning in a free society: "the art of prose is tied to the only regime in which prose holds any meaning: democracy".[76]

While Sartre's ideas are certainly contestable, Blanchot goes to the opposite extreme: what writers seek to accomplish is irrelevant, since the meaning of literature, its essence, its "one subject" is nothing more than language itself. For Blanchot, the question of literature only finds meaningful answers when it is "addressed to language, behind the man who writes and reads, to the language that becomes literature".[77] Literature says nothing except to affirm its own existence: "the work of art, the literary work—is neither completed nor unfinished: it is. What it says is only this: it is—and nothing more. Apart from that, it is nothing. Whoever wants it to express more, will find nothing, find that it expresses nothing".[78] This articulates a view of writing in which words

---

73 "On a constaté avec surprise que la question: 'Qu'est-ce que la littérature?' n'avait jamais reçu que des réponses insignifiantes" (Maurice Blanchot. "La Littérature et le droit à la mort". *La Part de Feu* [Paris: Gallimard, 1949], 294).
74 "pour celui-ci, l'art est une fuite; pour celui-la, un moyen de conquérir" (Jean-Paul Sartre. *Qu'est-ce que la littérature?* [Paris: Gallimard, 1948], 45).
75 "l'écrivain, homme libre s'adressant à des hommes libres, n'a qu'un seul sujet: la liberté" (*ibid.*, 70).
76 [l]'art de la prose est solidaire du seul régime où la prose garde un sens: la démocratie" (*ibid.*, 82).
77 "adressée au langage, derrière l'homme qui écrit et lit, par le langage devenu littérature" (Blanchot. "La Littérature et le droit à la mort", 293).
78 "l'œuvre d'art, l'œuvre littéraire—n'est nini achevé ni inachevée: elle est. Ce qu'elle dit, c'est exclusivement cela: qu'elle est—et rien de plus. En dehors de cela, elle n'est rien. Qui veut lui faire exprimer davantage, ne trouve rien, trouve qu'elle

do not and cannot represent any world in which writers and readers live: for Blanchot, the "writer must commit to [...] words rather than the things that words represent. This is nothing less than the writer's abandonment of representation's claim to be able truly to conjure things before the reader".[79]

This basic idea informs a great deal of modern criticism, much of it based in French thought of the latter half of the twentieth century. For example, Jacques Derrida argues that one cannot understand a text by referring to something outside it:

> Yet if reading must not simply redouble the text, it cannot legitimately transgress the text toward something other than itself, to a referent (metaphysical reality, historical, psycho-biographical, etc.) or to a signified outside text whose content could take place, could have taken place outside language, that is to say, in the sense that we give here to that word, outside of writing in general. This is why the methodological considerations that we risk here on an example are closely dependent on general propositions that we have elaborated above, as to the absence of the referent or the transcendental signified. *There is no outside-text.*[80]

Similarly, Jacques Lacan argues that language is a closed system, in which our signifiers cannot ever point to a "thing" that is somehow outside the system:

> Therefore, let me specify what language means in that which it communicates; it is neither signal, nor sign, nor even a sign of the thing as an external reality. The relationship between signifier and signified is entirely enclosed in the order of language itself, which completely determines the two terms.[81]

---

n'exprime rien" (Maurice Blanchot. "La Solitude Essentielle". *L'Espace Littéraire* [Paris: Gallimard, 1955], 12).

79   Eric Richtmeyer. "Maurice Blanchot: Saboteur of the Writers' War". *Proceedings of the Western Society for French History*, 35 (2007), 255.

80   Et pourtant, si la lecture ne doit pas se contenter de redouble le texte, elle ne peut légitimement transgresser le texte vers autre chose que lui, vers un référent (réalité métaphysique, historique, psycho-biographique, etc.) ou vers un signifié hors texte dont le contenu pourrait avoir lieu, aurait pu avoir lieu hors de la langue, c'est-à-dire, au sens que nous donnons ici à ce mot, hors de l'écriture en général. C'est pourquoi les considérations méthodologiques que nous risquons ici sur un exemple sont étroitement dépendantes des propositions générales que nous avons élaborées plus haut, quant à l'absence du référent ou du signifié transcendantal. Il n'y a pas de hors-texte.

Jacques Derrida. *De la Grammatologie* [Paris: Éditions de Minuit, 1967], 227.

81   "Précisons donc ce que le langage signifie en ce qu'il communique: il n'est ni signal, ni signe, ni même signe de la chose, en tant que réalité extérieure. La relation entre

These ideas can be traced back further to the ideas of the Swiss linguist Ferdinand de Saussure, whose work (first published in 1916) analyzes language as a system of signs, which "unite not a thing and a name, but a concept and a sound-image"[82] or what he will later refer to as a signified and a signifier, using ideas that date back to Sextus Empiricus (c. 160–210 CE) who claimed of the Stoics "three things, they say, are yoked with one another, the signified, the signifier, and the thing that happens to exist".[83] Saussure, unlike the Stoics, attempts to define linguistic signs purely internally, with as little reference as possible to any "thing that happens to exist". Such signs are not to be read in terms of any positive content or reference, but in terms of their difference from other signs in the overall system:

> When we say they correspond to concepts, we imply that these are purely differential, defined not by their positive content but negatively by their relations with other terms of the system.[84]

In fact, for Saussure, language is entirely composed of differential relationships, a series of differences without any positive terms:

> [I]*n language there are only differences*. Even more: a difference generally supposes positive terms between which it is established; but in language there are only differences *without positive terms*. Whether we take the signified or the signifier, language has neither ideas nor sounds that pre-exist the language system, but only conceptual differences and phonic differences issuing from the system.[85]

---

signifiant et signifié est tout entière incluse dans l'ordre du langage lui-même qui en conditionne intégralement les deux termes" ("Discours de Jacques Lacan". *La Psychanalyse*, 1 [1956], 243).

82 "unit non une chose et un nom, mais un concept et une image acoustique" (Ferdinand de Saussure. *Cours de Linguistique Générale*, ed. by Tullio de Mauro [Paris: Payot & Rivages, 1967], 98).

83 "τρία φάμενοι συζυγεῖν ἀλλήλοις, τό τε σημαινόμενον καὶ τὸ σημαῖνον καὶ τὸ τυγχάνον" (Sextus Empiricus. *Against Logicians*, 2.11, ed. by R. G. Bury [Cambridge, MA: Loeb Classical Library, Harvard University Press, 1935], 244).

84 "Quand on dit qu'elles correspondent à des concepts, on sous-entend que ceux-ci sont purement différentiels, définis non pas positivement par leur contenu, mais négativement par leurs rapports avec les autres termes du système" (Saussure, 162).

85 dans la langue il n'y a que des différences. Bien plus: une différence suppose en général des termes positifs entre lesquels elle s'établit; mais dans la langue il n'y a que des différences sans termes positifs. Qu'on prenne le signifié ou le signifiant, la langue ne comporte ni des idées ni des sons qui préexisteraient au système linguistique, mais seulement des différences conceptuelles et des différences phoniques issues de ce système.

Saussure's analysis treats language as a sealed system, internally-focused and without reference.[86] In Saussure's view, the basic unit of language, *le signe linguistique,* is arbitrary. It has no necessary link with the world of objects and actions outside of language, and is simply an association of sounds and concepts:

> The unifying link between the signifier and the signified is arbitrary, or again, as we intend by signs the whole that results from the association of a signifier with a signified, we can say it more simply: *the linguistic sign is arbitrary.*[87]

Blanchot views literature in much the same way Derrida, Lacan, and Saussure view language, and this view of the self-referentiality of both language and literature has been enormously important for later critics. "Blanchot [...] made possible all discourse on literature" in Foucault's view, reducing it to "an empty space that runs as a grand movement through all literary languages".[88] In so doing, Blanchot owes a significant debt to Hegel, who in his *Vorlesungen über die Aesthetik* argues that poetry, properly speaking, is disconnected from materiality or any concrete reference to the material world: "Poetry is the universal art of self-liberated spirit, not bound to external sensuous material for its realization, but moving only in the inner space and inner time of ideas and feelings".[89] However, Blanchot adds a twist to Hegel's

---

Ibid., 166.

86 It should be noted here that these observations apply to Sassure's discussion of what he calls *langue,* the system of language (or the abstract rules of a signifying system), as opposed to *parole,* the actions of speech and understanding though which that language is used by human beings. A great deal of so-called Saussurian and post-Saussurian theory seems to operate as if the latter did not exist.

87 "Le lien unisssant le signifiant au signifié est arbitraire, ou encore, puisque nous entendons par signe le total résultant de l'association d'un signifiant à un signifié, nous pouvons dire plus simplement: *le signe linguistique est arbitraire*" *(ibid.,* 100).

88 "Blanchot [...] rendu possible tout discours sur la littérature" [...] "un creux qui parcourt comme un grand mouvement tous les langages littéraires" (Michel Foucault. "Sur les façons d'écrire l'Histoire" [interview with Raymond Bellour]. *Les Lettres françaises,* 1187 (15–21 June 1967), 6–9. Reprinted in his *Dits et écrits,* Vol. 1: *1954–1975,* 593).

89 "Die Dichtkunst ist die allgemeine Kunst des in sich freigewordenen, nicht an das äußerlich-sinnliche Material zur Realisation gebundenen Geistes, der nur im inneren Raume und der inneren Zeit der Vorstellungen und Empfindungen sich ergeht" (Georg Wilhelm Friedrich Hegel. *Vorlesungen über die Aesthetik,* Vol. 1 [Berlin: Dunder und Humblot, 1835], 115, https://books.google.com/books?id=Fss9AQAAMAAJ&pg=PA115).

disconnection of poetry and materiality by working with an idea of language as an arbitrary yoking of words and ideas, pursuing an argument that ultimately derives from Plato in the dialogue *Cratylus*. In that work, Hermogenes disputes Cratylus's notion that words are derived directly from nature, by insisting that "on the contrary, for their origins, each name is produced, not by nature, but by the customs, habits, and character of those who are both accustomed to use it and called it forth".[90]

From Hegel's declaration that poetry is "not bound to external sensuous material", to Blanchot's idea that the question of poetry is properly "addressed to language" and "expresses nothing" is but a short step, and thus we find ourselves facing contemporary critics who advance the argument to insist that poetry is always and only about itself.[91] However, the linguistic ideas that underlie much of this (post-Hegel) have been seriously questioned by recent research:

> a careful statistical examination of words from nearly two-thirds of the world's languages reveals that unrelated languages very often use (or avoid) the same sounds for specific referents. For instance, words for tongue tend to have l or u, "round" often appears with r, and "small" with i. These striking similarities call for a reexamination of the fundamental assumption of the arbitrariness of the sign.[92]

---

90 "οὐ γὰρ φύσει ἑκάστῳ πεφυκέναι ὄνομα οὐδὲν οὐδενί, ἀλλὰ νόμῳ καὶ ἔθει τῶν ἐθισάντων τε καὶ καλούντων" (Plato. *Cratylus. Parmenides. Greater Hippias. Lesser Hippias*, ed. by Harold North Fowler [Cambridge, MA: Loeb Classical Library, Harvard University Press, 1926], 10).

91 In a discussion of Hans-Georg Gadamer's ideas about "propositional" versus "eminent" or "absolute" texts, Rod Coltman puts the case in the starkest possible terms: "Because it does not refer to anything outside of itself, there is nothing beyond the poem that is more important than the poem itself. The text of the poem remains, in other words, because the poem is not about anything, or rather, it is only about itself" (Rod Coltman. "Hermeneutics: Literature and Being". *The Blackwell Companion to Hermeneutics*, ed. by Niall Keane and Chris Lawn [Chichester: John Wiley & Sons, 2016], 550–51). Richard Klein makes a similar point, asserting that the "fragility of literature, its susceptibility to being lost, is linked to its having no real referent" ("The Future of Literary Criticism". *PMLA*, 125: 4 [October 2010], 920, https://doi.org/10.1632/pmla.2010.125.4.920).

92 Damián E. Blasia, Søren Wichmannd, Harald Hammarströmb, Peter F. Stadlerc, and Morten H. Christiansen. "Sound–meaning Association Biases Evidenced across Thousands of Languages". *Proceedings of the National Academy of Sciences*, 113: 39 (27 September 2016, https://doi.org/10.1073/pnas.1605782113).

These new findings threaten to unsettle the entire line of thought based on a long-held assumption, including the oft-repeated claims that language refers only to itself and that poetry refers only to poetry. Perhaps, at long last, such claims can be reconsidered.[93]

---

93 The irony of such claims is that a number of later thinkers who engage with Saussure rewrite him, covertly reversing his relation between the signifier and the signified. Saussure gives precedence to the concept over the sound-image: "One cannot reduce language to sound, [...] it is merely the instrument of thought, and does not exist for itself" ("On ne peut donc réduire la langue au son, [...] il n'est que l'instrument de la pensée et n'existe pas pour lui-même") (24). Jacques Lacan reverses Saussure's relation, representing it as S/s, with "S" referring to the signifier (Saussure's "sound-image") and "s" referring to the signified (Saussure's "concept"). But rather than acknowledge his wholesale reversal of the relation of the terms, Lacan ascribes *his own* formula to Saussure: "the sign thus written, deserves to be attributed to Ferdinand de Saussure" ("Le signe écrit ainsi, mérite d'être attribué a Ferdinand de Saussure") (*Écrits* [Paris: Seuil, 1966], 497). For Lacan, the signifier, in its most pristine state, is not what Saussure described as the instrument of thought; in fact, it signifies nothing at all: "all real signifiers, in themselves, are signifiers that signify nothing. [...] The more a signifier signifies nothing, the more indestructible it is" ("tout vrai signifiant en tant que tel est un signifiant qui ne signifie rien. [...] car c'est précisément dans la mesure où, plus il ne signifie rien, plus il est indestructible") (*Le Séminaire de Jacques Lacan, Livre III: Les Psychoses: 1955–1956*, ed. by Jacques Alain Miller [Paris: Seuil, 1981], 210). This conception of language had been rejected a decade before by the Danish linguist Louis Hjelmslev, for whom there can be no signifier without a signified because "expressional meaning" ("udtryksmening") is always connected to "expressional form as expressional *substance*" ("udtryksform som udtryks*substans*"), due to "the unity of content-form and expression-form established by the solidarity of what we have called the sign-function" ("den enhed af indholdsform og udtryksform der etableres af den solidaritet som vi har kaldt tegnfunktionen") (*Omkring Sprogteoriens Grundlæggelse* [Copenhagen: Bianco Lunos Bogtrykkeri, 1943], 51, 53).

Even before Lacan's sleight-of-hand rearrangment, Claude Lévi-Strauss had inverted Saussure's relation between the signifier and the signified: "symbols are more real than that which they symbolize; the signifier precedes and determines the signified" ("les symboles sont plus réels que ce qu'ils symbolisent, le signifiant précède et détermine le signifié") ("Introduction à l'œuvre de Marcel Mauss". In Marcel Mauss, *Sociologie et Anthropologie* [Paris: Presses Universitaires de France, 1950], xxxii). This latter view makes it possible to "read" language as wholly determinative of thought, which when combined with Barthes' and Foucault's differing formulations of the "death of the Author", renders literature—already denied any externally-referential ability—a mere function of language itself. Barthes traces this idea back to the French poet Stephan Mallarmé, claiming that "for Mallarmé, as for us, it is language that speaks, not the author; to write, is through a prior impersonality [...] to reach that point where only language acts, 'performs', and not 'me'" ("pour [Mallarmé], comme pour nous, c'est le langage qui parle, ce n'est pas l'auteur; écrire, c'est, à travers une impersonnalité préalable [...] atteindre ce point où seul le langage agit, 'performe' et non 'moi'") (Barthes, "La mort de l'auteur", 62). In summary, much literary theory and criticism over the last century is based on a questionable linguistic paradigm, the terms of which were

V
The Critics: The Author Is Dead (or Merely Irrelevant)

This idea is one we will encounter, among other places, in critical work on John Donne, a poet whose life and poetry might otherwise seem inseparable, so closely do the emotional themes of the poetry match the known struggles of the poet. The idea that emotions, thoughts, and experiences of the poet are immaterial to an understanding of the poem is one that has been with us since the advent of the so-called New Criticism. Wimsatt and Beardsley have argued that the author's intentions are both undiscoverable and irrelevant:

> [a] poem is not the critic's own and not the author's (it is detached from the author at birth and goes about the world beyond his power to intend about it or control it). The poem belongs to the public. It is embodied in language, the peculiar possession of the public, and it is about the human being, an object of public knowledge.[94]

From the idea that a poem is "embodied in language" and "detached from the author", it is but a short step to criticism that insists a poem is solely about language, and communicates no other meaning of any kind. At the time Wimsatt and Beardsley were writing this article, this argument was already being made across the Atlantic.

The irony of the authors' closing statement—"Critical inquiries are not settled by consulting the oracle"[95]—is that too much criticism of the last several decades has been written by those who have bypassed *consulting* the oracle by *becoming* the oracle. This idea can be seen in more highly developed form in the notion promulgated by Roland Barthes and Michel Foucault in the 1960s that the author does not exist for readers in any traditional sense—what exists or is perceived to exist is an *author function*. For Barthes, "we know that in order to give writing its future, the myth must be reversed: the birth of the reader must be

---

        inverted by its most prominent adherents to allow them to make claims for which there was otherwise no support.
94 W. K. Wimsatt Jr. and M. C. Beardsley. "The Intentional Fallacy". *The Sewanee Review*, 54: 3 (July–September 1946), 470.
95 Ibid., 487.

paid for by the death of the author".⁹⁶ In Foucault's view, writing refers primarily to two things—language, and the death of the author:

> We can say first that today's writing has freed itself of the theme of expression: it refers only to itself, and yet it is not caught in the form of interiority; it identifies with its own unfolded externality. [...] Writing unfolds like a game [...] where the writing subject constantly disappears. [...] The writing subject destroys all the signs of his particular individuality; the writer's hallmark is nothing more than the singularity of his absence; he must take the role of death in the game of writing. All of this is well known; and in its own good time, criticism and philosophy has taken note of this disappearance or this death of the author.⁹⁷

In turn, the entire concept owes a debt to the nineteenth-century French poet Stéphane Mallarmé, who in "Crise de Vers" argued for a pure form of poetry from which the author would be eliminated:

> The pure work implies the disappearance of the speaker of poetry, who yields the initiative to words, mobilized by the clash of their own inequality; they illuminate each other's reflections, passing like a virtual trail of fire on precious stones, replacing the breathing perceptible in the old lyrical verse or the enthusiastic personality that directed the phrase. The structure of a book of verse must be everywhere its own, innate, eliminating chance; still, the author must be omitted.⁹⁸

---

96 "nous savons que, pour rendre à l'écriture son avenir, il faut en renverser le mythe: la naissance du lecteur doit se payer de la mort de l'Auteur" (Roland Barthes. "La mort de l'auteur". In *Le Bruissement de la Langue. Essais Critiques IV* [Paris: Seuil, 1984], 67).

97 On peut dire d'abord que l'écriture d'aujourd'hui s'est affranchie du thème de l'expression: elle n'est référée qu'à elle-même, et pourtant, elle n'est pas prise dans la forme de l'intériorité; elle s'identifie à sa propre extériorité déployée. [...] l'écriture se déploie comme un jeu [...] où le sujet écrivant ne cesse de disparaître. [...] le sujet écrivant déroute tous les signes de son individualité particulière; la marque de l'écrivain n'est plus que la singularité de son absence; il lui faut tenir le rôle du mort dans le jeu de l'écriture. Tout cela est connu; et il y a beau temps que la critique et la philosophie ont pris acte de cette disparition ou de cette mort de l'auteur.

Michel Foucault. "Qu'est-ce qu'un auteur?" In his *Dits et écrits*. Vol. 1, 792–93.

98 L'œuvre pure implique la disparition élocutoire du poëte, qui cède l'initiative aux mots, par le heurt de leur inégalité mobilisés; ils s'allument de reflets réciproques comme une virtuelle traînée de feux sur des pierreries, remplaçant la respiration perceptible en l'ancien souffle lyrique ou la direction personnelle enthousiaste de la phrase. Une ordonnance du livre de vers poind innée ou partout, élime le hasard; encore la faut-il, pour omettre l'auteur.

Stéphane Mallarmé. "Crise de Vers". In *Divagations* (Paris: Bibliothèque-Charpentier, 1897), 246–47, https://fr.wikisource.org/wiki/Divagations/Texte_entier

This decades-long trend has marked a struggle in which critics have kidnapped poetry, subordinated it to their own imperatives, and reduced literature to the status of just one more cultural "text", or object of analysis, upon which to demonstrate their acumen. For Paul de Man, such criticism has a quasi-theological function akin to unmasking idolatry:

> Criticism [...] functions more and more as a demystification of the belief that literature is a privileged language. The dominant strategy consists of showing that certain claims to authenticity attributed to literature are in fact expressions of a desire that, like all desires, falls prey to the duplicities of expression. The so-called "idealism" of literature is then shown to be an idolatry, a fascination with a false image that mimics the presumed attributes of authenticity when it is in fact just the hollow mask with which a frustrated, defined consciousness tries to cover up its own negativity.[99]

Geoffrey Hartman speaks of this as a criticism that "liberates [...] critical activity from its positive or reviewing function, from its subordination to the thing commented on".[100] Hartman argues for infinite freedom for the critic, since "there is no absolute knowledge but rather a textual infinite, an interminable web of texts or interpretations", which needn't be subordinate to something called "literature" because, as Hartman puts it, "literary commentary is literature".[101]

With each new "reading" of a poem, or play, or novel, etc., the critics displace the original authors, making themselves supreme as both *author* and *interpreter*. But not quite all readers have given their assent to this state of affairs. With the poet John Donne, for example, what upsets a critic like Deborah Larson is that too many readers refuse to align themselves with this view, resulting in "the continuing interpretations of Donne's poetry through his life and of his life through his poetry".[102] Larson argues that such meetings of literature and life are wholly inappropriate, insisting that "Donne's poems should be recognized as a group of mainly unrelated monologues, spoken by several varying and

---

99 Paul de Man. *Blindness and Insight*, 12.
100 Geoffrey Hartman. *Criticism in the Wilderness: The Study of Literature Today* (New Haven: Yale University Press, 1980), 191.
101 *Ibid.*, 202.
102 Deborah Larson, *John Donne and Twentieth-Century Criticism* (London: Associated University Presses, 1989), 15.

contradictory *personae* playing a number of roles".[103] Note the language of compulsion, even duty—the poems should be read as unrelated, not only to the life of the poet, but to each other. The problem, however, is that too many readers are breaking the rules: otherwise we "would not have been arguing for the last hundred years over Donne's rakish youth and his conversion to 'sincere' love, nor would any one of his poses become the dominant one, as has often happened".[104]

This, in a nutshell, is what a great deal of literary criticism has become over the last several decades—an explicit argument that art should be held at a wide remove from life, that art has little or nothing to do with the artist except as a locus of linguistic, socio-historical, economic, and political forces, and that art reflects nothing more than a set of sterile techniques and conventions. This attitude of superiority of the critic to the poet, with its distancing of life from poetry, is aptly expressed by the poet-critic T. S. Eliot: "If Donne in youth was a rake, then I suspect he was a conventional rake; if Donne in age was devout, then I suspect he was conventionally devout".[105] The obvious gesture here is reduction—Donne's lived experience is described as "conventional", and therefore of small importance, scant account, and slight claim on the attention of the critic who tells readers *move along, nothing to see here*. But, as Larson complains, "[b]iographical interpretation [...] is difficult to escape from, even with a conscious effort".[106] Why should it be escaped from? Why may it not be one tool among many? Because *to the extent that the poet is allowed to exist, the free reign of the critic is threatened*.[107]

The authoritarian relationship between critic and poet goes back to the very beginnings of what we define as the Western tradition:

> Philosophy has long had a need to keep poetry in its place—as Plato, alluding to the "ancient quarrel" between the two, was among the first to tell us (Rep. 10.607b). But what is striking in Plato's attitude is that

---

103 *Ibid.*, 14.
104 *Ibid.*
105 T. S. Eliot. "Donne in Our Time". *A Garland for John Donne, 1631–1931*, ed. by Theodore Spencer (Cambridge: Harvard University Press, 1931), 10.
106 Larson, 71.
107 Many critics would sign on to *half* of Barthes' death-of-the-author formula, while ignoring the part that threatens their own profession: "criticism [...] should on this day be shaken off at the same time as the Author" (66) ("la critique [...] soit aujourd'hui ébranlée en même temps que l'Auteur").

[...] he regards poetry at all times and in all its uses with *suspicion*, as a substance inherently volatile.[108]

Such hostile criticism reduces poetry to mere "convention", or it views poetry as a secret code which plays "hide and seek" with its readers, as critics argue that the "real" meaning of the poetry is either wildly different from the apparent meaning, or is so lost in textual, contextual, and linguistic tangles as to be wholly undiscoverable.

This book argues for readings of love poetry that oppose such hostility, that challenge the free reign of the critics, and resist criticism's unrelenting interrogation of poetry. Along the way we will frequently encounter critics for whom love in poetry must be defined reductively as a "convention" or a "literary commonplace", or in one especially egregious case, as "a citation" of the perceived experiences of others. We will encounter eminent scholars who describe individual poets as "sick", and others who would—if only they could—literally rather than interpretively rewrite the poems and other texts upon which they expound.[109] This authoritarian approach to literary criticism is perhaps an understandable side-effect of what Noam Chomsky calls "the self-selection for obedience that is [...] part of elite education".[110] It reflects the goals that Fichte, the German Idealist philosopher, outlines for the new education (*der neuen Erziehung*):

> If you would have power over a man, you have to do more than merely address him; you must shape him, and shape him so that he cannot want otherwise than you would have him want.[111]

---

108 G. R. F. Ferrari. "Plato and Poetry". In *The Cambridge History of Literary Criticism, Vol. 1: Classical Criticism*, ed. by George Alexander Kennedy (Cambridge: Cambridge University Press, 1989), 92. Emphasis added.

109 The most famous example of this is Paul de Man, who in his work *Allegories of Reading* (1979), rewrote (by the simple insertion of *ne*) a passage from Rousseau's *Confessions*. As first pointed out by Ortwin de Graef, de Man "adds a negation to Rousseau's sentence, as if this did not make a difference, as if one was entitled to do so on the basis of the main clause" ("Silence to be Observed: A Trial for Paul de Man's Inexcusable Confessions". In (*Dis*)*continuities: Essays on Paul de Man*, ed. by Luc Herman, Kris Humbeeck, and Geert Lernout [Amsterdam: Rodopi, 1989], 61).

110 Noam Chomsky. Online discussion that took place on LBBS, Z-Magazine's Left On-Line Bulletin Board. Posted at rec.arts.books, 13 November 1995, 03:21:23, http://bactra.org/chomsky-on-postmodernism.html

111 "Willst du etwas über ihn vermögen, so mußt du mehr tun, als ihn blos anreden, du mußt ihn machen, ihn also machen, das er gar nicht anders wollen könne, als du willst, das er wolle" (Johann Gottlieb Fichte. *Johann Gottlieb Fichte: Fichtes Reden an*

Such critics often seem unable or unwilling to see poetry as anything other than a self-referential system of conventions, tropes, and signs, disconnected from life, irrelevant except for the urgent need felt by the critics to make sure that readers are trained to see as they see, and read as they read. Obedience, once selected, becomes the lens through which these critics read, and the method by which they would shape readers in their own image, so that they cannot want otherwise, a process we can see at work in the long history of the relation between literature and criticism, beginning with the allegorical readings of the Song of Songs.

A consideration of the Song of Songs and its interpretive history reveals that criticism claiming to expose the hidden has a very long history, shaping the way we have been taught to read and understand poetry and other literary forms for over two thousand years. The earliest examples are not rooted merely in suspicion, but in the openly-expressed desire to exercise authority over the hearts and minds of others, and many modern examples of suspicion-based criticism retain more than a trace of that original impulse. But if we can learn to hear their voices once again, the poems considered here have more than enough power to fight back against such entrenched ways of reading—not merely through the brilliance of their surfaces,[112] but through the passionate depths of their engagements with the love that was once called *fin'amor*. Such love—often forbidden by those who would be obeyed—is presented by the poets as a temptation, a seduction, a siren's call to the too-easily missed

---

die Deutsche Nation, ed. by Samantha Nietz [Hamburg: Severus, 2013], 32). Fichte's idea is reflected in Spivak's fairly recent description of Humanities education as an "uncoercive rearrangement of desires" (Gayatri Chakravorty Spivak. "Righting Wrongs". *The South Atlantic Quarterly*, 103: 2/3 [Spring/Summer 2004], 526). The "uncoercive" nature of such "rearrangement" is perhaps best attested by the experience of one of the current authors who had the occasion to observe a discussion of this idea among a group of Ph.D. students. One student noted the possibility that such "uncoercive rearrangement" might be a subtle means of stifling minority opinion. *Every other student in the group* condemned that idea, and the discussion was quickly dropped.

112 Though Stephen Best and Sharon Marcus claim that "[i]n the last decade or so, we have been drawn to modes of reading that attend to the surfaces of texts rather than plumb their depths" ("Surface Reading: An Introduction". *Representations*, 108: 1 [Fall 2009], 1–2), the trends of the last decade and a half seem ephemeral when compared to a style of reading and interpretation that has held sway for over two millennia.

experience of being truly and fully alive. As Goethe's Mephistopheles slyly observes: "Gray, dear Friend, is all theory, / And green is life's golden tree",[113] and in such beautifully mortal seductions lies the heart of love's response to its critics.

---

113 "Grau, teurer Freund, ist alle Theorie, / Und grün des Lebens goldner Baum" (Johann Wolfgang Von Goethe. *Faust*, Part I, ed. by Walter Kaufmann [New York: Anchor Books, 1990], 206, ll. 2038–39).

2. Channeled, Reformulated, and Controlled: Love Poetry from the Song of Songs to Aeneas and Dido

I
Love Poetry and the Critics who Allegorize: The Song of Songs

Susan Sontag, in her now-classic essay "Against Interpretation", protests against a form of criticism which reshapes texts like the Song of Songs into new and ideologically compliant forms:

> Interpretation [...] presupposes a discrepancy between the clear meaning of the text and the demands of (later) readers. It seeks to resolve that discrepancy. The situation is that for some reason a text has become unacceptable; yet it cannot be discarded. Interpretation is a radical strategy for conserving an old text, which is thought too precious to repudiate, by revamping it. The interpreter, without actually erasing or rewriting the text, is altering it. But he can't admit to doing this. He claims to be only making it intelligible, by disclosing its true meaning. However far the interpreters alter the text ([as in] the Rabbinic and Christian "spiritual" interpretations of the clearly erotic Song of Songs), they must claim to be reading off a sense that is already there.[1]

---

1   Susan Sontag. *Against Interpretation: And Other Essays* (New York: Farrar, Straus and Giroux, 2013), 5–6. This kind of interpretation-through-alteration has reached the point of altering (or suggesting alterations to) texts. Such critical rewriting by

One of the most powerfully erotic, celebratory, and secular love poems in all the world's literature, the Song of Songs (שיר השירים, or *Shir ha-Shirim*) has endured nearly two thousand years of interpretation that attempts to tame it and explain it away. Traditionally dated to sometime around 950 BCE, the Song has a complicated textual history.

Illumination for the opening verse of Song of Songs, the Rothschild Mahzor, Manuscript on parchment. Florence, Italy, 1492.[2]

Gerson Cohen suggests that "while the Song of Songs may contain very ancient strata, the work as we have it now cannot have been completed before the Macedonian conquest of the Near East and rise of the Hellenistic culture".[3] Likely written down between 400 and 100 BCE, it

---

those determined to save the reputations of poetry's gods has been going on since the days of Aristotle, who mentions a figure named Hippias of Thasos (unknown to us) who sought to solve the "problem" of Zeus' apparent dishonesty in Book Two of the *Iliad*, by "following prosody, as in Hippias of Thasos" "we grant to him that he achieve his prayer" ("κατὰ δὲ προσῳδίαν, ὥσπερ Ἱππίας ἔλυεν ὁ Θάσιος, τὸ "δίδομεν δέ οἱ εὖχος ἀρέσθαι"") (*Poetics*, 1461a, 22–23. In *Aristotle: Poetics. Longinus: On the Sublime. Demetrius: On Style*, ed. by Stephen Halliwell [Loeb Classical Library, Cambridge, MA: Harvard University Press, 1995], 30). As Richard Janko explains it, "[i]t was thought offensive that Zeus deceives Agamemmnon, e.g. by Plato (*Republic*, II 383A). By altering the accent on "grant" (from "δίδομεν" to "διδόμεν"), Hippias tried to shift the blame for the deceit away from Zeus" (Aristotle. *Poetics*. Trans. by Richard Janko [Indiannapolis: Hackett, 1987], 149, n. 61a21).

2   https://commons.wikimedia.org/wiki/File:Song_of_songs_Rothschild_mahzor.jpg
3   Gerson Cohen. "The Song of Songs and the Jewish Religious Mentality". In *Studies in the Variety of Rabbinic Cultures* (Philadelphia: The Jewish Publication Society, 1991), 13.

may be, as M. H. Segal argues, "a collection of love poetry of a varied character" preserved by "oral transmission through the generations",[4] a collection written in a popular, rather than classical Hebrew, a Mishnaic Hebrew more like Aramaic than the Hebrew of the prophets.[5] The Song looks back to details of city life and attitudes about relations between the sexes that reflect the Jerusalem of Solomon's time, as well as the Jerusalem of the Hellenistic period,[6] testifying to the power of love and desire, even staging a sex scene between its male and female lovers. It is wholly without disapproval and judgment, frank in its depiction of passion, and absolutely uninterested in a world beyond love—not only is God not discussed,[7] neither is the relationship of Israel to its religious traditions or the surrounding nations. As Zhang Longxi describes it: "[t]he language of the Song of Songs is the secular language of love. It speaks of the desire and the joy of love, [but not] of law and covenant, the fear and worship of God, or sin and forgiveness".[8]

For that very reason, on both the Judaic and Christian sides of the controversy, this Hellenistic text that treats of Bronze-age lovers has been made to wear the mantle of an allegory, cast as a poem describing the relationship between God and Israel by Rabbinic interpreters, or between God and the Christian Church by early Church Fathers. In one of the great ironies of literary history, the Christian tradition of de-eroticizing the Song is powerfully advanced by Origen[9] (c. 184–254 CE), a man who castrated himself to avoid the temptations of sexual desire. As the early Church historian Eusebius tells it:

---

4   M. H. Segal. "The Song of Songs". *Vetus Testamentum*, 12: 4 (October 1962), 477.
5   *Ibid.*, 478.
6   *Ibid.*, 481–82. The method and date of composition of the Song is a matter of ongoing controversy, and estimates vary from the 10th century BCE to the end of the 2nd century BCE. For a summation of the various positions, see Abraham Mariaselvam, *The Song of Songs and Ancient Tamil Love Poems: Poetry and Symbolism* (Rome: Editrice Pontificio Intituto Biblico, 1988), 43–44.
7   The only mention of the deity is embedded in the term שַׁלְהֶבֶתְיָה (*shalhevetyah*) in 8:6, which literally translated is "Yahweh-flame", but serves poetically as a way of intensifying the idea of flame—*shalhevet*—into the idea of a "colossal" or "roaring" flame, like a lightning strike.
8   Zhang Longxi. "The Letter or the Spirit: The Song of Songs, Allegoresis, and the Book of Poetry". *Comparative Literature*, 39: 3 (Summer 1987), 194.
9   Origen composed a ten-book commentary on the Canticle of Canticles [the Song of Songs], conscious of the work of the great Rabbi Akibah and with the explicit intent of showing how the Song was of relevance to the Christian canon of the Bible. [...] Origen continues the exegetical tradition of Akibah, who approached the love song allegorically.

In the time that he was applying himself to the work of teaching in Alexandria, Origen did a thing which gave surpassing proof of an incomplete and immature mind, though it also served as a supreme example of self-restraint. He gave the saying that "there are eunuchs who make themselves eunuchs for the kingdom of heaven" too absolute and violent an understanding, and thinking at once to fulfill the Saviour's utterance, as well as to shut down any suspicion and slander by unbelievers due to the fact that he, a young man, did not discourse about divine things only with men, but also with women, he rushed to complete the Saviour's words by his deeds.¹⁰

Origen's introduction to his commentary on the Song makes his attitude toward the text clear. It is absolutely not to be read in its literal sense.¹¹ A reader who cannot or will not transcend the literal meaning of the Song's words should not read it at all:

> One who does not know how to listen to the language of love with pure and chaste ears will distort what he hears and turn from the inner man to the outer man, and shall be converted from the spirit to the flesh; nourishing concupiscence and carnality within himself, brought to carnal lust by reason of the Scriptures. On this account, then, I warn and counsel everyone who is not yet rid of the molestations of flesh and blood, nor has

---

John Anthony McGuckin. "The Scholarly Works of Origen". *The Westminster Handbook to Origen*, ed. by John Anthony McGuckin (Louisville: Westminster John Knox Press, 2004), 31.

10 Ἐν τούτῳ δὲ τῆς κατηχήσεως ἐπὶ τῆς Ἀλεξανδρείας τοὔργον ἐπιτελοῦντι τῷ Ὠριγένει πρᾶγμά τι πέπρακται φρενὸς μὲν ἀτελοῦς καὶ νεανικῆς, πίστεώς γε μὴν ὁμοῦ καὶ σωφροσύνης μέγιστον δεῖγμα περιέχον. τὸ γὰρ "εἰσὶν εὐνοῦχοι οἵτινες εὐνούχισαν ἑαυτοὺς διὰ τὴν βασιλείαν τῶν οὐρανῶν" ἁπλούστερον καὶ νεανικώτερον ἐκλαβών, ὁμοῦ μὲν σωτήριον φωνὴν ἀποπληροῦν οἰόμενος, ὁμοῦ δὲ καὶ διὰ τὸ νέον τὴν ἡλικίαν ὄντα μὴ ἀνδράσι μόνον, καὶ γυναιξὶ δὲ τὰ θεῖα προσομιλεῖν, ὡς ἂν πᾶσαν τὴν παρὰ τοῖς ἀπίστοις αἰσχρᾶς διαβολῆς ὑπόνοιαν ἀποκλείσειεν, τὴν σωτήριον φωνὴν ἔργοις ἐπιτελέσαι ὡρμήθη.

Eusebius. *Ecclesiastical History*, ed. by J. E. L. Oulton (Loeb Classical Library, Cambridge, MA: Harvard University Press, 1932), 28.

11 Richard A. Layton differs, arguing that the literal sense is important, but only in support of the allegorical: Origen "pairs [his] allegorical reading with a pioneering literal interpretation of the Canticle. He interprets the lovers' exchanges in the Song as a drama that unfolds in dialogue among four characters: the bride, the groom and their respective entourages. [...] [T]he letter constitutes an indispensable and persistent experience in Origen's reading of the Song" (Richard A. Layton. "Hearing Love's Language: The Letter of the Text in Origen's *Commentary on the Song of Songs*". In *The Reception and Interpretation of the Bible in Late Antiquity: Proceedings of the Montréal Colloquium in Honour of Charles Kannengiesser, 11–13 October 2006*, ed. by Lorenzo DiTommaso and Lucian Turcescu [Leiden: Brill, 2008], 288).

withdrawn from the inclinations of the physical, to regulate themselves by entirely abstaining from the reading of this book.[12]

Origen probably did not use a knife to be "rid of the molestations of flesh and blood" merely in order that he might read the Song in peace. But he is at great pains to explain every sensual detail of the poem in terms of the relationship between Christ (the Bridegroom) and the Church (the Bride). Origen's comments on the famous opening of the Song illustrate his method. First, the poetry:

יִשָּׁקֵ֙נִי֙ מִנְּשִׁיק֣וֹת פִּ֔יהוּ כִּֽי־טוֹבִ֥ים דֹּדֶ֖יךָ מִיָּֽיִן׃[13]

Let him kiss me with the kisses of his mouth: for your lovemaking is better than wine.[14]

And now, Origen's ingenious attempt to explain what those "kisses" really mean:

> For this reason I beg you, Father of my spouse, pouring out this prayer that you will have pity for the sake of my love for him, so that not only will the angels and the prophets speak to me through his ministers, but that he will come, and "let him kiss me with the kisses of his mouth" by his own self, that is, to pour his words into my mouth with his breath, that I might hear him speak, and see him teach. For these are the kisses of Christ, who offered them to the Church when at his coming, he made himself present in the flesh, and spoke the words of faith and love and peace.[15]

---

12   Audire enim pure et castis auribus amoris nomina nesciens, ab interiore homine ad exteriorem et carnalem virum omnem deflectet auditum, et a spiritu convertetur ad carnem nutrietque in semet ipso concupiscentias carnales, et occasione divinae scripturae commoveri et incitari videbitur ad libendem carnis. Ob hoc ergo moneo, et consilium do omni qui nondum carnis et sanguinis molestiis caret, neque ab affectu materialis abscedit, ut a lectione libelli huius eorumque quae in eum dicentur penitus temperet.

       Origen. *Origene: Commentaire sur le Cantique des Cantiques. Vol. 1. Texte de la Version Latine de Rufin*, ed. by Luc Bresard, Henri Crouzel, and Marcel Borret (Paris: Éditions du Cerf, 1991), 84.

13   Song of Songs (Song of Solomon) 1:2.

14   Ariel and Chana Bloch point out that the Hebrew דֹּדֶיךָ (*dodeyka*) though often translated as "your love", should be more accurately rendered as "your lovemaking" in order to capture the sense of physical, sexual love that is being referred to in this verse, and in similar uses of the term in Prov. 7:18, Ezek. 16:8 and 23:17, as well as elsewhere in the Song of Songs 1:4, 4:10, 5:1, and 7:13 (*The Song of Songs: A New Translation and Commentary* [New York: Random House, 1995], 137).

15   Propter hoc ad te Patrem sponsi mei precem fundo et obsecro, ut tandem miseratus amorem meum mittas eum, ut iam non mihi per ministros suos angelos dumtaxat et prophetas loquatur,

The lengths to which Origen goes here to explain away the "kisses" of a lover are revealing. There was no need to wait for Ricoeur's hermeneutics of suspicion—the fundamentals of that tradition are here in Origen's work.

For Ann Astell, Origen's entire method is a flight from the literal toward the mystical, an attempt to leave behind the carnal in favor of a union with the Spirit:

> Origen's method of exegesis [...] moves away from the *Canticum*'s literal, carnal meaning to its *sensus interioris*, [while] the bridal soul, renouncing what is earthly, reaches out for the invisible and eternal [...] An almost violent departure from the body itself and from literal meaning energizes the soul's ascent.[16]

Gerson Cohen suggests something similar about Rabbinical interpretations of the Song, grounding his case in the marriage imagery used to describe the human-divine relationship in the Hebrew scriptures. Putting Israelite religion in the context of the religions of surrounding cultures, Cohen argues "the Hebrew God alone was spoken of as the lover and husband of his people, and only the house of Israel spoke of itself as the bride of the Almighty".[17] Perhaps the most famous example of this marital motif, however, is the negative example found in Hosea, where Israel is likened to a "wife of whoredom":

לֵךְ קַח־לְךָ אֵשֶׁת זְנוּנִים וְיַלְדֵי זְנוּנִים כִּי־זָנֹה תִזְנֶה הָאָרֶץ מֵאַחֲרֵי יְהוָה:[18]

> Go take to yourself a wife of whoredom and children of whoredom, for the land has committed great whoredom by departing from Yahweh.

Though a jealous God promises to take Israel back,

וְאֵרַשְׂתִּיךְ לִי לְעוֹלָם וְאֵרַשְׂתִּיךְ לִי בְּצֶדֶק וּבְמִשְׁפָּט וּבְחֶסֶד וּבְרַחֲמִים:
וְאֵרַשְׂתִּיךְ לִי בֶּאֱמוּנָה וְיָדַעַתְּ אֶת־יְהוָה:[19]

---

sed ipse per semet ipsum veniat et osculetur me ab osculis oris sui, verba scilicet in os meum sui oris infundat, ipsum audiam loquentem, ipsum videam docentem. Haec enim sunt Christi oscula quae porrexit ecclesiae, cum in adventu suo ipse praesens in carne positus locutus est ei verba fidei et caritatis et pacis.

Origen, 180.

16 Ann W. Astell. *The Song of Songs in the Middle Ages* (Ithaca: Cornell University Press, 1990), 3.
17 Cohen, 6.
18 Hosea 1:2.
19 Ibid., 2:19–20.

And I will wed you to me forever, in righteousness and justice, in loving kindness and compassion. I will wed you to me faithfully, and you shall know Yahweh.

such reconciliation will come only after the "husband" humiliates the "wife":

לָכֵן אָשׁוּב וְלָקַחְתִּי דְגָנִי בְּעִתּוֹ וְתִירוֹשִׁי בְּמוֹעֲדוֹ וְהִצַּלְתִּי צַמְרִי וּפִשְׁתִּי לְכַסּוֹת אֶת־ עֶרְוָתָהּ׃
וְעַתָּה אֲגַלֶּה אֶת־ נַבְלֻתָהּ לְעֵינֵי מְאַהֲבֶיהָ וְאִישׁ לֹא־ יַצִּילֶנָּה מִיָּדִי׃[20]

So I will return and take back my grain in its season, and my wine in its season, and I will strip away my wool and flax, which clothed her nakedness. And then I will uncover her shamelessness in her lovers' eyes, and none shall deliver her from my hand.

More disturbing than the angry-God-as-husband motif in Hosea, however, is the violently-abusive-God-as-husband of Ezekiel 16. Here, readers encounter "a fairy tale marriage that has gone horribly awry".[21] Ezekiel portrays God as a man who finds an infant girl (Israel) who has been exposed, thrown out upon the hills or fields to be killed and eaten by predators, one of the ancient world's forms of birth control (Athenians of the fifth century BCE exposed "10 percent or more of their newborn girls"[22]). Scholars often claim the Jews refused to engage in such practices. For example, Margaret King contends that "Jews and Christians [...] steadily opposed the linked practices of infanticide, exposure, and abortion by which the Greeks and Romans controlled population".[23] But despite such contentions, the picture in Ezekiel is plain:

וְאָמַרְתָּ כֹּה־ אָמַר אֲדֹנָי יְהוִה לִירוּשָׁלִַם מְכֹרֹתַיִךְ וּמֹלְדֹתַיִךְ מֵאֶרֶץ הַכְּנַעֲנִי אָבִיךְ הָאֱמֹרִי וְאִמֵּךְ חִתִּית׃
וּמוֹלְדוֹתַיִךְ בְּיוֹם הוּלֶּדֶת אֹתָךְ לֹא־ כָרַּת שָׁרֵּךְ וּבְמַיִם לֹא־ רֻחַצְתְּ לְמִשְׁעִי וְהָמְלֵחַ לֹא הֻמְלַחַתְּ וְהָחְתֵּל
לֹא חֻתָּלְתְּ׃ לֹא־ חָסָה עָלַיִךְ עַיִן לַעֲשׂוֹת לָךְ אַחַת מֵאֵלֶּה לְחֻמְלָה עָלָיִךְ וַתֻּשְׁלְכִי אֶל־ פְּנֵי הַשָּׂדֶה בְּגֹעַל
נַפְשֵׁךְ בְּיוֹם הֻלֶּדֶת אֹתָךְ׃[24]

---

20 Ibid., 2:9–10.
21 Nancy R. Bowen. "A Fairy Tale Wedding?" In *A God So Near: Essays on Old Testament Theology in Honor of Patrick D. Miller*, ed. by Patrick D. Miller, Brent A. Strawn, and Nancy R. Bowen (Winona Lake, IN: Eisenbrauns, 2003), 65.
22 Mark Golden. "Demography and the Exposure of Girls at Athens". *Phoenix*, 35: 4 (Winter 1981), 321.
23 Margaret L. King. "Children in Judaism and Christianity". In *The Routledge History of Childhood in the Western World*, ed. by Paula S. Fass, 39–60 (New York: Routledge, 2013), 47.
24 Ezekiel 16:3–5.

Thus says the Lord Yahweh to Jerusalem: your origin and your birth is of the land of Canaan; your father was an Amorite, and your mother a Hittite. At your birth, on the very day you were born, your navel was not cut, nor were you washed in cleansing water, massaged with salt, or wrapped in swaddling bands. No eye had pity on you to do any of these things for you, but you were cast into an open field, for you were hated on the day you were born.

Though it is blamed on the Amorites and Hittites, exposure clearly was not unknown in Israel, as Israel is described here as a baby girl left outside to die: "Ezekiel's allegory draws particular attention to the [...] cruel but often regrettably practised offense of leaving an infant girl to die at birth, because families preferred boys".[25] The man who rescues her describes seeing this baby girl "מִתְבּוֹסֶסֶת בְּדָמָיִךְ" — "polluted in [her] blood" before he says to her[26] "חֲיִי" — "Live!" and takes her home to raise her to womanhood. After raising her as his own daughter, he takes a fancy to her:

עֲדָיִים שָׁדַיִם נָכֹנוּ וּשְׂעָרֵךְ צִמֵּחַ וְאַתְּ עֵרֹם וְעֶרְיָה:[27]

For jewels her breasts were well-fashioned, and her hair grown, and [she] was naked and bare.

The note of father-daughter incest is disturbing enough, but what follows makes that pale into insignificance:

וָאֶעֱבֹר עָלַיִךְ וָאֶרְאֵךְ וְהִנֵּה עִתֵּךְ עֵת דֹּדִים וָאֶפְרֹשׂ כְּנָפִי עָלַיִךְ וָאֲכַסֶּה עֶרְוָתֵךְ וָאֶשָּׁבַע לָךְ וָאָבוֹא בִבְרִית אֹתָךְ נְאֻם אֲדֹנָי יְהוִה וַתִּהְיִי לִי: וָאֶרְחָצֵךְ בַּמַּיִם וָאֶשְׁטֹף דָּמַיִךְ מֵעָלָיִךְ וָאֲסֻכֵךְ בַּשָּׁמֶן: וָאַלְבִּישֵׁךְ רִקְמָה וָאֶנְעֲלֵךְ תָּחַשׁ וָאֶחְבְּשֵׁךְ בַּשֵּׁשׁ וַאֲכַסֵּךְ מֶשִׁי: וָאֶעְדֵּךְ עֶדִי וָאֶתְּנָה צְמִידִים עַל־יָדַיִךְ וְרָבִיד עַל־גְּרוֹנֵךְ: וָאֶתֵּן נֶזֶם עַל־אַפֵּךְ וַעֲגִילִים עַל־אָזְנָיִךְ וַעֲטֶרֶת תִּפְאֶרֶת בְּרֹאשֵׁךְ:[28]

When I passed by you and looked at you, behold, your season was the time for love. I spread my garment over you, covering your nakedness. I made an oath to you, and entered a covenant with you, declared the Lord Yahweh, and you belonged to me. Then I washed you with water, thoroughly washing your blood away, and anointed you with oil. I covered you in embroidered garments, and gave you leather sandals. I bound you in fine linens and covered you in silks.

---

25   Ronald E. Clements. *Ezekiel* (Louisville: Westminster John Knox Press, 1996), 74.
26   Ezekiel 16:6.
27   *Ibid.*, 16:7.
28   *Ibid.*, 16:8–12.

I decked you in jewelry, putting bracelets on your wrists, a necklace around your neck, a ring in your nose, earrings in your ears, and a glorious crown on your head.

Having taken the child he raised as a daughter and married her (converting incestuous thoughts into deeds), this much older man (God) explodes in rage over the infidelities of his young daughter-wife:

וַתִּבְטְחִי בְיָפְיֵךְ וַתִּזְנִי עַל־ שְׁמֵךְ וַתִּשְׁפְּכִי אֶת־ תַּזְנוּתַיִךְ עַל־ כָּל־ עוֹבֵר
[…]
יַעַן הִשָּׁפֵךְ נְחֻשְׁתֵּךְ וַתִּגָּלֶה עֶרְוָתֵךְ בְּתַזְנוּתַיִךְ עַל־ מְאַהֲבָיִךְ וְעַל־ כָּל־ גִּלּוּלֵי תוֹעֲבוֹתַיִךְ וְכִדְמֵי בָנַיִךְ אֲשֶׁר נָתַתְּ לָהֶם: לָכֵן הִנְנִי מְקַבֵּץ אֶת־ כָּל־
[…]
וְנָתַתִּי אוֹתָךְ בְּיָדָם וְהָרְסוּ גַבֵּךְ וְנִתְּצוּ רָמֹתַיִךְ וְהִפְשִׁיטוּ אוֹתָךְ בְּגָדַיִךְ וְלָקְחוּ כְּלֵי תִפְאַרְתֵּךְ וְהִנִּיחוּךְ עֵירֹם וְעֶרְיָה: וְהֶעֱלוּ עָלַיִךְ קָהָל וְרָגְמוּ אוֹתָךְ בָּאָבֶן וּבִתְּקוּךְ בְּחַרְבוֹתָם:[29]

But you trusted in your beauty, and played the whore because of your fame, and lavished your whorings on any passer-by. […] Because your filth was poured out and your nakedness uncovered as you whored with your lovers, and the abominations of your idols, and the blood of your children that you poured out to them, behold, I will bring together all your lovers, [and] I will give you into their hands, and they will throw down your defenses and break down your high places; they will strip you of your clothes and take your jewels and leave you naked and bare. They will bring a great multitude against you, and they will stone you with stones and thrust you through with their swords.

The young girl he had once saved from death, he now has beaten, stoned, and cut to pieces. Having saved her, claimed her, but been unable to keep her, God spends his truly impotent rage in the fashion of a violent cuckold: he turns her over to those men who will brutalize her for him, and only then will his rage be abated:

וַהֲנִחֹתִי חֲמָתִי בָּךְ וְסָרָה קִנְאָתִי מִמֵּךְ וְשָׁקַטְתִּי וְלֹא אֶכְעַס עוֹד:[30]

So toward you I will rest my fury, and abolish my jealousy, and I will be quiet and calm, and I will not be angry any more.

---

29 Ibid., 16:15, 36–37, 39–40.
30 Ibid., 16:42.

After her near-fatal beating, God's daughter-wife will return to him in shame—he will accept her back merely so that he may further humiliate her:

לְמַעַן תִּזְכְּרִי וָבֹשְׁתְּ וְלֹא יִהְיֶה־לָּךְ עוֹד פִּתְחוֹן פֶּה מִפְּנֵי כְּלִמָּתֵךְ בְּכַפְּרִי־לָךְ לְכָל־אֲשֶׁר עָשִׂית׃[31]

> So that you will remember and be ashamed, and never let it come to pass that you open your mouth because of your humiliation, when I am appeased concerning all that you have done.

It is tempting to think that the infant girl of so many years before might have been better off if only God had passed her by in that open field, leaving her to the mercy of beasts less systematically savage than himself. Hardly a story of love, this "fairy tale marriage gone horribly awry" is more akin to a tale of domestic abuse, as "the profile of YHWH in Ezekiel 16 matches that of real-life batterers in significant ways".[32]

There is no love in these allegorical accounts of what Cohen ominously calls "the inseverable *marital union* between God and Israel",[33] unless by "love" we mean ownership and domination, or vengeance and impotent wrath that uses others to inflict its bloody will, or the desire to silence and shame a daughter-bride into compliant and docile submission. This is the powerful impression given by the multiple instances to be found in the Biblical prophets of the marriage allegory. Whether in Hosea, or Ezekiel 16 and 23, or in Jeremiah 3 and 13, the portrait of the human-divine marriage is an overwhelmingly negative one, which the relative lightness of Isaiah 54 cannot atone for:

כִּי־כְאִשָּׁה עֲזוּבָה וַעֲצוּבַת רוּחַ קְרָאָךְ יְהוָה וְאֵשֶׁת נְעוּרִים כִּי תִמָּאֵס אָמַר אֱלֹהָיִךְ׃
בְּרֶגַע קָטֹן עֲזַבְתִּיךְ וּבְרַחֲמִים גְּדֹלִים אֲקַבְּצֵךְ׃
בְּשֶׁצֶף קֶצֶף הִסְתַּרְתִּי פָנַי רֶגַע מִמֵּךְ וּבְחֶסֶד עוֹלָם רִחַמְתִּיךְ אָמַר גֹּאֲלֵךְ יְהוָה׃ ס[34]

> For as a forsaken wife Yahweh has called you, pained in spirit like the wife of a man's youth when she is refused, said your God. For the briefest instant I left you, but with great mercy I will gather you. In an outburst of wrath, for a moment I hid my face from you, but with everlasting loving kindness I will have mercy on you, says Yahweh, your redeemer.

---

31 Ibid., 16:63.
32 Linda Day. "Rhetoric and Domestic Violence in Ezekiel 16". *Biblical Interpretation*, 8: 3 (July 2000), 218, https://doi.org/10.1163/156851500750096327
33 Cohen, 12.
34 Isaiah 54:6–8.

Far from being comforting, the latter passage sounds like the insincere apology uttered by a husband who has just beaten his wife—again.

The relationship described in the Song is radically different—there is no sense of punishment, and no dominant theme of domestic violence, rage and bloody revenge. What a reader encounters in this ancient love poem is something missing elsewhere in the Bible: "whereas the other books of the Bible do indeed proclaim the bond of love between Israel and the Lord, only the Song of Songs is a *dialogue* of love",[35] though Cohen insists that the dialogue is between "man and God".[36] However this very insistence, grounded as it is in the tradition of the Christian exegesis of Origen and the Rabbinic exegesis of Akiba (c. 50–137 CE), is just one more instance of the ongoing attempts to tame the Song, and force it to say what its guardians demand it should say. Such commentary on love poetry tries to "eliminate any implication of erotic love and to attach to poetry a significance that demonstrates [...] ethical and political propriety".[37] As Cohen explains, "if love could not be ignored, it could be *channeled*, *reformulated*, and *controlled*, and this is precisely what the rabbinic [and Christian] allegory of the Song of Songs attempted to achieve".[38] This attempt to channel, reformulate, and control is exactly what we will see love being subjected to in both poetry and criticism as we move through time.

One of the most evocative portions of the Song is a wonderfully explicit scene played out between the young man and woman of the poem. The young man comes to her door, calling for her in desire, but when she answers, he has slipped away:

פִּתְחִי־ לִי אֲחֹתִי רַעְיָתִי יוֹנָתִי תַמָּתִי שֶׁרֹאשִׁי נִמְלָא־ טָל קְוֻצּוֹתַי רְסִיסֵי לָיְלָה׃
פָּשַׁטְתִּי אֶת־ כֻּתָּנְתִּי אֵיכָכָה אֶלְבָּשֶׁנָּה רָחַצְתִּי אֶת־ רַגְלַי אֵיכָכָה אֲטַנְּפֵם׃
דּוֹדִי שָׁלַח יָדוֹ מִן־ הַחֹר וּמֵעַי הָמוּ עָלָיו׃
קַמְתִּי אֲנִי לִפְתֹּחַ לְדוֹדִי וְיָדַי נָטְפוּ־ מוֹר וְאֶצְבְּעֹתַי מוֹר עֹבֵר עַל כַּפּוֹת הַמַּנְעוּל׃
פָּתַחְתִּי אֲנִי לְדוֹדִי וְדוֹדִי חָמַק עָבָר[39]

---

35 Whereas in Hosea and Ezekiel there is no dialogue—the railed-upon woman gets no voice.
36 Cohen, 12.
37 Longxi, 207.
38 Cohen, 14. Emphasis added.
39 Song of Songs 5:2–6.

> Open to me, my sister, my darling, my dove, my perfect one: for my head is drenched with dew, my hair with midnight's drops. I have stripped off my garments; how shall I put them back on? I have washed my feet; how shall I soil them? My lover put in his hand by the hole, and my womb moved for him. I rose up to open to my lover; and my hands dripped with myrrh, and my fingers with sweet smelling myrrh, with my hands upon the bolt of the lock. I opened to my lover; but my lover had withdrawn, and he was gone.

We do not have commentary by Origen for this passage (of his ten original volumes, only four remain), so let's look at something from seemingly the opposite end of the exegetical spectrum, a book called *Song of Solomon for Teenagers*:

> Imagine the King of Kings. He is not just a great man. He is God! Imagine He loved you when you were unlovable. He cleaned you up and made you somebody. He wants to love you and protect you. He wants to enjoy you. He wants you to love and enjoy Him. How dare you say no. Don't you realize that without Him you can do nothing. [...] How dare you reject One who is altogether lovely. The problem we have is that He is the one that picks the time of visitation.[40]

Though the lack of question marks can be disconcerting, and the remarks about enjoying and being enjoyed are borderline disturbing, the allegorical method of interpreting the Song is essentially the same in this simple twenty-first-century text as it is in Origen's complex third-century writings. The young man in the poem is erased as a human being and turned into a symbol for God, while the young woman is denied her sexuality and made to serve as a metaphor for those who do not turn quickly enough to Him. The story of passion, sex, longing, and love is completely dismissed in favor of a meaning which is forced onto the text like the attentions of an unwanted suitor, and this forcing has a long history: "[t]he fundamental way to justify the canonicity of the Song of Songs, among both Jews and Christians, has always been to read the text as an allegory, a piece of writing which does not mean what it literally says".[41]

---

40 Chris Ray. *Song of Solomon for Teenagers: And Anyone Else Who Wonders Why They Are Here* (Bloomington: AuthorHouse, 2010), 29.
41 Longxi, 195.

But when the allegory is stripped away and the commentary is removed, what happens in this exquisite passage? A young man calls late at night at a girl's door: "open to me", he says, "for my head is drenched with dew, my hair with midnight's drops". The young man is expressing sexual desire for his "darling", his "perfect one". She hesitates: "I have washed my feet; how shall I soil them?" ("Feet" are often used in the Bible as a euphemism for more intimate parts of the body—the story of Ruth and Boaz is an excellent example). But he persists, putting "his hand by the hole", as her "womb moved for him". The Hebrew word here is מֵעַי (*meeh* or *me-yeh*), which when used about a woman, can generally be translated as "womb" just as it is at Ruth 1:11, where Naomi bemoans her age and infertility:

וַתֹּאמֶר נָעֳמִי שֹׁבְנָה בְנֹתַי לָמָּה תֵלַכְנָה עִמִּי הַעוֹד־לִי בָנִים בְּמֵעַי וְהָיוּ לָכֶם לַאֲנָשִׁים׃

Return, my daughters, why will you go with me? Are there yet sons in my womb that may become your husbands?

With her womb stirring, the young woman is suddenly wet with myrrh, her hands and her fingers dripping with the scented, sensual oil. As she slips her oiled fingers around "the bolt of the lock", she opens to him, and the consummation is near. Here, the Hebrew word is מַנְעוּל (*manul*), which, translated as "bolt", is like the deadbolt that is inserted between the door and the doorjamb, making the phallic reference of the verse obvious. Just as the young woman fondles the *manul* with her wet fingers, at that precise moment, the young man had "withdrawn, and he was gone", leaving the young woman open, wet with oil, and absolutely frustrated. In the terms of the Porter from *Macbeth*, the young man (and his *manul*) can stand to, or not stand to,[42] and in this case, he and it have done the latter.

Near the end of the Song, it appears that the relationship between the young man and young woman is illicit, for she wishes he could be as her brother, so that when they met in public there would be no suspicion:

מִי יִתֶּנְךָ כְּאָח לִי יוֹנֵק שְׁדֵי אִמִּי אֶמְצָאֲךָ בַחוּץ אֶשָּׁקְךָ גַּם לֹא־יָבוּזוּ לִי׃

---

42 *Macbeth* 2.3.32. All quotations from the plays are from *William Shakespeare: The Complete Works*, ed. by Stephen Orgel and A. R. Braunmuller (New York: Pelican, 2002).

אֶנְהָגֲךָ אֲבִיאֲךָ אֶל־ בֵּית אִמִּי תְּלַמְּדֵנִי אַשְׁקְךָ מִיַּיִן הָרֶקַח מֵעֲסִיס רִמֹּנִי׃
שְׂמֹאלוֹ תַּחַת רֹאשִׁי וִימִינוֹ תְּחַבְּקֵנִי׃[43]

> O that you were as my brother, who sucked the breasts of my mother! When I should meet you outside, I would kiss you, yes, and no one would despise me. I would lead you, and bring you to my mother's house, and she would teach me; I would give you a drink of the spiced wine of the juice of my pomegranate. Your left hand would be under my head, and your right hand would embrace me.

None of this makes any sense if seen through the allegorical lens of Origen. The young woman is wishing she could invite the young man home to have sex with her—with his left hand under her head, and his right hand embracing her, she is imagining them either making love or dancing the tango (arguably the same thing), and the image of drinking the spiced wine of the juice of her pomegranate could not be more obvious. It echoes an earlier scene which is clearly a reference to a sexual assignation:

אֲנִי לְדוֹדִי וְעָלַי תְּשׁוּקָתוֹ׃ ס
לְכָה דוֹדִי נֵצֵא הַשָּׂדֶה נָלִינָה בַּכְּפָרִים׃
נַשְׁכִּימָה לַכְּרָמִים נִרְאֶה אִם פָּרְחָה הַגֶּפֶן פִּתַּח הַסְּמָדַר הֵנֵצוּ הָרִמּוֹנִים שָׁם אֶתֵּן אֶת־ דֹּדַי לָךְ׃[44]

> I am my lover's, and his desire is for me. Come, my love, let us go into the field; let us spend the night in the village. Come, let us rise early and go to the vineyards; let us see whether the vines flourish, the tender grapes appear, and the pomegranates bud and blossom. There I will give my love to you.

If the "vines flourish" and the "pomegranates bud and blossom", then perhaps this love scene will work out better than the last one.

So how did we get to the point where a poem so obviously sexual as the Song of Songs is commonly tamed into submission as a religious allegory, where even teenagers are taught to read a poem that openly features youthful eroticism and unceasing sexual innuendo as if it were written by virgins, for virgins, and about virgins? For centuries after its composition—perhaps as long as a millennium, if the most generous estimates are correct—the Song appears to have been read and sung in the spirit of love and desire, for "there is no record of allegorization in

---

43 Song of Songs 8:1–3.
44 *Ibid.*, 7:11–13.

the earliest period".[45] The allegorical reading of the Song began under a Roman imperial rule that since the days of Caesar Augustus had been slowly tightening its grip on the sexual behaviors of its subjects,[46] developing at approximately the same time among the Jews and the Christians:

> At the council of Jamnia at the end of the first century, [...] Rabbi Judah argued that the Song of Songs defiled the hands, i.e., was taboo or sacred, hence canonical, while Ecclesiastes did not. Rabbi Jose then expressed his doubt about the propriety of including the Song in the canon, but Rabbi Aquiba made a powerful plea [and he] angrily denounced those who treated this holy Song as an ordinary song (*zemîr*) and chanted it in "Banquet Houses".[47]

Rabbi Akiba argued for the inclusion of the Song in the Hebrew canon by claiming "all the world is not as worthy as the day on which the Song of Songs was given to Israel, for all the writings are holy, but the Song of Songs is the holy of holies".[48] Arguing against other Rabbis who thought, based on a literal interpretation, that the text was obscene, Akiba seems to have been the earliest known advocate for an allegorical approach to the Song.

In the centuries that follow, allegory becomes orthodoxy. The *Babylonian Talmud* makes repeated allegorical references to the Song. In the Gemara (a section completed c. 500 CE) of the *Tractate Sanhedrin*, verses from the Song are interpreted as signifying the Sanhedrin, the judicial body appointed in each Israelite city:

---

45 Weston Fields. "Early and Medieval Interpretation of the Song of Songs", *Grace Theological Journal*, 1: 2 (Fall, 1980), 222, https://biblicalstudies.org.uk/pdf/gtj/01-2_221.pdf

46 The urge to allegorize the Song may well have developed in reaction to a changing imperial atmosphere, in light of a series of laws, penalties, and taxation measures designed to control the whos, whats, whys, and hows of marriage and sexuality (laws the poet Ovid seems to have been punished for violating).

47 Longxi, 194.

48 Benjamin Edidin Scolnic. "Why Do We Sing the Song of Songs on Passover?" *Conservative Judaism*, 48: 4 (1996), 55, https://www.rabbinicalassembly.org/sites/default/files/public/jewish-law/holidays/pesah/why-do-we-sing-the-song-of-songs-on-passover.pdf

שררך אגן הסהר אל יחסר המזג וגו' שררך-זו סנהדרי [...] בטנך ערימת חטים מה ערימת חטים
הכל נהנין ממנה אף סנהדרין הכל נהנין מטעמיהן⁴⁹

> *Your navel is like a round goblet which lacks no wine*: that navel—that is the Sanhedrin. [...] *Your belly is like a heap of wheat* [Song of Songs 7:2]: even as we profit from wheat, so also we profit from the Sanhedrin's reasonings.

Those reading the Song as a poem about love and desire are condemned as bringing evil to the world, and unless the Rabbis are condemning something wholly imaginary, this is evidence that there were still people who approached the Song in exactly this way:

הקורא פסוק של שיר השירים ועושה אותו כמין זמר והקורא פסוק בבית משתאות בלא זמנו מביא רעה לעולם מפני שהתורה חוגרת שק ועומדת לפני הקב״ה ואומרת לפניו רבונו של עולם עשאוני בניך ככנור שמנגנין בו לצים⁵⁰

> A reader of a verse from the Song of Songs who sings it at the wrong time, turning it into a festival song, brings evil into the world. The Torah, dressed in sackcloth, stands before the Holy One and cries out, "Lord of the Universe! Your children treat me as a lyre played by scornful fools".

For centuries, the perspectives of Akiba, Origen, and the Talmud remain the dominant mode of reading and understanding the Song. But a change comes at the end of the eleventh century, in France, at the same time the first of the troubadour poems are appearing in the world. Rabbi Solomon the Izakhite, known to history as Rashi, champions the *Peshat* method of Scriptural interpretation, "the interpretation of the text according to its 'plain meaning'".[51] Rashi has little use for the Talmudic idea that the Song should not be sung on festival days; rather than bringing evil into the world, he regards such singing as bringing good:

---

49 *Tractate Sanhedrin*. In *Hebrew English Edition of the Babylonian Talmud*, ed. by Rabbi Isidore Epstein (London: Socino Press, 1969), 37a.
50 *Ibid.*, 101a.
51 Sara Japhet. "Rashi's Commentary on the Song of Songs: The Revolution of the Peshat and its Aftermath". In J. Männchen and T. Reiprich, eds. *Mein Haus wird ein Bethaus für alle Völker genannt werden. Festschrift für Thomas Wille sum 75. Gerburgstag* (Neukirchen: Neukirchener Verlag, 2007), 202.

אבל אם אומרו בזמנו על המשתה, כגון שהוא יום טוב, ונוטל כוס בידו ואומר עליו
דברי הגדה ופסוקים מעניינו של יום—מביא טובה לעולם⁵²

> But I say the time for the feast is a good day, and for a man to take a glass in his hand and tell others the words of ancient legends and the verses relevant to the day—this always brings good to the world.

Rashi also gets right to the "plain meaning"[53] of the famous "kisses" of the Song, arguing that they are literal kisses being desired by an actual woman whose husband has become neglectful. The resulting view of the text is at once less strained (having no need to compare a woman's body to an all-male judiciary), more responsive to textual detail, and entirely more human than the interpretations of Akiba, Origen, and the innumerable commentators who follow them:

זה השיר אומרת בפיה בגלותה ובאלמנותה מי יתן וישקני המלך שלמה מנשיקות פיהו
כמו מאז לפי שיש מקומות שנושקין על גב היד ועל הכתף אך אני מתאוה ושוקקת
להיותו נוהג עמי כמנהג הראשון כחתן אל כלה פה אל פה⁵⁴

---

52 Rashi's commentary is quoted here from the *Tractate Sanhedrin* (101a), Part VII, Vol. 21. In *The Talmud: The Steinsaltz Edition*, ed. by Rabbi Adin Steinsaltz (New York: Random House, 1999), 52–53. As is traditional, Steinsaltz uses the semicursive Rashi script, rather than the more familiar square or block Hebrew script, to reproduce Rashi's commentary.

53 Edward L. Greenstein suggests that the "plain" meaning is often actually much more complex than the allegorical meaning. In arguing for historical context as a crucial element of Rashi's *peshat* method of reading, Greenstein makes Rashi sound like an early ancestor of today's historicists:

> Most secondary literature on Jewish exegesis defines *peshat* as the "simple", "plain", or "literal" approach, but these terms are misleading. The historical meaning of the biblical text may actually be complex and figurative, neither simple nor straightforward. [...] The *peshat* method, therefore, should perhaps be glossed in English as the direct, *contextual* mode of exegesis, not "plain" or "literal", which it often is not. The *derash* method is the acontextual approach because it disregards the constrictions of the historical, literary and linguistic condition in which the text first came to us.

Edward L. Greenstein. "Medieval Bible Commentaries". In *Back to the Sources: Reading the Classic Jewish Texts*, ed. by Barry W. Holtz (New York: Simon & Schuster, 2006), 219, 220.

54 *Mikraot Gedolot: Torah with Forty-Two Commentaries* (מקראות גדולות: חמישה חמישי תורה עם שניים וארבעים פרושים), Vol. 3 (The Widow and Brothers Ram: Truskavets/Glukhov, Ukraine, 1907), 418, https://books.google.com/books?id=fEUpAAAAYAAJ. Also in *Mikraot Gedolot* (מקראות גדולות), Vol. 4, ed. by Yaakov ben Hayyim. Printed by Daniel Bomberg (Venice, 1524), 130r, https://archive.org/stream/The_Second_Rabbinic_Bible_Vol_4/4#page/n261. Further discussed in Yehoshafat Nevo. *French Biblical Interpretation: Studies in the Interpretive Methods of the Bible Commentators in Northern France in the Middle Ages* (פרשנות המקרא הצפרתית עיונים בדרכי פרשנותם של מפרשי המקרא בצפון צרפת בימי הביניים) (Reḥovot: Moreshet Ya'akov, 2004), 274.

> She sings this song with her mouth, in exile and widowhood: "Would that King Solomon would kiss me, like he used to, with the kisses of his mouth, since in some places they kiss the back of the hand or the shoulder, but I long for the familiarity with which he first treated me, like a bridegroom with his bride, kissing mouth to mouth".

Rashi may be the first Rabbinical interpreter to apply this "plain meaning" method to the Song,[55] but he would not be the last. Two anonymous commentators of the twelfth century in France take the *Peshat* methodology to its logical conclusion, arguing that the Song was merely a song, was not sacred, and was included in the canon because it was popular. The first commentator, finally published for the first time in 1866,[56] makes the point directly:

> the interpretation of "the Song of Songs" is: This is one of the songs composed by Solomon, who wrote many songs, as it is said: "And his songs numbered one thousand and five" (1 Kgs 5:12). Why was this one written [written down and included in the canon] of all the others? It was written because it was loved by the people.[57]

The second twelfth-century commentator, first published in 1896, "explained the Song of Songs as a secular love song, did not present it as a parable, did not regard it as a prophecy, and did not include an allegorical interpretation".[58]

At the time the troubadours are working, it appears that the love poetry of the Song is being read and explained, by at least a few, as love poetry about human beings desiring each other, regardless of the laws of God or man. As Japhet explains, "this kind of commentary on the Song of Songs—an exclusive adherence to the plain meaning and total avoidance of any kind of allegory—is a unique phenomenon, with no parallel in the long history of Jewish exegesis of the Song of Songs until the modern period".[59] Sadly, this unique phenomenon does not last. In the thirteenth century, at about the same time the troubadour movement is being crushed by the Church, and the notably allegorical

---

55 Japhet, 202.
56 *Ibid.*, 211.
57 *Ibid.*, 212.
58 *Ibid.*, 214.
59 *Ibid.*, 215.

"sweet new style" (*dolce stil novo*) adopted by Dante is taking over, the *Peshat* school dies out, and the allegorical reading of the Song returns.

In some quarters, it never disappeared in the first place. For Richard of St. Victor, the twelfth-century mystical theologian, even the most erotic portions of the *Song* are to be interpreted in terms of the visitation of Grace, or "visitationem gratiae":

> My beloved put in his hand through the hole of the mind, and my belly is swollen to the touch thereof; and this visitation of grace, is sent through the hole by the hands that, as through a chink, infuse grace into the souls of the faithful.[60]

This is also evident in the work of Giles of Rome (Egidio Colonna), the thirteenth-and fourteenth-century cleric and Archbishop of Bourges, who argues that "the principal intention of [the Song] is to express the mutual desire between the bridegroom and bride, or between Christ and the Church".[61] Giles—who served in the same Provençal region whose theological, sexual, and poetical heresies the Church spent decades subduing during the Crusades and the Inquisition—insists that the language of opening to the lover is to be understood in terms of preaching:

> My bridegroom attracted me so much, that being unwilling or unable to resist him, I got up from contemplation to open to my beloved through preaching, and not only through preaching in word, but also through preaching in example. Therefore it continues: my hands, that is, my works, dripped with myrrh, that is, with the mortification of the flesh.[62]

---

60 "Dilectus meus misit manum suam per foramen, et venter meus intumuit ad tactum ejus, Quam visitationem gratiae, missionem manus per foramen vocat. Quasi enim per rimam gratiam infundit, cum non total animam perfundit" (Richard of St. Victor. *Exposition in Cantica Canticorum*. In *Patrologiae Cursus Completus: Series Latina*, Vol. 196, ed. by Jacques-Paul Migne [Paris, 1855], col. 503c, https://archive.org/stream/patrologiaecurs104unkngoog#page/n271).

61 "Intentio principalis huius opis est exprimere mutua desideria inter sponsum & sponsam, sive inter christum & ecclesiam" (Giles of Rome. *Librum Solomonis qui Cantica Canticorum Inscribitur Commentaria D. Aegidii Romani* [Rome: Antonium Bladum, 1555], 2v, https://books.google.com/books?id=ZcjIK13ZCXAC&pg=PP4).

62 "Ita sponsus attraxit me: unde non volens vel valens resistere ei, (surrexi) a contemplatione, (ut aperirem dilecto meo) per praedicationem; et non solum aperui ei praedicando verbo, sed etiam praedicando exemplo. Ideo subditur, (manus meae,) idest, operationes meae, (stillaverunt myrrham,) idest carnis mortificationem" (*ibid.*, 11v, https://books.google.com/books?id=ZcjIK13ZCXAC&pg=PP22).

This reading of the Song, insisting that what it really says is opposed to what it merely seems to say, served the immediate ideological needs of the Inquisition-era Church, and has remained dominant ever since.[63] Even now, the movement to restore the erotic sense of the verse is largely confined to academia, and has little impact on the way most readers encounter the poem.[64]

The story of the Song is a miniature reflection of the story of this book. Love, passionate and mutually chosen regard between two people, without concern for gods, laws, or institutions, has always struggled to survive in a hostile world. Its literary monuments have been appropriated for the purposes of those opposed to it, as verses speaking of desire and frustration, passion and joy, the sensual details of liquids, oils, and sweets, and open admiration of the body's form, are "channeled, reformulated, and controlled" into metaphors, allegories, and symbols of an *eros* redirected toward the sky. "It is amusing", as Longxi notes, "to see how the priggish commentators

---

63 Bart Vanden Auweele argues a different case, emphasizing the relatively recent academic voices that have challenged the secular reading of the Song of Songs:

> As long as the Song was read and understood allegorically, it was regarded as one of the most important, most inspiring and most used books of Scripture. Strangely enough, from the emergence of modern exegesis onwards, the poem fell gradually into a kind of oblivion as its obvious meaning became recognised. In the nineteenth and the first half of the twentieth century, the Song was scarcely read in Church and at university. [...] Moreover, modern exegetes approached the Song as a collection of diverse short erotic poems instead of being a coherent story with a well-constructed plot. [...] In recent years, however, the possibility and legitimacy of a reading of the Song according to its so-called "obvious and literal meaning" has been challenged. Modern interpreters such as Ricoeur, Patmore and Berder have criticised secular erotic readings of the Canticle for representing modern reader expectations rather than expressing a genuine biblical view on sexuality.

Bart Vanden Auweele. "The Song of Songs as Normative Text". In *Religion and Normativity Vol. 1: The Discursive Struggle over Religious Texts in Antiquity*, ed. by Anders-Christian Jacobson, Bart Vanden Auweele, and Carmen Cvetkovic [Aarhus: Aarhus University Press, 2009], 158). The irony is that Auweele's case is based on critics whose techniques stem from the interpretive strategies of those who reduced the Song to allegory in the first place. What exactly is "a genuine biblical view on sexuality" if the Song is not allowed to speak for itself on that matter? Here, we have a circular argument which insists that the Song is properly read as expressing a "genuine biblical view", while that "view" is imposed on the text by critics. The Bible says *what we say it says* (a statement to which the Inquisition would have been amenable).

64 For an excellent overview of this process, see J. Paul Tanner, "The History of Interpretation of the Song of Songs", *Bibliotheca Sacra*, 154: 613 (1997), 23–46, https://biblicalstudies.org.uk/article_song1_tanner.html, or http://www.paultanner.org/English HTML/Publ Articles/Hist Song of Songs - P Tanner.pdf

stretch the words out of all proportion [...]. Such farfetched exegeses [...] consistently read love songs as about anything but love".[65] We will see versions of this pattern repeatedly, as passion becomes worship, and desire becomes the decorous admiration of *objects* whose best use is to transport the admirer beyond the hated and distrusted flesh, and toward a union with what one cannot speak to, cannot draw near to, and most definitely cannot touch.

II
Love Poetry and the Critics who Reduce: Ovid's *Amores* and *Ars Amatoria*

Two collections of poetry that have no pretensions to being allegories of the sacred, the *Amores* and the *Ars Amatoria*, despite their often scurrilous reputations, are actually no more explicit in their passions and descriptions than the Song of Songs. But while the Song, after much debate, was included in the canons of Judaism and Christianity, the *Ars Amatoria*, and Ovid along with it, were banished from Rome to the shores of the Black Sea. Born in 43 BCE, Ovid was an established poet by his early twenties, and he "poured forth with uninterrupted regularity a series of elegiac works that far surpassed anything ever previously attempted in their open mockery of accepted sexual morality".[66] The *Amores* (an early work loosely centered around the poet's wry and self-aware fascination with a woman he refers to as Corrina) are completed by the time Ovid was twenty-eight, and by this time "he had established himself as Rome's foremost poet, and was the idol of the capital".[67]

The *Amores* have the feel of a young man's poetry, mixing bravado with uncertainty in their treatment of love and desire. The poems often talk of love as something that is sweeter when stolen, especially in poems like Elegy 1.4, "*Amicam qua arte*", and the famous Elegy 1.5

---

65 Longxi, 207.
66 G. P. Goold. "The Cause of Ovid's Exile". *Illinois Classical Studies*, 8: 1 (Spring 1983), 96, http://hdl.handle.net/2142/11861
67 *Ibid.*

"*Corrina Concubitus*". The former mockingly bemoans the fact that the lady's husband would be at dinner:

> Vir tuus est epulas nobis aditurus easdem—
> ultima coena tuo sit, precor, illa viro!
> ergo ego dilectam tantum conviva puellam
> adspiciam?[68]

> Your husband will be at the same supper with us—
> let that supper, I pray, be your husband's last!
> Shall I be so close to a girl I love
> and merely be a guest?

But the lover soon finds the husband's presence exciting, since it challenges him to remain undetected in public:

> ante veni, quam vir—nec quid, si veneris ante,
> possit agi video; sed tamen ante veni.
> cum premet ille torum, vultu comes ipsa modesto
> ibis, ut accumbas—clam mihi tange pedem!
> me specta nutusque meos vultumque loquacem;
> excipe furtivas et refer ipsa notas.
> verba superciliis sine voce loquentia dicam;
> verba leges digitis, verba notata mero.
> cum tibi succurret Veneris lascivia nostrae,
> purpureas tenero pollice tange genas.
> siquid erit, de me tacita quod mente queraris,
> pendeat extrema mollis ab aure manus.
> cum tibi, quae faciam, mea lux, dicamve, placebunt,
> versetur digitis anulus usque tuis.[69]

> Come before your husband, why not, come before,
> I don't see what's possible, but arrive before.
> When he lies on the couch, look, with modest
> demeanor recline beside him—secretly touch my foot!

---

68 Ovid. *Amores* 1.4. In *Ovid: Heroides and Amores*, ed. by Grant Showerman (Loeb Classical Library, Cambridge, MA: Harvard University Press, 1958), 328, ll. 1–4.
69 *Ibid.*, 328, 330, ll. 13–26.

> Look at me and my nods and my expressive face;
> catch my secrets and return them.
> Without saying a word, my eyebrows will speak to you;
> words from my fingers, words traced in wine.
> When you think of the pleasures of our love,
> with a tender thumb touch your cheeks.
> If you remember some silent complaint against me,
> gently grasp the bottom of your ear with your hand.
> When you are pleased, my light, with what I do or say,
> fiddle with the ring on your finger.

Ironically, the lover giving this advice descends into jealousy. What if the woman with whom he is cuckolding her husband, cuckolds *him* with her husband? An intolerable thought:

> nec femori committe femur nec crure cohaere
> nec tenerum duro cum pede iunge pedem.
> multa miser timeo, quia feci multa proterve,
> exemplique metu torqueor, ecce, mei.[70]

> Do not engage or touch him with the thigh
> not the tip of the foot with his hard foot.
> Alas, I fear much, because I have often been wanton,
> tormented, look you, by my own example.

The young man (Ovid himself?) wants to believe that his love (Corinna perhaps, though unnamed in this poem) is faithful to him, despite her marriage to another. And if necessary, he would prefer that she lie in order to maintain this belief:

> sed quaecumque tamen noctem fortuna sequetur,
> cras mihi constanti voce dedisse nega![71]

> Nevertheless, whatever the night's fortune proves,
> tomorrow, in a firm voice, deny that you gave yourself!

---

70   *Ibid.*, 330, ll. 43–46.
71   *Ibid.*, 332, ll. 69–70.

The more famous elegy, "*Corrina Concubitus*", reflects none of the teasing and self-tormenting doubts of the fourth elegy, and is filled with the delights of physical *eros*, desire and fulfillment. First, the poem gives voice to the delights of seeing:

> ecce, Corinna venit, tunica velata recincta,
> candida dividua colla tegente coma—
> qualiter in thalamos famosa Semiramis isse
> dicitur, et multis Lais amata viris.[72]

> Behold, Corinna comes, draped in a loose gown,
> hair parted over her white neck—
> just as Semiramis came to her bed,
> so they say, and Lais loved by many men.

Next, the poem moves to touch mixed with sight:

> Deripui tunicam—nec multum rara nocebat;
> pugnabat tunica sed tamen illa tegi.
> quae cum ita pugnaret, tamquam quae vincere nollet,
> victa est non aegre proditione sua.
> ut stetit ante oculos posito velamine nostros,
> in toto nusquam corpore menda fuit.
> quos umeros, quales vidi tetigique lacertos!
> forma papillarum quam fuit apta premi!
> quam castigato planus sub pectore venter!
> quantum et quale latus! quam iuvenale femur!
> Singula quid referam? nil non laudabile vidi
> et nudam pressi corpus ad usque meum.[73]

> I tore off her coat—it was thin, and covered little;
> but, she held the tunic, fighting to be covered,
> fighting as if she would win,
> or be conquered easily, but not by her own betrayal.
> As she stood before my eyes with drapery set by,
> she hadn't a flaw in her entire body.

---

72 *Amores* 1.5, 334, ll. 9–12.
73 *Ibid.*, ll. 13–24.

> What shoulders, what arms I saw and touched!
> The form of her breasts, how fit to be caressed!
> How flat is her belly, beneath her breasts!
> Her side's quantity and quality! What a thrilling thigh!
> Why refer to more? I saw nothing unpraiseworthy
> and pressed her naked body against mine.

Finally, as desire has played its scene, and quiet satisfaction remains, the poem turns to a wish for many more such afternoons as this one:

> Cetera quis nescit? lassi requievimus ambo.
> proveniant medii sic mihi saepe dies![74]

> Who knows not what followed? Weary, we rested.
> May such afternoons come for me often!

Corinna is neither a goddess, nor an allegory for the sacred. There has never been a critical impulse to explain *"Corrina Concubitus"* as if it were really portraying the relationship between humanity and the gods. Corinna is portrayed as a flesh-and-blood woman, desired and worried over by a flesh-and-blood man. If Corinna is a stand-in for anything or anyone, perhaps it is Julia, the daughter of Augustus, the Roman Emperor who would, some twenty-plus years after the publication of the *Amores*, banish Ovid from Rome for life. While this possibility has long been a matter of debate,[75] it does tie in with the overall feeling in many of the elegies of forbidden love—an *eros* that is more exciting because of the possibility of getting caught and severely punished. If Corinna is Julia, and the famous twofold reason for Ovid's banishment (*carmen et error*, the poem and the mistake Ovid refers to in his poem *Tristia*, 2.207) was "for writing the *Ars Amatoria* and for committing a transgression"[76] with her, then what a reader encounters in both the *Amores* and the *Ars Amatoria* is life and experience, transgression and joy, transformed into poetry that celebrated love and desire which was enjoyed in the shadow of condemnation and

---

74 *Ibid.,* ll. 25–26.
75 See John C. Thibault. *The Mystery of Ovid's Exile* (Berkeley: University of California Press, 1964), 38–54.
76 Goold, 107.

banishment. Rather than passion sublimated into a search for the divine, these poems are perhaps our first clear example, unsullied by the allegorizing and temporizing mood, of what the troubadours will call *fin'amor*, love as an end in itself.

Title page of a 1644 edition of Ovid's *Ars Amatoria*.[77]

However, in what will soon become a familiar move in the criticism of many different authors and periods, some commentary on Ovid's work returns it to the realm of allegory, not of the human-divine relationship, but, in this case, of poetry itself. Reducing Ovid's work to a series of conventions and tropes, Peter Allen argues that it amounts to little more than poetry gazing at its own reflection:

> The lesson is in fact a lesson in literary theory. The *Ars* and *Remedia* reveal (though often in indirect ways) that the love described in elegiac poetry is essentially the same as the poetry itself: both are artistic fantasies, constructed by the reader and the poetic lover together. Elegiac love depends for its existence on the presence of recognizable conventions, which help the reader situate it within a literary context, to recognize it as fiction. Through such conventions the poet involves the reader in the act of literary creation, which is itself an amatory relationship and,

---

77   https://commons.wikimedia.org/wiki/File:Ovid_Ars_Amatoria_1644.jpg

in fact, the most intimate relationship in these texts; the preceptor's true task is to teach the reader how to be a creator, like himself.[78]

Once, in the mid-twentieth century work of a critic like Blanchot, this kind of argument—reducing literature to a meta-discourse in which all that literature talks about is itself—might have seemed fresh, even profound. It draws loosely on the now-familiar idea that language refers only to language, and that only by a series of shared conventions do we credit it with an illusory signifying power. Such criticism categorically denies any possibility of poetry's intervention in the world, turning literature into a passive prop for political, military, economic, and epistemological regimes of power to which it cannot even refer, much less oppose. It presents an appearance of radicalism, while deliberately entangling itself in its own refusals and withdrawals.

Such an argument about Ovid insists that, "[d]espite the *Amores'* pose of sincerity, well-informed readers will recognize that each of their characters and situations are conventional".[79] Note the rhetorical pressure applied to the reader—to resist the critic's insistence that Ovid's work is merely conventional, relating only to the experience of *writing about love* and not *love itself*, puts the reader outside the camp of the "well-informed". Thus we are told how we should read Ovid, and how we should not read Ovid; "well-informed" readers will naturally obey such prescriptions and proscriptions. But this is all a symptom of an authoritarian strain in criticism that can be seen running all the way back through Origen, Rabbi Akiba, and Giles of Rome, for whom the Song of Songs had to be read with the ideological demands of empire and church in mind. To demand, even implicitly as Allen does, obedience in the reading of a poet whose delight in disobedience is reflected throughout his poetry, is more than faintly absurd. And here we see a new assertion—one we will encounter later in criticism of medieval poetry: that the "poetic 'I'" does not represent an individual point of view (neither that of a poet nor a narrative voice), but is instead a conventional and collective illusion. It would be ill-informed, according to such criticism, to believe otherwise:

---

78 Peter Allen. *The Art of Love: Amatory Fiction from Ovid to the Romance of the Rose* (Philadelphia: University of Pennsylvania Press, 1992), 20.
79 *Ibid.*

> The *amator* is little more than a convention himself, a reuse of the traditional Roman poetic "I", which derives from Propertius, Tibullus, Gallus, and Catullus, as well as Catullus's Alexandrian model, Callimachus. This poetic "I" is a ventriloquist's voice, a literary echo of an echo of an echo. Even the sincerity that post-Romantic readers, at least, traditionally attribute to the poet-lover is undermined by the *amator*'s confessions of infidelity and multifarious desire. His affirmations of love are "sincere" not in the sense that they unify the *amator*, the poet, and the historical Ovid, but in the sense that they create an effective illusion of a poet in love.[80]

From Allen's perspective, the "well-informed" reader will also reject the possibility that "Corrina" had any referent in the world of flesh-and-blood, regarding it as obvious that "she" is merely another literary convention:

> Corinna is no more real than her lover. Historical identities have been found for the women in earlier elegy, but literary history is silent on Corinna, and efforts to re-create her are not only fruitless but even irrelevant to an understanding of the *Amores*. Rather than existing as a person in her own right [...] she is the object of the *amator*'s desire, the grain of sand that provokes the poetic oyster to produce a string of literary pearls [...]. Poetry, not Corinna, is the true star of the *Amores*.[81]

And thus the "well-informed" and properly compliant reader will approach the *Amores* in order to read about poetry, not about love. We will see this same move made by other critics, though in different contexts, *ad infinitum*. Even a less apparently prescriptive critic like Alison Sharrock ultimately cannot resist turning Ovid's poetry into an allegory for the act of reading: "the *Ars* itself is a spell (a *carmen*) with great seductive power. [...] Just as texts are magically seductive, so is interpretation, so is theory. It is the act of reading that draws us into the poem. Reading about desire provokes the desire to read".[82] Such critics have become temperamentally averse to the idea of poetry speaking of anything but itself, as if it were the self-obsessed bore most of us try to avoid at parties.

---

80 Allen, 21.
81 *Ibid.*
82 Alison Sharrock. *Seduction and Repetition in Ovid's Ars Amatoria*, 2 (Oxford: Clarendon Press, 1994), 296.

But Ovid was anything but a bore. He was the kind of poet dedicated to "pushing the limits (of convention, genre, discretion) and refusing to be bound to or by anything other than his own genius".[83] Ovid gives every appearance of refusing to take seriously the pieties that surround love, and especially refuses to take seriously the laws that surround marriage and procreation in Augustus' Rome.[84] However, he does take quite seriously the joys of transgressive love itself. For example, "Ad Auroram", Elegy 1.13 from the *Amores*, shows a lover railing against the rising sun—in a way that foreshadows the passions of the *alba* form of twelfth-century Occitania[85]—for cutting short his time with his beloved:

> Quo properas, Aurora? mane!-sic Memnonis umbris
> annua sollemni caede parentet avis!
> nunc iuvat in teneris dominae iacuisse lacertis;
> si quando, lateri nunc bene iuncta meo est.
> nunc etiam somni pingues et frigidus aer,
> et liquidum tenui gutture cantat avis.
> quo properas, ingrata viris, ingrata puellis?[86]

> Where do you hurry, Aurora? Stay, so to Memmnon's shades
> his birds may make annual festival in combat!
> Now I delight to lie in the tender arms of my mistress;
> if at any time, now it is best that she lies close to me.
> now, too, sleep is deep and the air is cold,
> and slender-throated birds sing liquid songs.
> Why do you hurry, unwelcome to men, unwelcome to girls?

The lover berates the oncoming light, knowing his course is futile, but driven by passion and the desire to remain in his "girl's soft arms", crying out over how many times dawn has torn him away from them:

---

83 Barbara Weiden Boyd. "The *Amores*: The Invention of Ovid". In *Brill's Companion to Ovid*, ed. by Barbara Weiden Boyd (Leiden: Brill, 2002), 116.

84 The *Lex Iulia de Maritandis Ordinibus* of 18 BCE restricted marriage between the social classes, and the *Lex Iulia de Adulteriis Coercendis* of the same year made adultery punishable by banishment—the latter was applied to Julia in 2 BCE.

85 For a comprehensive survey of this theme across world literature, see *Eos: An Enquiry into the Theme of Lover's Meetings and Partings at Dawn in Poetry*, ed. by Arthur T. Hatto (The Hague: Mouton & Co.), 1965.

86 Ovid. *Amores*, 1.13, 368, ll. 3–9.

> optavi quotiens, ne nox tibi cedere vellet,
> ne fugerent vultus sidera mota tuos!
> optavi quotiens, aut ventus frangeret axem,
> aut caderet spissa nube retentus equus![87]

> often have I wished night would not give place to thee,
> so that the stars would not flee before your face!
> often have I wished the wind would break your axle,
> or that a thick cloud would trip and fell your horse!

Then, rehearsing the myth of Aurora, the goddess of dawn who is herself married to the eternally old Tithonus, the lover accuses the goddess of hypocrisy for wanting to stay with her young lover Cephalus, while repeatedly denying the lover of the poem the chance to stay in the arms of his beloved:

> Tithono vellem de te narrare liceret;
> fabula non caelo turpior ulla foret.
> illum dum refugis, longo quia grandior aevo,
> surgis ad invisas a sene mane rotas.
> at si, quem mavis, Cephalum conplexa teneres,
> clamares: "lente currite, noctis equi!"
> Cur ego plectar amans, si vir tibi marcet ab annis?[88]

> I wish Tithonus were licensed to tell about you;
> there is no more shameful story in heaven.
> Fleeing from him, for he is so many ages older than you,
> you rise early from the old man, to morning's chariot wheels.
> Whereas, if you had your beloved Cephalus in your embrace,
> then you would cry: "Run slowly, horses of the night!"
> Why must I suffer in love since your man is wasted with years?

It is especially notable that human desire and frustration are at the center of Ovid's poem, and the goddess Aurora, with her serial attractions to, and affairs with, mortal men, is a reflection of and comment upon the

---

87 Ibid., 370, ll. 27–30.
88 Ibid., ll. 35–41.

love between men and women, not a transcendent and otherwise body-denying goal for which lovers must strive.

Ovid mocks the pretensions of controlling husbands, and by extension those of Augustus in passing a law against adultery, in "Ad virum servantem coniugem", *Amores* 3.4. This poem laughs at the man who would too strictly defend the sexual fidelity of a woman; such a man makes himself a tyrant, a fool, and a cuckold:

> Dure vir, inposito tenerae custode puellae
> nil agis; ingenio est quaeque tuenda suo.
> siqua metu dempto casta est, ea denique casta est;
> quae, quia non liceat, non facit, illa facit!
> ut iam servaris bene corpus, adultera mens est;
> nec custodiri, ne velit, ulla potest.
> nec corpus servare potes, licet omnia claudas;
> omnibus exclusis intus adulter erit.[89]

> Harsh man, setting a guard over your tender girl
> gets you nothing; her own character is what will defend her.
> If she is chaste when free from fear, then she is pure;
> but if she doesn't sin because she's not allowed to, she'll do it!
> Even if you have well guarded the body, the mind is adulterous;
> no watchman has any power over her will.
> Neither can you guard her body, though you close every door,
> excluding all; for the adulterer will be within.

In Ovid's elegy, adultery is a natural response to the tyranny of unwanted husbands and absurdly impractical laws that create (or enhance) the very effects they seek to prevent. In fact, the strict laws of the husband or the emperor inculcate the desire to break those laws and achieve the forbidden (a motif familiar from *Genesis* 2–3):

> nitimur in vetitum semper cupimusque negata;
> sic interdictis imminet aeger aquis.
> centum fronte oculos, centum cervice gerebat
> Argus—et hos unus saepe fefellit Amor;

---

89   Ovid. *Amores*, 3.4, 458, 460, ll. 1–8.

> in thalamum Danae ferro saxoque perennem
> quae fuerat virgo tradita, mater erat;
> Penelope mansit, quamvis custode carebat,
> inter tot iuvenes intemerata procos.
> Quidquid servatur cupimus magis, ipsaque furem
> cura vocat; pauci, quod sinit alter, amant.[90]

> We strive for what is forbidden and desire what is denied;
> just as a sick man gazes over prohibited waters.
> A hundred eyes before, a hundred behind, had
> Argus—and these were often deceived only by Love;
> in a chamber of eternal iron and rock Danae was shut,
> though she had been shut in as a maid, she became a mother;
> Penelope remained steadfast, although without a guard,
> among many youthful suitors.
> Whatever is guarded we desire the more, the thief
> is invited by worry; few love what is permitted by another.

Finally, the elegy ends with a bit of advice for old husbands—pretend, as Shakespeare will write, to believe her when she says "she is made of truth", even though you know she lies. Pretend not to notice the dalliances, even the affairs, because unless you are willing to be rid of her, there is really nothing you can do about them:

> quo tibi formosam, si non nisi casta placebat?
> non possunt ullis ista coire modis.
> Si sapis, indulge dominae vultusque severos
> exue, nec rigidi iura tuere viri,
> et cole quos dederit—multos dabit—uxor amicos.
> gratia sic minimo magna labore venit;
> sic poteris iuvenum convivia semper inire
> et, quae non dederis, multa videre domi.[91]

> Why did you marry beauty if only chastity would please you?
> Those two things can never be combined.
> If you are wise, indulge your lady—and the stern looks?

---

90 Ibid., 460, ll. 17–26.
91 Ibid., 462, ll. 41–48.

> Ditch them. Do not rigidly insist on the rights of a husband,
> and cherish her very generous and loving…friends.
> You will receive great thanks, with little effort on your part;
> so in this way, you can always celebrate and feast with youths,
> and see many gifts at home which you did not give.

The last lines are a wry joke—those gifts the husband did not give to his much-younger wife may very well be gifts he can no longer give her: children resulting from sexual encounters with young men who can still "stand to" in a way that the husband has long since stopped being able to do.

Beyond pure social and sexual satire, the *Amores* are a work of pointed political critique. The passing of such laws as the *Lex Iulia de Maritandis Ordinibus* and the *Lex Iulia de Adulteriis Coercendis* (of 18 and 17 BCE) and the *Lex Papia Poppaea* (of 9 CE) represented an ongoing attempt to use the power of government to "reform Roman private morality".[92] Thus, more than merely claiming that the husband creates or encourages adultery in a wife over whom he keeps too strict a watch, the *Amores* make a political point we might characterize as libertarian today: the government encourages rebellion by being tyrannical. In such a reading of the *Amores*, Augustus is the cuckolded husband who foolishly creates the conditions and the impetus for his own cuckolding by trying to control what cannot be controlled—the social and sexual mores of his "wife", the Roman people. Read in this way, Ovid's poems can be seen as an allegory which describes the relationship between Augustus and Rome in the terms of relationships between men and women. But though they *can* be seen so, there are no powerful cultural forces that demand they *must* be seen so, and "[i]t is only in recent years, that Ovid's *Amores* has come to be viewed as a political work".[93] The poetry itself, unlike that of the *Song*, has not been "channeled, reformulated, and controlled" to the point that its frankly erotic content has been subjected to wholesale interpretive erasure, and that is an unqualifiedly good thing. But the suggestion (not mandate) for reading the *Amores* in a political light makes it easier for us to see the way in which love itself

---

92 These laws proscribed class intermarriage, fornication/adultery, and celibacy, respectively. P. J. Davis. "Ovid's Amores: A Political Reading". *Classical Philology*, 94: 4 (October 1999), 435, https://doi.org/10.1086/449457
93 *Ibid.*, 431.

is often "channeled, reformulated, and controlled" in order to serve the agendas of the powerful.

In passing laws designed to regulate sexuality, Augustus is trying to establish a Julian dynasty that will survive the vicissitudes of time and unforeseen circumstance. Just as the early critics like Xenophanes, Akiba, and Origen seek to control the reading of *eros*-driven poetry, Augustus seeks to control *eros* itself. But like the husband of "Ad virum servantem coniugem", he is trying to control the uncontrollable. Ovid even treats the myth of the founding of Rome, the story of Romulus and Remus, in a way designed to puncture the pretensions of an Augustus determined to control private behavior: "Ovid's treatment of the Romulus and Remus legend is similarly disrespectful. Where Virgil chooses his language carefully and speaks of Ilia as merely 'pregnant by Mars' [...], Ovid points to Romulus and Remus as the product of adultery".[94] As Ovid puts it:

> Rusticus est nimium, quem laedit adultera coniunx,
> et notos mores non satis urbis habet
> in qua Martigenae non sunt sine crimine nati
> Romulus Iliades Iliadesque Remus.[95]

> He is a rustic fool, who hurts over an adulterous wife,
> and he surely doesn't know the ways of *this* city,
> in which the sons of Mars were not born without crime,
> Romulus, and Remus, Ilia's twins.

To all the self-important men and women of the world who would legislate private morality, who would pass laws about who can do what to whom, with whom, under what circumstances, in what positions, and with what ends in mind,[96] Ovid's *Amores* say: *Oh please, get over yourselves.* In Ovid, we see love being both celebrated for its own sake and for its subversive potential as a private weapon against public tyranny.

---

94 *Ibid.*, 443.
95 Ovid. *Amores*. 462, ll. 37–40.
96 The *Lex Papia Poppaea* targeted both celibate people *and* childless couples.

This subversive potential is developed to extremes of sharpness and power in the *Ars Amatoria*, a work that "exudes urban hipness",[97] by identifying itself and its ethos with the cosmopolitan and imperial city of Rome. These are the poems of a sophisticated and experienced older man, a Pandar-like figure who tells a world full of young men how to find, approach, speak to, and seduce a world full of women, and in so doing, undermine the values of the Augustine state:

> The poem really is subversive—not in the challenge it offers to the new morality, or because it has the effrontery to claim for the lover the same "professional" status as the farmer, the soldier, the holder of high public office, but because it [...] establishes the lover/poet as the emperor of an alternative and privately constituted state.[98]

One can see why the Augustus, who was busily trying to clean up Roman morality, restore the wholly imaginary *mos maiorum*[99] (the good old ways of the good old days), and channel Roman sexuality into childbirth and the maintenance of social class distinctions, would find offense in a poem that valued the private over the public, the lover over the warrior, the poet over the emperor.

Subversive notes begin playing almost as soon as the poetry starts. The *Ars Amatoria* is "a book that, proposing to teach Romans how to love and be loved, in fact achieved the result of winning for its author the implacable hatred of the most important Roman of all", and is a major part of "Ovid's project of constructing his poetic career as a constant pain in Augustus' neck".[100] It isn't hard to see why, when Ovid's critique of Rome's self-mythologizing is so often front and center in his work. For example, while recommending that young men look for women in the theatre, Ovid compares the founding of Rome with rape and the (im)morality of a military empire:

---

97 Peter White. "Ovid and the Augustan Mileau". In *Brill's Companion to Ovid*, ed. by Barbara Weiden Boyd (Leiden: Brill, 2002), 12.
98 Ovid. *The Art of Love*. Trans. by James Michie. Introduction by David Malouf (New York: Modern Library, 2002), xii.
99 Karl-J. Hölkeskamp. *Reconstructing the Roman Republic: An Ancient Political Culture and Modern Research* (Princeton: Princeton University Press, 2010), 17.
100 Sergio Casali. "The Art of Making Oneself Hated: Rethinking (Anti-)Augustanism in Ovid's *Ars Amatoria*". In *The Art of Love: Bimillennial Essays on Ovid's Ars Amatoria and Remedia Amoris*, ed. by Roy Gibson, Steven Green, and Alison Sharrock (Oxford: Oxford University Press, 2006), 216, 219.

> Primus sollicitos fecisti, Romule, ludos,
> Cum iuvit viduos rapta Sabina viros.
> Tunc neque marmoreo pendebant vela theatro,
> Nec fuerant liquido pulpita rubra croco;
> Illic quas tulerant nemorosa Palatia, frondes
> Simpliciter positae, scena sine arte fuit;
> In gradibus sedit populus de caespite factis,
> Qualibet hirsutas fronde tegente comas.
> Respiciunt, oculisque notant sibi quisque puellam
> Quam velit, et tacito pectore multa movent.
> [...]
> Rex populo praedae signa petita dedit.
> Protinus exiliunt, animum clamore fatentes,
> Virginibus cupidas iniciuntque manus.
> [...]
> Siqua repugnarat nimium comitemque negabat,
> Sublatam cupido vir tulit ipse sinu,
> Atque ita "quid teneros lacrimis corrumpis ocellos?
> Quod matri pater est, hoc tibi" dixit "ero".
> Romule, militibus scisti dare commoda solus:
> Haec mihi si dederis commoda, miles ero.[101]

> You first instituted these games, Romulus,
> when the single men profited by raping the Sabine women.
> Back then no awnings hung over a marble theatre,
> nor was the platform stained with red saffron;
> there artless and thick Palatine branches
> were simply placed, while the stage was unadorned;
> the audience sat on steps made from turf,
> the branches covering their shaggy hair.
> Each cast his eyes around, noting the girls
> he wanted, and was deeply stirred in his silent heart.
> [...]
> The king gave the signal for the rape.
> Immediately they burst forth, shouting, betraying their
> virgins with greedy, lustful hands.

---

101 Ovid. *Ars Amatoria*, 1.101–10, 114–16, 127–32. In *Ovid: The Art of Love and other Poems*, ed. by J. H. Mozley (Loeb Classical Library, Cambridge, MA: Harvard University Press, 1962), 18, 20.

> [...]
> If a girl resisted too much, or refused her companion,
> lifted up on his lustful bosom, the man carried her,
> saying, "And what's that ruining your eyes with tears?
> What your father was to your mother, that will I be to you".
> Romulus, only you knew what was fitting:
> if you give me such advantages, I will be a soldier too.

The rape, or abduction (from the Latin *raptio*) of the Sabine women, is a well-known element of early Roman legend. As Livy tells the story:

> The Roman State was now strong enough in war, a match for any of its neighbors; but the absence of women, and the lack of the right of intermarriage with their neighbors, meant their greatness would last for a generation only, for they had no hope of offspring. [...] On the advice of the senate, Romulus sent envoys amongst the surrounding nations to ask for alliance and intermarriage on behalf of his new community. [...] Nowhere did the embassy get a friendly hearing. [...] Romulus, disguising his resentment, made elaborate preparations for the games in honor of equestrian Neptune, which he called Consualia. He ordered the spectacle proclaimed to the surrounding peoples, and the Romans began preparations, with every resource of their knowledge and ability, to celebrate, in order to create amongst the peoples a clear and eager expectation. [...] When the time came for the show, when the peoples' eyes and minds were together occupied, then the forceful attack arose. The signal was given for the young Romans to carry off the virgins. A great part of them were carried off indiscriminately, but some particularly beautiful girls were marked out for the prime leaders, to whose servants had been given the task to carry them to their houses.[102]

---

102 Iam res Romana adeo erat valida ut cuilibet finitimarum civitatum bello par esset; sed penuria mulierum hominis aetatem duratura magnitudo erat, quippe quibus nec domi spes prolis nec cum finitimis conubia essent. [...] ex consilio patrum Romulus legatos circa vicinas gentes misit, qui societatem conubiumque novo populo peterent. [...] nusquam benigne legatio audita est. [...] Romulus, aegritudinem animi dissimulans ludos ex industria parat Neptuno equestri sollemnis; Consualia vocat. indici deinde finitimis spectaculum iubet, quantoque apparatu tum sciebant aut poterant, concelebrant, ut rem claram exspectatamque facerent. [...] ubi spectaculi tempus venit deditaeque eo mentes cum oculis erant, tum ex composito orta vis, signoque dato iuventus Romana ad rapiendas virgines discurrit. magna pars forte, in quem quaeque inciderat, raptae: quasdam forma excellentes primoribus patrum destinatas ex plebe homines, quibus datum negotium erat, domos deferebant.

Livy. *Titi Livi Ab vrbe condita libri praefatio, liber primvs*, Vol. 1, ed. by H. J. Edwards (Cambridge: Cambridge University Press, 1912), 12–14, https://books.google.com/books?id=gsNEAAAAIAAJ&pg=PA12

Livy's tale is one of a necessary action taken out of the need for self-preservation, because Rome's "absence of women" meant its "greatness would last for a generation only". Brutal and dishonest and wicked as it was, it had a recognizable motive. The way Ovid transforms the tale, however, it becomes an extension of the Consualia games, a game in its own right. The women are "pay" for soldiers and Romulus is praised for knowing how to treat military men properly. With such rewards, the poem's narrator—a lover, not a fighter—would be willing to enlist right away. The journey from Livy's earnestness to Ovid's satire is a comment on how far Rome has fallen—what was once a republic is now an empire, a realm in which the emperor, far from being an establisher of new worlds, is the enforcer of people's bedrooms.

Later, Ovid continues the none-too-subtle undermining of Augustus, describing his vainglorious public re-staging of the naval battles between the Persians and Greeks as a fine place to seduce women:

> Quid, modo cum belli navalis imagine Caesar
> Persidas induxit Cecropiasque rates?
> Nempe ab utroque mari iuvenes, ab utroque puellae
> Venere, atque ingens orbis in Urbe fuit.
> Quis non invenit turba, quod amaret, in illa?
> Eheu, quam multos advena torsit amor![103]

> When Ceasar, in the manner of a naval battle,
> brought on Persian and Cecropian vessels?
> Of course, young men and girls came from both seas,
> Venus, the mighty world was in our city.
> Who did not find one they might love in that crowd?
> Alas, how many were tortured by love!

In ridiculing a mock battle by describing it as a seduction zone where foreign flames may burn the men who get too close to them, Ovid equates sex with conquest, and *eros* with war. From such a vantage point, an empire is a vast *screwing over* of the world, and its emperor the *screwer in chief*. The result of such accusatory descriptions was predictable: according to Lanham, "Ovid wanted to be honest and Augustus did

---

103 Ovid. *Ars Amatoria*, 1.171–76, 24.

not. No wonder Augustus banished him".[104] In a dictatorship, telling the truth can be, and often is, considered a subversive act, and "Ovid paid a political penalty for a political crime".[105]

In the final section of Book II, the sharp satire takes a new form, as "Ovid" becomes a character in the verse, and sets himself up as an alternative emperor whose name will be shouted throughout the world:

> Me vatem celebrate, viri, mihi dicite laudes,
> Cantetur toto nomen in orbe meum.
> [...]
> Sed quicumque meo superarit Amazona ferro,
> Inscribat spoliis "Naso magister erat".[106]

> Celebrate me as a poet, men, speak my praises,
> let my name be known through all the world.
> [...]
> But whoever shall overcome an Amazon with my steel,
> let him inscribe upon his spoils, "Ovid was my master".

And why not? According to the incisive logic of the poem, why shouldn't a poet be emperor of a world based on love, or at the very least desire? But critics have been in a rush to disapprove, as "'excess', 'irrelevance', 'narcissism', 'self-indulgence', [and] 'vacuity'", are "the standard accusations levelled against Ovid" and "Ovidian poetry"[107] more generally. It is nearly impossible to support such a reading of the poet or his poetry when both are returned to the context of an imperial dictatorship, but that doesn't stop critics from trying:

> The judgements of two influential critics may be taken as representative of the long and dominant tradition in Ovidian scholarship, which, although it has been challenged in recent years, remains the orthodoxy. Wilkinson says of Ovid's didactic poetry: "Quite apart from the sameness of tone, there is too much *crambe repetita*. Surely we have heard before, and more than once, of lovers communicating by writing on the table in

---

104 Richard A. Lanham. *The Motives of Eloquence: Literary Rhetoric in the Renaissance* (New Haven: Yale University Press, 1976), 63.
105 *Ibid.*
106 *Ibid.*, 2.739–40, 743–44, 116.
107 Sharrock, 87.

wine, exchanging glances and signs, drinking from the side of the cup where the other has drunk, and touching hands" (Wilkinson 1955: 143). This view is echoed by Otis (1966: 18): "so many of the same themes [as in the *Amores*] are repeated and so often repeated in a much less striking way". According to this view, the *Ars* is rather a heavy reworking of the well known *topoi* of Latin love elegy.[108]

To paraphrase the preacher of Nazareth, "the poor [in poetic spirit] we will always have with us". Despite those critics determined to diminish Ovid, his poems, even at their lightest-seeming, have a serious question to ask: why? Why must life be dominated by the Augustus Caesars of the world—who command with soldiers and laws, who banish their own daughters and granddaughters for adultery, and exile one of the finest poets in the history of the world for *carmen et error*, a poem and a mistake—rather than be gifted to us in all its imaginative possibility by the Ovids and Shakespeares and Shelleys? Why should not poets, the "unacknowledged legislators of the world",[109] be celebrated instead of emperors, soldiers, and all those who use the power of the sword and the state to forbid the actions and pursuits that bring men and women joy? Though Ovid died in exile far from Rome, his influence, his ideas, his words, even his jokes have survived the millennia in ways that Augustus, despite his power and the legions at his disposal, has not. The great man who would both rule the world and banish its adulterers from his sight, has himself been banished by death, while the poet of love and seduction, sly satire and disrespect for the rules, lives on in his verses, and in the works of countless other poets and writers who have been influenced by him. Ovid "attacks unnamed detractors, censors, thunderbolt-hurlers, who look suspiciously like Augustus",[110] the political moralists who condemn, and the academic critics who dismiss a body of poetic work that celebrates love and desire against the pinched and pursed-lipped claims of law and authority. Power and Law may have banished Ovid, but the poet of Love and Laughter has long since had the last word.

---

108 *Ibid.*, 3.
109 Percy Shelley. "A Defence of Poetry". In *Essays, Letters From Abroad*, Vol.1 (London: Edward Moxon, 1852), 49, https://babel.hathitrust.org/cgi/pt?id=wu.89000649913;view=1up;seq=77
110 Casali, "The Art of Making Oneself Hated", 221.

III
Love or Obedience in Virgil: Aeneas and Dido

From laughter we come to tragedy, from joy to tears. For in the *Aeneid*'s story of Aeneas and Dido, readers encounter one of the best and worst love stories the ancient world has to offer. Faced with the choice of human love, or divine will, Dido chooses love, while Aeneas—the epic's hero in the most unfortunate sense of the term—chooses as the tamers of the Song of Songs would have readers choose, and as Augustus would have Rome choose. *Pius* Aeneas chooses obedience to the will and law of the gods, and Dido is destroyed.

Having escaped from burning Troy, Aeneas and his brave but bedraggled followers have landed at Carthage, on the North African coast. In part, the story of Aeneas' devastation of Dido is a poeticizing of the military relations between Rome and Carthage in a later era, when after many battles, Carthage is razed to the ground by Rome, never to rise again. But in the time of the *Aeneid*, such conflict is a thousand years in the future: Carthage is rising, founded by exiles from Tyre who fled violence and bloodshed at home. Aeneas, an exile from the Trojan war, is in need of mercy. Dido gives it. Perhaps she shouldn't have.

Aeneas is the perfect hero for an empire busy tightening its grip at home while seeking to expand its reach abroad. The *Aeneid* is written during the early, expansionist portion of Augustus' time as emperor, approximately 29–19 BCE, when "campaigning was virtually continuous in western and southern Europe".[111] Unlike the later Ovid, who ridicules the puritanism of Augustus, Virgil flatters the emperor by creating a proto-Roman hero whose prime virtue is obedience.[112] Aeneas is not passionless, at least where love and sex are concerned, but he prefers to direct his strength, his emotions, his *eros* toward mourning for the loss of Troy and founding a new city

---

111 David Shotter. *Rome and Her Empire* (New York: Routledge, 2014), 218.
112 There is, in Virgil's portrayal of Aeneas, very little of the spirit with which he had once infused his character Gallus (based on his contemporary and friend Gaius Cornelius Gallus), for whom "Love conquers all; and we must yield to love" ("Omnia vincit amor; et nos cedamus Amori") (Eclogue 10.69. In *Virgil*, 2 vols, ed. by H. Rushton Fairclough [Loeb Classical Library, Cambridge, MA: Harvard University Press, 1960], 74).

for his descendants and those of the men who follow him. His cry, "Oh fatherland! Troy, home of the gods!"[113] has far more passion and pathos than does his recounting of the loss of his wife in the final battle at Troy. Escaping with his family, Aeneas sees to the safety of his father and son, but leaves his wife, Creusa, vulnerable:

> ergo age, care pater, cervici imponere nostrae;
> ipse subibo umeris nec me labor iste gravabit;
> quo res cumque cadent, unum et commune periclum,
> una salus ambobus erit. mihi parvus Iulus
> sit comes, et longe servet vestigia coniunx.[114]

> Come then, dear father, upon my neck;
> this task will not be too heavy for my shoulders;
> However things may fall, we two have one common peril,
> and we will have one salvation. My little Iulus
> come with me, and at a distance let my wife follow our steps.

Having his wife follow at a distance leads to the predictable result; Creusa is lost in the battle, killed by the Greeks:

> heu misero coniunx fatone erepta Creusa
> substitit, erravitne via seu lapsa resedit,
> incertum; nec post oculis est reddita nostris.
> nec prius amissam respexi animumue reflexi
> quam tumulum antiquae Cereris sedemque sacratam
> venimus: hic demum collectis omnibus una
> defuit, et comites natumque virumque fefellit.[115]

> Ah, wretched fate snatched Creusa.
> Did she stop for a while, lose the way, or slip and fall back?
> I am not certain; nor afterwards was she returned to our eyes.

---

113 "O patria, o divum domus Ilium" 2.241. All references are from *The Aeneid*. In *Virgil*, 2 vols, ed. by H. Rushton Fairclough (Loeb Classical Library, Cambridge, MA: Harvard University Press, 1960).
114 *Ibid.*, 2.707–11.
115 *Ibid.*, 2.738–44.

> Neither did I turn my mind or thought toward my lost one
> until to the ancient Ceres' hallowed home
> we came; when all were gathered, she alone
> was absent, lost to her son and her husband.

He does not lack emotion when describing her loss, even claiming that he went back into the battle zone trying to find her, crying out her name as he "rushed furiously and endlessly from house to house through the city".[116] However, the telling detail is that during the initial escape, he never gave her any thought, and only realized that his wife was missing after he had brought father and son to safety.

Aeneas is no Odysseus. Odysseus, even amid his serial philandering and flirting with witches, goddesses, and the daughters of kings, still longs to be reunited with Penelope, whom the goddess Calypso describes as "your wife, she that you ever long for daily, in every way",[117] and for whom "he cried out, still calling forth tears, / Crying as he held his beloved, trustworthy, and strong-minded wife".[118] It appears the feelings were mutual. From Penelope's point of view, theirs was a reunion of joy and passion: "Hers and her husband's tears mingle, her knees melt (that sure sign of Aphrodite's presence), [and] she proceeds formally to their bed with him, led by a maid with torches, as though to renew the days of their beginnings".[119] But far from pining for *his* wife, Aeneas can barely be bothered to remember her even as they are trying to escape from burning Troy. Later, he gives her no more thought while falling in "love" (or lust) with Dido than he gives Dido after issuing the orders to sail away from Carthage.

---

116 "quaerenti et tectis urbis sine fine furenti" (*ibid.*, 2.771).
117 "σὴν ἄλοχον, τῆς τ' αἰὲν ἐέλδεαι ἤματα πάντα" (Homer. *Odyssey*, 5.210. Vol. I: Books 1–12, ed. by A. T. Murray [Loeb Classical Library, Cambridge, MA: Harvard University Press, 1919]).
118 "ὣς φάτο, τῷ δ' ἔτι μᾶλλον ὑφ' ἵμερον ὦρσε γόοιο· / κλαῖε δ' ἔχων ἄλοχον θυμαρέα, κεδνὰ ἰδυῖαν" (Homer. *Odyssey*, 23.231–32. Vol. II: Books 13–24, ed. by A. T. Murray).
119 Jean H. Hagstrum. *Esteem Enlivened by Desire: The Couple from Homer to Shakespeare* (Chicago: University of Chicago Press, 1992), 58.

Dido and Aeneas. Ancient Roman fresco (10 BC–45 AC). Pompeii, Italy.[120]

The love story between the two is mostly one-sided, primarily on Dido's part. The deck is strangely stacked against her, as well. She falls in love unwillingly, forced by the gods to play the role that will destroy her, despite the fact that Juno regards Dido as dying an undeserved death. The gods — as is their usual course in Homer, Virgil, and most Greek and Roman mythology — play with human beings like chess pieces on a grand game board. Dido's passion comes over her against her will as part of an ongoing struggle between Juno and Venus that dates all the way back to the famous judgment of Paris, that Venus was more beautiful than Juno. Dido is not a tragic figure in the later Senecan model, whose wounds are often self-inflicted. No, Dido, like so many tragic figures from the earlier Greek tradition of Aeschylus, Sophocles, and Euripides, is made a victim by the gods as they play out their petty rivalries on the human stage, with mortals as their unwitting proxies. Dido is caught, as Hamlet would say, between "the pass and fell incensed points / Of mighty opposites":[121] Juno, who opposed Troy and opposes the founding of Rome, and Venus, who aids her son Aeneas wherever and whenever possible. Venus sends Cupid, in the guise of Aeneas' son, to pierce Dido's heart with the first fatal pangs of love for Aeneas:

---

120 https://commons.wikimedia.org/wiki/File:Affreschi_romani_-_Enea_e_didone_-_pompei.JPG
121 *Hamlet*, 5.2.60–61.

> Tu faciem illius noctem non amplius unam
> falle dolo, et notos pueri puer indue voltus,
> ut, cum te gremio accipiet laetissima Dido
> regalis inter mensas laticemque Lyaeum,
> cum dabit amplexus atque oscula dulcia figet,
> occultum inspires ignem fallasque veneno.[122]

> Do you, just for this one night,
> imitate his form, and boy as you are, take his familiar face,
> so that, when Dido takes you into her lap
> amidst the royal tables and flowing wine,
> and she embraces you and kisses you sweetly,
> breathe into her a hidden fire and secretly poison her.

The famous night that Aeneas and Dido spend in a cave while taking shelter from a rainstorm, the night of their first lovemaking, is arranged as a trap by the dueling goddesses, Juno and Venus. As Juno designs it:

> venatum Aeneas unaque miserrima Dido
> in nemus ire parant, ubi primos crastinus ortus
> extulerit Titan radiisque retexerit orbem.
> his ego nigrantem commixta grandine nimbum,
> dum trepidant alae saltusque indagine cingunt,
> desuper infundam et tonitru caelum omne ciebo.
> diffugient comites et nocte tegentur opaca:
> speluncam Dido dux et Troianus eandem
> devenient. adero et, tua si mihi certa voluntas,
> conubio iungam stabili propriamque dicabo.
> hic hymenaeus erit.[123]

> Aeneas and unhappy Dido, as one
> prepare to go hunting in the woods, where the first risings
> Of brilliant Titan will have raised his rays, lighting the world.
> I shall pour on them a black storm mixed with hail,
> whilst the hunters run back and forth with their nets,
> from above I will shake the whole sky with thunder.

---

122 *The Aeneid*, 1.683–88.
123 Ibid., 4.117–27.

> The comrades will scatter and be covered with opaque night:
> into a cave will Dido and the Trojan chief
> vanish. I will be present, and, if your will is firm,
> in a stable and proper marriage and wedlock,
> this will be a wedding.

Once word spreads of the love affair, as "Rumor runs through Libya's great cities",[124] the common people, King Iarbus (long a suitor for Dido's love), and the poem itself turn against the idea of the "marriage" into which Juno has bound the pair. The people's talk turns sour and critical, turning the night in the cave into something sordid and "shameful":

> venisse Aenean Troiano sanguine cretum,
> cui se pulchra viro dignetur iungere Dido;
> nunc hiemem inter se luxu, quam longa, fovere
> regnorum immemores turpique cupidine captos.
> haec passim dea foeda virum diffundit in ora.[125]

> Aeneas is come, born of Trojan blood,
> with whom in marriage fair Dido deigns to join;
> now, between them, in luxury they waste the length of winter,
> reigning heedlessly, enthralled by shameful desire.
> These tales the foul goddess spreads through men's mouths.

Soon enough (too soon, from Dido's perspective), Jove orders Aeneas to leave Carthage and sail across the Mediterranean in search of the shores where he will lay the foundations for the "kingdom of Italy and Rome".[126] Immediately, Aeneas "burns to depart in flight, and relinquish that pleasant land",[127] strategizing not how to leave, but how to make his excuses to Dido: "Ah, what could he do? What can he dare say now to the furious queen / to pacify her? What opening speech could he use?"[128] Aeneas is more concerned with how to manipulate Dido into approving of his sudden plan than he is with the effect his leaving will have on her.

---

124 "Libyae magnas it Fama per urbes" (*ibid.*, 4.173).
125 *Ibid.*, 4.191–95.
126 "regnum Italae Romanaque" (*ibid.*, 4.275).
127 "ardet abire fuga dulcisque relinquere terras" (*ibid.*, 4.348).
128 "heu quid agat? quo nunc reginam ambire furentem / audeat adfatu? quae prima exordia sumat?" (*ibid.*, 4.283–84).

As with Creusa, he never looks back, and she does not cross his mind, except as an immovable anchor he must cut loose and pull away from. The confrontation between them is heartbreaking and baffling to Dido, but merely embarrassing for Aeneas, whose eyes are now solely fixed on his dearly-beloved gods as he seeks to navigate the awkward final moments of his time with yet another woman he will leave behind on his journey. Dido begs him, uselessly, not to go:

> mene fugis? per ego has lacrimas dextramque tuam te
> (quando aliud mihi iam miserae nihil ipsa reliqui),
> per conubia nostra, per inceptos hymenaeos,
> si bene quid de te merui, fuit aut tibi quicquam
> dulce meum, miserere domus labentis et istam,
> oro, si quis adhuc precibus locus, exue mentem.[129]

> You're running from me? By these tears and by your hand,
> (since there is nothing else for my miserable self),
> through our marriage, by the way our wedding took place,
> if I have deserved well of you, or if there was anything
> sweet about me, have mercy on a falling house, and yet,
> I pray you, if there is room for prayers, change your mind.

But Aeneas, possessed by an immovable determination to obey the very gods who have so long betrayed him and his beloved Troy, gives an answer that sounds like little more than the *It's not you, it's me* cliché of innumerable modern breakup scenes:

> ego te, quae plurima fando
> enumerare vales, numquam, regina, negabo
> promeritam, nec me meminisse pigebit Elissae
> dum memor ipse mei, dum spiritus hos regit artus.
> [...]
> sed nunc Italiam magnam Gryneus Apollo,
> Italiam Lyciae iussere capessere sortes;
> hic amor, haec patria est.
> [...]

---

129 *Ibid.*, 4.314–19.

> desine meque tuis incendere teque querelis;
> Italiam non sponte sequor.[130]

> I will, because of many things which
> you are able to recount, never, queen, deny that you
> are deserving, nor shall I regret my memory of Dido
> while I am mindful of myself, while breath reigns in this body.
> [...]
> But now of great Italy has Grynean Apollo spoken,
> Italy, his Lycian lots order me to take hold of;
> this must be my love, this my fatherland.
> [...]
> Stop inflaming both of us with your complaints;
> I do not go to Italy of my own free will.

Virgil works especially hard here to make Aeneas sympathetic, despite the fact that such a move comes at the cost of making him seem weak and dishonest, denying the fact that he chooses to obey power—as he once did with Priam, and as he now does with Jove. He is at pains to deny that his relationship with Dido is a marriage—"I never held out the conjugal torch, / nor ever pretended to such a contract"[131]—despite the fact that Juno calls it a marriage from the very beginning. Virgil is so eager to excuse Aeneas, in fact, that his poem blames Dido for impropriety in getting involved in a relationship arranged by the gods who call the action "marriage" (this, in a Rome in which Augustus Caesar is legislating private relationships):

> pronuba Iuno
> dant signum; fulsere ignes et conscius aether
> conubiis summoque ululurant vertice Nymphae.
> ille dies primus leti primusque malorum
> causa fuit; neque enim specie famave movetur
> nec iam furtivum Dido meditatur amorem:
> coniugium vocat, hoc praetexit nomine culpam.[132]

---

130 *Ibid.*, 4.333–37, 345–47, 359–60.
131 "nec coniugis umquam / praetendi taedas aut haec in foedera veni" (*ibid.*, 4.422–23).
132 *Ibid.*, 4.166–72.

> Nuptial Juno
> gave the signal; fires flashed in the heavens
> witnessing the marriage, as Nymphs howl from the peaks.
> That day was the first of death and evil,
> the cause of woe; no longer does reputation concern her,
> nor does Dido dream of a secret love:
> she calls it marriage, and in this name covers her guilt.

Any guilt that Dido feels may come from her feeling that she has somehow betrayed the memory of Sychaeus, her long-dead husband, by falling in love with Aeneas:

> agnosco veteris vestigia flammae.
> sed mihi vel tellus optem prius ima dehiscat
> [...]
> ante, pudor, quam te violo aut tua iura resolvo.[133]

> I recognize the vestiges of the old flame.
> But may the earth open for me to its depths
> [...]
> before, Shame, I violate you or break your law.

But guilt aside, it is not only Dido that calls the relationship between herself and Aeneas a marriage. In this case, Aeneas, always so ready to align himself with the will of the gods, denies what the gods affirm. According to Macrobius (c. 400 CE), Virgil puts Dido into a completely untenable position, violently transforming a figure of legendary faithfulness into the passionate victim of love he portrays in the *Aeneid*:

> [Virgil] imitated whatever, and wherever he found; so that the fourth book of the *Argonautica* by Apollonius served as the model for his fourth book of the *Aeneid*, upon which he almost entirely formed the tale of Dido and Aeneas' love on the wildly incontinent passion Medea bore for Jason. [Virgil] so elegantly arranged this that his account of a lustful Dido, which he and all the world knows is false, has for many centuries maintained the appearance of truth.[134]

---

133 Ibid., 4.23–24, 27.
134 [Virgil] quidquid ubicumque invenit imitandum; adeo ut de Argonauticorum quarto, quorum scriptor est Apollonius, librum Aeneidos suae quartum totum paene formaverit, ad Didonem vel Aenean amatoriam incontinentiam Medeae circa Iasonem trasferendo. quod ita elegantius

There is a split tradition about Dido, a pre-Virgilian tradition "that represents her only as a leader"[135] and a post-Virgilian account in which she has been turned into a victim of passion. In the earlier tradition, "preserved among the fragments attributed to the Greek historian Timaeus of Tauromenium (*ca.* 356–260 BCE)" Dido is no one's victim, but "is a heroic figure [whose] suicide is an act of defiance that testifies to the nobility of her nature".[136] In this story, Dido dies in order to avoid dishonor to herself and Carthage:

> With the success of the opulent wealth of Carthage, Hiarbas of the Maxitani summoned ten African leaders in order to claim [Dido] in marriage under threat of war. The deputies, fearing to report this to the queen of the Carthaginians, acted falsely towards her with the news that the king asked for and awaited one who could teach he and his and Africans together a more cultured life; but who could be found, who would wish to leave his relations and cross over to live among the barbarians and wild beasts? Then, castigated by the queen, in case they refused a hard life for the salvation of the rest of the country, to which, if necessary, their life itself was owed, they disclosed the king's message, saying that she will have to act according to the precepts she gives to others, if she wishes to her city to have security. Taken by this deceit, in the name of Acerbas she called, for a long time and with many tears and piteous wailings. At last she replies that she will go where the fate of her city has summoned her. Taking three months, pyres were built in the outer quarter of the city, and many victims mounted and were consumed by the fires, as if she would placate the ghost of her husband, and make her offerings to him before the wedding; then with a sword she mounted the pyre, and looking at the people, said that she would go to her husband just as she was instructed, and ended her life with the sword.[137]

---

auctore digessit, ut fabula lascivientis Didonis, quam falsam novit universitas, per tot tamen saecula speciem veritatis.

Macrobius. *Saturnalia, Books 3–5*, ed. by Robert A. Kaster (Loeb Classical Library, Cambridge, MA: Harvard University Press, 2011), 408.

135 Marilynn Desmond. *Reading Dido: Gender, Textuality, and Medieval Aeneid* (Minneapolis: University of Minnesota Press, 1994), 24.
136 *Ibid.*
137 Cum successu rerum florentes Karthaginis opes essent, rex Maxitanorum Hiarbas decem Poenorum principibus ad se arcessitis Elissae nuptias sub belli denuntiatione petit. Quod legati reginae referre metuentes Punico cum ea ingenio egerunt, nuntiantes regem aliquem poscere, qui cultiores victus eum Afrosque perdoceat; sed quem inveniri posse, qui ad barbaros et ferarum more viventes transire a consanguineis velit? Tunc a regina castigati, si pro salute patriae asperiorem vitam recusarent, cui etiam ipsa vita, si res exigat, debeatur, regis mandata aperuere, dicentes quae praecipiat aliis, ipsi facienda esse, si velit urbi consultum. Hoc dolo

Virgil also stacks the deck against Dido by portraying her, though her Tyrian roots and Carthaginian power, as a passionate and irrational Eastern woman, the very model of the Parthian threat that Rome faced on its Eastern frontiers, and a clear and contemporary reference to the all-too-recent troubles brought upon Rome by the dalliance between Augustus' defeated rival Marc Antony and the Egyptian Queen, Cleopatra. She is cast as precisely the kind of "unstable" element (uncontrolled female desire) that Aeneas is supposedly well rid of, and that Augustus (in the persons of his daughter Julia, and his granddaughter Julia) will eventually banish from Rome. Her frenzied suicide is a far cry from the resigned calm of such Romans as Cato, who killed himself in a gesture designed to value liberty above life in the dying days of the Roman Republic:

> The night before his death Cato is calm and discusses Stoic philosophy over dinner with his companions. [...] Later that night he tries to kill himself with his own sword—but because his hand is injured, the blow is not quite powerful enough. His companions come to his rescue and his wound is sewn up by a surgeon. But such is Cato's determination that he tears open the wound again with his bare hands [...]. Cato's bravery and determination in taking his own life brought him immediate glory.[138]

Dido, on the other hand, is portrayed as wild, out of control, made insane with passion due to the poison of Cupid. First, she curses Aeneas, and calls for never-ending war between the people of Carthage and the future people of Rome:

> haec precor, hanc vocem extremam cum sanguine fundo.
> tum vos, o Tyrii, stirpem et genus omne futurum
> exercete odiis, cinerique haec mittite nostro

---

capta diu Acherbae viri nomine cum multis lacrimis et lamentatione flebili invocato ad postremum ituram se quo sua et urbis fata vocarent, respondit. In hoc trium mensium sumpto spatio, pyra in ultima parte urbis exstructa, velut placatura viri manes inferiasque ante nuptias missura multas hostias caedit et sumpto gladio pyram conscendit atque ita ad populum respiciens ituram se ad virum, sicut praeceperint, dixit vitamque gladio finivit

Marcus Junianus Justinus. *Epitoma Historiarum Philippicarum Pompei Trogi* (Leipzig: B. G. Teubner, 1886), VI. 1–7, 134–35), https://babel.hathitrust.org/cgi/pt?id=uiug.30 112023680843;view=1up;seq=202

138 Catherine Edwards. *Death in Ancient Rome* (New Haven: Yale University Press, 2007), 2.

> munera. nullus amor populis nec foedera sunto.
> exoriare aliquis nostris ex ossibus ultor
> qui face Dardanios ferroque sequare colonos,
> nunc, olim, quocumque dabunt se tempore vires.
> litora litoribus contraria, fluctibus undas
> imprecor, arma armis: pugnent ipsique nepotesque.[139]

> This is my prayer, with these words I pour out my blood.
> Then do you, O Tyrians, pursue his race, and his children
> with hatred, and to my dust offer this
> gift—let no love nor federation be between our peoples.
> Rise from my ashes, unknown avenger
> to fight with fire and sword the Dardan colonies,
> now, hereafter, whenever we have the strength.
> Let shore clash with shore, waves with waves clash.
> This is my curse: endless war between us and their children.

Then, climbing atop the burning pyre on which she will die, she cries out over the life she has lived, and bemoans the fate that brought Aeneas to the shores of Carthage:

> 'felix, heu nimium felix, si litora tantum
> numquam Dardaniae tetigissent nostra carinae'.
> dixit, et os impressa toro 'moriemur inultae,
> sed moriamur' ait. 'sic, sic iuvat ire sub umbras.
> hauriat hunc oculis ignem crudelis ab alto
> Dardanus, et nostrae secum ferat omina mortis'.[140]

> "I had been happy, indeed too happy, if only the
> Trojan ships had never touched our shores".
> She spoke, face pressed on the bed: "We die unavenged,
> but let us die. Thus, it pleases to go down to the shades.
> May he drink this fire with his eyes, from far at sea, that cruel
> Trojan, and carry with him omens of our death".

---

139 *The Aeneid*, 4.621–29.
140 *Ibid.*, 4.657–62.

Dido's fate, written by Virgil to glorify the authoritarian and imperial Rome of Augustus Caesar, is to die for love. Aeneas' fate is to live in the annals of poetry as the ultimate symbol of those who choose obedience, and the gods, over passion. An entire tradition of later poetry takes Aeneas to task, including John Milton, who writes his Adam as the founder of a world (not merely a city) who chooses love over God. This tradition has its deepest roots in the poet who most admired Virgil's skill, and most despised his politics: Ovid—whose more serious side is evident in his treatment of Dido, giving her a voice and a dignity that Virgil denied her.

IV
Love or Obedience in Ovid: Aeneas, Dido, and the Critics who Dismiss

Dido is a character Ovid would (and does) sympathize with. Aeneas, the curiously dispassionate son of the goddess of love, and the unquestioningly obedient servant of power, is the character that Virgil would have readers admire. We are assured by some classical scholars that those of us who sympathize with Dido (finding Aeneas a combination of inexplicable and abhorrent) are simply wrong, because all Romans read the poem in favor of Aeneas: "His speech, though we may not like it, was the Roman answer to the conflict between two compelling forms of love, an answer such as a Roman Brutus once gave, when he executed his two sons for treason against Rome".[141] But what of Ovid? What of the many Roman readers who read, enjoyed, and admired Ovid's verse? Were they not Romans as well? Despite Augustus, Rome was no more monolithic in its literary and political sympathies than had been Athens before it, or would be London after it.

Ovid's most famous treatment of the episode is quite short, but more in line with what might be expected from the author of the *Amores* than with the author of the *Aeneid*. His focus is on Dido, the pain she feels at the loss of Aeneas, and her death. Aeneas is given no more than a sidelong glance in the few lines Ovid spends on the story in his *Metamorphoses*:

---

[141] R. G. Austin. *P. Vergili Maronis Aneidos Liber Quartos* (Oxford: Clarendon Press 1955), 106.

> excipit Aenean illic animoque domoque
> non bene discidium Phrygii latura mariti
> Sidonis; inque pyra sacri sub imagine facta
> incubuit ferro deceptaque decipit omnes.[142]

> Aeneas received there her heart and home,
> but she could not abide parting from her Phrygian husband;
> on a fire intended for sacred rites, she fell upon her sword,
> deceiving all, as she had been deceived.

Ovid's treatment of the relationship, described as a marriage, takes on a more expansive and unqualifiedly pro-Dido tone in *The Heroides*, which appear to be "an early work, contemporary with the earliest *Amores*".[143] If so, the sensitivity displayed by a poet still in his twenties makes it hard to understand what those critics who regard Ovid as having "excessive desire for himself"[144] are seeing when they read his work. Far from reflecting anything like narcissism, Ovid's treatment of Dido "constitutes one of the earliest surviving reactions to the *Aeneid*, and one of the boldest [and most] scathing about Aeneas".[145]

A letter written from Dido's point of view, Ovid's *Heroides* 7, "Dido to Aeneas", is one of the single most heart-wrenching things that ever came from his pen, and gives the lie to scholarly insistence that the Roman answer to Dido would have been the one Virgil gave to Aeneas. Ovid writes Dido as someone who sees Aeneas, sees through the pro-imperial Roman propaganda of the Augustan regime, and no more reads things the single right Roman way than Ovid does himself:

> In the *Aeneid*, Dido seems never quite able to accept that wandering has now become a fundamental part of Aeneas' character. [...] Ovid's Dido, by contrast, can see that Aeneas is the kind of man who needs to keep moving, and who avoids facing up to the things he has done by simply

---

142 Ovid. *Metamorphoses*. 14.78–82 (Berlin: De Gruyter, 1998), 332.
143 Peter E. Knox. "The Heroides: Elegaic Voices". In *Brill's Companion to Ovid*, ed. by Barbara Weiden Boyd (Leiden: Brill, 2002), 120.
144 Sharrock, 293.
145 Richard Tarrant. "Ovid and Ancient Literary History". In *The Cambridge Companion to Ovid*, ed. by Philip R. Hardie (Cambridge: Cambridge University Press, 2002), 25.

leaving town. This Dido sees Aeneas as addicted to wandering, and doomed to the repetition of his mistakes.[146]

Ovid's Dido does not go wild with anger as does Virgil's, does not call down curses, and make predictions of catastrophic future wars; she merely tells Aeneas, sadly, that he will never find another love like hers:

> quando erit, ut condas instar Karthaginis urbem
> et videas populos altus ab arce tuos?
> omnia ut eveniant, nec di tua vota morentur,
> unde tibi, quae te sic amet, uxor erit?
> Uror ut inducto ceratae sulpure taedae,
> ut pia fumosis addita tura rogis.
> Aeneas oculis vigilantis semper inhaeret;
> Aenean animo noxque diesque refert.
> ille quidem male gratus et ad mea munera surdus
> et quo, si non sim stulta, carere velim.
> non tamen Aenean, quamvis male cogitat, odi,
> sed queror infidum questaque peius amo.[147]

> When will you establish a city like Carthage,
> and see the people from your own high citadel?
> Should all take place exactly in the event as in your prayers,
> where will you find the lover who loves as I do?
> I burn, like waxen torches covered with sulfur,
> as the pious incense placed upon a smoking altar.
> Aeneas, to you my waking eyes were always drawn;
> Aeneas lives in my heart both night and day.
> But he is ungrateful, and spurns my gifts,
> and were I not a fool, I would be rid of him.
> Yet, however ill he thinks of me, I cannot hate him.
> I complain of his faithlessness, but my love grows worse.

Ovid also catches Aeneas's odd remark about having not given his wife a single thought while helping his father and son escape the fires of

---

146 Rebecca Armstrong. *Ovid and His Love Poetry* (London: Bloomsbury Academic, 2005), 111.
147 Ovid. "Heroides VII: Dido to Aeneas". In *Ovid: Heroides and Amores,* ed. by Grant Showerman, 34, ll. 19–30.

Troy. He gives Dido a sharp, yet gentle response, far from the raving to which Virgil subjects her. In her Ovidian letter, she reproves Aeneas for his hypocrisy to his gods and to his previous wife:

> quid puer Ascanius, quid di meruere Penates?
> ignibus ereptos obruet unda deos?
> sed neque fers tecum, nec, quae mihi, perfide, iactas,
> presserunt umeros sacra paterque tuos.
> omnia mentiris; neque enim tua fallere lingua
> incipit a nobis, primaque plector ego:
> si quaeras ubi sit formosi mater Iuli—
> occidit a duro sola relicta viro![148]

> What has little Ascanius done to deserve this fate?
> Snatched from the fire only to be drowned in the waves?
> No, neither are you bearing them with you, false boaster;
> your shoulders neither bore the sacred relics, nor your father.
> You lie about *everything*; and I am not the first victim of your lies,
> nor I am the first to suffer a blow from you:
> do you ever ask, where Iulus' mother is?
> She died because her unfeeling husband left her behind!

In remarking that she is not the first that Aeneas has abandoned, Dido makes it clear that she regards herself as his second left-behind wife, a critique that Ovid employs both here and in the *Metamorphoses* to reject Aeneas' Virgilian excuse that he had never married her. Finally, describing the form her death will take, Dido places the blame squarely on Aeneas:

> scribimus, et gremio Troicus ensis adest;
> perque genas lacrimae strictum labuntur in ensem,
> qui iam pro lacrimis sanguine tinctus erit.
> quam bene conveniunt fato tua munera nostro!
> instruis impensa nostra sepulcra brevi.
> nec mea nunc primum feriuntur pectora telo:
> ille locus saevi vulnus amoris habet.[149]

---

148 *Ibid.*, 88, ll. 77–86.
149 *Ibid.*, 96, ll. 184–90.

> I write, and in my bosom the Trojan sword is here;
> over my cheeks the tears run, onto the drawn sword,
> which soon will be stained with blood rather than tears.
> How fitting is your gift in my fateful hour!
> You bring my death so cheaply.
> Nor is now the first time my heart feels a weapon's blow:
> it already bears the cruel wounds of love.

Ovid, unlike Virgil, doesn't lift a finger to make readers sympathize with Aeneas. Quite the opposite—he portrays his abandonment of Dido as the betrayal of life as it is lived by ordinary human beings who are neither emperors, nor the epic heroes meant to justify them:

> Ovid transfers Dido's story from an account of Rome's imperial origins to a collection of letters written by classical heroines lamenting erotic betrayals. A more intimate, cyclical view of history as repeated instances of male treachery replaces Virgil's portrait of it as a linear progress from Troy to Actium. From this feminine perspective, the crucial events are not the rise and fall of empires but the births, deaths, and love affairs of private individuals. By disregarding Aeneas's public accomplishments, Ovid undermines the official justification for Dido's abandonment. If Aeneas is a hero according to one account, he is a traitor according to the other.[150]

It should come as no surprise, however, that among Ovid's critics are those who would rather sympathize with Augustus, and his proxy figure Aeneas, than with Dido. Lancelot Patrick Wilkinson dismisses Dido in *Heroides* 7, and, in so doing, very neatly embodies a too-common condition among literary critics—the cultivated inability to respond emotionally to poetry (except, perhaps, with the impatience of a reader no longer able to respond other than as a literary-reference-detection machine):

> [T]he more Ovid tries to excel, the less he succeeds. The forced epigrams creak [...]. We are not really convinced when Virgil's Dido, exaggerating a curse that had come naturally in Homer, less naturally in Catullus, raves that Aeneas was the son of a Caucasian crag, nurtured by Hyrcanian tigresses; still less, when Ovid's Dido attributes his origin to stone and mountain-oaks, wild beasts or, better still, the sea in storm as now it is.

---

150 John Watkins. *The Specter of Dido: Spenser and Virgilian Epic* (New Haven: Yale University Press, 1995), 31.

> [...] So it goes on, argument after weary argument, conceit after strained conceit (to our way of thinking), for close on to two hundred lines.[151]

Here we have a glimpse inside the mind of a critic who, recounting "argument after weary argument", is no longer able, or willing—so impressed is he by the Virgilian virtues of warfare and obedience—to respond to anything in poetry which is not immediately redolent of masculine blood and iron.

Ovid was never the kind of poet an admirer of power and empire would find amenable, and such admiration is amply represented in the critical literature. For example, Howard Jacobson argues that "Ovid's [...] inability to separate out his personal feelings from the mythical situation is one reason why this poem fails".[152] Here a literary critic points to a poet and says that the poet's "inability" to get beyond "personal feelings" is a reason for poetic failure. It is difficult to think of a more perfect illustration of the unbridgeable chasm that often seems to separate poetry and its critics. But more than his "feelings", for Jacobson it is Ovid's politics that represent his real failing: "Ovid was congenitally averse to the Vergilian world-view and quite unable to sympathize with a *Weltenschauung* that could exalt grand, abstract—not to mention divine—undertakings over simple individual, human and personal considerations".[153] This is an extraordinary argument, brutal in its frank dismissal of the value of individual human life: *Ovid was wrong to the extent that he did not value empire over the individual heart; and so, too, are you.* For Jacobson, *Heroides* 7 is merely an agon, a struggle of one poet with another, "Ovid waging war against Vergil". Ovid, just as those who admire him, "is doomed to defeat from the start because of his incapacity and unwillingness to appreciate the Vergilian position".[154] Note the weasel word, *appreciate*. Not understand and reject: Ovid failed, as do readers for whom Ovid's treatment of Dido is more appealing than Virgil's, because of a failure to agree with and align with the obvious rightness of the imperial, the "grand, abstract [and] divine", rather than the "individual, human and personal".

---

151 L. P. Wilkinson. *Ovid Recalled* (Cambridge: Cambridge University Press, 1955), 93.
152 Howard Jacobson. *Ovid's Heroidos* (Princeton: Princeton University Press, 1974), 90.
153 *Ibid.*, 90.
154 *Ibid.*

But even critics not quite so imperially inclined find reason to dismiss Ovid's Dido: for David Scott Wilson-Okamura, "[c]ompared with Virgil's Dido, Ovid's Dido (in *Heroides* 7) is a simplification. A mere victim, she is sad, but somehow not tragic—not tragic because not strong. We pity her more and care about her less".[155] For such critics, compared with the martial glories of Virgil's Aeneas, and even the rage of Virgil's Dido, the quiet, sad, but ultimately not-to-be-deceived understanding of Ovid's Dido offers too little in the way of excitement or what is mistaken for strength. But Ovid's Dido is much stronger than Virgil's, for she sees what Aeneas really is (and by extension, what Rome and its servants really are, what any empire and its servants, even its academic servants, really are). Such critics ignore a crucial point, since the "difference between Virgil's Dido and Ovid's illuminates the differences in style and politics between epic and epistle. [...] In Ovid, national glory is irrelevant [...]".[156] All too many (primarily male) literary critics condescendingly dismiss Dido in the fashion of W. S. Anderson, who writes of what he calls "a contrast between a *heroic* and a *charming* Dido",[157] then goes on rather back-handedly to credit Ovid for freeing Dido "from the grandeur and majesty Virgil sought" while giving her "arguments [that] tend to produce an impression of a charming, even coquettish woman of passion".[158] If you listen carefully there, you can hear the *tsk tsk* being delivered along with a pat on the head. But as so often, the critic says more about himself here than about the poet or the poem. Perhaps it is ever thus.

For Ovid, and for many of his readers, "[y]ou cannot leave Dido behind. She will not oblige by sacrificing the private life, the life of feelings, to the greater glory of Rome".[159] And yet, from a practical and political point of view, perhaps Ovid should have left her behind. Perhaps the poet erred in writing his Dido as he did. In all likelihood, it was at least partly Ovid's own poetry, perhaps even his letter from Dido to Aeneas, that got him into trouble with the imperial dictator. It could

---

155 David Scott Wilson-Okamura. *Virgil in the Renaissance* (Cambridge: Cambridge University Press, 2010), 234.
156 Linda S. Kauffman. *Discourses of Desire: Gender, Genre, and Epistolary Fictions* (Ithaca: Cornell University Press, 1986), 48.
157 W. S. Anderson. "The Heroides". In *Ovid*, ed. by J. W. Binns (London: Routledge, 1973), 60.
158 *Ibid.*, 61.
159 Lanham, 63.

well be that "Ovid's version of an *impius* Aeneas predisposed Augustus against him and the *Ars*, was, as it were, the straw that broke the camel's back".[160] I. K. Horváth tells readers "to take a closer look at *Heroides* 7, the so-called Dido-letter, which was, in our opinion, written largely to offend and annoy Augustus, and is usually dismissed with the simple statement that in Ovid, 'Pius' Aeneas is a 'worthless liar'".[161]

If it is true that Ovid was making a deliberate jibe at Augustus and the Roman myth of Aeneas by writing from the point of view of a betrayed and abandoned Carthaginian queen, then we have in "Dido to Aeneas" a powerful example of love and its poetry standing up to power and saying "No". In giving Aeneas no reply to Dido's words, the poet of love, as opposed to imperial piety, throws his weight behind Dido. And so have countless readers and poets since.

---

160 Jacobson, 90, n. 26.

161 den VII. Gesang der Heroides näher ins Auge zu fassen, den sogenannten Dido-Brief, der unserer Überzeugung nach in hohem Masse dazu angetan war, bei Augustus Anstoss und Ärgernis zu erregen, und der zumeist mit der einfachen Feststellung dessen abgetan wird, dass aus dem "pius" Aeneas bei Ovid ein "nichtswürdiger Eidbrüchiger" wird.

I. K. Horvath. "Impius Aeneas". *Acta Antiqua: Academiae Scientarum Hungaricae*, ed. by A. Dobrovits, J. Harmatta, and G. Y. Moravcsik. Book 6, Vols 3–4 (1958), 390, http://real-j.mtak.hu/441/1/ACTAANTIQUA_06.pdf

3. Love and its Absences in Late Latin and Greek Poetry

I
Love in the Poetry of Late Antiquity: Latin

After Virgil and Ovid, the poetry of love begins to fade into the background of the literary scene. Many of the later Latin poets, like Claudian and Sidonius of the late fourth and the fifth centuries, follow Lucan rather than Ovid, in a poetic tradition that puts love aside entirely: "Lucan's poem, programmatically, declares the absence of 'love' at the outset. The *Bellum Civile* has no 'love'. It does not have an *Iliadic* part [...] or an *Odyssean* part. It has only war".[1] Lucan's epic *The Civil War* (or *Pharsalia*) is a lengthy account of the defeat of Pompey the Great by Julius Caesar, whose victory at the battle of Pharsalus in 48 BCE put Rome on the path to the empire it would hold for centuries: "in the Pharsalia [Lucan] universalized his personal grievance into all Rome's, and therefore the world's, loss of *libertas* [...] to the whimsy of a Caesar".[2] Though Lucan was not politically sympathetic either to Pompey or to Caesar, being instead a great admirer of Cato (a staunch defender of the old Roman Republic), he looks back with an odd nostalgia to the saner despot of the previous century. Lucan's poem is

---

1   Sergio Casali. "The *Bellum Civile* as an Anti-*Aeneid*". In *Brill's Companion to Lucan*, ed. by Paolo Asso (Leiden: Brill, 2011), 84.
2   Patrick McCloskey and Edward Phinney, Jr. "Ptolemaeus Tyrannus: The Typification of Nero in the Pharsalia". *Hermes*, 96 (1968), 80.

one in which "two incompatible attitudes are presented [...] at least as long as Lucan remained in Nero's circle: not only does he praise him, he does so against his own political beliefs".³

On the other hand, Lucan "did not object to monarchy, but to severe and despotic tyranny, as practiced in the Hellenized East and in Rome during Nero's later years. In the *Pharsalia*, tyranny was exemplified by Caesar and Alexander. Its emblem was the sword".⁴ Julius Caesar serves Lucan as "the prototype of the tyrant Nero [... though] Caesar had more virtues than Lucan cared or was able to attribute to Nero".⁵ And yet, despite his oddly ambivalent attitude toward Nero, Lucan's love for Rome, and his longing for the old days of the Republic, shine through the poem's portrayal of a charismatic Cato, the last line of defence, protecting a freedom Lucan had never known:

> Actum Romanis fuerat de rebus, et omnis
> Indiga servitii fervebat litore plebes:
> Erupere ducis sacro de pectore voces:
> "Ergo pari voto gessisti bella, iuventus,
> Tu quoque pro dominis, et Pompeiana fuisti,
> Non Romana manus? quod non in regna laboras,
> Quod tibi, non ducibus, vivis morerisque, quod orbem
> Adquiris nulli, quod iam tibi vincere tutum est,
> Bella fugis
> [...]
> nunc patriae iugulos ensesque negatis,
> Cum prope libertas?
> [...]
> O famuli turpes, domini post fata prioris
> Itis ad heredem.⁶

---

3   Nigel Holmes. "Nero and Caesar: Lucan 1.33–66". *Classical Philology*, 94: 1 (January 1999), 80, https://doi.org/10.1086/449419
4   McCloskey and Phinney, 82.
5   *Ibid.*, 83.
6   Lucan. *The Civil War*, 9.253–61, 264–65, 274–75, ed. by J. D. Duff (Cambridge, MA: Harvard University Press, 1962), 522, 524.

3. *Love and its Absences in Late Latin and Greek Poetry* 99

The campaign for Rome was nearly ended, and the mob,
on fire for servitude, swarmed across the beach.
Then from the leader's sacred breast, these words burst forth:
"So did you young men go to war, fighting for the same vows,
defending the masters—and were you the troops of Pompey,
and not of Rome? Now that you no longer labor for a tyrant;
now that your lives and deaths, belong to you, not your leaders;
now that you fight for no one else but yourselves, *now* you
fly from the war,
[...]
now you deny your country your swords and throats
when freedom is near?
[...]
Cowardly slaves! Your former master has met his fate,
and you go to serve his heir".

Lucan, who was eventually drawn into a plot to assassinate Nero, established a pattern, with *Pharsalia*, of celebrating the greater glories of an unrecoverable Roman past, longing for a world he portrayed as more civilized than the present age. At the same time, he perversely praises the dictator Nero—whom modern historians call "a Caesar worse than Caesar, a tyrant whose vices were compounded by the petulant inhumanity of a childlike man who acted thirteen even when he was as old as thirty-two"[7]—by describing him as the glorious final goal toward which all Roman history had been striving:

> Quod si non aliam uenturo fata Neroni
> [...]
> Multum Roma tamen debet ciuilibus armis
> Quod tibi res acta est. te, cum statione peracta
> Astra petes serus, praelati regia caeli
> Excipiet gaudente polo: seu sceptra tenere
> Seu te flammigeros Phoebi conscendere currus
> Telluremque nihil mutato sole timentem
> Igne uago lustrare iuuet, tibi numine ab omni
> Cedetur, iurisque tui natura relinquet
> Quis deus esse uelis, ubi regnum ponere mundi.[8]

---

7   McCloskey and Phinney, 87.
8   Lucan, 1.33, 44–52, 25, 27.

> Yet, if fate could in no other way bring Nero,
> […]
> much will Rome owe to these civil wars
> because they were conducted for you. When your task is done,
> and you go to seek the stars, the palaces of heaven will be yours,
> heaven will be joyful: and whether you hold a sceptre
> or choose to ride Phoebus' fiery chariot
> circling with moving fire the undisturbed earth,
> by the light of fire you will be given power, from all
> granted to you, and nature will leave you to decide
> what god to be, and where to put your universal throne.

We still see this combination of nostalgia and perversity nearly four centuries later in the work of Claudian, whose panegyrics to a failing Rome, and its forgettable (and essentially forgotten) ruler Honorius, show how far poets had declined into grateful subservience since the days of the banished Ovid:

> Agnoscisne tuos, princeps venerande, penates?
> haec sunt, quae primis olim miratus in annis
> patre pio monstrante puer
> […]
> teque rudem vitae, quamvis diademate necdum
> cingebare comas, socium sumebat honorum
> purpureo fotum gremio, parvumque triumphis
> imbuit et magnis docuit praeludere fatis.
> et linguis variae gentes missique rogatum
> foedera Persarum proceres cum patre sedentem
> hac quondam videre domo positoque tiaram
> summisere genu.[9]

> Do you recognize your house, adored Prince?
> It is the same that first you marveled at in the years of old
> When your pious Father, showed it to you as a child.
> […]
> Though your life was yet rude, and the crown had not yet

---

9   Claudian. "Panegyric on the Sixth Consulship of the Emperor Honorius". 28.53–55, 65–76. *Claudian: Vol. II*, ed. by Maurice Platnauer (Loeb Classical Library, Cambridge, MA: Harvard University Press, 1998), 78.

> enclosed your head, your father shared his honors,
> his royal purple, fondling you in his lap, sharing his triumphs,
> teaching you, in your youth, the overture to your mighty destiny.
> Peoples of different nations and languages sent requests,
> Persian nobles sought treaties while sitting with your father,
> but having once seen the crown on your head,
> they also bent their knees to you.

One can imagine Ovid's disdain for such flattery (even Virgil might find this level of obsequiousness embarrassing). For Claudian "no exaggeration, however gross, suggested to him that here he must, for the sake of decency, draw the line".[10] If it seems that the purpose of poetry in the Roman world of the early fifth century (404 CE) was the unseemly celebration of mediocrity in power, that is because of work like Claudian's fawning poem to Honorius, the first Roman Emperor to see Rome sacked during his reign:

> The ambitious Alaric comprehended Honorius' feebleness and again invaded Italy, intending to march on Rome. At the time, Honorius presided over the imperial court from a town on the Adriatic coast, Ravenna, surrounded by great protective marshes [...]. Alaric besieged Rome three times between 408 and 410, [and] in 410 venerable Rome finally fell.[11]

But later fifth-century poets would not fail to rise (or sink) to the challenge represented by Claudian's flattery. Sidonius Appolinaris, the fifth-century Bishop of Auvergne, writes his *Carmen II*, or *Panegyric on Anthemius* to address the late-fifth century ruler (the *Augustus*) of a nearly-collapsed Western Roman Empire. F. J. E. Raby describes Sidonius as "the most distinguished literary figure of his day", famous for "his panegyrics on successive emperors", before noting that "the poems themselves are poor in content", though they have an "ineffectual ingenuity".[12] It is not hard to tell why: Sidonius's work, like Claudian's, is pure propaganda designed to prop up a weak ruler:

---

10 F. J. E. Raby. *A History of Secular Latin Poetry in the Middle Ages* (Oxford: Clarendon Press, 1934), 90.
11 William E. Dunstan. *Ancient Rome* (Lanham: Rowman & Littlefield Publishers, 2011), 515.
12 F. J. E. Raby. *A History of Christian-Latin Poetry: From the Beginnings to the Close of the Middle Ages* (Oxford: Clarendon Press, 1927), 80, 81.

Claudian's panegyrics have been defined as propaganda, and Sidonius' panegyrics certainly have a definite political purpose, but [...] an important fact should always be borne in mind: Claudian wrote his imperial panegyrics for an apparently established dynasty, [while] Sidonius was writing half a century later and lived in a period of political chaos.[13]

By Sidonius's time, Rome had long since begun its decline. But Sidonius was loyal to the bitter end, presenting "what remained of the empire as a model society that was worthy of unquestioning loyalty. To be loyal to Rome was to be loyal to civilization itself".[14] Yet Rome, and its civilization, had passed its peak long before Sidonius was born. Diocletian had split the Empire into western and eastern portions in 285 CE, while Constantine had transferred the center of real power from Rome to Constantinople sometime between 324 and 330 CE. Since the move east, the west had become increasingly vulnerable to northern invaders, such as Alaric in 410, and by the time of Sidonius, it was under foreign domination: "The years from 456 to 472 saw the Roman west under the virtual rule of a German named Flavius Ricimer, a Suevian general whose maternal grandfather had ruled as a Visigothic king. Ricimer made and unmade a series of puppet emperors occupying the Ravenna throne",[15] one of whom was Anthemius. But despite Anthemius's status as Ricimer's pawn, Sidonius addresses this inconsequential ruler as if he were the great Augustus Caesar himself:

> Auspicio et numero fasces, Auguste, secundos
> erige et effulgens trabealis mole metalli
> annum pande novum consul vetus ac sine fastu
> scribere bis fastis; quamquam diademate crinem
> fastigatus eas umerosque ex more priorum
> includat Sarrana chlamys, te picta togarum
> purpura plus capiat, quia res est semper ab aevo
> rara frequens consul, tuque o cui laurea, Iane,
> annua debetur, religa torpore soluto

---

13 Lynette Watson. "Representing the Past, Redefining the Future: Sidonius Appolinaris' Panegyrics of Avitus and Anthemius". In *The Propaganda of Power: The Role of Panegyric in Late Antiquity*, ed. by Mary Whitby (Boston: Brill, 1998), 181.

14 Peter Brown. *Through the Eye of a Needle: Wealth, the Fall of Rome, and the Making of Christianity in the West, 350–550 AD* (Princeton: Princeton University Press, 2012), 404.

15 Dunstan, 518.

> quavis fronde comas, subita nee luce pavescas
> principis aut rerum credas elementa moveri.
> nil natura novat: sol hie quoque venit ab ortu.[16]

> Your fortunes, Augustus, and your second *fasces*,
> take up, and in your ceremonial robe gleaming with gold,
> open, as a veteran consul, the new year; without scorn
> write your name again in the rolls; though the diadem in your hair,
> and your sloping shoulders, are like those of your predecessors
> who wore Tyrian robes, your consul's togas painted
> purple might please you more, for since Rome's earliest years
> repeated consulships are rare; and you, Janus, whose laurel
> is due to you annually, bind up your weariness,
> bind up your hair with leaves, do not give in to sudden fear,
> or imagine the elements are all in motion.
> Nature is unchanged: the sun rises in the East, but also here.

There is something absurd in lauding a weak western Augustus in an era in which power has long since flowed east to Constantinople (where the sun of wealth and power really rises in Sidonius' era).[17] No one there likely knew or cared much about the rump emperors of the feeble and abandoned west. In all likelihood, no one outside an increasingly irrelevant Rome would ever have heard or read the propaganda produced by either Claudian or Sidonius: "whether or not Claudian found many readers in the East, his propaganda is not likely to have had much more effect there than communist propaganda in western capitals today".[18]

After such unseemly adulation of past power in a perilously fragile present, the rest is silence. By 476, with the deposition of the western Emperor Romulus by Flavius Odoacer, who proceeded to call himself (and reign as) the first king of Italy, the west fell into irrelevance. The

---

16   Sidonius. "Panegyric on Anthemius", 2.1–12. In *Poems and Letters*. 2 Vols, ed. by W. B. Anderson (Loeb Classical Library, Cambridge, MA: Harvard University Press, 1963), 1: 5, 7.
17   Sidonius seems to have known this, as "he dated his death by the reign of the eastern emperor, Zeno. Sidonius considered Zeno, as emperor at Constantinople, to be the sole surviving head of the legitimate Roman empire" (Brown, 406).
18   Alan Cameron. *Claudian: Poetry and Propaganda at the Court of Honorius* (Oxford: Clarendon Press, 1970), 246.

poems of praise written by a fifth-century bishop seem, in retrospect, like insincere love letters written to a dying world, as the age of secular civilization was about to begin its long struggle with the western Church Sidonius served. Theology would soon begin to dominate Latin writing, a development reflected in much of the new Christian poetry of the period. Christianity comes to have a transformative effect (and not often for the better) on both Latin and later vernacular poetry; its influence can be seen initially in the poetry of Prudentius, a Roman Christian of the fourth century. His *Hymnus Ante Somnum* (*Hymn Before Sleep*) is representative:

> Fluxit labor diei,
> redit et quietis hora,
> blandus sopor vicissim
> fessos relaxat artus.
> [...]
> Corpus licet fatiscens
> iaceat recline paullum,
> Christum tamen sub ipso
> meditabimur sopore.[19]

> The day's labor has flowed past,
> and the quiet hours return,
> the charms of sleep, in turn,
> relax our weary limbs.
> [...]
> The weary body may
> recline a short while,
> yet in Christ himself
> our sleeping thoughts will be.

Rather than the idea of human love being introduced after "the day's labor has flowed past" (as one might expect in Ovid), the turn here is away from the human and toward the divine. This turn is even more prominent in the sixth-century poet Venantius Fortunatus, who may

---

19 Prudentius. "Hymnus Ante Somnum". In *Patrologiae Cursus Completus*, Vol. 59, ed. by Jacques Paul Migne (Paris: Apud Garnier Fratres, 1855), cols. 831–41, ll. 9–12, 149–52, https://books.google.com/books?id=jnzYAAAAMAAJ&pg=RA1-PT325

well represent the high point of artistic achievement in the Christian Latin poetry of the period. His hymn, *Vexilla Regis*, is "one of the first creations of purely medieval religious feeling",[20] a sentiment expressed in words of joy over a human sacrifice. There is no trace here of the spirit of Ovid, or the *Song of Songs*, as all emotion is directed toward the heavens:

> Vexilla regis prodeunt,
> fulget crucis mysterium,
> quo carne carnis conditor
> suspensus est patíbulo.
> [...]
> Salve ara, salve victima
> de passionis gloria,
> qua vita mortem pertulit
> et morte vitam reddidit.[21]

> The Royal banner advances,
> the mystical Cross glows,
> where the maker of flesh, flesh was made,
> suspended on the gallows pole.
> [...]
> Hail the altar, hail the victim
> of the glorious passion,
> by which life suffered death,
> and life was delivered from death.

Here, poetry serves as a vehicle for worship, a means through which imagination and emotion can be "channeled, reformulated, and controlled" away from the here and toward the hereafter. At this point, poetry is approaching the condition Plato once envisioned, in which "only hymns to the gods and poems to great men"[22] can be written. Here

---

20   Raby, 89.
21   Venantius Fortunatus. *Venanti Honori Clementiani Fortunati Presbyteri Italici Opera Poetica*, ed. by Frederick Leo (Berlin: Apud Weidmannos, 1881), 34–35, ll. 1–4, 29–32, https://archive.org/stream/venantihonoricl00unkngoog#page/n68
22   "μόνον ὕμνους θεοῖς καὶ ἐγκώμια τοῖς ἀγαθοῖς ποιήσεως" (*Republic* 607a. In *Plato: Republic. Books 6–10*, ed. by Christopher Emlyn-Jones and William Preddy [Loeb Classical Library, Cambridge, MA: Harvard University Press, 2013], 436).

also we can see the way in which love poetry has often been redirected and repurposed, not only by such commentators and critics as Akiba and Origen, but by poets working in the spirit of their ideas (Dante will be one of the pre-eminent examples of this phenomenon). Christian-themed Latin poetry such as that of Prudentius and Fortunatus remained popular[23] despite the failed attempts of Italian humanists like Pietro Bembo in the fifteenth and sixteenth centuries to revive Latin as the dominant language of secular poetry.[24] Throughout the Europe of Bembo's time, and long before, many of the most talented writers of love poetry had shifted to the vernacular,[25] in a creative and poetic mood that started with the eleventh-century poets of the area we now know as the South of France.

There are, however, some notable exceptions to the overall trend. Among them is the fourth-century poet Ausonius (from Bordeaux), who wrote a wide variety of verse: descriptions of everyday life (the *Ephemeris*), epitaphs, idylls (the most famous of which is a loving description of the Mosel region in Germany, the *Mosella*), but perhaps the single most memorable piece he ever wrote was included among his epigrams, a poem called *Ad Uxorem* (*To My Wife*). Here, he celebrates love and the wife he would lose all too soon upon her death at the age of twenty-seven:

---

23 *Vexilla Regis* was "composed for the the solemn reception of [a] special relic of the Holy Cross sent by the Eastern Roman Emperor Justin II to Saint Radegund for a convent of nuns she had founded near Poitiers, and [it is] now [2010] used in the liturgy for Passiontide" (Gabriel Díaz Patri. "Poetry in the Latin Liturgy". In *The Genius of the Roman Rite: Historical, Theological, and Pastoral Perspectives on Catholic Liturgy*, ed. by Uwe Michael Lang [Chicago: Hillenbrand Books, 2010], 45–82, 57)

24 Bembo's poetry did not have the lasting appeal of the vernacular work of the time, and in the estimate of a later scholar, it was at least partly because Bembo's Latin poetry has "more elegance than vigour", resulting in a verse that seems "polished and cold" (John Edwin Sandys. *A History of Classical Scholarship Vol. II: From the Revival of Learning to the End of the Eighteenth Century in Italy, France, England and the Netherlands* [Cambridge: Cambridge University Press, 1903], 114, 115, https://archive.org/stream/historyofclassic02sandiala#page/114).

25 The theoretical justification for this move appears first in Dante: "[t]his concern first appears in *La Vita Nuova*, where Dante informs the reader that what drew him and Guido Cavalcanti together was their agreement that this work would be written entirely in the vernacular" (Richard J. Quinones. "Dante Alighieri". In *Medieval Italy: An Encyclopedia*, ed. by Christopher Kleinhenz [New York: Routledge, 2004], 281).

> uxor, vivamus quod viximus et teneamus
> nomina quae primo sumpsimus in thalamo,
> nec ferat ulla dies, ut commutemur in aevo,
> quin tibi sim iuvenis tuque puella mihi.
> Nestore sim quamvis provectior aemulaque annis
> vincas Cumanam tu quoque Deiphoben,
> nos ignoremus quid sit matura senectus:
> scire aevi meritum, non numerare decet.[26]

> Wife, let us live as we have lived and hold fast
> to those names we first took privately,
> and not be changed by transporting time.
> Why should I not be youthful, you a maiden in years?
> Though I should live longer than Nestor,
> though you should outstrip Cumaean Sibyl,
> let us be ignorant of maturity and age,
> and know Time's worth, not count its years.

Remember this poem, when we later encounter theological and academic critics who deride husbands for "uxoriousness", or being too much in love with their wives (and too little in love with God). Remember too, the pain Ausonius describes feeling—a full thirty-six years later—as he remembers his wife Sabina:

> te iuvenis primis luxi deceptus in annis
> perque novem caelebs te fleo Olympiadas,
> nec licet obductum senio sopire dolorem;
> semper crudescit nam mihi paene recens.
> [...]
> ...tu mihi semper ades.[27]

> In my youth, I mourned for you, cheated of the years,
> and I have wept, unmarried, for nine Olympiads.
> Growing old has not obscured or dulled my sorrow;

---

26 "Ad Uxorem", Epigram 20. In *Ausonius: Epigrams. Text with Introduction and Commentary*, ed. by Nigel M. Kay (London: Duckworth, 2001), 45.

27 Ausonius. "Attusia Lucana Sabina Uxor", Parentalia IX. In *Ausonius. Vol. I: Books 1–17*, ed. by Hugh G. Evelyn-White [Loeb Classical Library, Cambridge, MA: Harvard University Press, 1919], 70, ll. 7–10, 18.

> for me, the pain ever grows, always recent.
> [...]
> ...you are always with me.

These lines were written "thirty-six years after [Sabina's] death, when Ausonius was seventy years old; yet the wound caused by her loss is still fresh, and time, which to others brings relief, has but intensified his sorrow".[28] This is not a poem that speaks only of poetry itself.

Far from being merely conventional figures, "some of Latin amatory poetry's addressees probably were based on real people", and here we have a perfect example: "Ausonius's uxor [...] is no figment of his imagination: she is in fact his wife, nor is Epigram 20 the only occasion on which he refers to her. The ninth poem of his *Parentalia*, a collection of epitaphs for dead family members, tells of her death at the age of twenty-seven".[29] In referencing Catullus' Fifth Ode (*Vivamus mea Lesbia*), "Ausonius's matrimonial love poem is [...] noteworthy for its engagement with an inherently non-matrimonial tradition",[30] a note that we will hear again, in different ways, in both Shakespeare and John Donne, over a thousand years later.

The most famous examples of later Latin love poetry, however, do not appear for centuries after the periods of Claudian, Sidonius, and Ausonius. Alcuin, the late eighth-to early ninth-century poet and scholar in the court of Charlemagne, writes some curiously passionate verses to male friends. John Boswell argues that a "distinctly erotic element [...] is notable in the circle of clerical friends presided over by Alcuin at the court of Charlemagne. [...] The prominence of love in Alcuin's writings, all of which are addressed to males, is striking".[31] One notable example is found in the opening lines of *Pectus amor nostrum penetravit flamma*:

> Pectus amor nostrum penetravit flamma
> Atque calore novo semper inardet amor.

---

28 Sister Marie José Byrne. *Prolegomena to an Edition of the Works of Decimus Magnus Ausonius*. New York: Columbia University Press, 1916, 12.
29 Robert J. Sklenár. "Ausonius' Elegiac Wife: Epigram 20 and the Traditions of Latin Love Poetry". *The Classical Journal*, 101: 1 (October-November 2005), 52.
30 *Ibid.*, 51.
31 John Boswell. *Christianity, Social Tolerance, and Homosexuality: Gay People in Western Europe from the Beginning of the Christian Era to the Fourteenth Century* (Chicago: University of Chicago Press, 1980), 188–89.

Nec mare, nec tellus, montes nec silva vel alpes
Huic obstare queunt aut inhibere viam,
Quo minus, alme pater, semper tua viscera lingat,
Vel lacrimis lavet pectus, amate, tuum.³²

The flames of our love have penetrated my breast
And new heat always relights this love.
Neither sea, nor land, mountain nor forest, nor the Alps
Can obstruct or inhibit it
In the slightest, bountiful father, from always licking your flesh,
Or bathing your breast, my love, in my tears.

Though scholars after Boswell have been at great pains to explain away the apparent eroticism of such lines as "semper tua viscera lingat" ("always licking your flesh", or perhaps even more intimately, "always licking your inmost flesh"), it should come as no surprise to anyone familiar with the history of interpreting the *Song of Songs* that there are always ready arguments to explain what appears to be erotic passion as actually something else. Allen Frantzen, for example, argues that "such effusions [...] belong to a venerable tradition of 'Christian *amicitia*'³³ and need not have any direct relation to sexual passion", then does his best to argue that Alcuin "deplored same-sex intercourse",³⁴ although this claim is undermined because Frantzen mistakes references to masturbation in Alcuin's letters for references to sex. David Clark argues along similar lines, maintaining that while "Boswell is wrong to suggest that Alcuin did not condemn same-sex activity", what Alcuin is really doing is "euphemistically referring to the sin of masturbation",³⁵ in a

---

32 Alcuin. "Pectus amor nostrum penetravit flamma". *Monumenta Germaniae historica inde ab anno Christi quingentesimo usque ad annum millesimum et quingentesimum* (Berlin: Apud Weidmannos, 1881), Vol. I: 236, ll. 1–6, https://books.google.com/books?id=U6woAAAAMAAJ&pg=PA236

33 "Christian friendship" — we will see this argument resorted to again, when scholars need to explain away what appears to be an "inconvenient" passion in the Occitan poem "Na Maria".

34 Allen J. Frantzen. *Before the Closet: Same-Sex Love from "Beowulf" to "Angels in America"* (Chicago: University of Chicago Press, 1998), 198, 199.

35 David Clark. *Between Medieval Men: Male Friendship and Desire in Early Medieval English Literature* (Oxford: Oxford University Press, 2009), 79. Clark makes this argument based on a single passage in Alcuin's voluminous output. In *Interrogationes et Responsiones in Genesin*, Alcuin takes on the following question: "In the days of Noah, why were the sins of the world punished by water, but those

letter where he threatens one of his young students that such sinners will "burn in the flames of Sodom".[36] Clark insists that "[i]t is simply not possible to say whether Alcuin's [...] desires were the outward expression of personally recognised erotic feelings and whether those feelings were sexually expressed", then goes on to make this contrary claim:

> nor is the question important or productive. It is perfectly possible for an individual to feel and express homoerotic desires and yet be utterly opposed to, even repulsed by, their physical expression, just as it is possible for an individual to condemn same-sex acts and yet be homosexually active.[37]

When trying to understand the apparent passions expressed in a poem like *Pectus amor nostrum penetravit flamma*, how can knowledge of the passions of the author be deemed unimportant and unproductive? No proof is given for such a claim; readers are apparently simply supposed to accept this pronouncement without question. This is a prescriptive style of argument that we will see again and discuss in greater depth, especially in critical discussion of Donne's work. Here we will merely observe that such arguments, which separate the poet from the poem,

---

of the Sodomites were punished by fire?" ("Quare diebus Noe peccatum mundi aqua ulciscitur, hoc vero Sodomitarum igne punitur?") Alcuin answers by drawing the reliably orthodox conclusion that the sins of Noah's world were *natural*, while those of Sodom were *unnatural*: "Because the sin of lust with women is natural, it is condemned as though by a lighter element; but the sin of lust against nature with men is avenged by the harsher burning element; there the ground is washed with water and returns to fertility; but this one is made eternally barren, burned by fire" ("Quia illud naturale libidinus cum feminis peccatum quasi leviori elemento damnatur: hoc vero contra naturam libidinis peccatum cum viris, aeriois elementi vindicatur incendio: et illic terra aquis abluta revirescit; hic flammis cremata aeterna steriliate arescit".) (*Patrologiae Cursus Completus*, ed. by Jacques Paul Migne [Paris: Apud Garnier Fratres, 1863], Vol. 100, col. 543, https://books.google.com/books?id=-JqsZH3ajIgC&pg=PT202).

36 Frantzen, 199. This letter never explicitly references the sin being spoken of: "What is it, my son, that I hear of, not from one muttering in a corner, but from many publicly laughing about the story that you are still devoted to childish uncleanness, and have never been able to dismiss what you never should have wished to do?" ("Quid est, fili, quod de te audio, non uno quolibet in angulo susurrante, sed plurimis publice cum risu narrantibus: quod puerilibus adhuc deservias immunditiis, et quae nunquam facere debuisses, nunquam dimittere voluisses [velis]".) (Alcuin. "Epistola CCVI, Ad Disciplum". In *Patrologiae Cursus Completus*, Vol. 100, col. 481–82, https://books.google.com/books?id=-JqsZH3ajIgC&pg=PT171).

37 Clark, 80.

often serve to explain away the unruly and uncontrolled desires expressed in the poetry of love.

The anonymous lyric *Iam dulcis amica*, a late tenth-or early eleventh-century poem existing in three versions,[38] celebrates a love that will begin to sound very familiar when we consider the vernacular poems of the troubadours. Peter Dronke explicitly compares this poem to the *Song of Songs*, arguing that the "Song of Songs language emerges in the terms of endearment—soror, amica, electa, dilecta […] but most of all it belongs to the final strophe of the Paris version, with its linking of the melting snows and nascent greenness with the quickening warmth of love".[39] This can be seen in the final two stanzas of the Paris manuscript:

> Ego fui sola in silva
> et dilexi loca secreta:
> Frequenter effugi tumultum
> et vitavi populum multum.
> Iam nix glaciesque liquescit,
> Folium et herba virescit,
> Philomena iam cantat in alto,
> Ardet amor cordis in antro.[40]

> I was alone in the forest
> and I delighted in secret places:
> Frequently I fled from the tumult
> and avoided the popular crowds.
> Now, as snow and ice melt,
> Leaves and grass grow green,
> The nightingale sings from high above,
> While love burns in the cave of my heart.

As Dronke argues, this song reflects a woman's perspective, and this evocation of "the fear and longing, the emotional heights and depths of the woman in love" owes a great deal "to the Song of Songs", and

---

38 See Peter Dronke, *The Medieval Poet and His World* (Rome: Edizioni di Storia e Letteratura, 1984), specifically Chapter 8, "The Song of Songs and Medieval Love Lyric", 209–36.
39 *Ibid.*, 221–22.
40 *Ibid.*, 234–35. The original text from Paris BnF Latin 1118 fol 247v. is available online at http://gallica.bnf.fr/ark:/ 12148/btv1b8432314k/f504.item

"recur[s] spontaneously in similar forms in the ancient Near East, in medieval Spain [and] Anglo-Saxon England".[41]

Perhaps more famous still are the Latin poems from the *Carmina Burana*, a manuscript from the early thirteenth century collecting Latin and German songs of mockery, morality, drinking, and love. Among the best known now, due to the music of Carl Orff, is *Tempus est iocundum*, a lyric in the *carpe diem* tradition:

> Tempus est iocundum, o virgines,
> modo congaudete vos iuvenes.
> Oh-oh, totus floreo, iam amore virginali
> totus ardeo,
> novus, novus amor est, quo pereo.
> [...]
> Veni, domicella, cum gaudio;
> veni, veni, pulchra, iam pereo.
> Oh-oh, totus floreo, iam amore virginali
> totus ardeo,
> novus, novus amor est, quo pereo.[42]

> The time is now for happiness, O virgins,
> rejoice together now you young men.
> Oh, oh, I am blooming, now with my first love.
> totally on fire,
> new, new love is what I am dying of.
> [...]
> Come, my mistress, with joy;
> come, come, my beauty, for now I am dying.
> Oh, oh, I am blooming, now with my first love,
> totally on fire,
> new, new love is what I am dying of.

But here, we have reached both the time, and the spirit of the Occitan troubadours, and have left, properly speaking, the realm of late classical

---

41　*Ibid.*, 233.
42　*Carmina Burana: Lateinische und deutsche Lieder und Gedichte einer Handschrift des XIII Jahrhunderts aus Benedictbeuern auf der K. Bibliothek gu München*, ed. by Johann Andreas Schmeller (Stuttgart: Literarischen Vereins, 1847), 211–12, https://books.google.com/books?id=0XN3YW-EqacC&pg=PA211

and early medieval Latin poetry. In lyrics such as these, we can hear the voice of Ovid and the Song of Songs once again, and see something of the essence of *fin'amor*.

II
Love in the Poetry of Late Antiquity: Greek

Greek literature, by the early centuries of the Common Era, had long since been considered lesser than Latin poetry and prose. But for a time, Greek writers kept love alive in their work, especially through the work of a group of writers known as the *Erotici Graeci*, Greek writers of love stories. Of these, the most famous is Longus, "probably a rhetorician of the period known as the Second Sophistic, [who] reveals a crafted style, wide literary learning, and an unusually sophisticated, self-conscious narrative technique".[43] *Daphnis and Chloe*, Longus' verse novel of approximately 200 CE, tells the story of two infants, a boy and a girl, exposed to die on hillsides about two years apart. In the way of such stories, the children are rescued before they are eaten by wild animals, and they are raised by rural families who live in close proximity to each other. Over the years, the two—the boy Daphnis and the girl Chloe—fall in love (Chloe when she sees Daphnis bathing, and Daphnis some time later after Chloe kisses him). However, they haven't the slightest idea about the physical aspect of love—sex is a mystery to both of them, and neither of them knows anyone willing to explain it to them. An aging cowherd named Philetas, having accidentally encountered the naked god of love in his orchard, and remembered his long-ago love for a girl named Amaryllis as a result, tells the pair that the only cure for their condition is "kissing and embracing and lying down with naked bodies".[44] The young lovers take to this activity with regularity and enthusiasm, but find themselves confused about the "lying down with naked bodies" part,

---
43 Richard F. Hardin. *Love in a Green Shade: Idyllic Romances Ancient to Modern* (Lincoln, NE: University of Nebraska Press, 2000), 11.
44 "φίλημα καὶ περιβολὴ καὶ συγκατακλινῆναι γυμνοῖς σώμασι" (Longus. *Daphnis and Chloe*, ed. by Jeffrey Henderson [Loeb Classical Library, Cambridge, MA: Harvard University Press, 2009], 2.7.7, 68).

thinking that "in any case, there must be something in it stronger than kissing",[45] without knowing what that something might be.

In the meantime, a series of misadventures threaten to separate the pair, often menacing the two lovers through "the forms of sexual violence to which Chloe—and to a certain extent Daphnis—is subject".[46] Daphnis is kidnapped by Tyrian pirates, and is only rescued by Chloe's quick thinking in playing a cowherd's pipe that induces dozens of cows to jump from a low cliff into the water near the ship (and some even onto the ship itself), causing the ship to capsize and drown the heavily-armored pirates, enabling Daphnis to swim back ashore. A fellow shepherd tries to rape Chloe, and she is abducted by Methymnean raiders seeking revenge on Daphnis. (They blame him for the loss of their ship, since one of his goats chewed through the line with which they had moored their vessel, causing it to float away with the tide while they were on shore). Longus resorts to a *deus ex machina* here, having Pan rescue Chloe.[47]

After a number of misadventures—including an episode in which Daphnis tries to imitate goats in his absurdly ineffectual claspings with Chloe[48]—Daphnis is finally taught how to make use of the "lying down with naked bodies" advice that has puzzled him for so long:

> Finding a freedom from envy and a liberality in the goatherd that she had not expected, Lycaenium began then to teach Daphnis in this manner. She ordered him to sit down next to her, and to give her the customary kind and number of kisses, and to throw his arms around her as he kissed her, and lie down upon the ground. Then he sat down, and kissed her, and lay down with her, learning in action to be able and vigorous while lying upon his side, and as he raised himself up, she slipped beneath him skillfully, bringing him into that path he had sought for so long. From

---

45 "πάντως ἐν αὐτῷ τι κρεῖττόν ἐστι φιλήματος" (ibid., 2.9.2, 70).
46 John J. Winkler. *The Constraints of Desire: The Anthropology of Sex and Gender in Ancient Greece* (New York: Routledge, 1990), 103.
47 If the reader is beginning to catch a whiff of a later story like *The Princess Bride*, he or she is probably not alone—and yes, it is still probably good advice not to get involved in a land war in Asia, though your mileage may vary whether or not to go in against a Sicilian when death is on the line.
48 Stephen Epstein raises the serious, yet profoundly comic question: "What purpose does the text achieve by bringing its male protagonist into such close connection with goats?" ("The Education of Daphnis: Goats, Gods, the Birds and the Bees". *Phoenix*, 56: 1–2 [Spring-Summer 2002], 26, https://doi.org/10.2307/1192468).

that point on, there was no need to take more pains with him; Nature taught him the rest of what was necessary.⁴⁹

However, Lycaenion also tells Daphnis that the experience will be different with the virgin Chloe: "Chloe, if you wrestle with her in this way, will be injured, and cry aloud while bleeding",⁵⁰ advice which frightens Daphnis and nearly dissuades him from even kissing Chloe. Daphnis here shows a concern similar to that found in the poetry of the later troubadours, as well as the works of Shakespeare and Milton, a "mutuality in love, so crucial to the meaning of this story, [which] sets the Greek romances apart". Daphnis, "exercising restraint out of consideration for Chloe, shows a different kind of love",⁵¹ caring for her as an individual whose feelings and desires are just as important to Daphnis as his own.

In the background of the two young lovers's misadventures, Chloe's parents are trying to arrange a financially advantageous marriage for her, which leaves Daphnis, a poor goatherd, in desperation. In another *deus ex machina*, the nymphs of the fields give Daphnis three thousand drachmas for him to take to Chloe's father in order that he might be the chosen suitor. In a further development—as again, is the way with such stories—events are set in motion which reveal each of the two lovers to be of high and noble birth, and they are brought together in a marriage that brings joy to everyone. Finally, "Daphnis himself taught Lycaenium's lessons, and then Chloe learned that what had happened before in the the woods had been but shepherds' games".⁵² Their love,

---

49   Εὑροῦσα δὴ ἡ Λυκαίνιον αἰπολικὴν ἀφθονίαν, οἵαν οὐ προσεδόκησεν, ἤρχετο παιδεύειν τὸν Δάφνιν τοῦτον τὸν τρόπον. Ἐκέλευσεν αὐτὸν καθίσαι πλησίον αὐτῆς, ὡς εἶχε, καὶ φιλήματα φιλεῖν οἷα εἰώθει καὶ ὅσα, καὶ φιλοῦντα ἅμα περιβάλλειν καὶ κατακλίνεσθαι χαμαί. Ὡς δὲ ἐκαθέσθη καὶ ἐφίλησε καὶ κατεκλίνη, μαθοῦσα ἐνεργεῖν δυνάμενον καὶ σφριγῶντα, ἀπὸ μὲν τῆς ἐπὶ πλευρὰν κατακλίσεως ἀνίστησιν, αὐτὴν δὲ ὑποστορέσασα ἐντέχνως ἐς τὴν τέως ζητουμένην ὁδὸν ἦγε. Τὸ δὲ ἐντεῦθεν οὐδὲν περιειργάζετο ξένον: αὐτὴ γὰρ ἡ φύσις λοιπὸν ἐπαίδευσε τὸ πρακτέον.

Longus 3.18.3–4, 126. This episode was expurgated from translations of this text as recently as the 1950s by academics and publishers determined to protect the moral decency of their readers.

50   "Χλόη δὲ συμπαλαίουσά σοι ταύτην τὴν πάλην καὶ οἰμώξει καὶ κλαύσεται κἂν αἵματι κείσεται πολλῷ" (*ibid.* 3.19.2, 126).
51   Hardin, 15, 16.
52   "Δάφνις ὧν αὐτὸν ἐπαίδευσε Λυκαίνιον, καὶ τότε Χλόη πρῶτον ἔμαθεν ὅτι τὰ ἐπὶ τῆς ὕλης γενόμενα ἦν ποιμένων παίγνια" (Longus 4.40.3, 196).

now passionately and physically expressed, brings mutuality and desire together in the fashion of *fin'amor*.

In addition to pastoral comedies like *Daphnis and Chloe*, which Jean Hagstrum refers to as "one of the subtlest explorations of dawning love in literature",[53] Greek poetry of the first millenium also gives us Musaeus' version of the legend of Hero and Leander. Musaeus, a late fifth-or early sixth century poet, transforms the tale of "the nightly marriage of Hero" and "the swimming of Leander"[54] into the tragedy that will later inspire Renaissance English poets like Christopher Marlowe and George Chapman (who finishes the version Marlowe left at his death, and translates Musaeus' version in 1616). Musaeus' Hero is a "priestess of Aphrodite"[55] and is locked away each night by her father "in the Tower of her ancestors, dwelling as a neighbor to the sea",[56] ostensibly to serve the goddess, but really to keep her out of the reach of young men. Even so, Leander knows he must have her, "at once let me die, but let me spend my strength in Hero's bed",[57] because he is on fire after looking into her eyes: "by means of her eyes' light, his love rose high like flames".[58] Leander struggles with this new-found passion and tries to master it, even briefly thinking it shameful that he has been so overpowered by love, before he determines to venture whatever it takes to have Hero:

> εἷλε δέ μιν τότε θάμβος, ἀναιδείη, τρόμος, αἰδώς,
> ἔτρεμε μὲν κραδίην, αἰδὼς δέ μιν εἶχεν ἁλῶναι,
> θάμβεε δ' εἶδος ἄριστον, ἔρως δ' ἀπενόσφισεν αἰδῶ.[59]

> seized by astonishment, impudence, trepidation, shame,
> he trembled at heart, shame possessed him to be so conquered,
> but in amazement at her excellent form, love put shame asunder.

---

53 Hagstrum, 134.
54 "γάμον ἔννυχον Ἡροῦς" [...] "νηχόμενόν τε Λέανδρον" Musaeus. *Hero and Leander*, ed. by Thomas Gelzer (Loeb Classical Library, Cambridge, MA: Harvard University Press, 1973), ll. 4–5.
55 "Κύπριδος ἦν ἱέρεια" (ibid., l. 31).
56 "πύργον ἀπὸ προγόνων παρὰ γείτονι ναῖε θαλάσσῃ" (ibid., l. 32).
57 "αὐτίκα τεθναίην λεχέων ἐπιβήμενος Ἡροῦς" (ibid., l. 79).
58 "σὺν βλεφάρων δ' ἀκτῖσιν ἀέξετο πυρσὸς Ἐρώτων" (ibid., l. 90).
59 Ibid., ll. 96–98.

After Leander ventures, and wins Hero's love, there is still a problem: her father.

Hero laments Leander's eloquence, because her father's control over her marriage prospects means "these words are entirely spoken in vain".[60] She then outlines the basic dilemma that we will see frequently—children (especially daughters) are treated as the property of their fathers, and cannot love freely where they would:

> ...πῶς γὰρ ἀλήτης
> ξεῖνος ἐὼν καὶ ἄπιστος ἐμοὶ φιλότητι μιγείης;
> ἀμφαδὸν οὐ δυνάμεσθα γάμοις ὁσίοισι πελάσσαι·
> οὐ γὰρ ἐμοῖς τοκέεσσιν ἐπεύαδεν· ἢν δ᾽ ἐθελήσῃς
> ὡς ξεῖνος πολύφοιτος ἐμὴν εἰς πατρίδα μίμνειν,
> οὐ δύνασαι σκοτόεσσαν ὑποκλέπτειν Ἀφροδίτην·
> γλῶσσα γὰρ ἀνθρώπων φιλοκέρτομος, ἐν δὲ σιωπῇ
> ἔργον ὅ περ τελέει τις, ἐνὶ τριόδοισιν ἀκούει.[61]

> ...how, may a wanderer,
> a stranger, not to be trusted, unite with me in love?
> We are not able to draw near in holy marriage,
> for it is not my father's will and pleasure; if you wish
> as a far-roaming stranger to stay in my father's land,
> you will not be able to shroud Aphrodite in night,
> for the tongues of men are fond of jeering, and the silent
> deeds of a man are soon heard of in the marketplace.

Despite the fact that Hero is a "priestess of Aphrodite" she is not "the willingly chaste priestess who seeks the isolation of her tower and wants to appease the gods of love. According to Hero, it is because of her parents' hated decision [...] that she lives in the tower outside the city, with only wind and sea as her neighbours".[62]

The arrangement the lovers make, as anyone familiar with the legend has already anticipated, is a dangerous one, as Leander plans to come to

---

60 "ταῦτα δὲ πάντα μάτην ἐφθέγξαο" (ibid., l. 177).
61 Ibid., ll. 177–84.
62 Nicola Nina Dümmler. "Musaeus, *Hero and Leander*: Between Epic and Novel". In *Brill's Companion to Greek and Latin Epyllion and Its Reception*, ed. by Manuel Baumbach and Silvio Bär (Leiden: Brill, 2012), 427.

her at night by swimming across the Hellespont. All he asks is that Hero leave the light on:

> Παρθένε, σὸν δι' ἔρωτα καὶ ἄγριον οἶδμα περιήσω,
> εἰ πυρὶ παφλάζοιτο καὶ ἄπλοον ἔσσεται ὕδωρ.
> οὐ τρομέω βαρὺ χεῖμα τεὴν μετανεύμενος εὐνήν
> [...]
> μοῦνον ἐμοὶ ἕνα λύχνον ἀπ' ἠλιβάτου σεὸ πύργου
> ἐκ περάτης ἀνάφαινε κατὰ κνέφας, ὄφρα νοήσας
> ἔσσομαι ὁλκὰς Ἔρωτος ἔχων σέθεν ἀστέρα λύχνον.[63]

> Maiden, for your love, I will cross the wild waves,
> though fire boil them, and rain push back the ships,
> I fear no heavy storm, in pursuit of your bed.
> [...]
> Only light me a lamp from your high tower
> to shine above the darkness that I may see it;
> I will be love's sailing ship, guided by your light.

At first, it works. Their interval of passion and mutual desire begins as Hero leads Leander to her tower:

> καί μιν ἑὸν ποτὶ πύργον ἀνήγαγεν· ἐκ δὲ θυράων
> νυμφίον ἀσθμαίνοντα περιπτύξασα σιωπῇ
> ἀφροκόμους ῥαθάμιγγας ἔτι στάζοντα θαλάσσης
> ἦγαγε νυμφοκόμοιο μυχοὺς ἔπι παρθενεῶνος.[64]

> and she led him to her high tower, where at the doors
> her panting bridegroom she silently embraced,
> still foam-drenched and dripping from the sea
> she led him deep within her bridal chamber.

And for some time to come, Hero and Leander manage both to keep their love and their secret:

---

63 Musaeus, ll. 203–05, 210–12.
64 *Ibid.*, ll. 260–63.

> Ἡρὼ δ᾽ ἑλκεσίπεπλος ἑοὺς λήθουσα τοκῆας
> παρθένος ἠματίη, νυχίη γυνή. ἀμφότεροι δὲ
> πολλάκις ἠρήσαντο κατελθέμεν εἰς δύσιν Ἠῶ.[65]

> Hero of the long-trained robes, keeping secret from her father,
> maiden was day, but wife by night, and both
> often prayed for the setting of the sun.

Many nights that summer they enjoy each other's love, but as winter comes, the swim across the Hellespont grows more difficult, until one night, the waters are too rough to be crossed:

> πολλὴ δ᾽ αὐτόματος χύσις ὕδατος ἔρρεε λαιμῷ,
> καὶ ποτὸν ἀχρήιστον ἀμαιμακέτου πίεν ἅλμης.
> καὶ δὴ λύχνον ἄπιστον ἀπέσβεσε πικρὸς ἀήτης
> καὶ ψυχὴν καὶ ἔρωτα πολυτλήτοιο Λεάνδρου.[66]

> Great waves of water poured themselves into his throat,
> and he drank deep of the worthless, irresistible brine,
> and then the traitorous lamp was blown out by a sharp wind,
> and with it died the breath and love of long-suffering Leander.

When Leander does not come that night, Hero fears the worst, and upon seeing his body washed up on the shore, Hero strips off her robe and joins him:

> ῥοιζηδὸν προκάρηνος ἀπ᾽ ἠλιβάτου πέσε πύργου.
> κὰδ δ᾽ Ἡρὼ1 τέθνηκε σὺν ὀλλυμένῳ παρακοίτῃ,
> ἀλλήλων δ᾽ ἀπόναντο καὶ ἐν πυμάτῳ περ ὀλέθρῳ.[67]

> with a rushing sound, she fell head-first from her high tower.
> Hero died next to her dead husband,
> and at last in death, each had joy in the other.

---

65 Ibid., ll. 285–87.
66 Ibid., ll. 327–30.
67 Ibid., ll. 341–43.

As we will also see in poetry from the troubadours to Shakespeare and Milton, Musaeus emphasizes the "theme of love's mutuality", in which lovers are willing "to take deadly risks in a universe that is careless of their suffering".[68] They will risk all for love, whether the physical danger of the Hellespont, the death-threats of a god, or the social, legal, and financial dangers of defying a system of arranged marriages that leaves no room for any passion (except perhaps for greed), so dedicated is that system to the profitable gains to be had through marriage and children. Slowly but surely, however, it is that very pragmatism, combined with the increasing influence of the church in Europe, that brings the classical and early-medieval eras of love poetry to their conclusion.

Love and longing are vitally present in the poetry we have so far encountered, despite the best efforts of societal law-givers and the frequent attempts of the Akibas and Origens to erase, rewrite and reinterpret this poetry. There is much more such longing in the eleventh-and twelfth-century poetry of the troubadours. As we see love thrive, proving that "powerful passion will not be constrained by the normal bonds of society",[69] so we will also see the attempts to channel, reformulate, and control it grow stronger, more systematic, and infinitely more lethal.

---

68 Pamela Royston Macfie. "Lucan, Marlowe, and the Poetics of Violence". In *Renaissance Papers 2008*, ed. by Christopher Cobb and M. Thomas Hester (Rochester: Camden House, 2009), 49.

69 Audrey L. Meaney. "The Ides of the Cotton Gnomic Poem". *Medium Ævum*, 48: 1 (1979), 36, https://doi.org/10.2307/43628412

4. The Troubadours and *Fin'amor*: Love, Choice, and the Individual

In Erich Auerbach's view, "for the Provençal poets and the [Italian] poets of the new style [*dolce stil novo*], 'high love' was the only major theme".[1] Speaking of *die hohe Minne* (what French scholars call *amour courtois*, and English scholars "courtly love"), Auerbach gives voice to a critical consensus that over the last century-and-a half has dominated our understanding of the origins and development of western love poetry. Both the consensus, and Auerbach, are wrong.

I
Why "Courtly Love" Is Not Love

Start with adultery. Start, at least, with the idea of adultery. Breaking the rules, doing something you are not supposed to do. Doing some*one* you are not supposed to do. This is the key idea that allows us to understand a literary tradition that stretches from the troubadours through Petrarch to Shakespeare, Milton, and beyond. Illicit desire— whether celebrated in the passionate poems of medieval Occitania, or sublimated in the poetic tradition of idealized females worshiped by abject males in Dante, Petrarch and Sidney—is central to the energy of Shakespeare and the poetic tradition that follows in his wake. Love,

---

1   "[f]ür die Provenzalen und die Dichter des Neuen Stils war die hohe Minne das einzige große Thema" (Erich Auerbach. *Mimesis: Dargestellte Wirklichkeit in der abendländischen Literatur*. 2nd ed. [Bern: Francke, 1959], 180).

will, desire, and the willingness (even determination) to risk everything, up to and including death—these are the passions that draw readers and audiences back again and again.

Centuries of transformation have left many of us ill-equipped to recognize the frankness and passion of troubadour verse. Some of this change was wrought merely by time and changing customs, but some of it was brought about by the best efforts of historians and literary critics to understand and interpret the past through the expectations, reverences, and distastes of later eras. Perversely, we often approach these poems through the lens of late nineteenth-century notions of propriety and decency that are alien to our own time, and to the time of the troubadours. The dangerous, even life-risking, desires expressed in these poems have been carefully tamed, hidden behind the ill-fitting phrase "courtly love". This term, invented by Gaston Paris in 1881,[2] has become commonplace in critical analyses of troubadour poetry.[3] Paris argues that

> love is an art, a science, a virtue, which has its rules as chivalry and courtesy [...]. In no French work, as it seems to me, does this courtly love appear before *the Knight of the Cart*. The love of Tristran and Isolde is a different thing: it is a simple passion, ardent, natural, which does not know the subtleties and refinements of that between Lancelot and Guinevere. In the poems of Benoit de Sainte-Maure, we find gallantry, but not this exalted, almost mystical, yet still sensual, love.[4]

---

2   Appearing as *amour courtois* in his article "Études sur les romans de la Table Ronde" in *Romania*, 10: 40 (October 1881), 465–96, and in "Études sur les romans de la Table Ronde. Lancelot du Lac, I. Le Lanzelet d'Ulrich de Zatzikhoven; Lancelot du Lac, II. Le Conte de la charrette", *Romania*, 12: 48 (October 1883), 459–534.

3   Even so recent an analysis as that of William M. Reddy relies on this term. Reddy defines the troubadour conception of *fin'amor* in terms of "an opposition between love and desire" (*The Making of Romantic Love: Longing and Sexuality in Europe, South Asia, and Japan, 900–1200 CE* [Chicago: University of Chicago Press, 2012], 2), even aligning the troubadour concept with what he calls the "'courtly love' phenomenon [that] is well known to medievalists" (2). Reddy, does, however, note that the literature of so-called "courtly love", can "represent a kind of resistance", and an "escaping [from the mid twelfth-century Church's] blanket condemnation of all sexual partnerships as sinful and polluting" (26).

4   l'amour est un art, une science, une vertu, qui a ses règles tout comme la chevalerie ou la courtoisie [...] Dans aucun ouvrage français, autant qu'il me semble, cet amour courtois n'apparaît avant le Chevalier de la Charrette. L'amour de Tristran et d'Iseut est autre chose: c'est une passion simple, ardente, naturelle, qui ne connaît pas les subtilités et les raffinements de celui de Lancelot et de Guenièvre. Dans les poèmes de Benoit de Sainte-More, nous trouvons la galanterie, mais non cet amour exalté et presque mystique, sans cesser pourtant d'être sensual.

Tellingly, Paris bases his notion of *amour courtois* on the only tale by the northern trouvére Chrétien de Troyes that differs from his normal pattern: *the Knight of the Cart*, a story about the adulterous relationship between Lancelot and Guinevere. Ordinarily, Chrétien opposes the "new mode of love and the central theme of the Provençal Troubadours poetry", by "refusing the adulterous relationship [...] and the idolatrous passion which binds the lovers".[5] This refusal is "exemplified in all of Chrétien's romances except *Lancelot*",[6] and in all of his other work, Chrétien "proclaims a mode of love which, dominated by the rules of reason and the code of courtliness, should lead to marriage and exist only inside of marriage".[7] This bears repeating, for there is something odd and contradictory at work in the way Paris comes to define his most famous term: the critical definition of "courtly love" as a chaste and rule-bound mode of relationship is based on the only one of Chrétien's romances that breaks those rules, illustrating a love that "fell outside Christian teaching and was the exact opposite of the traditional view on marriage",[8] while at the same time, the critic comes to his definition by underplaying these transgressive features of the poem.

The effect of Paris' misbegotten definition can be seen by looking at Andreas Capellanus' twelfth-century treatise, *De amore* (*Of Love*), which is now (mis)leadingly translated as *The Art of Courtly Love*. Capellanus' text begins by addressing itself to a young man named Walter, and by defining what love is:

> Love is some kind of an inborn passion that proceeds from looking and thinking immoderately on the form of the opposite sex, a passion that makes one wish more than anything to embrace the other, and by mutual desire accomplish all of love's precepts in the other's embrace.[9]

Gaston Paris, "Études sur les romans de la Table Ronde" (1883), 519, http://www.persee.fr/doc/roma_0035-8029_1883_num_12_48_6277
5   Moshe Lazar. "Cupid, the Lady, and the Poet: Modes of Love at Eleanor of Aquitaine's Court". In *Eleanor of Aquitaine: Patron and Politician*, ed. by William W. Kibler (Austin: University of Texas Press, 1976), 42.
6   A common shorthand term for *The Knight of the Cart*.
7   Lazar, 43.
8   *Ibid.*
9   "Amor est passio quedam innata procedens ex vision et immoderate cogitatione formae alterius sexus, ob quam aliquis super Omnia cupit alterius potiri amplexibus et Omnia de ultriusque voluntate in ipsius amplexu amoris praecepta compleri" (Andreas Capellanus. *De amore libri tres: Von der Liebe. Drei Bücher* [Berlin and Boston: De Gruyter, 2006], 6).

Paris' idea of *amour courtois* has affected the way Capellanus' text is understood by rewriting it after the fact. The widely-used English translation by John Jay Parry reads as a courtly love treatise that often incorporates the main characteristic of this ethos—suffering. By translating the text in a way that supports this pre-existing interpretation, Parry has created a kind of circular argument. The word *passio* is translated as "suffering", although it can also be translated as "passion". If *passio* stood by itself, then either translation might suffice; however, an "inborn passion" makes more sense with what follows, even as Parry renders it: "[love] causes each one to wish above all things the embraces of the other".[10] In the following lines, Parry continues his translation in the same circular manner: "That love is suffering is easy to see, for before the love becomes equally balanced on both sides there is no torment greater".[11] The word "torment" is meant to stand in for the Latin *angustia*, which means narrowness, want, or perplexity. By far the better choice for translation is *want* (in the sense of desire and lack). The lover wants, more than anything else in the world, to gain the object of his desire. Capellanus makes this clear in a later protion of his work when he refers to the passion he is discussing as *pure love*:

> Pure love is that which joins and unites the hearts of the two lovers with the affection of love. This, however, consists in the contemplation of the mind and the affection of the heart; it proceeds as far as a kiss, the arms' embrace, and modestly touching the nude lover.[12]

The "pure love" spoken of is both of the body and of the mind, only "the final consolation is omitted",[13] though that, too, is allowed in what Capellanus calls *amor mixtus*, mixed, or compounded love. The flesh in *De amore* is not marginalized as it is in the later spiritualized poetry of the Dantean and Petrarchan traditions. The man in *De amore*

---

10 Andreas Capellanus. *The Art of Courtly Love*. Trans. by John Jay Perry (New York: W. W. Norton & Co., 1941), 28.
11 *Ibid*. The original is as follows: "Quod amor sit passio facile est videre. Nam antequam amor sit ex utraque parte libratus, nulla est angustia maior" (Capellanus, *De amore libri tres: Von der Liebe*, 6).
12 "Et purus quidem amor est, qui omnimoda directonis affection duorum amantium corda coniungit. Hic autem in mentis contemplation cordisque consistit affect; procedit autem usque ad oris osculum lacertique amplexum et verecundum amantis nudae contactum" (Andreas Capellanus. *De amore libri tres: Von der Liebe*, 282).
13 "extremo praetermisso solatio" (*ibid*.).

prays to God, not for wisdom, not for piety, but for the opportunity to see his lover again. The manner in which he makes this supplication resembles the open passions of troubadour poetry: "For not an hour of the day or night could pass that I did not beg God to allow me the bounty of seeing you close to me in the flesh".[14] *Amor purus* is both emotional and physical. It is not the stylized "courtly love" of the later scholarly tradition.

Perhaps C. S. Lewis did the most to popularize this term, as he traced "courtly love" in twelfth-century poetry from the southern troubadours to the northern *trouvére* Chrétien de Troyes. In so doing, Lewis identifies four marks—Humility, Courtesy, Adultery, and the Religion of Love[15]—that he claims characterize the "new feeling" that arose in the poets and the time and place in which they lived. However, though Lewis acknowledges that "courtly love necessitates adultery", he also insists that "adultery hardly necessitates courtly love".[16] This revealing turn of phrase captures the ambiguity, the division in feelings between excitement and disapproval that characterizes the long poetic tradition that springs from troubadour roots. Poems of desire that would be fulfilled, no matter the cost—if only the opportunity manifested itself— gave rise to later poems of decorous and often tormented sublimations of desire, using such Neoplatonic metaphors as the ladder of love.[17] Desire became worship, as flesh became once again an object of shame.

Lewis's ambivalent refusal to credit fully the significance of the troubadours and their poetry is exceedingly odd, given that he describes their work as "momentous" and "revolutionary" and "the background of European literature for eight hundred years".[18] For Lewis, "French poets, in the eleventh century, discovered or invented, or were the first to express, that romantic species of passion which English poets were

---

14 "Non enim poterat diei vel noctis hora pertransire continua, qua Deum non exorarem attentius, ut corporaliter vos ex propinquo videndi mihi concederet largitatem" (*ibid.*, 192).
15 C. S. Lewis. *The Allegory of Love: A Study in Medieval Tradition* (London: Oxford University Press, 1936), 2.
16 *Ibid.*, 14.
17 The idea that a lover's admiration for a beloved serves the lover as the first step on a ladder, in which each successive rung represents an increasingly refined notion of love, until by the top, the lover has left earthly love behind in favor of divine love.
18 *Ibid.*, 4.

still writing about in the nineteenth".[19] But his use of *French* rather than *Provençal* or *Occitan* is telling—Lewis spends as little time with the troubadours as possible, referencing none of their poetry specifically, preferring to spend his time with Ovid, the anonymous author of the twelfth-century *Concilium Romarici Montis* (a mock-council on love which references the classical poet as *Ovidii Doctoris egregii*[20]), Chrétien de Troyes, and Andreas Capellanus. As Lewis reads them, each of these sources are fixated on rules, codes, official judgments, and elaborate enactments of dominance and submission that parody the rituals of Catholicism. In his reading of Chrétien's *Lancelot*, for example, the issue is not "love [as] a noble form of experience [and] a theory of adultery",[21] but obedience given too slowly: "The Queen has heard of his [Lancelot's] momentary hesitation in stepping on to the tumbril, and this lukewarmness in the service of love has been held by her sufficient to annihilate all the merit of his subsequent labours and humiliations".[22]

Lancelot is momentarily ashamed to ride a cart whose driver promises to take him to the kidnapped Queen Guenivere, because the cart is used to carry prisoners, and any knight seen on such a transport will be shamed, and his reputation for honor destroyed. But though he hesitates, he climbs aboard, and willingly suffers the resulting shame (described in several following scenes), in order to be led to the Queen:

> Et li chevaliers dit au nain:
> «Nains, fet il, por Deu, car me di
> Se tu as veü par ici
> Passer ma dame la reïne».
> Li nains cuiverz de pute orine
> Ne l'an vost noveles conter,
> Einz li dist: «Se tu viax monter
> Sor la charrete que je main,
> Savoir porras jusqu'a demain
> Que la reïne est devenue».
> Tantost a sa voie tenue,

---

19 *Ibid.*
20 *Ibid.*, 19. The name translates as Ovid the Peerless [or Excellent] Doctor.
21 *Ibid.*, 37.
22 *Ibid.*, 28.

4. The Troubadours and Fin'amor: Love, Choice, and the Individual

> Qu'il ne l'atant ne pas ne ore.
> Tant solemant deus pas demore
> Li chevaliers que il n'i monte.
> Mar le fist et mar en ot honte
> Que maintenant sus ne sailli,
> Qu'il s'an tendra por mal bailli![23]

> And the Knight told the dwarf:
> Dwarf, for God's sake, tell me right away
> If you have seen here
> Pass by my lady the queen.
> The perfidious low-born dwarf
> Would not tell him the news,
> But merely said: If you want to ride
> On the cart that I drive,
> By tomorrow you'll be able to know
> What happened to the queen.
> With that, he maintained his way forward
> Without waiting for the other for a moment.
> For only the time of two steps
> The Knight hesitated to get in.
> What a pity he hesitated, ashamed to go,
> And he failed to jump without delay,
> For this will cause him great suffering!

The momentary delay earns him the displeasure of the Queen, who berates him for failing to immediately obey Love's promptings:

> Et la reïne li reconte:
> «Comant? Don n'eüstes vos honte
> De la charrete et si dotastes?
> Molt a grant enviz i montastes
> Quant vos demorastes deus pas.
> Por ce, voir, ne vos vos je pas
> Ne aresnier ne esgarder.[24]

---

23 Chrétien de Troyes. *Le Chevalier de la Charrette,* ed. by Alfred Foulet and Karl D. Uitti (Paris: Classiques Garnier, 1989), ll. 352–68.
24 *Ibid.*, ll. 4501–07.

> And the Queen replied:
> What? Were you not ashamed
> Of the cart and its lowly endowments?
> With much hesitation you mounted,
> Since you delayed two steps.
> For this, I did not want to see you,
> Nor speak to you, nor look at you.

And though Chrétien eventually brings the knight and the queen together physically, he remains somewhat coy (though not as purely "courtly" as Gaston Paris might suggest):

> Or a Lanceloz quanqu'il vialt
> Qant la reïne an gré requialt
> Sa conpaignie et son solaz,
> Qant il la tient antre ses braz
> Et ele lui antre les suens.
> Tant li est ses jeus dolz et buens
> Et del beisier et del santir
> Que il lor avint sanz mantir
> Une joie et une mervoille
> Tel c'onques encore sa paroille
> Ne fu oïe ne seüe;
> Mes toz jorz iert par moi teüe,
> Qu'an conte ne doit estre dite.[25]

> Lancelot now has everything he wants,
> Because the Queen accepts with joy
> His company and solace,
> Since he holds her in his arms
> And she holds him between hers.
> Their pleasure is so sweet and good,
> And the kisses and the caresses,
> What happened to them, without lying,
> Was a joy and a marvel
> As has never before been spoken
> Nor heard of, nor known;

---

25   *Ibid.*, ll. 4687–99.

> But still, I maintain the most perfect silence
> About what not to say in a story.

Despite this scene, however, there remains throughout the poem an ever-present sense that the issue is one of knightly obedience rather than human passion, that the knight and the queen of the tale are less individual than archetypal, less fully human than artfully allegorical. As Matilda Tomaryn Bruckner notes, the figure of Lancelot in Chrétien and the later prose romancers serves primarily as an object lesson in the relative inferiority and impurity of human desire, when compared to the purity of a love directed toward the heavens: "Across the large canvas of the Lancelot-Grail Cycle, the Cart episode remains at the center of Lancelot's story, even as it marks an important shift in Lancelot as hero, still the best of Arthurian chivalry, but not 'the good knight' who will achieve the Grail".[26]

Despite the note of desire in their story, Chrétien's knight and the queen he "serves" are ultimately, as Lewis highlights, more allegorical than human—high examples of what Lewis calls the "allegorical love poetry of the Middle Ages"[27] He is correct to call it so, but he is in a hurry to move past the troubadours for such authors as Chrétien precisely because the latter is writing allegory and the former are not. There is nothing allegorical about the passionate poems of Bernart de Ventadorn,[28] Guilhem IX, or the Comtessa de Dia, nor is there an emphasis on rules, ceremonies, mock judgments in high-church style, or demands for obedience—whether instantly or otherwise delivered. What Lewis finds discomfiting in the troubadour poetry is precisely that element of adultery that he repeatedly mentions, but consistently refuses to illustrate with quotation. He is much happier to tell us the

---

26 Matilda Tomaryn Bruckner. "'Redefining the Center' Verse and Prose Charrette". In *A Companion to the Lancelot-Grail Cycle*, ed. by Carol Dover (Cambridge, UK: Brewer, 2003), 95.
27 C. S. Lewis, 1.
28 "Bernart de Ventadorn provides one context in which to read the *Lancelot*—and with it, modern discussions of courtly love—since he and Chrétien appear to have known one another: they exchanged lyric poems in which they debate the passionate versus the rational aspects of love" (Sarah Kay. "Courts, Clerks, and Courtly Love". In *The Cambridge Companion to Medieval Romance*, ed. by Roberta L. Krueger [Cambridge: Cambridge University Press, 2000], 86.

opinions of Peter Lombard, Albertus Magnus, and Thomas Aquinas on love and passion[29] than he is to give the Occitan poets their voice.

Of course, Lewis is not the only figure at whose feet can be laid the blame for the oddly misbegotten notion of "courtly love", a notion all too often applied to the troubadours without actually being derived from their poetry or from an analysis of their poetry. This latter trend can also be seen in twentieth-century French psychoanalysis, in Jacques Lacan's use of the troubadours to develop his own ideas about desire. The effect of Gaston Paris's nineteenth-century recasting of *fin'amor* as *amour courtois* is evident in Lacan's work. Consistently using the term *amour courtois* in his own analysis, Lacan dismisses the work of the troubadours as anything other than "a poetic exercise, a fashion of playing with a certain number of idealizing and conventional themes, which could have no actual concrete reality".[30] What intrigues him is what he regards as a contradiction between the "idealizing and conventional themes" and the obviously non-idealizing behavior of a poet like Guilhem IX:

> The first of the troubadours is named Guilhem IX, seventh Earl of Poitiers, ninth Duke of Aquitaine, who appears to have been, before he devoted his inaugural poetic activities to courtly poetry, a most redoubtable bandit, the type that, my God, all nobleman could be expected to be at this time. In many historical circumstances that I will not pass on to you, we see him behave according to the standards of the most iniquitous shakedowns. These are the services that could be expected of him. Then at a certain point, he became a poet of this singular love.[31]

---

29 C. S. Lewis, 15–16.
30 "un exercice poétique, une façon de jouer avec un certain nombre de thèmes de convention idealisants, qui ne pouvaient avoir aucun repondant concret reel" (*Le Seminiare de Jacques Lacan. Livre VII. L'Éthique de la Psychanalyse* [1959–60] [Paris: Seuil, 1986], 177–78).
31 Le premier des troubadours est un nommé Guillaume de Poitiers, septième comte de Poitiers, neuvième duc d'Aquitaine, qui paraît avoir été, avant qu'il se consacrât à ses activités poétiques inaugurales dans la poésie courtoise, un fort redoutable bandit, du type de ce que, mon Dieu, tout grand seigneur qui se respectait pouvait être à cette époque. En maintes circonstances historiques que je vous passe, nous le voyons se comporter selon les normes du rançonnage le plus inique. Voilà les services qu'on pouvait attendre de lui. Puis, à partir d'un certain moment, il devient poète de cet amour singulier.

Ibid., 177.

But there is no contradiction at all between the poet of passion and the faintly criminal nobleman who practiced *rançonnage* (shakedowns for ransom) in order to fill his coffers, because the "idealizing and conventional themes" Lacan speaks of are largely a post-troubadour invention.[32] Lacan imposes an entirely extrinsic logic on the poetry of the troubadours, derived from his own concepts and those borrowed from Gaston Paris. The irony inherent in the positions of these two French intellectuals is that each imposes an interpretive violence on the southern poets from the perspectives of northern Parisian culture—and as we will see, such impositions, and such violence, reflect the pattern of a long and shockingly bloody history.

That "courtly love" has very little to do with the troubadours[33] can be seen not only in the way that Paris derives the concept from the northern poet Chrétien, but also because he slights the influence of the southern poets at every turn. In *La Poésie du Moyen Âge*, Paris tips his hand. First, only the literature of the north counts as properly "French" poetry: "the proper domain of Carolingian [eighth-to-twelfth-century] poetry was the north of France, the Ile-de-France, Orleans, Anjou, Maine, Champagne, the Vermandois, Picardy".[34] The literature produced south of the Loire

---

32 Lacan is engaged in a project that is less *exegetic* (reading out of) than it is *eisegetic* (reading on to) where his engagement with troubadour poetry is concerned. For Lacan "[t]he arbitrary Lady, who is coterminous with privation and inaccessibility [...] represents both negation and signification and [...] is not just a symbolic function, but a representaton of the rules and limits of the Symbolic" (Nancy Frelick. "Lacan, Courtly Love and Anamorphosis". In *The Court Reconvenes: Courtly Literature Across the Disciplines: Selected Papers from the Ninth Triennial Congress of the International Courtly Literature Society*, University of British Columbia, 25–31 July 1998 [Cambridge, UK: Brewer, 2003], 110). Rather than using his psychoanalytical categories to shed light on the poetry, Lacan is using the poetry to shed light on his categories. He is certainly not alone in approaching troubadour poetry (or any other poetry) in this way.

33 David F. Hult suggests that Paris' invention of the term *amour courtois* had much less to do with analysis of poetry than it did with "a personal and professional dilemma in Paris' career", arguing that the term's curious appeal to later generations can be explained by the "suggestions of a continuity between [...] academic life, its founding disjunction between pleasure and science, and the ideal scheme of an eroticism grounded in rules and progressive mastery" (David F. Hult. "Gaston Paris and the Invention of Courtly Love". In *Medievalism and the Modernist Temper*, ed. by R. Howard Bloch and Stephen G. Nichols [Baltimore: Johns Hopkins University Press, 1996], 216). In other words, Hult implies that "courtly love" is a notion only an academic could love.

34 "le domaine propre de la poésie carolingienne avait été le nord de la France, l'Ile-de-France, l'Orléanais, l'Anjou, le Maine, la Champagne, le Vermandois,

river valley, was that of an entirely different civilization: "all that was south of the Loire actually belonged to another civilization, where the Germanic element had penetrated less deeply, and where the language remained nearer the Latin",[35] and that which can be referred to as truly "French" was produced only in lands of the *langue d'oil*[36] in the north: "literature, like the French language, belongs to northern France".[37]

For Paris, Chrétien de Troyes was "the first master of French style",[38] and French literature was the premier vernacular expression in Europe, reaching even into southern Italy and the court of Sicily: "Southern Italy and Sicily also had Norman kings, and there again French literature found a homeland".[39] Paris credits French poetry with the flourishing of the poetic culture in the thirteenth-century Sicilian court of Frederick II, though he is forced to acknowledge the influence of that "autre civilisation" of the south, as he quickly, if reluctantly, mentions the poetry of Provençe. French poetry flourished "in Sicily, and it influenced in the thirteenth-century, as much as Provençal poetry, the birth of Italian poetry".[40] Paris further argues that the poetry of the north influenced the poetry of the south, setting up a hierarchy by which French poetry could be seen as the original high literary form in any of the European vernaculars, influencing even the troubadour poets: "the southern provinces had a language and a literature of their own, which had grown under conditions and with a quite different character.

---

la Picardie" (Gaston Paris. *La Poesie du Moyen Age* [Paris: Librarie Hachette, 1895], 8). Paris does not mention, however, that the vast majority of this period's poetry was written in Latin, not the vernacular, https://books.google.com/books?id=LdHs-jMItRQC&pg=PA8

35 "Tout ce qui se trouvait au sud de la Loire appartenait en réalité à une autre civilisation, où l'élément germanique avait moins profondément pénétré, et où la langue était restée plus voisine du latin" (*ibid.*, 9, https://books.google.com/books?id=LdHs-jMItRQC&pg=PA9).

36 The terms *langue d'oil* and *langue d'oc* refer to the way northerners and southerners, respectively, pronounced the word "yes".

37 "la littérature, comme la langue française, appartient à la France du nord" (Paris, *La Poesie du Moyen Age*, 9).

38 "le premier maître du style français" (*ibid.*, 18, https://books.google.com/books?id=LdHs-jMItRQC&pg=PA18).

39 "Le sud de l'Italie et la Sicile avaient aussi pour rois des Normands, et là aussi la littérature française retrouva une patrie" (*ibid.*, 36, https://books.google.com/books?id=LdHs-jMItRQC&pg=PA36).

40 "en Sicile, et elle y détermina peut-être, au XIIIe siècle, autant que la poésie provençale, l'éclosion de la poésie italienne" (*ibid.*).

It is true, however, that the first effect our literature had on a foreign literature was that it had on the poetry of the troubadours".[41]

Paris' preference is always for the trouvère poets of the north. He claimed that the troubadours were nourished by French poetry — "it is our poetry which the troubadours fed themselves on, and to which they made frequent allusions"[42] — and all the Romance lands fell under the influence of French literature, to which Paris subtly subordinates the poetry of the south: "the Romance nations [...] became as it were branches of the great French school".[43] The term *amour courtois*, or "courtly love", refers to the literature its inventor preferred, his much-favored poetry of the north, rather than the lyrics of that "autre civilisation" in the troubadour south. Paris' dismissive attitude reflects a long history of northern contempt for, and violence against the south (*le Midi*), its culture, languages, and poetry. This history stretches back to the tensions leading up to the Albigensian Crusade of the thirteenth century, in which the domination of the northern Franks was established with sword, fire, and blood. The imposition of the term *amour courtois* on a poetry that has nothing whatsoever to do with the concept is another in a long line of acts of domination and erasure. In such ways, often unnoticed, literary critics reiterate and support the violence of power and authority by denying poetry its voice.

Many modern scholars have questioned the idea of "courtly love". D. W. Robertson, for example, spent years waging war against the whole notion. Robertson's view is that the discussion of *De amore* through this concept is not only inaccurate, but confusing. Robertson argues that Capellanus does not reject "worldly delights", but looks on them as an unfortunate, if necessary, "malady". This idea is loosely based on the twelfth-century philosopher Bernardi Silvestris' notion that worldly

---

41 "Les provinces du Midi avaient une langue et une littérature à elles, qui s'étaient développées dans des conditions et avec des caractères assez différents. C'est donc, à vrai dire, la première action de notre littérature sur une littérature étrangère que celle qu'elle exerça sur la poésie des troubadours" (*ibid.*, 38, https://books.google.com/books?id=LdHs-jMItRQC&pg=PA38).

42 "ce sont nos poèmes dont les troubadours se nourrissaient et auxquels ils font de fréquentes allusions" (*ibid.*, 39, https://books.google.com/books?id=LdHs-jMItRQC&pg=PA39).

43 "les nations romanes [...] devinrent pour ainsi dire des succursales de la grande école française" (*ibid.*, 41, https://books.google.com/books?id=LdHs-jMItRQC&pg=PA41).

love is acceptable as long as it contributes to procreation. Silvestris, however, expresses this view in a fairly genial fashion:

> Corporis extremum lascivum terminat inguen,
> Pressa sub occidua parte pudenda latent.
> Iocundus que tamen et eorum commodus usus,
> Si quando, qualis quantus oportet, erit.
> [...]
> Cum morte invicti pugnamt genialibus armis,
> Naturam reparant perpetuant que genus.[44]

> The body ends in the lascivious groin,
> Where the use of these private parts, hidden away,
> Is pleasant and comfortable, so long as their use
> Is in quality, quantity, and opportunity, as it should be.
> [...]
> Against death they fight invincibly with nuptial arms,
> Repair our nature, and perpetuate our kind.

Robertson maintains that Capellanus does not fully embrace the sublimation and spiritualization of earthly love; in fact, Capellanus shows inclination for the "natural" Venus.[45] Cupidity, lust, and sensuality are only seen as maladies because these are "inborn", and they often go against reason. As Robertson puts it, "If 'Walter' becomes a lover by virtue of prolonged lascivious thought, his resulting uneasiness will be entirely self-engendered".[46]

In his famous essay "The Concept of Courtly Love", Robertson goes on to deny that the whole concept has any validity whatsoever, except as "an aspect of nineteenth and twentieth century cultural history". He insists that "[t]he subject has nothing to do with the Middle Ages, and its use as a governing concept can only be an impediment to our understanding of medieval texts".[47] Robertson's is a powerful argument—so far as it

---

44 Bernardi Silvestris. *De Mundi Universitate*, ed. by Carl Sigmund Barach and Johann Wrobel (Innsbruck: Verlag der Wagnerschen Universitaets-Buchandlung, 1876), 14.153–56, 161–62, https://archive.org/stream/bernardisilvest00silvgoog#page/n66

45 D. W. Robertson. "The Subject of the 'De Amore' of Andreas Capellanus". *Modern Philology*, 50: 3 (February 1953), 146–48, https://doi.org/10.1086/388953

46 *Ibid.*, 155.

47 D. W. Robertson. "The Concept of Courtly Love". In *The Meaning of Courtly Love*, ed. by F. X. Newman (Albany: State University of New York Press, 1968), 17. Emphasis added.

goes. But it performs an even more powerful surgical excision of the Occitan poets than had the arguments of Lewis and Paris. Robertson builds the "courtly love" concept that he then mockingly tears down, using the building blocks of French poetry (the *Roman de la rose*), Latin prose (Andreas Capellanus' *De amore*), and English poetry (Chaucer's *Troilus and Crysede*). The troubadours appear not at all, except in the faint echoes of their world glancingly referenced by Robertson's mocking of "pseudo-Albigensian heresies", and "pseudo-Arabic doctrines".[48] Robertson is partially right, but for the wrong reasons. "Courtly love" is an invention of "nineteenth and twentieth century cultural history", but the term describes a complicated phenomenon with roots that go back as far as the thirteenth-century writings of Matfré Ermengaud, whose work serves a very specific ideological purpose: to tame love and desire (by persuasion if possible, or violence if necessary) into service and obedience, to reduce the most powerfully anarchic part of the human spirit into quiescence and tractability. Robertson pursues this agenda by tacitly and through omission denying that any such love (or any such poetry) exists at all, except as irony; for Robertson, "if a poet *appears* to extol sexual passion his intentions will prove, on a closer inspection, to be ironical and moralistic".[49] This then allows Robertson to bludgeon "courtly love" into submission in service of a worldview in which the troubadours are defined out of the very possibility of existence.

Moshe Lazar, examining the stark differences between the terms most often used to describe and analyze love in this period—*courtoise*, *amour courtois*, and *fin'amor*—scoffs at the idea that these terms are interchangeable: "[These words] are used as though it were possible to lump together all the periods of the Middle Ages and to interchange the order of authors and works".[50] The invented phenomenon of "courtly love", in which a young man feels passionate love for an unavailable woman to whose service he dedicates himself in the absence of any possibility of sexual union,[51] is at best a parody of a love that does exist,

---

48 *Ibid.*
49 Roger Boase. *The Origin and Meaning of Courtly Love* (Manchester: Manchester University Press, 1977), 122.
50 Moshe Lazar. "Fin'amor". In *A Handbook of the Troubadours*, ed. by F. R. P. Akehurst and Judith M. Davis (Berkeley: University of California Press, 1995), 64.
51 For Jennifer Wollock, "courtly love" reflects the experience of Gaston Paris more than it does medieval social mores:

a love called *fin'amor*, written about by the eleventh-and twelfth-century troubadours. Calling it "the direct ancestor of romantic love as we know it today", Jennifer Wollock describes *fin'amor* as a radically subversive cultural force:

> [*Fin'amor*] gave medieval men and women a vent for their dissatisfaction with the institution of marriage as it then existed, holding up a different, much more exciting, and dangerous model of the male-female relationship. Its socially subversive force can still be felt today not just in the West but in cultures all across the world where traditional models of marriage as arranged by parents are still maintained.[52]

The frankly passionate, erotic, and embodied poetry of the troubadours is transformed into something decorous, pious, and bloodless by a later tradition of critics and poets. The work of the troubadours has been subjected to a systematic distortion, one that reflects the values of the distorters, but does violence to the poetry.

II
The Troubadours and their Critics

To begin seeing this in the poetry, let's linger for a moment with Paris' beloved trouvères, and consider a short snippet of an anonymous late twelfth-century song:

> *Soufrés maris, et si ne vous anuit,*
> *Demain m'arés et mes amis anuit.*
> *Je vous deffenc k'un seul mot n'en parlés*
> *—Soufrés, maris, et si ne vous mouvés.—*
> *La nuis est courte, aparmains me rarés,*
> *Quant mes amis ara fait sen deduit.*

For Gaston Paris, courtly love was defined by the lover's worship of an idealized lady. His love was an ennobling discipline, not necessarily consummated, but based on sexual attraction. Hult and Bloch have analyzed the psychology of Gaston Paris and his circle as it affected their understanding of medieval love literature, suggesting that the scholars' own experiences with unattainable ladies of the nineteenth century may have led them to stress the unattainability of the troubadours' objects of affection.

Jennifer G. Wollock. *Rethinking Chivalry and Courtly Love* (Santa Barbara: Praeger, 2011), 31.

52 *Ibid.*, 6.

> *Soufrés maris, et si ne vous anuit,*
> Demain m'arés et mes amis anuit.[53]

> *Suffer in silence husband, be not vexed tonight,*
> *Tomorrow I will be yours, but I am my lover's tonight.*
> I forbid you to speak a single word.
> — *Suffer in silence husband, and do not move.* —
> The night is short, soon I will be yours again,
> When my lover has had his senses' share.
> *Suffer in silence husband, be not vexed tonight,*
> Tomorrow I will be yours, but I am my lover's tonight.

These lines are not about rules and codes of "courtly" behavior, a disembodied love, or a sacramentalized *eros* given to ethereally disembodied devotion, as one might see in the works of Petrarch, for example. They do not reflect an ethos which is anti-body, anti-sex, anti-female. Even in the north, the spirit of a love that is neither courtly nor sacred is thriving.

Among the southern poets during this period there are a number of female writers, or trobairitz, though the majority are male. Many of the poets are famous for writing love poems (called *cansos*), though there are others who write often caustic verses of war and political conflict (called *sirventes*). Bertran de Born is the most exultant example of the latter:

> Be·m platz lo gais temps de pascor,
> que fai fuoillas e flors venir;
> e plai me qand auch la baudor
> dels auzels que fant retintir
> lo chant per lo boscatge;
> e plai me qand vei per los pratz
> tendas e pavaillons fermatz;
> qan vei per campaignas rengatz
> cavalliers e cavals armatz.[54]

---

53 Eglal Doss-Quinby. *Songs of the Women Trouvères* (New Haven: Yale University Press, 2001), 184–86.
54 Bertran de Born. *The Poems of the Troubadour Bertran de Born*, ed. by William D. Paden, Tilde Sankovitch, and Patricia H. Stablein (Berkeley: University of California Press, 1986), 339, ll. 1–9.

> I am pleased by the gay season of Spring,
> that makes the leaves and the flowers come;
> and it pleases me when I overhear
> the birds' faint echoes
> of song through the woods;
> and it pleases me when I see on the meadow
> tents and pavillions well-built;
> when I see the fields filled with ranks
> of armed knights and horses.

Bertran's love for war was such that Dante puts him into the *Inferno* as a sower of discord for his "persistence in dividing [King] Henry [II] from the *jove rei Engles*", Prince Henry.[55] Dante has Bertan accuse himself, as the warrior-troubadour stands amidst the flames:

> Io vidi certo, e ancor par ch'io 'l veggia,
> un busto sanza capo andar sì come
> andavan li altri de la trista greggia;
> e 'l capo tronco tenea per le chiome,
> pesol con mano a guisa di lanterna:
> e quel mirava noi e dicea: "Oh me!".
> [...]
> "E perché tu di me novella porti,
> sappi ch'i' son Bertram dal Bornio, quelli
> che diedi al re giovane i ma' conforti.
> Io feci il padre e 'l figlio in sé ribelli;
> Achitofèl non fé più d'Absalone
> e di Davìd coi malvagi punzelli.
> Perch' io parti' così giunte persone,
> partito porto il mio cerebro, lasso!,
> dal suo principio ch'è in questo troncone.
> Così s'osserva in me lo contrapasso".[56]

---

55 Ronald Martinez. "Italy". In *A Handbook of the Troubadours*, ed. by F. R. P. Akehurst and Judith M. Davis (Berkeley: University of California Press, 1995), 285.

56 *Inferno*. Canto 28.118–23, 133–42. In *La Divina Commedia. Inferno*, ed. by Ettore Zolesi (Rome: Armando, 2009), 470–71.

> I truly saw, and still seem to see it,
> a body without a head, walking just like
> the others in its dismal herd;
> the body carried its severed head by the hair,
> swaying in its hand, in the fashion of a lantern;
> and it looked at us and said: "Oh me!"
> [...]
> "And because you will carry news of me,
> know that I am Bertran de Born, he
> who gave comfort to the young King.
> I made father and son turn against each other;
> Achitophel did not do more with Absalom
> and David, through his malevolent provocations.
> Because I severed people so joined,
> severed now I bear my brain, alas!,
> from its origin, which is in this body.
> In this can be seen my retribution".

But many of the troubadour and trobairitz poems come from, and represent, the female perspective, and some break boundaries one might not initially expect. For example, consider a piece called *Na Maria*, attributed to a poet named Bietris (or Bieris) de Romans.

> Na Maria, pretz e fina valors,
> e·l joi e·l sen e la fina beutatz,
> e l'aculhir e·l pretz e las onors,
> e·l gen parlar e l'avinen solatz,
> e la dous car' e la gaja cuendansa,
> e·l dous esgart e l'amoros semblan
> que son en vos, don non avetz engansa,
> me fan traire vas vos ses cor truan.
> Per que vos prec, si·us platz que fin' amors
> e gausiment e dous umilitatz
> me posca far ab vos tan de socors,
> que mi donetz, bella domna, si·us platz,
> so don plus ai d'aver joi e'speransa;
> car en vos ai mon cor e mon talan,
> e per vos ai tot so qu'ai d'alegransa
> e per vos vauc mantas vetz sospiran.
> E car beutatz e valors vos enansa

> sobre totas, qu'una no·us es denan,
> vos prec, si·us platz, per so que·us es onransa,
> que non ametz entendidor truan.
> Bella domna, cui pretz e joi enansa,
> e gen parlar, a vos mas coblas man,
> car en vos es gajess'e alegranssa
> e tot lo ben qu'om en domna deman.[57]

> Lady Maria, for your esteem and pure worthiness,
> joy, wisdom, and pure beauty,
> graciousness and praise and distinction,
> noble speech and delightful company,
> sweet face and lively charm,
> the sweet glance and the amorous appearance
> that are in you without deception,
> I am drawn to you with nothing false in my heart.
> For this, I pray, please, let true love
> delight and sweet humility
> give me, with you, the relief I need,
> so you will grant me, beautiful lady, please,
> what I most hope to enjoy.
> Because in you, alas, are my heart and desire
> and for you, alas, are all my joys
> and for you, I go, freely sighing many sighs.
> And since beauty and merit advances you,
> superior to all others, for there is no one before you,
> I pray you, please, by all that brings you honor,
> do not love those false suitors.
> Beautiful Lady, whom praise and joy advances,
> and noble speech, my verses are for you,
> for in you is merriment and all delight,
> and every good thing one could want in a woman.

On an initial reading, this poem seems to be an erotic poem written by a woman to a woman. Though there are no explicitly sexual details, it appears to portray a jealous lover trying to fend off rivals, a poem in the tradition of Sappho, the ancient Greek poet who wrote much of her

---

57 Bietris de Romans. "Na Maria, prètz e fina valors". In *The Women Troubadours*, ed. by Meg Bogin (New York: Norton & Co., 1980), 132.

verse describing her erotic longings for beautiful women: "Toward you bare-shouldered beauties my mind / surely never changes".[58] Thus, *Na Maria* is not poetically unprecedented, nor in any way to be considered outside the realm of human erotic experience.

And yet, there is no shortage of claims that this poem is not what it seems. The apparent lesbian eroticism is explained away through the use of two arguments, which we will see again and again with only minor variations. Firstly, the religious or spiritualizing argument that sublimates love into worship:

This is a metaphor for the Virgin Mary.

This is Daniel E. O'Sullivan's argument.[59] He suggests that the line "so you will grant me, beautiful lady, please / what I most hope to enjoy" ("qe mi donetz, bella dompna, si·us platz, / so don plus ai d'aver esperansa") should be interpreted in the context of "Marian songs, [in which] the singer makes similar requests of the Virgin where the hoped-for reward is eternal salvation".[60] Though the critic acknowledges that "the question of asking Mary to shun deceitful lovers or suitors (*entendidor*) may seem odd given the Virgin's role in helping to save all of mankind",[61] he does not let that difficulty discourage him, and argues that the poet's entreaty has to do with prayer: "such requests for divine intercession must be made sincerely, thus the qualification that such people must not be deceitful (*truan*)".[62] Thus the critic erases the eroticism that seems evident on the text's surface, and allegorizes that eroticism in the traditional way (as seen in the case of the Song of Songs), by transforming its energy into an expression of divine love.

If that line of argument fails to convince, another line of attack comes in the form of an historicism that assumes every human expression of a particular time and place can necessarily be explained by and reduced

---

58 "ταὶς κάλαισ᾿ ὔμμιν <τὸ> νόημμα τὦμον / οὐ διάμειπτον" (Sappho, *Greek Lyric, Vol. I: Sappho and Alcaeus*, ed. by David A. Campbell [Loeb Classical Library, Cambridge, MA: Harvard University Press, 1982], Fragment 41, 86).
59 "Na Maria: Courtliness and Marian Devotion in Old Occitan Lyric". In *Shaping Courtliness in Medieval France: Essays in Honor of Matilda Tomaryn Bruckner*, ed. by Daniel E. O'Sullivan and Laurie Shepard (Cambridge, UK: Brewer, 2013), 184.
60 *Ibid.*, 195.
61 *Ibid.*
62 *Ibid.*

to the majority standards of that time and place. Such a position leaves no room for dissent or "non-normative" desires and points of view, thus dismissing the possibility of any such dissent or desires:[63]

> *This poem is merely expressing the contemporary reality of an affectionate, but non-sexual regard between women.*[64]

This is the argument of Angelica Rieger, who attempts to bury the passion of the poem through a series of remarks on its rhetorical reversals:

> [c]omposed by a woman and addressed to another, it acquires a special position not only within the works of the trobairitz but within the entire Occitan literature of the thirteenth century. Since the troubadour typically speaks to the domna, it is clear that the inversion of this configuration in the poems of the trobairitz may be regarded as a marginal phenomenon; that the masculine element should be eliminated, however, so that the lyrical dialogue takes place exclusively between one woman and another, is an extraordinary rarity.[65]

Rare though its female address to another female may be, and as apparently erotic as its language is, Rieger argues that we misread the poem if we see it as expressing sexual desire:

> The poem is indeed by a woman, addressed to another, but nevertheless does not concern a lesbian relationship. In addition to the [...] rejection of homosexuality within troubadour poetry, which makes a public, positive depiction of such a relationship very improbable, the poem does not contain any indecent passages either. Bieiris addresses Maria only in a manner customary for her time and her world; she expresses her sympathy for her in a conventionally codified form—which the choice of genre would also support—just as one, or better, a woman, speaks with a female acquaintance, friend, confidante, or close relative. In short, the

---

63 As Rita Felski has complained, historicism of this stripe has bound us into "a remarkably static view of meaning, where texts are corralled amidst long-gone contexts and obsolete intertexts, incarcerated in the past, with no hope of parole" (*The Limits of Critique*, 157).

64 This is a varation of the *amicitia* argument we have already seen used to explain away the apparent eroticism in Alcuin's poetry.

65 Angelica Rieger. "Was Bieiris de Romans Lesbian? Women's Relations with Each Other in the World of the Troubadours". In *The Voice of the Trobairitz: Perspectives on the Women Troubadours*, ed. by William D. Paden (Philadelphia: University of Pennsylvania Press, 1989), 73.

4. *The Troubadours and Fin'amor: Love, Choice, and the Individual*   143

colloquial tone used between women differed from that used today, and what modern readers deem erotic was simply tender.⁶⁶

As Rieger would have it, the poem "does not concern a lesbian relationship" because that would be "improbable", and therefore evidently impossible. But to speak of a "rejection of homosexuality within troubadour poetry" is a very careful circumscribing of the argument, since troubadour poetry exists within the context of a wider cultural and poetic practice in which same-sex desire is very much part of the picture. One need only look at Alain de Lille (Alanus ab Insulis), and his twelfth-century *De Planctu Naturae* for confirmation. Herein, Alain questions Nature about love and sexuality, and explains the prevalence of same-sex relations through a reference to the gods of Antiquity: "Jupiter, for the adolescent Ganymede, transferred him to the heavens, [...] and while he made him the governor of his drinks on the table by day, he made him the subject of his bed by night".⁶⁷ Though Alain portrays this state of affairs as the result of a fallen Nature who has "betrayed her God-given responsibility by placing sexuality in the hands of Venus [and her] moral licentiousness",⁶⁸ the very existence of the discussion makes Rieger's immediate dismissal of the possibility of homosexuality in *Na Maria* problematic.⁶⁹ Further evidence appears

---

66   *Ibid.*, 82. This is a variation of the *amicitia* argument we have already seen applied to Alcuin.
67   "Jupiter enim adolescentem Ganymedem transferens ad superna, [...] et quem in mensa per diem propinandi sibi statuit praepositum, in toro per noctem sibi fecit suppositum" (Alain de Lille. *Alani de Insulis doctoris universalis opera omnia*. In *Patrologiae Cursus Completus*, ed. by Jacques Paul Migne [Paris: Apud Garnier Fratres, 1855], Vol. 210, col. 451B, https://books.google.com/books?id=c10k8WCYMBoC&pg=RA1-PA470).
68   Barbara Newman. *Gods and the Goddesses: Vision, Poetry, and Belief in the Middle Ages* (Philadelphia: University of Pennsylvania Press, 2003), 87.
69   Alain de Lille only scratches the surface of the possibilities. For other examples, see the discussions of the anonymous twelfth-century poem "Altercatio Ganimedes et Helene" in Newman (2003), as well as in John Boswell's *Christianity, Social Tolerance, and Homosexuality* (Chicago: University of Chicago Press, 1980), and Rolf Lenzen, "Altercatio Ganimedis et Helene". Kritische Edition mit Kommentar. In *Mittellateinisches Jahrbuch*, 7 (1972), 161–86. As Thomas Stehling argues,

   [t]he recurrent reference to classical literature in medieval homosexual poetry represents more than just an appeal to a shared education; it may also be interpreted as an attempt to place homosexual love in a respectable context. [...] Engaged like other poets in this great revival of classical learning, poets writing homosexual verse learned to employ this respect in a particular way.

in the poetry of Hilarius, or Hilary the Englishman, four of whose five surviving love poems are written to boys.[70] *Ad Puerum Anglicum* makes the idea fairly clear:

> Puer decens, decor floris,
> Genma micans, velim noris
> Quia tui decus oris
> Fuit mihi fax amoris.[71]

> Demure boy, beautiful as a flower,
> Sparkling jewel, if only you knew
> That the glory of your eyes
> Has set my love on fire.

Such poetry makes plain that *Na Maria* exists in a context in which same-sex desires exist, and are expressed in powerful verse. But Rieger will have none of it. By trying to erase the very possibility of non-majority desires, she struggles mightily to force this female-voiced poem to revolve around a man, not as rival for the poet's sexual desires and affections (which would apparently require "indecent passages"), but as the wrong choice of man among what are presumably better choices of men. Thus the critic redefines the expressions of desire in the poem in terms of a wish that Lady Maria make the right choice among male suitors:

> Does Maria have a choice between several admirers, and is she to decide on the "right one", and are Bieiris's words spoken out of a sort of maternal concern that this young, beautiful, and intelligent woman might choose the wrong one? Or does the man in question stand between the two women, and is Bieiris's poem an appeal to Maria not to take him, thereby making herself and Bieiris unhappy? The list of possible situations could certainly go on, but the two cited may suffice to demonstrate that Bieiris's

---

Thomas Stehling. "To Love a Medieval Boy". In *Literary Versions of Homosexuality*, ed. by Stuart Kellogg (New York: Haworth Press, 1983), 167. Reddy insists, however, that "recent scholarship on courtly love has accurately characterized the strict heterosexuality" (25) of the Occitan poetry.

70 Stehling, 161.
71 Hilarius, "Ad Puerum Anglicum II". ll. 1–4. *Hilarii Aurelianensis Versus et Ludi Epistolae*. Mittellateinische Studien und Texte, ed. by Walther Bulst and M. L. Bulst-Thiele (Leiden and New York: Brill, 1989), Vol. 16, 46.

canso—following the feminine lyrical tradition—revolves around the absent third party, the man.[72]

But both O'Sullivan's and Rieger's decorous explanations get strained by the second stanza:

> Per que vos prec, si·us platz que fin' amors
> e gausiment e dous umilitatz
> me posca far ab vos tan de socors,
> que mi donetz, bella domna, si·us platz,
> so don plus ai d'aver joi e'speransa;
> car en vos ai mon cor e mon talan,
> e per vos ai tot so qu'ai d'alegransa
> e per vos vauc mantas vetz sospiran.[73]

> For this, I pray, please, let true love
> delight and sweet humility
> give me, with you, the relief I need,
> so you will grant me, beautiful lady, please,
> what I most hope to enjoy.
> Because in you, alas, are my heart and desire
> and for you, alas, are all my joys
> and for you, I go, freely sighing many sighs.

These lines are practically drenched in anxious longing—the voice we hear begs for relief, and the fulfilment of desire. In the meantime, she sighs as she walks abroad, praying that "fin' amors" will give her the heart of the woman she so desperately admires. It is tenuous, at best, to argue that what she prays her *bella domna* will grant her is to choose the right man. As the poem concludes, the feminine voice praises Maria as the embodiment of all that is desirable: "for in you is merriment and all delight, / and every good thing one could want in a woman". This, along with the warning "do not love those false suitors", especially when paired with the claim "I am drawn to you with nothing false in my heart"—sets the female voice of the poem directly in opposition to, and rivalry with those "entendidor", the (grammatically, at least) male

---

72 Rieger, 92.
73 Bietris de Romans, ll. 9–16.

wooers who will betray and lie to Maria. As Meg Bogin has observed, "Scholars have resorted to the most ingenious arguments to avoid concluding that [Bietris] is a woman writing a love poem to another woman",[74] and this, perhaps, is the best indication that Bietris is in fact writing a love poem to another woman: *the scholar doth protest too much, methinks.*

Rieger hedges her bets, admitting that "[t]he possibility of an element of female jealousy (which might even bear lightly homoerotic characteristics) need not be ruled out entirely". Nevertheless, she is determined to "substantiate that [Bietris's] poetic motivation does not spring from a lesbian relationship".[75] Alison Ganze, however, argues undauntedly in the familiar and predictable *what appears to be X is actually Y* style of the hermeneutics of suspicion, that it is a "faulty assumption [...] that the erotic language in the poem must be taken as a literal expression of sexual desire", before she goes on to assert that "'Na Maria' fits within the conventional mode expressing friendship between women".[76] Note how Ganze's gesture makes the poem safe, orthodox, predictable, and not at all disturbing to conservative sensibilities. *It's just about women being friends.* What appears to be erotic longing is actually just friendship. What *appears* to be [fill in the blank] is *actually* [fill in the blank differently]. William Burgwinkle argues along similar lines when he suggests that the poem *Tanz salutz e tantas amors*, perhaps by the mid-thirteenth century troubadour Uc de Saint Circ, "mocks all future discussions of whether ladies writing to ladies might be lesbians by simply pulling the linguistic rug from beneath *the supposed signs of sentiment, the words in question*"[77] Once a critic is in the habit of suspicion, regarding words as always or even usually meaning something other than they merely seem to mean, it appears that the habit is never broken. Thus Burgwinkle argues that love poems are not actually love poems, because they are really something else, in this case, a currency for exchange:

---

74 Meg Bogin. *The Women Troubadours* (New York: Norton & Co., 1980), 176.
75 Rieger, 92.
76 Alison Ganze. "'Na Maria, pretz e fina valors': A New Argument for Female Authorship". *Romance Notes*, 49: [1] (2009), 25–26, https://doi.org/10.1353/rmc.2009.0010
77 William E. Burgwinkle. *Love for Sale: Materialist Readings of the Troubadour Razo Corpus* (New York: Garland, 1997), 100. Emphasis added.

love songs should probably be seen more as a sort of currency in these Southern courts than as personal love missives. [...]. The "Lady" in such songs is often more an empty signifier than a flesh-and-blood woman. As in much of classical literature, the woman is an allegorical stand-in for something else. [This could be] an actual woman at court, the court itself, a fiefdom or castle, a male patron, or an empty category.[78]

With the inclusion of the "empty category", the critic claims that what appears to be X is not only not X, but is potentially anything in the world other than X. Burgwinkle decries the fact that troubadour love poems "continue to be read as personal love missives [...] rather than as musings on language", repeating the familiar critical move that reduces poetry only to language, or to a meta-discourse in which it always and only speaks of itself. He then declares that his argument will "show just how deeply representation, even of what seems to be the most personal nature, is imbued with issues of profit, marketing, and self-promotion".[79] Everything that comes after "seems" is the not-X of the formula. Troubadour love poems *seem* to be personal, but are *actually* [fill in the blank]. This same basic argument is made so often, about so many different poems, plays, novels, etc., that one begins to wonder if it is hard-wired into the academic psyche. What Harold Rosenberg once called "The Herd of Independent Minds"[80] is alive and well and publishing books and journal articles.

What we encounter in troubadour poetry, if we allow ourselves to see it, is a crossing of boundaries, love as resistance to, or rejection of, the ordinarily assigned categories or roles. It challenges the idea of faithfulness in marriage and questions the heteronormativity of our typical approaches to sex and desire.

In the spirit of crossing boundaries, let's look at the troubadours for a moment from outside the perspective of specialist scholars in the field. The popular myth and religion scholar Joseph Campbell wrote perceptively about the troubadours, and his analysis is acute: all too often writers, thinkers, theologians, poets, and academics treat love and desire as if they are definable only in terms of absolute antithesis,

---

78   *Ibid.*, 100–01.
79   *Ibid.*, 11. Emphasis added.
80   *Commentary*, 6 (1 Jan 1948), 244–52, https://www.commentarymagazine.com/articles/the-herd-of-independent-mindshas-the-avant-garde-its-own-mass-culture/

"writing of *agape* and *eros* and their radical opposition, as though these two were the final terms of the principle of 'love'".[81] It is as if love must be regarded in terms of extremes: "whatever is at hand, one loves—either in the angelic way of charity or in the orgiastic, demonic way of a Dionysian orgy; but in either case, religiously: in renunciation of ego, ego judgment, and ego choice".[82] Such thinking supports either the idea that impersonal principle is more important than personal choice, or that the drives of the body are more important than individual judgment. Campbell suggests that the primary poetic, philosophical, and cultural importance of this period, of the troubadour movement itself, is the elevation of the perspectives and choices of the individual over the impersonal claims of law and dogma and the body's claims of lust and desire. This stance often set the troubadours at odds with the theological ideas of their time:

> According to the Gnostic-Manichean view nature is corrupt [...] in the poetry of the troubadours [...] nature [...] is an end and glory in itself. [...] Hence, if the courtly cult of *amor* is to be catalogued according to heresy, it should be indexed rather as Pelagian than as Gnostic or Manichean, for [...] Pelagius and his followers absolutely rejected the doctrine of our inheritance of the sin of Adam and Eve, and taught that we have finally no need of supernatural grace, since our nature itself is full of grace; no need of a miraculous redemption, but only of awakening and maturation.[83]

This tension between worldviews, between the insistence that the world is corrupt, and the celebration of the world as full of its own grace, is reflected in the simultaneous existence of two groups that the twelfth- and thirteenth-century church regarded as heretical and dangerous: the troubadours—who celebrated the body—and the Cathars—who rejected that body as corrupt and fallen. The name Cathar comes from a Greek root meaning "purged" or "pure", and for them, the flesh needed to be "purged" and the entire physical world was a prison from which to escape. But the troubadours' "heresy" was not the more Gnostic, flesh-and world-denying belief characteristic of the Cathars who were the primary target of the Albigensian Crusade of the early thirteenth

---

81 Joseph Campbell. *Creative Mythology* (New York: Viking, 1968), 177.
82 Ibid.
83 Ibid., 176.

century: "there is little sign of Cathar influence on [troubadour] poetry. The delight in the senses found in much of the love-lyric is hardly compatible with the Cathar notion of the evil of matter".[84] If the troubadours were heretics, theirs was the more life-and world-affirming heresy (at its root, the word merely means "opinion") of Pelagius, a British monk who was a contemporary of the now-famous Augustine of Hippo. This obscure monk thought the doctrine of original sin was the single most pernicious thing he had ever heard of, and he devoted a great deal of his time and energy to arguing against the idea.

Imagine this: from the moment you are conceived, you are flawed, broken, and sick, while at the same time you are commanded to be well and denied the medicine that would cure you:

> O wearisome condition of humanity,
> Borne under one law, to an other bound,
> Vainely begot, and yet forbidden vanity,
> Created sicke, commanded to be sound.[85]

You are denied this medicine (unless you are one of a lucky few) by the will of a perfect, just, and unbending deity—and this denial comes as a result of no action or inaction, no deserving or failing of your own—in fact, you have not done, and cannot do anything either to elicit or forestall the pleasure or displeasure of this deity. Judgment was rendered upon you before the founding of the world into which you would one day be born as a helpless, broken, and already-condemned infant. Since you are fatally flawed from the very beginning, the only possibility that you have of salvation, joy, and fulfillment is the forcible manipulation of your sin-infected will by God (through a power known as grace), because you are entirely unable to take any positive responsibility for your life.[86] Pelagius opposed all of this in the name of human freedom:

---

84 Linda M. Paterson. *The World of the Troubadours: Medieval Occitan Society c.1100-c.1300* (Cambridge: Cambridge University Press, 1993), 342–43.
85 Fulke Greville. *The Tragedy of Mustapha* (London: Printed for Nathaniel Butler, 1609), "Chorus Sacerdotum", Sig. B2r, https://archive.org/stream/tragedyofmustaph00grev#page/n16
86 Jean de Meun's thirteenth-century reaction to this problem takes 625 lines of the *Roman de la Rose* to work through what might be called a semi-Pelagian solution, ending a discussion of free will with the idea that "It is above all destiny / no matter what will or will not be destined" ("Il est seur toutes destinees, / ja si ne seront

"the relationship of human freedom to divine grace was the crucial issue on which Augustine and Pelagius differed. [...] Augustine [refused] to admit that the debate was between freedom and determinism. Pelagius, on the other hand, was just as adamant in insisting that it was".[87]

For Pelagius, Augustine's doctrine of original sin contributes to the decay of society, and to the breakdown of the ordinary restraints that our sense of responsibility for our actions puts on our baser impulses. Pelagius regards "man's sin as the result not of an inheritance from Adam but of imitation of his *example*".[88] Pelagius believes that "each soul was created by God at the time of conception [...] and thus could not come into the world tainted by original sin transmitted from Adam. [...] Adam's sin did have disastrous consequences for humanity; it introduced death and the habit of disobedience. But the latter was propagated by example, not by physical descent".[89]

Pelagius argues that Augustine's doctrine acts as a *carte blanche*, a cosmic get-out-of-jail-free card that gives people perverse permission to abandon themselves to their baser, more aggressive and violent impulses, resulting in the chaos that Thomas Hobbes describes as the war of all against all, in which life is "solitary, poore, nasty, brutish, and short".[90] In a letter to a follower named Demetrias, Pelagius argues

---

destinees") (Lorris and de Meun [1965], v.3. ll. 17695–96). Robert Musil's modern reaction to this dilemma is fully Pelagian:

> If God predetermined and foreknew everything, how can a man sin? Yes, this is an early question, but you can see that it is still a very modern question as well. This has created an extremely intriguing representation of God. We offend him by his own consent; he even forces us to transgressions for which he will blame us. He not only knows about it beforehand [...], but he caused it!

> Wenn Gott alles vorher bestimmt und weiß, wie kann der Mensch sündigen? So wurde ja früher gefragt, und sehen Sie, es ist noch immer eine ganz moderne Fragestellung. Eine ungemein intrigante Vorstellung von Gott hatte man sich da gemacht. Man beleidigt ihn mit seinem Einverständnis, er zwingt den Menschen zu einer Verfehlung, die er ihm übelnehmen wird; er weiß es ja nicht nur vorher [...], sondern er veranlaßt es!

Der Mann Ohne Eigenschaften [*The Man Without Qualities*] (Berlin: Rowohlt Verlag, 1957), 485–86.

87 Brinley Roderick Rees. *Pelagius: Life and Letters* (Woodbridge: Boydell Press, 1998), 54.
88 Ibid., 76.
89 John Toews. *The Story of Original Sin* (Eugene, OR: Wipf and Stock Publishers, 2013), 76.
90 Thomas Hobbes. *Leviathan: Or, The Matter, Forme & Power of a Commonwealth, Ecclesiasticall and Civill* (London: Andrew Crooke, 1651), 62, https://books.google.com/books?id=L3FgBpvIWRkC&pg=PA62

that "the ignorant vulgar are at fault"[91] for allowing themselves to be persuaded "that mankind has not, in truth, been created good, because it is able to do evil",[92] insisting that we are "capable of both good and evil",[93] but that either involves an exercise of will: "neither good nor evil is done without the will".[94] And the will can be trained; it is not hopelessly corrupt as the result of an inherent fault, a fundamental brokenness or wickedness in human nature, but weakened as a result of "being instructed in evil",[95] in no small part by those, like Augustine, who preach that human nature is fundamentally evil due to inherited sin. Pelagius, like Rousseau, thinks people are basically good and need only a little development, maturation, and guidance. In the words of the seventeenth-century English Pelagian, John Milton, they require education. Milton's belief that human beings are not irretrievably wicked is made clear in his 1644 treatise *Of Education*, where he outlines the ultimate purpose of human education: "The end of learning is to repair the ruins of our first parents by regaining to know God aright, and out of that knowledge to love him, to imitate him, to be like him, as we may the nearest by possessing our souls of true virtue".[96]

The troubadours are more closely aligned to this Pelagian (and Miltonic) point of view that the world and its people are basically good. This is the heritage that the troubadours passed down to the Renaissance and eventually to our own time: the idea that nature is good and love is an end in itself, not something to be denied or escaped from, not a trap, not an object of shame, but a source of joy.[97] It contains a hint of later ideas to come, like the *carpe diem* motif of so much English

---

91 "imperitum vulgus offendit" (Pelagius. *Pelagii Sancti et eruditi monachi Epistola ad Demetriadem*, ed. by Johann Salomo Semler [Halae Magdeburgicae: Carol Herman Hemmerde, 1775], 14, https://books.google.com/books?id=uw5qbOfGtgoC&pg=PA14).

92 "non vere bonum factum hominem putes, quia is facere malum potest" (*ibid.*).

93 "boni et mali capacem etiam" (*ibid.*, 32, https://books.google.com/books?id=uw5qbOfGtgoC&pg=PA32).

94 "nec bonum sine voluntate faciamus, nec malum" (*ibid.*).

95 "mali etiam esse studuimus" (*ibid.*, 34, https://books.google.com/books?id=uw5qbOfGtgoC&pg=PA34).

96 John Milton. *Of Education* (London: 1644), Sig. A1v, https://books.google.com/books?id=7rJDAAAAcAAJ&pg=PP4

97 The more recognizably orthodox point of view is memorably expressed in the sixteenth-century English poet George Gascoigne's poem "Gascoigne's Good Morrow", where readers are informed that we must "deeme our days on earth, / But hell to heavenly joye" (*The Complete Works of George Gascoigne*: Vol. 1, The Posies, ed.

Renaissance poetry. From this point of view, the claims of this life, and this world, rather than the airy promises of a future existence, take on an urgency that is otherwise denied them. In the view of the troubadours, "not heaven but this blossoming earth was to be recognized as the true domain of love, as it is of life".[98] Hand-in-hand with this immediacy of earthly life and love, goes a concept of individualism that is vital for understanding the troubadours and their poetry:

> The troubadour's new time expresses a new individualism. [...] It is the Occitan troubadour, with his self-promoting songs of desperate love for the wife of his patron, who ignores war and nation to disguise a revolutionary individualist intent (whether as illicit desire or as social gain) behind the spiritual quality of true love. He is a figure who is from our perspective recognizably Keatsian, certainly Romantic, and therefore perceptively modern and out of his time.[99]

There is, of course, no shortage of critics who will deny such a proposition, arguing instead for the near-inaccessibility of medieval poetry. One such critic is Paul Zumthor, who insists that "A first obvious piece of evidence becomes clear to our eyes: the remoteness of the Middle Ages, and the irrecoverable distance that separates us [...]. Medieval poetry belongs to a universe that has become foreign to us".[100] For Zumthor:

> When a man of our century confronts a work of the twelfth century, the time that separates one from the other distorts, or even erases the relationship that ordinarily develops between the author and the reader through the mediation of the text: such a relationship can hardly be spoken of any more. What indeed is a true reading, if not an effort that involves both the reader and the culture in which the reader participates, an effort corresponding to that textual production involving the author and his own universe? In respect to a medieval text, the correspondence no longer occurs spontaneously. The perception of form becomes ambiguous. Metaphors are darkened, comparisons no longer make

---

by John W. Cunliffe [Cambridge: Cambridge University Press, 1907], 57, https://archive.org/stream/cu31924013121292#page/n68).
98 Campbell, *Creative Mythology*, 183.
99 Elizabeth Fay. *Romantic Medievalism: History and the Romantic Literary Ideal* (New York: Palgrave, 2002), 15.
100 "Une première évidence éclate aux yeux: l'éloignement du moyen âge, la distance irrécupérable qui nous en sépare [...] la poésie médiévale relève d'un univers qui nous est devenu étranger" (Paul Zumthor. *Essai de Poétique Médiévale* [Paris: Seuil, 1972], 19).

sense. The reader remains embedded within his own time; while the text, through an effect produced by the passage of time, seems timeless, which is a contradictory situation.[101]

But to give in to an idea like this, is to give in to an absolute and unprovable claim which is structurally identical to the *mentalités* idea of Lucien Febvre, who argued in 1947 that there was no such thing as an atheist in the Renaissance (despite the fact that many were accused of atheism, and even executed on the charge[102]) because "the mental equipment available in the sixteenth century made it as good as impossible for anyone to be an atheist, and, perhaps more important, [...] an atheist could only have been a solitary figure to whom nobody would have paid any significant attention".[103] Febvre's claim, in turn, has its roots in the work of Wilhelm Dilthey (1910), for whom

> one speaks of the spirit of a time, of the spirit of the Middle Ages, or the Enlightenment. At the same time, it is a fact that in such epochs limitations are met with in the form of a life-horizon. By that, I mean the limit on the people of a time in terms of their life's thinking, feeling, and will. There is a proportion of life, lifestyle, experience, and ability to form concepts, which tightly binds the individual within a certain range of modifications of opinions, value formation, and purposes. Inevitabilities rule herein over particular individuals.[104]

---

101 Lorsqu'un homme de notre siècle affronte une œuvre du XIIe siècle, la durée qui les sépare l'un de l'autre dénature jusqu'à l'effacer la relation qui, ordinairement, s'établit entre l'auteur et le lecteur par la médiation du texte: c'est à peine si l'on peut parler encore de relation. Qu'est-ce en effet qu'un lecture vraie, sinon un travail où se trouvent à la fois impliqués le lecteur et la culture à laquelle il participe? Travail correspondant à celui qui produsuit le texte et où furent impliqués l'auteur et son propre univers. A l'égard d'un texte médiéval, la correspndance ne se produit plus spontanément. La perception même de la forme devient équivoque. Les métaphores s'obscurcissent, le comparant s'écarte du comparé. Le lecteur reste engagé dans son temps; le texte, par un effet tenant à l'accumulation des durées intermédiaires, apparaît comme hors du temps, ce qui est une situation contradictoire.

Ibid., 20.

102 See Michael Bryson, *The Atheist Milton* (London: Routledge, 2012), 36–50.

103 Lucien Febvre. *The Problem of Unbelief in the Sixteenth Century: The Religion of Rabelais*. Trans. by Beatrice Gottlieb (Cambridge, MA: Harvard University Press, 1985), Translator's Introduction, xxviii.

104 [S]pricht man vom Geist einer Zeit, vom Geist des Mittelalters, der Aufklärung. Damit ist zugleich gegeben, daß jede solcher Epochen eine Begrenzung findet in einem Lebenshorizont. Ich verstehe darunter die Begrenzung, in welcher der Menschen einer Zeit in bezug auf ihr Denken, Fühlen und Wollen leben. Es besteht in ihr ein Verhältnis von Leben, Lebensbezügen, Lebenserfahrung und Gedankenbildung, welche die Einzelnen in einem bestimmten Kreis

Foucault makes a similar argument, insisting that "in a given culture and time, there is never more than one *episteme* that defines the conditions of possibility of all knowledge".¹⁰⁵ Such claims, if taken seriously, render it almost futile to read the poetry of any era or any culture that is separated from one's own by enough time, and geographic and/or linguistic difference, because of the differences between the *mentalités* and life-horizons (*Lebenshorizont*) and *epistemes* of the past and the present. Claims like this (commonly made, though rarely substantiated) allow the scholar to put up "No Trespassing" signs, warning away interested—though non-specialist—readers, and creating what amount to obscure literary fiefdoms ruled over by critics who have blanketed their subject areas in a forbidding darkness.¹⁰⁶

Zumthor insists that "the song is its own proper subject, without a predicate. [...] The poem is its own mirror".¹⁰⁷ From this point of view, Zumthor sees all poetry as "self-referential", a structure "in which the 'I' who speaks has a purely grammatical function, devoid of reference to anything other than the act of singing which it performs, records, re-enacts, and anticipates".¹⁰⁸ Though Zumthor says that "this is not a

---

    von Modifikationen der Auffassung, Wertbildung und Zwecksetzung festhält und bindet. Unvermeidlichkeiten regieren hierin über den einzelnen Individuen.

    Wilhelm Dilthey. *Der Aufbau der geschichtlichen Welt in den Geisteswissenschaften* (Frankfurt am Main: Suhrkamp, 1970), 217.

105 "Dans une culture et à un moment donné, il n'y a jamais qu'une épistémè, qui définit les conditions de possibilité de tout savoir" (*Les mots et les choses: Une archéologie des sciences humaines* [Paris: Gallimard, 1966], 179).

106 Rita Felski describes this impulse as one in which "the critic feels impelled to beat off the barbarians by raising the drawbridge—a too-drastic response that cuts off the text from the moral, affective, and cognitive bonds that infuse it with energy and life. Thus the literary work is treated as a fragile and exotic artifact of language, to be handled only by curators kitted out in kid gloves" (*The Limits of Critique*, 28). She then notes that "[s]uch a vision of reading remains notably silent on the question of how literature enters life" (28–29). R. Howard Bloch and Stephen G. Nichols describe a similar attitude, decrying what they see as the use of "philological expertise [...] not as a tool to make medieval literature accessible, but as a *cordon sanitaire* to prevent the reading of such works" ("Introduction". In *Medievalism and the Modern Temper*, ed. by R. Howard Bloch and Stephen G. Nichols [Baltimore: Johns Hopkins University Press, 1996], 3).

107 "Le chanson et ainsi son propre sujet, sans prédicat [...] Le poèmee est miroir de soi" (Zumthor, 218).

108 Simon Gaunt. "The Châtelain de Couci". In *The Cambridge Companion to Medieval French Literature*, ed. by Simon Gaunt and Sarah Kay (Cambridge: Cambridge University Press, 2008), 96.

claim for the freezing of the text",[109] that is, in effect, what has happened to a great deal of troubadour criticism. Zumthor's assertion that there is an unbridgeable gap between the medieval era and our own was followed by the insistence that the poems must not be understood as being about love and desire in any real and still-understandable sense, but about language and performance.[110] This tendency has been exacerbated by Zumthor's concomitant claim that any attempt by a modern reader to read twelfth-century work is doomed because "the period that separates one from the other distorts, or even erases the relationship" necessary for understanding. Despite the caveat Zumthor adds about not applying "simplified analogies and mythical justifications"[111] this is precisely what a number of critics of the last few decades have done, applying French feminist thought,[112] or making accusations of troubadour misogyny and narcissism,[113] or arguing that what appear to be love poems are actually disguised representations of political struggles. The latter is argued by Erich Köhler, for whom the more esoteric style of troubadour poetry (the closed song or *trobar clus*) indicates a class struggle between higher and lower levels of nobility: "the persistent element of esotericism in the attitude of the feudal nobility, becomes more and more a deliberate stance that crucially separates it from the lower nobility".[114] Köhler not only "argued vigorously that the troubadour lyric mediated the tension between the different sections of the nobility" but he also maintained

---

109 "On ne prétend pas en cela geler le texte" (Zumthor, 20).
110 This is a curious reworking of what Holmes calls a "Burckhardtian opposition of medieval conformism, or community values, and Renaissance individualism" (Olivia Holmes. *Assembling the Lyric Self: Authorship from Troubadour Song to Italian Poetry* [Minneapolis: University of Minnesota Press, 2000], 3).
111 "des analogies simplifiantes et des justifications mythiques" (Zumthor, 20).
112 See Tilde Sankovitch, "The Trobairitz". In *The Troubadours: An Introduction*, ed. by Simon Gaunt and Sarah Kay (Cambridge: Cambridge University Press, 1999), 113–26.
113 See Simon Gaunt, "Poetry of Exclusion: A Feminist Reading of Some Troubadour Lyrics". *The Modern Language Review*, 85: 2 (April 1990), 310–29.
114 "Das beharrende Element der esoterischen Haltung, der Feudaladel, wird sich mehr und mehr der Interessenverschiebung bewußt, die ihn vom Kleinadel immer entscheidender trennt" (Erich Köhler. "Zum 'Trobar Clus' Der Trobadors". *Romanische Forschungen*, 64: 1–2 [1952], 101). Köhler goes on to argue that the "trobar clus" serves as as "deepening of the conscious sense of one's own existence", and "as a mystical recovery and concealment of the sense of being" ("Vertiefenwollen des bewußt werdenden Sinns der eigenen Existenz, als ein mystisches Bergen und gleichzeitiges Verbergen der vom standischen Sein") (98).

that "the erotic love to which the songs were ostensibly devoted was invariably a metaphor for other desires, other drives".[115] As E. Jane Burns explains it, the passions expressed in the troubadour poems are merely masks, disguising the desire for wealth, status, and power:

> [T]roubadour poets' professed love of the domna actually masked a concerted social aspiration to be elevated to the status of her husband. Thus could poor, landless knights of the lower nobility attempt to attain higher standing (Köhler 1964). [...] Provencal love songs [have] less to do with eroticism, passion, or desire than with class conflict between the disenfranchised squirine and the established nobility (Köhler 1970).[116]

One has to marvel at the lengths to which scholars will go to rewrite poetry in order to "consistently read love songs as about anything but love".[117] And as one follows Burns' explanation a little further, the idea at work becomes clear—what is aimed at is nothing less than the dissolving of the text in the solvent of criticism: "The courtly lady dissolves further in Lacanian analyses of lyric and romance where she

---

115 Simon Gaunt and Sarah Kay. "Introduction". In *The Troubadours: An Introduction*, ed. by Simon Gaunt and Sarah Kay (Cambridge: Cambridge University Press, 1999), 4. Emphasis added.

116 E. Jane Burns. "Courtly Love: Who Needs It? Recent Feminist Work in the Medieval French Tradition". *Signs: Journal of Women in Culture and Society*, 27: 1 (Autumn 2001), 40. It is important to note, however, that for Köhler, this is not necessarily true of the troubadours who write in the "trobar leu" or open style. Speaking of the poet Guirat de Bornelh, Köhler argues for the importance of recognizing desire and joy in this style of troubadour poetry: "Whoever knows the meaning of "joy" in the troubadors, [...] in the interrelationship with the woman as the source, [...] who knows this notion as the dominant motif of Provençal poetry, is able to measure what the light style [or *trobar leu*] must mean for Guiraut" ("Wer um den Sinn des 'joy' bei den Trobadors weiß, [...] in der Wechselbeziehung zur Frau als ihrer Quelle [...] wer diese Vorstellung als das beherrschende Motiv der provenzalischen Dichtung erkennt, vermag zu ermessen, was der leichte Stil für Guiraut bedeuten muß") (Köhler, 91–92). In a later article, Köhler makes a clear distinction between the two styles, arguing that for the high nobility, obscurity served as an insiders' code from which the lower nobility (to say nothing of the common people) were excluded: "the obscure and difficult style, the trobar clus, is suitable for the high nobility, who speak an esoteric language to set up a barrier between the profane and the treasure of true love, to which they [the high nobility] alone must have access" ("le style obscur et difficile, le trobar clus, convient à la haute noblesse, qui parle une langue ésotérique pour mettre à l'abri des profanes le trésor du vrai amour, auquel elle seule doit avoir accès") ("Observations historiques et sociologiques sur la poésie des troubadours". *Cahiers de civilisation médiévale*, 7: 25 [1964], 31, http://www.persee.fr/doc/ccmed_0007-9731_1964_num_7_25_1296).

117 Longxi, 207.

becomes a textualized object of masculine desire, a metaphor for the enigma of femininity and a cipher for male poetic practice".[118] This argument has long been a paradigm in studies of troubadour poetry. Frederick Goldin argues that the women being addressed in troubadour poems are essentially mirrors that reflect the troubadour back to himself, showing him what he "wants to become" but also "what he can never be".[119] Burns argues that the apparent passions of the troubadour poems are actually "a misreading of the feminine in terms of the masculine",[120] while O'Sullivan states the case baldly, openly using the what appears to be X is really Y formula: "[t]he male-authored *canso* is narcissistic in nature: while it may be ostensibly about the praiseworthy Other, it's really about praising the Self".[121] Tilde Sankovitch turns the troubadours into auto-eroticists, claiming that Narcissus serves as a model for "the troubadours' self-referential erotic quest for beauty and perfection" while the poetry refers not to "the domna's intimate Otherness but to the poet's wish to penetrate into his own perfection's space".[122] All of these arguments follow Paris in furthering the trend of violent ideological impositions tracing back to the early thirteenth century, by subordinating the troubadours and their poetry to the concepts and dictates of outside authority. The pen and the sword are merely different means to the same end.

What is especially noteworthy is how closely the critics adhere to a basic paradigm, essentially repeating each other's arguments with some minor changes in terminology and theory. The effect is like listening to a chorus singing a song with only one verse, each singer replicating the others, with minor variations available only in the register and timbre of the voices, whose individuality is otherwise lost in the repetitiveness of the musical theme. And it has to be asked, if this is truly all that

---

118 Burns, 40.
119 Frederick Goldin. *The Mirror of Narcissus and the Courtly Love Lyric* (Ithaca: Cornell University Press, 1967), 75.
120 Jane E. Burns. *Courtly Love Undressed: Reading through Clothes in Medieval French Culture* (Philadelphia: University of Pennsylvania Press, 2002), 252, n. 14.
121 Daniel O'Sullivan. "The Man Backing Down from the Lady in Trobairitz Tensos". In *Founding Feminisms in Medieval Studies: Essays in Honor of E. Jane Burns*, ed. by Laine E. Doggett and Daniel E. O'Sullivan (Cambridge: Boydell & Brewer, 2016), 45.
122 Tilde Sankovitch. "Lombarda's Reluctant Mirror: Speculum of Another Poet". In *The Voice of the Trobairitz: Perspectives on the Women Troubadours*, ed. by William Paden (Philadelphia: University of Pennsylvania Press, 1989), 184, 185.

troubadour poetry is, why read any of it, much less any of the criticism which shows so much disdain for it? This kind of argument, despite its theoretical and secular sheen, is fundamentally religious in nature, reflecting the assumptions of the Akibas and Origens of the world for whom a text must be forced to obey, forced to yield a morally (or theoretically) edifying sense or be righteously and roundly accused, before being abandoned altogether. As Longxi points out, for such readers, this has long meant systematically turning away from the literal meanings of words and texts:

> As allegory etymologically means "speaking of the other", in reading this we should then understand it as that. Of the four levels (or the fourfold scheme) of meaning, which constitute the theoretical foundation of biblical allegory, the least important or relevant to true understanding, according to the allegorists, is the literal sense. The revelation of the Spirit must be at the cost of the suppression of the Letter. For Origen and his followers, the written word should be cast off and forgotten in order to free the spirit of the Logos from the shell of human language.[123]

Along similar lines, and with similar goals in mind, Gregory Stone uses what he calls a "grammatical" argument—similar to that of Zumthor, but based on categories from Dante's *De Vulgari Eloquentia*—to erase the individuality of the troubadour poets by claiming that it never existed in the first place. His argument is based on the notion of a "mature rejection of the new Renaissance model of the self-determining singular ego, a model with which the late Middle Ages is already quite familiar yet regards as a lie".[124] While one wonders how such notably retiring, self-effacing personalities as Guilhem IX and his famous granddaughter Eleanor of Aquitaine would react to such an idea, Stone goes on to maintain that "[t]he Middle Ages consciously insists that I am they: that the individual subject is never singular, is always in some essential sense general, collective, objective".[125] Miraculously, an entire era and all of its people can be described as insisting that "I am they", as if the scene in Monty Python's *Life of Brian* where Graham Chapman's Brian insists to the crowd "You are all individuals", while they respond in

---

123 Longxi, 200.
124 Gregory B. Stone. *The Death of the Troubadour: The Late Medieval Resistance to the Renaissance* (Philadelphia: University of Pennsylvania Press, 1994), 4.
125 *Ibid.*

unison, "Yes. We are all individuals" has been inverted and turned into an interpretive principle.[126]

As Daniel Heller-Roazen demonstrates, critics frequently claim that the "I" in medieval texts testifies to the absence of poetic individuality:

> [t]he critical works on the problem of the medieval poetic "I" concur precisely in their uncertainty about the referential status of the first-person pronoun; and in many instances they deny, implicitly or explicitly, the possibility of attributing the "I" of a medieval author to a historical individual. [...] the "I" is not the name of an actual individual but essentially the product of a rhetorical operation, [and] the significatum of the first-person pronoun in medieval poetry cannot be presupposed by criticism. [...] The "I", which for many recent critics of "literary subjectivity" is what names an actual being, is precisely what, for many medieval authors, appears to express a fundamental anonymity: something without any determined nature or properties, a work of artifice and fiction in every sense. The definition of the "I" as the sign of an existing subject, which appears almost self-evident today, is therefore foreign to the texts of medieval literature.[127]

The syllogistic argument here is as familiar as it is threadbare: 1) Critics concur about their "uncertainty" over the meaning of "I" in medieval poetry. 2) The "I" appears to such critics to "express a fundamental anonymity". 3) Therefore the "I" (as "the sign of an existing subject" or actual person) is "foreign to medieval texts". The conclusion simply does not follow from the premises, but in arguments of this type that is almost irrelevant; the authoritative tone is intended to carry the day. The "I" is simply asserted to be "the product of a rhetorical operation", without any argument or evidence being put forward to support this, and successive critics perform essentially this same maneuver in analyses of medieval poetry. Their thinking is is "governed to a remarkable degree by [Jacob] Burckhardt's apparently ineradicable [nineteenth-century] assumption that in the Middle Ages 'man was conscious of himself only as a member of a race, people, party, family,

---

126 https://www.youtube.com/watch?v=QereR0CViMY
127 Daniel Heller-Roazen. *Fortune's Faces: The Roman de la Rose and the Poetics of Contingency* (Baltimore: Johns Hopkins University Press, 2003), 30, 33. And so Heller-Roazen essentially repeats Stone's repetition of Zumthor. With such repetition careers are made. And so it continues…

or corporation'",[128] a case that critics like Zumthor, Heller-Roazen, and Stone repeat practically word-for-word,[129] and which forms one of the governing assumptions for Stephen Greenblatt's much-contested book *The Swerve*.[130] This repetition from one critic to the next functions as a kind of groupthink by which modern critics who mimic one another's voices deny the individuality of medieval men and women:

---

128 Lee Patterson. "On the Margin: Postmodernism, Ironic History, and Medieval Studies". *Speculum*, 65: 1 (January 1990), 95.

129 In Burckhardt's formulation, the condescension is nearly overwhelming:

> In the Middle Ages the two sides of consciousness—that turned toward the world and that turned toward the inner self of man—were dreaming or half awake under a common veil. The veil was woven of faith, childish partiality, and delusion, through which the world and its history appeared in miraculous hues, but Man recognized himself only as a race, a people, a party, a corporation, a family, or otherwise in any general or common form.

> Im Mittelalter lagen die beiden Seiten des Bewußtseins—nach der Welt hin und nach dem Innern des Menschen selbst—wie unter einem gemeinsamen Schleier träumend oder halbwach. Der Schleier war gewoben aus Glauben, Kindesbefangenheit und Wahn; durch ihn hindurch gesehen erschienen Welt und Geschichte wundersam gefärbt, der Mensch aber erkannte sich nur als Race, Volk, Partei, Corporation. Familie oder sonst in irgend einer Form des Allgemeinen.

> Jacob Burckhardt. *Die Cultur der Renaissance in Italien*: *Ein Versuch* (Basel: Schweighauser, 1860), 131, https://babel.hathitrust.org/cgi/pt?id=gri.ark:/13960/t7fr4fg3z;view=1up;seq=137

130 Greenblatt bases his case on the notion that the Renaissance is responsible for establishing a sense of individuality of which earlier periods were incapable: "Something happened in the Renaissance, something that surged up against the constraints that centuries had constructed around curiosity, desire, individuality, sustained attention to the material world, the claims of the body" (*The Swerve: How the World Became Modern* [New York: W. W. Norton & Co., 2011], pp. 9–10). But such expressions of "desire, individuality, sustained attention to the material world, [and] the claims of the body" are readily evident in the poetry of the troubadours, trobairitz, and Minnesingers, as well as the earlier work of the Greek *erotici*, Ovid, and the writer(s) of the Song of Songs. The historian John Monfasani describes Greenblatt's book as a "Burckhardtian, or, perhaps more accurately, Voltairean view of the Renaissance as an outburst of light after a long medieval darkness", and calls it an echo of Burckhardt's "caricature of the poor benighted medievals as incapable of conceiving of themselves other than as part of some corporate structure (as opposed to us liberated modern individualists)" ("The Swerve: How the Renaissance Began". *Reviews in History*, 1283, http://www.history.ac.uk/reviews/review/1283). Marjorie Curry Woods argues that Greenblatt "reinforces a tired old master-narrative, in which one or another renaissance man changes the world" ("Where's the Manuscript". *Exemplaria*, 25: 4 [Winter 2013], 322), while John Parker calls Greenblatt's account "a venerable and familiar story" ("The Epicurean Middle Ages". *Exemplaria*, 25: 4 [Winter 2013], 325), and Lee Morrissey and Will Stockton refer to it as a kind of monstrosity or caricature: "New Historicism on steroids (all anecdotes, all the time)" ("What Swirls around The Swerve". *Exemplaria*, 25: 4 [Winter 2013], 334, https://doi.org/10.1179/1041257313Z.00000000036).

> What this fashionable prose produces is of course that most reactionary of accounts, a hierarchical Middle Ages in which not merely alternative modes of thought but thought per se is proscribed—an account that at one stroke wipes out not merely the complexity of medieval society but the centuries of struggle by which medieval men and women sought to remake their society.[131]

Following obediently along with his scholarly tribe, Stone then takes from Dante the idea that "Grammar, which is nothing else but a kind of unchangeable identity of speech in different times and places [...] [has] been settled by the common consent of many peoples, [and] seems exposed to the arbitrary will of none in particular"[132] before going on to make the crucial gesture of erasure:

> The language of troubadour song is "grammatical" in the sense that it is universal: troubadour song, says Dante, "suffuses its perfume in every city, yet it has its lair in none". The locus of song is everywhere in general and nowhere in particular, its place is no place. [...] The language of troubadour love poetry does not permit the identification of its speaker as a certain historical and singular individual: the time and place of the *I* is no particular time and no particular place. Grammar or the language of song transcends the concrete historical situation; in Heideggerian terms, it is an ontological rather than an ontic language; it expresses Being in general rather than a certain particular being.[133]

And thus, rather neatly, individual poets can be erased, and the passions their poems expressed can be transformed from those of living men and women to generalized expressions of "Being", and love—a passion between individuals who have been lifted clean out of time and existence—no longer exists except as a function of "grammar".

Such arguments, reducing individuality to generality, bring to mind William Blake's statement that "[t]o generalize is to be an Idiot".[134] But to be fair, what is on display here is not so much idiocy as it is a carefully-constructed limiting of poetry's ability to reach potential readers. Readings like those of Zumthor or Stone cannot erase the

---

131 Patterson, 97.
132 G. B. Stone, 4.
133 *Ibid.*, 5.
134 William Blake. *The Works of William Blake*, Vol. 2, ed. by Edwin John Ellis and William Butler Yeats (London: Benard Quartich, 1893), 323, https://archive.org/stream/worksofwilliambl02blakrich#page/323

existence of the poems, and cannot prevent readers from reading the poems, but they do attempt to dictate the terms on which readers can understand those poems. This is one of the primary problems readers encounter in much of the literary scholarship and criticism of the last several decades—an insistence, exercised through analytical terms that seek to make disagreement either impossible or easily-dismissible as "naive" or "uninformed", that poetry must be read against its apparent grain, that its human life and light must be drained out of it as it is transformed into an allegory for whatever the critic seeks to impose on readers. In Stone's case, readers, if they are to avoid being naive, must understand these poems as mere artifacts of "an anonymous or universal language, as essentially identical to the language of others",[135] lifeless items that are "always repeating the same rather than saying something different, repeating the topoi, the conventions of courtly love poetry".[136] It comes as no surprise, then, that from this critical point of view, the expression of genuine human emotion is impossible, because for such a critic it seems that there is no genuine human emotion to be expressed in the first place. Making an argument that sounds like a distillation of Kafka's nightmare scenarios of bureaucratic imprisonment and Joseph Heller's Catch-22,[137] Stone argues that the attempt to express individual emotions makes one precisely not individual. Citing Jonathan Culler's work *On Deconstruction* as his authority, Stone delivers what he fancies is the death blow: "Saying 'I love you', [...] is always a convention, a citation; it does not so much distinguish an individual as it makes him resemble everyone else".[138]

Such a critical position takes a *for thee but not for me* stance, exempting itself as the special case to which its own reductive principles do not apply. My language, says the critic, signifies what I mean it to signify; as Humpty-Dumpty would have it: "When *I* use a word [...] it means just what I choose it to mean—neither more nor less".[139] The poet's language, however, is merely "conventional", a series of "tropes" that refer, not to

---

135 G. B. Stone, 6.
136 *Ibid.*
137 An infinitely expandable and flexible principle whereby anything can be defined into or out of existence at the whim of authority.
138 G. B. Stone, 6.
139 Lewis Carroll. *Through the Looking Glass: And what Alice Found There* (Philadelphia: Henry Altemus Company, 1897), 123.

any extra-linguistic reality, but to language itself.¹⁴⁰ Thus, poetry always and only refers to poetry, revealing the inherent impossibility of its doing otherwise. But the work of the critic is never conceived as being subject to the same limitations—*criticism* does not refer only to itself, but claims authority over any and all other forms of discourse, including—and especially—the discourse of poetry. And like Plato, it seems that critics would deny poetry a place in their carefully-wrought Republic.

There has been some resistance to this trend, notably from Sarah Kay, whose argument in *Subjectivity in Troubadour Poetry* tries to recover the notion that the "I" of troubadour lyric may, in fact, refer to actual persons:

> There is evidence of a relationship between the lyric first person and the characters of other medieval genres, which suggests that medieval readers were prepared to take the first person as referring to an ontological entity (a person). [...] The subject then, can be read not just as a grammatical position, but as articulating a self.¹⁴¹

Truly, a dizzyingly radical notion. Simon Gaunt and Sarah Kay have suggested that "perhaps the time has come now to reassess the nature of love in troubadour poetry and to take what the troubadours said about themselves seriously again".¹⁴² The fact that such a statement needs to be made at all is remarkable. The critics here admit that they have dismissed the troubadours' testimony about themselves, and confess that the trend has gone too far and gone on for too long: "[s]ince 1945 [...] concerted efforts have been made to downplay (or at the very least to reinterpret) the significance of what made troubadour poetry

---

140 This idea can be seen, among other places, in Paul de Man's assertion that language ultimately refers only to itself, because of a "discrepancy between the power of words as acts and their power to produce other words" (*The Rhetoric of Romanticism* [New York: Columbia University Press, 1984], 101), though he complicates his argument with the assertion that literature and criticism are one and the same, equally unreliable: "[l]iterature as well as criticism—the difference between them being delusive—is condemned (or privileged) to be forever the most rigorous and, consequently, the most unreliable language in terms of which man names and transforms himself" (*Allegories of Reading*, 19).

141 Sarah Kay. *Subjectivity in Troubadour Poetry* (Cambridge: Cambridge University Press, 1990), 212–13.

142 Simon Gaunt and Sarah Kay. "Introduction". In *The Troubadours: An Introduction*, ed. by Simon Gaunt and Sarah Kay (Cambridge: Cambridge University Press, 1999), 6.

famous in the first place: love".[143] Such efforts have a lengthy history, long preceding the period the critics here refer to, and a clear agenda in service of "the power which demands submission".[144]

But if the critics are set aside, it is easy to see that the troubadours celebrate love, often with a frank eroticism that is reminiscent of the Song of Songs. The troubadours celebrate love and desire in a way that is true to immediate experience, true to the life that men and women of flesh actually inhabit, an attitude that may have been an unexpected side-effect of the first Crusades:

> [T]he crusaders had discovered the marvels across the seas with their own eyes. A new world had revealed itself to them: a civilization that was not Christian, that accorded a positive attitude to life on earth, that gave free expression to love and sensual pleasures rather than dwelling on sin, contrition, and penitence.[145]

The troubadours are dedicated to an ethos that is "a secular unchristian idea of love [...] a love dominated by a strong expression of sensuality and eroticism, free from any principle of sin and guilt, achristian and amoral in the context of prevalent church standards".[146] And though, as Lazar bemusedly notes, "[a] good number of scholars have attempted to allegorize it and represent it as essentially religious and mystical in nature" these arguments are little more than "a wishful denial of the adulterous tenor of *fin'amor* and an exercise in literary exorcism".[147] The troubadours do not—as Dante and Petrarch will do—climb a Neoplatonic ladder of love in search of God. In fact, "[i]n the *fin'amor* tradition of the twelfth century, one might say that God is always on the side of the adulterous lovers and never on that of the deceived husband".[148]

The troubadours and trobairitz write a poetry that insists love and life is to be experienced now, here, without unnecessary delay and needless obstacles. The beauty they celebrate is here, in living and breathing

---

143 Ibid.
144 L. T. Topsfield. *Troubadours and Love* (Cambridge: Cambridge University Press, 1975), 39.
145 Lazar, 62.
146 Ibid., 71.
147 Ibid., 71–72.
148 Ibid., 74.

never-to-be-replicated individuals. In a sense, these poems illustrate the dynamic of the central scene in Raphael's painting *The School of Athens*, where Plato and Aristotle walk together, while Plato points up to the heavens and Aristotle points down to the Earth to indicate where each man saw truth, beauty, and reality as having its origin. Unlike so many of the Italian and English poets who will follow them, the troubadours point—with Aristotle—to the Earth beneath their feet. In these poems, you are invited to see, not through an allegory or the doctrines of a philosophical position, but through a pair of eyes; and what these eyes are gazing into is not a gateway to a soul, or a vision of the love that moves the sun and the other stars—they are gazing with rapture and delight into the eyes of another person just like you.

III
The Troubadours and Love

The roots of the troubadour poetic tradition are obscure. One prominent argument suggests that it is indebted to Spanish-Arabic poetry of the eleventh century in terms of its themes and motifs:

> Spanish-Arabian poetry [...] celebrates love as the highest form of happiness and the noblest source of inspiration; it sings of the beloved's beauty, the sorrow of the rejected lover and the cruelty of the lady. It introduces new fashions in composition, as in its hymns to Spring. Anticipating Provençal lyrics by close on two centuries, Hispano-Moorish poetry was the only one, in Europe, to cultivate those themes and to exhibit those characteristics.[149]

According to this interpretation, it was through "contacts with the courts of Aragon and Castile, [...] intermarriage such as that of Guilhem of Poitou with Philippa of Aragon in 1094, and [ongoing] political dealings that knowledge of Hispano-Arabic love philosophies and love poetry of the tenth and eleventh centuries came to the courts and poets"[150] of Occitania. We can see, if not direct influence, at least shared poetic

---

149 Robert S. Briffault. *The Troubadours* (Bloomington: University of Indiana Press, 1965), 25.
150 Elizabeth Salter. "Courts and Courtly Love". In *The Medieval World*, ed. by David Daiches and Anthony Thorlby (London: Aldus Books, 1973), 424.

genes, by looking at a Spanish Arabic poem contemporary to those of the troubadours. This twelfth-century work, "Gentle Now, Doves of the Thornberry and Moringa Thicket", by a poet named Ibn Arabi,[151] demonstrates many of the same themes of yearning and devotion to human, embodied love.

The poet fears the "sad cooing"[152] of the doves will betray him, and asks them not to "reveal the love I hide / the sorrow I hide away".[153] This love, and its sorrow, leads to thoughts of "a grove of tamarisks" where "spirits wrestled, / bending the limbs down over me, / passing me away", bringing him "yearning", and "breaking of the heart".[154] The tamarisks may reference the story of Abraham, or as the Qur'án refers to him, Ibrahim, who plants a tamarisk grove in Genesis 21 as a recognition of the struggle, negotiation, and coming to peace in a property dispute between Abraham and Abimelech. The wrestling of the spirits could be those of the two ancient patriarchs, or it could be something more like the struggle captured in the story of Abraham's grandson, Jacob, who wrestles, not with an angel, but with El (God) himself, reflected in the name he is given in Genesis 32:28 after the dusk-to-dawn wrestling match, "Israel", or, "he struggled with God". Perhaps this captures part of Arabi's suggestion, but references to "yearning" and "breaking of the heart", raise the possibility that something more intimate and personal is happening. Is it more of an internal struggle, the spirit who took me and forced me to struggle with and confront my own yearning? Perhaps the spirit Arabi is wrestling with is the difficulty he experiences in discovering the meaning of his own yearnings, the desires that dogmatic religion would tell him to reject.

This wrestling leads Arabi through images of a "faithless" woman "who dyes herself red with henna",[155] a person (perhaps a tradition) practiced in taking the devotion of another, soaking it up, and then throwing that other away. The image evokes a woman who soaks up a dying man's blood with her own hair, draining the life of a fool who gave

---

151 The translation used here is that of Michael Sells, in Maria Rosa Menocal, *Shards of Love: Exile and the Origins of the Lyric* (Durham, NC: Duke University Press, 1994), 70–71.
152 Ibid., l. 6.
153 Ibid., ll. 7–8
154 Ibid., ll. 13–18.
155 Ibid., ll. 39–40.

it in return for nothing. Finally, Arabi comes to the extremity of saying that "the house of stone" (a house of worship blessed by the Prophet of Islam) pales in comparison to "a man or a woman".[156] The Ka'bah, the cubic building in Mecca that is circled seven times counterclockwise — what does that mean, what significance does that hold, when compared to the living reality of the man or woman standing in front of you? Even the sacred books, the Torah, the Qur'án, are held lightly next to what Arabi calls "the religion of love", pledging that "wherever its caravan turns along the way, / that is the belief, / the faith I keep".[157] What the poem suggests is the necessity of struggling with and accepting one's own yearnings before coming to a place of peace. We are not sinful because we desire; we are not broken because we want. This is an emphatically humane vision.

While this poem is not exactly the same in its emphasis as the troubadour poems, it makes precisely the same kinds of people uncomfortable: "the poem is the 'yes and no' that makes the Averroist — and all other priests — blanch [...] [due to its] intractable and purposeful blurring of sacred and profane love".[158] The power in this work is that of the individual perspective, of singular passion, of the realization that there is something more important in this world than can be found in the traditional symbols and institutions of law, religion, state, and family. Each of these speak a language that essentially boils down to the same demand: "obey". But the "religion of love" is not about obeying. It is about being led where passion, insight, and desire lead you — the path Blake called "the road of excess" which "leads to the palace of wisdom".[159]

The road of excess was the favored highway of the first troubadour poet, Guilhem IX, the duke of Aquitaine and Count of Poitou (modern Poitiers). He was a man who did not care for any authority other than his own — twice excommunicated from the Church, on the first occasion he threatened to behead the bishop who pronounced the sentence, only to think better of it and tell the cleric whose neck was already extended for the sword's blow: "you shall never enter Heaven with the help of

---

156 *Ibid.*, ll. 35–36.
157 *Ibid.*, ll. 57–60.
158 Menocal, 75.
159 William Blake. "The Marriage of Heaven and Hell". In *The Complete Poetry and Prose of William Blake,* ed. by David V. Erdman (Berkeley and Los Angeles: University of California Press, 2008), 35.

my hand". The second time, Guilhem was excommunicated for refusing to give up his mistress, the Viscountess of Châtellraut, telling the bald bishop of Angoulême that "the comb shall curl your wayward hair before I give up the Viscountess".[160]

Guilhem was a man of action and of words, who had a "sardonic wit: he ordered that his mistress's portrait should be painted on his shield [...] declaring that 'it was his will to bear her in battle as she had borne him in bed'".[161] His poems combine frank enjoyment of sex with longing for love, but the clearest indication of his preference for love in deeds rather than merely in words can be seen in the final lines of his poem *Ab la dolchor del temps novel* (In the sweetness of the new times):

> Que tal se van d'amor gaban
> Nos n'avem la pessa e·l coutel.[162]
> Those others vainly talk of love
> But we have a piece [of bread], and a knife.

Love was not sublimated in worship for Guilhem—its passions were raw, and its excitements were those of the heart, the eyes, and the senses. In *Farai chansoneta nueva* (I will write a new song), Guilhem asks what the use could possibly be in withdrawing from the world of life, love, and pleasure:

> Qal pro y auretz, s'ieu m'enclostre
> E no·m retenetz per vostre?
> Totz lo joys del mon es nostre,
> Dompna, s'amduy nos amam.[163]

> What can it bring you if I cloister myself
> And you do not keep me for your own?
> All the joys of the world are ours
> Lady, if we love each other in turn.

---

160 Topsfield, 12–13.
161 Helen Castor. *She-Wolves: The Women Who Ruled England Before Elizabeth* (London: Faber and Faber, 2010), 133–34.
162 Guillaume IX. *Les Chansons de Guillaume IX, Duc d'Aquitaine*, ed. by Alfred Jeanroy (Paris: Honoré Champion, 1913), 26, ll. 29–30, https://archive.org/stream/leschansonsdegui00willuoft#page/26
163 *Ibid.*, 21, ll. 25–28, https://archive.org/stream/leschansonsdegui00willuoft#page/21

4. The Troubadours and Fin'amor: Love, Choice, and the Individual

This idea of lovers loving each other in turn is one of the first and most basic elements of the concept that will come to be called *fin'amor*. As the later poet Bernart de Ventadorn argues, love must be mutual in order for it to be true.

Though Guilhem wishes for a mutual love, he also wishes for a physical love, and the physicality of his desire is made clear in a number of places. In *Ben vuelh que sapchon li pluzor* (I want everyone to know), he writes of "a bawdy game" ("un joc grossier")—in which, after being told "your dice are too small" ("vostre dat som menudier"), he "raised the table" ("levat lo taulier") and then "tossed the dice" ("empeis los datz"), upon which toss "two of them rolled and the third plumbed the depths" ("duy foron cairavallier / e·l terz plombatz").[164] A poem in which a man attempts to prove that two of his "dice" are not too small for that third one to *plombatz* is not a poem with any great allegorical potential. Neither is *Companho faray un vers...convinen* (I will make a poem as it should be), in which Guilhem compares two mistresses to horses he greatly enjoys riding:[165]

> Dos cavalhs ai a ma selha ben e gen;
> Bon son e adreg per armas e valen;
> Mas no·ls puesc amdos tener que l'us l'autre non cossen.
> Si·ls pogues adomesjar e mon talen,
> Ja no volgra alhors mudar mon guarnimen,
> Que miels for' encavalguatz de nuill [autr'] ome viven.[166]

> I have two horses, noble and good for my saddle:
> Good and strong in combat and valor;
> But I can't keep both, because they hate each other.
> If I could tame them to my desire,
> I would not move my equipment anywhere else,
> For I would be mounted better than any man alive.

---

164 *Ibid.*, 15–16, ll. 45, 51, 57–60, https://archive.org/stream/leschansonsdegui00willuoft#page/15

165 As Peter Dronke asks, "would it ever have occurred to any reader or listener to interpret" such poems as this, or many other troubadour verses, "in any other than a sexual way if scholars had not invented the troubadours' 'platonic' love?" (Dronke, 242, n. 3).

166 Guillaume IX, 1, ll. 7–12, https://archive.org/stream/leschansonsdegui00willuoft#page/n24

In *Ab la dolchor del temps novel*, Guilhem prays for nothing so much as the gift of more life, and more erotic love—not in words, but in the deeds forbidden by the churchmen who speak in "foreign Latin":

> Enquer me lais Dieus viure tan
> C'aja mas manz soz so mantel.
> Qu'eu non ai soing d'estraing lati
> Que·m parta de mon Bon Vezi.[167]

> God give me a life long enough
> To get my hands beneath her dress.
> For I have no fear that foreign Latin
> Will part me from my Good Neighbor.

This is not "courtly love". This is the expression of frankly physical desire. The first troubadour was not a man who regarded love as a path to the divine, or the woman right in front of him as a window through which he should learn to see God. For the passionate and sometimes violent Guilhem, love was a crucial part of a life here and now that is to be celebrated without apology and without genuflection to gods above or devils below. Love—in all its emotional and physical glories—needed no justification. Guilhem was a man many modern academics would not like, and the feeling would probably be mutual.

Ab la dolchor del temps novel is a poem that openly praises "the physical love which can be desired, hoped for, shared and enjoyed".[168] The poem's "switch from delicacy" to "rough desire" is "characteristic of Guilhem and intentional"—especially in the "jest at those who talk and never do",[169] where Guilhem anticipated at least a few of his later critics. In *Mout jauzens me prenc en amar* (I take a great joy in love), a favorite of those commentators who try to squeeze Guilhem into the category of "courtly love",[170] he writes of keeping love for himself, "to

---

167 *Ibid.*, 26, ll. 23–26, https://archive.org/stream/leschansonsdegui00willuoft#page/26
168 Topsfield, 27.
169 *Ibid.*
170 Sarah Spence, for example, insists that "the lady here is presented as a Christ figure" (*Texts and the Self in the Twelfth Century* [Cambridge: Cambridge University Press, 1996], 91), basing this on the lines "And since I wish to return to joy / It is right, that I seek for the best" ("E pus en joy vuelh revertir / Ben dey, si puesc, al mielhs anar")

refresh the heart / and renew the flesh",[171] in verses that present "all excellence in physical reality".[172] And yet, Guilhem had something of the sceptic of Ecclesiastes about him, as if desire's fulfillment would never really bring him what he hoped for. In *Pus vezem de novel florir* (Since we see new blossoms), Guilhem complains:

> Per tal n'ai meyns de bon saber
> Quar vuelh so que no puesc aver[173]

> So I know less than any what is good
> Because I want what I cannot get.

This scepticism leads him to the position (adopted perhaps, only in his more reflective of moments) that *Tot is niens*—all is nothing, rather in the fashion of Koheleth, from Ecclesiastes 1:14:

> רָאִיתִי אֶת־ כָּל־ הַמַּעֲשִׂים שֶׁנַּעֲשׂוּ תַּחַת הַשָּׁמֶשׁ וְהִנֵּה הַכֹּל הֶבֶל וּרְעוּת רוּחַ׃

> I have seen all the works done beneath the sun; behold, all are vanity, a striving after the wind.

In Topsfield's view, "Guilhem appears to reject *Amors* as an embryonic regulated system of courtly wooing. He is dissatisfied with it and the small amount of *Jois* it affords. He stands to one side and looks for the *Jois* which is the reward of each individual man",[174] an individual man who loves, wholly and physically, an individual woman, but not in accordance with anyone's expected code of behavior, courtly or otherwise. Discussion of this poem has long been divided over whether it is "a burlesque" or "a serious love lyric".[175] The dichotomy is a false one, reflecting a Neoplatonic, anti-body, anti-sex bias. For Guilhem, the so-called burlesques (a term imposed by scholars) and the so-called

---

(Guillaume IX, 21–22, ll. 3–4). The lenses of "courtly love", once donned, appear to make it impossible to see otherwise.

171 "Per lo cor dedins refrescar / E per la carn renovellar" (Guillaume IX, 23, ll. 34–35, https://archive.org/stream/leschansonsdegui00willuoft#page/23).
172 Topsfield, 36.
173 Guillaume IX, 17, ll. 19–20, https://archive.org/stream/leschansonsdegui00willuoft#page/17
174 Topsfield, 30.
175 *Ibid.* Reddy repeats this distinction throughout his discussion of Guilhem's poetry (92–104).

serious love lyrics (another imposition) are expressions of different aspects of the same desire: "He desires the joys of shared love, and that the lady shall belong to him, and he to her".[176]

Guilhem was a man who bristled at restrictions, found the claims of those who would tell him what to do intolerable and absurd, and wanted to find a way to achieve and maintain *Jois*, an "individual happiness" in a world in which *Amor* was constantly threatened with extinction.[177] In that way, Guilhem embodies both the troubadours' distinctiveness and that which made them a threat to be eliminated by thirteenth-century Crusaders and Inquisitors, or an embarrassing excess to be allegorized away by the Akibas and Origens of the modern academy. These poets sought for a way to find *Jois* in a world of rules, laws, and demands for obedience; they sought—even in what many scholars insist on describing as "conventional" language—to find a way to express a new (or long-suppressed) desire, not for stability or order, not for matrimony and fidelity, but for love: mutual, embodied, and not to be abandoned at the commands of any bishop, bald or otherwise.

The mutuality of *fin'amor*, the love sought and celebrated by the troubadours, is wonderfully expressed by Marcabru, a poet often described as a moralist who condemned the excesses of court life. But in *Per savi·l tenc ses doptanssa* (Doubtless, I think him wise), he defines what he calls *bon'Amors* (good love, or the best love) as "two desires in a single longing" ("dos desirs d'un enveia"),[178] and further identifies *Jois* as one of the benefits of *fin'amor* or *bon'Amors*, which itself is "the assured happiness of a love which does not deceive", a love that is wholly "without deceit and cannot be degraded".[179] What Marcabru rails against is what he calls "false love against true" ("Falss' Amor encontra fina"), condemning "the group of liars" ("la gen frairina") who slander love, and the man "whose love lives by rape and pillage" ("car s'Amors viu de rapina").[180] Marcabru finally curses all such liars and defamers of *fin'amor*:

---

176 *Ibid.*, 39.
177 *Ibid.*
178 Marcabru., ed. by Jean Dejeanne (Toulouse: Édouard Privat, 1909), XXXVII, 178–83, l. 28, http://gallica.bnf.fr/ark:/12148/bpt6k4240c/f191.image
179 Topsfield, 83–84.
180 Marcabru, ll. 14, 20, 51, http://gallica.bnf.fr/ark:/12148/bpt6k4240c/f191.image and http://gallica.bnf.fr/ark:/12148/bpt6k4240c/f193.image

> La cuida per qu'el bobanssa
> li sia malaventura.[181]

> Let the ideas they are so proud of
> bring them to bad ends.

From the troubadours themselves, we see emerging at this point a definition of *fin'amor* that is comprised of mutual desire between lovers, honesty, and a refusal to let love be defined by social convention, or become a vehicle of self-interest and *rapina*.[182] As Topsfield explains:

> [B]ehind Marcabru's *Fin'amors* there is also the idea of man as part of the nature which was created by God, and able to respond entirely to this nature that has been given to him [...]. His merit is that he [...] can assimilate his carnal desire, which is his God-given *natura*, to a higher concept of love, *Fin'amors*, which is constant and free from deceit.[183]

Here we have a poet for whom human *natura* is not inherently wicked, for whom carnal sexuality is not fallen, and the body is not shameful. If there is a "heresy" here, it is not the "Gnostic" view of the Cathars, but the rather gentler "Pelagian" view—a belief that human nature is not fallen and that the world is a good and beautiful place. The fact that this is a "heresy" speaks volumes about the perversity of "orthodoxy".

From Marcabru, then, we can add another element to our definition of *fin'amor*: the mutuality of bodily and sexual desire between equal partners. The mutual desire between lovers is both physical and emotional. It is not merely a repressed or sublimated *eros*; it is the fully and powerfully physical expression of love and desire, combined with mutual choice and honesty. It is a love which does not live by *rapina*, by taking, forcing, pillaging, raping. It is a love in which we can see *dos desirs d'un' enveia*, one longing formed from two desires, one heart formed from two.

---

181 *Ibid.*, ll. 61–62, http://gallica.bnf.fr/ark:/12148/bpt6k4240c/f194.image

182 Charles Camproux argues that mutuality and equality are the primary characteristics of *fin'amor*: "Cette notion d'égalité entre les partenaires est une des plus importantes qui entrent dans la conception de l'amour chez les troubadours" [This notion of equality between partners is one of the most important that go into the concept of love in the troubadours] (Charles Camproux. *Le "joy d'amor" des troubadours. Jeu et joie d'amour* [Montpellier: Causse et Castelnau], 1965, 179).

183 Topsfield, 103.

One reason that Marcabru is often referred to as a moralist may be because of his oft-made distinction between *fin'amor* and *fals'amor* (or *Amar*). He is angry with those who would turn love into a tool of *rapina*, those for whom the pairings between lovers are either merely about lust (*Amar*), or for whom money and power are the primary motivations for their pairings (a dynamic that will become all too familiar in Shakespeare's plays). For Marcabru, such people see the world as fragmented, *frait*, rather than whole, *entier*. To adopt the path of wholeness requires both body and mind, sexual desire and honesty, a synthesis of the physical and spiritual that subordinates neither, an intermingling we will see best exemplified by the centuries-later poetry of John Donne, in a dynamic he calls a "dialogue of one". This search for wholeness and *Jois* was not a disguised religious quest. The troubadours wrote "a poetry of desire, telling of the poet's joy or sorrow as he waits for his [earthly and embodied] reward", a point perpetually—and it seems deliberately—misconstrued by critics who argue for "the conclusion that the poets, amid their perpetual longing, did not desire physical intercourse with the beloved. Most of them [...] frankly said that they did. The love of which they spoke was a physical one".[184]

Bernart de Ventadorn, perhaps the most passionate of all the troubadour poets, even regards love as a necessity for survival: in *Non es meravelha s'eu chan* (It is no marvel if I sing), Bernart writes that one who does not know love is already dead:

> Ben es mortz qui d'amor no sen
> al cor cal que dousa sabor.[185]

> He is truly dead who has no sense of love
> or its sweet savor in his heart.

Bernart further develops the theme of mutual love and desire that we have seen in Guilhem and Marcabru. In *Chantars no pot gaire valer* (A

---

184 Colin Morris. *The Discovery of the Individual, 1050–1200* (New York: Harper & Row, 1972), 113.
185 Bernart de Ventadorn. *Bernart von Ventadorn, seine Lieder, mit Einleitung und Glossar*, ed. by Carl Appel (Halle: Max Niemeyer, 1915), 188, ll. 9–10, https://archive.org/stream/bernartvonventad00bern#page/188

song can have no value), Bernart defines *fin'amor* as agreement and wanting between two lovers:

> En agradar et en voler
> es l'amors de dos fis amans.
> nula res no i pot pro tener,
> si·lh voluntatz non es egaus.[186]

> In pleasing and in wanting
> is the love of two noble lovers.
> Nothing in it can be good
> If the will is not mutual.

For Bernart, "[i]t was love which gave purpose to life.,[187] and for him, as for other vernacular poets of the twelfth century, the love poetry of Ovid had a tremendous influence, serving as "the highest authority in matters pertaining to love".[188] This poetic ethos differs from that of the later Italian poets, in whom one finds "the usual attempt to allegorize and point a moral".[189] Bernart, who "goes far outside the conventional into the language of passion",[190] is perhaps the best example among the troubadours of this passionate and non-allegorical ethos.

To see how Bernart both uses and transcends the "conventional", look at the first stanza of his poem *Can l'erba fresch'e·lh folha par*:

> Can l'erba fresch' e·lh folha par
> e la flors boton' el verjan,
> e·l rossinhols autet e clar
> leva sa votz e mou so chan,
> joi ai de lui, e joi ai de la flor
> e joi de me e de midons major;
> daus totas partz sui de joi claus e sens,
> mas sel es jois que totz autres jois vens.[191]

---

186 *Ibid.*, 86, ll. 29–32, https://archive.org/stream/bernartvonventad00bern#page/86
187 Morris, 115.
188 Charles Homer Haskins. *The Renaissance of the Twelfth Century* (Cambridge, MA: Harvard University Press, 1927), 108.
189 *Ibid.*
190 Morris, 113.
191 Bernart de Ventadorn, 220, ll. 1–8, https://archive.org/stream/bernartvonventad00 bern#page/220

> When fresh grass and leaves appear
> And flowers bloom among the orchards,
> And the nightingales, high and clear,
> Lift their voices, pouring out their songs;
> Joy to them and joy to the flowers,
> And joy to me, and to my Lady even more,
> Joy is all around me; Joy enfolds my mind,
> But here my joy quite overwhelms the rest.

By the time Bernart is writing this, in the mid to late twelfth-century, this is already a familiar opening. We see it reflected later in Chaucer: the opening reference to springtime, the budding of growth, and the reawakening of nature. Chaucer writes his famous opening lines to the *Canterbury Tales*, "Whan that April, with his shoures soote, / The drought of March hath perced to the roote", some two hundred and forty years after Bernart, but Bernart has already perfected the metaphor. The difference is that Bernart, unlike Chaucer, powerfully places himself (*pace* Zumthor and the "no-medieval-I" chorus) into the love narrative of his poems. The main theme is the repeated expression of the painful effect of the passion he feels, the desire that he has for a woman, the lady Aliu Anor, better known as Eleanor of Aquitaine. According to the *vida* (the later biography of Bernart, ostensibly written by Uc de Saint Circ), the love was mutual:

> Bernart de Ventadorn [...] went to the duchess of Normandy, who was young and of great merit, and devoted herself to reputation and honor and praise. And the songs and verses of Sir Bernart pleased her very much, and she received him and welcomed him warmly. He stayed in her court a long time, and fell in love with her and she with him, and he made many good songs about her. And while he was with her, King Henry of England took her as his wife and took her from Normandy and led her to England. Sir Bernart remained on this side [of the Channel], sad and grieving, and went to the good Count Raymond of Toulouse, and stayed with him until the count died. And because of that grief, Sir Bernart entered the order of Dalon, and there he died.[192]

The *vidas* are later and often fanciful accounts of the poets' lives, but "some elements of the *vida* may be true".[193] If true, Bernart finds himself

---

192 William D. Paden and Frances Freeman Paden, trans. *Troubadour Poems from the South of France* (Cambridge, UK: Brewer, 2007), 184.
193 *Ibid.*

in an impossible situation. He has developed an urgent passion for a woman of wealth, nobility, and power, a woman whose station far exceeds either his reach or his grasp. And though the poems suggest that *perhaps* this passion was requited at some point, Bernart often appears to berate himself over the ridiculous inequality in terms of rank, wealth, influence, and power between himself and his beloved.

The passion that is gently suggested in Arabi's poem is frank and open in Bernart's work. In *Can l'erba fresch'e·lh folha par*, Bernart fervently wishes for the opportunity to find his lover alone:

> Be la volgra sola trobar,
> que dormis, o·n fezes semblan,
> per qu'e·lh embles un doutz baizar,
> pus no valh tan qu'eu lo·lh deman.
> per Deu, domna, pauc esplecham d'amor![194]

> I yearn to find her all alone,
> Asleep, or merely seeming so,
> Because I'd steal the sweet kiss
> That I am not worthy to ask for.
> By God, my Lady, we have little success in love!

Bernart cannot act on his desires because of the difference in station between himself and his love:

> Tan am midons e la tenh char,
> e tan la dopt' e la reblan
> c'anc de me no·lh auzei parlar,
> ni re no·lh quer ni re no·lh man.[195]

> I so love and cherish my lady,
> That I am afraid and draw back;
> I do not speak of myself in her hearing,
> Nor do I ask for anything from her.

---

194 Bernart de Ventadorn, 222, ll. 41–45, https://archive.org/stream/bernartvonventad00bern#page/222
195 *Ibid.*, 221, ll. 25–28, https://archive.org/stream/bernartvonventad00bern#page/221

This poem is both sexually and socially transgressive. While many of the troubadours are knights and minor nobles, a number of them are referred to as *Joglars* (from which we get our word *juggler*), mere performers, like Bernart, who have nothing else to fall back on. Such performers, because of their art, are invited into circles to which they would normally have no access. In Bernart's case, the singer/poet has fallen in love with the epitome of the unattainable woman. And yet, desire cannot and will not be reasoned with:

> S'eu saubes la gen enchantar,
> mei enemic foran efan,
> que ja us no saubra triar
> ni dir re que·ns tornes a dan.
> adoncs sai eu que vira la gensor
> e sos bels olhs e sa frescha color,
> e baizera·lh la bocha en totz sens,
> si que d'un mes i paregra lo sens.[196]

> If I knew how to cast a spell;
> I'd turn my enemies into infants,
> So none of them could understand
> Gossip, or play its hurtful games.
> Then I could see how nobly she turned
> Her beautiful eyes, with their vibrant color,
> I'd kiss her mouth so sensually,
> The mark would show for a month.

Though one is tempted to paraphrase Rosalind from *As You Like It*—*try the day, without the month*—that final image is fascinating. How hard *would* you have to kiss someone for the effects to show after an hour, much less a month?

Such foolishness as Bernart's could have serious—even life and death—consequences. The most famous story that illustrates the high stakes of the loves the troubadour poets celebrate comes from the *vida* of Guilhem de Cabestanh:

> Guilhem de Cabestanh [loved] a lady who was called My Lady Sermonda, the wife of Sir Raimon del Castel de Roussillon, who was

---

196 *Ibid.*, 221–22, ll. 33–40, https://archive.org/stream/bernartvonventad00bern#page/221

very rich and noble and wicked and cruel and proud. [...] And the lady, who was young and noble and beautiful and pleasing, loved him more than anything else in the world. And this was told to Raimon del Castel de Roussillon, and he, like a wrathful and jealous man, investigated the story and learned that it was true and had his wife guarded closely. And one day, Raimon del Castel de Roussillon found Guillem eating without much company and killed him and drew his heart from his body and had a squire carry it to his lodging and had it roasted and prepared with a pepper sauce and had it given to his wife to eat. And when the lady had eaten it, the heart of Sir Guilhem de Cabestanh, Sir Raimon told her what it was. When she heard this, the lady lost sight and hearing. And when she came around, she said, "Lord, you have given me such a good meal that I will never eat another". And when he heard what she said, he ran to his sword and tried to strike her on the head, and she went to the balcony and let herself fall, and she died.[197]

This story is difficult to credit as anything like literal truth, but it does go hand in hand with other stories of the risks taken by troubadour poets in their declarations of adulterous love. Another poet, Peire Vidal, is said to have had his tongue cut out by the husband of his love: "a knight of Saint Gili cut out his tongue because he gave out that he was his wife's lover".[198]

The poetic evidence for the danger of the adulterous passions the troubadours celebrated comes through most strongly from the *alba*, the dawn song, in which two adulterous lovers are guarded by a watchman whose job it is to warn them of the coming of the first rays of morning.[199] The night, which has been the lovers' shelter and given

---

[197] Paden, 186.

[198] Barbara Smythe. *Trobador Poets: Selections from the Poems of Eight Trobadors* (New York: Cooper Square Publishers, 1966), 149.

[199] [In] the dawn song (Middle High German tagelied, Old Provençal alba, Old French aube) [...] two lovers embrace in the secrecy of the night before their necessary parting at the arrival of dawn. A watchman or a little bird may take the role of an ally warning the two of the encroaching daybreak, with dawn signalling the need for the reluctant lovers to separate in order to avoid discovery by the spies of courtly society. It is in this moment of anguish that joy and sorrow intermingle, and the lovers lament their impending separation by desperately embracing one last time. Then the man leaves his beloved while she expresses her longing to see him again soon. [...] In the forbidden nature of the tryst, the relationship is adulterous since the lady is married. Because the lovers possess no power to change their predicament, their desire for each other may be fulfilled only in secret.

Rasma Lazda-Cazers. "Oral Sex in the Songs of Oswald von Wolkenstein: Did it Really Happen?" In *Sexuality in the Middle Ages and Early Modern Times: New Approaches to a Fundamental Cultural-Historical and Literary-Anthropological Theme*, ed. by Albrecht Classen (Berlin: De Gruyter, 2008), 581–82.

them opportunity to act on their mutual desire, is too short, and the dawn, which comes all too soon, threatens to expose the lovers to the jealousy and violent reprisals of the angry husband. The most famous example is the anonymous poem, *En un vergier sotz fuella d'albespi*:

> En un vergier sotz fuella d'albespi
> tenc la dompna son amic costa si
> tro la gayta crida que l'alba vi,
> Oy Dieus! Oy Dieus! de l'alba tan tost ve.
> "Plagues a Dieu ia la nueitz non falhis
> ni·l mieus amicx lonc de mi no·s partis
> ni la gayta iorn ni alba no vis,
> Bels dous amicx, baizem nos yeu e vos
> aval e·ls pratz on chanto·ls auzellos
> tot o fassam en despieg de gilos,
> Oy Dieus! Oy Dieus! de l'alba tan tost ve.
> Bels dous amicx, fassam un ioc novel
> yns el iardi on chanton li auzel
> tro la gaita toque son caramelh,
> Oy Dieus! Oy Dieus! de l'alba tan tost ve.
> Per la doss'aura qu'es venguda de lay
> del mieu amic belh e cortes e gay
> del sieu alen ai begut un dous ray,
> Oy Dieus! Oy Dieus! de l'alba tan tost ve".
> La dompna es agradans e plazens
> per sa beutat la gardon mantas gens
> et a son cor en amar leyalmens,
> Oy Dieus! Oy Dieus! de l'alba tan tost ve.[200]
>
> In an orchard under leaves of hawthorn
> the lady holds her lover beside her
> until the watchman cries out the coming of dawn,
> O God! O God! the dawn, it comes too soon.
> Please God, do not let the night end already
> nor let my lover part from my side
> nor let the watchman see the dawn,

---

200 Matilda Tomaryn Bruckner, Laurie Shepard, and Sarah White, eds. *Songs of the Women Troubadours* (New York: Garland Publishing, 2000), 134.

4. The Troubadours and Fin'amor: Love, Choice, and the Individual

> Fair sweet friend, let us kiss, you and I,
> down in the meadow where the songbirds sing,
> let us do all this in spite of that jealous man.
> O God! O God! the dawn, it comes too soon.
> Fair sweet friend, let us play a new game
> in the garden where the songbirds sing
> until the watchman plays his pipe.
> O God! O God! the dawn, it comes too soon.
> For the gentle breeze which comes from there
> from my lover, beautiful, and courteous, and merry,
> of his breath I have drunk a sweet ray of sun.
> O God! O God! the dawn, it comes too soon.
> The lady is delightful and pleasing
> And many admire her for her beauty,
> and for her heart which is true in love.
> O God! O God! the dawn, it comes too soon.

The pathos of this poem is haunting, nearly nine centuries later. Two lovers, who choose each other in the face of law, arranged marriages, social convention, church doctrine, and the very real possibility of getting caught and punished, wish the night could last just a few moments longer. Only in the darkness is their freedom possible, only at night can they feel the one they love next to them, hear the rise and fall of breath, and know themselves as one and at peace. But with light comes the law, with light come the claims of ownership and property, church and state. The watchman cries out the coming of dawn so that the lovers can escape undetected, and hopefully, live to love again another night. The evident frustration in these poems is fueled by the absurdity of being unable to love the one of your choice except under the cover of darkness and lies. This poem expresses an idea we can see as early as the Song of Songs: the right to decide for oneself, and the insistence that love is a personal choice, a potentially risky enterprise engaged with, and embarked upon, by two partners.

The same constellation of ideas is powerfully expressed in the *tagelieder* (dawn songs) of the Minnesingers (love singers) from Germany, perhaps most memorably by the late-twelfth and early-thirteenth-century poet Wolfram von Eschenbach in his *Den morgenblic bî wahtaeres sange erkôs*:

Den morgenblic bî wahtaeres sange erkôs
ein froue, dâ si tougen
an ir werden friundes arme lac;
dâ von si... freuden vil verlôs.
des muosen liehtiu ougen
aver nazzen. sî sprach 'ôwê tac!
wilde und zam daz frewet sich dîn
und siht dich gerne,
wan ich ein. wie sol iz mir ergên!
nu enmac niht langer hie bî mir bestên
mîn vriunt: den jaget von mir dîn schîn'.
Der tac mit kraft al durh diu venster dranc.
vil slôze si besluzzen:
daz half niht: des wart in sorge kunt.
diu friundîn den vriunt vast an sich dwanc:
ir ougen diu beguzzen
ir beider wangel. sus sprach zim ir munt.
'Zwei herze und ein lip hân wir
gar ungescheiden:
unser triuwe mit ein ander vert.
der grôzen liebe der bin ich gar vil verhert,
wan sô du kumest und ich zuo dir'.
Der trûric man nam urloup balde alsus.
ir liehten vel diu slehten
kômen nâher. sus der tac erschein.
weindiu ougen, süezer frouen kus.
sus kunden sî dô vlehten
ir munde, ir brüste, ir arme, ir blankiu bein:
swelch schiltaer entwurfe daz
geselleclîche
als si lâgn, des waere ouch dem genuoc.
ir beider liebe doch vil sorgen truoc.
si pflâgen minne ân allen haz.[201]

The morning light shone, and the Watchman sang,
while a lady secretly
lay in the arms of her lover.

---

201 Wolfram von Eschenbach. *Werke*, ed. by Karl Lachmann (Berlin: G. Reimer, 1879), 3–4, https://books.google.com/books?id=-rwFAAAAQAAJ&pg=PA3

> Because of this, she lost all her joy,
> and her moist though beaming eyes
> filled with tears. She said, 'Alas, day!
> everything that lives, wild and tame, rejoices over you
> and longs to see you,
> except for me. What will become of me?
> Now my beloved can no longer stay here with me,
> for your light chases my lover away.
> The day shone powerfully through the windows,
> and though they bolted many locks,
> they were of no use against sorrow.
> The lady pressed her lover tight,
> and her eye's flowing tears
> made both cheeks wet. She spoke to him with her lips:
> "Two hearts and only one body we have.
> Inseparable,
> we remain truly connected to each other.
> My whole happiness in love is destroyed,
> unless you come back to me and I to you".
> The sorrowful man would soon have departed,
> but their bright, smooth bodies
> came close again, although the day already shone.
> With weeping eyes, and the sweet lady's kiss,
> they intertwined themselves,
> mouths, breasts, arms and their bright white legs.
> Any painter who wanted to represent
> their companionship
> as they lay beside each other, would be overwhelmed.
> Although their love caused them great care,
> they gave themselves entirely to each other.

In what may well be the earliest example of a *tagelied* poem,[202] *Slâfest du, friedel ziere*, Dietmar von Aist[203] powerfully expresses the pain of separation at dawn:

---

[202] "The type first appears in a poem by Dietmar von Aist [...], the earliest Minnesinger who seems to have an acquaintance with troubadour lyrics" ("Tagelied". In *Princeton Encyclopedia of Poetry and Poetics*, ed. by Alex Preminger, Frank J. Warnke, and O. B. Hardison Jr. [Princeton: Princeton University Press, 1972], 841).

[203] Dietmar von Aist and Wolfram von Eschenbach were two of the most crucial figures in the development of the tagelied in German poetry: "[a]round 1170

"Slâfest du, friedel ziere
man wecket uns leider schiere:
ein vogellîn sô wol getân
daz ist der linden an daz zwî gegân".
"Ich was vil sanfte entslâfen:
nu rüefestu kint Wâfen.
liep âne leit mac niht gesîn.
swaz du gebiutest, daz leiste ich, friundîn mîn".
Diu frouwe begunde weinen.
"Du rîtest und lâst mich einen.
wenne wilt du wider her zuo mir?
ôwê, du füerest mîn fröude sament dir!"[204]

"Do you sleep still, my dearest love?
Unfortunately, we will both soon awake.
A most beautiful songbird
Has flown into the branches of the tree".
"I slept gently in your arms,
until you called: *child, awake!*
Love without suffering cannot be:
what you command, I will do, my love".
The Lady began to cry:
"You ride away and leave me alone.
When will you return to me again?
Alas, you take my joy away with you!"

In the *alba* and the *tagelied*, the lady and her lover are opposed by the entire structure of the European world in which marriage is a contractual arrangement of property, while at the lower social and economic levels it finds its *raison d'etre* in the pretense of avoiding the "sin" of fornication.

Dietmar von Aist cultivated the *Tagelied* as a genre already well known; about 1200 Wolfram von Eschenbach turned its conventions upside down" (William D. Paden. "Introduction". In *Medieval Lyric: Genres in Historical Context*, ed. by William D. Paden [Urbana and Chicago: University of Illinois Press, 2000], 11).

204 Dietmar von Aist. "Slâfest du, friedel ziere". In *Des minnesangs frühling*, ed. by Friedrich Vogt (Leipzig: Verlag von S. Hirzel, 1920), 37, https://books.google.com/books?id=DcQPAAAAMAAJ&pg=PA37

4. *The Troubadours and Fin'amor: Love, Choice, and the Individual*   185

Codex Manesse, UB Heidelberg, Cod. Pal. germ. 848, fol. 314v Herr Günther von dem Vorste (between 1305 and 1315).[205]

It becomes a sacrament of the church, controlled by religion, government, and God.[206] As Matthew 19:6, written during the height of the Roman Imperial era, puts it, "What, therefore, God has joined together, let no man tear apart".[207] Where is the choice for those who are married? In the dawn songs like *En un vergier sotz fuella d'albespi*, and *Den morgenblic bî wahtaeres sange erkôs*, we see the awareness that there can be a choice.[208] But the awareness is painful because it comes with the knowledge of

---

205 https://commons.wikimedia.org/wiki/File:Codex_Manesse_314v_Günther_von_dem_Vorste.jpg
206 Catholic theologians are referring to marriage as a sacrament as early as the twelfth century, though it will not be until the Council of Trent in 1563 that this arrangement is formalized.
207 "ὃ οὖν ὁ Θεὸς συνέζευξεν, ἄνθρωπος μὴ χωριζέτω".
208 Though they are a minority, within the Church there are voices at this time beginning to speak up for individual choice in marriage. In the *Decretum Gratiani* (c. 1140 CE), a Benedictine monk named Gratian argues that "mutual consent makes a marriage" ("consensus utiusque matrimonium facit") (*Corpus Iuris Canonici, Vol. 1: Decretum Magistri Gratiani* [Leipzig: Bernhard Tauchnitz, 1879. Reprint Graz: Akademische Druck-u. Verlagsanstalt, 1959], 1091, http://www.columbia.edu/cu/lweb/ digital/collections/cul/texts/ldpd_6029936_001/pages/ldpd_6029936_001_00000604.html?toggle=image&menu=maximize&top=&left).

being profoundly trapped. *Two hearts and only one body we have, but O God, the dawn! It comes too soon!* The dawn comes, demands a return to obedience and conformity and custom, and the "one body" of the lovers torn back in two by the harsh light of day.

None of this is the "courtly love" of Victorian scholarly invention. Neither are the poems written by the two poets below, who each found love famously vexing. The twelfth-century troubadour, Raimbaut d'Aurenga writes with frank and playful passion. In *Non chant per auzel ni per flor* (I do not sing for bird or flower), Raimbaut references the conventional vernal opening to Troubadour poetry by renouncing it. He then writes directly and openly of his physical desire for his lover, and the joy he takes in her:

> Ben aurai, dompna, grand honor
> Si ja de vos m'es jutgada
> Honranssa que sotz cobertor
> Vos tenga nud'embrassada;
> Car vos valetz las meillors cen!
> Q'ieu non sui sobregabaire –
> Sol del pes ai mon cor gauzen
> Plus que s'era emperaire![209]

> It shall be, Lady, a great honor
> if you will grant me
> the benefit under the covers
> Of having you in naked embrace;
> for you are worth more than a hundred;
> And though I do not boast:
> At this thought alone my heart joys
> more than were I the emperor.

The trobairitz Comtessa de Dia writes in much the same frankly erotic fashion in the poem *Estat ai en greu cossirier*, in which she is explicit about her desire to replace her husband with her lover:

---

209 Victoria Cirlot, ed. *Antología de textos románicos medievales: siglos XII–XIII* (Barcelona: Edicions Universitat Barcelona, 1984), 151–52, ll. 17–24.

Estat ai en greu cossirier
per un cavallier qu'ai agut,
e vuoil sia totz temps saubut
cum ieu l'ai amat a sobrier.
Ara vei qu'ieu sui trahida
car ieu non li donei m'amor,
don ai estat en gran error
en lieig e quan sui vestida.
Ben volria mon cavallier
tener un ser en mos bratz nut,
qu'el s'en tengra per ereubut
sol qu'a lui fezes cosseillier;
car plus m'en sui abellida
no fetz Floris de Blancheflor;
ieu l'autrei mon cor e m'amor,
mon sen, mos huoills e ma vida.
Bels amics avinens e bos,
cora·us tenrai en mos poder,
e que iagues ab vos un ser,
e que·us des un bais amoros?
Sapchatz, gran talan n'auria
qu·us tengues en luoc del marit
ab so que m'aguessetz plevit
de far tot so qu'eu volria.[210]

I have been in great distress
about a knight I once had,
I want it known for all time
how much I loved him
but now, I feel betrayed
because I did not tell him of my love
and I am in great torment
naked in my bed or fully dressed.
If only I could hold my knight
naked in my arms until the dawn,
drunk with my beauty
he'd feel like he was in paradise;
for I am more in love with him

---

210 Bruckner, *et al.*, 10.

> than Floris was with Blancheflor;
> I give him my heart and my love,
> my mind, my eyes, and my life.
> Sweet lover, so charming and so good,
> when will I have you in my power
> to lie with you at night
> and give you all my passionate kisses?
> Know this for certain, I greatly desire
> to have you in my husband's place
> as soon as you will promise me
> to do everything I desire.

This isn't spiritualized adoration. These two poets do not sing for birds or flowers, and in this breaking away from the conventional opening of lyric poetry, these poets also break away from sexual, social, and even psychological convention. These poets write of lovers who choose. What else can those last lines mean, "as soon as you will promise me / to do everything I desire", except *come take me*, especially after the euphemistic line "to have you in my husband's place" (*qu·us tengues en luoc del marit*)? The poets express the anxiety that they may not get the opportunity to act on their desires. For Raimbaut:

> Qu'il fetz a son marit crezen
> C'anc hom que nasques de maire
> Non toques en lieis. —Mantenen
> Atrestal podetz vos faire![211]

> She made her husband believe
> That no man born of woman
> Could say he had touched her. Soon
> You will be able to prove the same thing of me!

In Raimbaut's poem, thinking of his lover, and comparing her situation to that of the legendary Isolde, he bases his hopes on a deception that may or may not succeed. In the Comtessa de Dia's poem, she has been "in great distress", feels "betrayed", and suffers "in bed or fully dressed".

---

211 Cirlot, 151–52, ll. 46–48.

The poems by the troubadours, even the myths that surround them, belie any notion that the love of which they write is a decorous matter of rules and codes, of obedience demanded and given. Their poems are filled with desire, frustration, joy, despair, and the tantalizing possibility of freedom, of choice, of life lived, not spent in mechanical compliance with the expectations of others. These are poems of rebellion, not obedience, of chaos, not conformity. Perhaps this can best be illustrated by returning briefly to Bertran de Born, the warrior troubadour more famous for poems of war than for poems of love and desire. Even Bertran reflects something of the larger troubadour ethos in *Be·m platz lo gais temps de pascor* (I Am Pleased by the Gay Season of Spring), a celebration of war and love in which he mocks the entire notion of sin:

>   Amors vol drut cavalgador
>   bon d'armas e larc de servir,
>   gen parlan e gran donador
>   e tal qi sapcha far e dir
>   fors e dinz son estatge
>   segon lo poder qi l'es datz.
>   E sia d'avinen solatz,
>   cortes e d'agradatge.
>   E domna c'ab aital drut jaz
>   es monda de totz sos pechatz.[212]

>   Love wants a knightly rider for a lover,
>   good with arms and generous in service,
>   noble in speech and a lavish giver
>   one who knows what to *say* and what to *do*
>   outside and inside his realm
>   according to the ability he has been given.
>   Let him be attractive, a good fit,
>   elegant and pleasing,
>   and the lady who lies with such a lover
>   is cleansed of all her sins.

For Bertran, love is not a sin; he laughs at the idea. Love is physical and vigorous—like war. Clearly, he doesn't think war is a sin; it's his

---

[212] Betran de Born, 343, ll. 51–60.

favorite thing on earth, the very reason for living. For Bertran, the lover should be a great warrior. The lady who is herself a great warrior in love, who "wins" her love the way a warrior defeats an honorable enemy, is cleansed of any foolishly-imagined "sin" of love to begin within. If there is "sin" here, it is in the attempt to reduce this poem (and the troubadour/trobairitz corpus in its entirety) to "a mirror of itself",[213] a "mature rejection of the new Renaissance model of the self-determining singular ego",[214] or "an ontological rather than an ontic language [which] expresses Being in general rather than a certain particular being".[215] With such formulations, scholars attempt to erase a soldier, poet, and lover who lived more fully than most of us ever will.

The young singer of the anonymous ballad *Coindeta Sui* would no doubt concur with Bertran. Though the song is playful, it expresses serious determination about a serious dilemma. The singer is caught in an arranged, loveless, and passionless marriage to a much older man. She is stewing in her own actively hostile emotions, as she is repulsed by her husband:

> Coindeta sui! si cum n'ai greu cossire
> per mon marit, quar ne·l voil ne·l desire.
> Q'eu be·us dirai per que son aisi drusa,
> Coindeta sui!
> qar pauca son, ioveneta e tosa,
> Coindeta sui!
> e degr'aver marit dunt fos ioiosa,
> ab cui toz temps pogues iogar e rire:
> Coindeta sui!
> Ia Deus mi·n sal se ia sui amorosa,
> Coindeta sui!
> de lui amar mia sui cubitosa,
> Coindeta sui!
> anz quant lo vei ne son tant vergoignosa
> qu'e prec la mort qe·l venga tost aucire.[216]

---

213 Zumthor, 170.
214 G. B. Stone, 4.
215 *Ibid.*, 5.
216 Bruckner *et al.*, 130, ll. 1–15.

> I'm pretty, and yet my heart's in distress
> for I have no desire for my husband.
> I'll tell you all of my longing for love:
> I'm pretty!
> I'm small, young and well-groomed,
> I'm pretty!
> and should have a husband who gives me joy
> with whom I climb, play and laugh all the time.
> I'm pretty!
> Now God save me if I ever loved him:
> I'm pretty!
> I have not the least passion for him,
> I'm pretty!
> yet seeing his age, I feel so ashamed,
> I pray Death will come kill him, and soon.

The song is about what she desires, how she will get it, and what others should learn from her getting it. After all, she sings so that "every lady will learn to sing / about my friend whom I so love and desire".[217] It is very much in the spirit of Bertran de Born. Imagine a girl of fifteen married to a man who is fifty. Imagine that they have nothing in common (unsurprisingly), that he is a tyrant, and that his body has decayed into undesirability, while his libido still tells him that he is a young man, so that he is a thoroughgoing combination of all things that would likely be considered disgusting and oppressive by a young girl. All too often, marriages in the medieval and early modern eras were arrangements of contentment, at best. At worst, they were hellish traps of jealousy, disgust, lack of desire, and differences in age or temperament. In the world of the troubadours, divorce was no longer the practical possibility it had once been in the Roman world. For most, the only way out of a failed marriage was through the death of the marriage partner.[218] Thus the young girl of *Coindeta Sui* sings the line "I pray Death will come kill him and soon". In such circumstances of lifelong passionless entrapment, one wonders how often death was willing and able to oblige.

---

217 "chant tota domna ensegnada, / del meu amic q'eu tant am e desire" (*ibid.*, ll. 28–29).
218 Even those "who divorced because of adultery by the other party" were forced to "remain unmarried so long as the first spouse lived" (James A. Brundage. Law, Sex, and Christian Society in Medieval Europe [Chicago: University of Chicago Press, 2009], 244).

Passion must and will have an out, especially in this period when a new way of thinking about life and the individual was emerging. But the movement these poems participated in was destroyed, as the troubadour culture and the courts that supported it were crushed in the Albigensian crusade (1209–29 CE). Due in large part to pressures applied after the establishment of the Inquisition in 1232, the emphasis changed in much of the poetry that followed:

> [A]fter the crusade against the Albigensians (the heretic Cathars), [...] there begins a process of psychological inhibition and repression in the domain of love songs, a trend toward spiritualization and allegorization that would eventually lead to the *Roman de la Rose*, to the *dolce stil novo* of Guido Guinizelli or Cavalcanti, and to the *Vita Nuova* of Dante.[219]

However, despite the fact that the spirit of poetry was changed and softened by a later tradition, the troubadour poems and their spirit survived, though in dormancy. The basic assumptions of the modern Western world have long rested on the foundational idea of individual choice that the troubadours fought for bravely, but unsuccessfully. We, through Shakespeare and the poets who followed him, now live, for better or worse, in the world of the troubadour ethos—a spirit which Shakespeare makes his own in his most powerful plays, and around which Milton centers his crucial scene of human choice in *Paradise Lost*. By the seventeenth century in England, the troubadours have won a victory more complete than the Crusaders of thirteenth-century France could ever have imagined.

Perhaps it should come as no surprise that a movement so radical as that of the troubadours was crushed. Perhaps it should be even less surprising that so many contemporary scholars have worked so hard to insist that there was nothing particularly remarkable about this poetry. Authority often has its way both by force and by deception, and those who stand against "the power which demands submission"[220] are often defeated. Though "Ovid defended love against the vulgar material Roman capitalists, [and] Bernart and his fellows seem to have faced down the Church",[221] each suffered the consequences. Ovid was banished for

---

219 Lazar, 92.
220 Topsfield, 39.
221 James J. Wilhelm. *Seven Troubadours: The Creators of Modern Verse* (University Park: Pennsylvania State University Press, 1970), 113.

life, never to see his beloved Rome again. And the troubadours, their way of life, and even their language, were all quite nearly removed from the Earth: "In 1539, the *Ordonnance de Villers-Cotterêts* established French as the only authorized language for official documents [while] Occitan was progressively banned from public and high-prestige contexts and relegated to private use".[222] This denigration of all non-*langue d'oil* forms reached new levels of intensity with the release of Abbé Grégoire's *Rapport sur la nécessité et les moyens d'anéantir le patois, et d'universaliser l'usage de la langue française* (Report on the Need and Means to Annihilate the Patois and to Universalize the Use of the French Language) to the French National Convention in 1794. There, Gregoire argues that the question of language use is properly to be determined by the winners of the centuries-long struggle between north and south in France, while acknowledging that the contest could have turned out differently: "probably, instead of the language of Trouvères, we would now be speaking the language of the Troubadours, if Paris, the center of government, had been located on the left bank of the Loire".[223]

Even today, while "Italian and Catalan scholars" are commonly taught Occitan because the language "remains a necessary step in the acquisition of philological expertise", in France the attitude is different: "The northern French academy [...] has gradually backed away from medieval Occitan studies [...] as something that either does not really concern it, or as a phenomenon that can simply be alluded to—a stepping stone to something better that replaced it'.[224] This dismissive attitude is hardly new, as demonstrated by Antoine de Rivarol's *Discours de l'Universalité de la langue Française* (1784), where he writes approvingly of "la Langue Latine", and "la Langue Toscane", while referring

---

222 Rafëu Sichel-Bazin, Carolin Buthke and Trudel Meisenburg. "Prosody in Language Contact: Occitan and French". *Prosody and Language in Contact: L2 Acquisition, Attrition and Languages in Multilingual Situations*, ed. by Elisabeth Delais-Roussarie, Mathieu Avanzi, and Sophie Herment (Berlin: Springer, 2015), 73–74.
223 "probablement, au lieu de la langue des Trouvères, nous parlerions celle des Troubadours, si Paris, le centre du gouvernement, avoit été situé sur la rive gauche de la Loire" (Henri Grégoire. *Rapport sur la nécessité et les moyens d'anéantir le patois, et d'universaliser l'usage de la langue française* [Paris: Imprimerie Nationale, 1794], 8, https://books.google.co.uk/books?id=8PB2RBNrLZYC&pg=PA8).
224 William Burgwinkle. "The Troubadours: The Occitan Model". In *The Cambridge History of French Literature*, ed. by William E. Burgwinkle, Nicholas Hammond, and Emma Wilson (Cambridge: Cambridge University Press, 2011), 21.

dismissively to "le patois des Troubadours".[225] With the educational reforms of Jules Ferry in 1881–82 came measures designed to prevent schoolchildren from speaking anything other than "standard" Parisian French.[226] Visitors to *le Midi* can still encounter evidence of this in a sign in an abandoned schoolhouse in Ayguatébia which says *Parlez Français, Soyez Propres*—"Speak French, Be Clean"—marking what locals call *la vergonha*, a policy of shaming people who speak one of the Occitanian languages. Such words illustrate how far the enemies of troubadour culture have been willing to go in order to "channel, reformulate, and control" its ideas, the language(s) in which they were expressed, and the human joys and freedoms they tried to convey. And yet, despite a history of theological, governmental, and critical disdain and erasure, the poetry survives.

---

225 12–13.
226 See R. Anthony Lodge. *French: From Dialect to Standard* (London: Routledge, 1993), 219.

5. *Fin'amor* Castrated: Abelard, Heloise, and the Critics who Deny

The brief flowering of the troubadours helps us to understand the love story, in twelfth-century Paris, of Peter Abelard and Heloise d'Argenteuil, who lived the passions and the dangers often spoken of in the poetry of the age. The letters between Abelard and Heloise are among the world's most vibrant embodiments of *fin'amor*,[1] as well as its most tragic testaments to the violence and determination of those who would prevent men and women from living and loving as they choose. Written around 1128, this Latin correspondence tells a story of love that is both of the body and the mind. It is a painful account of what Shakespeare would one day call the "marriage of true minds", as the lovers are separated by difficult circumstances including a jealous uncle, castration, character assassination, shame, inner conflict, and religion.

Abelard was an esteemed teacher and philosopher in Paris whose lectures drew students from all over Europe:

> [Abelard's] fame as a teacher and great reputation as a scholar helped establish the University of Paris as students arrived from all over Europe to study with him [...]. In Paris, Abelard was regarded as a young [star] among the schoolmen of the monastic orders, whose theological lectures were considered dusty and boring as they commented endlessly on the traditions of the church fathers and earlier medieval thinkers. Abelard's

---

1   Jean Hagstrum observes that the story of Abelard and Heloise is "an invaluable guide to what lies behind the imaginative literatures of love" (Hagstrum 203).

lectures challenged revered traditions, and his students were often rowdy and disrespectful to the accepted traditions of the church.[2]

During his time in the schools of Paris, Abelard was hired to tutor Heloise, the niece of one of the city's most influential citizens, a secular canon named Fulbert. According to Abelard, this new pupil Heloise, "in her outward appearance, was not the lowest; but for her wealth in letters, she was supreme".[3] Abelard tells the story of how they met in *Historia calamitatum* or *A Story of His Misfortunes*, which he addresses to a "Friend". Who exactly this piece was meant for is unknown, but it has long served to give readers an intimate and painful portrait of the significant details of Abelard's love for Heloise and the price both he and she paid for that love. In the *Letters*, Heloise remembers the secret and passionate love-making in the convents and in her uncle's house, clandestine meetings which resulted in Heloise getting pregnant. After "being found in bed together",[4] Abelard and Heloise secretly married, in a failed attempt to satisfy Fulbert, even though neither had a high opinion of the institution.[5] The Church disapproved of Abelard's marriage (during this period, clerical celibacy was slowly being imposed

---

2   Roger E. Olson. *The Story of Christian Theology: Twenty Centuries of Tradition & Reform* (Downers Grove, IL: InterVarsity Press, 2009), 326.

3   "Quae cum per faciem non esset infirma, per abundantium litterarum erat suprema" (Peter Abelard and Heloise d'Argenteuil. *Magistri Petri Abaelardi epistola quae est Historia calamitatum: Heloissae et Abaelardi epistolae*, ed. by Johann Caspar von Orelli [Turici: Officina Ulrichiana, 1841], 6, https://archive.org/stream/ magistripetriaba00abel#page/6).

4   Betty Radice. "Introduction". *The Letters of Abelard and Heloise*. Trans. by Betty Radice (London: Penguin, 1974), 16.

5   Heloise seems to have had an even lower opinion of marriage than did Abelard (practiced, as it was, primarily for *economic* reasons):

> This one is not better because he is richer or more powerful; the latter depends on fortune, the former on virtue. Nor should she be estimated as less than venal, who freely marries the rich man rather than the poor one, and desires what her husband *has* more than what he *is*. To such a one, certainly, pay is due rather than gratitude. Certainly it is true that she thinks more of his property than of him, and she, if she could, would prostitute herself to a richer man.

> [N]on enim quo quisque ditior sive potentior, ideo et melior; fortunae illud est, hoc virtutis. Nec se minime venalem aestimet esse, quae libentius ditiori quam pauperi nubit, et plus in marito sua quam ipsum concupiscit. Certe quamcunque ad nuptias haec concupiscentia ducit, merces ei potius quam gratia debetur. Certum quippe est eam res ipsas, non hominem sequi, et se, si posset, velle prostituere ditiori.

> Peter Abelard and Heloise d'Argenteuil, 33, https://archive.org/stream/ magistripetriaba00abel#page/n40

on the Western Church[6]), and his once-promising career ground to a halt (something we will see again centuries later in the story of John and Anne Donne).

In his later years, Abelard was accused of heresy by the French abbot Bernard of Clairvaux.[7] Bernard (the heresy-hunter[8] whose preaching

---

6   In 1031, the Council of Bourges declared that "[p]riests, deacons and subdeacons were to refrain from taking wives and concubines, and those already married were to separate from their wives, or face the threat of degradation" (Helen Parish. *Clerical Celibacy in the West*: *C.1100–1700* [Farnham: Ashgate, 2010], 96). By 1059, instructions were given that "the laity should refuse the sacraments of married priests" (97). In 1095, the Council of Clermont demanded that "any priest, deacon, or subdeacon who was married must refrain from the celebration of the Mass" (103), and by 1119, "Pope Calixtus II made further attempts to enforce the prohibitions on clerical marriage at the Council of Rheims [...], at which it was determined that all married clergy were to be expelled from their benefices, and threatened with the penalty of excommunication if they did not separate from their wives" (103). Abelard and Heloise's relationship takes place in a context in which the primary employer of intellectuals (the Church) is in the process of forbidding them to have anything like a "normal" sexual and emotional life. It is this same institution that will soon establish the Inquisition and come to dominate the university:

   Gregory IX, in 1231, endowed the University [of Paris] with the great Papal privilege that completed its organization. It was the self-same Pope, who in 1233 entrusted the Dominicans with the office of the Inquisition. The Church, that under the great Innocent III (1198–1216) had reached the peak of its power, regarded this as a necessary defense against the heretical movements of the twelfth century. But the Church also saw a danger in the laity's culture at the end of the twelfth century, so it felt it had to subject education to its control. Thus, there is a close internal link between the introduction of the Inquisition and the enforcement of papal supervision of the universities.

   [S]tattete Gregor IX. im Jahre 1231 die Universität mit dem großen päpstlichen Privileg aus, das ihre Organisation abschloß. Es was derselbe Papst, der 1233 den Dominikanern das Amt der Inquisition übertrug. Gegen die ketzerischen Bewegungen des 12. Jahrhunderts schien der Kirche, die unter dem großen Innozenz III (1198–1216) den Höhepunkt ihrer Machstellung erreicht hatte, diese Gegenwehr geboten. Sie durfte aber auch in der stark von Alterum befruchteten Laienkultur des ausgehenden 12. Jahrhunderts eine Gefahr sehen, mußte also das Bildungswesen ihrer Kontrolle unterwerfen. So hängt die Einführung der Inquisition und die Durchsetzung der päpistlichen Oberaufsicht über die Universitäten innerlich zusammen.

   Ernst Robert Curtius. *Europäische Literatur und Lateinisches Mittelalter*. Berlin: A. Francke, 1948, 63. Perhaps it should not come as a surprise that the methods of academic and theological critics of poetry can so often seem identical.

7   Joseph R. Strayer. *Western Europe in the Middle Ages: A Short History* (New York: Appleton-Century-Crofts, Inc., 1955), 130.

8   "Otto of Freising described Bernard of Clairvaux as rather too ready to pounce upon hints of heresy, and Bernard was instrumental in branding innovative philosophy as dangerous heresy" (Christine Caldwell Ames. *Medieval Heresies: Christianity, Judaism, and Islam* [Cambridge: Cambridge University Press, 2015], 199).

against Henry the Monk[9] was part of the long ideological buildup to the Albigensian Crusade) "considered that Abelard did not so much invent a new heresy, as reassert old heresies, whether that of Arius, Pelagius, or Nestorius, all of which had been condemned by the Fathers of the Church".[10] Abelard's acute and competitive interest in combining philosophical and theological questions got him into trouble: "his first theological work, on the Trinity", was "condemned as heretical".[11] During the course of his academic career, Abelard made enemies by being too willing to mock current teaching methods, while others were more reliably orthodox:

> Other men used methods which were essentially like his, and even borrowed directly from his work, without losing their reputation for orthodoxy. [...] They were less shocking than Abelard because they were not innovators and because they were careful not to claim too much for their methods. They admitted that some articles of the faith were beyond rational analysis and they were careful to find orthodox solution to problems in which they had cited conflicting authorities.[12]

In all likelihood, however, it was not primarily his innovative thinking and lecturing that got him into so much trouble, but rather his complicated, and impolitic personality: "[a]rrogant and abrasive—he could not find a teacher smarter than he, and made this blazingly clear".[13]

Abelard was a proudly independent thinker, who reveled in controversy, and "was not blindly submissive to his authorities [...]; he knew how to compare them, criticize them, and combine them", while letting reason have "the last word".[14] Abelard emphasized intellectual independence in his teaching, and his students were "enthralled by

---

9   "Henry led a popular anti-clerical uprising, proclaiming a reform of marriage and elimination of degrees of consanguinity" (Ryan P. Freeburn. *Hugh of Amiens and the Twelfth-Century Renaissance* [Farnham: Ashgate, 2011], 150–51).

10 Constant J. Mews. "Accusations of Heresy and Error in the Twelfth Century Schools: The Witness of Gerhoh of Reichersberg and Otto of Freising". In *Heresy in Transition: Transforming Ideas of Heresy in Medieval and Early Modern Europe* (London: Routledge, 2005), 44.

11 John Marenbon. *Medieval Philosophy: An Historical and Philosophical Introduction* (London: Routledge, 2007), 136.

12 Strayer, 130.

13 Ames, 199.

14 Jacques Le Goff, ed. *The Medieval World*. Trans. by Lydia G. Cochrane (London: Collins & Brown, 1990), 21.

the novelty of his pedagogy, which challenged them not just to absorb the definitive statements (*auctoritates*) in revered authors (*auctores*), but also to interrogate the texts and passages with the strength of their own logic".[15] Abelard's students, seemingly willing to follow him anywhere in order to learn from him, were often notably loyal, though none were finally more loyal than Heloise.

Abelard writes frankly of Heloise in his *Historia calamitatum*, revealing his fascination with her intelligence and determination. They are now thought to have met sometime in 1115,[16] at a time when Heloise was still fairly young.[17] Very few women of the time, much less women so young, knew how to read and write, especially in formal Latin, or were educated in the classics: "this gift of the science of letters, which is rare in women, highly recommended the young girl, and made her highly praised throughout the entire realm",[18] writes Abelard, describing Heloise's intelligence, the shared quality that aroused their passion and led to their perilous choice. "I began to hold an estimate of myself as the only philosopher in the world, with no reason to fear anyone, and so I relaxed and gave in to my lustful desires".[19] The negative emphasis he puts on his recollections, reducing his love for Heloise to "lustful desires", is understandable, given the mutilated state of his body while writing these lines. It is impossible fully to imagine the horror he must

---

15 Jan M. Ziolowski, editor and translator. *Letters of Peter Abelard, Beyond the Personal* (Washington: The Catholic University Press of America, 2008), xxii.
16 Denis de Rougemont differs, positing a first meeting in 1118. *L'Amour et l'Occident* (Paris: Plon, 1939), n. 12, 289.
17 The ages of Abelard and Heloise in 1115 are dated from a birthdate for Abelard of 1079, and for Heloise of 1100, making Abelard thirty six and Heloise fifteen. However, Constant Mews has recently argued that "[t]he tradition that she was born in 1100, and thus only a teenager when she met Abelard, is a pious fabrication from the seventeenth century, without any firm foundation. In 1115, she is more likely to have been around twenty-one years old" (Constant J. Mews, *Abelard and Heloise* [Oxford: Oxford University Press, 2005], 59).
18 "Nam quo bonum hoc, litteratorie scilicet scientiae, in mulieres es rarius: eo amplius puellam commendabat, et in toto regno nominatissimam fecerat" (Peter Abelard and Heloise d'Argenteuil, 6, https://archive.org/stream/magistripetriaba00abel#page/6).
19 "cum iam me solum in mundo superesse philosophum aestimarem, nec ullam ulterius inquietationem formidarem, frena libidini coepi laxare" (*ibid.*, 5–6, https://archive.org/stream/magistripetriaba00abel#page/5).

have experienced the night when, "sleeping in my private lodging",[20] hired thugs took Fulbert's revenge on him:

> They cut off those parts of my body with which I had committed the act about which they mourned. [...] First thing the next morning, the entire city gathered before my house, and the crying out stunned with wonder, the prostrated lamentations, the upsetting and exasperating moaning and weeping is difficult, even impossible to describe. Honestly, it was primarily the clerks and my students who crucified me with their intolerable grieving and lamenting, and I suffered more from their sympathy than from the pain of the wound, and I felt the shame more than the dismemberment. [...] From then on, I applied myself principally to the study of the sacred lessons, which to my present state was more convenient.[21]

What we see here is not the extinguishing or renouncing of Abelard's once-passionate love, but the words of a man who has built a protective wall behind which he can hide so that he will not be further harmed. *Historia calamitatum* reflects the guarded inner world that its author creates as a direct response to his mutilation and humiliation. In a way, it also reflects a painful internalization of the judgment rendered on him, and his love, by the world. A letter from his former teacher, Roscelin of Compiègne, provides powerful testimony to that judgment:

> I saw in Paris, in the house of a stranger, a certain clerk by the name of Fulbert received you and fed you with honor at his table, treating you as a member of his household and as an intimate friend. He also introduced you to his niece, a young girl of great abilities, and great prudence, engaging you to be her teacher. You were not unmindful, but contemptuous, in the way you treated that man of noble birth, your host and Lord, a clergyman, the canon of the church of Paris, who hosted you free of charge and with honor. Not sparing the virgin, whom you should have preserved and taught as a disciple, instead, with your spirit tossed about by unbridled lust, you taught her not to argue, but to commit

---

20 "dormientem in secreta hospicii mei camera" (*ibid.*, 11, https://archive.org/stream/magistripetriaba00abel#page/11).

21 eis videlicet corporis mei partibus amputatis, quibus id quod plangebant commiseram, [...] Mane autem facto, tota ad me civitas congregata, quanta stuperet admiratione, quanta se affligeret lamentatione, quanto me clamore vexarent, quanto planctu perturbarent: difficile, immo impossibile est exprimi. Maxime vero clerici ac precipue scolares nostri intolerabilibus me lamentis et eiulatibus cruciabant, ut multo amplius ex eorum compassione quam ex vulneris lederer passione, et plus erubescentiam quam plagam sentirem. [...] quod professioni meae convenientius erat, sacre plurimum lectioni studium intendens.

Ibid., 11–12, 13, https://archive.org/stream/magistripetriaba00abel#page/12

fornication. In this one fact you are guilty of many crimes: of treason, and fornication, and the filthiest violation of virginal modesty. But the Lord God, to whom vengeance belongs, has freely acted, depriving you of that part by which you sinned.[22]

Of his later escape to Troyes, Abelard describes himself as one hiding away from condemnation: "Here, hidden alone, except for one of our clerks, I could truly sing out to the Lord: 'Lo! I've become a fugitive from the world, and have found refuge in solitude'".[23] But even the solitude does not lessen his sense of shame or relieve his anguish. At some point he considers joining the "gentes" or "heathens" and "passing the boundaries of Christendom".[24]

Having been forcibly separated from Abelard for years, Heloise, now abbess of the Paraclete in Ferreux-Quincey, reads his *Historia calamitatum* only after it is brought to her by chance.[25] The letters Heloise writes in response reveal a passionate woman who agonizes over Abelard's misfortunes and "his life's continual persecutions".[26] Heloise, unlike Abelard, rejects the derision of society,[27] voicing that rejection

---

22   Vidi siquidem Parisius, quod quidam clericus nomine Fulbertus te ut hospitem in domo sua recepit, te in mensa sua ut amicum familiarem et domesticum honorifice pavit, neptim etiam suam, puellam prudentissimam et indolis egregiae, ad docendum commisit. Tu vero viri illius nobilis et clerici, Parisiensis etiam ecclesiae canonici, hospitis insuper tui ac domini, et gratis et honorifice te procurantis non immemor, sed contemptor, commissae tibi virgini non parcens, quam conservare ut commissam, docere ut discipulam debueras, effreno luxuriae spiritu agitatus non argumentari, sed eam fornicari docuisti, in uno facto multorum criminum, proditionis scilicet et fornicationis, reus et virginei pudoris violator spurcissimus. Sed Deus ultionum, Dominus Deus ultionum, libere egit, qui ea qua tantum parte peccaveras te privavit.
     Roscelin of Compiègne. "Epistola XV: Quae est Roscelini ad P. Abaelardum". *Patrologiae Cursus Completus*, Vol. 178, ed. by Jacques Paul Migne (Paris: Apud Garnier Fratres, 1885), col. 369, https://archive.org/stream/patrologia ecurs53unkngoog#page/n189
23   "ubi cum quodam clerico nostro latitans, illud vere Domino poteram decantare: 'Ecce elongavi fugiens et mansi in solitudine'" (Peter Abelard and Heloise d'Argenteuil, 19, https://archive.org/stream/magistripetriaba00abel#page/19).
24   "ut Christianorum finibus excessi" (*ibid.*, 23, https://archive.org/stream/magistri petriaba00abel#page/n31).
25   "Missam ad amicum pro consolatione epistolam, dilectissime, vestram ad me forte quidam nuper attulit" [Recently it chanced, most beloved, that the letter of consolation you sent to a friend was brought to me] (*ibid.*, 30, https://archive.org/stream/magistripetriaba00abel#page/n37).
26   "continuas vitae persecutiones" (*ibid.*, 30, https://archive.org/stream/magistripetri aba00abel#page/n37).
27   What made Peter Abelard so unusual in the eyes of Heloise was his gift for combining his skill in philosophy with a gift for composing and singing songs of love. When she read the Historia

in the words of two intensely passionate letters, and then a third, more philosophical and intellectual in its approach. In each case, what she appears to be seeking is not absolution, but a restored connection to Abelard, a return of words for words. As Barbara Newman describes the correspondence, it moves from passion to intellectual exchange:

> In the early 1130s Peter Abelard received three letters from Heloise, once his mistress and wife, now his sister and daughter in religion. The first two made such painful reading that he must have thought twice before scanning the third, in which Heloise resolutely turned from the subject of tragic love to the minutiae of monastic observance. For romantic readers, the correspondence lapses from titillation into tedium with this epistle. But Abelard was no doubt immensely relieved. Laying aside her griefs, Heloise now wrote to him as abbess to abbot, asking for only two things: a treatise explaining "how the order of nuns began", and a rule for her daughters at the Paraclete.[28]

And yet, one can imagine why Heloise asks for these things in her third letter—she had been, and was still, in love with Abelard's mind, and such a request would elicit more words, more thoughts, more of Abelard's voice to which Heloise could return in the most intimate of unions, hearing her long-absent husband in the quiet hours of night and morning as she scanned the words he would send her. They needn't be words of love—his words alone would sustain her.

But in her first two letters, Heloise's words overflow with passion and the bittersweet memories of the sensual and emotional delights she had shared with Abelard. She often reveals her sexual frustrations and longing, writing of her desire to be with the man she loves, despite the disapproval of the world. But only her memories will allow her that luxury:

> But those stimuli of the flesh, these instigators of sensuality, the very passions of youth, with the experience of longing and delight and pleasure, all greatly inflame [me]. [...] They praise me as chaste, when

---

calamitum, she reminded him of these public declarations of love and of the incessant letters he had showered on her in the past. From her perspective, a true relationship was not an illicit sexual encounter but a mutual profession of true love.

Constant J. Mews. *The Lost Love Letters of Heloise and Abelard* (New York: Palgrave MacMillan, 1999), 82.

28   Barbara Newman. *From Virile Woman to WomanChrist: Studies in Medieval Religion and Literature* (University Park: University of Pennsylvania Press, 1995), 19.

they do not see that I am a hypocrite. They think of the cleanness of the flesh as virtue, but virtue is not of the body, but of the soul.[29]

Nothing could sublimate or redirect Heloise's love, not even being a nun, for she says she feels "immoderate love"—"immoderato amore",[30] not for God, but for Abelard. She makes her preference for Abelard above all others on Earth or in Heaven clear when she tells him that "only you have the power to make me sad, or to bring me delight or comfort".[31] If her words were put to music, one could hear the troubadours and their songs of *fin'amor*. Bernart de Ventadorn's poem, *Tant ai mo cor ple de joya* (My heart is full of joy), in its treatment of love and comfort, echoes Heloise's paradoxical sense of naked exposure and warm reassurance in her confessions of love to Abelard:

> Anar posc ses vestidura,
> nutz en ma chamiza,
> car fin' amors m'asegura
> de la freja biza.[32]

> I walk undressed,
> naked in my shirt,
> for love secures me
> from the coldest winds.

Sometimes, Heloise's tone becomes more urgent, even demanding, as she desires to love and be loved despite Fulbert, the Church, or the jealous God himself. However, Abelard cannot respond in the way that Heloise yearns for. After his intial diffidence, Heloise's words become even more intensely heartfelt, revealing the passionate and courageous

---

29 "Hos autem in me stimulos carnis, haec incentiva libidinis ipse iuvenilis fervor aetatis, et iocundissimarum experientia volputatum, plurimum accendunt. [...] Castam me raedicant, qui non deprehenderunt hypocritum. Munditiam carnis conferunt in virtutem, cum non sit corporis, sed animi virtus" (Peter Abelard and Heloise d'Argenteuil, 43–44, https://archive.org/stream/magistripetriaba00abel#page/43).
30 *Ibid.*, 32, https://archive.org/stream/magistripetriaba00abel#page/n39
31 "Solus quippe es, qui me contristare, qui me laetificare seu consolari valeas" (*ibid.*)
32 Bernart de Ventadorn, 260–63, ll. 13–16, https://archive.org/stream/bernartvonventad00bern#page/260

person she has always been, determined to love fully, and on her own terms, despite a world that disdains her love for Abelard:

> God knows I have never required anything from you except for yourself; I only wanted you, not anything that belonged to you. [...] And if the name of wife appears more sacred and honorable, for me the word friend will always be sweeter, or—though you might be indignant—concubine or whore. [...] I preferred love to marriage, freedom to fetters. I call God as witness, if Augustus, the whole world's ruler, had deemed me worthy of marriage, and raised me to preside with him over the earth forever, it would have been dearer to me to be called your whore than his Empress.[33]

Heloise refuses the idea that she may only love Abelard for the sake of God, and in that way, she is more akin to the troubadours than to the later Italian poets who see love as a ladder by which to reach the divine: "[w]hen Heloise protested that she desired him for himself, [she] echoed the Ciceronium dictum that one should love a friend, for that person's sake—without reference to loving someone for the sake of God".[34] Heloise is unwilling to believe that such love is a sin: "I am innocent"—"sum innocens",[35] for she views love as something greater than anything the world can oppose it with:

> She wants freedom from compulsion in loving her paragon, who had every grace of mind and body, making her the envy of queens and great ladies. She wants him for herself alone, without the restraints or sanctions of marriage—her love is single, obsessive, possessive, eternal, extramarital. And nothing can overcome her passion, not his castration, not his unavailability, not his theological arguments, not her

---

33   Nihil unquam, deus scit, in te nisi requisiui; te pure, non tua concupiscens. [...] Et si uxoris nomen sanctius ac validius videtur, dulcius mihi semper exstitit amicae ocabulum, aut, si non indigneris, concubinae vel scorti. [...] sed plerisque tacitis, quibus amorem coniugio, libertatem vinculo praeferebam. Deum leslcm invoco, si me Augustus universo praesidens mundo matrimonii honore dignaretur totumque mihi orbem confirmaret in perpetuo praesidendum, carius mihi et dignius videretur tua dici meretrix, quam illius imperatrix.

    Peter Abelard and Heloise d'Argenteuil, 32–33, https://archive.org/stream/magistri petriaba00abel#page/n40

34   Constant J. Mews. "Abelard, Heloise, and Discussion of Love in the Twelfth-Century Schools". In Babette S. Hellemans, eds. *Rethinking Abelard*: *A Collection of Critical Essays* (Leiden: Brill, 2014), 26.

35   Peter Abelard and Heloise d'Argenteuil, 34, https://archive.org/stream/magistri petriaba00abel#page/n41

administrative duties in a convent, and certainly not her vows, which were far from freely or religiously taken.³⁶

She makes it painfully clear that she never chose the religious life, and that had she been free to make her own choices, both their lives would have been very different:

> Truthfully, the young girl had no calling for the monastic profession, nor any religious devotion, but I did this to obey you. And if, in that, I deserve nothing from you, be the judge yourself of how vain all my hardships are. I expect no reward from God, for certainly I have never done anything for the love of him. You hurried to God, and I followed in the habit; indeed, I went first. [...] I have never had the slightest hesitation, were it to run into the Vulcanian flames of Hell, to follow you or precede you at your bidding. My heart was not with me, but with you. Even now, if it is not wholly with you, it is nowhere. In fact, without you, it does not exist at all.³⁷

Heloise's love for Abelard, after many years of separation, shows no signs of having diminished. This is painfully clear in the way she begins and ends her letters. She addresses her first letter, "To her lord, or rather her father, to her husband, or rather her brother; his servant, or rather his daughter, his wife, or rather his sister; to Abelard, Heloise".³⁸ Abelard, in contrast, distances himself from Heloise by opening the letters with "To Heloise, his dearly beloved sister in Christ, Abelard her brother in the same".³⁹ The ending of the letters play almost the same notes: "Farewell, my only",⁴⁰ versus "Live, but in Christ I pray, remember

---

36 Hagstrum, 204.
37 quam quidem iuvenculam ad monastice conversationis asperitatem non religionis devotio sed tua tantum pertraxit iussio. Ubi si nihil a te promerear, quam frustra laborem, diiudica. Nulla mihi super hoc merces exspectanda est a deo, cuius adhuc amore nihil me constat egisse. Properantem te ad deum secuta sum habitu, immo praecessi. [...] Ege autem (deus scit) ad Vulcania loca te properantem praecedere vel sequi pro iussu tuo minime dubitarem. Non enim mecum animus meus sed tecum erat. Sed et nunc maxime si tecum non est, nusquam est: esse vero sine te nequaquam potest.

Peter Abelard and Heloise d'Argenteuil, 34, https://archive.org/stream/magistri petriaba00abel#page/n41
38 "Domino suo, immo patri; coniugi suo, immo fratri; ancilla sua, immo filia, ipsius uxor, immo soror" (*ibid.*, 30, https://archive.org/stream/magistripetriaba00abel#page/n37).
39 "Heloissae, dilectissimae sorori suae in Christo, Abaelardus, frater eius in ipso" (*ibid.*, 35, https://archive.org/stream/magistripetriaba00abel#page/n42).
40 "Vale unice" (*ibid.*).

me".⁴¹ As Newman notes, "Abelard's *Historia* is a quasipublic document [...]. But Heloise's letters are relentlessly private [...]. While Heloise, like an Ovidian heroine, gestures toward the whole world as witness to her woes, she addresses her appeal to Abelard alone".⁴²

There is, perhaps, a physical as well as emotional explanation for Abelard's detached style: "Disgust with his mutilated person may have made him want to shut the past out of his mind; he was changed, and [...] he may have been all too ready to believe that she was changed too".⁴³ Abelard's stiffness can easily be seen as selfishness on his part, and yet, his attempts at formality may well lie in his desire to shut out what he feels cannot be restored, passions he can remember but no longer feel physically, insisting, despite the pain of loss, on what he thinks is best for both of them. Perhaps he believed that if he kept holding on to the past, his suffering, and hers, would never diminish. However, in *Historia calamitatum*, when he is not yet corresponding with Heloise, and allows himself room for honesty, Abelard shows the true colors of his love; it is fleshly, sensual, and romantic:

> First we were joined together in one house, soon we joined by mind and spirit. Using her instruction as an occasion for privacy, we gave all our time to love, and the secret recesses that love chose, and that her studies afforded us. With our books open, we spent more words on love than on our readings; we shared more kisses than sentences. My hands found their way to her bosom more often than to our books. [...] No stage of love is skipped by cupid-struck people such as we. [...] It was incredibly irritating for me to have to go to the School, and equally irritating when I had to maintain nightly vigils to love, and then turn around and study all the next day.⁴⁴

---

41 "Vivite, sed Christo quaeso mei memores" (*ibid.*, 39, https://archive.org/stream/magistripetriaba00abel#page/39)
42 Newman, 56.
43 Radice, 27.
44 Primum domo una coniungimur, postmodum animo. Sub occasione itaque disciplinae amori penitus vacabamus, et secretos regressus, quos amor optabat, studium lectionis offerebat. Apertis itaque libris, plura de amore, quam de lectione verba se ingerebant, plura erant oscula, quam sententiae. Saepius ad sinus quam ad libros educebantur manus. [...] nullus a cupidis intermissus est gradus amoris. [...] Taediosum mihi vehementer erat ad scholas procedere, vel in eis morari; pariter et laboriosum, cum nocturnas amori vigilias et diurnas studio conservarem.

Peter Abelard and Heloise d'Argenteuil, 7, https://archive.org/stream/magistripetriaba00abel#page/7

Here, his passions are uninhibited, and his words belong to the pages that tell the story of *fin'amor*. Similar words and passions can be found in his songs. One notable development in Latin song, from about 1100 (thus co-existent with the songs of the troubadours and Minnesingers), is what are called *"planctus* or laments".[45] Abelard "wrote six *planctus*",[46] including one based on the laments of David over the deaths of Saul and Jonathan. But in the scriptural story, a reader can still hear Abelard's passion:

> Heu! cur consilio
> acquievi pessimo,
> ut tibi praesidio
> non essem in praelio?
> Vel confossus pariter
> morerer feliciter
> cum, quid amor faciat
> majus hoc non habeat,
> Et me post te vivere
> mori sit assidue
> nec ad vitam anima
> satis sit dimidia.[47]

> Alas! Why did I plan,
> acquiescing to debasement,
> that you would protect yourself
> and I would not be in the battle?
> Even pierced alike
> we would die happily
> when love would fashion it so.
> Greater than this we cannot have.
> And to live after you
> would be to die continually
> For with only half a soul
> Life is not enough.

---

45 Alice V. Clark. "From Abbey to Cathedral and Court: Music Under the Merovingian, Carolingian and Capetian Kings in France until Louis IX". *The Cambridge Companion to French Music* (Cambridge: Cambridge University Press, 2015), 12.
46 *Ibid.*, 13.
47 Latin text from Lorenz Weinrich. "'Dolorum solatium': Text und Musik von Abaelards Planctus". *Mittellateinisches Jahrbuch*, 5 (1968), 72, ll. 69–80.

His "letters of direction", as the latter highly didactic letters are called, might bear the mask of indifference, but as a result of Heloise's letters, Abelard throws himself into a frenzy of literary activity on her behalf: in addition to the famous, if painfully diffident letters, Abelard wrote "a hundred hymns, thirty-five sermons, [...] a substantial series of solutions of Heloise's theological problems [and a] half-dozen *Planctus* [...] which touch very closely on the state of mind of Heloise and himself". Through these works, "Abelard had found an acceptable medium in which to express his love for Heloise".[48] On top of all of this, it is evident that Abelard's heart remained with Heloise when he asked if she would bury him: "by whatever cause I go the way of all flesh, proceeding absent from you, I pray you to bring my body, whether it lie buried or exposed, to your cemetary".[49] Years later, "Peter the Venerable [...] made sure to return the body to Heloise" and when Heloise herself died, she "was laid to rest next to Abelard".[50] Her jealous uncle, his hired thugs, and the society in which they lived, may have separated the lovers physically, but they could not extinguish their love. Their words and cries of desire and suffering echo yet another poem by Bernart de Ventadorn, *Can vei la lauzeta mover* (When I see the lark move):

> Ai, las! Tan cuidava saber
> d'amor, e tan petit en sai,
> car eu d'amor no·m posc tener
> celeis don ja pro non aurai.
> Tout m'a mo cor, e tout m'a me
> e se mezeis e tot lo mon;
> e can se.m tolc, no·m laisset re
> mas desirer e cor volon.[51]

---

48 W. G. East. "This Body of Death: Abelard, Heloise and the Religious Life". In Peter Biller and Alastair J. Minnis, eds. *Medieval Theology and the Natural Body* (Woodbridge, Suffolk: Boydell & Brewer, 1997), 51.

49 "quocunque casu viam universae carnis absens a vobis ingrediar, cadaver obsecro nostrum, ubicunque vel sepultum vel expositum iacuerit, ad cimiterium vestrum deferri faciatis" (Peter Abelard and Heloise d'Argenteuil, 39).

50 Charles J. Reid. *Power Over the Body, Equality in the Family: Rights and Domestic Relations in Medieval Canon Law* (Grand Rapids: William B. Eerdmans, 2004), 130.

51 Bernart de Ventadorn, 250–54, ll. 9–16, https://archive.org/stream/bernartvon ventad00bern#page/250

5. Fin'amor Castrated: Abelard, Heloise, and the Critics who Deny

> Alas! So much, I believed I knew
> about love, and how little I really know
> because I cannot hold back from loving
> her, the lady I will not ever have.
> All my heart, and all of me,
> myself and the whole world,
> she has taken, and left behind nothing
> except desire and a yearning heart.

And yet, in a now-familiar pattern, literary critics devoted to a "thou shalt" and "thou shalt not" authoritarian style of interpretation have long insisted that these letters are not about love, with some going to the extent of arguing that the letters are not even genuine. Barbara Newman argues strenuously against those critics who deny the authenticity of Heloise's letters, identifying their aim as "not only the repression of Heloise's desire, but the complete obliteration of her voice", locating the urge to obliterate that voice "in a priori notions of what a medieval abbess could write, frank disapproval of what Heloise did write, and at times outright misogyny".[52] Newman takes D. W. Robertson as her prime example:

> Robertson's condescension toward Heloise is blatant. He refers to her twice as "poor Heloise" and once even as "little Heloise"; at least a half dozen times, he calls her discourse on marriage in the *Historia calamitatum* a "little sermon". In a display of stunning inconsistency, he manages to deny that "little Heloise actually said anything like" what Abelard records, and at the same time to ridicule her for saying it. Embodying all the negative stereotypes of the feminine, Robertson's Heloise is both minx and shrew.[53]

As Newman observes, "Robertson himself would read these letters, like all medieval texts that purport to celebrate erotic love, as witty and ironic; they form part of an exemplary conversion narrative authored by Abelard".[54] Robertson is a wonderful example of the kind of authoritarian reader Longxi refers to when he observes that critics attempt to transform literature into "a model of propriety and good conduct, something that carries a peculiar ethico-political

---
52 Newman, 47.
53 *Ibid.*, 49.
54 *Ibid.*, 50.

import".⁵⁵ In pointing out that the works of Marie de France, "one of the most celebrated erotic writers of the twelfth century", enjoyed widespread popularity in their day, Newman remarks that "some twelfth-century audiences were less fastidious in these matters than their modern interpreters".⁵⁶

The tradition of scholars and critics arguing that the love story of Abelard and Heloise is not what it seems to be has been active since Ignaz Fessler in 1806, who first suggested that the letters between Abelard and Heloise were a fraud.⁵⁷ In 1972, John Benton argued that the letters were the result of a collaborative forgery between two men, a "'twelfth-century epistolary 'novelist' and a 'thirteenth-century institutional scoundrel'".⁵⁸ Though Benton later abandoned this theory, Hubert Silvestre persisted, arguing in 1985 that:

> The *Historia* and the correspondence are […] the work of a late thirteenth-century forger, working on the basis of some authentic material, who wished to uphold the right of clerics to have a concubine, and who found a powerful way of doing so by putting the arguments for clerical concubinage not into the mouth of a man, as might be expected, but of an outstanding woman. This forger was none other than the famous poet Jean de Meun, whose vast completion of Guillaume de Lorris' *Roman de la Rose*, one of the most widely read French works of the later Middle Ages, contains a passage recounting the romance of Abelard and Heloise, and who translated the *Historia* and the correspondence into French.⁵⁹

But as John Marenbon notes, this theory is simply illogical:

> There are […] a number of instances in the Old French translation, not explicable by variants in the Latin text or defects in the manuscript of the French, where Jean de Meun, failing to grasp the meaning of a phrase in the correspondence, mistranslates it. How could Jean de Meun misunderstand a text which he himself had forged?⁶⁰

The compulsion that many critics have to "channel, reformulate, and control" texts that describe human love is enabled by "the wish, among

---

55 Longxi, 205.
56 Newman, 52.
57 Ignas Fessler. *Abälard und Heloise*, Vol. II (Berlin, 1806), 352.
58 John Marenbon. *The Philosophy of Peter Abelard* (Cambridge: Cambridge University Press. 1997), 83.
59 *Ibid.*
60 *Ibid.*, 83–84.

some literary theorists, to treat texts as if they were not the products of their authors, but independent signifiers, awaiting the reader to interpret them in one of the unlimited ways in which they can be understood".[61] That this wish drives the Bentons and Silvestres of the world to spin elaborate (and ultimately unsupportable) theories of fraud and conspiracy is at once sad and instructive. But such an impulse needn't drive us. Those who contend that the letters are a fraud because they were composed by Abelard himself, make claims that are entirely free of any actual evidence: "[t]here is nothing intrinsically impossible about the suggestion, but it requires strong evidence. This its supporters signally fail to provide".[62]

Abelard and Eloise confessing their love to his brother monks and her sister nuns. Coloured stipple engraving by Miss Martin after Perolia.[63]

The passionate love of Abelard and Heloise, with all its struggles and complications, is not a fraud perpetrated by "novelists", "scoundrels" or by Abelard himself. The sheer energy that has gone into constructing and defending such arguments (primarily by male critics) speaks eloquently of the determination to achieve "not only the repression of Heloise's

---

61 Ibid., 93.
62 Ibid., 90.
63 Wellcome Images, https://commons.wikimedia.org/wiki/File:Abelard_and_Eloise_confessing_their_love_to_his_brother_monk_Wellcome_V0033159.jpg

desire, but the complete obliteration of her voice".[64] What is it about the idea of a powerfully intellectual and passionately eros-driven Heloise that so disturbs such critics? It is "neither improbable nor anachronistic to attribute to Heloise the sentiments expressed in her letters",[65] despite the urge of moralizing critics to explain them away. Nor does the love of Abelard and Heloise fit the bloodless and library-bound scholarly idea of "courtly love", a passionless construct that reveals its adherents' disdain: "Abelard and Heloise speak a different language of sensuous frankness [...]. Their relationship found physical expression, and Heloise is neither cold nor remote but loving and generous, eager to give service and not to demand it".[66]

Far from being something so bloodless as Robertson's "exemplary conversion narrative authored by Abelard",[67] the story of Abelard and Heloise is defined by passion, desire, and loss. Their love cannot be confined to an academic's tale, a somnolent morality play that fits comfortably within the paradigm of "courtly love", with its emphasis on love as a flawed if necessary path to Heaven. Theirs is a tale of the delights and dangers of *fin'amor* in a world determined to control love and sexuality—a world in which too many seem determined to write such a story out of existence by insisting that it does not really mean what it says. But as Zang Longxi reminds us, in response to those critics who would torture texts into "saying" what they do not say, while vigorously denying what they do say: "the plain literal sense of the text must always act as a restraint to keep interpretation from going wild, [...] bringing the letter into harmony with the spirit, rather than into opposition to it".[68]

---

64 Newman, 47.
65 Marenbon, *The Philosophy of Peter Abelard*, 89.
66 Radice, 49.
67 Newman, 50.
68 Longxi, 215. The response to this position is predictable. As David Dawson argues,
   although the "literal sense" has often been thought of as an inherent quality of a literary text that gives it a specific and invariant character (often, a "realistic" character), the phrase is simply an honorific title given to a kind of meaning that is culturally expected and automatically recognized by readers. It is the "normal", "commonsensical" meaning, the product of a conventional, customary reading. The "literal sense" thus stems from a community's generally unself-conscious decision to adopt and promote a certain kind of meaning, rather than from its recognition of a text's inherent and self-evident sense.

   Allegorical Readers and Cultural Revision in Ancient Alexandria (Los Angeles: University of California Press, 1992), 7–8. Note how often the critic resorts to

The history of Abelard and Heloise is one of delight and suffering—real suffering, not the stylized variety of the courtly stories—and just perhaps, it is also a story of a new joy at being reunited, through words on a page (one can only imagine how many times Abelard read and read again those words Heloise had given him, and as for Heloise, she leaves us in no doubt). For beside the sensual delight each took in the other, what else more than their words, their intellects, their thoughts, brought Abelard and Heloise together as two sighted lovers amidst the eyeless crowds? Those who would condemn Heloise's passions, argue that her words were really not her own, or adopt any other tactic that might serve to explain her away, will always be with us. But they need no longer have any claim on our attention, much less our readerly obedience to their insistent demands that we read as they do. Abelard and Heloise loved as few ever will, and Heloise in particular stands above the mean and base denunciations of the passionless, and sanctimonious critics who would silence or shame her across the centuries. Heloise was a woman of strength, substance, and character who would merely laugh at her modern detractors, for her focus was always on love: "[m]ore than any ancient Roman, perhaps, Heloise fulfilled to perfection the classical ideal of the *univim*, the woman who belonged solely and wholly to a single man. Whatever the role she played, Abelard was always her *solus*, her *unicus*, he alone could grieve her, comfort her, instruct her, command her, destroy her, or save her".[69]

In the end, love found a way to thrive, through the lovers' passionate and painful lines, and through our own open and honest reading of those lines nearly a thousand years later. The love of Abelard and Heloise was neither ironic, nor faked—such claims say more about the critics than about the words of two twelfth-century lovers who, even now, face the condemnation of the moral scolds among us who never miss a chance to drain the joy out of life, love, and poetry.

---

condescending language that insists on the naïveté and "conventional" quality of readings that attempt to recover a literal sense of a text. Such readings are "unself-conscious", "conventional", "customary", and otherwise to be revealed, unmasked, and debunked by the clear-eyed, self-conscious, and most definitely *un*conventional critic. Who benefits from such relentless and widely-shared (in some sense also "conventional" and "customary") interpretive stances by critics? Other, that is, than the critics themselves?

69 Newman, 70.

6. The Albigensian Crusade and the Death of *Fin'amor* in Medieval French and English Poetry

I
The Death of *Fin'amor*: The Albigensian Crusade and its Aftermath

At the beginning of the thirteenth century, everything changed. In its earliest days, the mood in Provençe was ebullient and defiant. It radiates from the tale of *Aucassin et Nicolette*, which, though written in the northern dialect of Picardy, "gives a faithful picture"[1] of the attitudes held in Occitania—sensual, anticlerical, and fiercely independent:

> In Paradise what would I do? I do not seek to enter there, but only wish for Nicolette, my sweet friend that I love so much. For no one goes to Paradise except the kinds of people I will tell you about now: there is where the old priests go, crippled and maimed old men, who cower all day and night in front of the altars, and in the crypts; and people wearing old tattered cloaks, naked and with no shoes, covered in sores, diseased and dying of hunger and thirst and cold. These are the people who go to Paradise; I want nothing to do with them. I would rather go to Hell, where there are fine clerks and knights, who have died in tournaments and noble wars, brave soldiers and noble men. These are who I would

---

1   Briffault, 132.

go with. And there, also, are the beautiful and courteous women who have two or three lovers in addition to their husbands. There is to be found all gold, silver, fine furs, musicians and poets, and the prince of this world. Let me go with these, as long as I have Nicolette, my sweet love, with me.[2]

Marianne Stokes, *Aucassin and Nicolette* (1898).[3]

Better to love in hell, than serve in heaven. Such rhetorical bravery was still relatively easy in 1200, nine years before the opening of the Albigensian Crusade with the wholesale slaughter of the men, women, and children of the southern town of Béziers. Occitania was still cosmopolitan and

---

2   En paradis qu'ai je a faire? Je n'i quier entrer, mais que j'aie Nicolete, ma tres douce amie que j'aim tant. C'en paradis ne vont fors tex gens con je vous dirai. Il i vont ci viel prestre et cil viel clop et cil manke, qui tote jor et tote nuit cropent devant ces autex et en ces viés creutes, et cil a ces viés capes eraéses et a ces viés tateceles vestues, qui sont nu et decauç et estrumelé, qui moeurent de faim et de soi et de froit et de mesaises. Icil vont en paradis; avec ciax n'ai jou que faire; mais en infer voil jou aler. Car en infer vont li bel clerc, et li bel cevalier, qui sont mort as tornois et as rices gueres, et li boin sergant, et li franc home. Aveuc ciax voil jou aler. Et s'i vont les beles dames cortoises, que eles ont .ii. amis ou .iii. avoc leur barons. Et s'i va li ors et li argens, et li vairs et li gris; et si i vont harpeor et jogleor et li roi del siecle. Avoc ciax voil jou aler, mais quě j'aie Nicolete, ma tres douce amie, aveuc mi.

Aucassin et Nicolette, ed. by Francis William Bourdillon (London: Kegan Paul, Trench & Co., 1887), 14–17, https://archive.org/stream/AucassinEtNicoletteALoveStory/Aucassin_et_Nicolette_Bourdillon_1887#page/n102

3   https://commons.wikimedia.org/wiki/File:Marianne_Stokes05.jpg

tolerant, a place in which "the influence of the Church never went as deep [...] as it did in the Kingdom of the Franks".[4] The people were characterized by a "political particularism" which "was intensified by their traditional opposition to the religion of the French".[5]

All seemed well, especially because Occitan culture was successful and growing. The poetic culture of the troubadours had spread beyond the borders of Occitania into Italy and Spain. One of the most powerful areas of troubadour influence was in Germany, where a group of poets known as the Minnesingers followed in the footsteps of the troubadours "with a time lag of some fifteen years".[6] The most famous of these, Walther von der Vogelweide (*c*. 1170–1230) illustrates the spread of the idea of *fin'amor* as passionate, embodied, and often forbidden love from the lands of the *langue d'oc* to the valley of the Rhine:

> Under der linden
> an der heide,
> dâ unser zweier bette was,
> dâ mugent ir vinden
> schône beide
> gebrochen bluomen unde grass.
> vor dem walde in einem tal,
> tandaradei,
> schône sane diu nahtegal.
> Ich kam gegangen
> zuo der ouwe:
> dô was min friedel komen ê.
> dâ wart ich enpfangen,
> hêre frouwe,
> daz ich bin sælic iemer mê.
> kuster mich? wol tûsentstunt:
> tandaradei,
> seht wie rôt mir ist der munt.
> Dô hât er gemachet
> alsô riche

---

4   Briffault, 130.
5   *Ibid.*, 131.
6   Nigel F. Palmer. "The High and later Middle Ages (1100–1450)". In Hellen Watanabe-O'Kelly, ed. *The Cambridge History of German Literature* (Cambridge: Cambridge University Press, 1997), 47–48.

von bluomen eine bettestat.
des wirt noch gelachet
inneclîche,
kumt iemen an daz selbe pfat.
bî den rôsen er wol mac,
tandaradei,
merken wâ mirz houbet lac.
Daz er bî mir læge,
wessez iemen,
(nu enwelle got!), sô schamt ich mich.
wes er mit mir pflæge,
niemer niemen
bevinde daz, wan er unt ich,
und ein kleinez vogellîn,
tanderadei,
daz mac wol getriuwe sin.[7]

Under the Linden
Out on the heath,
Where our bed for two was,
You may still find
Beauty both
In broken blooms and grass,
Where, in a field at the forests' edge,
Tandaradei!
So sweetly sang the nightingale.
I came walking
Through the meadow:
My lover had come before.
And he greeted me,
Highest Lady!
So that my joy is always with me.
Did he kiss me? A thousand times:
Tandaradei!
See how red my mouth is.
He prepared for us a place

---

7   Walther von der Vogelweide. "Under der linden". In Karl Lachmann, ed. *Die Gedichte Walthers von der Vogelweide* (Berlin: George Reimer, 1891), 39–40, https://archive.org/stream/diegedichtewalt00lachgoog#page/n62

Of riches
A bed from flowers.
It made me laugh
With delight.
One who comes along the same path,
At the roses he may well
Tandaradei!
Mark where I lay my head.
That he lay with me,
If anyone knew,
God forbid—I would be shamed.
What there he did with me,
None must ever know,
Except for he and I,
And a little bird,
Tandaradei!
Who will probably be true.

What the lovers of *Under der linden* enjoy, and what the notably female voice describes, is the freedom to love each other passionately, and physically, removed from the constraints of the world of law, authority, and religion. This poem has none of the "sterile", and "exhausted" quality of poetry in which love "rested not on an emotion or even a noble heart but on a feudal concept of service".[8] It is, rather, a demonstration of Walther's idea that "true love [is] mutual and natural".[9] We have not yet reached the stage at which love and desire are wholly sublimated into service and worship, the stage that most comfortably fits the term "courtly love". *Under der linden* has nothing in common with the romances of Chrétien de Troyes, in which a figure like Lancelot can and will be punished by his lady for a failure of swift and cheerful obedience. "The song does not sing of spiritual frailty or squandered joy. Instead, it sings of the joys of consummated love".[10] Hovering over this poem's

---

8   W. T. H. Jackson. "Faith Unfaithful—The German Reaction to Courtly Love". In F. X. Newman, ed. *The Meaning of Courtly Love* (Albany: State University of New York Press, 1968), 74.
9   Jackson, 74.
10 Andreas Krass. "Saying It with Flowers: Post-Foucauldian Literary History and the Poetics of Taboo in a Premodern German Love Song". In Scott Spector, Helmut Puff, and Dagmar Herzog, eds. *After the History of Sexuality: German Genealogies with and Beyond Foucault* (New York: Berghahn Books, 2012), 64.

delight is a powerful awareness "of the moral taboo that looms over extramarital love affairs",[11] a sense of the ever-present shadow of the oppressive and disapproving world, precisely the kind of place, in fact, in which love and desire will be turned into service and obedience. The lady would be shamed if anyone knew of the love she and her lover shared, if anyone but the (probably) discreet birds could ever tell of her love. Even here, it seems, joy must be stolen in small moments hidden from a society determined to grind its inhabitants into a dry and near-lifeless compliance.

In Occitania, however, love, music, and passion were not yet lost. Located primarily between the Rhone and the Pyrenees, the world of the troubadours was a desirable one. The most powerful people of the time, including the lords of Montpellier, the viscounts of Narbonne, and the Trencavels, maintained tight political alliances, which along with strategic marriages between the powerful families of Poitiers and Toulouse, consolidated regional powers and rivalries that lasted until the Albigensian Crusade of the early thirteenth century:

> The counts of Poitiers arranged a marriage between Count William VII of Poitou (also known as William IX of Aquitaine, the first known troubadour) and Philippa, the daughter of Count William IV of Toulouse. Duke William X, Philippa's son inherited all the titles, and passed on to his only child, Eleanor of Aquitaine.[12]

Eleanor of Aquitaine's royal husbands, Louis VII of France and Henry II of England also had influence in the region. These men, along with Henry II's sons, Geoffrey, Henry, Richard, and John, knew many of the troubadours of the time, and one is known to have composed his own lyrics. Richard, who would later become Richard I, loved music, and "would stand alongside the choir at the royal chapel, urging them with his hands to sing louder".[13]

The era that gleamed with poetic inspiration was also a period of cosmopolitan spirit. It was a culture characterized by a sophisticated ethic of tolerance regarding opinion and belief, whose ethos could be

---
11 *Ibid.*
12 Frederic L. Cheyettee. *Ermengard of Narbonne and the World of the Troubadours* (Ithaca: Cornell University Press, 2001), 4.
13 David Boyle. *Troubadour's Song: The Capture, Imprisonment and Ransom of Richard the Lionheart* (New York: Walker & Co., 2005), 5.

summed up in the word *paratge*, a word meaning: "honor, righteousness, equality, denial of the right of the strongest, respect for the human person for itself and for others. *Paratge* applies in all fields, political, religious, and emotional".[14] Such a concept led "the lords of the South [...] against the Crusaders to defend and not to plunder".[15]

But in the background, under the bright surfaces of life in a relatively liberal and highly cultured Occitania, trouble was slowly coming to a boil. The First Crusade in 1099 brought turmoil to the region, including pogroms against the Jews[16] (a group that had long been treated relatively well in Occitan culture[17]). This period also saw the rise of heretical sects, especially a religious group known to present-day historians as the Cathars, who established themselves in the south, with an openly-run diocese in the town of Albi (thus the name "Albigensians"). Cathars, literally, "the cleansed" or "the purged", spread through Languedoc and into major cities of northern Italy. The religion of the Cathars—or "*boni homines*, 'good men', [...] the popular Occitan name for the Cathar 'Perfects'"[18]—allowed for something like gender equality,[19] and became so influential by the mid-twelfth century that they could hold public debates with the bishops of Albi and Toulouse. For powerful churchmen, such independence was intolerable, as "this was also a period when the centralized Church was turning its back on women again and found

---

14 "honneur, droiture, égalité, négation du droit du plus fort, respect de la personne humaine pour soi et pour les autres. Le paratge s'applique dans tous les domaines, politique, religieux, sentimental" (Ferdinand Niel, *Albigeois et Cathares* [Paris: Presses Universitaires de France, 1974], 67).

15 "Les seigneurs du Midi [...] contre les Croises pour la defendre et non pour la spolier" (Charles Camproux. *Le "joy d'amor" des troubadours. Jeu et joie d'amour* [Montpellier: Causse et Castelnau, 1965], 95).

16 On the massacres of Jews in Cologne, Metz, Trier and anti-Jewish hostilities brought about by the First Crusade toward the end of the eleventh century see Norman Golb, *The Jews in Medieval Normandy: A Social and Intellectual History* (NY: Cambridge, University Press, 1998).

17 *Paratge*, with its basic "respect for human beings was also applied to Jews", a state of affairs which did not sit well with the Catholic authorities under Innocent III, so "at the Council of Saint Gilles, Raymond VI, Count of Toulouse, and twelve of his major vassals had to swear they would stop giving official positions to Jews" (Henri Jeanjean. "Flamenca: A Wake for a Dying Civilization?", *Parergon*, 16: 1 [July 1998], 21, http://ro.uow.edu.au/cgi/viewcontent.cgi?article=2958&context=artspapers).

18 Cheyettee, 295.

19 Approximately 45% of Cathar ministers were female (Richard Abels and Ellen Harrison. "The Participation of Women in Languedocian Catharism". *Mediaeval Studies*, 41 [1979], 225, https://doi.org/10.1484/J.MS.2.306245).

the influence of the powerful women behind Cathar society particularly threatening".[20]

The widespread practice of a religion that so openly challenged social and political norms, while it rejected the orthodox claims of Rome, made the weak and indecisive Count Raymond V of Toulouse nervous enough that he wrote a letter in 1177 explaining the situation to Church authorities:

> The disease of heresy has grown so strong in my lands that almost all those who follow it believe that they are serving God... The priesthood is corrupted with heresy; ancient churches, once held in reverence, are no longer used for divine worship but have fallen into ruins; baptism is denied; the Mass is hated; confession is derided... Worst of all, the doctrine of two principles is taught.[21]

The "doctrine of two principles" refers to the dualist Cathar belief, familiar from various strands of Gnosticism, and Plato's *Timaeus*, that the creator of this world was a demiurge, an inferior—and for the Cathars, evil—god who "kept the divine souls of humans imprisoned in their physical bodies (or other warm-blooded animals), condemning them to perpetual reincarnation. This cycle could only be broken by adherence to Cathar beliefs".[22] The Cathar belief system, in its skepticism and refusal of Catholic authority, represented just the latest in a long line of rebellious sentiments in the Languedoc:

> Skeptical Provençe was the natural refuge of all heretics. From the ninth century, when the Adoptionist heresy spread from Toledo, where it originated, over Languedoc, down to the foretokenings of Protestantism, medieval heresies were primarily inspired by revolt against the spiritual and material tyranny of the Roman Church. [...] The teachings of the Cathars [were] affiliated with similar kernels of resistance scattered throughout Christendom, and deriving in direct continuity from the earliest years of the Church.[23]

This resistance was shared nearly across the board in Occitania, even by those who were not Cathar believers. The differences between the north

---

20 Boyle, 282.
21 Sean McGlynn. *Kill Them All: Cathars and Carnage in the Albigensian Crusade* (Stroud: The History Press, 2015), 16.
22 *Ibid.*, 17.
23 Briffault, 137.

and south were as much cultural and linguistic as they were religious: "for southerners, the *langue d'oil* of northern France was more of a foreign language".²⁴ The southerners, whose *langue d'oc* was closer to Catalan than to the language of Paris, regarded the northerners as uncultured barbarians: "crude, unrefined, brutish and bellicose, altogether lacking in manners and culture",²⁵ and the northerners regarded the residents of Languedoc as the twelfth-and thirteenth-century equivalents of Chardonnay-sipping elitists, "sybaritic, indulgent, indolent and effete".²⁶ Occitania was a rich land as well, and made a tempting prize for less wealthy northern nobles when the Church-sponsored invasion of the south began in 1209. The Cathar refusal of Catholic authority was certainly what rankled Pope Innocent III, who had attempted to rouse the northern nobles to a crusade against the south in 1205 and 1207 before his successful effort of 1209. But it was money, land, and power that motivated the warriors who besieged the towns of Béziers, Carcassone, and Albi (and others over the following decades). Occitania, as McGlynn notes, had a booming economy "boosted by trade across the Mediterranean, including with Egypt and Syria; they exported wine, dyed woollens, olive oil and grain while importing spices, silks and luxury items".²⁷

In the leadup to the Crusade, Pope Innocent III demanded both the submission of Raymond VI, and the turning over of Cathar heretics to Catholic authorities. Northern nobles like Simon de Montfort, as orthodox as they may have been, were primarily interested in wealth, seeing the chance to enrich themselves by dispossessing the southern nobility. The pope had bigger concerns, since he saw himself as inhabiting a unique position of power and responsibility: "no pope had ever envisioned himself with so magnificent a mandate over the world", and as he saw it, the heresy of the south had to be eliminated — "if it were not obliterated [...] then all Christian existence would come to an end. [...] The crusade against heresy in the lands of the count of Toulouse was a holy war for the very survival of Christendom".²⁸ But the pope

---

24 McGlynn, 24.
25 *Ibid.*
26 *Ibid.,* 24–25.
27 *Ibid.,* 25.
28 Simon Pegg. *A Most Holy War: The Albigensian Crusade and the Battle for Christian Freedom* (Oxford: Oxford University Press, 2008), 60–61.

was a practical man who knew how to win the princes and nobles of the north to his cause—money talks, then as now. In a letter of November 17, 1207, Innocent III appealed to King Philip II of France, complaining of what he called "[t]he age-old seduction of wicked heresy, which is constantly sprouting in the regions of Toulouse",[29] and promising both "remission of sins" for the crusaders and the confiscation "of all the goods of the heretics themselves".[30] The offer was clear: go to war in the south, clear out the heretics, and your reward will be their lands and possessions, with no need to worry about sin in the process. At Béziers, when the papal legate Arnaud Amaury was asked by the Crusaders how they would be able to tell heretics from the orthodox, he told them not to worry about it:

> Those who realized that Catholics and heretics were mixed together, said to the Abbot: "What shall we do, my lord? We can not discern between the good and the evil". Both the Abbot and the rest feared the heretics would pretend to be Catholics, from fear of death, and afterwards return again to their perfidy; so he is reported to have said: "Kill them. For the Lord knows who are his".[31]

According to Guilhem de Tudela, one of two early thirteenth-century authors of the *Cansó de la croisada*, or *Song of the Crusade*, the slaughter was meant to terrorize the entire region into submission to both the Church and the French King in Paris:

> Le barnatges de Fransa e sels devas Paris
> E li clerc e li laic li princeps els marchis
> E li un e li autre an entre lor empris
> Que a calque castel en que la o'st venguis
> Que nos volguessan redre entro que lost les prezis

---

29 Catherine Léglu, Rebecca Rist, and Claire Taylor, eds. *The Cathars and The Albigensian Crusade: A Sourcebook* (New York: Routledge, 2014), 64.
30 *Ibid.*, 65.
31 Cognoscentes ex confessionibus illorum catholicos cum haereticis esse permixtos, dixerunt Abbati: Quid faciemus, domine? Non possumus discenere inter bonos et malos. Timens tam Abbas quam reliqui, ne tantum timore mortis se catholicos simularent, et post ipsorum abcessum iterum ad perfidiam redirent, fertur dixisse: Caedite eos. Novit enim Dominus qui sunt eius.

(Caesarii Heisterbacences. *Dialogus Miraculorum*, ed. by Josephus Strange, 2 Vols. [Cologne: H. Lempertz & Co., 1851], 1, 302), https://archive.org/stream/caesariiheister00stragoog#page/n318

> Quaneson a la espaza e quom les aucezis
> E pois no trobarian qui vas lor se tenguis
> Per paor que aurian e per so cauran vist
> [...]
> Perso son a Bezers destruit e a mal mis
> Que trastotz los aucisdron no lor podo far pis
> E totz sels aucizian quel mostier se son mis
> Que nols pot gandir crotz autar ni cruzifis
> E los clercs aucizian li fols ribautz mendics
> E femnas e efans canc no cug us nichis
> Dieus recepia las armas sil platz en paradis
> Canc mais tan fera mort del temps Sarrazinis.[32]

> The lords of France and those of Paris
> And the clerics and princes and marquises
> And all others employed between them
> Were of the same mind: a castle whose owner
> Would not surrender to the gathered forces
> Should be put to the sword, even the animals.
> And then they would find no others to resist them,
> For fear of what had already been seen.
> [...]
> This is why those of Béziers were destroyed,
> For it was the most evil that could be done.
> And they killed all who fled into the church,
> No cross, nor altar, nor crucifix saved them,
> And the madmen killed the clerks like beasts,
> And women and children, I think none survived.
> May God please to take them in his arms to heaven:
> Such death has not been known since Saracen times.

Such slaughter often goes by the name of genocide today. The contemporary chronicler Peter of Vaux-de-Cernay defends and even celebrates the near-extermination by claiming that the population was consumed by "heretical depravity which infected the citizens of Béziers, who are not only heretics, but also robbers, lawbreakers, adulterers,

---

32 Guilhem de Tudela and Anonymous. *Historie de la Croisade contre les Hérétiques Alibgeois*, ed. by M. C. Fauriel (Paris: Imprimerie Royale, 1837), ll. 481–88, 492–99, https://archive.org/stream/histoiredelacroi00guil#page/36

and thieves, all of the worst sort, filled with every kind of sin".[33] After noting that nearly all of these "heretics" had been killed, Peter revels in the fact that "the city was captured on what is often called the feast day of Saint Mary Magdalene",[34] calling the timing of the mass murder of the men, women, and children of Béziers "a just measure of divine dispensation".[35]

Reports of the numbers of dead differ widely. "The Song does not give a number; William of Puylaurens simply and starkly says 'many thousands'; Peter of Vaux de Cernay claims '7,000' were killed in the church of St Mary Magdalene; in a letter to Rome the legates wrote that 'none was spared' and that 'almost 20,000' were put to the sword. William the Breton heard that 60,000 perished; others take it up to 100,000".[36] Estimates of the total number of dead in the years from 1209–1229 range from 200,000[37] to 1,000,000 or more.[38]

Such a massacre changes a world, and the southern region of Occitania, the land of *langue d'oc*, would never again be the same: "Béziers introduced the people of Occitania to the high stakes they faced. These included inevitable punishment, if not execution, for recalcitrant Cathars, changes in religious practices for those afraid to die for their beliefs, and political domination from the outside even for those who had always remained faithful to the church".[39] Those who had participated—and continued to participate—in the ongoing slaughter were rewarded: "On 24 June 1213, in a field outside the walls of Castelnaudary, between Toulouse and Carcassonne, Amaury of

---

33 "hereticae, pravitatis infecta nec solú haeretici cives Biterrenses, sed erant raptores iniusti, adulteri, latrones pessimi, pleni omni genere peccatorum" (Pierre de Vaux-Cernay. *Historia Albigensium et sacri belli in eos anno MCCIX* [Trecis: Venundantur Parisiis, Apud N. Rousset, 1617], 42). One detects the faintest hint of the *fin'amor* ethos of the troubadours in the reference to "adulterers", https://archive.org/stream/historiaalbigens00pier#page/n73
34 "Fuit autem capta civitas saepe dicta in festo S. Mariae Magdalenai" (*ibid.*, 44, https://archive.org/stream/historiaalbigens00pier#page/n75).
35 "justissima divinae dispensationis mensura" (*ibid.*).
36 McGlynn, 61.
37 Stephen Pinker. *The Better Angels of Our Nature: Why Violence has Declined* (New York: Viking, 2011), 141.
38 Michael C. Thomsett. *Heresy in the Roman Catholic Church: A History* (Jefferson: McFarland Publishers, 2011), 3.
39 Laurence W. Marvin. *The Occitan War: A Military and Political History of the Albigensian Crusade, 1209–1218* (Cambridge: Cambridge University Press, 2008), 45.

Montfort was knighted by Bishop Manasses of Orléans".[40] The close relationship between the crusaders and the Church, the military and theological powers of the day, is made evident in this gesture. Under a cloak of sanctity, the Church had its way by force of bloody arms. Four years before the ceremony, Simon de Montfort, Amaury's father, had been made the commander of the forces that would carry out the Albigensian Crusade. In order to be safe from any and all criticism for the slaughters, Simon urged the bishop to dub his son, Amaury, a knight of Christ. The father-son duo fully dedicated itself to Innocent III's vision of "sacred" violence, using bloodshed to restore the power of the Church in Occitania: "The Castelnaudary ceremony […] represented […] the rededication of the Montfort clan to Pope Innocent III's vision of holy violence by creating almost a fresh category of knight, dedicated to Christ's war yet without the religious vows of the military orders".[41] It was as much a political as an economic move, and the sanctifying of the knights meant one thing in particular:

> [It] emphasized the sanction of orthodox religion in the exercise of political authority, a crude identification of church and secular power that disconcerted the bishop of Orléans. Castelnaudary showed how Simon specifically identified his and his family's mission as holy. The primacy of the anti-heretical message that had inspired Innocent III to call for a crusade in 1208–9 was increasingly drowned out by the secular implications of Simon's conquests: the political reorganization of Languedoc.[42]

The brutal massacres of the Albigensian Crusade destroyed the once-optimistic and humanistic culture of Occitania, and "[r]epression now was the spirit of the age".[43] The Crusade granted new lands and wealth to the northern French nobility, who along with the Church, made sure that much of what remained of a vibrant culture in the south was rooted out over the next century. The Inquisition was established in 1229 precisely in order to ensure that heresy would be found wherever it was hiding, with confessions extracted and "heretics" burned, an effort

---

40 Christopher Tyerman. *God's War: A New History of the Crusades* (Cambridge, MA: Belknap Press of Harvard University Press, 2006), 563.
41 Ibid.
42 Ibid., 566.
43 Boyle, 284.

to enforce theological and political conformity that began with the slaughter at Béziers which Innocent III blandly referred to as *negotium pacis et fidei*,[44] a "business of peace and the faith" that looks like genocide:

> The pope argued that all peaceful efforts of the Church had failed because of the obstinacy of the heretics, and that only armed action could help to resolve the situation. This official "reconstruction" [...] aimed to impose the idea of the crusade as a *final solution*.[45]

It is difficult to pinpoint one cause of the atrocities that began in 1209, as there is no single factor that can be isolated. The troubadours and the Cathars, each in their different ways, contributed to what might be called a twelfth-century Renaissance, the ideals of which did not necessarily serve the interests of numerous powerful players in the region. Territorial greed, the ambitions of the northern French nobility, the blossoming of the Cathars and their independence, all played a role in triggering the Albigensian Crusade. Even the *Cansó de la croisada* takes two different points of view. The poem has two authors, one anonymous and one Guilhem de Tudela, and consists of two parts. Guilhem is eager to condemn heresy, and his verse energetically denounces the heretical sects in the south of France. In his accounts of Simon de Montfort's pillaging of the town of Lavaur, Guilhem often tries to depict de Montfort as a courteous and gentle knight, perfoming the most praiseworthy of deeds:

> Oi Dieus dizon trastuil dama santa Maria
> Co a fait gran proeza e granda cortezia![46]

> "Oh God, and our holy lady Mary,
> What a deed of great prowess and grand courtesy!"

---

44 Pierre de Vaux-Cernay, 296, https://archive.org/stream/historiaalbigens00pier#page/n327
45 "Le pape soutint que tous les efforts pacifiques de l'Église avaient échoué à cause de la pertinacia des hérétiques, et que seule une action armée pouvait permettre de résoudre la situation. Cette reconstruction officielle [...] visait à imposer l'idée de la croisade comme *extrema ratio*" (Marco Meschini. "'Smoking sword': le meurtre du legat Pierre de Castelnau et la premiere croisade albigeoise". In Michel Balard, ed. *La Papauté et les Croisades* [Farnham: Ashgate, 2011], 72).
46 Guilhem de Tudela and Anonymous. *Historie de la Croisade contre les Hérétiques Alibgeois*, ll. 1499–1500, https://archive.org/stream/histoiredelacroi00guil#page/108

But what underlines Guilhem's support for de Montfort and the crusaders is a powerfully authoritarian ideal:

> Lai doncas fo laor faita aitant grans mortaldat
> Quentro la fm del mon cug quen sia parlat
> Senhor be sen devrian ilh estre castiat
> Que so vi e auzi e son trop malaurat
> Car no fan so quels mando li clerc e li Crozad.[47]

> Then there was so great a mortal slaughter
> I believe it will be talked of to the world's end.
> My lords, it is right they should be chastised,
> For, unfortunately, as I have seen and heard,
> They refuse obedience to the clerks and crusaders.

The anonymous author, however, deplores the bloodthirsty attitudes of the crusaders and sides with the southerners. This author provides more dialogue and information from the other side, but most importantly, a certain sympathy for those who have chosen to live how their hearts desired, combined with a caustic cynicism toward the crusaders and the Church, whom he describes as having "shamed and disgraced Christianity".[48] One cleric, Folquet de Marselha—himself a former troubadour[49]—comes in for especially sharp criticism:

> E dic vos de lavesque que tant nes afortitz
> Quen la sua semblansa es Dieus e nos trazitz
> Quab cansos messongeiras e ab motz coladitz
> Dont totz hom es perdutz quels canta ni os ditz
> Ez ab sos reproverbis afdatz e forbitz
> Ez ab los nostres dos don fo enjotglaritz

---

47 *Ibid.*, ll. 1566–70, https://archive.org/stream/histoiredelacroi00guil#page/112
48 "totz crestianesmes aonitz abassatz" (*ibid.*, l. 2933, https://archive.org/stream/histoiredelacroi00guil#page/210).
49 This former troubadour understood the non-spiritual nature of *fin'amor*: he "displayed his awareness of the distinction between the kind of love he portrayed as *fin'amor*, and the spiritual love appropriate to religious sentiments, by doing penance whenever he heard the love songs he had written" (Nicole M. Schulman. *Where Troubadours Were Bishops* [London: Routledge, 2001], 18).

> Ez ab mala doctrina es tant fort enriquitz
> Com non auza ren diire a so quel contraditz.⁵⁰

> And of this bishop, so full of his own righteousness,
> He with his false-seeming betrayed God and us,
> With his chants and his smoothly-polished lies,
> And his songs, the damnation of any who sing them.
> And by his powerfully sharp and slick reproofs,
> And by our gifts whereby he lived like a celebrity,
> And by his evil doctrines, he has risen so high,
> That no one dares say anything to contradict him.

The author depicts the crusaders' opponent, Raymond VI, the count of Toulouse, in a notably positive light:

> Que sieu ai enemics ni mals ni orgulhos
> Si degus mes laupart eu li serei leos.⁵¹

> I defy the strongest and most wicked enemies,
> and I will be like a lion or a leopard unto them.

But the same author has withering contempt for the crusaders' leader, Simon de Monfort:

> Si per homes aucirre ni per sanc espandir,
> Ni per esperitz perdre ni per mortz cosentir,
> E per mals cosselhs creire, e per focs abrandir,
> E per baros destruire, e per Paratge aunir,
> E per Las terras toldre, e per Orgilh suffrir,
> E per los mals escendre, e pel[s] bes escantir,
> E per donas aucirre e per efans delire,
> Pot hom en aquest segle Jhesu Crist comquerir,
> El deu porta corona e el cel resplandir!⁵²

---

50 Guilhem de Tudela and Anonymous, ll. 3309–16, https://archive.org/stream/histoiredelacroi00guil#page/234
51 Ibid., ll. 3809–10, https://archive.org/stream/histoiredelacroi00guil#page/268
52 Ibid., ll. 8685–96, https://archive.org/stream/histoiredelacroi00guil#page/586

> If by killing men and spilling their blood,
> Or by wasting their souls and preaching murder,
> And by following evil counsel, and setting fires,
> And by destroying barons, and dishonoring *Paratge*,
> And by stealing lands and exalting pride,
> And by praising evil and scanting good,
> And by massacring women and their children,
> A man can win Jesus Christ in this world,
> Then he surely wears a splendid crown in heaven.

The decades-long crusade altered the course of the European world. But for our purposes, the most dramatic change brought about by Béziers and all the massacres that followed affected the poetry of the thirteenth century. No longer were poets free to flout the morality of the Church without trepidation. Fear now dominated the land, and in turn, the minds and hearts of those who would write of love. Decades after the Albigensian Crusade, poetry had lost its sensual edge, and repression had triumphed: "A manuscript of *trouvère* music in the British Library, dating from the middle of the thirteenth century, includes the songs of Blondel and his contemporaries, but some of the words have been scrubbed out and replaced with religious ones".[53] As the Church moved against heresy, poetry was immediately put under tighter controls: "The Papal Legate made noble knights swear never again to compose verses".[54] From now on, verse was to conform to the demands of Church orthodoxy, as evidenced by the example of the prior of Villemeir, "a zealous Dominican" who "published a theological poem addressed to recalcitrant poets, in which the truths of each article of faith [were] reinforced"[55] by the use of an ominous and repeated formula: "If you refuse to believe this, turn your eyes to the flames in which your companions are roasting. Answer forthwith, in one word or two; either you will burn in that fire or you will join us".[56] Given the sudden and violent changes brought by the crusaders, "[t]hese forcible arguments did not fail in their appeal. In the minds of the poets, inspired by holy

---

53 Boyle, 288.
54 Briffault, 148.
55 *Ibid.*
56 *Ibid.*, 149.

terror, they speeded with marvelous effect the transformation in their 'conception of love'".⁵⁷

The slaughter at Béziers changed everything: "Corpses fouled rivers. [...] Skulls were crushed. Murder was a path to redemption. Vines and fields were devastated. [...] Good men became heretics. [...] Heretics dangled from walnut trees. Very few who began the war lasted to the end. The world was changed forever".⁵⁸ As the world changed, so did poetry: "the activity of a few poets of Languedoc continued for a while on a much reduced scale, and in a form almost unrecognizable [...]. Prior to that date, nothing is to be found in the poetry of the troubadours that suggests a platonic idealization of passion".⁵⁹ After the violent destruction of Occitanian culture, troubadour poetry—what little was left of it—became a tool of Church-mandated morality. In so doing, the poetry all but died: "[t]he change took place in the corruption and dissolution of the grave".⁶⁰

The effects of this change can be seen in the work of Guilhem Montanhagol, who worked sometime between 1233 and 1268, during the time in which the Inquisition was established to finish the job the Albigensian Crusade had started. Montanhagol's poetry is a kind of adaptation-as-appeasement, reacting to the Inquisition's condemnation of *fin'amor* by recasting love in more "acceptable" terms:

> It is not only love, but the entirety of courtly life that Montanhagol's poems show us being transformed. The new doctrine of love is indeed a form of change in the spirit of the times. We cannot explain one without the other. They are the consequence of the domination of religious power. The theory of chaste love, as the new ideal of life, was born of a moral and religious idea. [...] This Provençal poetry, which is soon to succumb to the enmity of the clergy, first seems to have tried to disarm its opponent. Accused of immorality and prosecuted as an accomplice of heresy, it tries to comply with the moral orthodoxy of Christianity in order to survive. This is an interesting attempt and one of the most curious periods in the history of Provençal poetry.⁶¹

---

57 Ibid.
58 Pegg, 191.
59 Briffault, 104.
60 Ibid., 128.
61 Ce n'est donc pas seulement l'amour, mais la vie courtoise tout entière que les poésies de Montanhagol nous montrent transformée. La nouvelle doctrine de l'amour n'est à vrai dire qu'une forme du changement survenu dans l'esprit du temps. On ne peut l'expliquer l'une sans

Perhaps Montanhagol's most famous line is from his *canso* entitled *Ar ab lo coinde pascor*.[62] In this work, his claim is that "chastity comes from love", "d'amor mou castitatz" (l.18). This is a far cry from the earlier Guilhem IX, for whom *amor* led to anything but *castitatz*. But times have changed for Montanhagol, and the idea of love portrayed in the poetry of the thirteenth century has changed with them. This was a necessary transformation, if poetry was to survive:

> In reality, this transformation [...] was primarily from necessity; in order that love songs could survive, they had to accommodate themselves to the requirements of religious power. The troubadours now had to sing of a love consistent with Christian morality, rejecting evil desires for the essence of virtue and chastity.[63]

With poetry no longer free to celebrate *fin'amor*, Platonic love became the refuge to which new and conformist poets quickly learned to fly: "[t]he principles governing this remarkable reform are set forth in [...] the *Brevaries of Love*, by Master Matfré Ermengaud. The excellence of platonic love is therein demonstrated [and] supported with quotations drawn from the troubadours".[64] So old is the tradition of making the troubadours say what they do not say, and so old are the clearly identifiable and repressive purposes for doing so. Matfré's late-thirteenth-century work is an "encyclopedia describing the universe

---

l'autre. Elles sont la conséquence de la domination du pouvoir religieux. La théorie de l'amour chaste, comme le nouvel idéal de la vie, est née d'une idée morale et religieuse. [...] Cette poésie provençale, qui doit bientôt succomber sous l'inimitié du clergé, semble d'abord s'être efforcée de désarmer son adversaire. Accusée d'immoralité & poursuivie comme complice de l'hérésie, elle veut se conformer à l'orthodoxie & à la morale chrétiennes afin de conserver le droit de vivre. C'est une tentative intéressante & une des périodes les plus curieuses de l'histoire de la poésie provençale.

Jules Coulet, in Guilhem Montanhagol, *Le troubadour Guilhem Montanhagol*, ed. by Jules Coulet [Toulouse: Imprimerie et Librairie Édouard Privat, 1898], 54–55, 57, https://archive.org/stream/letroubadourguil00guil#page/54

62 *Ibid.*, 69–75, https://archive.org/stream/letroubadourguil00guil#page/70

63 En réalité, cette transformation [...] était avant tout une nécessité ; pour que la chanson d'amour pût vivre, il fallait qu'elle s'accommodât aux exigences du pouvoir religieux. Les troubadours ne pouvaient désormais chanter qu'un amour conforme à la morale chrétienne, ignorant des désirs mauvais & par essence vertueux chaste.

Ibid., 52, https://archive.org/stream/letroubadourguil00guil#page/52

64 Briffault, 151.

as emanating from God's love",⁶⁵ a nearly thirty-five-thousand-verse poem which "surveys the natural and moral orders and concludes with an exhortation to human marital love",⁶⁶ precisely the opposite of that *fin'amor* celebrated by the troubadours. Even more interesting, however, is the critical impulse behind Matfré's writing:

> He claims to be writing at the request of his fellow troubadours in order to expound what is worthwhile (and what reprehensible) in the poetry of *fin'amors*. [...] Sexuality, we are taught, has its place in human behavior so long as it is morally vitruous and oriented toward reproduction.⁶⁷

Matfré makes this emphasis clear, arguing that the highest forms of *amor* must be redirected from earth to the heavens:

> Si tôt nol connoisson lh'enfan,
> Mas ges en quascun home gran,
> Quez a de Dieu conoissensa,
> Non habita, ses falhensa,
> Si non l'ama d'aquel amor
> Qu'om deu amar son creator,
> Quar non habita mas els bos.⁶⁸

> An infant does not understand everything,
> But not so the noble man
> Who knows God:
> It is not life, but disloyalty,
> Nor is it true love, this love of women,
> For a man owes love to his creator,
> If he would live, not in evil, but in goodness.

For Matfré, *fin'amor* must be "chaste", and "prefer wisdom to the folly of the world", and "defend and praise ladies".⁶⁹ But, as must be painfully

---

65 Sarah Kay. *Parrots and Nightingales: Troubadour Quotations and the Development of European Poetry* (Philadelphia: University of Pennsylvania Press, 2013), 5.
66 Sarah Kay. *The Place of Thought: The Complexity of One in Late Medieval French Didactic Poetry* (Philadelphia: University of Pennsylvania Press, 2007), 23.
67 Ibid., 24.
68 Matfré Ermengaud. *Le Breviari d'Amor*, ed. by Gabriel Azaïs (Béziers: Secrétariat de la Société archéologique, scientifigue et littéraire de Béziers, 1862), ll. 1657–63, https://archive.org/stream/lebreviaridamor01ermeuoft#page/63
69 Sarah Kay, *The Place of Thought*, 33.

evident at this point, Matfré's notion of *fin'amor* is radically different from, even directly opposed to those of Guilhem IX, or Bernart de Ventadorn, or the Comtessa de Dia. For Matfré, the Holy Spirit "is the source and root of love".[70] Here we see the origins of the sublimated (and un-troubadour-like) version of love that Gaston Paris will come to define as "courtly" in the nineteenth century. When William Reddy describes the troubadours' "dissent against the Gregorian Reform doctrine that all sexual behavior [...] longing, [and] pleasure was bound up with the realm of sin"[71] he is right about the erotic dissent, but wrong to describe it as "courtly love". Especially as defined and used since Paris, that deliberately misleading term has been part of a rearguard action meant to declaw and domesticate the love the troubadours called *fin'amor* by deemphasizing its physical and illicit aspects, in order to "channel, reformulate, and control" desire.[72] This imperative can already be seen in the work of a thirteenth-century cleric who was determined, at the behest of a demonstrably violent and authoritarian Church, to rewrite troubadour poetry into a demure and acceptably Christian form, reflecting the belief that "only God is, and nothing else is",[73] that all things have their existence through God, and that all love is love of God. Matfré even claims authority for this rewriting of the troubadours by describing himself as a truer lover than any who have written, or been written about, before:

> [Doncx] pueis la natura d'amor
> Sabon li veray amador,
> Ne dey hien saber tot quan n'es,
> Quar plus fis aymans non veg ges,
> Ni fo anc plus fis en amor

---

70 "es d'amor fons e razitz" (Matfré Ermengaud, ll. 659–60, https://archive.org/stream/lebreviaridamor01ermeuoft#page/28).
71 Reddy, 106.
72 The effects of this can be seen in Reddy's insistence on reading *fin'amor* as something that somehow transcends "mere" desire: "Fin'amors, in its most developed form, combined [...] sublimity, patience, and loyalty [...] and the satisfactions it offered were a "hundredfold" greater than the satisfaction of mere desire" (162). With "sublimity", and its superiority to "mere desire", we enter the territory of Matfré Ermengaud and Gaston Paris, an over seven-century-long tradition of rewriting the troubadours.
73 "Sol Dieus es e non es res als" (Matfré Ermengaud, l. 1373, https://archive.org/stream/lebreviaridamor01ermeuoft#page/53).

> De me Floris am Blanca flor
> Ni Tisbes anc ni Piramus
> Ni Serena ni Elidus,
> Alion ni Filomena
> Ni Paris ni Elena
> Ni l bel' [Ise]uts ni Tristans.[74]

> Therefore, since the nature of love
> is known by true lovers,
> None should know everything better than me,
> For there is no lover alive,
> Who was ever truer in love
> Than me, neither Floris nor Blancheflor,
> Neither Thisbe nor Piramus,
> Neither Serena nor Elidus,
> Not even Filomena
> Or Paris, or Helen,
> Or beautiful Isolde, or Tristan.

Just in case there is any doubt about the extent and intensity of the priestly attitudes toward love and the status of women in the new world, in which the troubadours have been turned into the mouthpieces of Catholic orthodoxy, Matfré explains:

> Cert es qu'a luy la port naelhor;
> E qui Dieu per bes temporals
> Ama, l'amor non es corals
> Ni veraia ni certana,
> Ans es amors de putana.[75]

> Certain it is that he whose end is women;
> Who for God has but a temporal
> Love, whose love is not of the heart,
> Neither true nor certain,
> Follows after the love of whores.

---

74 *Ibid.*, ll. 27833–43, https://archive.org/stream/lebreviaridamor02ermeuoft#page/431
75 *Ibid.*, ll. 9330–34, https://archive.org/stream/lebreviaridamor01ermeuoft#page/318

From Bernart de Ventadorn, even from Guilhem IX, this is a fall from the heights of joy and sensuality into the depths of pious wickedness. Though he is writing decades after the violence of the Albigensian Crusade, the shadow of orthodoxy's war on heresy further darkens Matfré's verse beyond his frequent expressions of misogyny, increasing the disdain with which he regards those who would cling too tightly to the "sins" of life, love, and independently-chosen faith that the Crusade had attempted to destroy in the south:

> Writing in the third quarter of the thirteenth century in Languedoc, Matfre is surrounded by the continuing battles with heterodoxy and in particular with Cathar heresy. Matfre himself is a native of Béziers, which was the first city taken during the Albigensian crusade. [...] As a result, the *Breviari* reflects the contemporary anxiety of the thirteenth-century Church concerning widespread heterodoxy, particularly in southern France.[76]

Matfré regarded the troubadours as having been all too often the unwitting servants of the devil himself: "Satan [...] in his desire to make men suffer, inspires them with an idolatrous love for women. Instead of adoring their Creator [...] they entertain guilty passions for women, whom they transform into divinities".[77] Ironically, however, the latter part of Matfré's pious accusation can serve as a nearly-perfect description of exactly the path that love poetry will follow as it moves into its later French, Italian, and English incarnations, as women are removed from their bodies, denied their sexuality, idolized, dehumanized, and turned into goddesses of light and air.[78]

---

76 Michelle Bolduc. "The Breviari d'Amor: Rhetoric and Preaching in Thirteenth-Century Languedoc". *Rhetorica: A Journal of the History of Rhetoric*, 24: 4 (Autumn 2006), 419.

77 Briffault, 151.

78 The tendency in northern French poetry to portray women as idealized saints is traceable all the way back to the ninth century, though it comes to full flower in the thirteenth century. The ninth-century poem *Séquence de sainte Eulalie* tells the story of "a young Spanish maiden who was tortured and burned to death in Merida around the year 304", while it "exalts death by martyrdom as the ultimate Christian achievement" (Brigitte Cazelles. *The Lady as Saint* [University Park: University of Pennsylvannia Press, 1991], 27). There is something more than faintly pornographic about the narrative, as Eulalia's death puts her in the role of "a powerless victim whose death engenders life" for others (29), even as the poem makes note of her budding sexuality:

II
Post-*Fin'amor* French Poetry: The *Roman de la Rose*

This process, as well as hints of resistance to the process, can be seen in the thirteenth-century French poem *Roman de la Rose*. The *Roman* is the work of two authors, Guillaume de Lorris and Jean de Meun, whose writing styles are radically different, but whose attitudes towards love and its sublimation into worship have more in common than might initially appear. Their collaboration, although they were separated by decades and by death, produced the dream vision of a young man, Lover (*Amant*), who falls in love with a rosebud, Rose. In the dream, Lover wanders into a garden where he meets the God of Love (*Li dex d'Amors*), who shoots Lover with an arrow, subjecting him to great pain and suffering. At the same time, Lover sees and falls hopelessly in love with Rose, though he is kept at a distance from her by various characters, Resistance (*Dangier*), Shame (*Honte*), Jealousy (*Jalousie*), Fair Welcoming (*Bel Acueil*), and Chastity (*Chasteé*), among others. Lover does not want to give up on Rose, and as he pursues his desire, many other characters, including Venus and Reason (*Reson*) try to help, giving him different, and often contradictory advice. After much suffering,

---

> Buona pulcella fut eulalia.
> Bel auret corps bellezour anima
> Voldrent la ueintre li deo Inimi.
> Voldrent la faire diaule seruir
> […]
> Melz sostendreiet les empedementz
> Qu'elle perdesse sa virginitét.
>
> Eulalia was a good girl.
> She had a beautiful body, a more beautiful soul.
> They would force her will, the enemies of God.
> They would force her will to serve the devil.
> […]
> But she would rather endure prison and torture
> Than lose her virginity.

Léopold Eugène Constans. "Séquence de Sainte Eulalie". In *Chrestomathie de l'ancien français (IXe-XVe siécles)* (Paris and Leipzig: H. Welter, 1906), 28–29, ll. 1–4, 16–17), https://archive.org/stream/chrestomathiede00cons#page/28
    The poem treats Eulalia's subsequent burning and beheading as a substitute for sexuality, as an even more intense version of *le petit mort*, subjecting the girl's "beautiful body" to the sensations of burning flames rather than burning passion, with *le gran mort* as the climax, emphasizing what Cazelles refers to as "an ultimate exposure of the female body" (81), in service of "the traditionally sacrificial interpretation of female holiness" (83).

persuasion, and confusion, Lover finally possesses Rose. Much more than telling a simple story of desire, however, the poem creates a space within which both authors argue for love and condemn the Church and its violence to tell the story of *fin'amor*, its forceful sublimation, and the nostalgic urge to return to the days of "pure love". Ultimately, the goal of the poem is for "Lover to be successful in [his] defeat of Christian and courtly morality".[79]

A more conservative view of the *Roman* and its depictions of love suggests that "Lover's desire for the rose is the classic form of cupidity, a love of an earthly object for its own sake rather than for the sake of God".[80] Here, Charles Dahlberg expresses the doctrine of the thirteenth-century Church, which insisted that all love, properly channeled, was love of God. However, this is precisely the position we have already seen rejected by Héloïse d'Argenteuil, who references Cicero, not the Bible or any Christian thinker, in support of her view that love is both *of* and *for* the beloved, without reference to God: "How can friendship be possible, or who can be a friend to anyone, who does not love him for himself?"[81] The *Roman* hinges principally on these opposing views of love: love for the sake of God, or love for the sake of the beloved. This opposition controls the poem's development, and the way the poem shows love manifesting in different forms is its way of dealing with the transition from the *fin'amor* ethos present in the work of the troubadours to the Christianized form of love that comes to dominate post-Albigensian-Crusade poetry.

Guillaume de Lorris begins the poem with a cautionary statement about dreams seeming deceitful at first, solely because of the fact that they are dreams. However, Lover, who tells the story, asserts that dreams should be taken seriously, because Macrobius, a Roman philosopher from the fifth century, "did not think dreams at all deceitful".[82] Despite

---

79 Christine McWebb. "Hermeneutics of Irony: Lady Reason and the *Romance of the Rose*". *Dalhousie French Studies*, 69 (Winter 2004), 3–13, 411.
80 Guillaume de Lorris and Jean de Meun. *The Romance of the Rose*. Trans. and ed. by Charles Dahlberg. 3rd ed. (Princeton: Princeton University Press, 1971), 15.
81 "Amicitiae vero locus ubi esse potest aut quis amicus esse cuiquam, quem non ipsum amet propter ipsum?" Cicero. *De Finibus Bonorum et Malorum*. In Cicero, *On Ends*, ed. by H. Rackham (Loeb Classical Library, Cambridge, MA: Harvard University Press, 1914), 2.78, 168.
82 "ne tine pas songes a lobes" (Guillaume de Lorris and Jean de Meun. *Le Roman de la Rose*. 3 vols, ed. by Felix Lecoy [Paris: Honoré Champion, 1965], Vol. 1, l. 8).

the disbelief of others, Lover maintains that "most men dream at night / many hidden things / which later may be seen openly".[83]

Similar to the famous opening of the *Canterbury Tales*, the dream vision of the *Roman* begins with the description of spring when Lover, "in joyful May, so I dreamed, / the amorous time, full of joy",[84] wanders alone and enjoys the delights of nature. In poetry, such images of springtime have long been associated with rebirth, sex, and a time when "the trees recover their green".[85] Similarly, there are certain words that have become "code" for recognizing certain authors and their themes. We associate the word "pandemonium" with Milton, "prick" with Shakespeare, and so on. The word that appears frequently in both sections of the *Roman* is the word "joy". The relation to the work of the troubadours is immediately evident—if one opens a book of troubadour poetry to nearly any page, the word joy will appear. Sensual like the lyrics of the troubadours, the *Roman* has the perfume of *fin'amor*, disguised within a dream vision. Heather M. Arden, in her explication of the *Roman*, notes the connection between the poem and the troubadours, though with some diffidence:

> This new view of love had gone through three stages by the time it reached Guillaume de Lorris. It began at the end of the eleventh century in southern France and was expressed in the songs of the troubadours. [...] Several important themes in courtly songs recur in the first part of the Rose. The main theme of the songs is the lover's simultaneous feelings of great joy and great suffering.[86]

Arden's move is one often made in criticism of the troubadours. To assume that the troubadour poems were "courtly" is to assume that their songs had the characteristics of the later invention called "courtly love". But this is a typical, and, one begins to suspect, deliberate confusion, for *fin'amor* is highly sexual and earthly, while "courtly love" is spiritualized, sublimated, and censored.[87]

---

83 "li plusors songent de nuitz / Maintes choses couvertement / Que l'en voit puis apertement" (*ibid.*, ll. 18–20).
84 "qu'en may estoie, ce sonjoie, / el tens enmoreus, plain de joie" (*ibid.*, ll. 47–48).
85 "Li bois recueverent lor vedure" (*ibid.*, l.53).
86 Heather M. Arden. *The Romance of the Rose* (Boston: Twayne Publishers, 1987), 22.
87 This censored quality can be seen even in the love-making scene in Chrétien's *La Chevalier de la Charrette* (the romance upon which Gaston Paris constructed his idea

6. *The Death of Fin'amor in Medieval French and English Poetry* 241

Meister des Rosenromans, Dancing before the genius of love,
in *Roman de la Rose* (ca. 1420–1430).[88]

Writers often use their villains to assert certain inconvenient truths. Milton does this with his Satan; Shakespeare does this with his Edmund, and Guillaume de Lorris and Jean de Meun do this with a number of their characters. What can be confusing about the the *Roman*, however, is the fact that criticisms about a wide variety of things come from every character and even from the narration; the reader is left to decide what is "trifling" and what is truth. One common thread is hypocrisy, which is underscored in both sections of the poem, and often revisited directly or indirectly. Lover walks through the garden and sees a wall covered with images. He describes each one carefully, and when he gets to the image of Hypocrisy (*Papelardie*), he gives a particularly cutting description:

> C'est cele qui en reclee,
> quant nus ne s'en puet peure garde,
> de nul man fere n'est coarde;
> et fet dehors le marmiteus,

of *amor courtois*), where Chrétien slyly suggests, but will not speak of, the joys of Lancelot and Guinevere.

88 https://commons.wikimedia.org/wiki/File:Meister_des_Rosenromans_001.jpg

> s'a ele vis simple et pietus
> et semble seinte creature.[89]
>
> It is she who, in private,
> when no one can see her,
> of no evil-doing is afraid;
> In public faith she is an apostle,
> her face is simple and pious
> and she resembles a saintly creature.

This is an obvious criticism of the Church and its hypocritical repression of love and sexuality, clothed with terms like "pietus" and "semble",[90] and in this section of the *Roman*, it is not difficult to see a number of pointedly pro-*fin'amor* allusions being made. The songbirds that Lover admires during his walk sings of "les dances d'amors".[91] The description of "a girl / who was both gentle and beautiful"[92] whom Lover meets is not a "courtly" account; her "flesh more tender than a chick's"[93] is depicted in great detail. Lover tells his readers, "into a small gap / I entered where Delight [or Diversion] was",[94] where he meets another lady, named Joy, who has a "voice clear and pure".[95] Not only is the entire troubadour frame of reference in place here, but Lover even seems to see the troubadours, as he views the part of the garden where there are "flutists / and minstrels and jongleurs".[96] The perfect or "pure" garden of these loving singers, as the story shows, goes through a major change. Not only does the poem allude to the troubadours (in the references to "minstrels and jongleurs"), but also to the trobairitz, as "many ladies in the middle danced / and played on tambourines".[97]

However, in the middle of the festivities is a character named Diversion (*Deduiz*) who appears "with great nobility" ("par grant

---

89 Lorris and de Meun (1965), Vol. 1, ll. 408–13.
90 One also catches a whiff here of *pius Aeneas*, who can go toe-to-toe with anyone where hypocrisy is concerned.
91 *Ibid.*, l. 493.
92 "une pucele, / qui estoit assez gente et bele" (*ibid.*, ll. 523–24).
93 "char plus tender que poucins" (*ibid.*, l. 526).
94 "en un reduit / m'en entrai ou Deduiz estoit" (*ibid.*, ll. 716–17).
95 "voiz clere et saine" (*ibid.*, l. 733).
96 "fleüteors / et menestreus et jugleors" (*ibid.*, ll. 745–46).
97 "[m]out i avoit tableteresses / ilec entor et timberesses" (*ibid.*, ll. 751–52).

noblece"),⁹⁸ and the "courtly" sublimation and spiritualized redirection of *fin'amor* is clearly referenced as the "Diversion" that it really is. The moment another character, Courtesy (*Cortoisie*), who "was worthy in any court / to be an empress or queen",⁹⁹ enters the garden, the language shifts, and the scene changes from pleasant songbirds and joy to the "highly ornamented" description of Diversion. The earlier instances of the "flesh" and desire are sublimated to a "dance" and a mere "kiss" where Diversion courts Joy.

After the appearance of the God of Love, love in the *Roman* becomes about suffering. The grief comes from different obstacles, but Arden emphasizes two in particular: "social barriers due to the status of the beloved which is higher than the lover's, or barriers set up by the aloofness or coldness of the lady".¹⁰⁰ As a result, the experience of the lover is one of suffering until he receives the pity of his lady. In the *Roman*, pity becomes the key that will open the prison in which Lover finds himself, just as the character Pity softens up Resistance who guides and protects the Rose. Arden notes that the "rules guide the lover in his relations with others and with the beloved in particular, they condemn certain vices [...] and urge certain virtues".¹⁰¹ The "courtly lover" is imprisoned by a set of clearly-defined and rigidly-enforced codes, while "love" is a matter of regulated and controlled behaviors prescribed for anyone in the scripted role of "the lover" to follow. In the *Roman*, the God of Love commands Lover as just such a prisoner:

> Vasaus, pris estes, rien n'i a
> de destorner ne de desfendre,
> ne fai pas dangier de toi render.
> Quant plus volentiers te rendras,
> et plus tost a meri vendras.
> Il est fox qui moine dangier
> vers celui que doit losengier
> et qu'il covient a souplier.¹⁰²

---

98   *Ibid.*, l. 760.
99   "ert en totes corz bien dine / d'estre empereriz ou roïne" (*ibid.*, ll. 1241–42).
100 Arden, 22–23.
101 *Ibid.*, 25.
102 Lorris and de Meun (1965), Vol. 1, ll. 1882–89.

> Vassal, you are taken, do not hope
> for escape or defense,
> now faithfully surrender to my power.
> The more willingly you surrender
> the sooner you will have mercy.
> He is a fool who resists my power
> when he should flatter
> and desire to make supplication.

In the *Roman*, the description of the arrows used by the God of Love illustrate authority, but they also invoke images from the Albigensian Crusade and its horrific slaughter, as well as the Church's frequent use of "Bel Samblant" or "Fair Seeming" to achieve its goals:

> La meillor et la plus isnele
> de ces floiches, et la plus bele,
> et cele ou li melor penon
> furent ante, Biautez ot non.
> Une de cles qui plus bleice
> rot non, ce m'est avis, Simpleice.
> Una autre en i ot, apelee
> Franchise: cele iert empanee
> de valor et de cortoisie.
> La quarte avoit non Compaignie:
> en cele ot mout pesant saiete,
> el n'iere pas d'aler loig preste;
> mes qui de pres en vosist traire,
> il em peust assez mal feire.
> La cinquieme ot non Bel Samblant:
> ce fu toute la mains grevant;
> ne por quant el fet mout grant plaie;
> [...].
> .v. floiches i ot d'autre guise,
> qui furent laides a devise;
> li fust estoient et li fer
> plus noir que deables d'enfer.
> La premiere avoit non Orguelz;
> l'autre, qui ne valoit pas melz,
> fu apelee Vilennie:
> cele si fu de felonnie

tote tainte et envenimee;
la tierce fu Honte clamee,
et la quarte Desesperance;
Noviaus Pensers fu sanz doutance
Pelee la derreniere.[103]

The best and most swift
of these arrows, the most beautiful,
and the one with the best feathers
affixed to its tail, was called Beauty.
The one that gave the deepest wounds
was, in my view, Simplicity.
Another one there was, called
Freedom: this one was feathered
with valor and courtesy.
The fourth was called Company:
this arrow had a very heavy point,
it was not ready to fly far;
but if fired from close range,
could cause a terrible wound.
The fifth was named Fair Seeming:
and though of all, his was the least grievous,
nonetheless, it could leave a serious hurt;
[…]
Five arrows of another sort there were,
as ugly as you can imagine;
whose shafts and points were by far
blacker than all the devils of hell.
The first was known as Pride;
the other, which had no more value,
was named Villany:
that one was filled with crimes,
wholly tainted and venomous;
the third called Disgrace,
and the fourth Despair;
New Thought was without doubt
the name of the last.

---

103 Lorris and de Meun (1965), Vol. 1, ll. 935–69.

What the Albigensian Crusade accomplished was to divorce passion from the obedient minds of the faithful, and what was brought forth by the Crusade's horrific violence, was, as Lover says, a "New Thought". Despite Innocent III's hand-wringing about Cathar heresy, the lands and wealth of Occitania were major motivators of the Crusade, and Guillaume de Lorris does not disregard that kind of venality in his verse. In the passages on wealth and its rich purple robe, Lover uses a revealing phrase that alerts a reader to look carefully for a trick: "do not take this as a trick of flattery or deceit".[104] The trick, of course, is a reference to Diversion—the favored technique of a Church that would have its flock believe that human love is sinful, and that slaughter is *negotium pacis et fidei*, "the business of peace and faith".

Even though already well into the time of love's sublimation into piety, Guillaume de Lorris, through the character of Lover, includes vestiges of troubadour sensuality. Referring to Saracens and paganism, Lover describes a lady named Generosity, and finds it delightful that

> la cheveçaille ert overte,
> s'avoit sa gorge descoverte
> si que par outre la chemise
> li blancheoit la char alise"[105]

> her hood and collar were open,
> and her neck revealed
> so that beyond her blouse
> her soft flesh showed its whiteness.

Before being struck by an arrow and "poisoned" with sublimation, for a moment Lover describes couples who sang and danced together. Of them he speaks:

> Dex! Com menoient bone vie!
> Fox est qui n'a de tel envie!
> Qui autel vie avoir porroit,
> de meillor bien se soufreoit,

---

104 "nu tenez ore pas a lobe" (*ibid.*, l. 1052).
105 *Ibid.*, ll. 1169–72.

> qu'il n'est nus graindres paradis
> d'avoir amie a son devis.[106]

> God knows what a wonderful life they led!
> Only fools do not envy them!
> He who might live this way,
> can do without any greater good,
> since there is no grander paradise
> than to be with the love of one's choice.

It almost sounds nostalgic, as if the author is speaking here of something that has been lost, something precious that may already be unrecoverable. In the same yearning tone, the author alludes to the the topography of the south of France:

> Mes mout rembelissoit l'afaire
> li leus, qui ere de tel aire
> qu'il i avoit de flore planté
> tot jorz et iver et esté:
> violete i avoit trop bele.[107]

> But the best thing about the state of things
> was that the land would always
> have flowers and plants
> all through the winter and the summer:
> the violets were especially beautiful.

Even now, summer visitors to Provençe will see lavender fields full of the violet flowers the author speaks of—similar to those that perhaps inspired troubadour lyrics.

By this point of the *Roman*, Lover has lost touch with the *fin'amor* ethos of the troubadours, and is fully infected by "courtly love". By the fountain "which revealed to [Lover] the thousand things that appeared there",[108] a multitude of things Lover is no longer able to experience, he sits and sighs. Pierced by an arrow shot by the God of Love, Lover gives in to suffering,

---

106 *Ibid.*, ll. 1293–98.
107 *Ibid.*, ll. 1397–1401.
108 "qui me mostroient / mil choses qui entor estoinet" (*ibid.*, ll. 1603–04).

later claiming that "Death would not grieve me, / if I might die in the arms of my lover. / I am much grieved and tormented by Love".[109] Far from the *joi* spoken of by the troubadours, suffering consumes the courtly lover, since for him there is no greater pain (and perversely, no greater pleasure) than the desire for the unattainable beloved. Lover realizes that he can remove Love's arrow shaft "without great effort",[110] but no matter how hard he tries, he cannot remove the point or head of the arrow, for "the point remains within".[111] Lover is now "weak and defeated",[112] and in passage after passage, the descriptions of his condition mine the poet's vocabulary for words synonymous with "sad".

After the demise of *fin'amor*, love becomes sacrificial; this is one crucial aspect of diverted pure love (a diversion we can already see at work in Ermengaud). In later poetry, lovers are often portrayed as martyrs. In fact, the similarity between the treatments of love and sacrifice becomes so strong that some later English romances resemble another genre, saints' lives (*vita*). While every genre has its own vocabulary, "courtly love" romances are replete with such terms as suffering, pain, pity, mercy, angelic, courtesy, noble, and gentle. The language leaves no doubt that "courtly love", unlike *fin'amor*, is a Christianized and sublimated form of love. But scholars continue to blur the lines between the two ideas:

> In place of the theologian, courtly love has the troubadour. Instead of God (or in some instances Mary), courtly love posits the lady. In place of the monastery, monks, and contemplation, courtly love speaks of the courts, knights, and battle.[113]

The idea that "[i]n place of the theologian, courtly love has the troubadour" is risible when one thinks of actual troubadours like Guilhem IX. Such an interpretation does violence to the poetry, as can be seen when looking at Arnaut Daniel's *Lo ferm voler qu'el cor m'intra* (The firm will that enters my heart), which has precisely nothing to do with either Christianity or Platonic thought:

---

109 "la mort ne me greveroit mie, / se ge moroie es braz m'amie. / Mout me grieve Amors et tormente" (*ibid.*, ll. 2449–51).
110 "sanz grant contenz" (*ibid.*, l. 1745).
111 "la saiete remaint enz" (*ibid.*, l. 1746).
112 "foibles et vains" (*ibid.*, l. 1792).
113 Bernard V. Brady. *Christian Love* (Washington: Georgetown University Press, 2003), 152.

> Del cors li fos, non de l'arma,
> e cossentis m'a celat dinz sa cambra!
> Que plus mi nafra·l cor que colps de verga
> car lo sieus sers lai on il es non intra;
> totz temps serai ab lieis cum carns et ongla,
> e non creirai chastic d'amic ni d'oncle.[114]

> I would be of her body, not of her soul,
> if she would consent to hide me in her chamber!
> Since it wounds my heart more than blows of the rod
> that her servant is not entering there:
> with her I will be as flesh and nail
> and believe no chastisement of friend or of uncle.

The change from *fin'amor* to spiritualized and sublimated "courtly love" is not particularly subtle, and it involves an inordinate amount of violence—physical violence in the Crusade, physical, "moral", and psychological violence in the subsequent Inquisition, and intellectual violence in the long tradition of allegorically-inspired literary criticism dedicated to rewriting the poetry of love in its own passionless image. Such a change is not obscured in the *Roman*. The God of Love's commandments are just one aspect of this alteration, which Lover points out:

> Li diex d'Amors lors m'encharja,
> tot issi com vos oroiz ja,
> mot a mot ses copmmandemenz.
> Bien les devise cist romanz.[115]

> The God of Love then charged me,
> as you shall hear them now,
> word for word, with his commandments;
> this romance is an excellent device.

Before Lover was wounded with the arrow of (courtly) love, he referred to this poem as a "songes" or dream that was not to be considered a

---

114 Daniel, 112, ll. 13–18.
115 Lorris and de Meun (1965), Vol. 1, ll. 2055–58.

mere fable. Now, however, this has changed, as his story has become more serious, taking on a spiritual vocabulary and theme. When Love speaks to Lover, he says:

> Si maudi et escommenie
> touz ceus qui aiment Vilenie.
> [...]
> vilains est fel et sanz pitié
> sanz servise et sanz amitié.[116]

> I curse and excommunicate
> all those who love wickedness.
> [...]
> A wicked man is cruel and without pity;
> without service and without friendship.

Many things are forbidden to Lover, including obscene language: "Next, be on your guard that you never use / any filthy words or ribaldry. / Do not name base things, / and never open your mouth to disclose them".[117] Baseness does not only refer to language here, but also to passions, which are animalistic, and thus not highly regarded in the new, post-crusade and post-*fin'amor* world (the poems of Guilhem IX, would doubtless be regarded as "base" in this context—that, as much as anything else, illustrates the extent and nature of the change we are dealing with). The God of Love urges Lover, on many occasions, to serve well and be courteous, for decorum is expected (and in this case demanded). Resistance, who guards the Rose, gives similar advice: "You are free to love, as long as you keep / always far away from my roses".[118]

> Look, he says, but do not touch.

Passionate love is viewed negatively by many of the characters in this section of the *Roman*. Religious language becomes steadily more prominent toward the end of Guillaume de Lorris' portion, but in the

---

116 *Ibid.*, ll. 2073e-f, i-j.
117 "Aprés gardes que tu ne dies / ces orz moz ne ces ribaudies: / ja por nomer vilainne chose / ne doit ta bouche ester desclouse" (*ibid.*, ll. 2097–2100).
118 "Adés aime, mes que tu soies / loing de mes roses totes voies" (*ibid.*, ll. 3183–84).

midst of the poem's increasingly powerful air of sublimation, a burst of erotic passion shines through in this speech by Lover:

> Si con j'oi la rose apressie,
> un poi la trovai engroisie
> et vi qu'ele estoit puis creüe
> que quant je l'oi premiers veüe.
> La rose auques s'eslargissoit
> par amont, si m'abellissoit
> ce qu'el n'iere pas si overte
> que la graine fust descovierte;
> ençois estoit encor enclose
> entre les fueilles de la rose
> qui amont droites se levoient
> et la place dedenz emploient,
> si ne pooit paroir la graine
> por la rose qui estoit pleine.
> Ele fu, Diex la beneïe!
> asez plus bele espanie
> qu'el n'iere avant, et plus vermeille,
> dont m'esbahis de la mervoille;
> et Amors plus et plus me lie
> de tant come ele est embelie,
> et tot adés estraint ses laz
> tant con je voi plus de solaz.[119]

> When I approached the rose,
> I found it had grown
> and was larger than it had been
> the first time I had seen it.
> The rosebud was a little bigger
> at the top, but I was happy
> to see that it was not so open
> as to reveal its seed within,
> but was still enclosed
> by the leaves of the rose
> which made it stand upright

---

119 *Ibid.*, ll. 3339–60.

> and fill the place within
> so that the seed could not appear
> though the rose was full.
> And thanks be to God's blessing!
> it was even more beautiful,
> more open, and redder than before.
> I was amazed at the marvel;
> and Love more and more bound me,
> to the extent its beauty grew,
> the cords tightened to restrain me
> and my pleasure grew all the more.

Torn between his passions and courtesy, Lover still desires to possess the Rose. He meets Venus, the mother of the God of Love. Interestingly, mother and son differ in their principles, and with the mother's help, Lover "a kiss sweet and delicious / took from the rose immediately".[120] If Lover had strictly followed the "courtly" rules, then he would have been satisfied with the kiss; however, this is not the case, as he desires the Rose in more ways than permitted. Guillaume de Lorris, speaking through Lover, informs the reader that "[he] will pursue the whole history, / and never be lazy in writing it down".[121] This is exactly what he does: he writes about the love he and his forefathers knew, and what has become of it. It is a cautious portrait, replete with complexity and subtlety, and it ends with Lover's sorrow over his apparent frustration at not being able to love fully. He is in despair, but more than anything, he fears: "for my fear and pain, I think, means death".[122]

More satirical than Guillaume de Lorris, Jean de Meun continues the *Roman* from this point by pursuing the love theme that unifies the poem. De Meun's portion of the Roman is "a promotional treatise of procreative love versus […] chaste, regulated courtly love",[123] and his satire of courtly love is apparent from the opening lines which show Lover in great sorrow: "And if I have lost hope, / then I am at the point

---

120 "un besier douz et savoré / pris de la rose erraument" (*ibid.*, ll. 3460–61).
121 "Tote l'estoire veil parsuivre, / ja ne m'est parece d'escrivre" (*ibid.*, ll. 3487–88).
122 "qui me donront, ce croi, la mort" (*ibid.*, l. 4014).
123 McWebb, 10.

of despair. / Despair! Alas!"[124] Such exclamation recalls Shakespeare's treatment of the disingenuous hysteria in the Capulet household as they mourn over Juliet's (seeming) death on the day of her arranged marriage to the County Paris:

> CAPULET'S WIFE
> Alack the day, she's dead, she's dead, she's dead!
> CAPULET
> Ha! let me see her. Out alas!
> [...]
> NURSE
> O lamentable day![125]

This nearly comical grief goes on for another page, replete with exclamations that underscore the hysterics of the characters in the scene. Even the musicians who are there to play wedding music recognize the histrionics of the Capulet family: "Faith, we may put up our pipes and be gone".[126] Jean de Meun makes fun of such behavior throughout his portion of the *Roman*:

> Et se vos ne poez plorer,
> covertement sanz demorer
> de vostre salive pregniez,
> ou jus d'oignons, et l'esprengniez,
> ou d'auz ou d'autres liqueurs meintes,
> don voz palperes soient teintes;
> s'ainsinc le fetez, si plorrez
> toutes les foiz que vos vorrez.[127]

> And if you cannot cry,
> fake it without delay,
> mix your saliva
> with the juice of onions, and squeeze it out

---

124 "Et si l'ai je perdue, espoir, / a poi que ne m'en desespoir. / Desespoir! Las!" (Lorris and de Meun [1965], Vol. 1, ll. 4029–31).
125 *Romeo and Juliet*, 4.5.24–25, 30.
126 Ibid. 4.5.96.
127 Lorris and de Meun (1965), Vol. 1, ll. 7433–40.

> into your eyes (many other liquors will do),
> anoint your eyelids with these stains;
> if you make this preparation, you may cry
> as often as you like.

The difference that is apparent between the authors of the *Roman* is not only the treatment of the theme of love, but the writing style as well. When Guillaume de Lorris' Lover spoke of despair and sorrow, he did not use overwrought exclamations; Jean de Meun uses them to mock courtliness and decorum and the artificiality of the love they underscore. Jean de Meun's satirical verse opposes "the inhibitions of courtly and ecclesiastical moralism, and [seeks] to exempt vernacular poetry from euphemistic censorship and rigid rules of literary decorum".[128]

Intially, Jean de Meun maintains Guillaume de Lorris' take on sublimated, sacrificial love by portraying love as salvation, and Lover as a saint:

> Donc n'i a mes fors du soffrir
> et mon cors a martire offrir
> et d'atendre en bone esperance
> tant qu'Amors m'envoit alejance.
> Atendre merci me couvient.[129]

> So there is nothing for me to do but suffer
> and offer my heart and body to martyrdom
> and wait in good hope
> until Love sends me relief.
> I will wait for mercy to come to me.

Here, love is not for another person on Earth, but it is aimed toward martydom and Heaven. However, Jean de Meun, through his character Reason, defines for Lover a rather different kind of love. Reason's explication of love describes it as an emotion that cannot be easily explained:

---

128 Noah Guynn. *Allegory and Sexual Ethics in the High Middle Ages* (New York: Palgrave Macmillan, 2007), 138.
129 Lorris and de Meun (1965), Vol. 1, ll. 4145–49.

> Par mon chief, je la t'en veill prendre,
> puis que tes queurs i veust entendre.
> Or te demonstreré sanz fable
> chose qui n'est pas demonstrable,
> si savras tantost sanz sciance
> et connoistras sanz connoissance
> ce qui ne peut estre seü
> ne demonstré ne conneü.[130]

> By my head, I want to teach you,
> if your heart is ready to understand,
> I will give to you without falsehood
> things that are in no other way demonstrable,
> and you will know without science
> and understand without understanding
> What can in no other way be shown
> Demonstrated or understood.

Reason then goes on to describe love in the most negative terms she can muster as an irrational meeting of opposites:

> Amors, ce est pez haïneuse,
> Amors, c'est haïne amoureuse;
> [...]
> c'est reson toute forsenable,
> c'est forcenerie resnable;
> [...]
> c'est la soif qui toujors est ivre,
> ivrece qui de soif s'enivre.[131]

> Love is a peaceful hate,
> Love is a hateful affection;
> [...]
> It is a reason gone insane;
> It is insanity in reason;
> [...]

---

130 *Ibid.*, ll. 4247–54.
131 *Ibid.*, ll. 4263–64, 4269–70, 4279–80.

> It is the thirst that is always drunk,
> A drunkenness that always thirsts.

Replete with oxymorons, Reason's description conveys the essentially irrational truth—love is undefinable and unrestrainable. This assertion by Reason is in clear opposition to the commandments of the God of Love that dictate how Lover should feel, as if it were a rationally codifiable and controllable activity, a game that can and should be played by following prescribed rules. Such "courtly love" is a sanctified and sanctimonious fraud, but as Reason indicates, love does not wish to follow rules or play games, and realizes that "good lovers are found / in both coarse clothes and rich fabrics".[132] Lover patiently listens to Reason until she begins trying to dissuade him from the path he has chosen. Then Lover objects strongly:

> Dame, bien me voulez traïr.
> Doi je donques les genz haïr?
> Donc harré je toutes persones?
> Puis qu'amors ne sunt mie bones,
> ja mes n'ameré d'amors fines,
> ainz vivrai toujorz en haïnes?[133]

> Lady, your good to me is treason.
> Should I hate everyone?
> Must I despise all people?
> If Love is not favorable to me,
> Then must I not love purely,
> But live in hatred of all?

As Lover later says, "I cannot be other than I am".[134] What Lover desires is not the highly-codified and stylized artifice of "courtly love", but the reality—messy and irrational as it can be—of *fin'amor*, a love purged of religion, whose gaze is brought from the heavens back down to Earth. It is the human, and humane, version of the "natural love" of which

---

132 "car ausint bien sunt amoretes / souz bureaus conme souz brunets" (*ibid.*, ll. 4303–04).
133 *Ibid.*, ll. 4615–20.
134 "ne peut autre ester" (*ibid.*, l. 6871).

Reason speaks, when she says "This love, […] / deserves neither praise nor blame nor merit".[135] Reason then takes Lover on a journey through history, demonstrating how love underwent the process of sublimation, losing its passion along the way. Speaking of "pure love", Reason notes that

> Neïs Tulles, qui mist grant cure
> en cerchier secrez d'escripture,
> n'i pot tant son engin debatre
> qu'onc plus de .iii. pere ou de .iiii.,
> de touz les siecles trespassez
> puis que cist mond fu conpassez.[136]

> Even Cicero, who took great care
> in searching the secrets of ancient texts,
> could not find, no matter his ingenuity,
> more than three or four pairs of such loves
> in all the centuries that have passed
> since the world was composed.

Then Reason encourages Lover to pursue his desires:

> et s'ainsinc voloies amer,
> l'en t'en devroit quite clamer;
> et ceste iés tu tenuz a sivre,
> sanz ceste ne doit nus hom vivre.[137]

> And if you want to love in this way,
> men should not exclaim against you;
> for this is the love you must follow,
> and no man should suffer without it.

The reference to "men" instead of the "God of Love" or any other character standing in Lover's way, brings this dream vision back to reality. It is men using religion and violence who have created barriers

---

135 "Ceste amor, […] / n'a los ne blame ne merite, / n'en font n'a blamer n'a loer" (*ibid.*, ll. 5747–48).
136 *Ibid.*, ll. 5375–80.
137 *Ibid.*, ll. 5425–28.

for love. Reason then condemns Justice, for Justice has all too often been unjust, especially where love is concerned:

> […] Amor
> simplement que ne fet Joutice,
> […]
> car se ne fust maus et pechiez,
> dom li mondes est entechiez,
> l'en n'eüst onques roi veü
> ne juige en terre conneü.
> Si s'i preuvent il malement,
> qu'il deüssent premierement
> els meïsme justifier,
> […]
> Mes or vendent les juigemanz
> et bestornent les erremanz
> et taillent et content et raient,
> et les povres genz trestout paient:
> […]
> Tels juiges fet le larron pendre,
> qui mieuz deüst estre penduz.[138]

> […] Love
> alone is better than Justice,
> […]
> because without evil or sin,
> with which everyone is tainted,
> we would have never seen kings
> or judges on this Earth.
> Such men judge with malice
> where their first obligation
> is to judge and justify themselves,
> […]
> But they sell the judgments,
> and reverse the mistakes,
> and tally, and count, and erase,
> and the poor people pay for everything.

---

138 *Ibid.*, ll. 5532–33, 5537–43, 5549–52, 5554–55.

> [...]
> Such judges condemn thieves,
> when they ought to be hanged themselves.

Justice and judges are a none-too-subtle reference to the power and corruption of the Church, and in this obvious criticism of its workings, Jean de Meun does not hold back. According to Innocent III, "justice" was served by the Albigensian Crusade, which "tallied", "counted", and evidently, "erased", what it willed of the material and cultural wealth of the south, while the poor paid in blood. The criticism of the Church continues throughout the poem, though often in less direct form: "Now tell me, not in Latin, but in French, how you wish me to serve you?"[139] Latin, the language of the Church (and of scholarship), is here figured as the language of dishonesty and manipulation, in contrast to the truthful and straightforward vernacular.

Jean de Meun is most severely critical in his portrayal of the character False Seeming, equating the character and the Church:

> Faus Semblant, qui bien se ratorne,
> ot, ausinc con por essaier,
> vestuz les dras frere Saier.
> La chiere ot mout simple et piteuse,
> ne regardeüre orgueilleuse
> n'ot il pas, mes douce et pesible.
> A son col portoit une bible.
> Emprés s'en va sanz esquier,
> et por ses menbres apuier
> ot ausinc con par impotance
> de traïson une potance,
> et fist en sa manche glacier
> un bien trainchant rasoer d'acier
> qu'il fist forgier en une forge
> que l'en apele Coupe Gorge.[140]

---

139 "Or me dites donques ainceis, / non en latin, mes en françois, / de quoi volez vos que je serve?" (*ibid.*, ll. 5809–11).
140 Lorris and de Meun (1965), Vol. 2, ll. 12052–66.

> False Seeming, who arrayed himself well,
> had, as if to give it a try,
> dressed himself as a faithful friar.
> His features were simple, even piteous;
> nor was his gaze proud,
> but rather sweet and peaceful.
> And he had a Bible hanging from his neck.
> He went without a squire,
> but to support his members as he walked,
> he carried, against his weakness,
> a crutch of treason,
> and he slipped his into his sleeve
> a razor-sharp blade
> which he had made in a forge
> and named Cut-Throat.

The heavy censorship exercised by the Church and its ongoing Inquisition is here personified in the figure of the single most untrustworthy character of the *Roman*. Innocent III's "sharp steel razor" was the military force of northern French nobleman led by Simon de Montfort. This razor cut through Occitania, slicing through the land of *fin'amor* and its poetic expression. The violence inflicted on the citizens of Béziers is reenacted when the innocent-looking False Seeming commits a sudden atrocity against Foul Mouth as he

> par la gorge l'ahert,
> a .ii. poinz l'estraint, si l'estrangle,
> si li a tolue la jangle:
> la langue a son rasoer li oste.[141]

> grabbed [him] by the throat,
> and with two hands held and strangled him,
> then silenced his foolish talk
> by cutting his tongue out with a razor.

---

141 *Ibid.*, ll. 12334–37.

6. The Death of Fin'amor in Medieval French and English Poetry 261

In this scene, Foul Mouth—who accuses Lover of "a corrupt liason"[142]—is more than the malicious gossip of Guillaume's portion of the *Roman* as here he personifies those voices and ideas the Church would suppress, such as the troubadours and their free expression of love, whether of the mind or the body. Foul Mouth also recalls the religious liberty of the Cathars, and their free expression of a faith that fell afoul of the requirements of the Church for obedience in all matters of heart, mind, body, and conscience. The strangling and the cutting of the tongue are intentional and meaningful choices of attack. Like the troubadours, Foul Mouth is silenced in horrific circumstances by a corrupt authority. The troubadours before the Albigensian Crusade did not censor their lyrics, and through this incident, Lover is taught that such a free way of speaking will not be tolerated. A "courteous" society does not express itself in bawdy terms and phrases like those of Guilhem IX, Bernart de Ventadorn, or Bertran de Born, and it most certainly does not insist on liberty of conscience, as did the Cathars. The effect of all this can be seen in Lover in the *Roman*, who, manipulated by various authority figures in his dream, has been so addled by the process of attitude-shaping that he censures Reason for using the terms for genitalia:

> Si ne vos tiegn pas a cortaise
> quant ci m'avez coilles nomees,
> qui ne sunt pas bien renomees
> en bouche a cortaise pucele.
> Vos, qui tant estes sage et bele,
> ne sai con nomer les osastes,
> au mains quant le mot ne glosastes
> par quelque cortaise parole,
> si con preude fame en parole.[143]

> But I do not think of you as courteous
> when you have named the testicles to me,
> they are not well thought of
> in the mouth of a courteous girl.
> How can you, who are so wise and beautiful,

---

142 "un mauves acointement" (Lorris and de Meun [1965], Vol. 1, l. 3507).
143 *Ibid.*, ll. 6898–6906.

> name such things aloud
> without giving the word a euphemistic gloss,
> some courteous word instead,
> to fit the honest speech of a woman.

The apparent criticism here of the phenomenon of glossing and definition is important, and one we will later see in Chaucer. The sublimation of passionate love after the Albigensian Crusade was made possible not only through erasure, but also through the substitution of original words with a more "proper" language. This has been done to the songs of the troubadours, both through the imposition of the "courtly love" concept and, in some cases, through translations and interpretations that hide more than they reveal. Translations of the *Roman* have suffered likewise. The first modern English translation of the "entire" poem, done by Frederick Startridge Ellis, leaves its ending untranslated for reasons of "decency":

> With a view to justify the plan adopted of giving a summary conclusion to the story in place of following the author's text to the end, the original is here printed of the lines which the translator of the rest has forborne to put into English. He believes that those who read them will allow that he is justified in leaving them in the obscurity of the original.[144]

But Ellis does not merely refuse to translate the ending. He actually rewrites it:

> The remainder of the poem, in which the story of Pygmalion and the image is introduced, is mixed with a symbolism which certainly could not be put into English without giving reasonable offence, and the translator has therefore had the hardihood to bring the story to a conclusion by an invention of his own. Whether he is to be pardoned for so doing, apart from any defect in his work, those will be the most competent judges who take the trouble to read the original, which is given by way of appendix.[145]

Apparently, those "who take the trouble to read the original" in the Old French, are mature enough to be entrusted with the erotic secrets of Jean de Meun's conclusion, while those readers who have only English will have Ellis to protect their delicate moral state for them. The paternalistic

---

144 F. S. Ellis, trans. *The Romance of the Rose*. 3 Vols (London: J. M. Dent, 1900), 3, xii.
145 *Ibid.*

arrogance is overwhelming (and it should be noted that the era that gave us Ellis' morally improved version of the *Roman*, is the same Victorian era that gave us the concept of "courtly love").

The irony, of course is that the *Roman* anticipates such priggish bowdlerizing, by having Reason suggest that euphemistic and allegorical readings of texts, far from illuminating meaning, serve as a deliberate disguise behind which meaning is hidden:

> et qui bien entendroit la letre,
> le sen verroit en l'escriture,
> qui esclarcist la fable occure.[146]

> he that understands the letter well,
> can see the truth in the writing
> which clarifies the obscurity of the fable.

Jean de Meun censures this kind of hypocrisy frequently, often approaching it through criticisms of ecclesiastical dishonesty. The characters Hypocrisy and False Seeming frequently represent such views, since the *Roman* "suggests the continuity of love in order to highlight the corrupting effect that False Seeming has on it".[147] Nature's speech on mirrors brings the theme of hypocrisy into the visual realm of deception and illusion:

> Si font bien diverses distances,
> sanz mirouers, granz decevances:
> [...]
> Neïs d'un si tres petit home
> que chascuns a nain le renome
> font eus parair aus euz veanz
> qu'il soit plus granz que .x. geanz,
> [...]
> et li geant nain i resamblent
> par les euz qui si les desvoient
> quant si diversement les voient.

---

146 Lorris and de Meun (1965), Vol. 1, ll. 7132–34.
147 Joanna Luft. "The Play of Repetition and Resemblance in *The Romance of the Rose*". *The Romanic Review*, 102: 1–2 (2011), 50.

> [...]
> qui leur ont fet tex demontrances,
> si vont puis au peuple et se vantent,
> et ne dient pas voir, ainz mantent,
> qu'il ont les deables veüz.[148]

> The great differences between distances,
> with mirrors, can greatly deceive us:
> [...]
> One born a very small man
> who is called a dwarf by everyone
> can be made to watching eyes
> seem higher than ten giants,
> [...]
> and yet, Giants might resemble the dwarves
> because the eyes are deceived
> by the differences in appearances.
> [...]
> Those who have seen such things
> will go to the people and boast,
> and do not speak truths, but many lies,
> saying they have seen the devils.

Such mirrors and deceptions abound, not only in the poem, but in critical readings. A common critical move is to posit an endless multiplicity of possible readings and meanings; while this may be true in some cases, it is an argument that can be made to insist there is no particular value to any one reading: thus, troubadour poetry may just as well be about rivalry between different classes of Occitanian nobility as about love, and the Song of Songs may just as well be about the love of a god who plays no role in the text at all as about the love of human beings. Thus, for a critic like Joanna Luft, it is impossible to know just what the *Roman* shows us when Lover plucks his Rose:

> the account of the plucking cannot be fixed as either one type of sexual activity or another—as either heterosexual, homosexual, or autoerotic. All are possible readings of what the Narrator describes. While the allegorical meaning of the Lover's picking the rosebud cannot be reduced

---

148 Lorris and de Meun (1965), Vol. 3, ll. 18179–80, 18191–94, 18198–18200, 18204–07.

to one reading, this does not mean that no reading is valid. Rather, a number are. The indeterminacies that permeate the *Rose* create tensions that are irresolvable and force the reader to acknowledge that any one reading of the rosebud, and the allegory itself, is partial. [...] In its evasion of fixed meaning, the rosebud is a synecdoche of the poem itself. Like the rosebud, the poem cannot be pinned down to one reading.[149]

Those who argue for indeterminacy in readings of poetry which might otherwise be interpreted as challenges to power, serve the interests of that power by insisting that no such (defiant) reading can be established: if a critic is determined enough, "a text may be demonstrated to *mean* ever more fully, comprising even that which it is not, and *affording no resistance*".[150] To return for a moment to Longxi's observations about why there is such a thing as a better or worse reading of a text, it serves no reader well to be inculcated with the idea of the endless multiplicity of equally "valid" readings, any more than it serves a reader well to be hammered with the notion that there is always only one. When used well, interpretation contributes to a reader's experience and understanding of a text a basis for making choices between readings: "To put it simply, one reading is better than another if it accounts for more details of the text, bringing the letter into harmony with the spirit, rather than into opposition to it".[151] It is only through the ability to *choose* that we have any hope of resisting the blandishments of False Seeming and the threatenings of those who would demand our obedience as readers, and as citizens, in things both small and great.

Curiously, however, one thing critics have not been shy about fixing beyond notions of indeterminacy or multiplicity have been accusations of misogyny and immorality in Jean de Meun's portion of the *Roman*. The poet has been on the receiving end of such criticism ever since the fourteenth-and fifteenth-century author Christine de Pizan objected to his treatment of women and equality in the *Roman*:

> Christine took issue with essentially three interrelated aspects of the work: its verbal obscenity and the indecency of the concluding allegorical description of sexual intercourse; the negative portrayals of women,

---

149 Luft, 60–61.
150 Alan Sinfield. *Shakespeare, Authority, Sexuality: Unfinished Business in Cultural Materialism* (London: Routledge, 2006), 92. Emphasis added.
151 Longxi, 215.

which tended to treat them as a group and not as individuals, thereby making their "vices" natural and universal; the work's ambiguity, the absence of a clear authorial voice and intention which would serve as a moral guide to susceptible or ignorant readers.[152]

For Pizan, the issue is one of decency and of the attitudes of some of the characters toward women (while she conflates the author and his characters):

> In my opinion, which seems to be accordant with facts not to be contradicted, he speaks most dishonestly in certain parts, and especially through the person he calls Reason, who names the secret members plainly by name. [...] Since he blames all women generally, for that reason, I am constrained to believe that he never had the acquaintance of any honorable or virtuous women, but having haunted the paths of dissolute and evil women (as is common with lustful men) he believes that all women are like this, for he has had no knowledge of others. And if only he had blamed dishonest women alone, advising others to flee from them, this would have been a good and just lesson. But no, he accuses all without exception. But having gone so far past the limits of reason, the author's charges and accusations and false judgments of women should not be imputed to them, but to the one who tells such lies (so incredible and wildly off the mark), since the opposite is plainly manifest.[153]

For Pizan's contemporary, the theologian Jean Gerson, de Meun's work was of a kind with the "writings, words, and pictures that are

---

152 David F. Hult. "*The Roman de la Rose*, Christine de Pizan, and the *querelle des femmes*". In Carolyn Dinshaw and David Wallace, eds. *The Cambridge Companion to Medieval Women's Writing* (Cambridge: Cambridge University Press, 2003), 186.

153 Mais en accordant a l'oppinion a laquelle contrediséz, sans faille a mon avis, trop traicte deshonnestment en aucunes pars—et mesmement ou personnage que il claime Raison, laquelle nommes les secréz membres plainement par nom. [...] Mais vrayement puis que en general ainsi toutes blasma, de croire par ceste raison suis contrainte que oneques n'ot accoinctance ne hantise de femme honnourable ne vertueuse, mais par pluseurs femmes dissolues et de male vie hanter—comme font communement les luxurieux—, cuida ou faingny savoir que toutes telles feussent, car d'autres n'avoit congnoissance. Et se seullement eust blasmé les deshonnestes et conseillié elles fuir, bon enseignement et juste seroit. Mais non! ains sans exception toutes les accuse. Mais se tant oultre les mettes de raison se charga l'aucteur de elles accuser ou jugier nonveritablement, blasme aucun n'en doit estre imputé a elles, mais a cellui qui si loing de verité dit la mençonge qui n'est mie creable, comme le contraire appere manifestement.

Christine de Pizan. *Le Débat sur le Roman de la Rose*, ed. by Eric Hicks (Paris: Honoré Champion, 1977), 13, 18.

provocative, libidinous, and lacivious that should be utterly abhorred and excluded from a Christian republic".[154]

A modern critic like Noah Guynn aligns himself with this morally condemnatory tradition of reading Jean de Meun's poetry by rejecting the idea that the "attacks on women in the *Rose* are neutralized by the poem's dialectical structure, its relativist, ironic critique of opinion, or its avoidance of an overarching, sovereign authorial voice".[155] Despite the "dialectical structure" of the poem, its "relativist, ironic critique", and its deliberate "avoidance" of a "sovereign authorial voice", for Guynn, the entire poem is to be accused and convicted of misogyny because of the attitudes of individual characters (like the jealous husband). This should probably come as no surprise from a critic who also argues that the poem appears to do one thing, while it really does another: "the poem appears to celebrate unfettered, procreative desire and offers a formidable critique of celibacy", but it actually "seeks a shelter for male power in the apparent disruption and demystification, but also the subtle affirmation and perpetuation, of a variety of patriarchal cultural codes".[156]

The poem, according to the critic, apparently disrupts and demystifies, but actually affirms and perpetuates. As Rita Felski remarks, "we are regularly apprised", by critics inclined to this maneuver, "that what looks like difference is yet another form of sameness, that what appears to be subversion is a more discreet form of containment, that any attempt[s] at inclusion spawn yet more exclusions".[157] By such logic, the speech Shakespeare will give Shylock ("Hath not a Jew eyes?") subtly supports,

---

154 "scripta, verba et picturas provacatrices libidinose lascivie penitus excecrandas esse et a re publica christiane religionis exulandas" (Christine McWebb, ed. *Debating the Roman de la Rose: A Critical Anthology* [London: Routledge, 2007], 352).
155 Guynn, 138.
156 *Ibid.*, 140. This X-is-actually-Y move has been made even by defenders of the poem. In a strategy that goes all the way back to the original guardians of Homer, Jean Molinet, the late-fifteenth century author, "accuses Gerson of having misread" the work, whose "actual meaning [...] is sweet, savory, and moral" (Renate Blumenfeld-Kosinski. "Jean Gerson and the Debate on the Romance of the Rose". In Brian Patrick McGuire, eds. *A Companion to Jean Gerson* [Leiden: Brill, 2006], 355). "For Molinet" the "text means whatever Molinet wants it to mean" (366).
157 Felski, *The Limits of Critique*, 128.

rather than vigorously contests, anti-Semitism—and for anyone, poet or otherwise, to write or say "X" is really to mean "not-X".[158]

In the case of the *Roman*, however, the jealous husband's "misogynistic" point of view is rejected, even mocked, by the character Friend in his "equality" speech about husbands and wives:

> Ja ses vices ne li reproche
> ne ne la bate ne ne toche,
> car cil qui veust sa fame batre
> por soi mieuz en s'amour enbatre,
> quant la veust aprés rapesier,
> c'est cil qui por aprivesier
> bat son chat et puis le rapele
> por le lier en sa cordele.[159]

> He must not reproach her with her vices
> Nor must he ever beat or touch her.
> For he who beats a women
> To make her love him better,
> When he wants to soothe her later,
> Is like one who tries to tame
> His cat by beating it, and calls it back
> To try to get it to wear a collar.

---

158 David F. Hult argues that

> the most outrageous (and most frequently criticized) instance of antifeminist haranguing occurs in the speech of the "jealous husband" that is used as an illustrative example by the allegorical character Friend (Ami), who is, in turn, interacting with the Lover inside the allegorical dream construct. No fewer than three distinct fictional frames separate him from the voice of the narrator. What justification, then, do we have for deeming Jean de Meun a misogynist?

> David F. Hult. "Jean de Meun's Continuation of Le Roman de la Rose". In Denis Hollier, ed. *A New History of French Literature* [Cambridge: Harvard University Press, 1989], 101). The answer to Hult's question is that there is no justification, other than the desire of the critics to put the text on trial and find it guilty. As previously noted, Rita Felski traces this desire back to "the medieval heresy trial", a practice that emerged from the Inquisition, which was itself established shortly after the Albigensian Crusade to deal with heresy in southern France ("Suspicious Minds". *Poetics Today*, 32: 2 [Summer 2011], 219). Where earlier inquisitors tortured bodies, our modern variety torture texts, https://doi.org/10.1215/03335372-1261208

159 Lorris and de Meun (1965), Vol. 2, ll. 9703–10.

6. The Death of Fin'amor in Medieval French and English Poetry 269

Love, additionally, should be about equality of regard, not one-sided worship. In fact, Friend warns quite specifically against the danger of "courtly love" based on service and obedience, warning that it is little more than an illusion that will quickly spoil:

>li conmandast: "Amis, sailliez!"
>ou: "Ceste chose me bailliez",
>tantost li baillast sanz faillir,
>et saillist s'el mandast saillir.
>Voire neïs, que qu'el deïst,
>saillet il por qu'el le veïst,
>car tout avoit mis son desir
>en fere li tout son plesir.
>Mes quant sunt puis entrespousé,
>si con ci raconté vous é,
>lors est tornee la roële,
>si que cil qui seut servir cele
>conmande que cele le serve
>ausinc con s'ele fust sa serve,
>et la tient courte et li conmande
>que de ses fez conte li rande,
>et sa dame ainceis l'apela![160]

>If she commanded: "Lover, Jump!"
>Or: "Give that thing to me'",
>He would give it to her immediately,
>and jump whenever she ordered him.
>In fact, whatever she might demand,
>he would jump for her sight,
>because he had invested all his desires
>in doing her pleasure in everything.
>But after they get married,
>as I have told you before,
>the wheel turns,
>so that he who was used to serving her
>commands her to serve him,
>treating her exactly like his slave,

---

160 *Ibid.*, ll. 9427–43.

> holding her with a short leash,
> demanding that she account for her doings.
> She whom he used to call his lady!

Friend preaches against the dangers of "courtly love", and explains how it can turn into (and may very well start out as) misogyny. However, Friend expresses great admiration for true lovers, for whom "love [...] is honest and free in the heart".[161] Referring to the passionate lovers, Abelard and Heloise, and speaking particularly of Heloise's boldness and passion, Friend says, "I can hardly credit, by my soul, / that there ever lived another such woman".[162]

After that note of homage to Heloise, Friend finishes his speech on a liberating and optimistic note:

> uant vos en serez en sesine,
> si conme esperance devine,
> et vostre joie avrez pleniere,
> si la gardez en tel maniere
> con l'en doit garder tel florete.
> Lors si jorrez de l'amorete
> a cui nul autre ne comper;
> vos ne troveriez son per
> espoir en .xiiii. citez.[163]

> When at last you are in possession,
> As your hope divines,
> And your joys are plentiful,
> Guard it in the manner
> In which one should guard such a flower.
> Then will you enjoy a little love
> With which no other can compare;
> You will not find its like,
> Perhaps, in fourteen cities.

The passage echoes Shakespeare in one of his most outstanding manifestations of earthly love, the closing couplet of his sonnet 130:

---

161 "Amor [...] en queur franc et delivre" (ibid., ll. 9411–12).
162 "Mes je ne croi mie, par m'ame, / c'onques puis fust nule tel fame" (ibid., ll. 8795–96).
163 Ibid., ll. 9961–69.

"And yet, by heaven, I think my love as rare / As any she belied with false compare". What Friend refers to as "a little love / With which no other can compare" is akin to Shakespeare's declaration that the quite ordinary "she" of his sonnet is, in fact, anything but ordinary at all. She is beyond compare, not a symbol of higher love, not a gateway to God, and not to be loved for the sake of God. She is her own argument for love, and her equal will not be found "in fourteen cities" or fourteen thousand.

In that speech by Friend, Jean de Meun gives away the game. No longer is he writing about the love that must be directed toward the heavens, offered to a jealous God who cannot stand the idea that any affection in the universe might be directed anywhere other than him. This "little love" is the kind that topples such gods, and changes worlds. But in the thirteenth century, it is still something that must be carefully hidden, kept safe from the prying eyes and savage hands, arms, and armories of the post-Albigensian-Crusade world. To keep love safe will require wisdom, and the advice and strategies of those old enough to remember how different the past had been—here, the somewhat cynical Old Woman fits the bill nicely. La Vielle, whose later equivalent will be found in Chaucer's Wife of Bath, speaks of "the games of Love",[164] passing on what she has learned:

> Bele iere, et jenne et nice et fole,
> N'onc ne fui d'Amors a escole
> ou l'en leüst la theorique,
> mes je sai tout par la practique.[165]

> I was beautiful, and young, wild and foolish,
> And never went to any school of Love
> Or read in its theory,
> But I know it all through practical experience.

She emphasizes the same point throughout her speech in which she underscores the importance of nature. Loving is a natural act, and as Old Woman says, "Nature cannot lie, / who makes a man feel

---

164 "des geus d'amors" (*ibid.*, l. 12733).
165 *Ibid.*, ll. 12771–74

freedom, / [...] / A most powerful thing is Nature; / she surpasses even nurture".[166]

Finally, despite all obstacles of obedience, violence, and outright dishonesty, Lover reaches the Rose, and he is in ecstasy. Once again, the description of spring returns, and Lover advises young people who seek its pleasures:

> quant la douce seson vandra,
> seigneur vallet, qu'il convandra
> que vos ailliez cueillir les roses,
> ou les ouvertes ou les closes.[167]

> When the sweet season comes again,
> You will find it necessary
> To go plucking roses yourselves,
> Whether they be opened or closed.

There is no more insistence here on "courtly" codes and mannerisms. In an openly erotic speech reminiscent of Guilhem IX, Lover describes his initial misadventures:

> Par la santele que j'ai dite,
> qui tant iert estroite et petite,
> par ou le passaige quis ai,
> le paliz au bourdon brisai,
> sui moi dedanz l'archiere mis,
> mes je n'i antrai pas demis.
> Pesoit moi que plus n'i antraie,
> mes outre poair ne poaie.
> Mes por riens nule ne lessasse
> que le bourdon tout n'i passasse.[168]

---

166 "Mes Nature ne peut mentir, / qui franchise li fet sentir, / [...] / Trop est fort chose que Nature, / el passe neïs nourreture" (*ibid.*, ll. 13987–88, 14007–08).
167 *Ibid.*, ll. 21647–50.
168 *Ibid.*, ll. 21607–16.

> But this passage I have told you of,
> which was both narrow and small,
> through which I sought to pass,
> I broke down the barrier with my staff,
> placed myself inside the opening,
> but I could not enter more than halfway.
> I was peeved at being unable to enter further,
> but I did not have the power to go on.
> I would slacken for nothing
> though, till I had pushed my staff in all the way.

And after that brief comic interlude, Lover relates his final success:

> Par les rains saisi le rosier,
> qui plus sunt franc que nul osier;
> et quant a .ii. mains m'i poi joindre,
> tretout soavet, san moi poindre,
> le bouton pris a elloichier,
> qu'anviz l'eüsse san hoichier.
> Toutes an fis par estovoir
> les branches croller et mouvoir,
> san ja nul des rains depecier,
> car n'i vouloie riens blecier;
> et si m'an convint il a force
> entamer un po de l'escorce,
> qu'autrement avoir ne savoie
> ce don si grant desir avoie.[169]

> By its branches I seized the rosebush,
> fresher and more noble than any willow;
> and when I could grasp it with both hands,
> I began, gently, and without pricking myself,
> to slowly shake the bud,
> for I wanted to disturb it as little as possible.
> Though I could not help but cause
> the branches to shake and move,

---

169 Ibid., ll. 21765–88.

> I did not destroy any of them,
> for I did not wish to wound anything;
> and yet, I had to force my way a little,
> but did little damage to the bark,
> for I did not know how else to enjoy
> the beauty which I so much desired.

Within a dream filled with images of "courtly love" and all the cultural, clerical, and even military authority behind it, glimpses of *fin'amor* shine through, telling readers that the love celebrated by the troubadours has not completely disappeared, though it is now well-hidden and to be found only by the few. The *Roman* carefully, but compellingly, condemns love's sublimation and those responsible for it. In a dream vision created for a courtly and controlled world, the authors hold out hope for love's return in and through future generations (and ongoing generation):

> Mes nature, douce et piteuse,
> quant el voit que Mort l'envieuse,
> antre lui et Corrupcion,
> vienent metre a destrucion
> quan qu'el treuvent, dedanz sa forge
> torjorz martele, torjorz forge,
> tourjorz ses pieces renovele
> par generacion novele.[170]

> When Nature, sweet and piteous,
> through her vision sees envious Death
> join together with Corruption,
> to measure out destruction
> to whatever the find within her forge,
> she continues to hammer and forge,
> always renewing the pieces of life
> through new generation.

---

170 Lorris and de Meun (1965), Vol. 2, ll. 15975–82.

III
Post-*Fin'amor* English Romance: Love of God and Country in *Havelok the Dane* and *King Horn*

In the *Roman de la Rose*, something of the old spirit of the troubadours can still be felt. Across the water to the west, however, in early English romances, we find the sublimated and spiritualized forms of love so enthusiastically approved by the Akibas, Origens, and Ermengauds of the world, the authoritative glossators and critics for whom poetry and passion must be turned to higher purposes.

Laud Misc. 108 (a late thirteenth-century manuscript referred to hereafter as L) contains a collection of saints' lives—the *South English Legendary* (*SEL*), the two Middle English romances *Havelok the Dane*[171] and *King Horn*,[172] the poems *Somer Soneday* and *Sayings of St. Bernard*, the dream narrative *Vision of St. Paul*, and the *Dispute Between the Body and the Soul*.[173] The sanctification of love is a common element found among the various tales and protagonists of the manuscript, and the possible differences between saints and lovers do not seem to have preoccupied the authors of the texts. Although seemingly very distinct genres, the presence in L of both the saints' lives and the romances suggests that there was more in common between the two than might be supposed, and together they further explain how human love had been transformed into worship and earthly gazes redirected toward the heavens.

A common misconception about England after the Norman Conquest is that English was the silenced language, at least when it came to legal, political, religious, and literary use. This is only partially true, even in the eleventh and twelfth centuries, and the evidence of a thirteenth-century manuscript such as L, written entirely in English, demonstrates that the use of English was significant, not only in oral practice, but also as a written medium. The preparation of such a manuscript in terms of its copying and ornamentation, and the assembling of texts of different

---

171 All quotations are from "Havelok the Dane". In Ronald B. Herzman, Graham Drake, and Eve Salisbury, eds. *Four Romances of England* (Kalamazoo: Medieval Institute Publications, 1999), 73–160.
172 All quotations are from "King Horn". In *Four Romances of England*, 11–57.
173 See Kimberly K. Bell and Julie Nelson Couch. *The Texts and Context of Oxford, Bodleian Library, MS Laud Misc. 108* (Boston: Brill, 2011), especially the Introduction and Part One, for an insightful analysis on the manuscript, its compilation and provenance.

genres therein, reflect a clear sense of purpose, and suggest that it was intended for a wide audience and not merely for private use.[174] These works seem to have served a pedagogical function, and though originally such collections were for clerical reading in the context of the church, by the thirteenth century, manuscripts of saints' lives were made available to the laity.

This period in England saw great efforts by the Church to dominate, order, and unify the English people. This was necessary for the Church to implement its agenda in a more peaceful fashion than it had used in the chaotic environment of early-thirteenth century Occitania. If, during the Albigensian Crusade, the motto was "for the love of God, get rid of heresy", in England it was "for the love of the nation, get rid of heresy". Thus, in the lives of these saints, their connection with England is strongly emphasized; in this way, the agenda of the Church is wrapped in the flag of nationalism, and human passions are directed away from love and toward Nation and Deity. St. Augustine, for example, begins with "SEint Augustin, þat cristendom: brouhte in-to Engelonde",[175] stating this connection outright. A few lines down, the *vita* introduces St. Gregory, who "pope was of Rome, / Engelond he louede muche".[176] References to England are many, and the focus on everything English is quite consistent. It is not surprising that the Roman pope's love for England abounds, as does his eagerness to "love" it even more by Christianizing it and subordinating it to his will.[177] Upon his arrival in England, Augustine is rather saddened, "for he ne couþe: þe speche of

---

174 For a detailed explanation on medieval manuscript culture, text, and audience, see Chapter 6 of Peter Brown, ed. *A Companion to Medieval English Literature and Culture: c.1350–1500* (Malden: Blackwell, 2007). Such purposes can be seen in a text's physical form: "a text acquires new meanings within the physical context of the codex. The manuscript's illustrations, rubrics, and other paratextual features, as well as any other texts that are transmitted along with it, influence the reception of a text by its readers" (Lori J. Walters. "'The Foot on Which He Limps': Jean Gerson and the Rehabilitation of Jean de Meun in Arsenal 3339". *Digital Philology*, 1: 1 [Spring 2012], 112, https://doi.org/10.1353/dph.2012.0006).

175 Carl Horstmann, ed. "St. Austyn". *The Early South English Legendary or Lives of Saints* (London: N. Trubner, 1887), 24, l. 1, https://archive.org/stream/earlysouthenglis00hors#page/24

176 *Ibid.*, ll. 3–4.

177 As Innocent III tried to do in 1213, taking control of England from King John only to restore it, on John's submission, as a papal fiefdom—a humiliating agreement John promptly broke in 1214.

Engelonde".[178] This line points out the fact that Augustine was initially an outsider, sent by Pope Gregory the Great to undertake the mission of Christianizing England. Augustine's non-Englishness is indicated by the author's choice of not giving Augustine any direct lines. In order to create an atmosphere in which the English king and his people appear to be fully self-determining, the king has more lines than the saint. This is a subtle technique to make readers feel that the king is one of them, and as he receives the Christian faith, they receive it through him.

In L, one might think that the romances would be different from the saints' lives, that their distinguishing feature would be love; however, that is the subject with which the romances are least concerned. As a whole, L suggests a sacralizing and nationalist agenda. The most important subjects are England, the sanctifying of a newly-formed nation, and God: "The writers and audience of L acknowledge their own innate, inherited, God-given power of identity and defining that identity in terms of Englishness".[179] Some scholars have even suggested that the two romances of L can be seen as continuations of the saints' lives: "the rubricator who titled many of the lives in red ink titled *Havelok* as a *vita*: [*Incipit*] *Vita Hauelok quondam Rex Anglie. Et Denmarchie*".[180] This is not accidental, for Havelok acts as a saint and a martyr, building monasteries and going through suffering in order to restore the two nations England and Denmark. Havelok is also often portrayed as a Christ figure who has a special destiny, indicated by the "kynmerk" on his right shoulder and the fiery light that shines from his mouth while he is sleeping; these traits are common romance devices, emphasizing the special destiny of the person to whom they are attributed, despite any outward changes of state the character may have to endure due to villainy, usury, or other aspects of fortune or malice. This distinctiveness is also seen through the poet's constant use of the adjectives "fair" and "bold" when describing Havelok. These features are also used to describe the saints, who are martyrs, endowed with celestial identity, who sacrifice themselves for a specific cause.

There is, in fact, some ambiguity about the genre of *Havelok*. Many editors have treated it as an English equivalent of the Anglo-Norman

---

178 Carl Horstman, ed. "St. Austyn", l. 15.
179 Bell and Couch, 250.
180 *Ibid.*, 9.

Lai d'Haveloc. That poem is in fact called a "lai" in its opening lines, and there might be reasons for composing a Breton lay about a Danish prince, considering the fact that after the death of Edmund Ironside in 1016, England was ruled by Danish kings for about thirty years,[181] though *Havelok* could also be derived from Geoffrey Gaimar's *Estoire des Engleis* (c. 1136–1140).[182] Toward the end of the poem, *Havelok* calls itself a *gest*: "Nu have ye heard the gest al thoru / Of Havelok and of Goldeboru";[183] it is the *gesta*, the doings, the history of these two that bring about religious order. But while there is ambiguity here about genre, there is none about purpose. Although the poem opens in a leisurely fashion, a firmly didactic tone is consistently maintained throughout, making it clear that the poem and its lessons will concern virtues and villains, law and disorder. *Havelok* is not intended only for a noble audience, but for all types of people; in the beginning, the narrator addresses "gode men—/ wives, maydnes, and alle men",[184] solidly planting the poem in an everyman's England where religious order and peace are the predominant factors upon which a nation is founded. Ordinary life is described in great detail, and the poem extols Havelok's humble nature. Havelok possesses Christ-like features, and lives in a similarly simple way, despite his royal origins. Havelok grows up with the people, and it is the people who nourish and care for him, which enables Havelok's eventual defeat of his enemies, and the restoration of England as a Christian nation.

The narrative of *King Horn* is quite similar, as the heroes in both romances appear first as vulnerable children who are in danger of being killed, but grow to be bold and strong men who defeat their enemies. Horn and Havelok take their thrones as rightful heirs, and each restores order. At first, *King Horn* appears to be about the love of Horn and Rymenhild, but soon it becomes clear that Horn is more saint than lover: he is "well kene", "gret and strong, / Fair and evene long",

---

[181] See Peter Hunter Blair, *Ango-Saxon England* (Cambridge: Cambridge University Press, 1959), Chapter 2, "England and the Vikings", for more on the Danish rule and Danish presence in English life.

[182] On the reworkings of *Havelok* and its speculative history, see Scott Kleinman, "Animal Imagery and Oral Discourse in Havelok's First Fight", *Viator: Medieval and Renaissance Studies*, 35 (2004), 311–27, https://doi.org/10.1484/J.VIATOR.2.300201

[183] Herzman, "Havelok", ll. 2984–85.

[184] *Ibid*., ll. 1–2.

and his fairness reflects the goodness of God.[185] Horn's Christian piety is reflected in his defeat of the Saracens, and in the fact that England and Christianity always come first for him, whereas his love for the lady Rymenhild is never more than a secondary concern. The lovers do finally get married and rule the realm of Suddene together in happiness, but their marriage takes place only after all other pressing matters are resolved. Before departing to regain his father's lands from the pagans, Horn tells Rymenhild, "beo stille! / Ich wulle don al thi wille", but "I schal furst ride, / And mi knighthod prove".[186] Rymenhild must wait for seven years, until Horn restores the stability that Suddene had enjoyed during his father Athulf's reign. Any love Horn has for Rymenhild is completely sublimated here into the "higher" concerns of Christianity and the English nation, while Rymenhild must wait patiently with religion as her solace, an increasingly common situation in the period: "[f]rom the Anglo-Saxon period through the Middle Ages, [...] Christian religion was increasingly central to the routines of women's daily lives and to the ways in which their culture viewed women as a group".[187]

Christianity has contributed to a very long tradition of seeing women as inferior beings, and though a prominent thinker like Augustine argues "that women are created human and in the image of God, [...] ultimately sexual difference stands at the foundation of his theology".[188] It is that sexual difference which is thrown into sharp focus in post *fin'amor* poetry and prose, as no longer do women have the voice given them by the trobairitz poets, nor even the sympathetic portrayals of them as desiring and desirable human beings created by the troubadours. The status of women may well mirror the status of love (and poetry) itself, and in the time of *Havelok* and *King Horn* women are supporting players at best, existing at a time in which the love written of in poetry is not directed from person to person, but to the Nation, the Church, and God.

---

185 Herzman, "King Horn", ll. 95, 97–98.
186 *Ibid.*, ll. 545–46, 548–49.
187 Theresa D. Kemp. *Women in the Age of Shakespeare* (Santa Barbara: Greenwood Press, 2010), 12.
188 *Ibid.*

IV
Post-*Fin'amor* English Poetry: Mocking "Courtly Love" in Chaucer—the Knight and the Miller

By the late fourteenth century in England, things are beginning to change. Geoffrey Chaucer was by that time certainly aware of the approach to love that would later be described by scholars as "courtly". His works often parody this attitude, and in the *Canterbury Tales*, Chaucer provides rich soil for just such a parody in the "Knight's Tale" a long and highly stylized romance that is reworked by the bawdy Miller. The tension between mind and matter, soul and body, is at the root of much of the poetry written after the decline of *fin'amor*, until the ideas of the troubadour ethos slowly begin to reappear in Chaucer's works. Chaucer satirizes the sublimated, desexualized, and "courtly" love of the "Knight's Tale" through the raucous and unapologetic celebration of sexuality and the senses in the "Miller's Tale". The Knight recounts a medieval romance with "courtly" lovers, daring battles, and a beautiful and worship-inspiring lady named Emily. After hearing the tale, Chaucer's pilgrims all agree that they regard it as a "noble storie".[189]

Canterbury Tales mural by Ezra Winter (1939). North Reading Room, west wall, Library of Congress John Adams Building, Washington.[190]

The beloved in such "noble storie[s]" is a perfect, or near-perfect being, and "in character, she is distinguished for her courtesy, kindness, refinement, and good sense".[191] Arcite cannot go anywhere in the world that would require him to leave behind the sight of Emily: "Oonly the sighte of hire whom that I serve, / Though that I nevere hir grace may

---

189 Geoffrey Chaucer. *The Canterbury Tales: Complete*, ed. by Larry D. Benson (Boston: Wadsworth, 2000), I. 3111.
190 https://commons.wikimedia.org/wiki/File:Canterbury-west-Winter-Highsmith.jpeg?uselang=en-gb
191 William George Dodd. *Courtly Love in Chaucer and Gower* (Gloucester: Peter Smith, 1959), 9.

deserve, / Wolde han suffised right ynough for me".[192] Similarly, Palamon is a hapless and helpless worshiper of Emily. Both are madly in love with her, or with the idea of her. As Theseus describes Palamon to Emily, he is her servant: "That gentil Palamon, youre owene knyght, / That serveth yow with wille, herte, and myght / And ever hath doon syn ye first hym knewe".[193] This dynamic is common in "courtly" tales: "[a]mong the most familiar devices taken into romance is the address to an absent and uncaring object of love".[194] In the "Knight's Tale", Chaucer parodies the extreme sublimation of love in romances of his time, and sets up both Palamon and Arcite for further suffering and heartache, ensuring that readers will not miss the ridiculousness of the many situations in which the two "courtly" lovers find themselves. Arcite, when praying to Mars, complains that Emily does not seem to care whether he lives or dies: "For she that dooth me al this wo endure, / Ne reccheth nevere wher I synke or fleete".[195]

Emily's portrayal, as the female object of courtly adoration, is replete with religious symbolism; she appears in the garden on a May morning, singing "as an aungel hevenysshly",[196] embodying purity, beauty, and inaccessibility. Here, springtime is not about eroticism and the awakening of sensual desires, but about the transcendence of such things with heaven as the ultimate goal. It is unclear to Palamon and Arcite "wheither she be a woman or goddesse!"[197] For the courtly lover, "[the beloved] can never be reduced to a mere object of physical gratification",[198] nor, it seems, even be thought of in terms of anything like human love and desire.

Courtly love, as depicted in the "Knight's Tale", is a Neoplatonized and Christianized caricature of *fin'amor*. Unlike the lovers in troubadour poetry, the lovers in the "Knight's Tale" relegate the object (not subject) of their love to a position of near-irrelevance. Palamon and Arcite are so eager to find out whether Emily is "my lady" or "thy lady" that they are

---

192 Chaucer, I. 1231–33.
193 *Ibid.*, I. 3077–79.
194 Susan Crane. *Gender and Romance in Chaucer's Canterbury Tales* (Princeton: Princeton University Press, 1994), 51.
195 Chaucer, I. 2396–97.
196 Chaucer, I. 1055.
197 *Ibid.*, I. 1157.
198 Margaret Hallissy. *A Companion to Chaucer's Canterbury Tales* (Westport: Greenwood Press, 1995), 59.

willing to die without any response from her. In contrast, the "Miller's Tale" tells a story in which a response is definitely expected from the lady, and physical fulfillment is not denied, though the common critical reaction is tellingly reductive: "Love [in the "Miller's Tale"] is a matter not of the heart, mind, and spirit as it is in the romance, but of the body only".[199] By pairing the Knight's and Miller's tales, Chaucer strongly suggests that love must be a matter of heart, mind, spirit, and body all at once—a combination of elements that is much closer to the spirit of *fin'amor* than to that of "courtly love".

Generally categorized as an example of the *fabliaux*, a genre whose inventor may have been Guilhem IX, the first troubadour,[200] the "Miller's Tale" satirizes the courtly attitudes of the "Knight's Tale". In contrast with romances, such tales:

> exaggerate the real as much as allegory exaggerates the ideal. Their heroes are clever tricksters; their victims are the naïve and the stupid. All women in the *fabliaux* are lustful; all priests are gluttons or lechers; most representatives of public authority are corrupt. The peasant who makes a fool of his priest, the woman who makes a fool of her husband, and the priest who makes a fool of his bishop are glorified.[201]

The reader is comically warned about the Miller and his less-than-courtly sensibilities in advance of the tale: "What sholde I moore seyn, but this Millere / He nolde his wordes for no man forbere, / But tolde his cherles tale in his manere".[202] The reader is also encouraged to "turne over the leef and chese another tale" if he prefers "storial thyng that toucheth gentillesse, / And eek moralitee and hoolynesse",[203] a rhetorical move designed to increase the transgressive appeal of the tale that follows. What a reader who does not "chese another tale" will find, however, is that the "courtly idealism of love, initially a theme picked up from the Knight's Tale, is present throughout the Miller's Tale as an implied and ludicrously inappropriate standard of conduct",[204] which enables the laugh-out-loud humor of the story. What had been initially elevated

---

199 Hallissy, 75.
200 Reddy suggests that Guilhem IX was "the author of the first fabliau" (101–02).
201 Joseph R. Strayer. *Western Europe in the Middle Ages: A Short History* (New York: Appleton-Century-Crofts, 1955), 183.
202 Chaucer, I. 3167–69.
203 *Ibid.*, I. 3179–80.
204 Derek Pearsall. *The Canterbury Tales* (New York: Routledge, 2002), 178.

almost to the heavens in the language and content of the "Knight's Tale" topples to the ground in the "Miller's Tale", and is brought back to more recognizably earthly matters. Elements of courtly love are taken out of the context of romance and put into a frame where the celebration of "divine" ideals and figures seem like the ridiculous obsessions of the "naïve and the stupid".[205] A look at the main characters of the "Miller's Tale" offers ample evidence for this conclusion.

After the Knight's long story, the Miller will tell a "legend and a lyf",[206] not of a saint-like figure or a Platonic lover, but "of a down-to-earth, here-and-now lover, who wins a real flesh-and-blood woman".[207] The female character of the "Miller's Tale", Alison, is not an Emily, and the younger men showing interest in her do not act like Arcite or Palamon. The Miller tells of two lovers, just like the Knight does, but with a difference: the Miller portrays one of his tale's lovers, Nicholas, as a realist who knows what he wants and goes after it without illusions. The other lover, Absolon, is afflicted with self-delusion and pretensions to grand manners and high style, and is both tricked, and foiled in his planned revenge for the trick. In all this, we can see a small victory for *fin'amor* over "courtly love".

In dramatic contrast to the goddess-like, yet absent Emily, Alison has a mind of her own: she is an unmistakably human creature. In her genteel protestations and appeals to Nicholas's "curteisye",[208] she embodies a deliberate parody of a courtly lady. While the introduction of Alison is "modeled after the *descriptio feminae* which would traditionally introduce the heroine of a romance",[209] one should not miss the description of Alison in terms of animal imagery at the beginning of the tale,[210] comparisons which illustrate the physical passions highlighted by the *fabliau*. Alison knows the rules of that world, and lives her life in accordance with nature, without pretense and affectation. She does what she wants, chooses and refuses whom she pleases.

Alison is most definitely not the courtly lady who is described in religious terms, and although this "goode wyf" attends church to "Cristes

---

205 Strayer, 183.
206 Chaucer, I. 3441.
207 Bernard F. Huppé. *A Reading of the Canterbury Tales* (Albany: SUNY Press, 1964), 76.
208 Chaucer, I. 3287.
209 Pearsall, 176.
210 Chaucer, I. 3233–70.

owene werkes for to wirche", church is not the setting of an episode of courtly love here as it might have been in a traditional romance.[211] She is not the heroine of such a romance, nor is the absurd and preening Absolon, whom she meets at the church, its hero. Religious allusions in this story are placed in an entirely different context from that of the "Knight's Tale"; they are not celebrations of courtly love, but devices indicating the distance of the *fabliau* characters from the world of the "sacred" and "spiritual", where physical desires are objectionable, since these characters live in an unabashedly fleshly world in which such body-denying ideals are viewed as comical.

The humour of the treatment of courtly ideals in the "Miller's Tale" increases when one remembers the extreme length and artificiality of the wooing of Emily by Palamon and Arcite; thousands of lines pass during which no thoughts of sexual desire ever cross either of the two knights' minds. In the "Miller's Tale", sexual thoughts are present right from the beginning, starting with the way Chaucer plays with the knowledge and established expectations of his audience in the case of Absolon. His biblical namesake, Absolom the rebellious son of King David, is described as incomparably fair:

וּכְאַבְשָׁלוֹם לֹא־ הָיָה אִישׁ־ יָפֶה בְּכָל־ יִשְׂרָאֵל לְהַלֵּל מְאֹד מִכַּף רַגְלוֹ וְעַד קָדְקֳדוֹ לֹא־ הָיָה בוֹ מוּם:[212]

And as for Absolom, there was no man for beauty in all Israel so much to be praised; from the sole of his foot to the crown of his head, there was no defect in him.

Absolom is also described as someone more than willing to use his nearly-uncontrollable lust as a weapon:

וַיַּטּוּ לְאַבְשָׁלוֹם הָאֹהֶל עַל־ הַגָּג וַיָּבֹא אַבְשָׁלוֹם אֶל־ פִּלַגְשֵׁי אָבִיו לְעֵינֵי כָּל־ יִשְׂרָאֵל:[213]

They spread for Absolom a tent on the roof, and Absolom went in to his father's concubines before the eyes of all Israel.

Chaucer's Absolon is not nearly so ambitious as the son of Israel's king, though he is quite nearly as lustful and deceptive. Although Absolon "assume[s] all the poses of the courtly lover (more music, sleepless

---

211 *Ibid.*, I. 3308, I.3307.
212 II Sam. 14: 25.
213 *Ibid.*, 16: 22.

nights, gifts)",²¹⁴ and uses "high style language [...] right out of the courtly love tradition",²¹⁵ he is not quite what anyone would expect a courtly lover to be. It is through Absolon that Chaucer satirizes the pain and suffering involved in the concept of courtly love by displaying the young man's wooing of Alison in all its comic absurdity. Absolon's "unfortunate kiss [of Alison's unwashed rear] is preceded by a lovesong", which is "charged with the echoes of the Song of Songs".²¹⁶ Absolon's singing and ass-kissing bring the parody of courtly love to an absurdly comic climax.

The "song" element can also be seen with Nicholas, whose initial wooing of Alison includes an angel's song that salutes the Virgin: "And *Angelus ad virginem* he song".²¹⁷ Nonetheless, what might seem like courtliness is deflated when "prively he caughte hire by the queynte".²¹⁸ Once more, a religious and sacred image is taken out of its context, and put in the realm of its non-spiritual, fleshly opposite. Although described "lyk a mayden meke for to see",²¹⁹ Nicholas is anything but maiden-like or meek, as far as his behavior toward Alison is concerned. He is attracted to her, and with no signs of hesitation, he makes his attraction known.

The "Miller's Tale" certainly stands as a work on its own; however, its context in the *Canterbury Tales* gives it greater satirical power than it might otherwise have, by serving as a direct contrast with the "Knight's Tale". The description of Alison establishes her as the sensuous contrast to the remote and saint-like Emily. The Neoplatonized and Christianized love of the "Knight's Tale" is parodied in the "Miller's Tale", where the "courtly" ideals are treated as a joke and the pointless, and seemingly-endless suffering of Palamon and Arcite is implicitly mocked. Romance entertains the illusion that humans are more angel than animal, all mind and heart and soul, while the fabliau declares that humans are animals, bodies whose passions and sensual desires are not to be restrained.

---

214 Hallissy, 78.
215 *Ibid.*, 81.
216 Winthrop Wetherbee. *Chaucer: The Canterbury Tales.* 2nd ed. (Cambridge: Cambridge University Press, 1989), 58.
217 Chaucer, I. 3215.
218 *Ibid.*, I. 3276. For those unfamiliar with the meaning of "queynte" (kānt), simply change the first vowel sound. The meaning will become clear.
219 *Ibid.*, I. 3202.

Chaucer's attitude toward the "courtly" idealizing of love, on the whole, is a critical one, and the pairing of the Knight's and Miller's tales strongly suggests an ideal that is to be found in the real, a combination of mind, heart, soul, and body. In this respect, Chaucer's treatment of love is closer to the spirit of *fin'amor* than to that of "courtly love".

V
Post-*Fin'amor* English Poetry: Mocking "Auctoritee" in Chaucer—the Wife of Bath

The sublimation and spiritualization of love that took place between the times of the troubadours and Chaucer was not only accomplished through the Inquisition and the Albigensian Crusade's wholesale slaughter. It was also effected in a subtler fashion, through the glossing and alteration of what had once been an openly sensual literature (a practice that continues in too much modern criticism). Many authors no longer wrote in the fashion of Guilhem IX or Bernart de Ventadorn, but told tales of miracles, citing Christian authority figures in order to add weight to their lines. Chaucer's pilgrims, for example, often quote Christian figures. The Middle English word "auctoritee" is often used in the *Canterbury Tales*, and is a key term in the "Wife of Bath's Prologue and Tale". The word comes from the Latin *auctōritās*, meaning authority, reputation, credibility. To medieval readers, this word signified the important thoughts of the past as recorded and glossed in texts. However, the education required to become familiar with the ideas of previous *auctōrēs* was the privilege of a small minority. The majority of texts were in Latin, and illiteracy rates in medieval England were extremely high, running to about 90 per cent of males and 99 per cent of females.[220] Even among that ten per cent of literate men, however, only the clergy were educated in the languages of scholarship; thus, the books of the great authority figures were mainly read by clerics. However, these clerics did more than just read and study; they aimed to interpret and gloss, which in many cases amounts to a revision and rewriting of the texts in question (as we have seen with the Song of Songs).

---

220 Helen M. Jewell. *Women in Medieval England* (Manchester: Manchester University Press, 1996), 16.

6. The Death of Fin'amor in Medieval French and English Poetry

Opening page of the "Prologue of the Wife of Bath's Tale", from the Ellesmere manuscript of Geoffrey Chaucer's Canterbury Tales (early fifteenth century).[221]

To medieval readers, this pool of writing, which the Wife of Bath calls "auctoritee", was not to be questioned lightly, though the challenging spirit of Wycliffe and the so-called Lollards can already be seen in Richard II's rejection of the petition of the Commons in 1391 which sought to restrict education to the nobility, "that no neif or villein shall henceforth put his children to school in order to advance them".[222] This was part of a movement that by 1406 resulted in the Statute of Education in which "Parliament declared that 'every man or woman, of what state or condition that he be, shall be free to set their son or daughter to take learning at any school that pleaseth them within the realm' [...] a triumph for Wycklifism".[223] Though formal education had formerly been considered strictly a matter of men teaching authoritative men's thoughts and glosses to other men, things were slowly changing.

---

221 https://commons.wikimedia.org/wiki/File:Wife-of-Bath-ms.jpg
222 James Edward Geoffrey De Montmorency. *The Progress of Education in England: A Sketch of the Development of English Educational Organization from Early Times to the Year 1904* (London: Knight & Co., 1904), 27.
223 *Ibid.*, 28.

Chaucer illustrates some of this change by having the Wife seize "auctoritee", and as a result, appropriate the interpretive authority of the masculine, clerical glossators (the academics and critics of Chaucer's day).[224] The post-Albigensian period gave rise to an energetic proliferation of such glosses, in which the marginal commentary often undermined the primary text.[225] What is notable about glossing in this period is that Scripture is not the only work that is being glossed; secular writing is also undergoing heavy glossing. "To give a false appearance", one of today's definitions of the term gloss, conveys the self-interestedness that is potentially expressed in the act of glossing, which can be understood as a form of appropriation. The glosser speaks the text, asserts authority over it, provides an explanation, and consequently, limits (and even seeks to prevent) the possibility of other meanings.[226] As the friar from the "Summoner's Tale" testifies, "Glosynge is a glorious thyng, certeyn, / For lettre sleeth, so as we clerkes seyn",[227] describing a process in which he "twists the text of Scripture to serve his own material needs

---

224 The word "gloss" today has a few different meanings: "luster", "sheen", or "to give false a false appearance of acceptableness". The Greek word for gloss, γλώσσα, and the Latin word, *glossa* both mean "tongue, speech" (Francis E. Gigot. "Glosses, Scriptural—I. Etymology and Principal Meanings". In *The Catholic Encyclopedia: An International Work of Reference on the Constitution, Doctrine, Discipline, and History of the Catholic Church: Father to Gregory*, ed. by Charles G. Herbermann, et. al. [New York: Robert Appleton Company, 1907], Vol. 6, 588, https://archive.org/stream/07470918.6.emory.edu/07470918_6#page/n665). More broadly, the term means an "interpretation or explanation of isolated words. [...] A glossary is therefore a collection of words about which observations and notes have been gathered, and a glossarist is one who thus explains and illustrates given texts" (Gigot, 588). In its early usage, the term was assigned to "words of Greek texts that required some exposition" (Gigot, 588). It was only later that "gloss" came to refer to the interpretation itself.

225 Early Greek grammarians and Christian writers, who commented on Scripture, adopted the word "gloss" to indicate ambiguous verbal usage, whether foreign or obsolete, as opposed to an interpretation of difficult doctrinal or theological passages. Such glosses were mainly written on the margins of manuscripts. However, as glossing became more popular, the word "gloss" referred to more elaborate explication of Scripture, ranging from interpretative sentences to large commentaries on entire books that would either be marginal or interlinear. The exemplum of glossing, *Glossa Ordinaria*, or *The Gloss*, was a compilation of all glosses on the Bible, which itself consisted of layers of glosses (Gigot, 587).

226 On this point, see C. S. Lewis, who in *A Preface to Paradise Lost* (Oxford: Oxford University Press, 1942), openly states that his aim is to "prevent the reader from ever raising certain questions" (69).

227 Chaucer, III. 1793–94.

and those of his brother friars".²²⁸ "Glosynge" subordinates the text to the desires of the critic: "it is all too easy for this act of interpretation to become a matter of reading something *into* the text [...]. The text then becomes no more than a tool to serve the interests of the interpreter, meaning whatever he or she wishes it to".²²⁹

The Wife rebels against all of this, but especially against the idea that other people (notably men) are entitled to tell her how she should read and understand the texts of her day, which in turn influence how she lives (and understands) her life. The Wife is an earth-bound woman who wants to control her own existence and her own loves, rather than submit to another's pre-scripted role, courtly or otherwise. In pursuit of this control, the Wife of Bath defies the walls built by "auctoritee" and its attempts to rewrite poetry.

However, though the Wife's prologue and tale can be understood as her attempts to address the misogynistic assumptions, and the misrepresentations of women found in "courtly love", some critics view her narrative as ambiguous, regarding it as both feminist and antifeminist. Other arguments insist that in her prologue, the Wife is merely enacting an anti-feminist stereotype of the rapacious and imperious wife, and rather than being the embodiment of what misogynistic discourse *can't say*, she is embodying precisely what it *does say*. According to Catherine Cox, for example, the Wife of Bath does not, in any sense, produce what can be described as feminine discourse: "This sense of the narrative becomes clearer when we consider the Wife to be a textual 'feminine' representation, one constructed within the parameters of 'masculine' discourse and articulated in masculine terms".²³⁰ From this point of view, the Wife's arguments are not essentially different from those of her cleric husband, Jankyn, who often quotes "auctoritee" in his anti-feminist literature in order to justify his actions toward the Wife, reading to her from his book of "wicked wives" that contains passages from *Adversus Jovinianum*, *Dissuasio Ad Rufinum*, the *Golden Book on Marriage*, *Tertulan*, and other misogynistic works.

---

228 Alastair Minnis. *Fallible Authors: Chaucer's Pardoner and Wife of Bath* (Philadelphia: University of Pennsylvania Press, 2008), 261.
229 Jill Mann. *Life in Words: Essays on Chaucer, the Gawain-Poet, and Malory* (Toronto: University of Toronto Press, 2014), 82.
230 Catherine S. Cox. *Gender and Language in Chaucer* (Tampa: University Press of Florida, 1997), 19.

But far from being confined to the thralldom of an anti-feminist discourse, the Wife speaks as the dismissed "other", explicitly mimicking the operations of patriarchal (and explicitly anti-*fin'amor*) discourse in order to mock it, defuse it, and deny it any power over her. When she delivers her tirade against her three previous husbands, she repeats the very words anti-feminist writers have used about domineering wives: "When [Alison] accuses her old husbands [...] she cites the stereotype within her performance of it, establishing a link but also a distinction between the proverbial 'chidying wyves' and her own chiding objection to the proverb".[231] The Wife's performance is an instance of imitation designed to defuse the rhetorical attacks made against her, "a strategic repetition of sanctioned positions on gender from the crucially different position of a feminine voice".[232] The Wife refuses to play the roles assigned to her by the "courtly" and other misogynistic discourses of her era, and so she becomes, through imitation and appropriation, her own "auctour", her own "auctoritee".

The Wife's defiance goes beyond language, expressing itself also through her clothing and outward presentation. At the time of the pilgrimage that frames the *Canterbury Tales*, she is a widow. As such, she is expected "to wear widow's garb [and] modest attire in a somber hue",[233] and even more importantly, "her demeanor should match her clothing".[234] And yet, the Wife's exterior defies those expectations: "Hir coverchiefs ful fyne weren of ground; / [...] Hir hosen weren of fyn scarlet reed, / Ful streite yteyd, and shoes ful moyste and newe".[235] The Wife is not about to accept anyone else's terms, and by being flamboyant in demeanor and assertive in speech, the Wife defies *auctoritee*, while at the same time claiming her own, and reveling in her seductive and vibrant appearance. She is not afraid of sensuality, nor is she willing to have it "glossed" for her by any dry-as-dust and cloistered clerics (like Ermengaud, for example) who presume to counsel men and women of the world about human sexuality. She is the "other" that the gloss, written by clerical, anti-body and anti-pleasure men, opposes—the gloss

---

231 Susan Crane. *Gender and Romance in Chaucer's Canterbury Tales* (Princeton: Princeton, University Press, 1994), 116.
232 *Ibid.*
233 Hallissy, 103.
234 *Ibid.*
235 Chaucer, General Prologue, 453, 456–57.

that runs on the notion that all women are functionally interchangeable. The Wife, though her opposition to and appropriation of this patriarchal hermeneutic, turns the tables and puts men in the same position: "Yblessed be God that I have wedded five! / Welcome the sixte, whan that evere he shal".[236] The Wife of Bath, through her imitation and appropriation, makes it abundantly clear what "auctoritee" refuses to acknowledge, or reluctantly acknowledges only by seeing it as "other".

The beginning of the Wife's prologue repeats the points of the unorthodox theologian Jovinian (a fourth-century-CE opponent of Christian asceticism), but it also mimics the rather drearily orthodox, anti-feminist (and ascetic) Jerome. If the Wife's reasoning is inconsistent, a point that provokes a number of critics to reprove her, it is because there is inconsistency and disagreement in the texts from which she quotes, especially, perhaps, in the anti-feminist texts: "Commenting on Saint Paul's statement that it is good for a man to be unmarried [...] Jerome contends, 'If it is good for a man to be so, then it is bad for a man not to be so'".[237] Impeccable logic, to be sure. It is thus unsurprising that the Wife revamps biblical passages to fit her arguments; she is but imitating the techniques of the male glossators who adjust and alter texts to fit their ideology.

Toward the end of her prologue, in her descriptions of her last marriage, the Wife not only speaks of joys and woes in a marriage, but also depicts a relationship between women and (male) glossators. The conclusion of her prologue suggests that despite her appropriation of "auctoritee" and talk of "maistrie", and "soveraynetee", what the Wife most wants is mutuality and satisfaction of desires, much like the ideal expressed by Marcabru as "dos desirs d'un enveia" — "two desires in a single longing" and by Bernart de Ventadorn when he writes that love requires mutuality between the lovers: "Nothing in it can be good / If the will is not mutual" ("Nula res no i pot pro tener, / Si·lh voluntatz non es egaus"). She is yearning for the equality written of by Jean de Meun, for whom "love and lordship / do not keep each other company".[238] But

---

236 *Ibid.*, III. 44–46.
237 Carolyn Dinshaw. *Chaucer's Sexual Poetics* (Madison: University of Wisconsin Press, 1989), 124.
238 "amor et seigneurie / ne s'entrefirent compaignie" (Lorris, Guillaume and Jean de Meun, ll. 8421–22).

the Wife of Bath lives in a different time, a post Albigensian-Crusade era dominated by religious dogma, and so such equality is hard, perhaps even impossible, to find. However, once Jankyn apologizes and burns the misogynistic book with which he has has caused her so much "wo" and "pyne",[239] she becomes loving and kind to him, and she gains "soveraynetee" (the key term of her tale). But the question of whether or not she actually has attained her desire, despite her positive declaration of the fact, is made difficult to answer because of the very language in which she makes her declaration: it is the language of a fairy tale; as the Wife says, it is "in this matere a queynte fantasye".[240] There is no equality; there is no *fin'amor*. These are (yet) things of the past. And yet, in her words, there is a return of at least the imagined possibility for full understanding between husband and wife.

When the Wife of Bath manipulates authoritative texts, she suggests something about glossing and its misogynistic strategy: it deprives the female of her significance and therefore completely undermines both female and male sexuality. In this light, her tale of the knight and the Loathly Lady is a tale of resistance, an instance of the interpreted siezing control of the act of interpretation. The domestic sphere of the tale has as its main participants a married couple—King Arthur and his queen—and a knight who, overcome with lust and his own sense of entitlement, has raped a young maiden, and is to be executed for his crime.[241] But after intercession on his behalf by the queen and other ladies of the court, the knight is given one chance to save his life. If he is to do so, he must find the answer to the question, "what thyng is it that women moost desiren".[242] As the tale goes on, the answer is revealed: "Wommen desiren to have sovereynetee / As wel over hir housbound as hir love, / And for to been in maistrie hym above".[243] By the tale's end, the rapist knight, who both embodies and enacts the patriarchal power structure of female oppression (and the glossator's/critic's structure

---

239 Chaucer, III.787.
240 *Ibid.*, III.516. The potential double meaning here of "queynte' also presents difficulties.
241 Jean Hagstrum argues that "[t]he raped solitary country girl of the Arthurian landscape in the tale surely symbolizes what society had done to Alisoun in her loveless marriages" (271).
242 Chaucer, III.905.
243 *Ibid.*, III.1038–40.

of poetic oppression), must learn his lesson and act in deference to feminine desire.

For the Wife, "*Auctoritee* involves not only being an author, but also a master or a teacher".[244] This state, seldom achieved by females in the medieval period, is the one to which both the Wife of Bath and the Loathly Lady aspire. The Wife has been a student of marriage through five unions, and though she claims, "Experience, though noon auctoritee / Were in this world, is right ynogh for me / To speke of wo that is in marriage",[245] she still quotes authority, realizing that experience alone is not enough to adopt "auctoritee". The Loathly Lady lectures her husband by quoting great "auctours", such as Dante, Seneca, Boethius, and others. Her monologue, also known as the "pillow lecture", argues that women should be valued not only for their beauty and youth, but also for their intelligence. The knight does not learn his lesson from authoritative texts, or from "courtly" tales that strip the flesh-and-blood humanity from women, but by listening to his wife's lecture. He learns from the real woman who is right there in front of him.

However, the tale ends with a contradiction. Despite the tale's declaration, "And thus they lyve unto hir lyves ende / In parfit joye",[246] the lines before it contend that "she obeyed hym in every thyng / That myghte doon hym plesance or liking".[247] This ending seems to bring the reader back to the realm of romance and "courtly love" literature, where the beloved is only exalted in the wooing period. But the Wife ends her tale with a hint of the mutuality of which Marcabru and Bernart wrote, a relationship in which each renders to each "every thyng / That myghte doon hym [and her] plesance or likyng", and in which love is, as Jean de Meun described it, "en queur franc et delivre", honest and free in the heart.

By Chaucer's time, the troubadours had been gone for well over a century. Since that time, passionate, embodied, and erotic love had often been treated as a dangerous element, one which Christian "auctors" had laboriously identified as a sin. In Chaucer's world, book learning

---

244 Crane, 131.
245 Chaucer, III.1–3.
246 *Ibid.*, III.1257–58.
247 *Ibid.*, III.1255–56.

conveyed "auctoritee", and in his portrayal of the Wife, the Loathly Lady of her tale, and the anti-feminist discourse the Wife rails against, Chaucer imagines patriarchy from the "other's" perspective, carefully reckoning the costs of misogynistic clerical and "courtly" discourse. Chaucer, through the Wife of Bath, maintains that women's desire, and desire in general, cannot be denied.

7. The Ladder of Love in Italian Poetry and Prose, and the Reactions of the Sixteenth-Century Sonneteers

I
The Platonic Ladder of Love

Despite the changes that are beginning to appear in fourteenth-century England, by the same time in Italy the sublimation and spiritualization of love has long established itself as the dominant theme of European poetry, a theme that is exported to England in the sixteenth century, briefly sweeping aside much of the spirit we have seen developing in Chaucer. To understand how and why this happened, we will have to circle back and spend a little time with Plato.

Perhaps the single most basic element of Platonic metaphysical thought is the separation between the world we see and the world we do not see, a temporal world of motion and change, and an eternal realm of stasis. This idea stems from earlier Greek philosophers, such pre-Socratics as Heraclitus, for example, who is most famous for trying to illustrate the difference between the two realms, as well as their interdependence, with the image of a river (stasis) in which new waters continually flow (motion). But in Plato, this theme of the relation between the eternal and the temporal reaches its most powerfully articulated form, and his ideas are traceable through the history of thought in literature and art in the Western world.

In the *Symposium* this theme takes shape in an argument that posits an idea of Forms and Copies—not merely the idea of a realm of eternal Forms or Ideas which are the templates for the individual and ephemeral Copies we see here in the world of flux and change, but the idea that there are higher and lower, nobler and baser ways of using those Copies as ways to understand those eternal Forms. The *Symposium* regards the baser ways of understanding with suspicion, because they are stuck within the changing conditions of a world in which, as Shakespeare says, "everything that grows holds in perfection but a little moment", but they are also necessary, a means to an end. In what becomes the well-worn image of a "ladder of love", the dialogue pictures such baser understandings as the lower rung on a ladder that leads to higher understandings, a progression in which lower forms of love lead to higher loves, and eventually the highest love of all—the love of the Forms.

Organized around a series of speeches offering competing definitions of love, the *Symposium* reaches its philosophical climax when Socrates tells the story of his conversation with the prophetess Diotima. Diotima first defines what love *is*, then moves on to an elaborate description of how love may be realized or achieved: "think not that love is of the beautiful",[1] rather, love "is for the engendering and producing offspring upon beauty".[2] Why?

> That is because it is an undying thing in our mortal life. Immortality constrains us to set our hearts upon it even as we pursue the good, and so it comes about that love always exists as one's highest good. Necessarily then, from this reckoning, love is of immortality.[3]

But how can we fulfill such longing for immortality? In Diotima's conception, we do so through generation. As Diotima puts it, "the mortal condition always desires to enter an immortal existence. This is possible only through engendering, so that in the future, a young generation

---

1 "ἔφη, οὐ τοῦ καλοῦ ὁ ἔρως, ὡς σὺ οἴει" (Plato. *Symposium*, ed. by W. R. M. Lamb [Loeb Classical Library, Cambridge, MA: Harvard University Press, 1925], 206e).
2 "γεννήσεως καὶ τοῦ τόκου ἐν τῷ καλῷ" (*ibid.*).
3 ὅτι ἀειγενές ἐστι καὶ ἀθάνατον ὡς θνητῷ ἡ γέννησις. ἀθανασίας δὲ ἀναγκαῖον ἐπιθυμεῖν μετὰ ἀγαθοῦ ἐκ τῶν ὡμολογημένων, εἴπερ τοῦ ἀγαθὸν1 ἑαυτῷ εἶναι ἀεὶ ἔρως ἐστίν. ἀναγκαῖον δὴ ἐκ τούτου τοῦ λόγου καὶ τῆς ἀθανασίας τὸν ἔρωτα εἶναι.
Ibid., 206e-207a.

can take the place of the old one".[4] But the generation—or "increase"—being referred to is of two different kinds, a lower and higher. There is the physical generation engaged in by those who are "pregnant in the body".[5] These "turn toward women"[6] and "through begetting children they achieve immortality".[7] The higher example, however, is a spiritual generation, engaged in by those with "the pregnancy of the spirit".[8] It is to these that wisdom truly belongs, and their realm is that of Beauty itself: they have "prudence and goodness, which exist in all poets and creators and skilled craftsmen who are called inventors".[9]

This splitting of "pregnancy" into attempts to achieve immortality through the flesh and through the spirit leads Diotima to describe—using the metaphor of a ladder—a pedagogical process by which a student of Love and Beauty may move from first lessons to a final revelation. This process starts at the lowest rung of the ladder, where the student needs "to devote himself to the beautiful and good in the body".[10] The student then must

> thereupon in his true self understand that the beauty of that body is that of many associated bodies that exist, and he if means to pursue the idea and form of beauty, it would be great foolishness not to consider and establish for himself the whole, how the beauty of one body is like the the beauty of all bodies.[11]

Stepping from the first rung to the second rung of the ladder involves moving from individual example to collective examples—but it does not yet involve moving from example to concept, from concrete to abstract. That is the work of the third and fourth steps. Step three demands that

---

4   "θνητὴ φύσις ζητεῖ κατὰ τὸ δυνατὸν ἀεὶ τὸ εἶναι ἀθάνατος. δύναται δὲ ταύτῃ μόνον, τῇ γενέσει, ὅτι ἀεὶ καταλείπει ἕτερον νέον ἀντὶ τοῦ παλαιοῦ" (ibid., 207d).
5   "ἐγκύμονες [...] κατὰ σώματα" (ibid., 209a).
6   "πρὸς τὰς γυναῖκας" (ibid.).
7   "διὰ παιδογονίας ἀθανασίαν" (ibid.).
8   "δὲ κατὰ τὴν ψυχήν" (ibid.).
9   "φρόνησίν τε καὶ τὴν ἄλλην ἀρετήν· ὧν δή εἰσι καὶ οἱ ποιηταὶ πάντες γεννήτορες καὶ τῶν δημιουργῶν ὅσοι λέγονται εὑρετικοὶ" (ibid.).
10 "ἑνὸς αὐτὸν σώματος ἐρᾶν καὶ ἐνταῦθα γεννᾶν Βλόγους καλούς" (ibid., 210b).
11 ἔπειτα δὲ αὐτὸν κατανοῆσαι, ὅτι τὸ κάλλος τὸ ἐπὶ ὁτῳοῦν σώματι τῷ ἐπὶ ἑτέρῳ σώματι ἀδελφόν ἐστι, καὶ εἰ δεῖ διώκειν τὸ ἐπ᾽ εἴδει καλόν, πολλὴ ἄνοια μὴ οὐχ ἕν τε καὶ ταὐτὸν ἡγεῖσθαι τὸ ἐπὶ πᾶσι τοῖς σώμασι κάλλος· τοῦτο δ᾽ ἐννοήσαντα καταστῆναι πάντων τῶν καλῶν σωμάτων ἐραστήν.
    Ibid.

"besides this, in the meantime he must understand what is the soul's beauty, worthiness, and value over that of the body",[12] and learn to see "beauty in the laws".[13] This definitively moves the student's focus beyond the individual and toward the collective and conceptual: no longer will he direct his love toward "beauty in a boy or a man",[14] but he will instead turn "toward the mighty sea of beauty".[15] Here, at last, the student is ready to climb to the top of the ladder, ready for the final revelation of the true nature of beauty as eternity: "indeed it always existed, and neither comes into being nor is destroyed".[16] Finally, Diotima gives a summary description of how the student learns to move from lower to higher forms of devotion:

> Beginning with the beauty of the individual, the quest for beauty always rises, even as it were using the steps of a ladder, from one to two, and from two to all beautiful bodies, and from the beauty in all bodies to the beauty of of customs and observances, and from the customs and observances to the beauty of knowledge and mathematics, and from such knowledge to the individual learning that has its end solely in the knowledge of the existence of beauty itself.[17]

From Plato we come to the later Neoplatonist philosopher, Plotinus. The modification Plotinus makes to Platonic thought pushes it to the point of religiosity, transforming Platonic philosophy into a theology in all but name that is first cousin to Christianity. Plotinus describes the reality of everything that exists in a layered or structured form, like that presented in the *Symposium*, but with an extra twist. There is an ultimate level of reality, beyond all description, conception, idea, and imagination. Plotinus calls this level τὸ ἕν, or the One:

---

12 "μετὰ δὲ ταῦτα τὸ ἐν ταῖς ψυχαῖς κάλλος τιμιώτερον ἡγήσασθαι τοῦ ἐν τῷ σώματι" (ibid., 210c).
13 "τοῖς νόμοις καλὸν" (ibid.).
14 "παιδαρίου κάλλος ἢ ἀνθρώπου" (ibid., 210d).
15 "ἐπὶ τὸ πολὺ πέλαγος τετραμμένος τοῦ καλοῦ" (ibid.).
16 "μὲν ἀεὶ ὂν καὶ οὔτε γιγνόμενον οὔτε ἀπολλύμενον" (ibid., 211a).
17 τῶνδε τῶν καλῶν ἐκείνου ἕνεκα τοῦ καλοῦ ἀεὶ ἐπανιέναι, ὥσπερ ἐπαναβαθμοῖς χρώμενον, ἀπὸ ἑνὸς ἐπὶ δύο καὶ ἀπὸ δυοῖν ἐπὶ πάντα τὰ καλὰ σώματα, καὶ ἀπὸ τῶν καλῶν σωμάτων ἐπὶ τὰ καλὰ ἐπιτηδεύματα, καὶ ἀπὸ τῶν ἐπιτηδευμάτων ἐπὶ τὰ καλὰ μαθήματα, καὶ ἀπὸ τῶν μαθημάτων ἐπ᾽ ἐκεῖνο τὸ μάθημα τελευτῆσαι, ὅ ἐστιν οὐκ ἄλλου ἢ αὐτοῦ ἐκείνου τοῦ καλοῦ μάθημα.
Ibid., 211c.

In this manner we can proclaim a Principle, which exists beyond Being—the One. [...] Existing next in order to the One is Mind. Third is Spirit, and then physical Nature, which by this procession is shown and brought to light.[18]

All things proceed from the One. From this indescribable source the next level *emanates*, in what Plotinus describes as an unwilled process of creation in which lower levels come from higher levels, but not due to any purpose held by those higher levels. This next level is called *Nous*, or Mind. Here is where all thought, reason, ideas exist. *Nous*, for Plotinus, is the level Plato described as the realm of the Forms. *Nous* then produces *Psyche* or Spirit, the level of soul, engagement, and (willed) creative activity. Finally, from *Psyche*, comes the physical world of matter. Everything emanates from the one ultimate, indescribable, non-understandable source. Emanation proceeds downward, but is part of a cyclical process, conducted within a self-contained environment.

How? Because, according to Plotinus, the proper motion of emotional, intellectual, and spiritual life is never a focus here, on the world in which we live as physical and mortal beings, but above, to the realms from which matter emanated. Plotinus paints a picture of yearning and desire, though not of bodies for other bodies. The yearning Plotinus describes is of the mortal for the immortal, the temporary for the permanent, the changing for the changeless. As Plotinus describes it, this yearning is for one's origin:

> Everything longs for, and in this way loves its engenderer, and especially whenever they are solitary the engendered seeks the engenderer; but when the engenderer is the highest good, the engendered does so out of necessity, divided, existing alone in its otherness and distinction.[19]

We desire, if properly oriented and instructed, that level of existence that exceeds our own, and this upward-focus is reflected in the process of emanation (non-willed creation that descends from higher to lower

---

18 "Ὅτι δὲ οὕτω χρὴ νομίζειν ἔχειν, ὡς ἔστι μὲν τὸ ἐπέκεινα ὄντος τὸ ἕν, [...] ἔστι δὲ ἐφεξῆς τὸ ὂν καὶ νοῦς, τρίτη δὲ ἡ τῆς ψυχῆς φύσις, ἤδη δέδεικται" (Plotinus. *Ennead*, Vol. V, ed. by A. H. Armstrong [Loeb Classical Library, Cambridge, MA: Harvard University Press, 1984], 5.1.10, 44, 46).

19 "Ποθεῖ δὲ πᾶν τὸ γεννῆσαν καὶ τοῦτο ἀγαπᾷ, καὶ μάλιστα ὅταν ὦσι μόνοι τὸ γεννῆσαν καὶ τὸ γεγεννημένον· ὅταν δὲ καὶ τὸ ἄριστον ᾖ τὸ γεννῆσαν, ἐξ ἀνάγκης σύνεστιν αὐτῷ, ὡς τῇ ἑτερότητι μόνον κεχωρίσθαι" (*ibid.*, 5.1.6, 32).

levels) and return (a willed focus that ascends from lower to higher levels). For the Neoplatonists who follow Plotinus, love is properly understood as an ascent through higher levels of experience, thought, and awareness, with a corresponding move away from a focus on or attachment to the here and now. According to this way of thinking, love is not love for an individual. It seeks to leave behind the embodied physical experiences of life. This movement away from the individual and physical, and toward the eternal and ethereal leads to something divine. In the *Symposium* it leads to the finest sense of knowledge. In Plotinus—and in the Christian thinkers and writers who incorporate his thought into their own—it becomes something like a God beyond God, what the thirteenth-century German mystic Meister Eckhart called the God that you must leave for God's sake.[20] Where Plato stops a step short of that, Plotinus's structure puts an unknowable "divine" principle at the top. This idea of love as a yearning for the divine and immortal, a yearning which must be shaped and trained away from individuals, is taken up by Dante, Petrarch, and other Italian poets, and passed down through them to English sixteenth-century authors. This idea works against the destabilizing effect of individual choice in love (which itself undermines the force of Church, State, and marital and social conventions) that is so powerfully emphasized in troubadour poetry.

II
Post-*Fin'amor* Italian Poetry: The Sicilian School to Dante and Petrarch

Among the earliest poetry in the Italian tradition was the work of the Sicilian poets in the court of Frederick II (1194–1250). Frederick's was a court that anticipated many of the great aesthetic and academic achievements of the Renaissance:

---

20 "The highest and final thing that a man may leave is this: that he leaves God for God" ("Daz hœhste unde daz nêhste, daz der mensche gelàzen mac, daz ist, daz er got dur got làze" ["Qui audit me, non confundetur"]). Franz Pfeiffer, ed. *Deutsche Mystiker des Vierzehnten Jahrhunderts: Bd. Meister Eckhart. Erste Abtheilung* (Leipzig: G. J. Göschen, 1857), 310, ll. 34–35, https://books.google.com/books?id=-78FAAAAQAAJ&pg=PA310

The Holy Roman Emperor Frederick II, who ruled from 1208 to 1250 [...], was an absolute ruler, but an enlightened and (for those days) tolerant one [...]; the philosophy and literature of the Arabs, of the Sicilian and Byzantine Greeks, of classical and neo-Latin Italy, and of southern France and Spain, all flowed into Frederick's realm [...]. [A] patron of scholars, translators, poets and musicians, as he moved about among his various cities and castles, [...] he required the centralised control of the imperium to be administered by a highly loyal staff of professional legal administrators [...]. It was to this secular corps that the inventor of the sonnet belonged.[21]

This new poetry was written in a style heavily influenced by the troubadours, as the poets "modeled their songs on the Occitan [...] themes, but composed in the Sicilian dialect".[22] However, these poets added three crucial elements: first, their radically enhanced "descriptions of the pain and sorrow of love, which had enormous emotional power", and second, their "invention of the sonnet, which became the dominant form for love poetry, not only in renaissance Italy but all over Europe".[23] The third element, however, is the most important: the Sicilian poets wrote in service and deference to imperial authority: "It was probably Frederick II [...] who encouraged the composition of poetry on the model of that of the troubadours at his Sicilian court. [...] Thus the foundations of the Italian lyric were laid".[24] In this more deferential poetry, something new appears—the tendency, which grows more pronounced in the poetry that follows, to turn love into worship and women into divine objects of adoration:

> The Sicilians followed closely in the track of the Provençal poets [...]. The subject matter of this imitative poetry was love—but love that bore a peculiar relation to ordinary human feeling. Woman was regarded as an ideal being, to be approached with worship bordering on adoration. The lover derived personal force, virtue, elevation, energy, from his

---

21 Michael R. G. Spiller. *The Development of the Sonnet: An Introduction* (London: Routledge, 1992), 14.
22 Ffiona Swabey. *Eleanor of Aquitaine, Courtly Love, and the Troubadours* (Westport: Greenwood Press, 2004), 67.
23 *Ibid.*
24 Olive Sayce. *Exemplary Comparison from Homer to Petrarch* (Cambridge, UK: Brewer, 2008), 289.

enthusiastic passion. [...] Love was the consummation of spiritual felicity, which surpassed all other modes of happiness in its beatitude.[25]

One of the best examples of the Sicilian style survives in the work of the man usually credited with the invention of the sonnet form, Giacomo da Lentini.[26] Working at the court of Frederick in the early thirteenth century, Giacomo's lyrics straddle the line between troubadour sensuality, and the later spiritualization of the poets of the *dolce stil novo*, a style that "owed much to the Sicilian school, [but most of whose practitioners] were from Florence and wrote in the Tuscan dialect".[27] In perhaps his most famous poem, *Io m'aggio posto in core a Dio servire*, Giacomo writes of being torn between love of God and love of his Lady, and is not at all sure that the former outweighs the latter:

> Io m'aggio posto in core a Dio servire
> com'io potesse gire in paradiso,
> al santo loco c'aggio audito dire
> si mantien sollazo, gioco, e riso.
> Sanza mia donna non vi voria gire
> (quella c'a blonda testa e claro viso)
> che sanza lei non poteria gaudire,
> estando da la mia donna diriso.
> Ma non lo dico a tale intendimento
> perch'io pecato ci volesse fare,
> se non veder lo suo bel portamento,
> lo bel viso, e l[o] morbido aguardare:

---

25 John Addington Symonds. *Renaissance in Italy*, Vol. 4, part 1 (London: Mith, Elder & Co., 1881), 59–60, https://books.google.com/books?id=K4sTAQAAIAAJ&dq=Symonds+Renaissance+in+Italy+1881&pg=PA59

26 Sayce 290. See also Martin J. Duffell's brief outlining of the history of the sonnet form in *A New History of English Metre* (London: Modern Humanities Research Association and Maney Publishing, 2008), 117–18, and Ernest Hatch Wilkins' account in *The Invention of the Sonnet and Other Studies in Italian Literature* (Rome: Edizioni de Storia e Letteratura, 1959), 14–17, as well as Pierre Blanc's account of the cultural and political forces that shaped the sonnet in the court of Frederick II, in "Sonnet des origines, origine du sonnet: Giacomo da Lentini". Yvonne Bellenger, ed. *Le Sonnet a la Renaissance: Des Origenes au XVIIe Siecle* (Paris: Aux Amateurs de Livres, 1998), 9–18. Finally, and most importantly, see Paul Oppenheimer's account of the origin of the sonnet in *The Birth of the Modern Mind: Self, Consciousness, and the Invention of the Sonnet* (Oxford: Oxford University Press, 1989), and his earlier article "The Origin of the Sonnet", *Comparative Literature*, 34: 4 (Autumn 1982), 289–304.

27 Swabey, 67–68.

> che lo mi teria in gran consolamento,
> vegiendo la mia donna in ghiora stare.[28]

> I have it deeply in my heart to serve God,
> so that I will come into paradise,
> The holy place I hear everywhere spoken of,
> where always is solace, joy and laughter.
> Without my lady I would not want to go,
> she with the blond hair and bright face,
> for without her, I could take no pleasure,
> being separated from my lady.
> Although I do not intend to say
> that I would sin with her there;
> if I did not see her beautiful bearing,
> and her beautiful face and soft look,
> I could not have great consolation
> unless I saw my lady standing there in glory.

The poet bargains with God over the love he has for his lady—assuring heaven's monarch, or trying to, that he means not to "sin", but insisting that if she were not in heaven, he "would not want to go", and would "take no pleasure". The sentiments of Giacomo's poem and those of Aucassin in *Aucassin et Nicolette* seem to have rather more in common than might appear at a first glance. While Aucassin speaks harshly of the corruption of heaven and of those who are ticketed for that particularly joyless destination, a place of "naked folks and shoeless, and covered with sores, perishing of hunger and thirst, and of cold, and of little ease", Giacomo's lover speaks more quietly, perhaps a bit timorously, but no less determinedly of his distaste for a heaven in which his lady might not be found.

Elsewhere, however, the developing tendency to idealize the lady, to both raise and reduce her by comparing her to jewels, the stars, the sun, can be seen in Giacomo's sonnet *Diamante, né smeraldo, né zaffino*. The lady is worth more than any jewel, and is like the stars themselves:

---

28 Giacomo da Lentini. *A Critical Edition of the Poetry of Giacomo da Lentini*, ed. by Stephen Popolizio (Ph.D. dissertation, Indiana University, 1975; Ann Arbor Michigan: University Microfilms, 1980), 156.

> [D]iamante, nè smiraldo, nè zaffino,
> nè vernul'altra gemma prezïosa,
> topazo, nè giaquinto, nè rubino,
> nè l'aritropia, ch'è sì vertudiosa,
> nè l'amatisto, nè'l carbonchio fino,
> lo qual è molto risprendente cosa,
> non àno tanta beleze in domino,
> quant'a in se la mia donna amorosa.
> E di vertute tutte l'altre avanza,
> somigliante [a stella è] di splendore
> co la sua conta e gaia innamoranza;
> e più bellè[sti] che rose e che frore.
> Cristo le doni vita ed alegranza,
> e sì l'acresca in gran pregio ed onore.[29]

> Diamonds, nor emeralds, nor sapphires,
> nor any other precious gems,
> topaz, nor pearl, nor rubies,
> neither heliotrope, so great in power,
> nor amethyst, nor the finest stones,
> the things which are most resplendent,
> none have beauty and power,
> so much as is in my beloved lady.
> And her virtue advances beyond all others,
> it shines like the stars in its splendor
> through her cheerful and charming face.
> She is more beautiful than a rose, or a flower.
> Christ give her the gifts of life and joy,
> and may she grow great in praise and honor.

At the same time, she exceeds the stars in brilliance; indeed, she is the sun itself in Giacomo's *Dolce cominciamento*:

> Dolce cominciamento
> canto per la più fina
> che sia, al mio parimento
> d'Agri infino in Messina,
> ciòe la più avenente,

---

29 *Ibid.*, 193.

'O stella rilucente,
che levi la maitina.
quando m'apar davanti,
li tuo' dolzi sembianti
mi'ncendon la corina'.[30]

Sweet beginning,
I sing for the finest
there is, in my opinion,
from Agri, all the way to Messina,
that is the most charming and fair.
"Oh shining star,
that rises at dawn!
When you appear before me,
your sweet face
sets fire to my heart".

As beautiful as this is, what has gone missing, even at this early stage, is precisely what goes missing from the poetry of a post-Crusade troubadour like Guilhem Montanhagol: the open description and celebration of physical passion and sexual desire as an element of love. Even in Giacomo's verse, whose lover seems on the precipice of refusing heaven if his lady is not to be there, the ideas of God and heaven and future punishment and reward are working their way prominently into the poetry. Here, we are entering a period in which poetry withdraws from individual passions, taking refuge in idealized descriptions: "Love became an art, with its code of laws and customs. There was no longer this or that particular woman, but a woman with fixed shapes and features, as conceived in books of chivalry. All women were alike".[31] This is a distinct departure from the work of the Occitan poets: Giacomo is "deliberately turning away from the kinds of songs made and sung by

---

30 Ibid., 107.
31 "L'amore divenne un'arte, col suo codice di leggi e costumi. Non ci fu più questa o quella donna, ma la donna con forme e lineamenti fissati, così come era concepita ne' libri di cavalleria. Tutte le donne sono simili" (Francesco De Sanctis. *Storia della letteratura italiana*, Vol. 1 [Neaples: Morano, 1870], 11, https://books.google.com/books?id=VtuDUIv5cvUC&pg=PA11).

the troubadours".[32] His poems are not expressions of person-to-person love, but "lyric[s] sung by the soul to the soul, in the silent music of the soul", songs that "echo those celestial and silent proportions and ratios described by Plato", constructed "according to the architecture of the soul and of heaven".[33] One can imagine Guilhem IX snorting at such ideas, but such was the change from the late eleventh to the early thirteenth centuries, as the Church grew more powerful, and learned to exert more control over the lives of those under its sway, even dictating what would, and would not, be appropriate in the realm of art and poetry:

> The Church proscribed the poets of antiquity; and it had become an axiom that poetry was the art of lies. Poetry was hardly suffered to exist except as a veil to cloak some hidden doctrine; and allegory presented a middle way of escape, whereby the pleasure of art could be enjoyed with a safe conscience.[34]

The effects of this increasing control can be seen as we move from the Sicilians to the practitioners of what Dante calls the *dolce stil novo*. Guido Guinizelli (*c.* 1230–1276) is writing at about the same time as Montanhagol, while the last of the old troubadour spirit in Occitania is dying. In Guinizelli's poems, a transition between the embodied love of the troubadours and the spiritualized love of the emerging allegorical and Neoplatonist tradition is evident. There is still a powerful sense of bodily desire, but in *Chi vedesse a Lucia un var cappuzzo* (Who sees Lucia in her fur hat) something has gone wrong, and become twisted into the foul deformity of a rape fantasy:

> Ah, prender lei a forza, ultra a su' grato
> e bagiarli la bocca e 'l bel visaggio
> e li occhi suoi, ch'èn due fiamme de foco!
> Ma, pentomi, però che m'ho pensato,
> ch'esto fatto poria portar dannaggio
> ch'altrui despiaceria forse non poco.[35]

---

32 Paul Oppenheimer. "The Origin of the Sonnet". *Comparative Literature*, 34: 4 (Autumn 1982), 297, https://doi.org/10.2307/1771151
33 *Ibid.*, 304.
34 Symonds, 81, https://books.google.com/books?id=K4sTAQAAIAAJ&pg=PA81
35 Guido Guinizelli. *The Poetry of Guido Guinizelli*, ed. by Robert Edwards (New York: Garland Publishing, 1987), 54, ll. 9–14.

> Oh, to take her by force, even against her will,
> And kiss her mouth and beautiful face
> And her eyes, like two flames of fire!
> But I repent that thought,
> For this would cause harm and sorrow,
> And displease her not a little.

The violent lust of this poem may partly explain why Dante puts Guinizelli in hell: "In canto XXVI, amidst a band of the lustful, sodomites and others, Dante meets Guido Guinizelli. He salutes him by the name of the 'father', because he was both the initiator and [Dante's] master in the [*dolce stil novo*'s] third way, sensual and scholarly".[36] Alongside the hellish note, there is a ring of the future in Guinizelli's poem, a hint of the poetry that will follow a Neoplatonic path, with the increasingly intense sublimation of the physical into the spiritual, the rhetorical excesses of the comparisons of the beloved's eyes to the stars of heaven, the beloved's voice to the music of angels, or the beloved's eyelids to flame. The women of these poems will be described in ways that separate them from the realm of physically identifiable human beings. The woman is light, a star, radiant; she is not embodied, but a spiritual figure who draws the male poet toward heaven. In the above example, we can clearly see that the "Lucia" of the poem is not regarded by the narrator as a fully human woman; rather, she is an object—either of rape fantasies, or of worship—not a desired and desiring subject. The change in the lady's status in Guinizelli (as opposed to Marcabru or Bernart de Ventadorn) is already obvious.

The sublimation and spiritualization that is merely hinted at elsewhere is openly expressed in Guinizelli's *Al cor gentil* (Of the gentle heart):

> Splende 'n la 'ntelligenzïa del cielo
> Deo Crïator più che 'n nostr' occhi 'l sole:
> ella intende suo fattor oltra 'l cielo,
> e 'l ciel volgiando, a lui obedir tole,
> e con' segue al primero

---

36 "Au chant XXVI, parmi une bande de luxurieux, sodomites et autres, Dante rencontre Guido Guinicelli. Il le salue du nom de 'père', lui qui fut son initiateur et son maître dans sa 3 e manière, sensuelle et savante" (René Lavaud, in Daniel, 133, https://archive.org/stream/lesposiesdarna00arna#page/133).

> del giusto Deo beato compimento,
> così dar dovria, al vero,
> la bella donna, poi che 'n gli occhi splende
> del suo gentil, talento
> che mai di lei obedir non si disprende.[37]

> So shines in the Intelligence of heaven
> God the creator, more than sun in our eyes;
> She understands her maker beyond heaven,
> And turning to heaven, prepares to obey;
> And in first consequence thereof,
> As God blesses the just
> So in her true duty
> The beautiful lady, whose eyes shine
> On the gentle, and talented,
> Blesses those who do not cease to obey her.

Here, the lady is a conduit between the poet and God, a spiritual figure in whose eyes truth is glorified, and to whose service the poet is dedicated. In this poem, the beloved is barely a woman at all; instead, she is something more like a saint, an object of devotion and praise whose main purpose is to bring the poet to God. The shift—even as early as Guinizelli—is evident and profound: rather than being regarded as an individual (as a subject) who is desired by the male for her own beauties and merits, as in the troubadour poems, this woman is portrayed as the personification of an abstract principle—truth—and is desired primarily for her function or utility (as an object) in bringing the poet to God.

This is an idea we can trace to an Inquisition-era troubadour, Uc de Saint Circ, who was writing in northern Italy in the mid-thirteenth century, perhaps a generation before Guinizelli. Uc writes of aspiring to heaven through a lady:

> De ma vida·m faitz esmenda,
> Bella de dura merce,
> Ab sol que soffratz de me
> Qu'eu per vos al cel entenda.[38]

---

37 Guinizelli, 22, ll. 41–50.
38 "Servit aurai longamen", ll. 46–49. In Alfred Jeanroy, ed. *Poesies de Uc de Saint-Circ* (Toulouse: Édouard Privat, 1913), 30–34, https://archive.org/stream/

> Take my life in homage,
> Beautiful unmerciful one,
> As long as you suffer me
> To aspire through you to heaven.

This is the point at which the emphasis of love poetry clearly changes, shifting its focus from *here* to the *hereafter*. Though it may well be true that "Guinizelli [...] refuses to define sacred and profane love as mutually exclusive", this merely leads us back to Diotima's notion that human love is nothing more than a transitional stage in the seeking of divine love, especially since Guinizelli appeals to "a subtle Augustinian philosophical sense of love as a continuum from human to divine", and "treats the amatory situation as an inward and high-mindedly ethical event, connected with the larger process of order and purpose in God's universe".[39] In Guinizelli's poetry, the woman praised by the poet is not an end in herself, but a glorified means to an end. In fact, Guinizelli expresses anxiety lest he had at any point slipped up and paid too much regard to the woman, and therefore not enough to God: "It was not my fault, to fall in love with her".[40]

God is portrayed here as jealous because not all praise and love is going to him. Part of it may have, in quiet moments, gone too directly to the unnamed "her" of Guinizelli's song, making that "her" a rival to God, another deity. Such a gesture makes clear that this woman is not a woman, or at the very least is not treated so by the poem. This woman is a paragon, no mere fleshly mortal, and the poem goes to great lengths to give love a Christian doctrinal basis:

> The dramatized self-justification leaves the lady still enhanced and angel-like and at the same time allows a distant analogy to the Virgin. Thus [Guinizelli] by his mode of argument puts the love situation on an inward ethical basis, connects it with the macro-cosmic process of God's universe, and gives it a Christian justification.[41]

---

posiesdeucdesa00ucde#page/32
39 William J. Kennedy. "European Beginnings and Transmissions: Dante Petrarch, and the Sonnet Sequence". In A. D. Cousins and Peter Horwarth, eds. *The Cambridge Companion to the Sonnet* (Cambridge: Cambridge University Press, 2011), 87.
40 "non me fu fallo, s'in lei posi amanza" (Guinizelli, 22, l.60).
41 Lowry Nelson. *Poetic Configurations: Essays in Literary History and Criticism* (University Park: Penn State University Press, 1992), 100.

Guinizelli's sonnet *Io vogl' del ver la mia donna laudare* is less blatant in its treatment of the "lady" as a means rather than an end than is *Al cor gentil*. But even here, the reader encounters a meditation on a subject that serves to ennoble the meditator, and represents the woman as a glorious means to a higher and even more glorious end:

> Io vogl' del ver la mia donna laudare
> ed asembrarli la rosa e lo giglio:
> più che stella dïana splende e pare,
> e ciò, ch'è lassù è bello a lei somiglio.[42]

> I will in truth praise my lady,
> Comparing her to the rose and the lily.
> She shines brighter than Diana's star;
> And so, all that is beautiful, resembles her.

Again, we see the comparison of the woman to heaven, to "Diana's star" (Venus, or the "morning star") which the unnamed lady exceeds. It's lovely. The poetry of this period and place is aesthetically at least equal to, and arguably an advance beyond, much of the earlier troubadour poetry. But it also represents a significant shift in point of view and philosophical orientation. Far from being desirable for beauty, from passion, and through disregard for the consequences attending a nearly-always adulterous inclination and arousal, the woman is treated as an exemplar, a spiritual guide for the righteous man, and a transcendent agent of shame and reproach for the unrighteous man:

> e fa 'l di nostra fè se non la crede.
> e non la pò appressare om che sia vile;
> ancor ve dirò c'ha maggior virtute;
> null'uom pò mal pensar fin che la vede.[43]

> She makes you of our faith, if you do not believe.
> For no man can be near her, if he is vile:
> I tell you, she has an even greater strength;
> No man can think evil who has seen her.

---

42   Guinizelli, 40, ll. 1–4.
43   *Ibid.*, ll. 11–14.

All of this eloquence is put into the service of an argument which is essentially this: love is only that which leads to, and is finally revealed as having always been, love of God: "To Guido Guinizelli love, always guided by reason, is a pure form of man's aspiration toward God. Originating largely in the aesthetic admiration of physical beauty, love thereafter turns to the moral beauty which is its true goal. In the *cor gentil* the beautiful lady may induce a blessedness that is the image of the beatitude of heaven".[44] The love of another, the love of a freely chosen individual, a flesh and blood man or woman, is next door to idolatry. Such love of another is only excusable if it leads you to the love of God. And while the veils between idolatry and love of God here might seem thin, that is only because they *are* thin. The early Italian poets, much like the late troubadour Montanhagol, are trying to shoehorn notions of *eros* (from a tradition that spans from Ovid through the high-period troubadours) into the new dispensation, the rules set down by the post-Albigensian-Crusade Church (in which the theological and military powers-that-be demonstrated that they were ready and willing to turn against Europeans, not just a distant Muslim "other"). How far, at this point, we have come from the letters of Héloïse, and the poems of the troubadours.

One final poem from Guinizelli brings a number of ideas together in one place. In *Tegno di folle 'mpres', a lo ver dire*, the poet distinguishes his love from other women by resorting to the now familiar comparison to the sun: "Among others she is a shining sun".[45] The woman of this *canzone*, however, is also proud, perhaps a touch too proud, in the poet's view:

> ella non mette cura di neente
> ma vassen disdegnosa,
> ché si vede alta, bella, e avvenente.
> Ben si pò tener alta quanto vòle;
> ché la plu bella donna è che si trove[46]

---

44 Marianne Shapiro. *Woman Earthly and Divine in the Comedy of Dante* (Lexington: University Press of Kentucky, 2015), 28.
45 "Ed infra l'altre par lucente sole" (Guinizelli, 2, l.23).
46 *Ibid.*, ll. 18–22.

> She does not care about a single thing,
> But walks away disdainfully,
> Seeing herself as beautiful and fair.
> Well, she can have all the pride she wants,
> For she is the most beautiful woman anywhere.

The implication is that because the lover loves, the beloved is supposed to have mercy on, extend favor to, and in some cases reciprocate the love of the lover. When she does not, she is described as haughty, even imperious, while the man who loves her is a helpless fool:

> Tegno di folle 'mpres', a lo ver dire,
> chi s'abandona inver' troppo possente,
> si como gli occhi miei che fér esmire
> nincontr' a quelli de la più avenente.
> che sol per lor è vinti
> senza ch'altre bellezze li dian forza,
> ché a ciò far son pinti.[47]

> I think him foolish, truthfully,
> who abandons himself to a power too strong,
> like I, with my eyes, have done in this sort
> to the power of those eyes most fair,
> and by them are overcome.
> No need for other beauties to lend their force,
> To what had gone before.

This idea of the proud and unmerciful lady who refuses her love to the young male who pines for it is one that appears often in the later poetry of Petrarch, and in the verses of English poets like Philip Sidney. In Guinizelli, we can see an early example of what will become a well-worn pairing: *the ladder of love,* and *the pride or intractability of the beloved.* This pairing strongly suggests that the female is responsible for the spiritual life and death of the male. If the woman is the conduit through which the man is to learn to ascend to heaven on the ladder of his own increasingly refined, and upward-directed thoughts and emotions, and the woman is too proud to be as affable and obedient as the male would have her be,

---

47   *Ibid.*,11.1–7

then the man will fail to ascend, suffer spiritual death, and end up in a hell of eternal judgment and torment. From this develops the idea that love is something you die for, or die of, rather than live for. In his work, Petrarch makes frequent use of this idea, and Shakespeare will often mock characters who give voice to such weeping and gnashing of teeth.

Guinizelli's contemporary, Guido delle Colonne, develops the idea of the lady's pride and failure to be "affable" in *Amor, che lungiamente m'hai menato* (Love, which so long has driven me):

> Non dico c' a la vostra gran bellezza
> orgoglio non convegna e stiale bene,
> c'a bella donna orgoglio ben convene,
> che si mantene—in pregio ed in grandezza.
> Troppa alterezza—è quella che sconvene;
> di grande orgoglio mai ben non avene.
> Però, madonna, la vostra durezza
> convertasi in pietanza e si rinfreni:
> non si distenda tanto ch'io ne pèra.
> Lo sole è alto, e sì face lumera,
> e tanto più quanto 'n altura pare:
> vostr' argogliare—donqua e vostra altezze
> facciami prode e tornimi in dolcezze.[48]

> I do not say, that with your great beauty
> Pride does not agree, it serves you well;
> That pride in a beautiful woman is fitting
> Which maintains esteem and grandeur.
> But too much pride, that is not fitting;
> A great and haughty pride is never attractive.
> But my lady, your harshness
> Convert to pity, and restraint;
> Do not stretch so much, to seem so posh.
> The sun is high, and brilliantly lighted,
> And even more so, the higher it seems:
> So let your pride and your haughtiness
> Turn its face to me in sweetness and delight.

---

48 Piero Cudini, ed. *Poesia Italiana. Il Duecento* (Milan: Lampi di Stampa, 1999), 27, ll. 27–39.

In the terms of these lines, if the poet does not gain the love of the figure he refers to possessively as "my lady", then he will rail at length about her "haughty pride" and "harshness", berating her for her lack of "pity", while never considering her desires even for a moment. Nowhere is it clearer than in these lines that the beloved is a means, not an end in herself. In the troubadour poems, what is different is the idea of individual value and mutual desire. In those poems, the will is mutual, as is the choice. Where is the volition of the women being spoken of in the poems of Guinizelli and Colonne? Where is the voice of the female? She has become a beautifully spoken-of but slightly-regarded object, a consistent feature of Colonne's larger body of work, where "[h]is tone is overtly moralizing and didactic [and] he muses on the instability of human affairs, the unpredictable workings of Fortune, and [...] the fickleness of women and their dangerous and corrupting influence".[49] This crucial shift in perspective lays down the foundations of ideas and imagery that work their way through a developing poetic tradition that has enormous influence on the poetry of later centuries. Colonne's final lines bring this point home:

> Gli occi a lo core sono gli messaggi
> de' suoi incominciamenti per natura.
> Dunqua. madonna, gli occhi e lo meo core
> avete in vostra mano, entro e di fore,
> c'Amor me sbatte e smena, che no abento,
> sì come vento—smena nava in onda:
> voi siete meo pennel che non affonda.[50]

> The eyes bring messages to the heart
> Of all that begins by nature.
> Therefore, my lady, my eyes and my heart
> You have in your hand, inside and out;
> That love leads my life into battle,
> And beats, as the winds against a ship,
> But you are my banner, which will not sink.

---

49 Jane E. Everson. *The Italian Romance Epic in the Age of Humanism: The Matter of Italy and the World of Rome* (Oxford: Oxford University Press, 2001), 44.
50 Cudini, 28, ll. 54–60.

And yet where is this lady in those gorgeous lines? She is a thing that exists in his emotions, in his head, in his thoughts, in his language, in his verse. She is given no detailed description, no voice or validity or ability to speak back except as an adjunct to his desires or an aid to what he would have. If we look at the poem as a powerful expression of what the poet most desires, aesthetically it is beautiful. But when we consider how that desire is spoken, what use the poems make of the idea of the beloved, that desire, and that poem, become dark and troubling things.

By the time we come to the poetry of Dante, written in the late thirteenth and early fourteenth centuries, we are on ground that is more familiar to many readers. His collection *La Vita Nuova* (The new life) contains even clearer alterations of troubadour themes than do the works of his predecessors. These verses describe the effect on the poet that is wrought by seeing a young girl named Beatrice, who will become the muse of *La Divina Commedia*, or *The Divine Comedy*. The sonnet *Negli occhi porta la mia donna Amore* makes the effect especially clear:

> Negli occhi porta la mia donna Amore;
> Per che si fa gentil ciò ch' ella mira:
> Ov' ella passa ogni uom ver lei si gira:
> E cui saluta fa tremar lo core;
> Sì che bassando il viso tutto smore,
> E d'ogni suo difetto allor sospira:
> Fugge davanti a lei superbia, ed ira.
> Aitatemi voi, donne, a farle onore.
> Ogni dolcezza, ogni pensiero umile
> Nasce nel core a chi parlar la sente;
> Ond' è beato chi prima la vide.
> Quel ch'ella par quando un poco sorride
> Non si può dicer, nè tenere a mente,
> Sì è nuovo miracolo e gentile.[51]

> The door to love is in my lady's eyes,
> So where she looks all things grow gentle;
> And where she passes all men turn to her,

---

51 Dante. *The Canzoniere of Dante Alighieri*, ed. by Charles Lyell (London: James Bohn, 1840), 36, https://books.google.com/books?id=E6JWAAAAcAAJ&pg=PA36

> And those she blesses tremble to their core,
> Cast their faces down in shame, wholly pale,
> And instantly confess their every sin in sighs.
> Pride and anger flee before her,
> Help me honor her, noble ladies.
> All sweetness, all humble thoughts
> Be born in the hearts that hear her speak;
> And blessed be they who have once known
> How she appeared with a little smile;
> Nor words nor thoughts can describe her,
> She is so new and noble a miracle.

Dante describes this young girl as a "miracle" more than she is a flesh-and-blood human being; her value is not in her humanity, but in her function. Beatrice transforms ("where she looks all things grow gentle") the wicked hearts of evil men, who, as they "[c]ast their faces down in shame, wholly pale, / And instantly confess their every fault in sighs", become suddenly aware of their insufficiency in the face, not of a girl, but of a goddess. This sacramental function that Dante assigns to Beatrice is even clearer in the following lines from *Io mi sentii svegliar dentro a lo core*:

> Io mi sentii svegliar dentro a lo core
> Un spirito amoroso che dormia,
> E poi vidi venir di lungi Amore,
> Allegro sì che appena il conoscìa,
> Dicendo: or pensa pur di farmi onore;
> E ciascuna parola sua ridia:
> E, poco stando, meco il mio signore,
> Guardando in quella parte ond' ei venia,
> Io vidi monna Vanna e monna Bice
> Venire in verso il loco dov' io era,
> L'una appresso dell' altra meraviglia.
> E sì, come la mente mi ridice,
> Amor mi disse: questa è Primavera,
> E quella ha nome Amor, sì mi somiglia.[52]

> I felt awakening in my inmost heart
> Love's spirit, sleeping there.

---

52 *Ibid.*, 50, https://books.google.com/books?id=E6JWAAAAcAAJ&pg=PA36

> And I saw Love himself approach from afar,
> So cheerfully, I scarcely recognized him,
> He said, think now to give me honor;
> And with every word he laughed.
> And, when my Lord had stayed a little while,
> I gazed in the direction from which he came
> And saw lady Vanna and lady Beatrice
> Coming to the place where I stood,
> The one surpassing the other as a marvel,
> And now, as memory brings back their words
> Love said to me, this lady is the Springtime,
> But this one is called Love, she so resembles me.

Beatrice, as were the various "ladies" of the Guinizelli and Colonne poems, is made an abstraction, stripped of humanity in order better to serve to stir the poet's heart, and work him into an attitude of worship.

In the sonnet *Di donne io vidi una gentile schiera*, Dante takes the deifying and sacralizing of Beatrice even further. Here, Beatrice is not merely Love itself, no mere miracle—rather, she is "an angel through whom man reaches God",[53] accompanied by Love as by an attendant, a lady birthed in Heaven itself:

> Di donne io vidi una gentile schiera
> Quest' Ognissanti prossimo passato;
> Ed una ne venia quasi primiera,
> Seco menando Amor dal destro lato.
> Dagli occhi suoi gittava una lumiera,
> La qual pareva un spirito infiammato;
> Ed i' ebbi tanto ardir, che la sua cera
> Guardando, vidi un angiol figurato.
> A chi era degno poi dava salute
> Con gli occhi suoi quella benigna e piana,
> Empiendo il core a ciascun di virtute.
> Credo che in ciel nascesse esta soprana,
> E venne in terra per nostra salute:
> Dunque beata chi l'è prossimana.[54]

---

53 Hagstrum, 236.
54 Dante, *Canzoniere*, 378, https://books.google.com/books?id=E6JWAAAAcAAJ&pg=PA378

> I saw a group of gentle ladies
> On All Saint's Day just past;
> And one, without apology, as if the prime,
> Led Love along at her right hand.
> From her eyes shone forth a light,
> That seemed a spirit burning in flame;
> With great daring, at her form
> I gazed, and saw an angel's figure.
> Then with dignity and calm she blessed
> With her eyes, kindly and simply, all those
> Wicked at heart, filling them all with virtue.
> I believe she was born in highest heaven,
> And came to earth to be our blessing,
> So blissful are those who are close to her.

Here again, love for the "woman" is not love of a human being, but worship of an angel, and a conduit for salvation: "Beatrice gradually becomes a bearer not only of health and of salutation [...] but of salvation. Dante's overwhelming experience of love [...] for Beatrice becomes transformed into a sacred spiritual force".[55]

Ary Scheffer, *Dante and Beatrice* (1851). Museum of Fine Arts, Boston.[56]

---

55 Nelson, 100.
56 https://commons.wikimedia.org/wiki/File:Ary_Scheffer_-_Dante_and_Beatrice.jpg?uselang=en-gb

At this point, we have long since left behind the idea of love as a radically destabilizing force, between two people who have no business choosing each other, yet do, despite all the boundaries that separate them. We have moved from that, to a poetry that describes love in sacred terms, a love that is amenable to being channeled within the Church, a love that is not an anarchic threat. The love described by Guinizelli and Colonne, and even more powerfully by Dante, is not a two-way choice, but something that begins to reflect increasingly a single point of view: the desires of the male heart, the male voice, and the male passions, while the female heart, voice, and passions are set aside, and the female herself is increasingly dehumanized, dematerialized, and deified:

> Dante may be said to have rediscovered the Platonic mystery, whereby love is an initiation into the secrets of the spiritual world. [...] In proportion as Beatrice personified abstractions, she ceased to be a woman even for her lover; nor was it possible except by diminishing her individuality, to regard her as a symbol, of the universal. She passed from the sphere of the human into the divine.[57]

One of the most outstanding examples of Dante's sublimation of love into a spiritual value is found, not in his sonnets, but in his epic. In *Inferno*, Dante rehearses the then-already-famous story of the lovers Paolo and Francesca. Brought together by the circumstances of an arranged marriage between Francesca da Rimini and Paolo's brother Gianciotto de Malatesta, the lovers carried on an affair for years before getting caught in the bedroom by Gianciotto, who stabs them to death, affixing them both on his sword at the same time. As Dante's pilgrim is guided through Hell by Virgil, he encounters Francesca, who tells her story:

> "Noi leggiavamo un giorno per diletto
> di Lancialotto come amor lo strinse;
> soli eravamo e sanza alcun sospetto.
> Per più fiate li occhi ci sospinse
> quella lettura, e scolorocci il viso;
> ma solo un punto fu quel che ci vinse.
> Quando leggemmo il disïato riso
> esser basciato da cotanto amante,

---

57 Symonds, 90, https://books.google.com/books?id=K4sTAQAAIAAJ&dq=Symonds Renaissance in Italy 1881&pg=PA90

> questi, che mai da me non fia diviso,
> la bocca mi basciò tutto tremante.
> Galeotto fu 'l libro e chi lo scrisse:
> quel giorno più non vi leggemmo avante".
> Mentre che l'uno spirto questo disse,
> l'altro piangea; sì che di pietade
> io venni men così com'io morisse.
> E caddi come corpo morto cade.[58]

> "We were reading, one day, to our delight,
> Of Lancelot, held tightly by love;
> We were alone, without doubt or suspicion.
> Many times, our eyes were drawn together
> By that reading, and the color left our faces:
> But one point only had defeated us.
> When we read of the longed-for lips
> Being kissed by the happy lover,
> He, from whom may I never be parted,
> Kissed me, trembling, on the mouth.
> A Galahad was the book and its author,
> But that day we read no further".
> While the one spirit said this,
> The other wept, and from pity
> I grew sick, as if to die,
> And I fell as a dead body falls.

Dante is playing a sly game of poetic sleight-of-hand here. As so often in the *vidas*, the imaginative biographies of the troubadours, the costs of passion between two people who choose each other in the face of law, marriage, church, and other institutional impediments, can be enormous. Viewed from that perspective, Dante has written, in this scene with Francesca, the most devastatingly romantic *vida* of them all. But from the perspective of those Dantean poems which regard love as a vehicle for disembodied sublimation and worship, Dante has given Paolo and Francesca the most lasting of punishments for having dared to love each other rather than God, for having dared to be devoted

---

58 Dante. *Inferno*, Canto 5.127–42. In *La Divina Commedia. Inferno*, ed. by Ettore Zolesi (Rome: Armando, 2009), 124–25.

to each other rather than to the laws, codes, and expectations of their time and place. They will spend an eternity in Hell, suffering infinite punishment for a finite period of human sin, at the hands of a God who also arranges for them to regret and weep eternally over the love they had shared.

As far as some literary critics are concerned, this is all to the good, for such lovers, in the eyes of our rigid moralists, deserve to be punished, and tormented for eternity: Barbara Reynolds argues that Dante puts Francesca in hell "for a reason; [her words] are a key to her character, as is her use of poetry to justify her adultery and of Arthurian romance to blame for its influence".[59] Edoardo Sanguineti condemns Francesca as "a [Madame] Bovary of the thirteenth century, who dreams of kissing Lancelot, and who enjoys, in tragic reduction, the embraces of her brother-in-law".[60] Elspeth Kennedy blames not only poor moral choices but also faulty reading habits for Paolo and Francesca's consignment to an eternity of torment: "If Paolo and Francesca had read the whole of the cyclic romance, they too might have seen the kiss of Lancelot and Guinevere in a different way and resisted their own desire to imitate it".[61] Antonio Enzo Quaglio dismisses Francesca as an immoral dilettante, who should have left reading to her moral betters, sneering at "this bookish woman, this creature of print, [who,] projecting shadows on the pilgrim's own moral ambivalence, seems drawn as an ancient cartoon [...] from the poetic prehistory of the *Commedia*".[62] And in a move so dismissive it reads as high comedy, Mary Kay-Gamel reduces Francesca and her eternal torment to the (apparently deserved) agonies of a failed graduate student:

---

59 Barbara Reynolds. *Dante: The Poet, the Political Thinker, the Man* (London: I. B.Tauris, 2007), 135.
60 "una Bovary del Duecento, che sogna i baci di Lancillotto, e fruisce, in tragica riduzione, degli abbracciamenti del cognate" (Edoardo Sanguineti. *Il Realismo di Dante* [Florence: Sansoni, 1966], 28).
61 Elspeth Kennedy. "The Rewriting and Re-reading of a Text: The Evolution of the *Prose Lancelot*". In Alison Adams, Armel H. Diverres, and Karen Stern, eds. *The Changing Face of Arthurian Romance: Essays on Arthurian Prose Romance in Memory of Cedric E. Pickford* (Cambridge, UK: Brewer, 1986), 9.
62 "questa donna libresca, questa creatura cartecea, che proietta sul pellegrino le ombre della propria ambivalenza morale, sembra disegnata su antichi cartoni [...] nella preistoria poetica della Commedia" (Antonio Enzo Quaglio. *Al di là di Francesca e Laura* [Padova: Liviana Editrice, 1973], 29).

> Francesca is not a well-trained student of literature. She doesn't finish the work, she misremembers an important detail (Guinevere kisses Lancelot, not vice versa), she is guilty of the intentional fallacy, and her interpretation is entirely too mimetic. If she had read further, she would have discovered how grave, in emotional and spiritual terms, were the consequences of Lancelot and Guinevere's illicit love, and she might have acted differently. Francesca is a female reader who does not adequately question the *object* of her reading, the *method* she uses to read, and the *use* to which she puts her reading.[63]

But far from being the conventionally moral tale that satisfies the instincts of the moral scolds within academia (or the moral scold within Dante himself), the speech of Francesca da Rimini powerfully illustrates the immorality at the heart of the Christian myth, and the shocking cruelty of the "moral" codes that take their inspiration from it. Greater than all the *Inferno*'s scenes of torture and pain, greater even than the agony of Count Ugolino, who will spend eternity chewing on the bloody skull of his most hated rival, the passion and punishment of Paolo and Francesca walks a tightrope between fascination and condemnation, between the old attitudes of the troubadours, and the new dispensation in which love will be disembodied, tamed, and turned toward the very God who sentences human beings to an eternity of agony for a finite lifetime of human "error", a God whom Dante describes in the final line of *Paradiso*, as *l'amor che move il sole e l'altre stelle*, the love that moves the sun and the other stars. From *fin'amor*, we have now come to the kind of *amor* that consigns lovers to Hell and torment forever.

Less famously, but perhaps even more astoundingly, the forced Christianizing of the poetic tradition, and the shoehorning of the troubadours into the new, spiritualized poetry of love, is nowhere made more evident than in Dante's treatment of Arnaut Daniel, the poet among the troubadours whom he most admired. In *Purgatorio*, "Arnaut boasts of achieving the impossible",[64] while Dante has the troubadour speak as though he regrets his life and work, and looks forward only to being fully purged of his sin as he ascends toward God:

---

63 Mary-Kay Gamel. "This Day We Read Further: Feminist Interpretation and the Study of Literature". *Pacific Coast Philology*, 22: 1–2 (November 1987), 8.
64 "Arnaut se vante de réaliser l'impossible" (René Lavaud, in Daniel, 134).

> Tan mabellis vostre cortes deman,
> qu'ieu no me puesc ni voill a vos cobrire.
> Ieu sui Arnaut, que plor e vau cantan;
> consiros vei la passada folor,
> e vei jausen lo joi qu'esper, denan.
> Ara vos prec, per aquella valor
> que vos guida al som de l'escalina,
> sovenha vos a temps de ma dolor![65]

> I am so pleased by your courteous question,
> That I am not able or willing to hide from you.
> I am Arnaut, who goes weeping in song;
> Grieving, I look back on my past folly,
> And I foresee with joy the hope before me.
> So now I beg you, by that brave merit
> That guides you to the summit of the stairway,
> Remember, when the time comes, my sorrow.

In the eloquence and economy of this gesture, and in the pathos of the scene, a reader may miss the enormity of what Dante has just done. He has reduced an entire world, an entire language, an entire way of life, an entire experience of love and delight to the status of benighted sin. And though he could not bring himself to condemn to Hell the poet he so admired (whom he has another of his heroes, Guinizelli, describe as "the greater maker" ("il miglior fabbro"), he reduces him to a mouthpiece for the newly-ascendant orthodoxy of an Inquisition-era Roman Church. In this moment, and through this gesture, Dante—among the greatest poets our world has ever seen, or will ever see—climbs his mountain of Purgatory, and the new literary mountain of the *dolce stil novo*, as a traitor to poetry.

At the peak of this new literary mountain, we find the later figure of Petrarch. Though he is one of the towering figures in the Western literary tradition, Petrarch is not a solitary genius who establishes a new poetic point of view, creating *ex nihilo* a poetic form that had not existed before. His original contribution is more evident in terms of emphasis than form: it is not the choice to write about love, sublimated

---

65 Dante. *Purgatorio*, Canto 26.139–48. In *La Divina Commedia. Purgatorio*, ed. by Ettore Zolesi (Rome: Armando, 2003), 428–29.

into a passion for heaven, but rather to make the subject of sublimated, spiritualized love the dominant focus of his verse, and to change the vocabulary of love poetry. "Petrarch effected the first major stage in the spiritualization of love and beauty through his insistence upon the spiritual nature of womanly beauty—he contributed, as well, a unique vocabulary which permeates most of the love poetry which follows his: the beloved as tormenter, [and] the lover as sufferer".[66]

Much of the imagery and point of view in Petrarch's poetry is similar to what we have already seen. The idea of personified love appears first in Sonnet 3: captured and unable to defend himself because "your eyes, lady, had bound me",[67] Petrarch's narrator complains that "Love found me altogether disarmed / and opened the way to the heart through my eyes / which have become the doors and gates of tears".[68] Captured by Love, and bound by the eyes of the "lady" the reader will soon know as Laura, Petrarch's poetic voice grows increasingly pained and desperate. In Sonnet 11 it begins to appear evident this love is not returned. In fact his expression of love gets in the way and makes the beloved weary of him:

> Mentr'io portava i be' pensier' celati,
> ch'ànno la mente desïando morta,
> vidivi di pietate ornare il volto;
> ma poi ch'Amor di me vi fece accorta,
> fuor i biondi capelli allor velati
> et l'amoroso sguardo in sé raccolto.
> Quel ch'i' piú desiava in voi m'è tolto.[69]

> While I kept my loving thoughts hidden,
> that brought my mind to wish for death,
> I beheld Pity's face adorned;
> but when Love made you notice me,

---

66 Neal L. Goldstien. "*Love's Labour's Lost* and the Renaissance Vision of Love". In Stephen Orgel and Sean Kellen, eds. *Shakespeare and the Literary Tradition* (London: Routledge, 1999), 205.

67 "vostr' occhi, Donna, mi legaro" (Francesco Petrarca. *Il Canzoniere*, ed. by Paola Vecchi Galli [Milan: Rizzoli, 1954], 3.4). All further references to Petrarch's *Canzionere* will be to this volume.

68 "Trovommi Amor del tutto disarmato, / et aperta la via per gli occhi al core, / che di lagrime son fatti uscio et varco" (*ibid.*, 3.9–11).

69 *Ibid.*, 11.5–11.

> you hid your blond hair behind a veil,
> and drew back your loving gaze.
> What I wanted most in you, he took from me.

Sonnet 12 describes his life as one of "bitter torment" ("l'aspro tormento")[70] that might yet afford him the opportunity to gaze once more upon:

> cape' d'oro fin farsi d'argento,
> et lassar le ghirlande e i verdi panni,
> e 'l viso scolorir che ne' miei danni
> a llamentar mi fa pauroso et lento[71]
>
> a head of golden hair spun like silver,
> and the garlands laid by and green cloth,
> and your pale face that wounds me
> making my lamentations slow and fearful.

At other, more optimistic moments, Petrarch's narrator is less pained by than grateful for the opportunity to worship his beloved from afar: "I bless the place, the time and the hour / that brought so high the gazing of my eyes".[72] But more often, it is pain that characterizes love in Petrarch's verse. Sonnet 36 meditates on the possibility of escaping this agony by dying:

> S'io credesse per morte essere scarco
> del pensiero amoroso che m'atterra,
> colle mie mani avrei già posto in terra
> queste mie membra noiose, et quello incarco.[73]
>
> If I believed that by death I could be released
> from amorous thoughts that bind me to earth,
> with my hands I would already have buried
> these my tiresome limbs, and that burden

---

70   Ibid., 12.1.
71   Ibid., 12.5–8.
72   "I' benedico il loco e 'l tempo et l'ora / che sí alto miraron gli occhi mei" (ibid., 13.5–6).
73   Ibid., 36.1–4.

But by Sonnet 90, Petrarch is reliably trading on the imagery of earlier poets like Guinizelli, Colonne, and Dante, including the kinds of objectification and idealisation that will be a staple of the English poets who model themselves after Petrarch in the sixteenth century:

> Non era l'andar suo cosa mortale,
> ma d'angelica forma; et le parole
> sonavan altro che pur voce humana:
> uno spirito celeste, un vivo sole
> fu quel ch'i' vidi; et se non fosse or tale,
> piagha per allentar d'arco non sana.[74]

> The way she moved was not a mortal thing,
> but in the form of the angels, and her speech
> soared higher than any human voice.
> A celestial spirit, a living sun
> was what I saw there; if she is no longer so,
> my wound, though the bow be slack, will not heal.

Like his predecessors, Petrarch does not write of love for a woman. He writes of passion incited by an object in female form, whose embodied reality he is all too ready to transform into a living goddess.

Petrarch and Laura. Fresco in Petrarch's house in Arquà Petrarca.[75]

---

74 Ibid., 90.9–14.
75 https://commons.wikimedia.org/wiki/File:Affresco_di_Petrarca_e_Laura,_Casa_del_Petrarca_(Arquà_Petrarca).JPG?uselang=en-gb

The same transformation is evident in Sonnet 106, where the poet's beloved is "a new little angel on graceful wings",[76] who captures the poet in "a silk-woven net",[77] while "a sweet light issued forth from her eyes".[78] In Sonnet 121 we see the now-familiar idea that the beloved is haughty for not returning love. In this case, the beloved should be punished by Love for this failure:

> Or vedi, Amor, che giovenetta donna
> tuo regno sprezza e del mio mal non cura,
> e tra duo ta' nemici è sì secura.
> Tu se' armato, et ella in treccie e 'n gonna
> si siede, e scalza, in mezzo i fiori e l'erba,
> vèr' me spietata, e 'n contra te superba.
> I' son pregion; ma se pietà ancor serba
> l'arco tuo saldo, e qualcuna saetta,
> fa di te, e di me, signor, vendetta.[79]

> Now see, Love, how this young lady
> despises your rule, cares not for my pain,
> and between two enemies is so secure.
> You are in arms, and she in tresses and gown
> sits barefoot amidst flowers and the grass,
> without pity for me, set against you in pride.
> I am in prison, but if some mercy still keeps
> your bow strong, with a few arrows,
> for yourself and me, my Lord, take revenge.

The popular image of Petrarch is that of the long-suffering lover who pines with desire, but a recurring feature of his poetry is resentment. The lover in his poems expresses resentment over the refusal of the beloved to love in return, and expresses the desire that the beloved be made to pay for this.

---

76 "Nova angeletta sovra l'ale accorta" (ibid. 106.1).
77 "un laccio che di seta ordiva" (ibid., 106.5).
78 "sí dolce lume uscia degli occhi suoi" (ibid., 106.8).
79 Ibid., 121.1–9.

Sonnets 133 and 183 are similar expressions of another common idea: the lover is wounded by the experience of love and by the mere glance of the beloved. In Sonnet 133, the beloved is blamed for failing to have mercy:

> […] son già roco,
> donna, mercé chiamando, e voi non cale.
> Da gli occhi vostri uscìo 'l colpo mortale,
> contra cui non mi val tempo né loco;
> da voi sola procede, e parvi un gioco,
> il sole e 'l foco e 'l vento ond'io son tale.[80]

> […] I am already hoarse,
> lady, from begging mercy, and you disregard me.
> From your eyes issued the mortal blow
> from which I've no help, not time or place;
> from you all proceeds, and you think it a joke,
> the sun, fire, and wind that make me so.

In Sonnet 183, the beloved can kill the poet with the merest look,[81] for "that sweet glance of hers can kill me, / and her gentle shrewd little words",[82] and women in general are berated for being unreliable and fickle in love:

> Femina è cosa mobil per natura;
> ond'io so ben ch'un amoroso stato
> in cor di donna picciol tempo dura.[83]

> A woman is changeable by nature;
> And I know well that love's state
> in the heart of a lady lasts but a short time.

---

80 Ibid., 133.3–8.
81 This idea of the woman's ability to kill her lover by failing to return his affections is already present in *Le Roman de la Rose*, where they are warned that God will punish them for cruelty: "Ladies, learn from this example, / those of you who mistreat your lovers, / for if you let them die, / God will know well how to repay you" ("Dames, cest essample aprenez, / qui vers vos amis mesprenez; / car se vos les lessiez morir, / Dex le vos savra bien merir") (Vol. 1, l. 1505–08).
82 "'l dolce sguardo di costei m'ancide / et le soavi parolette accorte" (Francesco Petrarca. *Il Canzoniere*. 183.1–2).
83 Ibid., 183.12–14.

As Petrarch's sequence of poems nears its end, it becomes evident that the beloved Laura is now dead. Sonnet 364 makes reference to having been held, "burning", for "twenty-one years" before her death:

> Tennemi Amor anni vent'uno ardendo,
> lieto nel foco, e nel duol pien di speme;
> poi che madonna e 'l mio cor seco inseme
> saliro al ciel, dieci altri anni piangendo.[84]

> Love held me burning twenty-one years,
> happy in the fire, in my grief, full of hope;
> then, when my lady took my heart with her
> rising to Heaven, another ten years crying.

As the lover asks to be released by God, it is distressingly clear that the thirty-one years of focus testified to by the poems were not spent meditating upon an individual in a relationship of mutual choice, passion, and regard. Those years were spent instead in something like worship, not of an individual, but of a paragon, an idol, or a goddess. By the end of Petrarch's less-famous collection, the *Triunfi*, the poet looks to Laura as a promise of heaven itself:

> Amor mi diè per lei sì lunga guerra
> che la memoria ancora il cor accenna.
> Felice sasso che 'l bel viso serra!
> ché, poi ch'avrà ripreso il suo bel velo,
> se fu beato chi la vide in terra,
> or che fia dunque a rivederla in cielo?[85]

> Love gave to me for her so long a war
> that the memory still marks my heart.
> Happy the stone that covers her face!
> For now that she has resumed her beautiful veil,
> if he was blessed who saw her on Earth,
> What will it be to see her again in heaven?

---

84 *Ibid.*, 364.1–4.
85 "Trionfo della Divinita, Capitolo Unico". ll. 140–45. In *Triunfi*, ed. by Cristoforo Pasqualigo (Venezia: Giuseppe Bresciani, 1874), 116, https://books.google.com/books?id=5_0FAAAAQAAJ&pg=PA115

Beautiful but unattainable, the beloved Laura of Petrarch's poems serves as a passion-drenched metaphor, a stairway to heaven, salvation, and God. She was never loved as a woman, at least not by Petrarch. She was an object, not a subject, a means, not an end. She was merely a rung on the ladder of love for the poet to climb.

III
Post-Fin'amor Italian Prose: *Il Libro del Cortegiano* (*The Book of the Courtier*)

As we can see in *Il Libro del Cortegiano*, by the Italian courtier and author Baldassarre Castiglione, Diotima's ladder of love becomes a powerful inspiration to the thinking of the Italian *literati*. Written some time after 1507 (the year during which its conversations take place), and first published in 1528, it is a relatively late, though still useful, encapsulation of Neoplatonic thought in the Italian Renaissance. For the English Renaissance, however, it arrived right on time. First translated into English by Thomas Hoby in 1561, *The Book of the Courtier* became enormously influential on English literature. In the work's famous final section, the main speaker is an actual Italian courtier named Pietro Bembo, who was thirty-seven years old at the time of the writing. When Bembo describes the difference between the young and old courtiers, it is important to remember that the old Courtier is still relatively young, and that he is speaking from the perspective of high Neoplatonism.

Bembo is at pains to define love as a spiritual and idealized force corrupted by its association with human bodies and physical beauty. Already, we can see how forceful is the retreat from the frank eroticism and individualism of troubadour poetry:

> [A]fter a steady dialectical movement that respects man *and* woman, soul *and* body, the humanist and Neoplatonist Pietro Bembo's climactically placed hymn to love turns out to be another grand evasion of the human and an exaltation of angelic beauty and virtue in the tradition of Dante [and] Petrarch.[86]

---

86 Hagstrum, 300.

For Bembo's ideal courtier, sexual passion and the love of an individual woman is dangerous, something that needs to be tightly reined in by the firm hand of philosophy, and this is why he says of courtiers that "the old can not only love without blame, but more happily than the young".[87] By "the young", he means boys of an age with Shakespearean teenagers such as Romeo, Lysander, and Valentine. For Bembo, a man in his mid-thirties can love more happily than a boy in his mid-teens because young men lack the capacity Bembo assumes he has—a capacity to resist physical and emotional desires and redirect them onto something like a sacred path.

What the Romeos of the world have to do (according to Bembo) is learn how to transcend the love engaged in by ordinary people who adore what is right in front of them. This will enable foolish young men to become wise courtiers, who know how "to love outside the custom of the profane [and] vulgar",[88] by turning their attention away from beautiful individuals to Beauty itself:

> The Courtier, feeling caught, must get rid of every ugliness and totally escape vulgar love, and so enter into the divine way of love with the guidance of reason; and first consider that the body in which that beauty shines, is not the source from which it is born; indeed that beauty is an incorporeal thing, and (as we have said) a divine ray, and it loses much of its dignity being combined with that vile and corruptible subject, because it is the more perfect, the less it participates in matter, and it is most perfect, when entirely separate.[89]

With this sense of the vileness of the flesh established, the rest of the Courtier's mental and emotional journey is a sequential and upward bound chain: "remove from yourself the blind judgment of sense [...]

---

87 "i vecchi possano non solamente amar senza biasimo, ma talor più felicemente che i giovani" (Baldassarre Castiglione. *Il Libro del Cortegiano* [Milano: Giovanni Silvestri, 1822], 448, https://archive.org/stream/illibrodelcorteg00cast#page/448

88 "amar fuor della consuetudine del profano vulgo" (*ibid.*, 462, https://archive.org/stream/illibrodelcorteg00cast#page/462).

89 il Cortegiano, sentendosi preso, deliberarsi totalmente di fuggir ogni bruttezza dell'amor vulgare, e così entrar nella divina strada amorosa con la guida della ragione; e prima considerar che'l corpo, ove quella bellezza risplende, non è il fonte ond'ella nasce; anzi che la bellezza, per esser cosa incorporea, e (come avemo detto) un raggio divino, perde molto della sua dignità trovandosi congiunta con quel subietto vile e corruttibile perchè tanto più è perfetta, quanto men di lui participa e da quello in tutto separata è perfettissima.

Ibid., 463, https://archive.org/stream/illibrodelcorteg00cast#page/463

and love her no less for the beauty of her soul than of her body".[90] The point is to "devour sweet food for his soul [...] without going to the body with appetites anything less than honest".[91] And while loving the beauty of the soul is a wonderful thing, that love takes on an oddly pedagogical tone, for the Courtier must become the moral instructor of the woman who has inspired him with the passion he is trying to deny in himself by turning it to "higher" purposes:

> But let him be careful not to let her run into some error, but with admonitions and good reminders always try to induce in her modesty, temperance, true honesty; and be sure that in her mind there come to be no thoughts but those that are candid and alien to all ugliness and vice; and thus spreading virtue in the garden of her soul, he will reap beautiful fruits, and taste them with wonder and delight; and this will be the true generation and expression of beauty in beauty, which is said by some to be the purpose and purity of love.[92]

This directly echoes Pausanius' speech on the Heavenly and Earthly Aphrodites in the *Symposium*. For Pausanius, as for Bembo, the higher love revolves around education and development of the capacities — moral, intellectual, ethical — of the beloved (though for Pausanius, the beloved is a young male rather than Bembo's young female). While the male is to be the patient, reason-driven teacher, the female is to be the pliant and willing pupil:

> she always will show herself obedient and respectful, sweet and affable, and as eager to please him, as to be loved by him; and the desires of each

---

90 "Rimovasi adunque dal cieco giudizio del senso [...] e in lei ami non meno la bellezza dell'animo, che quella del corpo" (*ibid.*, 463–64, https://archive.org/stream/illibrodelcorteg00cast#page/463).

91 "pascerà di dolcissimo cibo l'anima [...] senza passar col desiderio verso il corpo ad appetito alcuno men che onesto" (*ibid.*, 464, https://archive.org/stream/illibrodelcorteg00cast#page/464).

92 però tenga cura di non lasciarla incorrere in errore alcuno, ma con le ammonizioni e buoni ricordi cerchi sempre d' indurla alla modestia, alla temperanza, alla vera onestà; e faccia che in lei non abbian mai luogo se non pensieri candidi e alieni da ogni bruttezza di vizi; e cosi seminando virtù nel giardìn di quel bell'animo, raccorrà ancora frutti di bellissimi costumi, e gusteragli con mirabil diletto; e questo sarà il vero generare, ed esprimere la bellezza nella bellezza, il che da alcuni si dice esser il fin d'amore.

Ibid., 464, https://archive.org/stream/illibrodelcorteg00cast#page/464

will be in harmony with those of the other; and consequently they will both be happy.[93]

A great deal of Italian and English poetry plays with this notion of the male who expects the female to be both "obedient" and "affable" where the pedagogical efforts of his love are concerned, although he is often disappointed in this regard. Bembo suggests that even kissing should be regarded as part of this drive toward the spiritual and moral education of both the male and the "obedient" female. The reasonable lover knows that mouths are where speech comes from, which reflects rational thoughts and interprets the soul. Kissing as an erotic act is, for Bembo, something to be feared, but kissing as a spiritual act is something very much to be desired:

> Because a kiss is the conjoining of body and soul, the danger is that the sensual lover may be more inclined to the body, than to the soul, but the rational lover knows that though the mouth is part of the body, it is the source of words, which are interpreters of souls, [...] and because of this a man delights in bringing his mouth to the mouth of his beloved lady, not for dishonest desires, but because he feels that the bond is a transfusion of souls from one body to another [...] the kiss, you could say, is the union of souls instead of bodies; because it has so much force, that it pulls the soul, and almost separates it from the body; which is why all chaste lovers want a kiss, as a union of souls.[94]

Any physically-based passion is described as dishonest, filthy, a distraction, so a kiss isn't engaged for desire, nor does it raise any. The kiss, when properly understood by the Courtier, does not take place at the level of flesh, but points lovers upward on the ladder of love.

---

93 "essa sempre se gli mostrerà ossequente, dolce e affabile, e così desiderosa di compiacergli, come d'esser da lui amata; e le voglie dell un e dell'altro saranno onestissime e concordi; ed essi conseguentemente saranno felicissimi" (*ibid.*, 464, https://archive.org/stream/illibrodelcorteg00cast#page/464).

94 perchè per essere il bacio congiungimento e dei corpo e dell'anima, pericolo è che l'amante sensuale non inclini più alla parte dei corpo, che a quella dell'anima, ma l'a mante razionale conosce che ancora che la bocca sia parte del corpo, nientedimeno per quella si dà esito alle parole, che sono interpreti dell'anima, [...] e perciò si diletta d'unir la sua bocca con quella della donna amata col bacio, non per moversi a desiderio alcuno disonesto, ma perchè sente che quello legame è un aprir l'adito alle anime, che tratte dal desiderio l'una dell'altra si trasfondono alternamente ancor l'una nel corpo dell'altra [...] il bacio si può più presto dir congiungimento d'anima, che di corpo; perchè in quella ha tanta forza, che la tira a sé, e quasi la separa dal corpo; per questo tutti gi' innamorati casti desiderano il bacio, come congiungimento d'anima.

Ibid., 466–67, https://archive.org/stream/illibrodelcorteg00cast#page/466

Through Peter Bembo's speech, Castiglione repeatedly makes the point that love of an individual, appreciation for human beauty and erotic attraction are impure and degraded forms of love,[95] which the Courtier is wise to reject in favor of Beauty itself:

> To escape torment, then, and enjoy beauty without passion, it is necessary that the Courtier, with the help of reason, revokes entirely his desire to enjoy beauty in the body, and, as much as he can, meditates on beauty as something simple and pure, and in the imagination abstract its form from matter, making it friendly and dear to his soul, and there enjoy it, keeping it day and night, in any time and place without ever losing it; always remembering that the body is something very different from beauty, and not only does not increase it, but decreases its perfection.[96]

For the Courtier who is well-instructed and who governs his passions appropriately, love leads beyond the mortal and fleshly beloved, directly to God:

> Therefore, we must direct all the thoughts and powers of our souls to this most holy light that shows us the way that leads to heaven, and following it, strip off the affects in which we were dressed as we fell, and by the lowest rung on the ladder that bears the image of sensual

---

95 There are voices that oppose this notion at the time. One especially notable example can be found in the work of Tullia d'Aragona, in her *Dialogo dell'infinità d'amore* of 1547, where the eponymous character claims that erotic love is not to be blamed, since it arises wholly from nature:

> At first I say, that I know well that of those things that we are by nature, we can be neither blamed nor praised; and therefore, neither plants nor animals can be blamed or praised for such love; neither should it be called lascivious, or dishonest in them, nor even in men.

> Al primo dico, che io so bene che di quelle cose, che ci vengono dalla natura, non possiamo essere biasmati, né lodati; e perciò né nelle piante, né negli animali non si può biasmar cotale amore; né in loro si chiama lascivo, o disonesto, né negli uomini ancora.

Tullia d'Aragona. *Dialogo della infinità d'amore* (1547). In *Della infinita d'amore dialogo di Tullia D'Aragona* (Milan: G. Daelli & Co., 1864), 67, https://archive.org/stream/bub_gb_1FOekK6PUbsC#page/n103

96 Per fuggir adunque il tormento di questa assenza, e goder la bellezza senza passione, bisogna che l Cortegiano con l'aiuto della ragione, revochi in tutto il desiderio dal corpo alla bellezza sola, e, quanto più può, la contempli in sé stessa semplice e pura, e dentro nella im imaginazione la formi astratta da ogni materia e così la faccia amica e cara all'anima sua, ed ivi la goda, e seco l'abbia giorno e notte, in ogni tempo e luogo senza dubbio di perderla mai; tornandosi sempre a memoria che l corpo è cosa diversissima dalia bellezza, e non solamente non le accresce, ma le diminuisce la sua perfezione.

Castiglione, 469, https://archive.org/stream/illibrodelcorteg00cast#page/469

beauty, ascend to the sublime rooms where the heavenly, lovable, and real beauty lives, secreted in the hidden chambers of God, so that the profane eye cannot see it.[97]

In such thought the individual is valuable only in terms of its connection to the universal. The beauty of an individual person is only of any significance in that it points beyond that individual, serving as a symbol for the universal concept of beauty.

From this point of view, the body is a prison to be escaped from. For Bembo, a focus on the body distracts lovers from the holy way of love dependent on reason, which leads them from the world of matter, through the higher contemplative stages, on a spiritual approach to the divine. As Agnolo Firenzuola expressed it in 1548:

> a beautiful woman is the most beautiful object you will ever see, and beauty is the greatest gift God has given all human creatures; and through its virtue, the soul is guided to contemplation, and through contemplation to the desire of all the things of heaven.[98]

From this point of view, love is reason coupled with informed desire for the highest beauty, the highest reality, for God himself. In short, for the wise older Courtier, love is a spiritual exercise that is approached through bodies that are left behind as soon as possible.

---

97 Indrizziamo adunque tutti i pensieri e le forze dell'anima nostra a questo santissimo lume che ci mostra la via che al ciel conduce, e drieto a quello, spogliandoci gli affetti che nei descendere ci eravamo vestiti, per la scala che neìl' infimo grado tiene l'ombra di bellezza sensuale, ascendiamo alla sublime stanza ove abita la celeste, amabile e vera bellezza che nei secreti penetrali di Dio sta nascosta, acciocché gli occhi profani veder non la possano.
    Ibid., 474, https://archive.org/stream/illibrodelcorteg00cast#page/474
98 "la donna bella, è il piu bello obietto che si rimiri: et la belleza è il maggior dono che faceβe Iddio all humana creatura. Concio sia che per la di lei uirtù, noi ne indiriziamo l'animo alla contemplatione, et per la contemplatione al desiderio delle cose del Cielo" (Agnolo Firenzuola. "Belleza delle Donne". In *Prose di M. Agnolo Firenzuola Fiorentino* [Florence: Bernardo Guinta, 1548], 62, https://archive.org/stream/bub_gb_hdGH5df6NxIC#page/n127).

IV
The Sixteenth-Century: Post-*Fin'amor* Transitions in Petrarchan-Influenced Poetry

It was eventually in England that the troubadour spirit—quite nearly destroyed by the ascendancy of the Inquisition in Europe—once again found rich soil in which to take root and thrive. In a nation of "heretics" the idea of human love was resurrected from the pious grave into which Innocent III had tried to have it eternally immured. Ironically, the Occitan poets disappeared quite nearly without a trace in France, where Neopetrarchism took hold in the sixteenth-century work of, among others, Maurice Scève and Louise Labé. Scève's work, in ten-line units called *dizains*, is thematically modeled after Petrarch's *Canzoniere*, and faithful to the traditions of Plato and Diotima:

> Bien que raison soit nourrice de l'ame,
> Alimenté est le sens du doulx songe
> De vain plaisir, qui en tous lieux m'entame,
> Me penetrant, comme l'eau en l'esponge.
> Dedans lequel il m'abysme, & me plonge
> Me suffocquant toute vigueur intime.
> Dont pour excuse, & cause legitime
> Je ne me doibs grandement esbahir,
> Si ma tressaincte, & sage Dyotime
> Tousjours m'enseigne a aymer, & hair.[99]

> Though reason is nursemaid to the soul,
> The sweet power of my sensuous dreams
> Of vain pleasure, follows me everywhere,
> Penetrating me, like water in a sponge,
> Thrusting and plunging me into the abyss,
> Suffocating me in my inmost heart.
> This for excuse, although legitimate
> Cannot amaze me or leave me in shock,
> If my holy and wise Diotima
> Still teaches me to love, and how to hate.

---

99 Maurice Scève. "Délie 439". In I. D. McFarlane, ed. *The Délie of Maurice Scève* (Cambridge: Cambridge University Press, 1966), 360.

Labé, on the other hand, writes a Petrarchan style of verse that reverses the typical gender roles of the genre: the voice of the lover who burns unrequitedly is female, while the cruel and unforthcoming beloved is male. In her sixteenth sonnet, *Apres qu'un tems la gresle et le tonnere*, she laments what appears to be her lover's sexual impotence:

> Après qu'un tems la gresle et le tonnerre
> Ont le haut mont de Caucase batu,
> Le beau jour vient, de lueur revêtu.
> Quand Phebus ha son cerne fait en terre,
> Et l'Ocean il regaigne à grand erre,
> Sa seur se montre avec son chef pointu.
> Quand quelque tems le Parthe ha combatu,
> Il prent la fuite et son arc il desserre.
> Un tems fay vù et consolé pleintif,
> Et defiant de mon feu peu hatif;
> Mais, maintenant que tu m'as embrasée
> Et suis au point auquel tu me voulois,
> Tu as ta flame en quelque eau arrosée,
> Et es plus froit qu'estre je ne soulois.[100]

> After a time in which hail and thunder
> Have beaten the top of Mount Caucasus,
> A beautiful day comes, clothed again in light.
> When Phoebus encircles his land again,
> And dives into the sea, his pale sister
> Moves back into our view with pointed crown.
> When for too long the Parthian warrior fights,
> He turns from his arc and loosens his bow.
> I consoled you once when I saw you sad,
> And that aroused my long slow-burning fire;
> But now that you have brought me to a burn
> And brought me to the point you wished,
> You've doused your flame with flowing drink,
> And yours is colder than mine can ever be.

---

[100] Louise Labé. "Sonnet 16". *Oeuvres de Louise Labé*, ed. by Prosper Blancheman (Paris: Librarie des Bibliophiles, 1875), 124, https://books.google.com/books?id=w_fl8BM3_SUC&pg=PA124

Here, the woman pines in vain desire for the man, and must, like poor Petrarch, rest in unrest, and abide in perpetual frustration. Still, despite the change of gender roles, the song remains the same—the beloved remains just as inaccessible in the sixteenth-century Lyonaisse poetry of Labé as in the fourteenth-century Tuscan poetry of Petrarch. Even in her famous eighteenth sonnet, *Baise m'encor, rebaise moy et baise,* a reworking of Catullus' fifth ode *Let Us Live, My Lesbia, and Let Us Love* (*Vivamus, mea Lesbia, atque amemus*), Labé writes of a love that is passionate, but frustrated and impossible to encompass fully:

> Baise m'encor, rebaise moy et baise;
> Donne m'en un de tes plus savoureus,
> Donne m'en un de tes plus amoureus:
> Je t'en rendray quatre plus chaus que braise.
> Las! te pleins tu? Ça, que ce mal j'apaise,
> En t'en donnant dix autres doucereus.
> Ainsi meslans nos baisers tant heureus,
> Jouissons nous l'un de l'autre à notre aise.
> Lors double vie à chacun en suivra;
> Chacun en soy et son ami vivra.
> Permets m'Amour penser quelque folie:
> Tousjours suis mal, vivant discrettement,
> Et ne me puis donner contentement
> Si hors de moy ne fay quelque saillie.[101]

> Kiss me again, kiss and kiss me once more;
> Give me one of your most savory,
> Give me one of your most amorous,
> I'll return them four times hotter than coals.
> Does sadness fill you? I'll appease that pain,
> By giving you ten other sweets;
> Thus mixing our happy kisses
> We may enjoy each other at our ease.
> Then we will live twice:
> Each ourselves, and each in the other's love.
> Love, let me dream about such foolish things:
> It hurts me, living so discreetly,

---

101 Labé. "Sonnet 18", 126, https://books.google.com/books?id=w_fl8BM3_SUC&pg=PA126

> And nothing will give me contentment
> Unless I break outside myself.

Despite the open eroticism of this sonnet, with the double meaning of "baise" (kiss and/or fuck—make the latter choice and the poem feels somewhat different), the troubadour notes are overwhelmed by the Petrarchan score: "Permets m'Amour penser quelque folie"—human love will only be a dream, and a foolish one at that. There will be no kisses, and no contentment. Compare this to Catullus' poem, in which there is no dominant note of frustration, though condemnation is reserved for the old moralists who would prevent lovers from enjoying each other:

> Vivamus mea Lesbia, atque amemus,
> rumoresque senum severiorum
> omnes unius aestimemus assis!
> soles occidere et redire possunt:
> nobis cum semel occidit brevis lux,
> nox est perpetua una dormienda.
> da mi basia mille, deinde centum,
> dein mille altera, dein secunda centum,
> deinde usque altera mille, deinde centum.
> dein, cum milia multa fecerimus,
> conturbabimus illa, ne sciamus,
> aut ne quis malus invidere possit,
> cum tantum sciat esse basiorum.[102]

> Let us live, my Lesbia, and let us love,
> and the rumors of the old and strict
> all value as a single penny!
> The sun sets and dies but will return again:
> But for us, when our brief light has died,
> The night is eternal sleep.
> Give me a thousand kisses, then a hundred,
> then another thousand, then a second hundred,
> then yet another thousand, then a hundred.
> Then, when we have made many thousands,

---

102 Gaius Valerius Catullus. *Catullus. Tibullus. Pervigilium Veneris*, ed. by F. W. Cornish (Loeb Classical Library, Cambridge, MA: Harvard University Press, 1913), 6,8.

> jumble the count, refuse to know the total,
> lest anyone judge with an evil eye,
> when he knows how many have been our kisses.

By way of contrast, in a distant area of the continent where the Inquisition had been relatively weak,[103] and the urge to transform the passion of love poetry into the piety of worship had not found expression in a *dolce stil novo*, love poetry has much of the passionate essence found in troubadour verse, without the note of frustration and failure often found in Labé. The sixteenth-century Armenian poet Nahaphet Quchak, known for his short lyric poems of love, or *hayren*, writes in a frankly passionate and physical manner that is reminiscent of Guilhem IX:

> Իմ սիրծ ի զո վար սիրդ՝
> զետ աշնան խազել կւ դոխայ։
> Արծւնք ի յերեսա Ի վեր՝
> զետ զարնան անձրեվ կւ ծոխայ։
> Հոգիս ի յիսնե եյավ՝
> մեկ մի զո ծոծոյդ ճար արա։
> Ծոծիկս ե ծոծիդ սովոր՝
> այլ ւհնդ վոր յերտայ՝ մեկ ասա՛.[104]

> From your burning love,
> my heart trembles like an autumnal leaf:
> My tears streaming down my face:
> as if a spring rain drizzles.
> My soul is being tortured,
> Give me the cure of your bosom.
> My breast is used to your breasts,
> Tell me, how will I live if they leave?

---

103 "About 1370 Gregory XI appointed the Dominican Friar John Gallus as inquisitor in the East, who in conjunction with Friar Elias Petit planted the institution [...] in Armenia" (Henry Charles Lea. *A History of the Inquisition of the Middle Ages*, Vol. 1 [New York: Macmillan, 1906], 355). Gregory "regarded the members of the Armenian Church in Cilicia as schismatics" (Krzysztof Stopka. *Armenia Christiana: Armenian Religious Identity and the Churches of Constantinople and Rome* [Krakow: Jagiellonian University Press, 2016], 270), but the fall of the Cilician Kingdom in 1375 placed the area under Muslim rule, and beyond the reach of any Pope.

104 Hayren 20. Nahaphet Quchak, *Haryur u mek hayren*, ed. by Arshak Madoyan and Irina Karumyan (Yerevan: Sovetakan Grokh, 1976).

For Quchak, love is physical and joyful, not something to be sublimated into spiritual devotion, or made to serve as a means to an end, the merest first rung on a ladder of love leading from Earth to Heaven. For Quchak, as for the troubadours, heaven is here, and its temple is the body of his beloved:

>Քանի մարն զիս բերեր՝
>զպհանի ձեմ խոստովաներ։
>Իրտեխ զպհանայ տեսեր՝
>նայ ծրեր ձամպւս ւ յելեր։
>Վորտեխ մեկ ախվոր տեսել՝
>գիրկ ւ ծոծ վի դեմ գնածեր։
>Ծոծիկն եմ ձամպտուն արել՝
>ծիծերւն եմ խոստովաներ։[105]

>How many faults are born,
>I haven't confessed to the priest:
>Wherever a priest I've seen,
>I've changed my route and left:
>Wherever a beauty I've seen,
>I've straight gone to her bosom and embrace,
>Made her bosom my altar,
>To her tits I've made my confessions.

In the final line, the refusal of euphemism drives home the point: love is its own justification, and needn't apologize to anyone or pretend its desires are in any way shameful. Quite the opposite, in fact; love is to be celebrated in wine and song:

>Իմ բարծրագնած լւսին՝
>շատ բարեվ տար իմ կիվսելին։
>—Ձ բարեվդ յես Ի ւր տանեմ՝
>ձեմ գիտեր իհգուևն կիվգելին։
>—Գնա Ի վերայ տախին՝
>բարձր պատ ւ ծարն Ի միձին։
>Նստեր Ի ծարի շգին՝
>կ խմե իր լւրձ ապիկին՝

---

[105] Ibid., Hayren 65.

Խմէ և հայրեն կ՚ասէ:
տ՚ <<Ի՞նձ անւշ և սէրն և գինին>>.¹⁰⁶

> My high and noble moon,
> Take many greetings to my beauty
> —Where should I take your greeting?
> I don't know the house of your beauty.
> —Go to the upper neighborhood
> Where she sits between high wall and tree:
> Sitting in the shadow of the tree,
> Drinking with seriousness,
> Drinking and singing hayrens:
> As "How sweet are love and wine!"

It is this spirit—this unapologetic celebration of passion and desire, so like that of the troubadours—that French and Italian poetry lost, and English poetry would successfully struggle to recover: "the Provençal tradition was much more continuous and lasting in England than in France. [...] The manner, style, metrical models, and the very themes and conceits of the troubadour tradition, [were] transported bodily one might say, into England".¹⁰⁷ For decades, however, the influence of Petrarch, and not the troubadours, was the dominant force in the English poetry of the sixteenth century before Shakespeare. Such early Tudor sonneteers as Thomas Wyatt and Henry Howard, the Earl of Surrey, and later Elizabethan figures like Philip Sidney both borrow from and struggle against Petrarch, creating a new vocabulary of poetry in English. These poems often reveal their Petrarchan roots, as they treat such subjects as the impossibility of being loved in return by the chosen object of the poet's love. Wyatt made extensive use of Petrarch in his own poetry:

> Of the Italian poets it was Petrarch whom Wyatt copied most freely. From Petrarch he derived the sonnet and certain conventional sentiments, which, once introduced into English love poetry, formed its staple subject-matter, with certain interruptions and revolts, for about a century and a half.¹⁰⁸

---

106 *Ibid.*, Hayren 81.
107 Briffault, 193–94.
108 E. M. W. Tillyard. In E. M. W. Tillyard, ed. *The Poetry of Sir Thomas Wyatt* (London: The Scholartis Press, 1929), 23.

For example, Wyatt's famous 1557 sonnet, "Whoso List to Hunt", makes clear the poet's painful longing, his extensive borrowings from Petrarch, and his acute awareness of how love and desire are affected by rank and station:

> Whoso list to hunt, I know where is an hind,
> But as for me, helas, I may no more.
> The vain travail hath wearied me so sore,
> I am of them that farthest cometh behind.
> Yet may I by no means my wearied mind
> Draw from the deer, but as she fleeth afore
> Fainting I follow. I leave off therefore,
> Sithens in a net I seek to hold the wind.
> Who list her hunt, I put him out of doubt,
> As well as I may spend his time in vain.
> And graven with diamonds in letters plain
> There is written, her fair neck round about:
> 'Noli me tangere for Caesar's I am,
> And wild for to hold, though I seem tame'.[109]

Wyatt's sonnet, a loose adaptation of Petrarch's Sonnet 190, borrows the Petrarchan model while changing its terms:

> Wyatt's [Caesar] is secular, possessive and tyrannous, but his Diere is also secular and arguably powerful herself. Wyatt's added description of her as "wylde for to hold: though I seme tame" hints at a powerful duplicity not present in Petrarch. There is a suggestion that this duplicity might equally be exercised against the speaker, his rivals, or [Caesar] himself.[110]

The "hind" in all likelihood was Anne Boleyn, the paramour, later the wife, of Henry VIII, and Wyatt's poem captures the angst of a man who desires a high-placed woman whom he can never have, in much the same way that Bernart de Ventadorn's twelfth-century poem, *When Fresh Leaves and Shoots Appear (Can l'erba fresch'e·lh folha par)*, describes the passionate devotion of Bernart for Eleanor of Aquitaine. Just as Bernart's poem describes the impossibility of loving the Queen of

---

109 Thomas Wyatt. *Sir Thomas Wyatt: The Complete Poems*, ed. by R. A. Rebholz (New Haven: Yale University Press, 1978), 77.
110 Rachel Falconer. "A Reading of Wyatt's 'Who so list to hunt'". In Michael Hattaway, ed. *A Companion to English Renaissance Literature and Culture* (London: Blackwell, 2003), 181.

Henry II, Wyatt's poem recognizes the futility and danger of crossing the power of Henry VIII, the "Caesar" of the poem.[111]

Wyatt's sonnets often feature the kinds of woman-as-cruel-angel imagery seen in Petrarch, including the comparisons of the beloved's eyes with fire, or sparks, or the stars and sun. In "Such Vain Thought as Wonted to Mislead Me", the beloved is described as "her whom reason bids me flee"[112] before the poet cries out in resignation, "She fleeth as fast by gentle cruelty / And after her my heart would fain be gone, / But armed sighs my way do stop anon, / 'Twixt hope and dread locking my liberty".[113] In another sonnet, "The Lively Sparks that Issue from those Eyes", Wyatt's lines bemoan the power of the beloved's gaze:

> Was never man could any thing devise
> Sunbeams to turn with so great vehemence
> To daze man's sight, as by their bright presence
> Dazed am I; much like unto the guise
> Of one stricken with dint of lightning,
> Blind with the stroke, and crying here and there.[114]

---

111 Though the question of whether or not Wyatt had an affair with Anne Boylen has been long debated, it does not seem likely ever to be proven on the positive side. "There is no evidence that Wyatt's verses or his attention ever deeply moved Anne, for she played for higher stakes, with the crown as her goal" (Retha M. Warnicke. "The Eternal Triangle and Court Politics: Henry VIII, Anne Boleyn, and Sir Thomas Wyatt". *Albion: A Quarterly Journal Concerned with British Studies*, 18: 4 [Winter, 1986], 578, https://doi.org/10.2307/4050130). There is also "no record linking Anne's name to Wyatt's [...] prior to the date of his imprisonment in 1536 when five other men were executed for committing adultery and incest with her" (Retha M. Warnicke. *The Rise and Fall of Anne Boleyn: Family Politics at the Court of Henry VIII* [Cambridge: Cambridge University Press, 1991], 65). Modern scholarship denies the latter charges, seeing them as part of the vicious push and pull of Tudor politics, as illustrated in Adam Blackwood's pamphlet broadside: "The marriage of the King with Anne Boleyn could not stand by any law in the world, Anne being his natural daughter. [It is] an illegitimate marriage, and that which it begot a bastard [...], Elizabeth" ("Le mariage du Roy avec Anne Boullen ne pouvoit subsister par aucune loy du monde, estant icelle Anne sa filie naturelle, [c'est un] mariage illegitime, & celle qui en estoit procree bastarde [...], Elizabet") (*Martyre de la Royne d'Escosse*. Edimbourg, 1587, Sig. C3v, 37 [misprinted as 73], https://books.google.com/books?id=_mZUAAAAcAAJ&pg=PA37).
112 Wyatt (1978), 84, l. 4.
113 *Ibid.*, ll. 5–8.
114 *Ibid.*, 84, ll. 5–10.

Wyatt's poems also work the theme of the lady who cruelly fails to be "tractable" and "willing" where a man's professions of love are concerned. In "Behold, Love, Thy Power How She Despiseth" (a loose translation of Petrarch's Sonnet 121), the beloved who refuses love in return is to be punished:

> Behold, Love.
> I am in hold. If thee pity moveth,
> Go bend thy bow that stony hearts breaketh
> And with some stroke revenge the displeasure
> Of thee and him that sorrow doth endure
> And, as his lord, thee lowly entreateth.[115]

At times, however, Wyatt will depart from his Petrarchan model in serious and purposeful ways: "Wyatt was writing from within a culture in which erotic love was not a celebrated subject of contemplation", and that fact "needs to be fully accounted for when we consider the changes he made to Petrarch's poems".[116] One of the most striking differences is the attitude taken toward the woman in the works:

> Whereas Petrarch famously idealizes Laura's virtues in a manner comparable to Dante's depiction of the heavenly Beatrice in *La Vita Nuova*, Wyatt is reluctant to praise his mistress, either physically or spiritually. There are almost no descriptions of Wyatt's mistress in any of his poems—no blazons or paeans to her beauty—and she is certainly not treated as a flawless angelic creature.[117]

Another major difference is that "Wyatt conspicuously avoids [...] Petrarch's notion that dying of love is the desired end. [...] Thus in the sonnet that begins, 'Eche man me telleth I chaunge moost my devise', Wyatt informs his mistress that he shall remain steadfast in his affection so long as his body and soul remain together", but no longer.[118] Nor does Wyatt write of human love as a ladder or pathway to divine love: "When Wyatt wants to write about love of God, he does not move through the vehicle of loving an earthly woman. Instead, in a pattern that becomes

---

115 *Ibid.*, 71, ll. 9–13.
116 Raimie Targoff. *Posthumous Love: Eros and the Afterlife in Renaissance England* (Chicago: University of Chicago Press, 2014), 50.
117 *Ibid.*
118 *Ibid.*, 66.

typical of sixteenth-and seventeenth-century English poets, he shifts decisively from erotic to devotional poetry".[119] Wyatt's verse will also turn to bitter humor, as it casts a cynical eye on the subject of truth and lies in a poem written to his tongue, "Because I have thee still kept from lies and blame", in which Wyatt berates that often-speechless organ for failing to keep faith with him, like an intractable and unwilling beloved:

> Unkind tongue, right ill hast thou me rendered,
> For such desert to do me wreak and shame.
> [...]
> Then are ye gone when I should make my moan.
> And you so ready sighs to make me shright,
> Then are ye slack when that ye should outstart,
> And only my look declareth my heart.[120]

Where Wyatt both uses and resists Petrarch, altering his themes in critical ways, the Earl of Surrey, Henry Howard, is at once more faithful and more whimsical an imitator of his Italian model, often letting flights of fancy loose while expressing the familiar themes of the cruel lady, the blazing power of her eyes, and the pain of the rejected lover. In "Each Beast can Choose his Fere According to his Mind", first published in *Tottel's Miscellany* in 1557, Howard creates a beast fable to dramatize the cruelty of a lady who refused to dance with a man who asked her. The man is described as a noble lion, while the woman is a coy wolf:

> A lion saw I late, as white as any snow,
> Which seemed well to lead the race, his port the same did show.
> Upon the gentle beast to gaze it pleased me,
> For still methought he seemed well of noble blood to be.
> And as he pranced before, still seeking for a make,
> As who would say, 'There is none here, I trow, will me forsake',
> I might perceive a Wolf as white as whalèsbone,
> A fairer beast of fresher hue, beheld I never none;
> Save that her looks were coy, and froward eke her grace.[121]

---

119 *Ibid.*, 78.
120 Wyatt (1978), 79, ll. 3–4, 11–14.
121 Henry Howard, Earl of Surrey. *The Poetical Works of Henry Howard, Earl of Surrey*, ed. by Robert Bell (Boston: Little, Brown & Co., 1854), 79, ll. 3–11, https://archive.org/

On asking her to dance, the lion is repulsed by the wolf in no uncertain terms:

> 'Lion', she said, 'if thou hadst known my mind before,
> Thou hadst not spent thy travail thus, nor all thy pain for-lore.
> Do way! I let thee weet, thou shalt not play with me:
> Go range about, where thou mayst find some meeter fere for thee'.[122]

The lion's response is at once indignant and impotent, filled with the rage of the lover who expects the beloved to be compliant and responsive to his advances:

> 'Cruel! you do me wrong, to set me thus so light;
> Without desert for my good will to shew me such despite.
> […]
> And thus farewell, Unkind, to whom I bent and bow;
> I would you wist, the ship is safe that bare his sails so low.
> Sith that a Lion's heart is for a Wolf no prey,
> With bloody mouth go slake your thirst on simple sheep, I say'.[123]

Elsewhere, Howard is more typically Petrarchan, as in a poem that bemoans a young woman's refusal to show her face or hair to a man who has declared his love for her. In "I Never Saw my Lady Lay Apart" (a translation of Petrarch's Sonnet 11, *Lassare il velo per sole o per ombra*), the poet writes of the pain of being refused the sight for which he longs:

> Yet since she knew I did her love and serve,
> Her golden tresses clad alway with black,
> Her smiling looks that hid thus evermore,
> And that restrains which I desire so sore.[124]

Here, the reader is at home in the familiar language and imagery of the Italian sonnets of the thirteenth and fourteenth centuries. The lover

---

stream/poeticalworkshe00vauxgoog#page/n89
122 *Ibid.*, 80, ll. 18–21, https://archive.org/stream/poeticalworkshe00vauxgoog#page/n90
123 *Ibid.*, 81–82, ll. 26–27, 68–71, https://archive.org/stream/poeticalworkshe00vauxgoog#page/n91
124 *Ibid.*, 52–53, ll. 8–11, https://archive.org/stream/poeticalworkshe00vauxgoog#page/n62

is denied access to even the sight of his beloved; the lady is described as cruel—denying the lover specifically because he loves, the ultimate in intractable and unwilling behavior. Love is described as painful, dangerous, and next door to fatal in these poems, and as Howard ends his poem "When summer took in hand the winter to assail", the poet warns readers away from love: "A mirror let me be unto ye lovers all; / Strive not with love; for if ye do, it will ye thus befall".[125]

But though Wyatt and Howard are important, by far the more famous, and still more widely-read poet is Philip Sidney. Soldier, courtier, diplomat, and poet, Sidney packed more into his not-quite thirty-two years than many of us do into a span of seventy or eighty. He defended poetry, in *The Defence of Poesie*, against anti-theatricalists and moralists like Stephen Gosson (himself a failed playwright). He wrote one of the most popular and influential prose romances in the English language—*The Countess of Pembroke's Arcadia*—which exists in multiple forms due to his death mid-revision. But most famously, he is the author of the first of the so-called sonnet sequences in English. Sidney's *Astrophil and Stella* (first printed in 1591, five years after his death), took the passion and pain, the devotion and loneliness, the hope and despair of Petrarch's poetry and made them English. However, what Michael Drayton would, in 1619, call a "Muse […] rightly of the English strain",[126] is not quite what we see in Sidney. Though he was—along with Spenser—the most brilliant lyric poet of his time, he was heavily in debt to his Petrarchan model, no matter how powerfully he reworked it into English verse.

The physical imagery with which Sidney has Astrophil (star-lover) describe Stella (star) demonstrates the debt. Right away, we see the focus on the eyes of the beloved, in sonnet 7: "When Nature made her chiefe worke, *Stella's* eyes, / In colour blacke why wrapt she beames so bright?"[127] Stella's eyes are so bright, in fact, that if "if no vaile those brave gleames did disguise, / They sun-like should more dazle than delight".[128]

---

125 Ibid., 47, ll. 47–48, https://archive.org/stream/poeticalworkshe00vauxgoog#page/n57
126 Michael Drayton. "To the Reader of these Sonnets", l. 13. *Idea*. In Arundell Esdaile, ed. *Daniel's Delia and Drayton's Idea* (London: Chatto & Windus, 1908), 67, https://books.google.com/books?id=mOiobc0PmsgC&pg=PA67
127 Philip Sidney. *The Poems of Sir Philip Sidney*, ed. by William A. Ringler, Jr. (Oxford: Clarendon Press, 1962), 168, ll. 1–2.
128 Ibid., ll. 7–8.

Sonnet 12 describes Stella in terms that fit squarely within the tradition seen in Bembo's speech and Petrarch's poetry of regarding the beloved as cruel and intractable for refusing to return the love of the young man who worships her: "O no, her heart is such a Cittadell, / So fortified with wit, stor'd with disdaine, / That to win it, is all the skill and paine".[129]

The "cruelty" of the beloved who rejects the lover leads, in Sonnet 48, to a declaration that the lover will die from his wounds, and a plea for the beloved to kill him quickly if she cannot love him: "Yet since my death-wound is already got, / Deare Killer, spare not thy sweet cruell shot: / A kind of grace it is to kill with speed".[130] We can hear echoes of Petrarch's Sonnets 133 and 183 in these lines, in which the lady can kill with a look.

Perhaps the most famous of Sidney's sonnets, Sonnet 71, appears initially to be a sublime mix of Petrarchan ingredients: Stella's eyes are like the sun ("inward sun in thine eyes shineth"); love for Stella is soon turned toward away from physical desire and toward love for the spiritual good ("So while thy beauty draws the heart to love, / As fast thy virtue bends that love to good":); and Astrophil is in pain for the lack of Stella, the physical absence of Stella metaphorized as food ("'But ah', Desire still cries, 'give me some food'".):

> Who will in fairest booke of Nature know
> How Vertue may best lodg'd in beauty be;
> Let him but learne of *Love* to reade in thee,
> *Stella*, those faire lines which true goodnesse show.
> There shall he find all vices' overthrow,
> Not by rude force, but sweetest soveraigntie
> Of reason, from whose light those night-birds flie;
> That inward sunne in thine eyes shineth so.
> And not content to be Perfection's heire
> Thy selfe, doest strive all minds that way to move,
> Who marke in thee what is in thee most faire.
> So while thy beautie drawes the heart to love,
> As fast thy Vertue bends that love to good:
> "But ah", Desire still cries, "give me some food".[131]

---

129 Ibid., 171, ll. 12–14.
130 Ibid., 189, ll. 12–14.
131 Ibid., 201, ll. 1–14.

But in this poem, one can hear a touch of the troubadour melody mixed into the Petrarchan score. While Astrophil extravagantly praises his beloved, he does not necessarily idealize her, describing Stella's virtues as impediments to his desire. This conflict is clearly evident in Sonnet 72:

> Desire, though thou my old companion art,
> And oft so clings to my pure Love, that I
> One from the other scarcely can descrie,
> While each doth blow the fier of my hart;
> Now from thy fellowship I needs must part,
> Venus is taught with Dian's wings to flie:
> I must no more in thy sweet passions lie;
> Vertue's gold now must head my Cupid's dart.
> Service and Honor, wonder with delight,
> Feare to offend, will worthie to appeare,
> Care shining in mine eyes, faith in my sprite,
> These things are left me by my only Deare;
> But thou Desire, because thou wouldst have all,
> Now banish art, but yet alas how shall?[132]

Sidney makes his Astrophil suffer from unsatisfied desire, no matter how purifying his love for Stella should be from the Neoplatonist or Petrarchan point of view. In the tension between Astrophil's often-Petrarchan attitudes and his powerful desire, we can also see the influence of Dante, for whom Beatrice's beauty was figured as a solemn promise of heavenly reward. Astrophil's contemplation of Stella's beauty educates him as a lover, but it also spurs his will and desire: "No matter how fallen Astrophil's will becomes, he remains valiant and ready for self-sacrifice, although he cannot resolve the psychic tension resulting from the opposing demands of love and virtue in his mind".[133]

It is in Sidney's later sonnets where the carefully-constructed Neoplatonic balance between "love and virtue" topples to the ground. Sidney does this by changing the poems' focus from the divine powers of the beloved's beauty to the human anguish of the lover's emotional conflict. The poems of Sidney's sequence read like a painful exercise in

---

132 *Ibid.*, 202, ll. 1–14.
133 Katona Gábor. "The Lover's Education: Psychic Development in Sidney's 'Astrophil and Stella'". *Hungarian Journal of English and American Studies*, 1: 2 (1995), 4.

a young man's trying (and failing) to tamp down physical desire — a desire that will never be sated, consummated, or satisfied — while attempting to convince himself that it is acceptable to sublimate or spiritualize that desire for a woman he will never have, against whom he now and then breaks out into resentful accusation, and for whom his physical and emotional desires never slacken even in the slightest. The orthodox Neoplatonist position outlined by Peter Bembo in *The Book of the Courtier* insists that such a resolution is not only acceptable, but decidedly preferable. But as Astrophil bids farewell to the world, at the end of the sequence, the stated preference for "Eternal Love", the love of heaven, seems forced: "Then farewell world; thy uttermost I see: / Eternal Love, maintain thy life in me". One cannot help but hear, if faintly, the earlier plea of Desire: "give me some food".

8. Shakespeare: The Return of *Fin'amor*

I
The Value of the Individual in the Sonnets

The true recovery of the troubadour tradition comes with Shakespeare, the poet and playwright who "towers like a mountain peak above the surrounding foothills, but is one substance and structure with them".[1] Most truly "of the English strain", Shakespeare's sonnets are a reversing, even a mocking of the Petrarchan mode and the Neoplatonic sublimation of passion into worship that sometimes marks the poetry of Sidney. Rather than treating the individual as a means to an end, the lowest rung on the ladder of love, Shakespeare's sonnets reverse this emphasis, valuing the individual as an end in itself, not a means to some higher goal.

In effecting this reversal, Sonnet 1 begins with a recognizably Platonic image, "beauty's rose", which is something like the form of rose, rather than the tangible flower which, for a good Platonist or Neoplatonist, is merely a copy of the higher reality. In the terms of the sonnet, "we" want to see a proliferation of such copies in order that the form or idea will not disappear from the world:

> From fairest creatures we desire increase,
> That thereby beauty's rose might never die,

---

1   Briffault, 197.

> But as the riper should by time decease,
> His tender heir might bear his memory;²

In the following lines the young man addressed in the sonnet is chided for not reproducing himself and his beauty, thus removing that beauty from the world, and limiting the ability of others to perceive the higher form due to the slow degradation of the copy.

> But thou contracted to thine own bright eyes,
> Feed'st thy light's flame with self-substantial fuel,
> Making a famine where abundance lies,
> Thy self thy foe, to thy sweet self too cruel:³

The young man is accused of being what we might call a narcissist today. He is "contracted" (married, bound) to his own eyes, rather than the brilliantly blazing eyes of a Petrarchan beloved; he seems in love with himself, like someone who wakes up, looks in the mirror, and falls in love all over again every morning. So far, the sonnet seems to fit the religious and allegorical frame with which Helen Vendler surrounds it:

> When God saw his creatures, he commanded them to increase and multiply. Shakespeare, in this first sonnet of the sequence, suggests we have internalized the paradisal command in an aestheticized form [...] We are also educated in the speaker's culture—here, in such stock figures as the medieval Rose of beauty, [...] the command from Genesis to increase and multiply, the dynastic obligation to produce heirs, and so on.⁴

However, as the sonnet continues, it becomes clear that the religious and allegorical frame does not fit; the poet regards this young man's beauty as something both important and tragically ephemeral, a moment's brightness that will soon be overwhelmed by the darkness of the grave.

---

2   William Shakespeare. "Sonnet 1", ll. 1–4. *William Shakespeare: The Complete Works*, ed. by Stephen Orgel and A. R. Braunmuller (New York: Pelican, 2002), 67. All further references to the sonnets will be from this edition, and will be referenced in the notes by sonnet number and line number(s).
3   1. 5–8.
4   Helen Vendler. *The Art of Shakespeare's Sonnets* (Cambridge, MA: Belknap Press of Harvard University Press, 1997), 46.

8. Shakespeare: The Return of Fin'amor

> Thou that art now the world's fresh ornament,
> And only herald to the gaudy spring,
> Within thine own bud buriest thy content,
> And tender churl mak'st waste in niggarding:
> Pity the world, or else this glutton be,
> To eat the world's due, by the grave and thee.[5]

The shift in emphasis is already clear—rather than being primarily concerned with "beauty's rose", the form of beauty, or with any God-given command to reproduce, this poem is concerned with the preservation of the individual rose (the young man himself), or at least with the preservation of the memory of that rose.

The next several sonnets make that concern obvious. Their power depends on the tragic sense of watching as a beautiful individual slowly but surely fades away. These sonnets focus on the value inherent in the person, not on preserving the form of Beauty for the next generation. That can take care of itself; the poems speak of preserving the all-too-ephemeral beauty of an individual subject to time, decay, and death. As with the troubadour poems, the individual takes center stage here, a flesh-and-blood mortal who is of worth in himself.

In Sonnet 3 the young man is placed in a sequence of acts of memory—each generation's beauty serving, not to remind onlookers of Beauty itself, but to remind them of the beauty of those individuals Time and Death have taken or will soon take. The young man is asked to consider his mother:

> Thou art thy mother's glass and she in thee
> Calls back the lovely April of her prime.[6]

Your mother's beauty, the poem suggests, is preserved in you. In turn, it is important that the young man have a child, in order to pass on the memory of his own beauty. The concern here is for the memory of individuals, the attempt to preserve what a Diotima or Bembo would regard as copies of the real, not the real itself. But the sonnets disagree—what is important is precisely the individual, the so-called

---

5   Shakespeare, 1. 9–14.
6   Ibid., 3.9–10.

copy, the unique manifestation of beauty, not a philosophical ideal. In taking action—through reproduction—to preserve the memory of his own beauty, the young man will ensure that he does not disappear, like tears in rain, in the never-ceasing flow of Time:

> So thou through windows of thine age shalt see,
> Despite of wrinkles this thy golden time.
> But if thou live remembered not to be,
> Die single and thine image dies with thee.[7]

By Sonnet 15, however, Time has become a more pressing factor. How long can the memory of individual beauty can be preserved merely through reproduction? Edmondson and Wells insist that nothing has changed:

> Sonnets 1–17 are concerned with procreation, with breeding and re-creating the image of oneself in another living and autonomous being in order to combat the ravages of Time and so vicariously to achieve everlasting life. In this respect they are grounded firmly in the Platonic ideal of procreative love expressed in the *Symposium*, "because procreation is the nearest thing to perpetuity and immortality that a mortal being can attain". It is through procreation that Shakespeare wills the re-creation and transcendence of his lover through time.[8]

But something has changed. Reproduction through children, though still encouraged in this poem, and a number of those that follow, is no longer put forward as the most effective preservation technique. In Goethe's formulation, "Art is long! And our life is short".[9] Everything and everyone, in the terms of Sonnet 15, is a thing of a moment, soon to disappear. In Neoplatonic terms, even in Petrarchan terms, this is only a problem of incorrect perception and valuation. What Diotima teaches, what Bembo describes, and what Sidney's Astrophil struggles to believe and act upon, is the idea that individual beauty—no matter how compelling—is only a doorway to wider spaces and greater wonders, a

---

7   *Ibid.*, 3.11–14.
8   Paul Edmondson and Stanley Wells. *Shakespeare's Sonnets* (Oxford: Oxford University Press, 2004), 65.
9   "Die Kunst ist lang! Und kurz ist unser Leben" (Goethe. *Faust*, Part I, 106, ll. 558–59). Goethe reverses the emphasis of Hippocrates of Cos (460–370 BCE): "Life is short, and art is long" ("Ὁ βίος βραχύς, ἡ δὲ τέχνη μακρή").

window through which one can see the light, though it is not the light itself. Sonnet 15 rejects these ideas in no uncertain terms. It starts with a seemingly orthodox statement of the ephemerality of all things in this world of flux and change:

> When I consider every thing that grows
> Holds in perfection but a little moment.[10]

Everything that grows, eventually dies. Our peak moments, our moments of "perfection", are but "little", consigned to the past as soon as they arrive in the ever-changing present:

> When I perceive that men as plants increase,
> Cheered and checked even by the self-same sky:
> Vaunt in their youthful sap, at height decrease,
> And wear their brave state out of memory.[11]

None of us are exempt. No philosophical or theological conceits of being somehow one with a larger universe, an emanation of a larger One, or the creation of an immortal God who promises mortals an eternity of blessing or punishment, can stop even the simplest movement of one moment to the next, or the loss of a single hair in the perceptible process of aging and eventual death. This idea of inevitable loss brings the poem to Art, to poetry itself:

> Then the conceit of this inconstant stay,
> Sets you most rich in youth before my sight,
> Where wasteful time debateth with decay
> To change your day of youth to sullied night,
> And all in war with Time for love of you,
> As he takes from you, I engraft you new.[12]

In a war against Time itself, who can do anything but lose? Each of us will die, and many of us will go through the process of saying goodbye to the things and people we love. If we have enough time, we will bid

---

10   Shakespeare, 15.1–2.
11   *Ibid.*, 15.5–8.
12   *Ibid.*, 15.9–14.

farewell to ourselves, to our sense of who and what we have been in a world into which we were thrown without preparation, and from which we are taken without remorse. It is a war we all lose, eventually. But the war this poem, and this poet, fights is slightly different. Art cannot keep the young man from aging and eventually dying. But it can lift a moment out of Time, describe it, keep it, and pass it on to those who will live their own all-too-short lives in the future. This is the power the sonnet describes—poetry as immortalization: "[t]he theme of Horace's Censorinus ode, *Donarem pateras*, often reappears: [...] the gifts bestowed by the poets will endure forever".[13]

It may be a Pyrrhic victory, achieved at great cost and impossible to hold for long, but it is the only victory the artist, the poet, the mortal can win. To say to Time and Death, *No. Not this one. Not this moment. You can't have him. You can't have her. You can't have this. This we will save. This we will preserve, as best we can, against you*—this is the "war with Time" the sonnet fights.[14] Far from valuing the young man as a Beatrice, or as a Laura, or as a Stella, as a means to higher ends, this sonnet, and others that follow, value the temporary over the permanent, the ephemeral over the eternal. The fight to recognize, revalue, and preserve the individual is powerfully expressed in one of the most famous of all the sonnets, number 18:

> Shall I compare thee to a summer's day?
> Thou art more lovely and more temperate:
> Rough winds do shake the darling buds of May,
> And summer's lease hath all too short a date:[15]

---

13 J. B. Leishman. *Themes and Variations in Shakespeare's Sonnets* (London: Routledge, 1961), 41.
14 The most profound of modern work often shares the same spirit. It can be found, for example, in Ingmar Bergman's 1957 film *Det sjunde inseglet*, or *The Seventh Seal*, especially in the scene where the Crusades-era knight Antonius Bloch realizes how precious the ordinary moments can be in a life much too intimately engaged with death: "I will remember this moment. The stillness, the twilight, the bowl of strawberries, the bowl of milk, your faces in the evening light. [...] And it will serve as a sign for me, and it will be enough" ("Jag ska minnas den här stunden. Stillheten, skymningen, skålen med smultron, skålen med mjölk, era ansikten i kvällsljuset. [...] Och detta ska vara mig ett tecken och en stor tillräcklighet".) (55:39–56:25)
15 Shakespeare, 18.1–4.

A summer's day is the perfect comparison to the beauty of the young man. The day will not last, and neither will he or his beauty. It is here for a moment, then gone forever, and though other days may follow, none of them are *that* day, none are quite the same. From the perspective of this sonnet, it is *that* day, *that* beauty, *that* individual that must be preserved in the face of inevitable loss. Since summer days are not equal in their beauty, they are not interchangeable:

> Sometime too hot the eye of heaven shines,
> And often is his gold complexion dimmed,
> And every fair from fair sometime declines,
> By chance, or nature's changing course untrimmed:[16]

Therefore, *this* one must be kept, no matter the cost, using every power and technique at the poet's disposal:

> But thy eternal summer shall not fade,
> Nor lose possession of that fair thou ow'st,
> Nor shall death brag thou wand'rest in his shade,
> When in eternal lines to time thou grow'st,
> So long as men can breathe or eyes can see,
> So long lives this, and this gives life to thee.[17]

Perhaps the cliché is true—perhaps the pen really is mightier than the sword, for who has gone to war with Time, wielding, as Hamlet puts it, "a bare bodkin"? Though the troubadours do not speak of fighting against time and death in their poetry, their spirit is here, much more than is the spirit of the Dante who would put Paolo and Francesca in Hell, or the spirit of the Petrarch who transforms a young girl into a symbol for heavenly transcendence. These sonnets value one man's life far more than they value philosophical or theological abstractions.

This is not to say, however, that the philosophical heights of a Bembo have no place in Shakespeare's sonnets—such heights are scaled, most notably in a sonnet often used in perhaps the most inappropriate context of all: wedding ceremonies. It seems a rare experience to attend a wedding in an English-speaking country in which Sonnet 116 does

---

16   Ibid., 18.5–8.
17   Ibid., 18.9–14.

not make an appearance, and it has been popular with "[g]enerations of readers [who] have understood this poem to constitute a lyrical definition of true love, that is, love that transcends time and is unperturbed by age and change".[18] This famous sonnet is often included beside the words of Paul from 1 Corinthians 13:4–8, which is usually read aloud from a modern translation that renders the central term as "love". For example, the popular New International Version (NIV) translation expresses the passage this way:

> Love is patient, love is kind. It does not envy, it does not boast, it is not proud. It does not dishonor others, it is not self-seeking, it is not easily angered, it keeps no record of wrongs. Love does not delight in evil but rejoices with the truth. It always protects, always trusts, always hopes, always perseveres. Love never fails.

A lovely sentiment, this passage as it is usually read seems to establish "love" as the basis for a marriage between two people who have chosen each other freely, and are solemnizing that choice in a modern marriage ceremony. The only problem is that the translation is misleading—while the word "love" is not, strictly speaking, inaccurate, the word "charity" would be closer to the mark. The King James Bible (or Authorized Version of 1611) renders the passage with "charity" in place of "love":

> Charity suffereth long, and is kind; charity envieth not; charity vaunteth not itself, is not puffed up, Doth not behave itself unseemly, seeketh not her own, is not easily provoked, thinketh no evil; Rejoiceth not in iniquity, but rejoiceth in the truth; Beareth all things, believeth all things, hopeth all things, endureth all things. Charity never faileth.

The English sense of the two passages is quite different. Love may, or may not, be "patient" or "suffereth long". But *charity*, from the Latin *caritas*, definitely is, and does. The difference is found in the shadings of meaning offered by the three classical Greek words used for love: *eros* (desire, lack, a need to have an emptiness filled), *philia* (friendship, familial affection, close familiarity and warmth), and *agape* (a love based on principle, respect and acknowledgment of the value of another—in that sense, a very unPetrarchan love).

---

18 Dympna Callaghan. *Shakespeare's Sonnets* (Malden: Blackwell, 2007), 62.

The "charity"[19] of the King James rendition, based on the Latin *caritas*, which is itself a translation of the Greek *agape*, comes much closer to the sense of "love" as it appears in Sonnet 116. As John Kerrigan cynically notes, "[t]his sonnet has been misread so often and so mawkishly that it is necessary to say at once, if brutally, that Shakespeare is writing about what cannot be attained".[20] While it may be too much to insist that the "love" of Sonnet 116 "cannot be attained", it is important to understand that, rather than being a celebration of desire, or even of friendship, Sonnet 116 celebrates the relative permanency of a "love" defined in terms of principle and an unchanging recognition of the inherent value of another person:

> Let me not to the marriage of true minds
> Admit impediments, love is not love
> Which alters when it alteration finds,
> Or bends with the remover to remove.[21]

The union is not between true hearts or bodies (though these are by no means incompatible), but "true minds". Even here, it is the individual that is valued for his or her own sake, for the value and truth of the mind each brings to the other. Each is regarded as an end in itself, and love, in the sense of *agape*, *caritas*, and charity is fixed and constant:

> O no, it is an ever-fixed mark
> That looks on tempests and is never shaken;
> It is the star to every wand'ring bark,
> Whose worth's unknown, although his height be taken[.][22]

The passage of time will not, cannot, alter this love, for it is both freely given, and freely received, a love of choice, of mutual recognition of

---

19 *Charity*, however, has taken on a rather different sense in the twenty-first century than the seventeenth century, and there may not be a one-word translation in contemporary English that can capture the complexity in the orginal term ἀγάπη [*agape*]. The closest analog available may be the Hindu concept of *bhakti*, a word that, though usually translated as devotion, is probably better rendered as participation. Thus, *agape* or *caritas* might be most accurately translated as "the love that participates in highest things".

20 John Kerrigan. *The Sonnets; and A Lover's Complaint* (New York: Penguin, 1986), 53.

21 Shakespeare, 116.1–4.

22 *Ibid.*, 116.5–8.

each other as inherently valuable, an appreciation of truth, substance, and goodness as found in each other, not as a guidepost to something or someone greater. Those who give and receive this love will not be dissuaded from it:

> Love's not Time's fool, though rosy lips and cheeks
> Within his bending sickle's compass come,
> Love alters not with his brief hours and weeks,
> But bears it out even to the edge of doom:
> If this be error and upon me proved,
> I never writ, nor no man ever loved.[23]

As Héloïse d'Argenteuil proves in her letters, and as Milton demonstrates in *Paradise Lost*, those who love with even a spark of this unalterable regard, will defy God himself in its name.

As we have seen, and will often see again, there are any number of literary critics dedicated to diminishing poetry's power, telling readers that poems do not mean what they merely *seem* to say (or that they do not mean at all, in some extreme cases). Dypmna Callaghan has remarked on this phenomenon with Sonnet 116, and "the many ways in which critics and editors have argued that this poem does not mean what it says",[24] a point borne out by both Vendler and Stephen Booth. Booth argues that the virtues of Sonnet 116 "are more than usually susceptible to dehydration in critical comment. The more one thinks about this grand, noble, absolute, convincing and moving gesture, the less there seems to be to it",[25] while Vendler regards Sonnet 116 as a statement against love by a faithless lover:

> The young man has, after all, said, "I did love you once, but now impediments have arisen through alterations and removes". The speaker argues by means of the couplet that the performative speech-act of Platonic fidelity in quasi-marital mental love cannot be qualified; if it is qualified, it does not represent love. [...] The poem entertains, in the couplet, the deconstructive notion of its own self-dissolution; the impossibility of error is proved by the contrary-to-fact hypothesis, I never writ. [...] The young man, by his mentioning of "impediments", has

---

23 *Ibid.*, 116.9–14.
24 Callaghan (2007), 61.
25 Stephen Booth. *Shakespeare's Sonnets* (New Haven: Yale University Press, 1977), 387.

announced the waning of his own attachment to the speaker, dissolving the "marriage of true minds".[26]

Where the sonnet speaks of a love that does not admit impediments, the critic has rewritten it into a scenario in which impediments are the very thing that has altered—even ended—a love that was not of "true minds". With that familiar what-*seems-to-be-X-is-actually*-Y move, the sonnet is inverted, and made to represent the opposite of what its words seem to convey. This is not the first time, nor will it be the last, that a critic has become so deeply engaged with his or her terms of analysis that a text has simply become invisible under the bright light of the critic's scrutiny. But it is not necessary to submit to the idea "that the consensus of generations of readers is so completely wide of the mark as some recent editors suggest".[27]

Shakespeare's sonnets are not always concerned with so high and noble a conception of love as is Sonnet 116. Their feet are more likely to tread on the ground, to paraphrase another of the most famous sonnets, number 130. This poem is "a clever piece of literary satire" in which "we see [Shakespeare's] amused and discerning awareness of Petrarchan excess".[28] In this poem, Shakespeare openly mocks the Petrarchan mode, holding up most of its major themes for ridicule: "Shakespeare proclaims his independence from convention in Sonnet 130 in which, while declaring love for his mistress, he mocks the standard vocabulary of praise".[29] For example, the beloved, here rendered as "mistress", thus discarding the sense of a woman who is angelic and unapproachable, does not have, as do so many Petrarchan and Neopetrarchan beloveds, eyes like the sun or hair like flaxen strands of gold:

> My mistress' eyes are nothing like the sun,
> Coral is far more red, than her lips red,
> If snow be white, why then her breasts are dun:
> If hairs be wires, black wires grow on her head:[30]

---

26 Vendler, 491, 493.
27 Callaghan (2007), 64.
28 Philip Martin. *Shakespeare's Sonnets: Self, Love and Art* (Cambridge, Cambridge University Press, 1972), 123.
29 Edmondson and Wells, 15.
30 Shakespeare, 130.1–4.

His mistress' eyes are nothing like the sun, and a good thing too. A woman with eyes like the sun would be well and truly unapproachable, for who could make eye contact with a woman whose eyes had the power to strike one blind? In the very first line of the sonnet, Shakespeare has dismantled the most common of the Petrarchan conceits—the lady as somehow heavenly or divine—and the next lines proceed to dismantle poetic notions of the lady's physical perfection. As the sonnet continues, the embodied reality of the mistress is celebrated, while the poetic cliché is mocked:

> I have seen roses damasked, red and white,
> But no such roses see I in her cheeks,
> And in some perfumes is there more delight,
> Than in the breath that from my mistress reeks.
> I love to hear her speak, yet well I know,
> That music hath a far more pleasing sound:
> I grant I never saw a goddess go,
> My mistress when she walks treads on the ground.[31]

Here we have a woman whose breath stinks,[32] whose voice is delicately described as being less pleasing than music, and whose feet, unlike those of a goddess, walk on English dirt. This description has sometimes caused readers to react negatively, so accustomed are they to the inflated praise of the "divine lady" in the tradition of poetry beginning with Giacomo da Lentini and working its way through Petrarch to Sidney: "Shakespeare's mock-blazon has sometimes been thought misogynistic, in part because readers have formed their idea of it from its octave, where nothing positive is predicated of the mistress".[33] But this is a mistake, for all of the criticisms that come before the closing couplet are rejections of Petrarchan clichés, not of the woman herself. The woman being described in these lines is no poetic ideal, no angel or goddess. This is a real woman with faults of the flesh. But the last two lines of the

---

31 *Ibid.*, 130.5–12.
32 The modern bristle toothbrush, though invented by the Chinese Tang dynasty of 609–917 CE, did not make its first appearance in England, even among the wealthy, until 1690. See Michael Olmert. *Milton's Teeth & Ovid's Umbrella: Curiouser and Curiouser Adventures in History* (New York: Touchstone, 1996), 62.
33 Vendler, 557.

sonnet, even more than the previous twelve, blow the Petrarchan mode of idealized description right out of the water:

> And yet by heaven I think my love as rare,
> As any she belied with false compare.[34]

Perhaps the most romantic lines in all of English literature, this final couplet declares for the individual over the ideal, for the flesh over the spirit, for immediate desire over sublimated worship. The woman described in this poem exists in the world where everything that grows holds in perfection but a little moment, and she is very probably past that little moment. But she is "rare", more singular and valuable than any of the laughably false "shes" of the post-troubadour poetic tradition who have been misrepresented through the "false compare" of poets less attuned to the beauty of this world than to the imperious demands of worlds beyond. The final couplet "effects a shift from the lyrical to the colloquial register in order to demonstrate that even goddesses are overrated".[35]

Even more cutting in its rejection of the Petrarchan mode is the description of a relationship between a man and a (much younger) woman in Sonnet 138. This poem gives us a picture of compromise and lies as the basis for an apparently successful relationship. No ladder of love or pathway to the divine here: this poem describes a union in which each deceives the other in order to keep the other reasonably, if not ecstatically, happy. The lies, such as they are, seem thin, relatively harmless, and perhaps even necessary if the two are going to stay together:

> When my love swears that she is made of truth,
> I do believe her, though I know she lies,
> That she might think me some untutored youth,
> Unlearned in the world's false subtleties.[36]

We begin with the depiction of two lies: the speaker's lover "swears that she is made of truth" (a more obvious lie is almost inconceivable), and the speaker knows that she lies; but the speaker also pretends to "believe her", to give an impression of simplicity and youthfulness

---

34 Shakespeare, 130.13–14.
35 Callaghan (2007), 57.
36 Shakespeare, 138.1–4.

in order to manipulate her thinking: "That she might think me some untutored youth". He pretends to believe her lies because it is useful to him to have her believe that he is falling for those lies. The subject of her lies is probably his greater age (and possibly her desire for a younger man), as evidenced by the following lines:

> Thus vainly thinking that she thinks me young,
> Although she knows my days are past the best,
> Simply I credit her false-speaking tongue,
> On both sides thus is simple truth suppressed:[37]

The speaker is both vain (trying to pretend to himself that he is still young, and that she is buying into his pretense), and thinking in vain, thinking thoughts which are obviously not true, as neither he nor she really regard him as young, because "she knows" his days are "past the best". But he pretends to believe her when she says he is young, both simply (without criticism or confrontation about what each knows is a lie) and as if a simpleton (thus furthering his own lie of being too naïve to catch on to her lies). When the speaker thinks about this, he gets angry for a moment, but then recovers his balance, and remembers his reasons for compromise:

> But wherefore says she not she is unjust?
> And wherefore say not I that I am old?
> O love's best habit is in seeming trust,
> And age in love, loves not to have years told.[38]

Why don't they just drop the masks, stop lying, and tell each other the truth? Because that would upset the delicate balance of a relationship that neither one of them is apparently willing to see come to an end. She is unjust, and he is old (and unjust in his own way), but honesty in love is not always the best policy. This couple, who have found something in each other (perhaps once it was *eros*, and perhaps *philia* has settled in, and there might even be a touch of *agape* or *caritas* in there somewhere), clearly do not intend to upset the delicate balance they have achieved

---

37 Ibid., 138.5–8
38 Ibid., 138.9–12.

by insisting on absolute truth between them. In fact, "seeming trust" is their love's "best habit" (best repeated action, and best guise or disguise), and since neither one of them broaches the topic of "age in love", those "years" will not be "told". The final couplet makes the compromise clear:

> Therefore I lie with her, and she with me,
> And in our faults by lies we flattered be.[39]

Here is no Astrophil agonizing over a Stella, Dante worshiping a Beatrice, or Petrarch gazing to the point of idolatry on his own carefully-wrought "she belied with false compare". The love described in this poem does not point the way to heaven or to higher philosophical truth. It merely enables two people to keep and maintain companionship in an often lonely world where at least one of the poem's figures held "in perfection but a little moment" a very long time ago. Sonnet 138 portrays a relationship in which two people compromise the ideal in favor of the real. Without the rhetorical heights of more famous poems like Sonnet 18 or Sonnet 116, and without the visual humor and obvious mocking of Petrarchism in Sonnet 130, Sonnet 138, in its quiet way, is the most thorough rejection of the Beatrices, Lauras, and Stellas of Italian and English poetry. It returns, as does Shakespeare's larger body of work, to the spirit of the troubadours, and to the spirit of Ovid, for whom love may have involved compromise and lies, but was always love of an individual. It returns to love as it was in the Song of Songs—love of a man or woman of flesh and blood, rather than a God.

II
Shakespeare's Plays: Children as Property

In Shakespeare's plays love thrives, not as allegory, but as the passionate desire and regard between two who choose each other, often in the face of fierce resistance. To trace the power and presentation of love, we will consider two elements: the treatment of children as property by fathers, and the claims of love, individual choice, and agency that defy paternal

---

39   *Ibid.*, 138.13–14.

demands in order to assert the rights of one's own heart. In so doing, we will look at three daughters—Silvia, Hermia, and Juliet—whose desires are regarded as impediments to the plans, purposes, and passions of the fathers who begot them, before turning to the occasionally successful, sometimes disastrous, but always disruptive challenges that love and lovers will make to the forces that demand the exclusive right to obedience, fidelity, and life itself.

Shakespeare is not staging his plays of love in the face of resistance in order to demonstrate, as the historian Lawrence Stone would have it, that "the tragedy of Romeo and Juliet, [lay] in the way they brought destruction upon themselves by violating the norms of the society in which they lived".[40] Many members of Shakespeare's audience may have thought as Stone thinks—initially. But others did not. And during the 1590s and 1600s, Shakespeare's plays consistently present characters that reject the forces of tradition:

> In the comedies and romantic tragedies, love emerges as a force of inspiration and renewal for individuals and the enduring bond that comprises human society. Time and again, he presents young men and women who marry for love, rejecting the traditional arrangements of their parents. The moral vision in Shakespeare's plays is not ironclad obedience to the *ancién regime* but a new moral order based on free will, choice, and commitment, a personal bond of love and trust between two individuals that becomes an inspiration to their world.[41]

Shakespeare's *Romeo and Juliet* does not condemn its title characters, but sympathizes with the lovers whose disobedience brings them momentarily to the brink of a truly chosen life, only to be crushed by the forces of obedience, law, and profit. Such a work does not criticize those who violate the norms of society; rather, it criticizes the norms themselves.

Shakespeare writes during a time of transition. His life and career cross over the end of the sixteenth-century Elizabethan world into the beginnings of the seventeenth-century Stuart dynasty, which will eventually see a people rise against its king, a gentleman farmer become the Lord Protector of England, and a poet of revolution become

---

40 Lawrence Stone. *The Family, Sex, and Marriage in England 1500–1800* (New York: Harper and Row, 1977), 87.
41 Diane Dreher. *Domination and Defiance: Fathers and Daughters in Shakespeare* (Lexington: University Press of Kentucky, 1986), 38.

the country's international voice. Even as he is writing his earliest plays, such as *Two Gentlemen of Verona*, England is already beginning to stir with discontent and the unmistakable signs of future rebellion. The resentment of Catholic citizens at being forced to conform to the doctrines and disciplines of a new faith, denying the dictates of their consciences, will soon enough burst out into the attempt to assassinate a king and a parliament together in the infamous Gunpowder Plot. The discontents of many Protestants with the quasi-Catholic ceremonies, hierarchies, and vestments of the English Church break out into vituperative pamphlet broadsides such as the Marprelate controversy of 1588–89. Elizabeth's last Archbishop of Canterbury, John Whitgift, uses his position to enforce conformity in religion, attempting to crush the Presbyterian and Independent church movements, even as he moves to codify and mandate English belief in the Calvinist doctrine of predestination with the Lambeth Articles of 1595. Francis Walsingham, Elizabeth's spymaster, makes the 1570s and 1580s a period of repression and abject terror for the country's Catholics, who can be jailed for celebrating Mass or hiding a priest (who was himself liable to execution for carrying out his then-illegal function). England undergoes tremendous upheaval during Shakespeare's lifetime, moving from majority Catholic at his birth to majority Protestant at his death, while matters of faith, family, marriage, and emotion are all too often matters of conformity and obedience to the imperious demands of authority: whether that of God, the monarch, or the father.

In a sense, Stone may be right—"an Elizabethan courtier [who saw] where duty lay"[42] may have condemned the disobedience of a character like Juliet. But courtiers were a minority among the public theatre audiences of the 1590s and early 1600s,[43] for whom the distinctly uncourtly scenario presented in *Arden of Faversham* (1592)[44] was already

---

42 L. Stone, 87.
43 For detailed discussions of the composition of such audiences (in terms of economics, gender, and numerous other factors), see Andrew Gurr, *Playgoing in London* (Cambridge: Cambridge University Press, 2004).
44 The as yet unsolved question of the authorship of this play revolves primarily around two candidates: William Shakespeare and Thomas Kyd. Arguments for Kyd go back to Charles Crawford and Walter Miksch in the early twentieth century (in, respectively, "The Authorship of Arden of Faversham". In *Jahrbuch der Deutschen Shakespeare-Gesellschaft*, 39 [1903], 74–86, and *Die verfasserschaft des Arden of Feversham* [Breslau: H. Fleischmann, 1907]), and have recently been championed

familiar. In that play, a wife named Alice is willing—even eager—to murder her husband in order to be with her lover, Mosby. And despite the fact that this is presented as a crime which will be punished, the idea is still present that marriage without love is a despotism in which the husband is an illegitimate usurper, whose fate is to be cast out and overthrown. As Alice expresses it:

> Sweet Mosby is the man that hath my heart,
> And he [Arden] usurps it, having nought but this,
> That I am tied to him by marriage.
> Love is a god, and marriage is but words;
> And therefore Mosby's title is the best.[45]

Shakespeare's audiences filled the Globe Theatre for spectacles of disobedience and passionate assertions of the right to choose, performances which enabled them to imagine themselves, not as criminals, but as living and loving in the same free and chosen manner as those men and women they saw enacted on the stage. Far from being a bastion of convention-confirming conservatism—as Stephen Greenblatt contends through his idea of subversion and containment, a process which continually produces rebellion and tames it at the same time (thus subverting and containing the rebellious force)[46]—Shakespeare's

---

by Brian Vickers ("Thomas Kyd, Secret Sharer". *Times Literary Supplement* [18 April 2008], 13–15). The most recent argument for Shakespeare's authorship (especially of the middle section of the play) has been made by MacDonald P. Jackson in *Determining the Shakespeare Canon: "Arden of Faversham" and "A Lover's Complaint"* (Cambridge: Cambridge University Press, 2015), while the editors of *The New Oxford Shakespeare* (Gary Taylor, et al., 2016) include the play, listing its authorship as by Anonymous and Shakespeare.

45 *Arden of Faversham*. In Martin Wiggins, ed. *A Woman Killed with Kindness and Other Domestic Plays* (Oxford: Oxford University Press, 2008), 1.98–102.

46 See Greenblatt's argument—published in several different forms—in *Shakespearean Negotiations: The Circulation of Social Energy in Renaissance England* (Berkeley and Los Angeles: University of California Press, 1998); 'Invisible Bullets: Renaissance Authority and its Subversion', in *Glyph 8: Johns Hopkins Textual Studies* (Baltimore: Johns Hopkins University Press, 1981), 40–61; 'Invisible Bullets: Renaissance Authority and its Subversion, *Henry IV* and *Henry V*', in *Political Shakespeare: New Essays in Cultural Materialism*, eds, Jonathan Dollimore and Alan Sinfield (Manchester: Manchester University Press, 1985), 18–47; and in "Invisible Bullets: Renaissance Authority and its Subversion", in eds. Peter Erickson and Coppélia Kahn, *Shakespeare's 'Rough Magic': Renaissance Essays in Honor of C. L. Barber* (Newark: University of Delaware Press, 1985), 276–302. This argument, as Gabriel

plays not only encourage, but as we will see in *Two Gentlemen of Verona*, *A Midsummer Night's Dream*, and *Romeo and Juliet*, they celebrate disobedience in the name of love, the power of men and women to choose their own hearts' path, and the right to live as they see fit. The driving force behind this celebration of disobedience, this rejection of the notion that children are the property of their parents and citizens are the helpless subjects of their monarch, is the power of an old idea—*fin'amor*:

> Beginning as a purely extra-marital emotion in troubadour literature of the twelfth century, it was transformed by the invention of the printing press and the spread of literacy in the sixteenth and seventeenth centuries. It was a theme which dominated the poetry, theatre and romances of the late sixteenth and seventeenth centuries and found its way into real life in the mid-eighteenth century.[47]

However, the mid-eighteenth century is far too late a period to identify as the time in which the love described in poetry, theatre, and romances works its way into real life. One only need look at the story of John Donne and Anne More, discussed in Chapter 9, to be disabused of that notion. This is very much a development of the literature of Shakespeare's time, and "the movement of lovers toward each other may well be the most important single motive force in Elizabethan literature".[48] Love is not "a reality which existed in one very restricted social group", nor is it merely "the subject of much poetry of the sixteenth and early seventeenth centuries, and of many of Shakespeare's plays".[49] For many, both in Shakespeare's audience and his larger world, love is an urgent concern. It is here and now that love enters "real life", as art and life engage in a mutually affirming, mutually embracing dance of cultural, intellectual, and philosophical upheaval which moves the world from one in which all human devotion is directed upward—to God, monarch, and father— to one in which love is shared between relative equals; a move away

---

Egan explains, insists that any resistance to authority portrayed in Shakespeare, Marlowe, and others was merely illusory, because "the theatre industry of Shakespeare's time was a special device for the containment of progressive forces precisely because it appeared to produce subversion" (Gabriel Egan. *Shakespeare and Marx* [Oxford: Oxford University Press, 2004], 95).

47 L. Stone, 490–91.
48 Roger Stilling. *Love and Death in Renaissance Tragedy* (Baton Rouge: Louisiana State University Press, 1976), 148.
49 L.Stone, 103.

from a world in which love, beauty, and other people are means to an end, steps on a ladder leading to the divine, and to a world in which love, beauty, and all our beloveds are ends in themselves. In his way, Shakespeare helps to push the intellectual world from Plato to Kant, from the forms to the things in themselves, from a focus on the abstract idea of a rose, to the beauty of the rose that is right in front of us. Harold Bloom, that old Falstaff of American literary criticism, was at least partly right: Shakespeare helped to invent the modern sense of what it means to be a human being in the Western world.[50]

Unfortunately, it is not hyperbolic to describe the parent-child relationships of Early Modern England as proprietary. Though Stone's thesis of the cold emotional detachment of parents from their children in the period may have been overstated,[51] the hierarchical relationships within families are well-documented. As late as 1658, in an era of revolution and upheaval, the *pater familias*-style conservatism of parent-child relations, though beginning its decline, is still alive and well and speaking with a clear voice about the rights of parents to determine the marital and family futures of their children. From this perspective, for sons or daughters to choose their own mates is among the worst kinds of disobedience possible:

---

50 As Bloom lays out the case,

> [t]he idea of Western character, of the self as a moral agent, has many sources: Homer and Plato, Aristotle and Sophocles, the Bible and St. Augustine, Dante and Kant, and all you might care to add. Personality, in our sense, is a Shakespearean invention, and is not only Shakespeare's greatest originality but also the authentic cause of his perpetual pervasiveness. Insofar as we ourselves value, and deplore, our own personalities, we are the heirs of Falstaff and of Hamlet, and of all the other persons who throng Shakespeare's theater of what might be called the colors of the spirit.

Harold Bloom. *Shakespeare: The Invention of the Human* (New York: Penguin, 1998), 4.

51 For a review and critique, see Linda A. Pollock. *Forgotten Children: Parent-Child Relations from 1500 to 1900*. Cambridge: Cambridge University Press, 1983, 1–67. See also Lois G. Schwoerer, "Seventeenth-Century English Women Engraved in Stone?" *Albion*, 16.4 (1984), 389–403, who analyzes Stone's work from a feminist perspective; Alan MacFarlane, "The Family, Sex, and Marriage in England", *History and Theory*, 18 (1979), 103–26, who critiques Stone's readings of secondary material; Philippe Ariès, "Lawrence Stone. The Family, Sex and Marriage in England, 1500–1800", *American Historical Review*, 83 (1978), 1221–24, who, in an otherwise complimentary review, argues that Stone distorts early modern child-rearing practices; and John Gillis, "Affective Individualism and the English Poor", *Journal of Interdisciplinary History*, 10 (1979), 121–28, who argues that Stone ignores the lower economic levels of society in his work.

But of all acts of *disobedience*, that of *marrying* against the consent of the Parent, is one of the highest. Children are so much the goods, the possessions of the Parent, that they cannot without a kind of theft, give away themselves without the allowance of those, that have the right in them.[52]

From this point of view, children are portable wealth; not as fixed as land, though not so permanent either, children represent an opportunity to improve the family's fortunes through advantageously-arranged marriages. And the fathers of the respective families that were matched in such a union were not about to allow the romantic notions of their children to interfere with business. The era struggled with

> a clear conflict of values between the idealization of love by some poets, playwrights and the authors of romances on the one hand, and its rejection as a form of imprudent folly and even madness by all theologians, moralists, authors of manuals of conduct, and parents and adults in general.[53]

It was the fathers who stood most to gain from the marriages they arranged for their children: "[t]he marital *pactum* was too important to be created by the individuals concerned; instead it was forged by the two men who headed the two families involved. Negotiations resembled statecraft on a smaller scale".[54] For many generations, marriage had been treated as a business deal, an economic exchange between families—or more precisely, between *fathers*, in what Foucault describes as "a deployment of alliance: a system of marriage, of the securing and developing of kinship ties, of the transmission of names and possessions".[55] As a result

---

52 Richard Allestree. *The Practice of Christian Graces, or The Whole Duty of Man* (London: Printed by D. Maxwell for T. Garthwait, 1658), 291, https://quod.lib.umich.edu/cgi/t/text/pageviewer-idx?cc=eebo;c=eebo;idno=a23760.0001.001;node=A23760.0001.001%3A19;seq=318;vid=96830;page=root;view=text

53 L. Stone, 181.

54 Hagstrum, 220.

55 "un dispositif d'alliance: système de mariage, de fixation et de développement des parentés, de transmission des noms et des biens" (Michael Foucault. *Histoire de La Sexualité Vol. 1: la Volonté de Savoir* [Paris: Gallimard, 1976], 140). Foucault opposes this "deployment of alliance" not with the concept of *fin'amor* that we are identifying here as a combination of love, mutual recognition, and mutual choice between lovers, but with what he calls "the *deployment of sexuality*" ("le *dispositif de sexualité*") (140), a concept he defines as operating "based on techniques of power that are mobile, polymorphous, and cyclical" ("d'après des techniques mobiles, polymorphes et conjoncturelles de pouvoir"), and as concerned with "the body's sensations, the quality of its pleasures, and the nature of its impressions, as tenuous

of this system of alliance-forming, "[m]ost marriages in the sixteenth and early seventeenth centuries were arranged by parents or guardians [and] economic interests and parental pressures prevailed, [though] the poor, with no considerations of lineage and property, could often choose for themselves".[56] The idea that money was often, if not always, at the root of such arranged marriages is supported by English court documents, in which "[o]f all the depositions studied for the period 1542–1600, at least a third sufficiently illustrates the weighting of financial considerations in the making of marriages".[57]

It was not, of course, the situation that no child ever had any input into the choice of his or her eventual spouse. But neither were theirs the voices that spoke most persuasively on the matter: "'I must be ruled by my friends', said Elizabeth Fletcher of Canterbury, 'as well as by myself'".[58] Even in cases where individual expression was accommodated, children were expected, in keeping with their role as goods and possessions, to maintain obedience. This expectation was especially pronounced where the subject of marriage was concerned:

> The choice of marriage partner concerned both boys and girls and was especially important in a society where there were large financial and political stakes in marriage and where divorce was virtually impossible. Almost all children until the end of the sixteenth century were so conditioned by their upbringing and so financially helpless that they acquiesced without much objection in the matches contrived for them by their parents.[59]

While "[t]he notion of children as property", seems inhumane to us, it "was deeply imbedded in Renaissance thought. Children were their

---

or imperceptible as these may be" ("les sensations du corps, la qualité des plaisirs, la nature des impressions aussi ténues ou imperceptibles qu'elles soient") (140). But far from being anything like an avenue for resistance to the authorities of a given time and place, for Foucault, this alliance of sexuality is merely one more means of control: "The deployment of sexuality does not have its reason for being in reproduction, but in [...] controlling populations in an ever more global manner" ("Le dispositif de sexualité a pour raison d'être non de se reproduire, mais de [...] contrôler les populations de manière de plus en plus globale") (141).

56 Dreher, 28.
57 Diana O'Hara. *Courtship and Constraint: Rethinking the Making of Marriage in Tudor England* (Manchester: Manchester University Press, 2000), 215.
58 *Ibid.*, 32.
59 L. Stone, 180.

parents' goods, to be used as they saw fit, and owed them lifelong obedience for begetting them".[60] Even titled children, who outranked their parents in the hierarchy of the nation, were expected to perform acts of fealty and submission that seem incredible today. For example, the playwright, translator, and author Elizabeth Cary (*née* Tanfield), became Lady Falkland the Viscountess Falkland, when her husband was made Viscount in 1634. And yet she was still required to show, not merely respect, but outright submission to her mother: "Elizabeth, Countess of Falkland, always knelt in her mother's presence, sometimes for an hour at a time, despite the fact that she had married above her parents into the peerage, and that she was 'but an ill kneeler and worse riser'".[61] And though Cary's case seems especially counter-intuitive today, it was far from uncommon in her time:

> [the] stress on domestic discipline and the utter subordination of the child found expression in extraordinary outward marks of deference which English children were expected to pay to their parents in the sixteenth and early seventeenth centuries. It was customary for them when at home to kneel before their parents to ask their blessing every morning, and even as adults on arrival at and departure from the home. This was a symbolic gesture of submission which John Donne believed to be unique in Europe.[62]

As John Aubrey describes conditions of the period:

> The child perfectly loathed the sight of his parents as the slave his torture. Gentlemen of 30 and 40 years old were to stand like mutes and fools bareheaded before their parents; and the daughters [...] were to stand at the cupboard-side, during the whole time of the proud Mother's visit [until] they had done sufficient penance in standing.[63]

Failure to obey, especially in the matter of marital choice, could have serious negative consequences even with one's siblings, much less one's parents:

> No amount of pleading would move some kinsmen. The widow Christine Marsh fell down on her knees before her brother George

---

60 Dreher, 21.
61 L. Stone, 171.
62 *Ibid.*
63 John Aubrey. *Wiltshire. The Topographical Collections of John Aubrey, 1659–70*, ed. by John Edward Jackson (London: Longman, 1862), 16, https://archive.org/stream/wiltshiretopogra00aubr#page/16

Coppyn, desiring him to be a good brother unto her and a friend also, for he had rebuked and threatened her for the promise she had made to George Gaunt.[64]

To marry without permission often brought financial repercussions, as displeased parents would use the threat of disinheritance to prevent and/or punish the "disobedience" involved in making one's own choice. Elizabeth Evelyn was punished in precisely this way by her father, who describes with a certain methodical and self-righteous tone the reasons for his decision to disinherit his eldest child:

> [July] 27 This night when we were all asleep went my daughter Elizabeth away to meet a young fellow, nephew to Sir John Tippet (Surveyor of the Navy, and one of the Commissioners), whom she married the next day, being Tuesday, without in the least acquainting either of her parents, or any soul in the house. [...] This accident caused me to alter my will, as was reasonable; for though there may be a reconciliation upon her repentance, and that she suffered her folly; yet I must let her see what her undutifulness in this action deprives her of, as to the provision she else might have expected, solicitous as she knew I now was of bestowing her very worthily.[65]

The fathers of Shakespeare's plays, who may well seem to modern readers and spectators like so many tinpot dictators, were not at all unusual for their time. To Shakespeare's contemporaries, they would have been entirely familiar, on-and off-stage. Hamlet explains why: art serves "to hold, as 'twere, the mirror up to nature; to show virtue her own feature, scorn her own image, and the very age and body of the time his form and pressure".[66] In giving this speech to the players, he is not telling them that art uncritically mirrors the values and practices of a civilization to its members while encouraging them to remain compliant. His entire purpose for the play-within-the-play is angry and accusatory. That is what art—Shakespeare's art—is when at its best. Art holds up the mirror to show the time and place within which it appears, to which it reacts, and against which it often struggles, that the

---

64 O'Hara, 33.
65 Ralph A. Houlbrooke, ed. "'Stealing a Marriage': The Marriage of Elizabeth Evelyn in 1685 Described by Her Father". *English Family Life, 1576–1716: An Anthology from Diaries* (Oxford: Blackwell, 1988), 39.
66 *Hamlet* 3.1.21–24.

"customs of [its] island and tribe are [not] the laws of nature".[67] Thus, when portraying the Duke of Milan in *The Two Gentlemen of Verona*, or Egeus in *A Midsummer Night's Dream*, or Capulet in *Romeo and Juliet*, Shakespeare is not soothing, he is savaging, He is holding them up for scorn as images of *what not to do* rather than as examples of the idea that *Father knows best*. The play's the thing, in which he will catch the consciences of countless fathers who think themselves king.

The plots initially revolve around marriage as a bond, not between a young man and a young woman, but between two men over and through the body of a woman. In what Eve Sedgwick describes as a dynamic of homosociality,[68] the fathers in these plays bond themselves to men of their choosing (often quite a bit older than their daughters), who offer advantages in terms of wealth, land, and power. Sedgwick, following Gayle Rubin, describes this as "traffic in women", or "the use of women as exchangeable, perhaps symbolic, property for the primary purpose of cementing the bonds of men with men".[69] In this claim, she rearticulates the argument of the French anthropologist Claude Lévi-Strauss:

> [t]he overall relationship of exchange which constitutes marriage is not established between a man and a woman, in which everyone has rights and everyone gets something: it is between two groups of men, and the woman figures as one of the objects of exchange, and not as one of the partners between whom exchange occurs.[70]

In just this fashion, the fathers in Shakespeare attempt to partner with other men, while using their daughters as "objects of exchange". Love—passionate and mutually chosen attachment between those who would otherwise be caught up in the pattern—serves as the primary means of resistance. Silvia and Hermia choose their loves despite their fathers,

---

67 George Bernard Shaw. "Caesar and Cleopatra". *Three Plays for Puritans* (New York: Brentano's, 1906), 119, https://babel.hathitrust.org/cgi/pt?id=hvd.32044014213078;view=1up;seq=167

68 A term originally coined in 1976 by Jean Lipmen-Blumen to describe a social, rather than sexual, preference for members of one's own sex.

69 Eve Kosofsky Sedgwick. *Between Men: English Literature and Male Homosocial Desire* (New York: Columbia University Press, 1985), 26.

70 [l]a relation globale d'échange qui constitue le mariage ne s'établit pas entre un homme et une femme qui chacun doit, et chacun reçoit quelque chose: elle s'établit entre deux groupes d'hommes, et la femme y figure comme un des objets des objets de l'échange, et non comme un des partenaires entre lesquels il a lieu.

Claude Lévi-Strauss. *Les Structures Élémentaires de la Parenté* (Berlin: De Gruyter), 2002).

and would likely do so again, despite the hardships that ensue. Romeo and Juliet choose each other in the face of family hatred and violence, even enacting their own version of a dawn song in which they lament the coming of day and the short moments they have left to be together. In many of his most powerful plays, Shakespeare casts love and its pursuit in the light of rebellions that are both justified and long overdue. As wielded in Shakespeare's plays, love serves as the primary challenge to the authority of fathers and rulers who claim obedience from children and subjects alike.

III
Love as Resistance: Silvia and Hermia

As the Troubadour poet Giraut de Borneilh (1138–1215) describes it, love enters through the eyes:

> Tam cum los oills el cor ama parvenza
> Car li oill son del cor drogoman
> E ill oill van vezer,
> Lo cal cor plaz retener.[71]

> So through the eyes love enters the heart,
> Because the eyes are the agents of the heart
> And the eyes go forth to gaze,
> On what the heart would like to own.

For Giraut, love cannot be tamed and controlled, nor does it develop as an emotional balm to heal the frictions of an arranged marriage between strangers; rather it is something that hits from the outside and works its way inwards in a near-immediate process of transformation. Gottfried Von Strassburg's image for this is the effect of the love-drink: meant to provide the bond between King Mark and his young bride-to-be Isot (Iseult or Isolde in other versions of the story), it instead transforms

---

71 John Rutherford, ed. *The Troubadours: Their Loves and their Lyrics* (London: Smith, Elder & Co., 1873), 34, ll. 1–4, https://archive.org/stream/troubadoursthei01ruthgoog#page/n48

Tristan and Isot from two into one, "who had both one heart".⁷² It is this transformative power that causes Gottfried's lovers to defy King Mark, and this power is shown again and again in Shakespeare as the driving force behind the resistance to the homosocial structure of exchange.

Such resistance can be seen initially in the early comedy *The Two Gentleman of Verona*. In this relatively light, yet humorously bizarre and revealing play, the triangular pattern of fathers matching themselves to men through their daughters is evident. But Shakespeare uses an old comic device, the cuckolding plot, to add a fourth element: a young man who will try to break up the sexual match between the often-older man and the daughter by stealing her away (with her enthusiastic assistance), thus scotching the proposed partnership between the men. The Duke of Milan wishes to match his daughter Silvia (whom he keeps locked in a tower at night) to a wealthy, if otherwise unappealing man named Thurio. He is swayed in this choice because Thurio is rich, despite an evident lack of any other desirable qualities. As Valentine describes Thurio, he is a "foolish rival, that her father likes / Only for his possessions are so huge".⁷³ But in arranging this match, the Duke has a problem: Silvia *despises* Thurio, and has fallen in love with Valentine. As Valentine is busily arranging to run away with Silvia by using a rope ladder (which he is hiding underneath his cloak), he encounters the Duke, who complains of his daughter's disobedience:

> she is peevish, sullen, froward,
> Proud, disobedient, stubborn, lacking duty,
> Neither regarding that she is my child
> Nor fearing me as if I were her father;
> And, may I say to thee, this pride of hers,
> Upon advice, hath drawn my love from her;
> And, where I thought the remnant of mine age
> Should have been cherished by her child-like duty,
> I now am full resolved to take a wife
> And turn her out to who will take her in:

---

72 "si heten beide ein herze" (Gottfried Von Strassburg. *Tristan*, l. 11,731, ed. by Karl Marold [Leipzig: E. Avenarius, 1906], https://archive.org/stream/gottfried vonstr00unkngoog#page/n240).

73 *Two Gentlemen of Verona* 2.4.172–73.

> Then let her beauty be her wedding-dower;
> For me and my possessions she esteems not.[74]

In this speech, we encounter elements we will see again. The father demands his daughter's obedience, in this case specifically to his will in terms of *his* choice for *her* marriage partner. When she does not comply with his will, he threatens to disown her, despite the fact that he had planned to rely on her as a caretaker as he aged, and resolves to throw her out of his house and let her fend for herself by living the life of an early modern vagrant.[75]

However, the perspective the Duke either does not understand or does not care to understand—his daughter's side of the question—is exactly what the play highlights for its audience, showing "the very age and body of the time his form and pressure". Silvia regards the match with Thurio, not merely as undesirable, but as *unholy*. In pleading with a gentleman to help her escape, she describes the match as one worthy of punishment by heaven itself:

> Thou art not ignorant what dear good will
> I bear unto the banished Valentine,
> Nor how my father would enforce me marry
> Vain Thurio, whom my very soul abhors.
> [...]
> Urge not my father's anger, Eglamour,
> But think upon my grief, a lady's grief,
> And on the justice of my flying hence,
> To keep me from a most unholy match,
> Which heaven and fortune still rewards with plagues.[76]

This is no mere foolery, or adolescent madness, nor is Shakespeare here running "directly across the norms and practices of [his audience]".[77] This is Shakespeare showing his audience that "the norms and practices" of their society run "directly across" their hearts. Silvia wants and needs to be stolen from her father, in a "theft' that involves giving herself away

---

74 Ibid., 3.1.68–79.
75 See Linda Woodbridge. *Vagrancy, Homelessness, and English Renaissance Literature* (Urbana: University of Illinois Press, 2001).
76 *Two Gentlemen of Verona* 4.3.14–17, 27–31.
77 L. Stone, 180.

"without the allowance of those, that have the right in [her]".[78] But in their mutual defiance of her father's will, Valentine and Silvia seek no harm each to the other, nor any dominance one over the other. The same cannot be said of the "lover" Proteus.

Proteus' love is destructive, and actively seeks to subordinate the will of others. Proteus does not so much rebel against the authority of the Duke of Milan as try to sneak around it, pretending to serve the Duke while imposing himself on Silvia, who absolutely does not want him. Proteus, who feared his father at the beginning of the play,[79] fears any honest confrontation with the Duke as much or more, and takes the coward's way out consistently. Determining to betray his friendship with Valentine because "I to myself am dearer than a friend",[80] and because the merest sight of Silvia has "dazzled [his] reason's light",[81] Proteus behaves as if Silvia owes him *her* love because of the frequent, though unwelcome, declarations he makes of *his* love.

It is in Proteus' threat to rape Silvia, and the odd way that threat plays out—not between himself and Silvia, but between himself and Valentine—where this play's most unusual twist on love can be found. Despite the fact that Silvia has declared that she would rather be eaten, digested, and then presumably excreted by a "hungry lion"[82] than have anything to do with Proteus, the perversely determined young man simply will not take "no" for an answer. Insisting that he will finally bend Silvia's will to his own, and not about to be satisfied with any courtly tricks or delays, Proteus declares that he will love Silvia "'gainst the nature of love" by forcing her to submit to his desire.[83] Whatever else may be said of *fin'amor*, it is not rape. The ultimate in *fals'amor*, rape seeks, not mutual choice in a one-to-one relationship, but a perverse form of obedience. Rape seeks exactly the opposite of that sought by love. Where love wishes to be free from the authority of the father, rape *reimposes* that authority by the most intimately violent means, changing the agent or enactor of that authority from the father to the rapist. In

---

78   Allestree, 291.
79   *Two Gentlemen of Verona* 1.3.78–87.
80   *Ibid.*, 2.6.23.
81   *Ibid.*, 2.4.208.
82   *Ibid.*, 2.4.33.
83   *Ibid.*, 5.4.59.

essence, Proteus does not seek to rebel *against* the Duke so much as *become* the Duke: declaring his authority over the flesh, the sexuality, of Silvia.

Even odder, and to many contemporary readers less explicable, is Valentine's reaction. Rather than show any concern for Silvia, he directs his emotional investment—not merely anger, but what looks like the genuine disappointment of a jilted lover—toward Proteus:

> [...] Proteus,
> I am sorry I must never trust thee more,
> But count the world a stranger for thy sake.
> The private wound is deepest: O time most accurst,
> 'Mongst all foes that a friend should be the worst![84]

Valentine is less worried about the trauma inflicted on Silvia than he is about his own feelings of betrayal. If it is true that the ones we love the most also have the power to hurt us most deeply, then it is apparent that Valentine's "true" love is Proteus, not Silvia. He demonstrates that by quickly accepting the thinnest of apologies from Proteus—whom the play has been at pains to portray as genuinely untrustworthy—and then simply *giving* Silvia to him: "that my love may appear plain and free, / All that was mine in Silvia I give thee".[85] In this gesture, Valentine behaves as if Silvia's love, and his "right" to it, is a transferable property. Far from being the mutual partner she was with Valentine in their earlier plan of escape, Silvia is now given no voice at all, leaving many readers and audiences wondering if something has gone wrong:

> To a modern audience accustomed to a sex/gender system that clearly designates cross-sex marriage as more important than same-sex friendship and furthermore sees same-sex and cross-sex affection as linked to mutually exclusive categories of identity, Valentine's valuation of his love of Proteus over his love of Silvia is unexpected, and has struck many critics and directors of the play as simply erroneous.[86]

We are on firmer ground, however, if we see this ending, not as a mistake, but as part of the play's design. Far from being erroneous,

---

84 *Ibid.*, 5.468–72.
85 *Ibid.*, 5.4.82–83.
86 Jeffrey Masten. "The Two Gentlemen of Verona". *A Companion to Shakespeare's Works*, Vol. III (Malden: Blackwell, 2003), 273.

the odd ending of this play suggests that we have been following the misadventures of young people who *play* at love, whether cross-sex *or* same-sex, without ever really understanding it, or lending themselves to its power. The "Gentlemen" neither choose their female loves, nor ever have the courage to do anything more than faintly and indirectly choose each other, through Valentine's declaration that their wedding days shall be "One feast, one house, one mutual happiness".[87] Their rebellions are in form only, resisting the "property" claims of older men to women that they themselves go on to treat as exchangable property, and the two "Gentlemen" seem especially happy to be received back into the arms of authority at the end, as the Duke declares:

> [...] Sir Valentine,
> Thou art a gentleman and well derived;
> Take thou thy Silvia, for thou hast deserved her.[88]

Rather than challenge authority as Silvia does, Proteus and Valentine adopt its roles, acting as the fathers and older males act, by exchanging (or intending to exchange) Silvia between them, just as the Duke had meant to do with Thurio. Not yet the love of mutual choice in defiance of authority, the loves toyed with by Valentine and Proteus are but that—toys.

A more powerful resistance to the "between men" structure can be seen in *A Midsummer Night's Dream*. Love and marriage—not always in tandem—are central to the play. But of the human pairs presented therein, only one is not brought together by violence or an authoritarian insistence on obedience to the force of another's will, sword, or magic. Theseus and Hippolyta, the ruling pair of the play, are the couple of the will crossed with the sword, as Theseus "wooed [her] with [his] sword, / And won [her] love doing [her] injuries",[89] while the eventual pairing of Demetrius with Helena is the result of an herb which "[t]he juice of it on eyelids laid, / Will make man or woman madly dote".[90] What the play illustrates and condemns through these pairings is an

---

87 *Two Gentlemen of Verona* 5.4.175.
88 Ibid., 5.4.145–47.
89 *A Midsummer Night's Dream* 1.1.16–17.
90 Ibid., 2.1.170–71.

"obedience [...] enforced with brutality".[91] Only Hermia and Lysander freely choose each other—in the midst of the delightful chaos of this play, is that supposed to be the example of what Stone calls love's "imprudent folly and even madness"?[92] Or, as Alan Sinfield suggests, is it merely the *illusion* of choice?

> If I were directing the play [...] the more effective move would be to disclose the tragedy in the conventional ending. This would involve presenting the boys and girls as manifestly brainwashed and infantilized by Puck's manipulations of their minds and bodies into cross-gender pairings. [...] Puck could be shown putting electrodes on to their heads; they would lose their vigour and engagement with life, and sink into marriage as into a stupor.[93]

These critics' urge to discount and dismiss Hermia's choice is cut from the same cloth as the tyranny of her father. Critic and father are closer together than it might initially seem. One may not expect a literary critic to adopt the emphatic physical presence of an actor. Neither might one expect a dramatic character to express himself in the terms of academic prose. But the dismissal of Hermia's will features prominently in the thinking of both figures. Egeus storms into the presence of the Duke, demanding that the public State enforce his private authority: he is "full of vexation" and "complaint" with Hermia,[94] who has refused his choice of marriage partner for her—the "spotted and inconstant" Demetrius[95]— and has further defied his will by, in "a kind of theft",[96] giving her love to Lysander. Egeus rages at Lysander for having used witchcraft (Sinfield's "manipulations") to steal his daughter away from him:

> This [man] hath bewitched the bosom of my child;
> Thou, thou, Lysander, thou hast given her rhymes,
> And interchanged love-tokens with my child:
> Thou hast by moonlight at her window sung,
> With feigning voice verses of feigning love,
> And stolen the impression of her fantasy

---

91 L. Stone, 112.
92 *Ibid.*, 181.
93 Sinfield, 109.
94 *A Midsummer Night's Dream* 1.1.22.
95 *Ibid.*, 1.1.110.
96 Allestree, 291.

> With bracelets of thy hair, rings, gawds, conceits,
> Knacks, trifles, nosegays, sweetmeats, messengers
> Of strong prevailment in unharden'd youth:
> With cunning hast thou filch'd my daughter's heart,
> Turn'd her obedience, which is due to me,
> To stubborn harshness.[97]

Egeus demands either that his daughter be forced to obey him, or be forced to face the death penalty:

> Be it so she will not here before your grace
> Consent to marry with Demetrius,
> I beg the ancient privilege of Athens,
> As she is mine, I may dispose of her:
> Which shall be either to this gentleman
> Or to her death, according to our law
> Immediately provided in that case.[98]

Even harsher than the Duke of Milan, Egeus would rather that his daughter die than be allowed to exercise a will and judgment independent of, or even slightly different from his own. Egeus' demands appear to put Theseus—with the conspicuously silent Hippolyta beside him—in something of an awkward position. He can give Egeus his will, and sit back while the raving old man makes a mockery of the authority of his state by demanding that public justice be meted out for private faults. He can simply dismiss Egeus, possibly creating trouble for himself with the patrician class of Athens. Or, he can do what so many of Shakespeare's characters do: *seem* to do, say, or think one thing while acting in an entirely different manner. In this case, Theseus *seems* to take Egeus' side, telling Hermia that she must subordinate her judgment (and her eyes—thus, her attraction to Lysander) to her father. When Hermia says "I would that my father looked but with my eyes",[99] a line practically calculated to appeal to the anti-authoritarian sentiments that the poetry and drama of this period are increasingly trading on,

---

97 *A Midsummer Night's Dream* 1.1.27–38.
98 *Ibid.*, 1.1.39–45.
99 *A Midsummer Night's Dream* 1.1.56.

Theseus responds with the conservative instruction: "Rather your eyes must with his judgment look".[100] So far, so predictable.

But the Thesean "fix" is in, though Egeus is too dull-witted to see it. As the conversation between the warrior duke and the spirited daughter of a tyrant-father proceeds, it becomes evident that Theseus is looking for a loophole, a way to bend the rules. When Hermia asks what the worst-case scenario is if she refuses to obey Egeus, Theseus subtly alters the terms of the old man's demands: Hermia will be forced "Either to die the death *or* to abjure / For ever the society of men".[101] There is the loophole. Hermia has a choice—limited though it is—of three options: obedience, "austerity and single life",[102] or death. It is not nearly as draconian a choice as the obedience or death ultimatum that Egeus would impose.

As the scene progresses, Egeus' absurdity, and Demetrius' unsavory character, each becomes more evident. In a clever mocking of the entire "between men" structure, Lysander turns to Demetrius and demands that he leave off his pursuit of Hermia: "You have her father's love, Demetrius; / Let me have Hermia's: do you marry him".[103] And why not? Why not just cut out the middle woman? If this bond is to be one between Egeus and Demetrius, what need for so obvious an object of exchange as Hermia? And though this is a laugh-line, and a big one, Egeus steps right into the role of the butt of the joke, insisting on his right to dispose of both his love and his property as he sees fit:

> Scornful Lysander! true, he hath my love,
> And what is mine my love shall render him.
> And she is mine, and all my right of her
> I do estate unto Demetrius.[104]

Demetrius has Egeus' "love", and as a sign of that soon-to-be-bonded love between men, Egeus will "estate" (like the value of moveable goods that can be passed from one owner to another) his daughter upon the man of his love's choice. The joke here, if the audience has ears to

---

100 *Ibid.*, 1.1.57.
101 *Ibid.*, 1.1.65–66. Emphasis added.
102 *Ibid.*, 1.1.90.
103 *A Midsummer Night's Dream* 1.1.91–92.
104 *Ibid.*, 1.1.95–98.

hear, and the reader has eyes to see, is that it is not "love" that is being portrayed here as folly or madness—it is the absurdity of allowing the *eros* of the father to be the sole legitimate and determining factor in the making of a marriage. "Do you marry him", indeed.

Another notable point about the ridiculous nature of Egeus' insistence on estating his daughter unto Demetrius, is that Demetrius has a reputation as what we might now call *a player*. As Lysander charges, with no self-defense whatsoever coming from the accused:

> Demetrius, I'll avouch it to his head,
> Made love to Nedar's daughter, Helena,
> And won her soul; and she, sweet lady, dotes,
> Devoutly dotes, dotes in idolatry,
> Upon this spotted and inconstant man.[105]

Demetrius has cruelly dallied with Helena, and is now, apparently to be "estated" with another young girl for his troubles. As Theseus, somewhat perturbed at this, notes: "I must confess that I have heard so much, / And with Demetrius thought to have spoke thereof".[106] At this point, Theseus goes from finding the loophole to finding the escape clause. He tells both Demetrius and Egeus to come with him:

> I must employ you in some business
> Against our nuptial and confer with you
> Of something nearly that concerns yourselves.[107]

In so doing, he creates the situation in which, being left utterly alone, Hermia and Lysander can do as they will—obey, escape, or pursue whatever other options occur to them. Theseus has worked his way out of an awkward, ridiculous, and unwanted situation, and given himself a layer of plausible deniability as a shield against any further trouble. From this point, "the course of true love" may not "run smooth",[108] but at least it has a fighting chance.

---

105 *Ibid.*, 1.1.106–10.
106 *Ibid.*, 1.1.111–12.
107 *Ibid.*, 1.1.123–126.
108 *Ibid.*, 1.1.134.

The relation of judgment to the eyes, seeing, sight, and insight, and their association with love are the dominant themes of the mix of magic and comedy that plays out in the forest scenes in the middle of the play. It is through the eyes, manipulated with herbal magic, that love is changed, conjured out of nothing, and (for some) restored. The comic action suggests both the fragility and the power of love, the ease with which surfaces can be mistaken for depths, especially for the young men of the play—though even the fairy queen Titania finds herself "enamored of an ass".[109]

Edwin Henry Landseer, *Scene from A Midsummer Night's Dream. Titania and Bottom* (1848–1851).[110]

The fairy king Oberon, who orders his servant Puck to fetch "a little western flower" on which "the bolt of Cupid fell", determines to use "the juice of it, on sleeping eyelids laid"[111] to control who will pair with whom. In so doing, he acts as a satire on Egeus and the entire structure of a society in which marriage and love not only "keep little company together nowadays",[112] but are regarded as incompatible, while "love" is regarded as madness, and marriage—arranged, of course, by the father—is thought

---

109 *Ibid.*, 4.1.76.
110 https://commons.wikimedia.org/wiki/File:Edwin_Landseer_-_Scene_from_A_Midsummer_Night's_Dream._Titania_and_Bottom_-_Google_Art_Project.jpg
111 *Ibid.*, 2.1.165–66, 70.
112 *Ibid.*, 3.1.139.

to be the "reasonable" and "sane" alternative. In the *Comedy-of-Errors*-style identity confusion that the plot relies on, Puck ends up squeezing the juice into the eyes of *both* young men, rather than merely putting Demetrius under its magic spell, and then the game is on. Lysander, in love with Hermia at the beginning, now wakes up and finds Helena irresistible, and is filled with the urge to fight Demetrius for her love:[113]

> Transparent Helena! Nature shows art,
> That through thy bosom makes me see thy heart.
> Where is Demetrius? O, how fit a word
> Is that vile name to perish on my sword![114]

When Helena, naturally enough, is shocked by Lysander's sudden outburst, and reminds him of his love for Hermia, the formerly stable young man illustrates the extremes of thought and behavior to which the drug can lead (in a comic illustration of the effects of authority and obedience):

> Content with Hermia! No; I do repent
> The tedious minutes I with her have spent.
> Not Hermia but Helena I love:
> Who will not change a raven for a dove?
> The will of man is by his reason swayed;
> And reason says you are the worthier maid.
> Things growing are not ripe until their season
> So I, being young, till now ripe not to reason;
> And touching now the point of human skill,
> Reason becomes the marshal to my will
> And leads me to your eyes, where I o'erlook
> Love's stories written in love's richest book.[115]

Reason, as much or more than love, is mocked by this speech. Reason, which as John Milton will write, "also is choice", cannot operate when the will is overridden, when it is "[u]seless and vain, of freedom both

---

113 The drug apparently makes Lysander forgetful of more than his love for Hermia, as he seems to have forgotten the fact that Demetrius—until he is also drugged—wants nothing to do with Helena.
114 *A Midsummer Night's Dream* 2.2.103–07.
115 *Ibid.*, 2.2.111–22.

despoiled, / Made passive", and made to serve "necessitie".[116] Under the influence of the drug that has been applied to his eyes, Lysander is less free to use, as Bertram would, "[t]he help of [his] own eyes"[117] than he was when confronting the authority of Egeus and Theseus. Lysander, who while pursuing the goals of *fin'amor* was willing to stand with Hermia before the authority of the father and the state, is now, while under the influence of *fals'amor*, a toady, a lackey, a slave who speaks and acts as authority—the drug—would have him speak and act. This is especially obvious to Hermia, when Lysander explains his sudden transformation:

> HERMIA What love could press Lysander from my side?
> LYSANDER Lysander's love, that would not let him bide,
> Fair Helena, who more engilds the night
> Than all you fiery oes and eyes of light.
> Why seek'st thou me? could not this make thee know,
> The hate I bear thee made me leave thee so?
> HERMIA You speak not as you think: it cannot be.[118]

Hermia is right for two reasons: Lysander speaks not as he thinks because he is not actually *thinking*, merely reacting obediently to the power of the drug—the former rebel now a comically absurd conformist—and Lysander speaks not *as himself*, but as someone under the influence, not of a chosen love, a *fin'amor*, but of a drug that renders his will "useless and vain". Hermia knows Lysander; her sight is insight, as Lysander's had been before the drug. Thus, far from being a lover like Proteus, who can find in one object the same superficial attractions he finds in any other object, Hermia is the kind of lover of whom the troubadours wrote—one who knows the beloved, and chooses, despite the trouble it may cause, love over obedience.

Demetrius and Helena are at the opposite end of the spectrum. Neither of them appears to have any insight whatsoever, as Helena continues to chase a man who has little but contempt for her, and

---

116 John Milton. *Paradise Lost* 3.108, 109–10. All citations of Milton's poetry are from *John Milton: Complete Poems and Major Prose*, ed. by Merritt Hughes (New York: Odyssey Press, 1957).
117 *All's Well that Ends Well* 2.3.106–07.
118 *A Midsummer Night's Dream* 3.2.185–91.

Demetrius—before being drugged—continues to chase a woman who wants nothing to do with him. Demetrius' reasons for his behavior— venal and mercenary as they are—are at least rational. Helena, on the other hand, is the one of the four who is portrayed as helpless in the face of an *unchosen* passion, almost as if she were a female version of Sidney's Astrophil, or of Petrarch himself, chasing an always-uncatchable Stella or Laura. The effect of this unfortunate sickness is to make her think herself uniquely undesirable in comparison with Hermia:

> [...] I am as ugly as a bear;
> For beasts that meet me run away for fear:
> Therefore no marvel though Demetrius
> Do, as a monster fly my presence thus.
> What wicked and dissembling glass of mine
> Made me compare with Hermia's sphery eyne?[119]

Demetrius, in contrast, suffers no such negative self-opinion. His beloved is not, like a heavenly principality, beyond his grasp, nor would it be sullied by his touch, because his beloved is Egeus and his money. As the play makes clear, *that* love is most certainly requited. But under the influence of the drug, Demetrius becomes just as untrue to money as Lysander becomes to Hermia:

> O Helena, goddess, nymph, perfect, divine!
> To what, my love, shall I compare thine eyne?
> Crystal is muddy. O, how ripe in show
> Thy lips, those kissing cherries, tempting grow!
> That pure congealed white, high Taurus snow,
> Fann'd with the eastern wind, turns to a crow
> When thou hold'st up thy hand: O, let me kiss
> This princess of pure white, this seal of bliss![120]

The effect of the drug is to override the will, rendering it compliant to the demands of the one who administers it, and in a sense, of the readers and audiences who look on in mirth. Underneath the laughter is a dark thread of reflection on just how fragile love can be as a challenger to the

---

119 *Ibid.*, 2.2.93–99.
120 *Ibid.*, 3.2.137–44.

claims of authority and power, when the human will can so easily be manipulated, even in those cases in which it could not be intimidated. Lysander, who like Hermia, is a good judge of character, a young man with insight (it was he, after all, who "outed" Demetrius as the unsavoury man he is), does not have that ability beaten out of him, but drugged out of him. Egeus would likely give a pretty penny to have the juice of that magic flower with which to cancel his daughter's will, and bring her back to heel.

Beyond the mere enforcement of the administrator's will, the drug serves a punitive function when it is administered to Titania, who has dared defy Oberon over his request for "a little changeling boy / To be [his] henchman".[121] As they argue and then part, Oberon darkly mutters "[t]hou shalt not from this grove / Till I torment thee for this injury".[122] Titania's refusal to obey is punished by having her sight manipulated and her will stripped away by being made a foolish slave to the effects of the flower whose "liquor" is squeezed upon her eyes:

> Having once this juice,
> I'll watch Titania when she is asleep,
> And drop the liquor of it in her eyes.
> The next thing then she waking looks upon,
> [...]
> She shall pursue it with the soul of love.[123]

The first thing Titania sees on awakening, of course, is the comic character Bottom, who has been transformed by Puck so that he has the head of an ass. Titania's drugged reaction is to do exactly as Oberon had demanded: "on the first view", she says while gazing into the eyes of the ass, "I love thee".[124] This is, of course, *not* love, and that is exactly the joke. So much of what passes for love in a culture of arranged marriages is a command performance, intended to gloss the ugly reality of having been bought and sold into a relationship and a life not of one's own choosing, from which there are few avenues of escape, except for perhaps "the ecclesiastical separation *a mensa et thoro*"—a separation from bed and

---

121 *A Midsummer Night's Dream* 2.1.120–21.
122 *Ibid.*, 2.1.136–37.
123 *Ibid.*, 2.1.176–79, 182.
124 *Ibid.*, 3.1.136.

board under which an "ecclesiastical judge permitted a man and wife to live apart, but without granting them the right to remarry".[125] Unlike comedy, in the real world no one was magically released from arranged marriages from which only death (theirs or their spouse's) would release them. But in *A Midsummer Night's Dream*, Lysander is released to be himself again, and once more be able to choose Hermia. Titania is released from her punishment of foolish illusion, and is shown the very ass of whom she thought she had been enamored. Even Egeus' claims of "the law, the law"[126] are swept away in a grand gesture by Theseus, who tells the old tyrant that "I will overbear your will".[127] Everything is made right, and all is restored.

Except that it isn't. One man, Demetrius, is left under the influence of the drug, forced to love Helena, while at the same time, Helena is trapped in a situation in which the man she loves—for whatever inexplicably pathetic Petrarchan reasons—does not really love her. Oh certainly, he plays the part well, unbeknownst even to himself, but Demetrius does not *choose* Helena. In effect, he is left under the spell of authority and obedience for the rest of his life. Readers and audience members who approve this as part of a "happy ending" should ask themselves if they would like to have their own wills rendered useless, or whether that is a treatment they would reserve strictly for people of whom they disapprove. *For thee, but not for me.*

IV
Love as Resistance: Juliet and the Critics who Disdain

Moving from comedy to tragedy, we see the same pattern at work. A father seeks to match himself to another man, using the daughter as a medium of exchange, while a fourth element—the younger man—interferes with the planned match, aided by the enthusiastic participation of the daughter. In *Romeo and Juliet*, the father is Capulet, the leader of one of the two rival families in Verona. His family's ongoing contention

---

125 Monique Vleeschouwers-Van Melkebeek. "Separation and Marital Property". In Mia Korpiola, ed. *Regional Variations in Matrimonial Law and Custom in Europe, 1150–1600* (Leiden: Brill, 2011), 81–82.
126 *A Midsummer Night's Dream*, 4.2.154.
127 Ibid., 4.2.178.

with the Montague family—expressed in Capulet's early determination to strike because "Old Montague is come / And flourishes his blade in spite of me"[128]—has caused enough trouble that the Prince has warned both houses: "If ever you disturb our streets again, / Your lives shall pay the forfeit of the peace".[129] Capulet needs a way to best "Old Montague", and what better way than by matching himself to a foreign nobleman who is kinsman to the Prince—the County Paris—in order to raise the status of his family, trump Montague, and do a little flourishing in spite of him? Capulet's daughter, Juliet, will be the glue that seals the two men together, if only Paris will be patient enough to let her grow up a little more. Capulet says that she is too young:

> My child is yet a stranger in the world;
> She hath not seen the change of fourteen years,
> Let two more summers wither in their pride,
> Ere we may think her ripe to be a bride.[130]

Paris thinks she is old enough at thirteen, an idea with more than adequate precedent in English history, even among the Tudors—Henry VII's mother, Margaret Beaufort, was thirteen while pregnant with the child that would eventually win the kingship at Bosworth Field.[131] As Paris notes: "Younger than she are happy mothers made",[132] a position indirectly supported by Juliet's mother, who tells the girl that she had already been her mother "much upon these years / That you are now a maid",[133] and that younger girls than Juliet "in Verona, ladies of esteem, / Are already made mothers".[134] This kind of early marriage, while shocking today, is not unusual in Shakespeare's time:

> Child betrothals and adolescent marriages are a source for scandal in the West today […] but were quite normal for much of our history. Catherine

---

128 *Romeo and Juliet* 1.1.76–77.
129 Ibid., 1.1.95–96.
130 Ibid., 1.2.8–11.
131 See Michael K. Jones and Malcolm G. Underwood. *The King's Mother: Lady Margaret Beaufort, Countess of Richmond and Derby* (Cambridge: Cambridge University Press, 1993), 95.
132 *Romeo and Juliet* 1.1.12.
133 Ibid., 1.3.72–73.
134 Ibid., 1.3.70–71.

of Aragon was betrothed at age three to Arthur, son of Henry VII of England, and married to him when she was fifteen.[135]

But Capulet is reluctant: "And too soon marred are those so early made".[136] At this point in the play, the father seems at least as concerned with his daughter's welfare, even with her heart and will, as he is with making the match between himself and Paris. He tells the suitor to take his time, get to know Juliet, and see if something develops organically. He, Capulet, cannot or will not *force* his daughter's heart, so Paris will have to appeal to Juliet on his own:

> But woo her, gentle Paris, get her heart,
> My will to her consent is but a part;
> An she agree, within her scope of choice
> Lies my consent and fair according voice.[137]

Capulet will play a quite different tune, of course, when matters grow more urgent later in the play.

Juliet's mother is working, not the other side of the match, but the proposed object of exchange for the match, as she questions Juliet. "How stands your disposition to be married?"[138] she asks, telling Juliet "[t]he valiant Paris seeks you for his love".[139] Unlike Silvia and Hermia, who find their fathers' choices repellent, Juliet appears amenable. When her mother presses the point—"Speak briefly, can you like of Paris' love?"[140]—Juliet responds as a model of obedience and cooperation: "I'll look to like, if looking liking move: / But no more deep will I endart mine eye / Than your consent gives strength to make it fly".[141] All of this, of course, flies out of the proverbial balcony window after she meets, falls in love with, and secretly marries Romeo—a state of affairs about which her parents are entirely unaware.

---

135 Hanne Blank. *Virgin: The Untouched History* (New York: Bloomsbury, 2007), 14.
136 *Romeo and Juliet* 1.2.13.
137 Ibid., 1.2.16–19.
138 Ibid., 1.3.65.
139 Ibid., 1.3.74.
140 Ibid., 1.3.96.
141 Ibid., 1.3.97–99.

Frank Dicksee, *Romeo and Juliet* (1884). Southampton City Art Gallery.[142]

When her initial willingness to cooperate changes into what seems to him an inexplicable and moody resistance, Capulet makes it clear what Juliet's position is:

> Hang thee, young baggage! disobedient wretch!
> I tell thee what: get thee to church o' Thursday,
> Or never after look me in the face:
> Speak not, reply not, do not answer me;
> My fingers itch.[143]

Because of the tumult that has arisen in Verona over the street brawl that resulted in the deaths of Tybalt and Mercutio, as well as the banishment of Romeo, Capulet acts quickly to seal the match between himself and Paris. There is now no time for wooing, and Capulet's will is now the whole, not just a part, of Juliet's consent. Or so he thinks, as he threatens to beat his daughter for her disobedience. All the while, Juliet finds herself unable—out of fear—to tell him why she is suddenly refusing the marriage to Paris. Her stammerings further enrage Capulet, who—having reached a nearly Jehovean state of wrath—tells his daughter that she will obey, or else be thrown out with the trash:

---

142 https://commons.wikimedia.org/wiki/File:DickseeRomeoandJuliet.jpg
143 *Romeo and Juliet* 3.5.161–65.

> Look to't, think on't, I do not use to jest.
> Thursday is near; lay hand on heart, advise:
> An you be mine, I'll give you to my friend;
> And you be not, hang, beg, starve, die in the streets,
> For, by my soul, I'll ne'er acknowledge thee,
> Nor what is mine shall never do thee good:
> Trust to't, bethink you; I'll not be forsworn.[144]

In this outburst, Capulet makes it perfectly clear what Juliet is—*property*. At this point, even his wife thinks that he is "too hot", while the Nurse tells him that he "is to blame [...] to rate her so".[145] But these proxies for audience reaction are nowhere near powerful enough to change Capulet's mind. His daughter—who in his mind owes him obedience for her begetting, and should be to him as creation is to its god—will either obey the commandments wrapped in his titanic thundering, or she will be thrown out into the streets. *An you be mine, I'll give you to my friend*. A starker statement of proprietary relationship can scarcely be found. Juliet is capital, a movable good that can be used as a medium of exchange in the purchase of something lasting and valuable. To Capulet, her lack of obedience lowers her value to nothing, and he finds her assertion of will enraging and confusing all at once—as if a man's cash suddenly lost all of its value, even announcing that it was not going to be used to make purchases. Capulet, in his moment of rage, would rather see Juliet in prison, in alehouses, a criminal, than allow her to make up her own mind and exercise her own heart's will. Juliet's "scope of choice" is the same the Father will later give Adam and Eve in Milton's *Paradise Lost*.

Obey or be cast out.

Capulet may seem less extreme than Egeus, since he is not openly demanding his daughter's death. However, Juliet's fear hints that Capulet may be more dangerous than he appears. Even as she begs her "[g]ood father" to hear her "but to speak a word",[146] she is terrified of telling him that she is already married—contracted in the presence of witnesses, solemnified by the Friar, and consummated through a

---
144 *Ibid.*, 3.5.191–97.
145 *Ibid.*, 3.5.176, 170.
146 *Ibid.*, 3.5.159–60.

clandestine night's passion—and for her to marry Paris would be a crime and a sin. But she is so afraid of her storming, raging father, that she would rather fake her own death than tell him the truth.

She has good reason to be afraid. His "fingers itch" in a time and place in which the killing of "disobedient" daughters was far from unheard of. The phenomenon known as "honor killing" was well-known in sixteenth-century Italy, with a particularly famous instance of it occurring in the killing by Giovanni Battista of his wife, Vittoria Savelli on 26 July 1563: "He first hit her forehead and then slit her throat, cutting her head half off, [...] the method used to dispatch livestock".[147] Another such incident, in 1555, involved a father killing his daughter in the same fashion: "the father took his [pregnant] daughter by the elbow and, under the eyes of the whole village, led her across the field to her lover's corpse. There, as all watched, as if she were his heifer, he slit her throat".[148] Having been told by her father to "Graze where [she] will",[149] as if she were an animal, Juliet is right to be afraid, and she is never fully able to break out of the role of "baggage" that her father assigns her. The audiences that watched this play for the first time were being "offered an alternative model to that of blind obedience to paternal dictate",[150] but they were also being shown with what violent fury paternal dictate will defend its prerogatives.

In terror and confusion, Juliet seeks the intervention of Friar Lawrence, a significantly less powerful advocate than the one Hermia finds in Theseus. Even more manipulative than the "fantastical duke of dark corners" who spends his time posing as a friar in *Measure for*

---

147 Thomas V. Cohen. *Love and Death in Renaissance Italy* (Chicago: University of Chicago Press, 2004, 27).
148 Elizabeth S. Cohen and Thomas V. Cohen. *Daily Life in Renaissance Italy* (Westport: Greenwood Press, 2001), 93. Astonishingly, "the notion of honor killing disappeared from the Italian Penal code only as recently as 1981 with the law no. 442 of 5 August called 'Abrogazione della rilevanza penale della causa d'onore e del matrimonio riparatore' [Abolishment of the 'honour motive' and of 'shotgun' marriages in criminal proceedings]" (Donatella Barazzetti, Franca Garreffa, and Rosaria Marsico. *National Report: Italia. Daphne Project: Proposing New Indicators: Measuring Violence's Effects*. University of Calabria, Rende: Italy, 2007, 3, http://www.surt.org/gvei/docs/national_report_italy.pdf). Credit for this insight is due to Modje Taavon, who in conversation pointed out the similarities between the Renaissance and modern practices of "honor killing".
149 *Romeo and Juliet* 3.5.190.
150 L. Stone, 218.

8. Shakespeare: The Return of Fin'amor

Measure,[151] Friar Lawrence is at once more than faintly disreputable, and nearly as afraid of direct confrontation as Juliet is. His plan is practically the archetype of a cowardly and foolish brand of Machiavellian scheming:

> Tomorrow night look that thou lie alone;
> Let not thy nurse lie with thee in thy chamber:
> Take thou this vial, being then in bed,
> And this distilled liquor drink thou off;
> [...]
> Each part, deprived of supple government,
> Shall, stiff and stark and cold, appear like death:
> And in this borrow'd likeness of shrunk death
> Thou shalt continue two and forty hours,
> And then awake as from a pleasant sleep.[152]

The plot has its intended effect, getting her out of the marriage to Paris, but at the cost of sowing the seeds of Juliet's real, rather than merely pretended, death.

Even upon discovering her "dead", however, the grief Capulet expresses centers more on the loss of his match with Paris, than it does on the loss of his daughter. Paris will now not be his son-in-law, since that position is already taken (though by someone other than he assumes):

> Death is my son-in-law, Death is my heir;
> My daughter he hath wedded: I will die,
> And leave him all; life, living, all is Death's.[153]

His concern here is over the question of the "heir" to whom he will leave his wealth and estate. He grieves that he has been unable to match himself with Paris, and has instead matched himself with Death (to whom all are matched in the end): "I will die, / And leave him all; [...] all is Death's". He has lost the one thing that mattered most to him in life—the mechanism though which he would be able to pass on his property, wealth, and inheritable legacy. Juliet, while valuable, is

---

151 *Measure for Measure* 4.4.156–57.
152 *Romeo and Juliet* 4.1.91–94, 102–06.
153 Ibid., 4.5.38–40.

enumerated as merely a possession, now lost, among all those that will be bequeathed to Death.

Through the tragic outcome of *Romeo and Juliet*, we can easily see how love functions as a challenge to and a rejection of the authority of the father. Romeo starts out unpromisingly, as the young man in love with Love, more Neopetrarchan than neo-troubadourian, moping, sighing and crying in a way that makes some want to reassure him and others to smack him. According to his father, Romeo spends most of his pre-dawn mornings in a competition with himself over how intensely he can grieve:

> With tears augmenting the fresh morning dew.
> Adding to clouds more clouds with his deep sighs;
> But all so soon as the all-cheering sun
> Should in the furthest east begin to draw
> The shady curtains from Aurora's bed,
> Away from the light steals home my heavy son,
> And private in his chamber pens himself,
> Shuts up his windows, locks far daylight out
> And makes himself an artificial night.[154]

All this excessive emotion is related to Romeo's unsuccessful courting of a girl named Rosaline, whose identity we learn from Romeo's friend, Benvolio, rather than from Romeo himself. She will simply not cooperate with, or be impressed by, any of Romeo's shopworn techniques. First, Romeo claims that the as-yet-unnamed Rosaline will "not be hit / With Cupid's arrow; she hath Dian's wit".[155] Diana, the Roman goddess of the hunt who is strongly associated with images of lesbian love in the Renaissance, if "subtly authorized under the idiom of chastity",[156] serves as Romeo's shorthand explanation to Benvolio for his failure. Romeo seems unable (or unwilling) to imagine that his failure to attract Rosaline has anything to do with him. It must be her. In Romeo's mind, she apparently also has a deaf ear for poetry: "She will

---

154 *Ibid.*, 1.1.131–39.
155 *Ibid.*, 1.1.207–08.
156 Valerie Traub. *The Renaissance of Lesbianism in Early Modern England* (Cambridge: Cambridge University Press, 2002), 237. See especially her discussion of Thomas Heywood's 1609 play *The Golden Age*.

not stay the siege of loving terms".¹⁵⁷ How is it that his verses—staged as they are in military terms as weapons with which to force his way past the defenses of the walled town of Rosaline's assent—are unable to conquer her resistance? It must be that *she hath Dian's wit*. That same "wit" must be why she will not "bide the encounter of assailing eyes" or "ope her lap to saint-seducing gold"¹⁵⁸ either. Romeo cannot talk his way, stalk his way, or buy his way into Rosaline's affections.

Wisely, Benvolio does not comment on any of this nonsense, except by telling his ridiculous young friend to turn his attention elsewhere, "[b]y giving liberty to thine eyes", and examining "other beauties".¹⁵⁹ Romeo's response is straight out of the Petrarchan lover's handbook. Rosaline—whom he has just absurdly implied is a tin-eared lesbian—is also the unreachable measure of all other beauties, any one of whom would serve merely as "a note / Where [he] may read" of his beloved's beauty, as if Rosaline (whose name Romeo never actually pronounces) were the Platonic form of which all other women were merely copies.¹⁶⁰ Romeo is made idiotic as he follows the path of superficial, sight-without-insight *fals'amor*. But he will soon learn what Giraut de Borneilh meant when he wrote "through the eyes love enters the heart", as what Romeo terms "the devout religion of mine eye"¹⁶¹—an image of obedience, doctrine, and authority—gives way to *fin'amor*, whose only doctrines are wonder and desire.

At the feast Capulet gives to mark what is meant to be the matching of Juliet to the County Paris, Romeo sees something he claims, at least, never to have seen before: true beauty. Watching Juliet dance, possibly with Paris himself, Romeo is flabbergasted:

> O, she doth teach the torches to burn bright!
> It seems she hangs upon the cheek of night
> Like a rich jewel in an Ethiope's ear;
> Beauty too rich for use, for earth too dear!
> So shows a snowy dove trooping with crows,
> As yonder lady o'er her fellows shows.

---

157 *Romeo and Juliet* 1.1.211.
158 Ibid., 1.1.212–13.
159 Ibid., 1.1.226–27.
160 Ibid., 1.1.234–35.
161 Ibid., 1.12.90.

> The measure done, I'll watch her place of stand,
> And, touching hers, make blessed my rude hand.
> Did my heart love till now? forswear it, sight!
> For I ne'er saw true beauty till this night.[162]

At this point, it is hard to know how much of this is genuine passion, the entering of love through the eyes, and how much of it is Romeo's established mode of framing everything in terms of poetic opposites, filtering lived experience through the "devout religion" of his eye. Does he truly *see* here, and if so, what can he possibly be seeing? A beautiful girl, with every grace imaginable, dancing with another man—thus adding a hint of the adulterous, or quasi-adulterous angle of so much troubadour and trobairitz poetry—Juliet is, to this point, someone with whom he has never exchanged so much as a single word. What does he know of her? What *can* he know of her? As the scene reveals, he does not even know her name when he approaches her, and speaks to her for the first time.

And then, something remarkable happens. In true troubadour and trobaritz fashion, this young man and young woman, who do not know each other at all, discover that they have "one joy in two hearts" ("zweier herzen wünne"),[163] as they compose a sonnet, together, as their first meeting and first words. Romeo approaches, and begins:

> If I profane with my unworthiest hand
> This holy shrine, the gentle fine is this:
> My lips, two blushing pilgrims, ready stand
> To smooth that rough touch with a tender kiss.[164]

Admittedly, it is difficult not to wonder whether or not this is an example of the "siege of loving terms" that had worked so poorly with Rosaline. Is this a stanza that Romeo has memorized, and keeps for occasions such as these? Perhaps. But even if so, perhaps especially if

---

162 *Ibid.*, 1.5.45–54.
163 Walther von der Vogelweide. "Saget mir ieman, waz ist minne?" In Karl Lachmann, ed., *Die Gedichte Walthers von der Vogelweide* (Berlin: George Reimer, 1891), 69, https://archive.org/stream/diegedichtewalt00lachgoog#page/n92
164 *Romeo and Juliet* 1.5.94–97.

so, what he then encounters—in Juliet's like-for-like response—has to be all the more amazing.

> Good pilgrim, you do wrong your hand too much,
> Which mannerly devotion shows in this;
> For saints have hands that pilgrims' hands do touch,
> And palm to palm is holy palmers' kiss.[165]

Some might argue that this exchange is merely conventional. Even so respected a critic as Ralph Berry argues in this way. For him the sonnet that Romeo and Juliet compose together is part of "a tranced process of courtly reciprocity", an "inward-turning, acquiescent" phenomena that reflects "the fluency, the intensity, and the superficiality of the means through which this society orders its experience, and its relationships".[166] One of the current authors had a graduate professor some years ago who professed to be thrilled during the first few minutes of the 1993 Kenneth Branagh film of *Much Ado About Nothing* because, "someone has finally figured out that love is merely a construct in Shakespeare, a conventional game". She then related her disappointment at the way the film departed from her reading of the play. The remark made in response to her observations, "Shakespeare doesn't belong to academics", did not go over well. But it is just as true now as it was then.

Literary critics are too often, despite pretensions to be defenders of the unfettered intellect, among the most conformist members of society. We follow the fashionable codes of our "discourse communities" in looking for ways to tame our material, to allegorize it—if not through the categories of religion, then through those of history or theory—into saying something very different from what a "naive" or "surface" reading of the text might suggest to an ordinary reader, one less artfully trained in the ways of interrogating a literary object in order to bend it to one's will, or make it disappear entirely. Regardless of whether or not Romeo's first stanza is a memorized performance piece, a Petrarchan pick-up line that he has at the ready, Juliet's response is not preplanned, rehearsed, or otherwise the kind of utterance that Nietzsche argues is only possible because the sentiment it expresses is already dead in

---
165 *Ibid.*, 1.5.98–101.
166 Ralph Berry. *The Shakespearean Metaphor* (New York: Macmillan, 1978), 38.

our hearts.¹⁶⁷ Juliet's response is only *conventional* in the sense that it uses a known form in order to express thoughts and emotions of her own—in that same sense, the guitar solo in Carlos Santana's *Europa* is "conventional", as is the fourth movement of Tchaikovsky's Symphony No. 6, the *Pathetique*.

Juliet's response does not indicate that she is a slave to convention; she is a mere girl who has yet to become sophisticated enough to be knowing and jaded about the poetical and musical forms of her time. Juliet gives us an example of what a more generous critic like Regina Schwartz calls a "communication [that] is instantaneous and complete", which teaches both lovers to "[leave] behind the Petrarchan lover's conventions", in favor of "a devotion without guile and without measure".¹⁶⁸ In fact, what makes Juliet's response at once more bracing and delightful is that she gets the form of the sonnet ever so slightly wrong—a deliberate cue, it seems, on the author's part to the freshness and originality of her response to Romeo. Where Romeo is predictably correct in following his author's ABAB rhyme scheme (hand, this, stand, kiss), Juliet's improvised response, while beautiful, is written as a *mistaking* of the typical scheme for the second stanza of a Shakespearean sonnet. Rather than CDCD, introducing two new rhymes to the mix, Juliet introduces only one new rhyme, while re-using one of Romeo's in a CBCB scheme (much, this, touch, kiss). However, one might read this, not as a mistake, but as an adaptation of the form that makes Juliet's second stanza even more responsive to Romeo's first than a purely "conventional" second stanza might have been. In this case, far from a girl who is merely giving the expected, "acquiescent" response her

---

167 "Whatever we have words for, we are already beyond" ("Wofür wir Worte haben, darüber sind wir auch schon hinaus") (Friedrich Nietzsche. *Zur Genealogie der Moral* [1887] *Götzendämmerung* [1889] [Hamburg: Felix Meiner Verlag, 2013], 244). Robert Musil expresses a similar idea: "The truth between two people cannot be spoken. As soon as we speak, we close doors; words are best used for insubstantial messages; we speak in the hours in which we are not alive" ("Die wahre Wahrheit zwischen zwei Menschen kann nicht ausgesprochen werden. Sobald wir sprechen, schließen sich Türen; das Wort dient mehr den unwirklichen Mitteilungen, man spricht in den Stunden, wo man nicht lebt") (Musil, 516). The Russian poet Fyodor Tyutchev makes much the same observation in his poem *Silentium*: "The thought, spoken, is a lie" ("Мысль изреченная есть ложь") (Stephen Prickett, ed. *European Romanticism: A Reader* [London: Bloomsbury, 2010], 638, l. 10).
168 Regina Schwartz. *Loving Justice, Living Shakespeare* (Oxford: Oxford University Press, 2016), 50, 51.

culture demands, we have an artist, a poet in her own right, who then matches Romeo line by line in composing the sonnet:

> ROMEO   Have not saints lips, and holy palmers too?
>
> JULIET   Ay, pilgrim, lips that they must use in prayer.
>
> ROMEO   O, then, dear saint, let lips do what hands do; They pray, grant thou, lest faith turn to despair.
>
> JULIET   Saints do not move, though grant for prayers' sake.
>
> ROMEO   Then move not, while my prayer's effect I take.[169]

The couple then starts another sonnet, this time getting through only the first four lines, before they are interrupted. But even though Romeo may, as Juliet observes, "kiss by th' book",[170] and though Juliet may be expressing herself with unnecessary emphasis by declaring that if Romeo is "marriéd, / My grave is like to be my wedding bed",[171] it hardly seems necessary to dismiss them as mere puppets of structural expectations and conventions:

> The young lovers feel intensely that which the [sonnet] mode incites them to feel. Confronted with the image of the ideal lover, each reverts to stereotype. What we have here is an existential drama of sonnet-life. The world of Romeo and Juliet [...] is a world of fixed relations and closed assumptions. They appear as quotations, and they speak in quotations: the cliché, of which the sonnet is exemplar, is the dominant thought-form of Verona.[172]

Here we have a touch of the Zumthor/Stone/Heller-Roazen argument that seeks to erase individuality. One begins to wonder what it is in this argument that appeals to the academic mind. Understood in this way, one *also* wonders why anyone would bother paying the price of admission to see this play. Kiernan Ryan, in a brilliant chapter on *King Lear*, addresses the reductive nature of too much critical writing about these plays, and about literature and art in general, and boils the problem down into three ingredients that are applicable to any number of other plays:

---

169 *Romeo and Juliet* 1.5.102–07.
170 Ibid., 1.5.111.
171 Ibid., 1.5.135–36.
172 Berry, 40.

> The first is [the critics'] supposition that the tragedy is the symptom of some ulterior phenomenon, whether it be language, the unconscious, patriarchy, or power. The play's autonomy and integrity as a work of art are ditched by critics bent on recruiting it to confirm their theoretical assumptions or preconceptions of the past. The second reason is endemic to critics raring to immure [the play] in its early modern matrix: a blindness to the possibility that the tragedy may not be fully intelligible in terms of its time, because its gaze is fixed on horizons that still lie ahead of our time. Even when radical historicists like Patterson hold [the play] must have been subversive in Shakespeare's day, it remains the imprint of an obsolete era, the pawn of a purely retrospective viewpoint. And the third reason is the failure to engage in detail with the poetic language and dramatic form [...], which in some cases, as Greenblatt's essays demonstrate, simply furnishes a pretext for expounding another text altogether.[173]

But there is no shortage of interesting material in the plays, despite the desire of many critics to rewrite the texts, or, as Ryan suggests, abandon them for others. In *Romeo and Juliet*, Juliet addresses fundamental questions of identity, politics, and love's tenuous existence in a world in which so many will fight for so long over what finally amounts to so little. In asking "wherefore art thou Romeo?" and "What's Montague?"[174] Juliet shows that her thinking is already more advanced than is Romeo's, who is still half caught in his own facility with Petrarchan poetic imagery, as he compares her to the sun and the stars, and wishes—rather than to be with her at the moment—to be a glove upon her hand so that he might touch her cheek:

> But, soft! what light through yonder window breaks?
> It is the east, and Juliet is the sun.
> [...]
> It is my lady, O, it is my love!
> O, that she knew she were!
> [...]
> Two of the fairest stars in all the heaven,
> Having some business, do entreat her eyes

---

173 Kiernan Ryan. "King Lear". In *A Companion to Shakespeare's Works, Vol. 1, The Tragedies*, ed. by Richard Dutton and Jean E. Howard (Maldan, MA: Blackwell, 2003), 376–77.

174 *Romeo and Juliet* 2.2.33, 40.

> To twinkle in their spheres till they return.
> [...]
> See, how she leans her cheek upon her hand!
> O, that I were a glove upon that hand,
> That I might touch that cheek![175]

In contrast, Juliet is already thinking about the practical obstacles to their ability to be together, and how those obstacles might be overcome, *pace* Denis De Rougemont's argument that it is the *obstacles themselves* that are the incitements to love.[176] In Juliet's speech, "'Tis but thy name that is my enemy",[177] and the obstacles of name and position can be overcome if the lovers will see beyond the historically contingent categories of politics and Veronese identity to the nature or essence of what each person is, or can be In referring to body parts like hand and foot, arm and face,[178] Juliet argues that in moving beyond what a Renaissance thinker, following Aristotle, would call "the accidental",[179] she and Romeo can find love *in spite* of the obstacles that stand between them.

Whether or not this is possible, or even desirable, is contested. For some, like Callaghan, *Romeo and Juliet* serves to create and impose "a certain formation of desiring subjectivity attendant upon Protestant and especially Puritan ideologies of marriage and the family required by

---

175 *Ibid.*, 2.2.1–3, 10–11, 15–17, 23–25.

176 Between joy and its external cause there is always some separation and some obstacle: society, sin, virtue, our bodies, our separate selves. And from this arises the heat of passion. And from this comes the fact that our wish for total union is bound indissolubly with a desire for the death that frees us.

> Entre la joie et sa cause extérieure il y a toujours quelque séparation et quelque obstacle: la societé, le peché, la vertu, notre corps, notre moi distinct. Et de là vient l'ardeur de la passion. Et de là vient que le desir d'union totale se lie indissolublement au désir de la mort qui libere.

Denis de Rougemont. *L'Amour et l'Occident* (Paris: Plon, 1939), 176.

177 *Romeo and Juliet* 2.2.38.

178 *Ibid.*, 2.2.40–41.

179 Al-Ghāzalī, an eleventh-and twelfth-century interpreter of Aristotle explained the distinction as a matter of prior and latter categories:

> In the sentence: "This human being is white and an animal", the predication of "white" and "animal" of "human being" is quite different. Al-Ghāzalī calls the first accidental and the second essential. [...] He seems to mean, as Aristotle indeed thought, that what is essentially tied to each other is also ordered in a special way, namely in the sense that animal is prior to human being [and thus prior still to white].

Henrik Lagerlund. "The Assimilation of Aristotelian and Arabic Logic up to the Later Thirteenth Century". *Medieval and Renaissance Logic*, ed. by Dov M. Gabbay and John Woods (Amsterdam: Elsevier, 2008), 288.

[...] the emergent economic formation of capitalism".[180] Callaghan also argues that the play has served as a powerful artifact that supports the "dominant ideology of romantic love", which oppressively "relegates homosexuality to the sphere of deviance, secures women's submission to the asymmetrical distribution of power between men and women, and bolsters individualism by positing sexual love as the expression of authentic identity".[181] For Julia Kristeva, the play's portrayal of love disguises a dark undercurrent in which, if Romeo and Juliet had survived, their passion would have revealed "the whole range of sadomasochism that both partners had already announced in the relatively quiet version of the Shakespearean text".[182] But if that is what *Romeo and Juliet* depicts, if Callaghan's argument about the play being oppressive is correct, or Kristeva's contention about its love's perversity is correct, then what should the play portray instead? Rather than presenting what these critics regard as an oppressively heterosexual and/or sadomasochistic "romantic love", should it, after all, proceed with the orderly demonstration of Juliet's obedience to her father? Would unfettered patriarchy be preferable? Or should it show Romeo and Mercutio running off together, while Juliet finds happiness with Rosaline or expresses her "authentic identity" through celibacy, or perhaps a hobby of some sort? Perhaps, as Sinfield suggests, it would be more interesting if the play were rewritten in order that "every man or woman may have his or her Jack *and* his or her Jill", so that we might have combinations that go beyond "even same-gender couples"?[183] Maybe it would be preferable to "amputate" the play, after the fashion of the avant-garde writer/director Carmelo Bene, who, in Gilles Deleuze's view, opens up amazing possibilities by eliminating Romeo altogether?

> CB [Carmelo Bene] [...] subtracts something from the original piece. [...] For example, he amputates Romeo, neutralizes Romeo in the original piece. [...] If you ampute Romeo, you will witness an amazing

---

180 Dympna Callaghan. "The Ideology of Romantic Love: the Case of Romeo and Juliet". *The Weyward Sisters: Shakespeare and Feminist Politics* (Cambridge, MA: Blackwell, 1994), 59.
181 *Ibid.*, 60.
182 "la gamme du sado-masochisme que les deux partenaires avaient annoncé déjà dans la version pourtant relativement paisible du texte shakespearien" (Julia Kristeva. *Histoires d'amour*. Paris: Denoël, 1983, 210).
183 Sinfield, 112, 111.

development. Mercutio was only a virtuality in Shakespeare's play. Mercutio dies quickly in Shakespeare, but in [Carmelo Bene's version] he does not want to die, cannot die, cannot reach the point of dying, since he is going to constitute the new play.[184]

Or should it, perhaps, remain exactly as it is, serving as an object of scorn tied to the critical whipping-post while modern, morally superior critics vent their spleens? At long last, it becomes impossible to tell whether there is any sense of decency left in criticism, as so many of us pound a work until it threatens to die beneath our urgent bludgeoning. This entire dynamic of morally outraged criticism is wonderfully described by Ryan:

> One of the least appealing features of literary studies today is the smug diagnostic attitude that has swept through them like foot-and-mouth disease through a fine herd of Friesians. It is this attitude that reduces Shakespeare's drama to an allegory or appendix of something else and then passes sentence on it from the supposedly superior vantage point of hindsight. It thereby denies the plays the power not only to arraign the world in which they were first forged and the world in which we now encounter them, but also to foreshadow futures that would otherwise remain intangible. It is an approach that goes hand in hand with a scorn for close reading, a contempt for the belief that there is something special about the creative use of language and form in imaginative writing at its best that sets it apart from other kinds of discourse and gives us ways of seeing the world which no other kind of writing can deliver.[185]

Perhaps it is in the dawn-song scene of Act 3 where *Romeo and Juliet* might mount a defense against its more disdainful critics. In a scene in which two young people, who about to be separated forever, have fallen in love—not to injure anyone, and certainly not to "relegate" anything or anyone "to the sphere of deviance"—and now face the full power of the father and the state arrayed against them, perhaps

---

184 CB [Carmelo Bene] [...] soustrait quelque chose de la pièce originaire. [...] Mais, par exemple, il ampute Roméo, il neutralise Roméo dans la pièce originaire. [...] Si vous amputez Roméo, vous allez assister à un étonnant développement, le développement de. Mercuzio, qui n'était qu'une virtualité dans la pièce de Shakespeare. Mercuzio meurt vite chez Shakespeare, mais, chez CB, il ne veut pas mourir, il ne peut pas mourir, n'arrive pas à mourir, puisqu'il va constituer la nouvelle pièce.

Gilles Deleuze. "Un manifeste de moins". *Superpositions* (Paris: Éditions de Minuit, 1979), 87–88.

185 Ryan, "King Lear", 377–78.

here some redeeming value might be found in the play. The scene is nearly a point-by-point recreation of the *alba* form of the troubadour poets. The genre assumes an oppressive and tightly-controlled world of social, financial, and political power. It includes marriage, not, as De Rougemont would have it, as the happy cure to love,[186] but as the oppressive institution through which love's flourishing is strangled in its cradle. And yet, authority fails. Love flourishes in spite of the power of the jealous husband (*lo gilos*), as the eyes go forth to gaze and desire (*ill oill van vezer*) despite the demands of authority and obedience. The lovers, invariably adulterous, can only meet in secrecy, under cover of darkness, and they need a watchman or guard to warn them as soon as the first rays of the too-quickly rising sun appear.

These poems are not biographical, of course, though the situations they describe are well within the range of human experience. They are literary constructions—as is *Romeo and Juliet*—whose effect depends on their contact with lived events and emotion. However, if regarded as *merely* literary constructions, or the occasions for formal dramatic performances, or as self-ironizing and self-aggrandizing pieces reflecting the narcissism and misogyny of the poets,[187] then they are just as dead as their authors. If were are to believe that "[a] poet wrote *albas*, not because he had experienced the situation depicted by the *alba*, and *not even because he fancied himself experiencing it with a particular woman* he was in love with, but simply because it was one of the current literary genres",[188] then we are being asked to believe that the most passionate poems written at the very dawn of the modern Western literary tradition can, and should, be coolly regarded as mere exercises in form, a day's work at the poet's office in eleventh-and twelfth-century Occitania.

---

186 "Then anguish satisfied by response, longing satisfied by presence, we cease to call for a sensitive and delicate happiness, cease to suffer, accept our day. And then marriage is possible, for we two are contented" ("Alors l'angoisse comblée par la réponse, la nostalgie comblée par la présence cessent d'appeler un bonheur sensible, cessent de souffrir, acceptent notre jour. Et alors le mariage est possible. Nous sommes deux dans le contentement") (Denis de Rougemont, 273).

187 See Simon Gaunt. "Poetry of Exclusion: A Feminist Reading of Some Troubadour Lyrics". *The Modern Language Review*, 85: 2 (April 1990), 310–329, https://doi.org/10.2307/3731812

188 Jonathan Saville. *The Medieval Erotic Alba: Structure as Meaning* (New York: Columbia University Press, 1972), 122. Emphasis added.

With friends like these, what need has poetry of enemies? Finally, what comes to mind are these lines by William Butler Yeats:

> Bald heads forgetful of their sins,
> Old, learned, respectable bald heads
> Edit and annotate the lines
> That young men, tossing on their beds,
> Rhymed out in love's despair
> To flatter beauty's ignorant ear.
> All shuffle there; all cough in ink;
> All wear the carpet with their shoes;
> All think what other people think;
> All know the man their neighbour knows.
> Lord, what would they say
> Did their Catullus walk that way?[189]

Yeat's riposte is one of the classic examples of a poet speaking back to critics, and is of a piece with the picture the novelist Fyodor Dostoevsky gives of a particular critic, a character named Stepan Verkhovensky, who represents a "creed [that] unavoidably involves a degree of alienation—from the concrete immediacy of life, from our feeling for what is".[190] As Dostoevsky describes him, this critic is all surfaces and no depths, a proto-nihilistic *poseur* who has little real use for either poetry or scholarship. Verkhovensky is "the cleverest man and a gifted man, so to speak, even a scholar, though, indeed, in scholarship... well, in a word, in scholarship, he did not so much, and it seems, nothing. But with the scholarship we have in Russia this very often happens".[191] Despite the "Old, learned, respectable bald heads", whose work both the poet and the novelist appear to regard as "not so much, and it seems, nothing", passionate poetry is not mere form, no matter how many books and journal articles pile up claiming that it is so, nor is it

---

189 William Butler Yeats. *The Scholars* [1929 version], in *Yeats's Poetry, Drama, and Prose: Authoritative Texts, Contexts, Criticism*, ed. by James Pethica (New York: W. W. Norton & Co., 2000), 60.
190 Ewan Fernie. *The Demonic: Literature and Experience* (New York: Routledge, 2013), 88.
191 "человек умнейший и даровитейший, человек, так сказать, даже науки, хотя, впрочем, в науке... ну, одним словом, в науке он сделал не так много и, кажется, совсем ничего. Но ведь с людьми науки у нас на Руси это сплошь да рядом случается" (Fyodor Dostoevesky. *Бесы* [*Demons*, aka *The Possessed*, or *The Devils*] [St. Petersburg: Azbuka, 2008], 20).

reducible to ideology, nor, finally, is it merely biography (which could be seen, in a mean-spirited way, as narcissism). It is an attempt to reflect, capture, transmit, and communicate at least some part of the experience (or range of experiences) that people have when they love, for good or ill, another than themselves in a passionate, vulnerable, sometimes possessive and insecure, and erotic way. It is not mere lust these poems describe. It is not mere poetic form that they rehearse. If the latter were all that such poetry had to offer, few besides Yeats' imagined scholars would read any of it.

But such has not been the fate of the troubadour *albas*, nor has it been the fate of *Romeo and Juliet*, whose *alba*, or dawn-song, is among the most affecting moments in the play despite the attempts of authority—that of Capulet in the play, and that of too many academic critics in the modern world—to eliminate its power. As Aileen Ann Macdonald observes:

> The *alba* [...] recounts the continuing events of a love affair after it has been initiated, for it describes the lovers' clandestine meetings at night, culminating in their passionate and poignant parting as dawn breaks. [...] It has been suggested [...] that the *alba* was in the beginning another woman's song, where the lady laments that dawn is coming to part her from her lover—just as does Juliet in the most famous *alba* of all after her night of love with Romeo.[192]

Juliet's *alba* is the emotional core of a play designed to take audiences and readers on a wrenching journey of what Aristotle once called *catharsis* (κάθαρσις)—the raising of intense emotion that is held, and then released during the play.[193] Far from being rendered merely "conventional", Juliet's emotions and predicament are even more

---

192 Aileen Ann Macdonald. "A Refusal to be Silenced or to Rejoice in any Joy that Love may Bring: The anonymous Old Occitan canso, 'Per ioi que d'amor m'avegna'". *Dalhousie French Studies*, 36 (Fall 1996), 10.

193 In Aristotle's definition:

> Tragedy, then, is imitation of an elevated action that is both great and complete, in language embellished by distinctive forms in each section, rendered by action and not by recitation, accomplishing through pity and fear the catharsis of such sufferings.

> ἔστιν οὖν τραγῳδία μίμησις πράξεως σπουδαίας καὶ τελείας μέγεθος ἐχούσης, ἡδυσμένῳ λόγῳ χωρὶς ἑκάστῳ τῶν εἰδῶν ἐν τοῖς μορίοις, δρώντων καὶ οὐ δι' ἀπαγγελίας, δι' ἐλέου καὶ φόβου περαίνουσα τὴν τῶν τοιούτων παθημάτων κάθαρσιν.

Aristotle, *Poetics*, ed. by Stephen Halliwell. In *Aristotle: Poetics. Longinus: On the Sublime. Demetrius: On Style* (Loeb Classical Library, Cambridge, MA: Harvard University Press, 1995, 46, 1449b 24–28).

powerfully expressed through the use of the *alba*, especially since she and her husband do not belong in the situation the genre describes. Romeo and Juliet are married, not an adulterous couple, and the jealous male here (*lo gilos*) is a father, not a husband.

Though the couple's marriage is clandestine and not yet formalized with a church ceremony, it is legally-binding, and would be known to be so by the English audience watching this play for the first time:

> *Consensus facit nuptias* had been a principle of Roman and early canonical law [...]. The church wanted a union of hearts as well as hearths, and so private vows and promises with or without consummation were understood to constitute a valid marriage, and the *desponsatio* (betrothal) became more important than the final ceremony.[194]

There were forces that opposed such marriages, but "clandestine contracts" remained part of the tapestry of marriage practices, in spite of the opposition:

> A note of "matters to be moved by the clergy" in the Parliament and Synod of 1563 included pleas [...] for the raising of the age of consent for girls to fifteen; for sterner punishments of adulterers, fornicators, and abductors; and pleas that both the marriage of minors without parental permission and "all clandestine contracts" be made void.[195]

The anger such clandestine marriages caused fathers who were thereby deprived of their ability to control—and profit from—the marriages of their children is attested to by a letter, dated June 3 1587 and written by Richard Bagot to Richard Broughton. In the letter, Bagot complains bitterly about his daughter Margaret's secret marriage, describing his "daughters lewde dealings in this her match, [which] hath not a little trobled me and her mother". Bagot then wonders how he will ever be able to "digest such a villainy", before wishing that "god give them joye and some sorrowe, as they have given us cause of grief".[196] The secret—

---

194 Hagstrum, 221.
195 R. B. Outhwaite. *Clandestine Marriage in England, 1500–1850* (London: Hambledon Press, 1995), 7.
196 Richard Bagot. "Letter from Richard Bagot to Richard Broughton, 1587 June 3". *Papers of the Bagot Family of Blithfield, Staffordshire, 1428–1671 (bulk 1557–1671)*. Folger MS L.a.68 (Folger Shakespeare Library, Washington, http://luna.folger.edu/luna/servlet/workspace/handleMediaPlayer?lunaMediaId=FOLGERCM1~6~6~361296~130605).

and not-so-secret—rebellions that Shakespeare presents on stage are already beginning to take root in the England from which he derives his audiences and readers.

Romeo and Juliet should not be in this position, and yet, due to the authority of Prince Escalus, who has banished Romeo over the killing of Tybalt, the overbearing authority of Capulet, and Juliet's fear of confronting him, here they are—in a strangely misplaced *alba*, hoping that it is not the dawn's first light they are seeing, light that will separate them forever. The female voice—Juliet—begins, noting and denying the coming of day:

> Wilt thou be gone? it is not yet near day:
> It was the nightingale, and not the lark,
> That pierced the fearful hollow of thine ear;
> Nightly she sings on yon pomegranate-tree:
> Believe me, love, it was the nightingale.[197]

And as they had begun, composing their poetry in the scene of their first meeting, so they end, writing the final poem of their vanishingly brief marriage. Romeo responds by acknowledging the light, and framing his choice between life and banishment, or love and death:

> It was the lark, the herald of the morn,
> No nightingale: look, love, what envious streaks
> Do lace the severing clouds in yonder east:
> Night's candles are burnt out, and jocund day
> Stands tiptoe on the misty mountain tops.
> I must be gone and live, or stay and die.[198]

After several more lines of back and forth, during which they switch rhetorical and emotional positions, with Juliet now urging Romeo to escape, Romeo pledging to stay and die, and each bemoaning how little time they have left together, the watchman of the *alba* enters. Juliet's nurse, who has aided and abetted the relationship between Romeo and Juliet to the best of her ability, comes in to warn them of the coming of day: "Your lady mother is coming to your chamber: / The day is

---

[197] *Romeo and Juliet* 3.5.1–5.
[198] Ibid., 3.5.6–11.

broke; be wary, look about".[199] With each wondering if they "shall ever meet again",[200] Romeo says *Adieu, adieu!* as he escapes out the balcony window, and they are never truly together again.

What renders this scene so powerful is the feeling of helplessness in the face of hostile and jealous authority that the *alba* genre brings with it, amplified by Shakespeare's modification of the marital situations usually found therein. These are lovers who should be together, who have every right to be together, and whom every single person in an audience wants to see together. The sense of love and unjust interference is palpable, powerful, and profound. To remark, as if there were some particularly insightful observation contained therein, that Shakespeare is merely making use of "one of the current [or past] literary genres" is to miss, even actively to obscure, the point. It does not matter whether, while writing these words, Shakespeare was, or had recently been, experiencing the emotions his work evokes. What matters is that the emotions *are* evoked, that art and an audience have similar enough frames of reference ("conventional" thoughts and objects of thought, if one must use such ground-to-dust terminology) that sympathy, empathy, even pity and fear can be evoked — that lived experience can be recalled, reframed, and made new again, even if only for a moment. Art "reveals in a more concentrated or intense way what ordinary life reveals in its expressive aspects".[201] This is what Dostoevsky refers to when he describes everyday people as "разбавляется водой"[202] — "diluted with water", or "watered-down" versions of literary characters — not that human beings in their ordinary lives are less than real, but that our artistic representations of ourselves and our experiences are concentrated and

---

199 *Ibid.,* 3.5.39–40.
200 *Ibid.,* 3.5.51.
201 Colin Falck. *Myth, Truth and Literature: Towards a True Postmodernism* (Cambridge: Cambridge University Press, 1989), 122.
202 So, without going into a more serious explanation, we will say only that, in reality, the typicality of persons is, as it were, diluted with water, and all those Georges Dandins and Podkoleosins are actually there scurrying and running in front of us every day, but as if in a somewhat liquefied state.

Итак, не вдаваясь в более серьезные объяснения, мы скажем только, что в действительности типичность лиц как бы разбавляется водой, и все эти Жорж-Дандены и Подколесины существуют действительно, снуют и бегают пред нами ежедневно, но как бы несколько в разжиженном состоянии.

Fyodor Dostoevsky. *Идиот* [*The Idiot*] (St. Petersburg: A. Suvorin, 1884), 452.

sharpened to a point. Just as we depend on our art for an intensified experience of life, our art depends on us for contact with everyday reality. Art, perhaps especially narrative and dramatic art, depends on its ability to refer to and represent the lived experience of human beings in order for it to have any power at all. It cannot be locked away inside the structures of language, or inside a self-referentiality of techniques and formal elements from which it cannot escape. Denied that contact with "ordinary life", literature, music, painting, sculpture, dance, dies, just as do Romeo and Juliet, alone, and with no one to mourn until it is too late.

The love between the young pair has served as their impetus to defy authority and social convention, while risking the sharp disapproval (and possible violence) of their families. But it has not given them the strength to stand up, and openly acknowledge what they have done. Romeo's banishment, and Juliet's faked death, show each of them turning in fear from the face of authority, as their celebrated love is not enough to enable them to face the wrath of those to whom they have long been in the habit of submissiveness. And *that* is their tragedy, not in "violating the norms of the society in which they lived",[203] but in failing to sufficiently honor love, and each other, by bringing their disobedience and rejection of those norms out into the open. Juliet, who is in some ways the stronger of the two, is still too young, and is not yet sure-footed and strong-willed enough to defy Capulet; she "possesses the strength to choose a Montague for her husband, but not to stand up to her father".[204] Given Capulet's wrath and potential for violence, it is all too easy to understand why.

One of the starkest differences between this pair, who are otherwise presented as having "zweier herzen wünne", is revealed in their death scenes. Romeo still has a bit too much of the Petrarchan sonneteer about him, and despite his love for Juliet, has not yet learned to see her apart from his own poetic fantasies of the ideal love she represents to him. Had he only been given time, he might have grown beyond his idealizing tendencies; but time is what the play—and all its sources, from the works of Arthur Brooke, to Pierre Boaistuau, to Matteo Bandello—will not give

---

203 L. Stone, 87.
204 Evelyn Gajowski. *The Art of Loving: Female Subjectivity and Male Discursive Traditions in Shakespeare's Tragedies* (Cranbury, NJ: Associated University Presses, 1992), 52.

him. In the heart of the Capulet mausoleum, with Juliet's awakening face and form in front of him, Romeo does not *see*. Her "two and forty hours"[205] of unconsciousness are all but up, and Romeo's own remarks indicate that she is warming and nearly surfacing past the waters of unconsciousness even as he looks at her. Far from being a cold corpse that will suddenly reanimate, Juliet is ruddy of cheek and lip; she looks alive, and Romeo finds that puzzling:

> O my love! my wife!
> Death, that hath sucked the honey of thy breath,
> Hath had no power yet upon thy beauty:
> Thou art not conquered; beauty's ensign yet
> Is crimson in thy lips and in thy cheeks,
> And death's pale flag is not advanced there.[206]

But rather than stop for a moment with Juliet, he turns and speaks to the body of Tybalt, lying in a "bloody sheet",[207] though perhaps something now registers with him about the contrast between the two bodies. He turns back to Juliet, and asks—as if speaking to her one last time—why she looks so much like she is still alive:

> Ah, dear Juliet,
> Why art thou yet so fair? shall I believe
> That unsubstantial death is amorous,
> And that the lean abhorred monster keeps
> Thee here in dark to be his paramour?[208]

The simple solution to the problem, of course, is that Juliet *is* alive. But Romeo, overwhelmed by a grief the like of which he has never experienced, that he can only understand through the Petrarchan and Platonic images and concepts he has not yet had time enough to master and move beyond, does not adopt the simple solution. In fact, it does not even occur to him. Instead, he mythologizes and poeticizes Juliet's death-which-is-not-death, by casting Juliet in the part of Eurydice in

---

205 *Romeo and Juliet* 4.1.105.
206 Ibid., 5.3.91–96.
207 Ibid., 5.3.97.
208 Ibid., 5.3.101–05.

the myth of Orpheus, especially perhaps, the version from Phaedrus' speech in Plato's *Symposium*:

> The gods let loose their wonder for the works of love, and haste to hold valour in high honor. Orpheus, son of Oeagrus, they sent away unsuccessful from Hades, showing him only the ghost of the wife he had come for, and did not deliver her true self to him. For they regarded him as soft of purpose, like a mere player and singer of songs, because he lacked the courage to die for love as Alcestis had, but sought to enter Hades alive.[209]

Perhaps with the idea of "the ghost of [his] wife" in mind, and not wanting to be thought "soft" like Phaedrus' version of Orpheus, Romeo proceeds to die for love, while indulging in one last poetic speech:

> Eyes, look your last!
> Arms, take your last embrace! and, lips, O you
> The doors of breath, seal with a righteous kiss
> A dateless bargain to engrossing death!
> Come, bitter conduct, come, unsavoury guide!
> Thou desperate pilot, now at once run on
> The dashing rocks thy sea-sick weary bark!
> Here's to my love! [*Drinks*] O true apothecary!
> Thy drugs are quick. Thus with a kiss I die.[210]

As he kisses her, is he so wrapped up in the poetry of the Orphean myth[211] that he does not feel the warmth of Juliet's lips? It is impossible to know, but given the focus on himself and his own emotions Romeo has shown throughout the play, it seems the likely answer is "yes".

---

209 ἀνεῖσαν ἀγασθέντες τῷ ἔργῳ οὕτω καὶ θεοὶ τὴν περὶ τὸν ἔρωτα σπουδήν τε καὶ ἀρετὴν μάλιστα τιμῶσιν. Ὀρφέα δὲ τὸν Οἰάγρου ἀτελῆ ἀπέπεμψαν ἐξ Ἅιδου, φάσμα δείξαντες τῆς γυναικὸς ἐφ᾽ ἣν ἧκεν, αὐτὴν δὲ οὐ δόντες, ὅτι μαλθακίζεσθαι ἐδόκει, ἅτε ὢν κιθαρῳδός, καὶ οὐ τολμᾶν ἕνεκα τοῦ ἔρωτος ἀποθνῄσκειν ὥσπερ Ἄλκηστις, ἀλλὰ διαμηχανᾶσθαι ζῶν εἰσιέναι εἰς Ἅιδου.

Plato. *Symposium*, ed. by W. R. M. Lamb (Loeb Classical Library, Cambridge, MA: Harvard University Press, 1925), 179D.

210 *Romeo and Juliet*, 5.3.112–20.

211 Romeo is a kind of inverted Orpheus—one who loses his Eurydice, not because he looks back at her, but because he cannot get his head out of his songs.

Juliet, on the other hand, sees Romeo. As she awakes and takes stock of where she is and what is going on, she sees Romeo's lifeless body, mere moments after it had crossed over into death. As she kisses him, she feels traces of life: "Thy lips are warm!"[212] In that moment, more than any other in the play, the full tragedy of love, fear, and authority hits home, and catharsis kicks into high gear. These two never had a chance, to love, to live, even to grow up past the initial blooming of their passions and potential. The story of their lives and deaths does not bolster "individualism by positing sexual love as the expression of authentic identity";[213] rather, it shows how an attempt to use such love as an expression of identity can be ruthlessly crushed by the "dominant ideology", not of love, but of (usually male) authority and its demands for "submission to the asymmetrical distribution of power" between fathers and daughters, fathers and sons. The Gramscian *hegemon* in this play, which embodies the cultural norms promoted by an elite class to maintain dominance over everyone else,[214] is hardly "romantic love", nor does that love relegate anything to "the realm of deviance". It is that love itself which is regarded as deviant by the authority figures of the play, only to have the play turn the tables on them by showing them to be blind and tyrannical murderers of their own children. As Prince Escalus bitterly sums up:

> Where be these enemies? Capulet! Montague!

---

212 *Ibid.*, 5.3.167.
213 Callaghan (1994), 59.
214 In Gramsci's thought, literary critics—at least as much as, if not more than, poets and playwrights and and novelists—are complicit in the dissemination of the ruling ideas of a given time and place. Gramsci proposed what he called "a study of how, in fact, the ideological structure of the dominant class is organized" ("Uno studio di come è organizzata di fatto la struttura ideologica di una classe dominante"), before noting that "the most remarkable and dynamic part of it is the press in general: publishers (that have implicit and explicit programs, and support a determined, or pre-given, current), political journals, and magazines of all kinds, scientific, literary, philological, popular, etc., various periodicals even down to church parish bulletins" ("La parte più ragguardevole e più dinamica di esso è la stampa in generale: case editrici (che hanno implicito ed esplicito un programma e si appoggiano a una determinata corrente), giornali politici, riviste di ogni genere, scientifiche, letterarie, filologiche, di divulgazione ecc., periodici vari fino ai bollettini parrocchiali") (Antonio Gramsci. *Quarderi del carcere, Vol. I, Quaderni 1–5*, ed. by Valentino Gerratana [Turin: Giulio Einaudi, 1977], Q3§ 49, 332–33).

> See, what a scourge is laid upon your hate,
> That heaven finds means to kill your joys with love.
> And I for winking at your discords too
> Have lost a brace of kinsmen: all are punished.[215]

It is as if Shakespeare is making the argument of a prosecutor in a courtroom in which, rather than the lovers, their parents, their city, their world are on trial: "Shakespeare [...] is making a closing demonstration: 'Look at the corpses in front of you—your own son and daughter! Why are they dead? For God's sake think!' And he is requiring his audience to do the same".[216] Far from being any kind of dominant ideology, in *Romeo and Juliet*, love is portrayed as a breathtaking, bittersweet, but doomed challenger to paternal authority and its demands for obedience. Love, unsublimated passion for another human being, the *fin'amor* of the troubadour and trobairitz poets of the eleventh and twelfth centuries, is no idle game in Shakespeare. It is a tool of resistance in a contest between generations that is all too often, a matter of life and death.

---

215 *Romeo and Juliet*, 5.3.291–95.
216 John Vyvyan. *Shakespeare and the Rose of Love* (London: Shepheard-Walwyn, 1960), 134.

9. Love and its Costs in Seventeenth-Century Literature

The theme of love as resistance to authority is transformed and amplified in the lyric poetry of John Donne and Robert Herrick. In work filled with a sense of the fragility and shortness of life, these poets contribute to an ethos that has come to be known by the name *carpe diem*, a phrase made famous by Horace, "who in Ode, I. xi, tells his mistress that […] life is short, so they must 'enjoy the day', for they do not know if there will be a tomorrow".[1] Horace's line, "carpe diem quam minimum credula postero"[2] ("Seize the day, put little trust in tomorrow"), tells Leuconoe, and all who have followed since, to live now, and love now, because each second of scruple, doubt, and delay brings men and women closer to a death that is non-negotiable and eternal. In poetry, and in life, the idea of death becomes love's greatest ally in its battle against the demands of authority, convention, and law.

Death hovers over the poetry of this period, and "English love poetry evolved through an understanding of human love as mortal", a perspective that shines clearly through *carpe diem* poetry. These poems "magnify the pleasures of this world at the expense of the next", drawing much of their power from "the nothingness that awaits lovers in the afterlife" as a means to persuade readers to live now and "embrace

---

1 Ruth F. Glancy. *Thematic Guide to British Poetry* (Westport: Greenwood Press, 2002), 43.
2 Horace. *Horace: Epodes and Odes*, ed. by Daniel H. Garrison (Norman: University of Oklahoma Press, 1998), 39.

what this life has to offer".[3] We can explicitly connect this poetry to the earlier work of Shakespeare, as "English *carpe diem* poetry [follows] in the path of *Romeo and Juliet*, [imagining] the intensification of erotic experience by virtue of its temporal limits".[4] This intensification played upon an emerging sense of what we would now call atheism, rejecting the authority of father and state, religion and church:

> For English Renaissance poets, the act of writing *carpe diem* lyrics required a decisive break with Christian metaphysics. There could be no mention of the soul's eventual journey to heaven in poems that urge an immediate seizing of the present; there could be no deferral of joy in poems that imagine this day as the lovers' only chance for bliss.[5]

In a worldview that rejects the notion of an afterlife, that breaks with "Christian metaphysics", and sees love in terms of "an immediate seizing of the present", we see an intensification of the troubadour ethos. The *carpe diem* poems are revolutionary, "a stripping from the afterlife of all forms of pleasure that could compensate for erotic loss, [...] overturning both Petrarchan ideas of heavenly continuity and English reactions to this Petrarchan paradigm".[6] In the *carpe diem* poets, the reactionary and flesh-denying poetics of the tradition running through Akiba and Origen to Dante and Petrarch meets its strongest challenge yet. Love, though it cannot prevent death, becomes the primary power behind the urge to live one's own life and to make one's own choices before that "necessary end"[7] finally comes.

I
Carpe Diem in Life and Marriage: John Donne and the Critics who Distance

John Donne is perhaps the most famous writer of love poetry in the English language, a man who lived the *carpe diem* motif even more powerfully than he used it in his poetry; however, to dig to any depth

---

3   Targoff, 165.
4   *Ibid.*, 166.
5   *Ibid.*, 171.
6   *Ibid.*, 176.
7   *Julius Caesar* 2.2.36.

in the commentary that surrounds him is to wander into territory filled with dramatic conflicts. Some critics—like Ilona Bell—portray a flawed but fascinating writer whose work is filled with passionate desire for beautiful women, and devoted love for a particular woman, while others—like Stanley Fish—regard Donne's work as "sick", and the poet himself equally so, someone who can be read only through "the pleasures of diagnosis".[8] Such extremes of analysis probably tell us more about the analysts than about Donne, as John Roberts observes: "I often feel that many books and essays on Donne tell me more about the critics writing them than they do about Donne's poetry".[9] For Roberts, the goal of criticism should be to make "Donne's poetry more, not less accessible to an even wider reading audience than he enjoys at the present time".[10] One wonders how declaring the poet and his work "sick" helps accomplish that goal.

John Donne, portrait after Isaac Oliver (possibly late 17th century, based on a work of 1616).[11]

---

8 Stanley Fish. "Masculine Persuasive Force: Donne and Verbal Power". In Elizabeth D. Harvey and Katharine Eisaman Maus, eds. *Soliciting Interpretation: Literary Theory and Seventeenth-Century English Poetry* (Chicago: University of Chicago Press, 1990), 223.
9 John Roberts. "John Donne's Poetry: An Assessment of Modern Criticism". *John Donne Journal*, 1 (1982), 60.
10 *Ibid.*, 67.
11 https://commons.wikimedia.org/wiki/File:John_Donne_by_Isaac_Oliver.jpg

To understand Donne and his poetry, we will need to engage with his critics, but not, as William Empson remarks, on their terms: "The habitual mean-mindedness of modern academic criticism, its moral emptiness combined with incessant moral nagging, its scrubbed prison-like isolation, are particularly misleading in the case of Donne; in fact, we are the ones who need rescuing, not the poet".[12] Where the critics enlighten, and even where they usefully enrage, we will look to them. But the weakness of such critical and scholarly communities is that they tend to talk primarily to each other, despite the best intentions of scholars such as Achsah Guibbory, who tries to make her work "accessible to the educated, interested general reader and the intelligent student".[13] Donne did not seek to be read by scholars, any more than Yeats or his imagined Catullus did, nor do "interested general reader[s]" often seek to approach his work through the various lenses of academic literary criticism rather than what Nietzsche calls "the lens of life" ("der Optik [...] des Lebens").[14] Critical work insisting that a poem like "Elegy 19: To His Mistress Going to Bed" is merely an instance of "scopophilic male narcissism",[15] or that "the love poems of John Donne" express the "imperatives of empire" in which "[d]esire is boundless [and] formulated in a series of imperatives that do not invite debate",[16] has little or no interest in making "Donne's poetry more, not less accessible". Such work is primarily concerned with establishing the credentials of its various authors as properly "serious" and "professional" members of an academic literary establishment that long ago signaled its lack of concern with "the educated, interested general reader" who reads love poetry as something other than a coded expression of all the darkest impulses of the human species.

---

12 William Empson. "Rescuing Donne". In John Haffenden, ed. *Essays on Renaissance Literature, Vol. One: Donne and the New Philosophy* (Cambridge: Cambridge University Press, 1993), 159.

13 Achsah Guibbory. *Returning to John Donne* (Farnham: Ashgate, 2015), 3.

14 *Die Geburt der Tragödie aus dem Geiste der Musik* (Leipzig: C. G. Naumann, 1894) 4, https://books.google.com/books?id=lSk2AQAAMAAJ&pg=PA4

15 Anthony Easthope. *Poetry and Phantasy* (Cambridge: Cambridge University Press, 1989), 193.

16 Catherine Belsey. *Desire: Love Stories in Western Culture* (Oxford: Oxford University Press, 1994), 133.

Donne's passionate poetry reflects his turbulent life. Though the poetry is not a straightforward biography (a simple account of his life in verse), it is an emotional representation (impressionist, if not photorealist) of the complex man who wrote it. And while Donne's poems engage with and challenge pre-existing literary forms like the Ovidian elegy and the Petrarchan sonnet, they are no more reducible to those forms than they are to "imperatives of empire" or "scopophilic male narcissism". To read poetry in this way, reduced to "the pleasures of diagnosis", is more lawyerly than literary, more prosecutorial than poetic. Poetry treated in this way is essentially a corpse undergoing an autopsy, dead to the very readers that academics as teachers ostensibly hope to reach, if as Guibbory argues, "the survival of the humanities"[17] is of any concern.

It is in the life of the poet that we will find the life of the poetry. Born in 1572 to a Catholic family in a militantly Protestant England, John Donne spent a lifetime never quite fitting in, never quite belonging to any group or institution to which he attached himself. By his late twenties, Donne had been a sailor on military expeditions, a student of law at the Inns of Court in London, and had already shown the tendency to restlessness and contradiction that would characterize him throughout his life. Donne was "not dissolute, but very neat; a great visiter of Ladies, a great frequenter of Playes, a great writer of conceited Verses" who later in life "became so rare a Preacher, that he was not only commended, but even admired by all that heard him".[18] The "great visiter of Ladies" can perhaps be seen in the famous—and critically oft-abused—Elegy 19, "On His Mistress Going to Bed". In urging "His Mistress" to remove her clothes just a little more quickly ("in a series of imperatives" that according to Catherine Belsey apparently should have invited "debate"—one can only imagine the Parliamentary-style bedroom encounter the critic imagines as more appropriate), Donne praises the glories of nakedness:

---

17 Guibbory, 3.
18 Richard Baker. *A Chronicle of the Kings of England* (London: Printed by George Sawbridge at the Bible on Ludgate-hill, 1670), 447, https://books.google.com/books?id=BnIVsU0RtzUC&pg=PA447

> Full nakedness, all joys are due to thee.
> As souls unbodied, bodies unclothed must be
> To taste whole joys [...].[19]

Here, Donne matches two ideas he will often pair in his writing—the Neoplatonic concern (seen in Peter Bembo's speech from *The Courtier*) with ascending beyond the body to experience the fullness of joy, and the more radical idea of experiencing "whole joys" in and through the body itself. This pairing is incredibly important for understanding the dynamics of love, especially erotic love in Donne's poetry. His insistence that bodies are not shameful fleshly prisons inside which noble souls are entrapped, but beautiful and worthy of celebration, exploration, and desire, is the next step in the journey we have already seen Shakespeare taking, away from the nearly disembodied idolatry expressed by the poetry of Dante and Petrarch. Donne returns to the open eroticism, the fleshly sexuality and passion of the troubadour and trobairitz poetry. We see further evidence of this ethos in the Elegy, when Donne's speaker both uses and mocks the religious imagery of love:

> Now off with those shoes, and then safely tread
> In this love's hallowed temple, this soft bed.
> In such white robes, heaven's angels used to be
> Received by men; thou, angel, bring'st with thee
> A heaven like Mahomet's paradise; and though
> Ill spirits walk in white, we easily know
> By this these angels from an evil sprite,
> Those set our hairs, but these our flesh upright.[20]

While the male speaker very likely has his "flesh upright" here, the phrase has a less humorously salacious meaning as well: flesh is "upright", good, worthy to be praised and not condemned. It is not the flesh and its desires that come in for mocking here so much as the urge to cloak that flesh in the robes of religion—the joke is made rather obvious by the reference to "Mahomet's Paradise", an image of "infidelity" (from a

---

19 John Donne. *John Donne: The Complete English Poems*, ed. by A. J. Smith (New York: Penguin, 1971), 125, ll. 33–35. Further references to this volume will be by line number, Donne, and page number.
20 ll. 17–24, Donne, 125.

Christian perspective) that both satirizes and amplifies the philosophical and theological unease of *bien pensant* readers, whose "right thinking" takes human sexuality and warps it into sin, while promising—in "Paradise"—to reward abstinence with delight (referencing the myth of the seventy-two virgins—*houris*—promised in the Islamic concept of heaven, loosely derived from the *Qur'an*, 56:35–37). Here the idea of *carpe diem* is presented as opposing the claims of religion—though with the safety of hiding behind the notion of "false" religion, as an English reader would see it. Erotic love, practiced with "Full nakedness", not only redeems flesh (or demonstrates that it never needed redemption in the first place) by showing it "upright", but it renders "angels" (whether from good or evil "sprite[s]") unnecessary.

However, it is the motif of exploration that catches the eye of many critics today. Donne's speaker requests permission to "explore' the naked body of "His Mistress" like a Walter Raleigh licensed by Elizabeth I:

> Licence my roving hands, and let them go
> Before, behind, between, above, below.
> O my America, my new found land,
> My kingdom, safeliest when with one man manned,
> My mine of precious stones, my empery,
> How blest am I in this discovering thee!
> To enter in these bonds is to be free;
> Then where my hand is set, my seal shall be.[21]

Guibbory argues that this is a masculine power play, and a metaphor for politics: "Donne repeatedly in these poems envisions relations between the sexes as a site of conflict, thereby mirroring a larger society in which there is considerable anxiety about the lines and boundaries of power".[22] Where the present authors see love in Donne (and others) as anti-authoritarian, Guibbory sees its use as authoritarian and as part of a pattern of "persistent misogyny",[23] as the male speaker subjugates both the mistress and the "new-found-land":

---

21 ll. 25–32, Donne, 125.
22 Achsah Guibbory. "'Oh Let Mee Not Serve So': The Politics of Love in Donne's *Elegies*". *English Literary History*, 57: 4 (Winter 1990), 812, https://doi.org/10.2307/2873086
23 *Ibid.*

> At the beginning of this passage the woman is the monarch, providing a license, but the moment she gives this license she loses her sovereignty. [...] The man becomes not only explorer but conquerer, and she becomes *his* land and kingdom. The repeated possessives reinforce the sense of his mastery, and by the end of this passage he has now become the monarch, setting his "seal".[24]

Guibbory goes on to argue that Donne's poetry "betrays a discomfort with (indeed, a rejection of) the political structure headed by a female monarch. Intimate private relations between man and woman and the power structure of the body politic mirror and reinforce each other".[25] But in her drive to read the Elegy as mysognistic and patriarchal, Guibbory underplays any sense of the mutuality of the power dynamic—dominance *and* submission[26]—in her own description of the poem. The speaker asks for "License", performing his exploration of the woman who is figured as both Queen *and* land, dominant *and* submissive. The speaker remains licensed throughout—that formal permission is neither usurped nor withdrawn—and is thus submissive, while he remains the explorer, and is thus dominant. The logic is one of contraries as complements, a yin-yang of eroticism whose key can be found in the line "To enter in these bonds is to be free". Bound *and* free—on both sides.

The "licensing" power of the woman is further enhanced by being transformed from monarchical to *divine* power; all women, including the "Mistress" being spoken to here, "are mystic books, which only we / Whom their imputed grace will dignify / Must see revealed".[27] The idea of "grace" here places the male speaker in a position distinctly inferior to that of the woman being addressed, who is figured as God reaching out in mercy toward a sinner. Grace, the divinely-given power that compensates for the inability of "fallen man" to "save himself in his own corrupt nature" repairs the ability of the sinner to reach toward

---

24 Ibid., 822.
25 Ibid., 821.
26 Here, the observation of Foucault is useful: "The relationship of power and the rebelliousness of freedom cannot be separated" ("La relation de pouvoir et l'insoumission de la liberté ne peuvent donc être séparées") ("Le Sujet e le Pouvoir". In his *Dits et Écrits*. Vol. IV: *1980–1988*, 237).
27 ll. 41–43, Donne, 125.

the good, as "freedom of will is precisely what grace restores".[28] Having grace "imputed" to them, the "we" who are so gifted are treated *as if* worthy of the gift, much in the same manner that a sinner who has grace imputed to him is treated as if he is worthy of God.[29] Not only do we not have an image of masculine subjugation of the feminine here, but we have something entirely different: an image of nearly-godlike female power over a male supplicant.[30]

Readers and interpreters who are determined — for professional or political reasons — to see this poem as "evidence" that John Donne rejects "the political structure headed by a female monarch" transform his poetry into a tool of oppression (while arguing that they are merely "revealing" the oppression already inherent therein). Such critics reflect the voices of the *gilos* (the jealous and controlling spouses), rather than those of the lovers in troubadour and trobaritz poetry. But "On His Mistress Going to Bed" is only evidence of imperialistic misogyny if one can no longer see the poetic forest for the critical trees. Psychologists describe such thinking as confirmation bias, a filtering of ideas whereby we "seek confirmation rather than disconfirmation of what we already believe". For example, "a doctor [who] assumes that a patient has condition X, [...] may interpret the set of symptoms as supporting the diagnosis" without regard to any counter-evidence of any kind.[31] In other words, we see what we are determined to see. So, at least, does Bell describe recent trends among Donne's critics:

> For theoretical or ideological reasons, twentieth-[and twenty-first-] century critics generally assume that the woman in Donne's poems is a shadowy figure, the object or reflection of male desire, a pretext for self-fashioning, a metaphor [...]. a sex object [...]. In the last two decades

---

28 R. V. Young. *Doctrine and Devotion in Seventeenth-century Poetry: Studies in Donne, Herbert, Crashaw, and Vaughan* (Cambridge: Boydell & Brewer, 2000), 75.

29 For further discussion, see Michael Bryson, *The Tyranny of Heaven: Milton's Rejection of God as King* (London: Associated University Presses, 2004), 119–22.

30 Here we can see in Donne a reworking of the idea of the woman as angel, found in so much Italian poetry of the period between Lentini and Petrarch, through the recovery of the idea of eroticism and desire in a dynamic in which power is mutual.

31 Robert Sternberg. *Cognitive Psychology* (Belmont: Wadsworth Cengage, 2009), 512. This kind of thinking is rampant in what Karl Popper calls *"pseudo-science"*. Popper maintains that "It is easy to obtain confirmations, or verifications, for nearly every theory — if we look for confirmations", but that "[e]very genuine test of a theory is an attempt to falsify it, or to refute it" (Karl Popper, 36, 37).

> [...] it has become clear that it was not Donne, but the critics who disembodied and disregarded the women in Donne's poems.[32]

What critics see—and authoritatively present to students and general readers as *that which there is to see*—in poetry and other forms of literature changes with the passing of the years, decades, and centuries. But the poetry remains, its words unchanged by the changing fashions of academic and cultural authority.

Even Bell, whose readings of Donne are less pinched than those of other critics, cannot resist describing the dynamics of "On His Mistress Going to Bed" as a matter of "masculine desire to conquer and control", and "masculine dominion" over the woman,[33] while ignoring the line in which the speaker sues for "Licence" from the woman. It is the woman—in the role of monarch and grace-giving deity—who grants that "Licence" to the male explorer, whose exclamations of joy at his "kingdom" and "empery"[34] are made over "dominion" (to borrow Bell's term) which is merely on loan, not owned by the male of the poem. One begins to wonder at the unanimity of critics who insist on morally condemning the poem and its male speaker, as if there is a misandrist imperative at work which demands that male sexuality (at least in relation to women) be regarded and described negatively. When even an obvious admirer of Donne and his poetry seems compelled to describe male sexuality in the poem as "a military campaign", as "control", and as "dominion", it is tempting to think that there are barely-suppressed whispers of *rape* in the background. Would a poem by Sappho, or a diary entry by Anaïs Nin be treated in the same way?

Perhaps Donne himself can be looked to for some guidance. In his third Satire, he emphasizes the need to judge in terms of particulars. He gives two examples: "Careless Phrygius", who "doth abhor / All, because all cannot be good, as one / Knowing some women whores, dares marry none",[35] and "Gracchus", who "loves all as one, and thinks that so / As women do in divers countries goe / In divers habits, yet

---

32 Ilona Bell. "Gender Matters: The Women in Donne's Poems". In Achsah Guibbory, ed. *The Cambridge Companion to John Donne* (Cambridge: Cambridge University Press, 2006), 201.
33 *Ibid.*, 208.
34 ll. 28–29, Donne, 125.
35 ll. 62–64, Donne, 162.

are all still one kind".³⁶ Phrygius mistakenly thinks all women bad, while Gracchus mistakenly believes all women good. But reason demands that we throw off such indiscriminate "blindness"³⁷ and value the particular, the individual, while leaving behind the generalizing patterns of ideology and ignorance: "and forced but one allow".³⁸ Far from there being any "persistent misogyny" in his poetry, Donne's verse often shows us women *and* men who choose each other under circumstances of extreme duress, neither one using the other in any kind of power play, but facing the consequences of their mutual choice together. Donne's shortest poems, his epigrams, show us "clandestine lovers whose daring and devotion triumph over the death they incur".³⁹ This can easily be seen in "Hero and Leander":

> Both robbed of air, we both lie in one ground,
> Both whom one fire had burnt, one water drowned.⁴⁰

And in "Pyramus and Thisbe":

> Two, by themselves, each other, love and fear
> Slain, cruel friends, by parting have joined here.⁴¹

"Disinherited" paints a rather stark portrait of the economic consequences that could ensue for such "clandestine lovers" in Donne's own day:

> Thy father all from thee, by his last will,
> Gave to the poor; thou hast good title still.⁴²

This latter situation is exactly what Donne experienced when he became just such a clandestine lover as Leander or Pyramus. No longer content to be a "great visiter of Ladies", Donne fell in love with Anne More, the daughter of Sir George More (the Chancellor of the Garter), and the niece by marriage to Sir Thomas Egerton (the Lord Keeper of the Great

---

36   ll. 65–67, Donne, 162.
37   l. 68, Donne, 162.
38   l. 70, Donne, 162.
39   Bell, 204.
40   ll. 1–2, Donne, 149.
41   ll. 1–2, Donne, 149.
42   ll. 1–2, Donne, 151.

Seal, and Donne's own employer). Socially, Anne More was of a much higher rank than Donne, and any officially sanctioned match between the pair was impossible. The growing love between the mismatched couple (also mismatched in age, as Donne was in his late twenties, while More was in her mid-to-late teens when their relationship began), and the difficult position that their affection put the lovers in, is reflected in Donne's poetry, where he writes of "two situations which he had never experienced before and which changed the course of his life: courting a young woman whom he desperately wanted to marry despite the obvious difficulties, and being married in defiance of society's code of conduct and at the cost of his career".[43] Getting marrried cost them everything: money, career, and future prospects. But like the lovers of his epigrams, John and Anne chose each other in spite of the worst the rule-bound world of fathers and monarchs could throw at them.

In late 1601, "about three weeks before Christmas",[44] John Donne and Anne More married in a secret ceremony. The anxiety that ensued "about the trouble that he and [Anne] had now brought on themselves" resulted in the circulation of "a joke about the furtive couple's situation":

> Doctor Donne after he was married to a Maid, whose name was *Anne*, in a frolick (on his Wedding day) chalkt this on the back-side of his Kitchin-door, *John Donne, Anne Donne, Undone*.[45]

The consequences were as severe as they were immediate when George More found out about the clandestine marriage, from Donne's own letter to him on 2 February 1602. After informing More of the marriage, Donne tries to explain why he and Anne had deceived him by marrying secretly, and asks More not to be *too* angry with either Anne or himself:

> I knew my present estate lesse then fitt for her; I knew, (yet I knew not why) that I stood not right in your Opinion; I knew that to have giuen any intimacion of yt had been to impossibilitate the whole Matter. [...] But for her whom I tender much more, then my fortunes, or lyfe (els I would I might neyther ioy in this lyfe, nor enioy the next) I humbly beg of yow, that she may not, to her danger, feele the terror of your sodaine anger. [...] if yow incense my lordship [Thomas Egerton], yow Destroy her and me; that yt is easye to give vs happines, And that my Endevors

---

43 David Edwards. *John Donne: Man of Flesh and Spirit* (New York: Continuum, 2001), 282.
44 John Stubbs. *John Donne: The Reformed Soul* (New York: W. W. Norton & Co., 2006), 154.
45 Ibid., 154.

and industrie, if it please yow to prosper them, may soone make me somewhat worthyer of her.[46]

The letter simply enraged More, setting him on to do exactly what Donne had hoped he would not do: turn Egerton against Donne, who was immediately fired from his position as Egerton's secretary, imprisoned, and on his release, left without any practical prospects for employment.

A poem like "The Canonization" reflects this experience of forbidden love, punished by all the forces a society determined to control the marriages of its (adult) children can bring to bear. Its first stanza captures the sense of frustration and helplessness at being punished for following one's own heart:

> For God's sake hold your tongue, and let me love,
> Or chide my palsy, or my gout,
> My five grey hairs, or ruined fortune flout,
> With wealth your state, your mind with arts improve,
> Take you a course, get you a place,
> Observe his Honour, or his Grace,
> Or the King's real, or his stampèd face
> Contemplate; what you will, approve,
> So you will let me love.[47]

A critic like Nancy Andreasen reduces this poem to a mere rehearsal of conventional elements, claiming that "Donne is dramatizing the stock comic situation of an extramarital love affair between an aging man of the world and a youthful mistress, an affair which further injures the debilitated rake's already-ruined fortune".[48] But this shrinking of the poem from a howl of protest against an unjust world (in which daughters are the property of fathers, marriages are economic arrangements made by and for those fathers, and lives can be ruined by the simple, yet radical, act of choosing for oneself) to a rather tired exercise in comic convention is of a piece with many of the readings we

---

46   L.b.526: Letter from John Donne, The Savoy, London, to Sir George More, 1601/1602 February 2. *Early Modern Manuscripts Online*, http://emmo.folger.edu/view/Lb526/semiDiplomatic
47   ll. 1–9, Donne, 47.
48   Nancy Jo Coover Andreasen. *John Donne: Conservative Revolutionary* (Princeton: Princeton University Press, 1967). Quoted in Larson, 164.

have already encountered. It is a perfect example of how critics often *rewrite* poems. But the "five grey hairs" of the third line are not those of an aging man of the world—whose worldliness and age would have gifted him with many more than five—nor is the "ruined fortune" that of a rake who has simply spent too much keeping up with the young girls he likes to entertain and be entertained by. All of this can be seen in the references to official positions, the kind Donne depended on, and has now lost: "get you a place", but "let me love"; "Observe his Honour, or his Grace", but "let me love". It can also be seen in the mention of approval, a social currency the "rake"[49] actively disdains, but on whose continuance Donne had absolutely relied: "what you will, approve", but "let me love".

The poem's second stanza raises another howl of protest. Whom have we injured with our love? The answer, of course, in an economy in which daughters are valuable property, is George More:

> Alas, alas, who's injured by my love?
> What merchant's ships have my sighs drowned?
> Who says my tears have overflowed his ground?
> When did my colds a forward spring remove?
> When did the heats which my veins fill
> Add one more to the plaguy bill?
> Soldiers find wars, and lawyers find out still
> Litigious men, which quarrels move,
> Though she and I do love.[50]

---

49 The most infamous of the "rakes" was John Wilmott, the 2nd Earl of Rochester, whose life and poetry was a scandal in the court of Charles II. As Samuel Johnson describes his life and death:

[I]n a course of drunken gaiety, and gross sensuality, with intervals of study, perhaps, yet more criminal, with an avowed contempt of all decency and order, a total disregard of every moral, and a resolute denial of every religious obligation, he lived worthless and useless, and blazed out his youth and his health in lavish voluptuousness, till, at the age of one-and-thirty, he had exhausted the fund of life, and reduced himself to a state of weakness and decay [and] died July 26, 1680, before he had completed his thirty-fourth year.

Samuel Johnson. *The Lives of the Most Eminent English poets, with Critical Observations on Their Works*, Vol. 1. (London: J. Fergusson, 1819), 150–51, https://books.google.com/books?id=e_sTAAAAQAAJ&pg=PA150).

50 ll. 10–18, Donne, 47.

Lawyers and litigious men trying to move quarrels began to interfere in Donne's situation immediately: "Sir George determined to extricate his daughter from Donne if it was humanly and legally possible. He had instigated proceedings, and a hearing was due at the High Commission to assess the legality of the marriage".[51] But both Anne and John Donne insisted that they had not only plighted troth (a standard of commitment often held to be as binding as a public marriage ceremony), but were legally married. Some weeks later, "the Archbishop of Canterbury himself finally ruled that the marriage was valid in the eyes of the established Church".[52] For the Donnes, however, the economic struggles had only just begun, as John Donne would be turned down for every position to which he applied, with the exception of a temporary job as the traveling secretary to Sir Robert Drury in 1611–12, until he took orders in the church in 1615. For fourteen years, the Donnes struggled, as the society of their time and place punished them for choosing each other, rather than allowing a father (or fathers) to choose instead. In this context, the fourth stanza of "The Canonization" takes on a meaning wholly alien to Andreasen's scenario of a ruined rake with a young mistress:

> We can die by it, if not live by love,
> And if unfit for tombs and hearse
> Our legend be, it will be fit for verse;
> And if no piece of chronicle we prove,
> We'll build in sonnets pretty rooms;
> As well a well-wrought urn becomes
> The greatest ashes, as half-acre tombs,
> And by these hymns, all shall approve
> Us canonized for love.[53]

The "pretty rooms" are refuges against the bruising demands of a world that sneers at the foolishness of lovers, and if the world will afford no place for love, at least "a well-wrought urn" will give the lovers a final unified resting place, much after the fashion and feeling of those resting places afforded to the lovers in the epigrams. As the poem ends, the idea of it being reducible to a stock comic situation becomes contemptible and

---

51 Stubbs, 170.
52 *Ibid.*, 174.
53 ll. 28–36, Donne, 47–48.

absurd. After their deaths, the lovers become a pilgrimage destination for future lovers who are still struggling with the Egeuses, Capulets, and Mores of the world. At the grave, these new lovers pray that their own fathers will learn from the example of the dead couple, now canonized as saints, and grow mild: "Countries, towns, courts: beg from above / A pattern of your love!"[54]

But as powerfully evocative as "The Canonization" is, we do not have a precise date for its composition, which opens the door to those critics who wish to separate the poet from the poem. As Guibbory argues:

> Readers have long identified the "mutual love" poems with Donne's secret courtship and marriage to Anne More. [...] Certain lyrics that privilege the sacred space of clandestine love and describe the world's opposition fit with what we know of Donne's situation at the time. Yet so long as we lack evidence for the dates and occasions of Donne's lyrics, poems like "The Relique" or "The good-morrow" [or "The Canonization"] must frustrate the autobiographical readings they invite.[55]

Must? Note the language of compulsion and authoritative limitation. The poems may "fit with what we know of Donne's situation at the time", yet we are told, *ex cathedra*, that "we lack evidence" (or what the critic considers admissable as evidence, a dated manuscript), and we must continue to hold off identifying the life of a poet who lived *fin'amor*, from the poetry which describes *fin'amor*, love between individuals who face all the consequences the world can throw at them for making their choice. Just as much current scholarship on the troubadours would deny readers the ability to see love poems as anything other than documentary evidence of misogyny and performative narcissism, so it would seem that many specialists in John Donne are determined to tell us to reject the evidence of the words in the poems themselves, and reject what we know about the correlation between those words and the known facts of the love and life of John and Anne Donne. The argument is an oddly familiar one, that correlation is not causation. But while such reasoning is valid in the realm of statistics, it is a great deal shakier in other realms (there is a reason that the argument is often resorted

---

54 ll. 44–45, Donne, 48.
55 Achsah Guibbory. "Erotic Poetry". In her, ed. *The Cambridge Companion to John Donne* (Cambridge: Cambridge University Press, 2006), 138.

to by tobacco companies and climate-change deniers), and it sounds especially jarring coming from literary critics.

But despite his critics, Donne's passions will not be contained—even the long Platonic tradition of regarding human love as the lowest rung on a ladder leading to the divine are made to serve the purposes of a poet who will not be reduced to quiet submission and conformity. In "The Extasie", Donne writes of a love between two who are one, a passion at once reflective and active, spiritual and embodied. Beginning with a description of "A pregnant bank swell'd up to rest"[56] where the lovers "Sat we two, one another's best",[57] the poem portrays these two who are one as being both in and out of their bodies as they silently gaze at one another. Their hands and eyes are joined:

> Our hands were firmly cemented
> With a fast balm, which thence did spring,
> Our eye-beams twisted, and did thread
> Our eyes upon one double string;
> So to' intergraft our hands, as yet
> Was all our means to make us one,
> And pictures in our eyes to get
> Was all our propagation.[58]

At the same time, their "souls" are suspended outside of their bodies, in the same silent contemplation of each other:

> As 'twixt two equal armies Fate
> Suspends uncertain victory,
> Our souls (which to advance their state
> Were gone out) hung 'twixt her and me.
> And whilst our souls negotiate there,
> We like sepulchral statues lay;
> All day, the same our postures were,
> And we said nothing, all the day.[59]

---

56   l.2, Donne, 53.
57   l.4, Donne, 53.
58   ll. 5–13, Donne, 53–54.
59   ll. 14–20, Donne, 54.

There is no "masculine desire to conquer and control" or "masculine dominion" here, despite the metaphor of souls as armies. Instead, we have silent mutuality, a communication that does not require words, as painfully sincere yet artfully deceitful as words can so often be. We have a sense of souls and bodies that are—like the lovers—themselves two-who-are-one. The souls can come forth from, but are always grounded in the bodies that are crucial parts of the "We" who "like sepulchral statues lay". The bodies are not mere objects, not fallen flesh to be derided and condemned, but a crucial part of the entire two-in-one reality that is being described. Each dynamic is fueled by love—between the two lovers, and between the bodies and souls themselves. The pairing is mutually desired and mutually sustaining, and *that* is the secret referred to by the following lines:

> If any, so by love refined
> That he soul's language understood,
> And by good love were grown all mind,
> Within convenient distance stood,
> He (though he knew not which soul spake
> Because both meant, both spake the same)
> Might thence a new concoction take
> And part far purer than he came.[60]

The "soul's language" is silence—mutually understood—a touch that is offered and accepted, felt both with and without the bodies of the lovers. The imagined audience here is someone who understands that these bodies and souls are not opposites, but necessary complements, ingredients or elements of a far more complex synthesis, a "new concoction" (using the language of alchemy as psychological and/or spiritual transformation and purification as well as physical transmutation). Observing this, even hearing this, the imagined other is himself or herself transformed through the realization that the binary division between body and soul is an illusion, just as is the binary between lover and lover. The two are one, for those with ears to hear and eyes to see.[61]

---

60 ll. 21–28, Donne, 54.
61 A similar spirit is found in Shakespeare's poem "The Phoenix and the Turtle" (published in Robert Chester's *Loves Martyr* of 1601), where two lovers "lov'd, as

The poem then goes on to make explicit that bodies and souls are a synthesis of elements that forms the individual self of each lover, who are themselves one, a union that forms the highest and most profound whole:

> But O alas, so long, so far
> Our bodies why do we forbear?
> They are ours, though they are not we, we are
> The intelligences, they the sphere.
> We owe them thanks, because they thus,
> Did us, to us, at first convey,
> Yielded their forces, sense, to us,
> Nor are dross to us, but allay.[62]

Their bodies are a necessary part of the synthesis, the whole. The "intelligences" without "the sphere" are like an energy without a vehicle through which to express itself, thus the bodies are not "dross" (unnecessary trash) but "allay" (part of an alloy, two substances combined into a stronger and more complex whole). Returning once again to the imagined other who sees, hears, and understands all of this, the poem concludes by erasing the difference between the disembodied and embodied lovers:

> To our bodies turn we then, that so
> Weak men on love revealed may look;
> Love's mysteries in souls do grow,
> But yet the body is his book.
> And if some lover, such as we,
> Have heard this dialogue of one,
> Let him still mark us, he shall see
> Small change, when we'are to bodies gone.[63]

This "dialogue of one" is a dialogue of oneness: the oneness of opposites that are not opposites. The "lover" who understands this, who sees "Small change" between the language spoken in silence between the lovers without and within their bodies, understands the both sacred

---

love in twain / Had the essence but in one; / Two distincts, division none: / Number there in love was slain" (ll. 25–28).
62 ll. 49–56, Donne, 55.
63 ll. 68–76, Donne, 55–56.

and radically secular point this poem makes about love: the highest form of love is that which is had here, now, with that he or she who is right in front of you.

Much of the essence of "The Extasie" is expressed in that idea, and much of the challenge this poem makes to Platonic and Neoplatonic orthodoxies about love can be understood through this idea as well. There is no need to climb a "ladder of love", no need to turn one's focus away from those beloveds in the here and now, in the world of flesh and blood, in order to experience the "true" or "transcendent" love that will allow the lover, as Diotima argues, to come to know "the soul's beauty".[64] There is no need to believe, in Peter Bembo's terms, that "the body is something very different from beauty, and not only does not increase beauty but lessens its perfection".[65] "The Extasie" sweeps all of this aside as so much body-shaming, flesh-hating, life-denying nonsense. The love portrayed in "The Extasie" is already fully embodied and fully spiritual, passionately physical and supremely sacred all at once. Let those understand who are able, the poem suggests, and they will part more pure and whole than when they came.

And yet, this poem has caused more arguments between the critics than perhaps any other of Donne's works. With "The Extasie", the critical drive to allegory, to diagnosis, to a hermeneutics of suspicion, to seeing the poem in terms of anything other than open, embodied passion becomes crystal clear. As far back as 1932, Merritt Hughes is arguing that the poem is not passionate at all, but is "merely the dramatisation of a conflict and reconciliation of ideas which had long been familiar in Italy and France, if not in England".[66] Hughes works hard to put "The Extasie" back in the cramped box of convention by insisting that it is a "minor heresy [to believe] that *The Extasie* was felt by its author as a revolt against Platonism",[67] and by arguing that "we owe *The Extasie* to the stream of tradition rather than to an original dramatic impulse on Donne's part".[68] In this last gesture, we can see the early

---

64 "ταῖς ψυχαῖς κάλλος" (Plato. *Symposium* 210c).
65 "l corpo è cosa diversissima dalia bellezza, e non solamente non le accresce, ma le diminuisce la sua perfezione" (Castiglione, 254–55).
66 Merritt Hughes. "The Lineage of 'The Extasie'". *Modern Language Review*, 27: 1 (January 1932), 2, https://doi.org/10.2307/3716215
67 Ibid.
68 Ibid.

stages of the "death of the author" impulse at work. "Tradition" wrote the poem, not Donne. By 1934, Frank Doggett is reclaiming the poem for passion by describing "The Extasie as "Donne's most complete declaration of the nature of love, and of the part taken by soul and by body in that passion",[69] arguing that "[t]he inner meaning of Donne's thought, here, is the necessity of the functions of both soul and body for complete love".[70] At the same time, however, Doggett contends that Donne's poem is essentially in agreement with the anti-body mysticism of Bembo in *The Courtier*.[71]

By the 1960s, Charles Mitchell argues that "The Extasie" portrays a love in which body and soul are indispensable parts of a larger whole. But Mitchell's emphasis is Neoplatonic, for "The Extasie" does its work by showing "how the outward union of man and woman effects the union of body and soul within man".[72] Lovers (and observers) are shown in the poem as having "grown inwardly from a mere body to a synthesis of body and soul by the outgoing power of love".[73] Katherine Thompson reverses that emphasis in 1982, making an argument that serves as a counterpoint to those who try to shoehorn "The Extasie" into a tidy Neoplatonic container:

> Even the initial stroke of wit in "The Extasie" depends on Donne's turning the tables on the conventional Neoplatonists, or one should say, it depends on Donne's inversion of their ladder of love. [...] Donne, by fiat, begins with ecstasy achieved [...then proves] the compatibility of the lovers at the level of soul; and then has his speaker argue for descent on the ladder rather than ascent.[74]

As Catherine Gimelli Martin observes, modern critical reaction to "The Extasie" has tended toward a reductive and cynical view:

---

69 Frank A. Doggett. "Donne's Platonism". *The Sewanee Review*, 42: 3 (July–September 1934), 285.
70 *Ibid.*, 288.
71 *Ibid.*, 289–90.
72 Charles Mitchell. "Donne's 'The Extasie': Love's Sublime Knot". *Studies in English Literature, 1500–1900*, 8: 1, The English Renaissance (Winter 1968), 92, https://doi.org/10.2307/449412
73 *Ibid.*, 100.
74 T. Katharine Thomason. "Plotinian Metaphysics and Donne's 'Extasie'". *Studies in English Literature, 1500–1900*, 22: 1, The English Renaissance (Winter 1982), 93–94, https://doi.org/10.2307/450219

most modern critics seem to agree that [Donne's poetry] is typically or even universally put to cynically seductive purposes. But this consensus is both newer and more tenuous than it seems; only a generation ago, literary critics regularly followed Herbert J. C. Grierson and Helen Gardner in regarding the major love lyrics as sincere [...]. This view first faded under the influence of Pierre Legouis, whose rereading of "The Extasie" as a seduction poem proved broadly influential among second-generation New Critics, for whom the ironic mode was fast becoming the insincere mode later canonized in Stephen Greenblatt's *Renaissance Self-Fashioning*.[75]

What Martin calls "the new orthodoxy"[76] insists that readers discount the presence of love and desire in Donne's poetry as nothing more than a cynically seductive lie. But "The Extasie" shows us a Donne who cannot be contained by criticism that reduces sincere passion to tattered convention, turning "all forms of inwardness [...] into mere social constructions".[77] Again, one wonders what it is about such reductively life-denying arguments that appeals to so many critics. It is as if we have trained several generations of academics to be like the man who, as Blake puts it, "sees the Ratio only" and thus "sees himself only",[78] so incapable or unwilling are they to see past what the troubadour poet Marcabru calls the fragmented, *frait*, in order to glimpse the whole, *entier*. Donne's work demands that we see past the Ratio, past the fragmented, past the commitments of any contemporary critical school, in order to understand his desire. Perhaps a little less dissection and a little more synthesis is in order. As Martin argues, "[m]ore than any other poet of the period, Donne represents his inner search for religious and erotic authenticity"[79] through the passionate intensity of his work.

---

75 Catherine Gimelli Martin. "The Erotology of Donne's 'Extasie' and the Secret History of Voluptuous Rationalism". *Studies in English Literature 1500–1900*, 44: 1 (2004), 123, https://doi.org/10.1353/sel.2004.0008
76 *Ibid.*, 123.
77 *Ibid.*
78 William Blake. "There is No Natural Religion". In *The Complete Poetry and Prose of William Blake*, ed. by David V. Erdman (Berkeley and Los Angeles: University of California Press, 2008), 3.
79 Martin, 123, quoting from Robert Watson, *The Rest Is Silence: Death as Annihilation in the English Renaissance* (Berkeley and Los Angeles: University of California Press, 1994), 164.

Donne, like Shakespeare, like Milton, is an entire world—a writer of astonishing virtuosity and versatility, a poet who can inhabit experience, emotion, and passion, yet maintain an ironic distance—he is at once an artist of the inside and the outside, the "is" and the "seems" of Hamlet's retort to Getrude.[80] One thing remains consistent, however. Donne's poetry, far from being the merely conventional fare described by those critics who "wear the carpet with their shoes", gives love its due. A more immediately playful poem like "The Sun Rising", shows us a Donne who regards love and its pleasures and demands as far more important, and far worthier of respect, than the demands of the world and its temporary rulers. Starting with a variation on the *alba* form of the troubadours, the poem decries the presence of the sun, and its interference with the pleasures of love:

> Busy old fool, unruly sun,
> Why dost thou thus,
> Through windows, and through curtains, call on us?
> Must to thy motions lovers' seasons run?[81]

In the *alba*, the rising of the sun threatens to betray the lovers, and calls an end to the all too brief night they have spent together, out of the reach and beyond the prying eyes of jealous spouses and a controlling world. Donne captures that sense of resentment against the sun, against the demands of the daylight world of law, loveless marriages, and obedience which ends only in death, by calling the sun a "fool" that serves the interests of the hateful and powerful, enforcing the schedule of a world that demands conformity. The question "Must to thy motions lovers' seasons run?" has only one practical answer: *yes*. But Donne rejects and mocks the practical answer, insisting that such drudgery is for those even more foolish than the sun their messenger:

> Saucy pedantic wretch, go chide
> Late school-boys and sour prentices,

---

80 *Hamlet* 1.2.76.
81 ll. 1–4, Donne, 80.

> Go tell court-huntsmen that the King will ride,
> Call country ants to harvest offices;
> Love, all alike, no season knows, nor clime,
> Nor hours, days, months, which are the rags of time.[82]

The "pedantic" sun (fussy, punctilious, and over-eager to obey times and seasons) is a fit alarum for children and workers chained to the drudgery of low pay and long hours, a proper herald for foolish kings and the greater fools who serve them, a necessary prompter for the activities of insects, but it is no authority for those men and women who love. Love transcends the petty rules and forms, the bowings and scrapings of lives spent jostling for position in a hierarchical society, the strict schedulings of time into "hours, days, months", man-made concepts which are merely "rags". Love rejects the calls of the world for obedience, for Love is its own law, its own world, as Donne tells the unwelcome and too-bright morning star that has intruded upon love's peace and quiet: "Princes do but play us; compared to this, / All honour's mimic, all wealth alchemy".[83]

Finally, love makes lovers a world entire unto themselves, their own rulers, their own subjects, beholden to no one but each other. And it is in this state that true human happiness can be sought and found:

> Thou sun art half as happy as we,
> In that the world's contracted thus;
> Thine age asks ease, and since thy duties be
> To warm the world, that's done in warming us.
> Shine here to us, and thou art everywhere;
> This bed thy center is, these walls, thy sphere.[84]

Where the lovers of "The Extasie" are two who are one, united each with the other in body and soul, the lovers of "The Sun Rising" become an entire world in their private room, within whose walls no laws but those of love hold sway.

---

82   Ibid., ll. 5–10.
83   ll. 23–24 Donne, 81.
84   Ibid., ll. 25–30.

II
The Lyricist of *Carpe Diem*: Robert Herrick and the Critics who Distort

Though his name may not be as well-recognized as Donne's, there are probably more readers who recognize fragments of the poetry of Robert Herrick than almost any other English poet save Shakespeare.

Robert Herrick, portrait by Edward Everett Hale, in *The Hawthorne Readers*, Book 4 (1904).[85]

His most famous poem, "To the Virgins to Make Much of Time", is for many readers the very definition of the *carpe diem* poem:

> Gather ye Rose-buds while ye may,
> Old Time is still a-flying:
> And this same flower that smiles to day,
> To morrow will be dying.
> The glorious Lamp of Heaven, the Sun,
> The higher he's a-getting;
> The sooner will his Race be run,
> And neerer he's to Setting.
> That Age is best, which is the first,

---

85 https://commons.wikimedia.org/wiki/File:Robert_Herrick_(poet).jpg

> When Youth and Blood are warmer;
> But being spent, the worse, and worst
> Times, still succeed the former.
> Then be not coy, but use your time;
> And while ye may, goe marry:
> For having lost but once your prime,
> You may for ever tarry.[86]

The famous *carpe diem* lyric is also a *carpe florem* poem: pluck the flower (of virginity) before it begins to fade. As Shakespeare observes in the opening lines of Sonnet 15, "everything that grows / Holds in perfection but a little moment", and Herrick here asks, why wait? What are you waiting for? This deceptively simple poem challenges everything. In the absence of an afterlife (and the irony must be noted that Herrick was an Anglican minister, having been ordained at the age of 32 in 1623), life must be lived now, and time lost will never be regained, thus it is absolutely vital to "use your time". Those who choose to be "coy", holding back out of fear of consequences for "sin" or disobedience, will be punished by the only authority that matters: death. In a world for which there may be no heaven that looks on and takes anyone's part,[87] Herrick's famous exhortation is no mere literary cliché, no mere exercise in convention. It is a powerful and beautiful statement of the outrageous, sad, and ultimately fatal predicament we all find ourselves in.

Yet, for some critics, Herrick's most famous poem is curiously removed from life, and, as Sarah Gilead argues, incapable of anything other than pointing to "the deceptive capacity of language to contain experience".[88] The intellectual genealogy of this idea is clear enough, partaking as it does of the flavor of Paul de Man's assertion that "Language always occurs within a range of deceptive appearances which it created itself; for that reason, it always endangers its own

---

86 Robert Herrick. *The Complete Poems of Robert Herrick*, ed. by Alexander B. Grosart. 3 vols. (London: Chatto & Windus, 1876), Vol. 1, 144–45, ll. 1–16, https://books.google.com/books?id=n14JAAAAQAAJ&pg=PA144. Further references to these volumes will be by line number, Herrick, volume number, and page number.
87 *Macbeth* 4.3.230–31.
88 Sarah Gilead. "Ungathering 'Gather ye Rosebuds': Herrick's Misreading of *Carpe Diem*". *Criticism*, 27: 2 (Spring 1985), 135.

innermost being, that is, the authentic act of saying".[89] Consistent with the "hermeneutics of suspicion", the idea Gilead shares with de Man is that language conceals what it pretends to reveal, and thus poetic language does not actually say what it seems to say. This idea that language conceals, that language is an unstable and untrustworthy medium, is widely shared in mid-to-late twentieth-century continental (and continentally-influenced) thought. For philosophers like Maurice Merleau-Ponty and Martin Heidegger, "it is in language that the unconcealment of things happens. Yet every disclosure, every revelation, is, at the same time, a concealment; language covers things over in the very process of thematization or unconcealment".[90] Jacques Derrida falls right in line by declaring that we have reached a point in which "the simple signifying nature of language appears very uncertain, partial, or inessential".[91] Literary criticism that takes such ideas as a starting point regards poetry as a pretense of meaning that needs to be exposed as meaningless in order that the machinations of languguage and ideology might be revealed.

Making use of these ideas with enough ingenuity and determination, a remorselessly skilled critical practitioner can quite nearly destroy any sense of life-affirmation in Herrick's poem, rewriting it to the point of turning it into a verse tract on suicide. The first step is to assert and then emphasize the contradictory nature of Herrick's theme:

> A *carpe diem* poem exists within an established literary subcategory, inhabits an enclosed ontological and significatory space. […] the meanings of the poem are secured by both external traditions (conventional motifs, arguments, moods and tropes) and by the poem's internal patterning. And yet the *carpe diem* theme itself celebrates not the rule-bound realms of art, conventionality, contextualization, but rather pure sensory experience. That is, it recommends that which by its form it denies. Pure experience is precisely what language does not offer; experience is always processed, mediated by the cultural forms (including language and art) through which we apprehend it. The *carpe*

---

89   Paul de Man. *The Paul de Man Notebooks*, ed. by Martin McQuillan (Edinburgh: Edinburgh University Press, 2014), 174.
90   Martin C. Dillon. *Merleau-Ponty's Ontology* (Evanston: Northwestern University Press, 1997), 179.
91   "la nature simplement signitive du langage paraît bien incertaine, partielle ou inessentielle" (Jacques Derrida. *L'Ecriture et la Différence* [Paris: Seuil, 1967], 9–10).

diem poem seems to point to, even provide access to, a mysteriously life-enhancing realm of experience but simultaneously substitutes a highly artificial construct—itself—for such experience.[92]

Let's break that last sentence down. In order to do that, we will move from direct statements to indirect statements, and as Polonius would say, "by indirections find directions out".[93] First, let's look at the simplest and most direct level of meaning available: "The *carpe diem* poem [...] point[s] to [...] a [...] life-enhancing realm of experience". That would be a direct, straightforward, and relatively uncontroversial statement. But note how the critic builds (or tears down) from that basis. The simple suggestion of *seeming* is added: "The *carpe diem* poem *seems* to point to [...] a life-enhancing realm of experience". Though still quite straightforward, this version introduces the smallest of doubts. Next, the critic adds a disingenuous claim about the poem's power, an absurd strawman: "The *carpe diem* poem *seems* to point to, *even provide access to*, a [...] life-enhancing realm of experience". It is easy to see how a poem might point to such a thing, but how could a poem provide access thereto? The obvious answer is that it cannot. Through the sly suggestion that a poem might *seem* to have powers that it cannot have, our critic establishes a "sensible" or "common sense" doubt about the poem's *seeming* in general. From here, the critic adds more doubt: "The *carpe diem* poem *seems* to point to, *even provide access to*, a *mysteriously* life-enhancing realm of experience". This introduces the idea that the *seeming* is not limited to the poem, but to the world of experience that the poem only *seems* to point to (and with each move, Herrick's verse recedes further and further to invisibility). Finally, the finishing touch is added: "The *carpe diem* poem *seems* to point to, *even provide access to*, a *mysteriously* life-enhancing realm of experience *but simultaneously substitutes a highly artificial construct—itself—for such experience*". This last move relies on meaningless inflation of its terms. What is "a highly artificial construct"? As all constructs are "artificial" (made by and through art and artifice), how is it possible for such a construct to be highly artificial, as opposed to simply and plainly artificial? The effect looked for, however, is not precision of definition, so much as it is the

---

92 Gilead, 135.
93 *Hamlet*, 2.1.65.

enhancement—through rhetorical inflation—of an already threadbare line of reasoning. The last assertion—as no evidence whatsoever is given for the notion that the poem *substitutes for experience*—completes the trick whereby Herrick's poem is replaced by an absurd version written by the critic, for the critic, with the express purpose of being deconstructed by the critic.

Rewritten in this way, Herrick's "To the Virgins" is merely a tiresome rehearsal of "established" literary forms and ideas, trapped within an old-fashioned and no-longer-negotiable set of conventions regarding life and the communication of emotions and ideas. For the critic, the "meaning" that "naive" readers take from this poem is a philosophical version of fast food: prepackaged in familiar wrapping (the "conventional motifs, arguments, moods and tropes") with standardized cooking and presentation techniques ("the poem's internal patterning"). As refashioned by the critic, the product does not, indeed cannot, deliver on its promises.

With the first, and most crucial step now taken (the construction of a strawman version of the poem), the second step is to distance it from any aspect of life that does not somehow refer to poetry itself, and is not somehow about the acts of writing and meaning. For Gilead, Herrick's poem can be reduced to "a metaphor for the act of reading and interpreting ('gathering' a message)". For the critic, "the persuasion to pleasure of Herrick's *carpe diem* may be read as a persuasion to seek signification: textuality replaces sexuality".[94] This move makes it possible to claim that Herrick's lyric is an artifact of ruthless competitiveness, a testament to the demands of the male poet's ego (an idea borrowed from T. S. Eliot's essay "Tradition and the Individual Talent" and Harold Bloom's book *The Anxiety of Influence*): "Herrick's 'To the Virgins' is compensatorily self-effacing, quiet, small, innocent, easy, almost anonymous-seeming. But its modesty, its virginal unaggressiveness conceals, perhaps, a kind of textual ruthlessness".[95] This critical formula relies heavily on the use of "shocking" reversals and combinations of ideas, images, and even sound patterns all strung together on the extremely thin thread of "perhaps". "Textual" is intended to remind the reader of "sexual", and "virginal [...] ruthlessness" is designed to

---

94   Ibid.
95   Ibid., 140.

raise the spectre of violence, even rape. Naturally, what else would we expect to find concealed behind "virginal unaggressiveness", other than "textual ruthlessness"? For the critic, that "ruthlessness" reveals itself in an Oedipal competition in which Herrick establishes his poetic persona as an "aggressive rival to and replacement of the poetic father" through the "acts of textual castration that create 'To the Virgins' from the bits and pieces of precursor texts" from "the classical age which produces the literary genera Herrick follows".[96]

As the critical assertions mount ever higher, the third step is to employ the "hermeneutics of suspicion" to argue that the poem does not mean what it merely seems to mean, and may, in fact, mean quite the opposite:

> By illustrating the unstoppable rush of time, the need to seize the day is made manifest. But the poem's "aging" also undermines the *carpe diem* assertion, for if the linear succession from "best" to "worst" is absolutely impervious to human will, action, or decision, then the choice between seizing the day or letting it pass is no choice at all. Not to tarry, not to defer the gathering of rosebuds, is not to defer death, the final gathering, the end of the race. Thus the poem simultaneously illustrates both the wisdom and the folly of heeding its message.[97]

Again, the argument relies on unsubstantiated claims that present themselves as authoritative critical judgments. The critic supplies no evidence at all for the "shocking" conclusion that "the poem simultaneously illustrates both the wisdom and the folly of heeding its message". It is true, of course, that "not to defer"[98] gathering rosebuds "is not to defer" death itself. But that is not what the poem claims. Instead it asserts that to defer gathering rosebuds is to defer (possibly until it is too late) the all-too-short experience of the most pleasurable aspects of life. Death is not the question of the poem—the question is what each of us will do with the time left *before* death. To argue seriously that there is "no choice at all" between grabbing experience and allowing it to pass

---

96 Gilead, 141.
97 *Ibid.*, 146.
98 Note how the critic uses the negation, the inversion there to add the *appearance* of complexity: "not to defer gathering", rather than merely "gathering". *Gathering rosebuds does not defer death*—this is a simple, straightforward statement. *Not to defer gathering* rosebuds *is not to defer* death—this statement cloaks itself, through its negations and convolutions, in an appearance of profundity, which lends a kind of thinly-woven authority to the statement that follows.

by, between living actively in the face of inevitable death and waiting passively and obediently for that death to arrive, is to reveal oneself as incapable of (or uninterested in) coherent argument. Only a critic who cannot or will not see past his or her ideological commitments could expect to be taken seriously when advancing this argument. But this is the kind of reasoning required by the step-by-step, paint-by-numbers process of the hermeneutics of suspicion method of reading.

Finally, the fourth and most crucial step is to reveal the "hidden" meaning of the poem, which in this case means rewriting the entire *carpe diem* motif. For the critic, far from urging that life be lived to the fullest while there is yet time, Herrick's famous poem rushes headlong toward death, driven by its own desire into a form of suicide:

> The *carpe diem* strategy posits sexual pleasure as life-intensifying, and thus a defense against mortality; intense pleasure, whether in anticipation, experience, or memory, in a sense displaces the consciousness or fear of death. But sexuality viewed not as pleasure but as reproduction makes the individual, his experiences, his consciousness, and his very existence, superfluous, expendable. The only perfect defense against fear of death, against the paralyzing anxiety of the coy virgin, is death itself. [...] *Carpe diem* urges "satisfaction" of desire, the feeding of it, but to satisfy desire is to get rid of desire, to destroy desire in the total discharge of need that is accomplished by death. The final rosebud to be gathered is death itself [...] Aggression against the self thus occurs both in rejecting desire and in seeking it; the first denies to the self a range of possible experiences [...]; the second is that impulse through which is created the replacement for the self in the next generation [...] — to seek desire is thus, paradoxically, a form of indirect suicide.[99]

Here we have a veritable *tour de force* of sleights-of-hand,[100] reversals, and unsupported assertions dressing themselves up as arguments. *Sexuality as reproduction makes the individual expendable.* Proof? None is offered. *The only perfect defense against the fear of death is death itself.* Proof? None. *Seeking desire is a form of "indirect suicide"*. Proof? Of course not. The point of that final statement lies, not in any actual truth claim, but in its rhetorical effect. Dress up a series of counter-intuitive reversals

---

99 Ibid., 147–48.
100 Note the sly way in which the critic shifts the ground beneath sexuality from "pleasure" to "reproduction", before making the unsupported assertion that "reproduction makes the individual [...] expendable".

in negations and inverted syntax, repeat those reversals in forceful language, backed up by the "authority" lent by the reputable journal or publishing house which has printed the piece in which the reversals appear, and wait for compliant, graduate-school-trained readers to fall in line, and start repeating your claims in their presentations, papers, and other "intellectual" productions. After being put through this process, the poem that generations of readers thought they had read has nearly disappeared,[101] and the most famous of *carpe diem* poems has been transformed into a *carpe mortem* poem. From the critical point of view offered by Gilead, there is no call to life and love in "To the Virgins", only literary convention, the remorseless progress of time, and the inevitability of death.

Inherent in much of the criticism this book discusses are the twin ideas that literature inevitably serves the interests of the powerful, and that resistance is impossible. Jacques Lacan, for example, insists that resistance always traps one inside the discourse of the power one is resisting, "the revolutionary aspiration has only one possible outcome, always, the discourse of the master. This is what experience proves. What you aspire to as revolutionaries is a Master. You will have one".[102] From this point of view, criticism like Gilead's ends up arguing that the *appearance* of a radically life-affirming spirit in Herrick's poem actually undermines itself, and ends up affirming death. What is perhaps even more astonishing than these oddly authoritarian ideas is how little thought is necessary to put them to use in an interpretive process whose template-driven results are determined in advance of the reading: follow the steps, complete the formula, and *voilà*, the critic has "revealed" that a poem long-thought to say "X" actually says "not-X".

Gilead's article is an artifact of its time, the mid 1980's, and its place, a Ph.D. written at Northwestern University in 1980, during the peak of the

---

101 This is consistent with the "nothingness" de Man claims is at the heart of literature: "Here the human self has experienced the void within itself, and the invented fiction, far from filling the void, asserts itself as a pure nothingness, *our* nothingness stated and restated by a subject that is the agent of its own instability" (*Blindness and Insight*, 19).

102 "l'aspiration révolutionnaire, ça n'a qu'une chance d'aboutir, toujours, au discours du maître. C'est ce que l'expérience en a fait la preuve. Ce à quoi vous aspirez comme révolutionnaire, c'est à un Maître. Vous l'aurez" (Jacques Lacan. *Le Séminaire de Jacques Lacan, Livre XVII: L'envers de la Psychanalyse*, ed. by Jacques Alain Miller [Paris: Seuil, 1991], 239).

fascination with deconstruction that swept through English departments in American academia. But it is part of a much longer story in literary criticism and interpretation, one that stretches back all the way to Akiba and Origen and their insistence that the Song of Songs be read against its own text. Theological interpreters of the Song of Songs take great care in telling us that the poem's frankly erotic treatment of love between a man and a woman is really a metaphor for loving God. Modern academic criticism of the troubadours is at pains to assure us that the poetry does not actually mean what it merely appears to mean. Much new historicist and cultural materialist criticism of Shakespeare aims to convince us that despite their anti-authoritarian appearances, Shakespeare's plays are part of the apparatus of Elizabethan and Jacobean state control.[103] Many Donne scholars are particularly concerned with separating the poet's life from the poet's written work, as part of a strategy of larger claims that insist that the poems are misogynist and imperialist. And a critic like Gilead tells us that the message of the *carpe diem* motif in Herrick's "To the Virgins" is impossible to find: "The longer the reader searches for the *carpe diem* message in Herrick's obviously *carpe diem* poem, the greater difficulty she has in finding it. […] Herrick's poem disintegrates into a tangle of conflicting concepts, images, and tropes".[104]

Not to put too fine a point on it, this is a form of critical violence that works to undermine poetry's potential for resistance, and dismiss the sense that poetry is something that might be enjoyed. Such criticism is often written in the kind of deliberately obtuse language that illustrates Montaigne's maxim: "Difficulty is the currency that the learned employ, like tricksters, in order not to reveal the vanity of their art, and which human stupidity is easily led to take as payment".[105] Things do not seem

---

103 One notable exception to this trend has been Alexander Leggatt, who regrets what he calls "a current tendency to see society as a structure of oppression and exploitation, and to read Shakespeare accordingly" (Alexander Leggatt. *Shakespeare's Political Drama: The History Plays and the Roman Plays* [New York: Routledge, 2003], viii).

104 Gilead, 150.

105 "La difficulté est une monoye que les sçavans employent, comme les joueurs de passe-passe, pour ne descouvrir la vanité de leur art, et de la quelle l'humaine bestise se paye ayséement" (Michel de Montaigne. "Apologie de Raimond de Sebonde". In *Les Essais de Michel de Montaigne*, Vol. 2, ed. by Fortunat Strowski [Bordeaux: Pech, 1906], 234, https://archive.org/stream/lesessaisdemi02mont#page/234). Montaigne goes on to quote from Lucretius' *De Rerum Natura* 1.639, 641–42, speaking of the famously obscure Heraclitus, who was:

to have changed since Montaigne's time: as Felski notes, the "sheer difficulty [of a work] accentuate[s] its allure to a certain kind of critic, convinced, akin to Burke commenting on the sublime, that the obscure is inherently more affecting and awe-inspiring than the clear".[106] There is "a fannish dimension" to this work, "evidenced in a cult of exclusiveness and intense attachment to charismatic figures".[107] What this kind of literary criticism reveals is an antagonism toward poetry, or as Derrida describes it, with an eye on the tradition stretching back to Plato, an intolerance for poetry as a threat to the dominance of the prose-bound philosopher:

> the history of philosophy is the history of prose; or, if you will, the *prosifying* of the world. Philosophy is the invention of prose. Philosophy speaks in prose. [...] Before writing, verse served as a kind of spontaneous engraving, a writing *before* the letter. Intolerant of poetry, philosophy took writing to *be* the letter.[108]

        Clarus, ob obscurum linguam, magis inter inanes,
        Omnia enim stolidi magis admirantur amantque
        Inversis quae sub verbis latitantia cernunt.

        Celebrated for his obscurity, especially among the inane,
        For all the stupid greatly admire and love
        That which is concealed beneath inverted words.

    Aristotle makes a similar comment when he notes that "knowing themselves ignorant, men worship those whose speech lies above their reckoning" (συνειδότες δ᾽ ἑαυτοῖς ἄγνοιαν τοὺς μέγα τι καὶ ὑπὲρ αὐτοὺς λέγοντας θαυμάζουσιν) (Aristotle. *Nichomachean Ethics I*, ed. by H. Rackham [Loeb Classical Library, Cambridge, MA: Harvard University Press, 1926], 10, ll. 26–27). In writing of the Paul de Man affair, Robert Alter sounds like a modern (if somewhat angrier) Montaigne, as he describes the situation as one in which "to his American admirers, with their cultural inferiority complex, it seemed that if things were difficult to grasp, something profound was being said", and that de Man "got away with it because of the gullibility of American scholars" ("Paul de Man Was a Total Fraud". *New Republic*. April 5, 2014, https://newrepublic.com/article/117020/paul-de-man-was-total-fraud-evelyn-barish-reviewed).

106 Felski, *The Limits of Critique*, 27. This kind of devotion to the difficult can be seen in the almost *de rigueur* political contempt for the idea of clarity expressed (with ironic clarity) by Trink T. Minh-ha: "Clarity is a means of subjection, a quality both of official taught language and of correct writing, two old mates of power: together they flow, together they flower, vertically, to impose an order" (Trink T. Minh-ha. *Woman, Native, Other* [Bloomington, Indiana: Indiana University Press, 1989, 16–17).
107 Felski, *The Limits of Critique*, 27.
108 l'histoire de la philosophie est l'histoire de la prose; ou plutôt du devenir-prose du monde. La philosophie est l'invention de la prose. Le philosophe parle en prose. [...] Avant l'écriture, le vers serait en quelque sorte une gravure spontanée, une écriture avant la lettre. Intolérant à la poésie, le philosophe aurait pris l'écriture à la lettre.

Jacques Derrida. *De la Grammatologie*, 406. Emphasis added.

As de Man approvingly defines it, such criticism is "a methodologically motivated attack on the notion that a literary or poetic consciousness [...] can pretend to escape, to some degree, from the duplicity, the confusion, the untruth that we take for granted in the everyday use of language".[109] In the critic's terms, the old claim of the English Puritan William Prynne is revived: poetry is a lie, and a dangerous one at that.

Criticism dedicated to a "hermeneutics of suspicion" gives us no exit, no recourse as it continually rewrites poetry as compliant with authority (a move the critic couches in the guise of "unmasking" or "revealing" poetry's hidden ideological nature). In transforming or rewriting such poetry as appears to offer even the slightest glimmer of resistant possibility, the critic makes him or herself into an agent of the oppressive structures of authority, part of a vicious circle of ideology in which "the subject acts as it is acted by the system".[110] He or she does this through a criticism that is tinged with both compulsion and violence in a project which seems to disdain the very poetry it works with: witness the critic's celebration of violence in her reading of Herrick: "an interrogative reading [of Herrick's poem] parries with its anti-textual analytical violence the poem's assertion of its own innocence, and of the reader's innocent desire to preserve inviolate the simplicity, integrity, and obvious good sense of *carpe diem*".[111]

But a poem like "To the Virgins" *is* innocent, in the etymological sense of *harmless*. No virgins are oppressed or subjugated by being encouraged to live a little before they die; not even if the poem is interpreted as a seduction lyric is its advice harmful to anyone except to the extent to which they are locked within systems of control in a society in which female sexuality is regarded as a valuable commodity to be bought and sold by fathers and (father-chosen) husbands. A short, epigrammatic poem like "To Live Freely", condenses "To the Virgins" into two lines which only a critic devoted to suspicion could read with interrogative violence:

---

109 Paul de Man, *Blindness and Insight*, 9.
110 "le sujet agit en tant qu'il est agi par le système" (Louis Althusser. "Idéologie et Appareils Idéologiques d'État" [1970]. *Les Classiques des Sciences Sociales* [Quebec: Université du Québec à Chicoutimi], 44, http://classiques.uqac.ca/contemporains/althusser_louis/ideologie_et_AIE/ideologie_et_AIE.pdf).
111 Gilead, 150.

> Let's live in hast; use pleasures while we may:
> Co'd life return, 'twod never lose a day.[112]

"Let's" (let us) is directed toward all, male and female, young and old alike. "Pleasures" may, of course, be sexual pleasures, but they needn't be limited thereto (unless a critic has a particular ideological point to hammer home). A considerable effort will have to be invested in this short lyric to ensure that it "disintegrates into a tangle of conflicting concepts, images, and tropes" or becomes intelligible primarily as "a form of indirect suicide". Here, perhaps, the reading method of Rashi is what best serves: the plain meaning of this text is an exhortation to enjoy each day, each moment, because we are all running out of time. And could "life return", were we given, after the diagnosis of a fatal illness, a short reprieve, an extra week or month, or even year of life, how many of us would waste even a day on drudgery, obedience, and ascetic self-denial?[113] Perhaps those who read the poetry of life and love as being actually about a desire for death, but not many others.

In similar fashion, a poem like "To Daffadills" expresses grief at the shortness of life, and the fading of beauty, not to hide anything from the reader by disintegrating into "a tangle", not to seduce anyone, nor even to persuade, but merely to commiserate across time and distance, one mortal writer with countless equally mortal readers:

> Faire Daffadills, we weep to see
> You haste away so soone:

---

112 ll. 1–2, Herrick, Vol. 2, 115, https://books.google.com/books?id=C21DAQAAMAAJ&pg=PA115

113 These are the same kinds of questions that Dostoevsky's novel *The Idiot* (*Идиот*) poses as Prince Myshkin tells the story (based on Dostoevsky's own experience of a narrowly-averted execution) of a man who faced what he believed would be the last moments of his life, and suddenly thought of how precious time would be to him, if only he were spared:

What if I did not die! What if I came back to life-what infinity! And all this would be mine! I would then treat every minute as a century, not losing anything, calculate every minute, so as to spend none of them in vain!

Что, если бы не умирать! Что, если бы воротить жизнь,-какая бесконечность! И всё это было бы моё! Я бы тогда каждую минуту в целый век обратил, ничего бы не потерял, каждую бы минуту счетом отсчитывал, уж ничего бы даром не истратил!'

Fyodor Dostoevsky. *Идиот* [*The Idiot*] (St. Petersburg: A. Suvorin, 1884), 62.

> As yet the early-rising Sun
> Has not attain'd his Noone.
> Stay, stay,
> Untill the hasting day
> Has run
> But to the Even-song;
> And, having pray'd together, we
> Will go with you along.
> We have short time to stay, as you,
> We have as short a Spring;
> As quick a growth to meet Decay,
> As you, or any thing.
> We die,
> As your hours doe, and drie
> Away, Like to the Summers raine;
> Or as the pearles of Mornings dew
> Ne'r to be found againe.[114]

In the face of such awful and meaningless ephemerality, in a world where beauty is born seemingly for the purpose of decaying and dying and disappearing forever, how can anyone take seriously the idea that the *carpe diem* motif needs to be subjected to an "interrogative reading [that] parries with [...] analytical violence the poem's assertion of its own innocence"? The *carpe diem* poem *is itself* what interrogates the real (not merely interpretive) violence of a world in which life exists only to be snuffed out. The *carpe diem* motif in English poetry is a response to a world which seemed to many to be falling apart:

> [T]he instability of the political climate leading up to and during the English Civil War created more incentives for seizing immediate and temporary pleasures; the idea that the world was coming to its end had a sufficiently wide reach [...]. Many responded to this threat by devoting themselves to repentance and prayer, but others translated this anxiety into a kind of seductive energy, urging the pleasures of the day before the day was no more.[115]

---

114 ll. 1–19, Herrick, Vol. 2, 35, https://books.google.com/books?id=C21DAQAAMAAJ&pg=PA35
115 Targoff, 176.

With death lurking seemingly around every corner, and with the Christian promises of heaven seeming ever more remote to many,[116] who, like Hamlet, regarded death as the "undiscovered country from whose bourn / No traveller returns",[117] *carpe diem* made sense to many contemporary readers in an urgent, visceral way that transcends the cool detachments of our own frames of reference in reading and criticism. The daffodils of Herrick's poem are not merely a metaphor, they are a frailly beautiful but relentless reminder of death. From the speaker's point of view, the demise of daffodils is senseless, too hasty, and without any redemptive point or purpose, just like human death, for which there is no remedy, and to which there is no point. Humanity, in Shakespeare's terms, is "noble in reason, […] infinite in faculty!" But we are also merely a "quintessence of dust".[118] Herrick captures this tragic and perplexing quality by showing the aspiration and uselessness of prayer to a god for whom the deaths of human beings and daffodils appear to be matters of equally depraved indifference: "And, having pray'd together, we / Will go with you along".

From the daffodil to the man, death is the end of all lives and all joys, and while the Neoplatonized and Christianized poetic tradition of Dante and Petrarch assumed an afterlife in which greater joys (or greater torments) would be had by all, the *carpe diem* tradition is rather closer to the metaphysics on offer in *King Lear*, where "nothing", and "never" sum up the hopes for life and love after death. Thus, a poem like "To Youth" offers what is, from this perspective, the best possible advice. What point is there in sacrifice and prayer, when heaven seems indifferent to all living things below? Far better to

> Drink Wine, and live here blithefull, while ye may:
> The morrowes life to late is, Live to-day.[119]

---

116 This is the period in which the first stirrings of what we consider the modern form of Atheism are developing. For further discussion, see Michael Bryson, *The Atheist Milton* (London: Routledge, 2012).
117 *Hamlet* 3.1.81–82.
118 *Ibid.*, 2.2.273, 278.
119 ll. 1–2, Herrick, Vol. 2, 209, https://books.google.com/books?id=C21DAQAAMAAJ&pg=PA209

Herrick's poetry often displays a disregard for social and literary convention, exercising an imaginative freedom that allows him to portray the "imaginary mistresses" of his poems in ways that flout the expectations of his time and place:

> The subversive quality of Herrick's imaginary mistresses derives from their existence in a space imaginatively removed from the conventional restraints that limited women's freedom [...]. This device of creating imaginary women who exist outside social reality enables Herrick [to] be innovative, disruptive, even subversive in his depictions of gender roles.[120]

This freedom is created by the *carpe diem* theme itself. In a world in which "nothing" and "never" are our defining expectations of the afterlife, what does it matter if people disobey the conventions set by their societies and peers? Donne serves as an excellent example of the consequences that can ensue from flouting the customs of one's time and place, but in terms of the eternal death waiting for all of us, how much did it really matter that John Donne and Anne More married without something so temporal as the permission of a father who would soon be, and is now, dead forever? In Herrick's hands, the *carpe diem* motif begins to seem like the only rational response to a temporary existence for men and women who would not live as slaves to geographically and temporally fixed authority, and recognised that the "customs of [their] island and tribe are [not] the laws of nature".[121] Neither Herrick nor the *carpe diem* tradition can be fully understood without recognizing this subversive element:

> Trying to understand Herrick's poetry dealing with women without recognizing this subversive, parodic element only leads one into a pathless quagmire as far as interpretation goes. Herrick defies the limits of standard interpretation [...] using text and language, using poetic liturgy, as a means by which accepted injustices might be mollified and eventually perhaps even corrected.[122]

Rather than regarding Herrick through a more jaundiced lens as "the voyeuristic, effeminate pervert that many critics have suggested",[123]

---

120 David Landrum. "Robert Herrick and the Ambiguities of Gender". *Texas Studies in Literature and Language*, 49: 2 (2007), 195, https://doi.org/10.1353/tsl.2007.0012
121 Shaw, 119.
122 Landrum, 205–06.
123 *Ibid.*, 187.

or as the old man who inflicts his "geriatric gaze" on the "bouncing mistress" whom he expects to increase "the effort she must make to rouse his manhood"[124] when he can no longer "stand to" so quickly as he once did in his youth, seeing Herrick as both parodic and disrespectful of convention helps us understand the urgency of what is perhaps his second most famous poem, "Corinna's going a Maying".

In "Corinna" (whose titular mistress is a reference to the Corrina of Ovid's *Amores*), we have the entire *carpe diem* theme and all of its implications put together in a powerful and beautiful whole. In encouraging Corrina to "goe a Maying", Herrick's poem stands up for the joys of the May Day festival, a celebration of spring, fertility, and life, against the increasingly powerful efforts of Puritan authority figures to shut it down. On a day such as this, the poem suggests it would be a sin to refrain:

> When all the Birds have Mattens seyd,
> And sung their thankfull Hymnes: 'tis sin,
> Nay, profanation to keep in,
> Whenas a thousand Virgins on this day,
> Spring, sooner than the Lark, to fetch in May.[125]

For the Puritans, however, the "sin" was in the keeping of the celebration itself, given the dancing, sexual play, and occasional gender-bending that would go on:

> May Day was condemned by Puritan writers for the sexual license it encouraged; the phallic symbolism of the maypole was noted by many. [...] These processions contained a strong element of role reversal, for in some the [chimney] sweeps dressed as females [,] but music and collecting contributions from bystanders were common to all.[126]

By Herrick's day, the authorities had been trying, with limited success, to shut down the May Day celebrations for decades. Elizabethan

---

124 Ceri Sullivan. "The *carpe diem* topos and the 'geriatric gaze' in early modern verse". *Early Modern Literary Studies*, 14: 3 (January 2009), 8.1–21 http://extra.shu.ac.uk/emls/14–3/Sullcarp.html
125 Lines 10–14, Herrick, Vol. 1, 116, https://books.google.com/books?id=n14JAAAAQAAJ&pg=PA116
126 Joan Lane. *Apprenticeship in England, 1600–1914* (London: University College London Press, 1996), 95.

constables gave orders on several occasions for the maypoles to be pulled down, the festivals themselves to be prohibited, and any resisters to be arrested:

> In Shrewsbury in 1588, the maypole was banned and members of the shearmen's guild were jailed for opposing the order. At Banbury, Oxon, a Puritan center whose M. P. was Anthony Cope, the high constable ordered the parish constables to take down all maypoles and prohibit festivities in May 1589.[127]

By the 1630s, the political mood in England had grown dark and contentious, with many of the Puritan faction condemning nearly all entertainments as the works of the Devil. The year 1633 saw the publication of William Prynne's *Histriomastix*, a broadside against everything the author thought sinful in an England rapidly moving toward revolution and civil war. Prynne censures "prophane, and poysonous" plays as "the common Idole, and prevailing evill of our dissolute and degenerous Age",[128] describing them as "the Workes, and Pompes of the very Devill"[129] which deal with "nothing else but the Adulteries, Fornications, Rapes, Love-passions, Meritricious, Unchast, and Amorous practices of Lacivious Wicked men",[130] and have "the Divell himselfe for their author".[131] Prynne condemns dancing as "unavoydably sinfull and abominable",[132] and further denounces all "obscene, lacivious, lust-provoking Songs and Poems",[133] "effeminate, amorous, wanton Musicke",[134] and "May-games, Revels, dancing, and other unlawfull pastimes on the Lords day".[135]

In this environment, "Corinna's going a Maying" is hardly a light, conventional piece which can be dismissed as being about merely "the deceptive capacity of language to contain experience", or as a piece in which "textuality replaces sexuality" but all too soon "disintegrates into

---

127 Richard L. Greaves. *Society and Religion in Elizabethan England* (Minneapolis: University of Minnesota Press, 1981), 426.
128 William Prynne. *Histriomastix* (London: Printed by E. A. and W. I. for Michael Sparke, 1633), Sig. B1v, https://archive.org/stream/maspla00pryn#page/2
129 *Ibid.*, Sig. G2r, https://archive.org/stream/maspla00pryn#page/43
130 *Ibid.*, Sig. K3v, https://archive.org/stream/maspla00pryn#page/70
131 *Ibid.*, Sig. S1v, https://archive.org/stream/maspla00pryn#page/130
132 *Ibid.*, Sig. Ii1r, https://archive.org/stream/maspla00pryn#page/241
133 *Ibid.*, Sig. Ll3r, https://archive.org/stream/maspla00pryn#page/261
134 *Ibid.*, Sig. Nn4r, https://archive.org/stream/maspla00pryn#page/279
135 *Ibid.*, Sig. Kkkkk4r, https://archive.org/stream/maspla00pryn#page/n922

a tangle of conflicting concepts, images, and tropes". In the dark and dangerous mood of an increasingly agitated and Puritan-influenced England, "Corinna's going a Maying" is a radical affirmation of the simple, flesh-bound, sensual delights of being alive. Celebrating life against death—especially in an environment in which life is denigrated as sinful, while death is lauded as a final release from human wickedness—is in itself a revolutionary act. Herrick's point of view, far from being the conventional tangle of predictable, if contradictory tropes to which Gilead would reduce it, is far-reaching enough that it anticipates the radical freedom asserted by the twentieth-century existentialist Albert Camus, for whom the only sin was the sin against life itself, committed by refusing to live now because of promises or hopes of another life to come: "For if there is a sin against life, it is perhaps not so much in despair, as in hoping to have another life, and evading the implacable grandeur of this one".[136] For Camus, just as for Herrick, we are physical creatures whose loves, lives, and pleasures are neither beastly *nor* angelic, but fundamentally human; and the only truth worthy of the name lies in the acknowledgement of the ephemeral, and therefore precious, quality of human life:

> I realize that there is no superhuman happiness, no eternity outside of the arc of time. These trivial and basic necessities, these relative truths are the only things that move me. The others, the "ideals", I don't have soul enough to understand them. Not that we should be like beasts, but the happiness of angels is meaningless to me.[137]

For Herrick, the life here and now is perhaps the only truly sacred thing, and the only "sin" is found in refusing the joys of the sacredness of each never-to-be-repeated moment:

> Can such delights be in the street,
> And open fields, and we not see't?

---

[136] Car s'il y a un péché contre la vie, ce n'est peut-être pas tant d'en désespérer que d'espérer une autre vie, et se dérober à l'implacable grandeur de celle-ci.

Albert Camus. "L'été à Alger". In his *Noces suivi de L'été* (Paris: Gallimard, 1959), 49.

[137] J'apprends qu'il n'est pas de bonheur surhumain, pas d'éternité hors de la courbe des journées. Ces biens dérisoires et essentiels, ces vérités relatives sont les seules qui m'émeuvent. Les autres, les "idéales", je n'ai pas assez d'âme pour les comprendre. Non qu'il faille faire la bête, mais je ne trouve pas de sens au bonheur des anges.

Ibid., 47–48.

> Come, we'll abroad; and let's obey
> The Proclamation made for May:
> And sin no more, as we have done, by staying;
> But my Corinna, come, let's goe a Maying.[138]

Should they delay, or miss their chance, they will be showing themselves unworthy of the precious and rare gifts that this all too brief existence "rounded with a sleep",[139] offers to those reverent enough to appreciate them:

> Come, let us goe, while we are in our prime;
> And take the harmlesse follie of the time.
> We shall grow old apace, and die
> Before we know our liberty.
> Our life is short; and our dayes run
> As fast away as do's the Sunne:
> And as a vapour, or a drop of raine
> Once lost, can ne'r be found againe:
> So when or you or I are made
> A fable, song, or fleeting shade;
> All love, all liking, all delight
> Lies drown'd with us in endlesse night.
> Then while time serves, and we are but decaying;
> Come, my Corinna, come, let's goe a Maying.[140]

The passion for life, for love, for the sheer joy of sensation and experience overflows from this poem like a floodtide overwhelming the shore. Or so it does, at least, from the point of view of a *Peshat* style of reading, based on the "plain sense" hermeneutic of Rashi. However, from the point of view of Rabbi Akiba, or the early Church father Origen, or the theological readers devoted to the allegorical reading of texts, or the countless academic critics who practise a hermeneutics of suspicion, the poem is a blank canvas, to be written over in ways that suit the ideological demands of the particular and present moment. Such was

---

138 Lines 37–42, Herrick, Vol. 1, 118, https://books.google.com/books?id=n14JAAAAQAAJ&pg=PA118
139 *The Tempest* 4.1.158.
140 Lines 57–70, Herrick, Vol. 1, 119, https://books.google.com/books?id=n14JAAAAQAAJ&pg=PA119

the interpretive method approved by William Prynne, a man for whom no expressions of moral condemnation could go too far:

> [T]he obscenity, ribaldry, amorousnesse, heathenishnesse, and prophanesse of most Play-bookes, Arcadiaes, and fained Histories that are now so much in admiration, is such, that it is not lawfull for any (especially for Children, Youthes, or those of the female sex, who take most pleasure in them) so much as once to read them, for feare they should inflame their lusts, and draw them on to actuall lewdnesse, and prophanesse. Hence Origen, Hierom and others informe us that in ancient times Children and Youthes among the Jews were not permitted to read the Booke of Canticles [the Song of Songs] before they came to the age of 30 years, for feare they should draw those spirituall love passages to a carnall sence, and make them instruments to inflame their lusts.[141]

If the old saying is true that you can know someone by the company he or she keeps, then what are we to make of literary critics (and schools of criticism) whose working methods and assumptions are so compatible with those of William Prynne, a man who would shut down theaters, eliminate dancing, and deny even the reading of poetry to anyone who is not a male of thirty or older? William Kerrigan once observed that such ideologically-driven criticism had "disdain for the personal sphere of existence", and told an interesting story of a conversation between academics to illustrate his point:

> In the days when New Historicism was first in the air a prominent scholar explained to me over a beer that Herrick's lyrics on silks and petticoats were really about the vestment controversies. I must have chuckled. "What do you think they're about?" the scholar demanded. I shrugged. "Women's clothes?" Her icy expression let me know in no uncertain terms that great lyrics could not be attached to such unworthy objects.[142]

The "icy expression" of the humorless critic is the telling detail. We need, as Kerrigan notes, to find a way of writing about poems that "allows them to be what they seem to be",[143] because too many critics no longer read poetry so much as pillage it, occupy it, and force it to submit. When we end up looking and sounding like William Prynne,

---

141 Prynne, Sig. Aaaaaa2r-Aaaaaa2v, https://archive.org/stream/maspla00pryn#page/912
142 William Kerrigan. "Kiss Fancies in Robert Herrick". *George Herbert Journal*, 14: 1–2 (Fall 1990), 157, https://doi.org/10.1353/ghj.1990.0014
143 *Ibid.*

a humorless Puritan fanatic and ideologue, perhaps it really is time to pull back from gazing into the abyss.

Carpe diem poetry poses a simple choice. Will you live now, as you would if there were no laws—either human or divine, secular or theological—against the joys of life, the joys of love, the joys of living uninhibitedly in the fullest and most human and embodied sense? Or will you obey, do as you are told, refrain from the physical and passionate side of a life that you have been taught is sinful and shameful, spending your only years on Earth apologizing for being alive, apologizing for wanting the things you want but are convinced that you should not want? Will you take off the mind forg'd manacles? Or will you wear them, for the rest of your life, as you patiently and obediently wait for death?

Choose.

10. Paradise Lost: Love in Eden, and the Critics who Obey

To choose is not so easy as it sounds. "All choice is frightening, when one thinks about it: a terrifying liberty, unguided by a greater duty".[1] Choices open some doors, while closing others. New lives, new possibilities, often come at the expense of other lives now foreclosed or lost. The wages of *choice* are death, as every life leads, eventually, to that ending that may be the only true universal of the human experience—not the understanding or the experience of the end, but the physical cessation itself, the transition from animate to inert, from you to it. Authority figures—the imperious gods and kings, the angry Egeuses and Capulets of the world—insist that choice must be circumscribed, that only certain choices are allowable or legitimate, even when, as in the case of the Father in *Paradise Lost*, they insist that choice itself must remain free:

> Not free, what proof could they have giv'n sincere
> Of true allegiance, constant Faith, or Love,
> Where only what they needs must do appear'd,
> Not what they would? What praise could they receive?
> What pleasure I, from such obedience paid,
> When Will and Reason (Reason also is choice)
> Useless and vain, of freedom both despoil'd,

---

[1] "Tout choix est effrayant, quand on y songe: effrayante une liberté que ne guide plus un devoir" (André Gide. *Les Nourritures terrestres* [Paris: Gallimard, 1921], 14).

> Made passive both, had serv'd necessity,
> Not mee.[2]

From this perspective, however, the key function of choice is to elicit praise—praise for one's obedience, delivered by the authority figure who takes pleasure in being obeyed. Choice in the ruled, which includes by design the possibility of choosing not to obey, enhances the pleasures of power for the ruler. Subjects without choice, without free will, or with wills so broken as to be no longer functional, offer this kind of sublimely sadistic ruler no satisfaction: *what pleasure I, from such obedience paid*? The pleasure is precisely in the sensation of an active and functioning will submitting to your own. In the case of those who choose incorrectly, those who disobey, the necessary and enjoyable response for the ruler is to inflict punishment, up to and including death:

> He, with his whole posterity must die,
> Die hee or justice must;[3]

At first glance, *Paradise Lost* might seem an odd choice with which to illustrate the primacy of human love and choice, over the imperious demands of authority that even the most arbitrary of dictates be unquestioningly obeyed. After all, does not Milton's epic poem relate the "tragic" consequences of disobedience to God, representing Adam's choice to eat the forbidden fruit along with Eve as foolish, and uxorious—the result of an excessive and misguided love for Eve over God? Such is the impression given by much of the criticism of Milton's poem, which the English historian Christopher Hill describes as a self-confirming enterprise "whose vast output appears to be concerned less with what Milton wrote [...] than with the views of Professor Blank on the views of Professor Schrank on the views of Professor Rank on what Milton may or may not have written".[4] William Empson compares such criticism to the kinds of groupthink that insist "a man ought to concur with any herd in which he happens to find himself".[5]

---

2   John Milton. *Paradise Lost* 3.103–11.
3   *Ibid.*, 3.209–10.
4   Christopher Hill. *Milton and the English Revolution* (London: Faber and Faber, 1977), 3.
5   William Empson. *Milton's God* (Norfolk, CT: New Directions, 1961), 231.

In this case, the "herd" has spent decades of scholarly and interpretive energy convincing itself that Adam's choice in *Paradise Lost*, Book 9, is the "fallen" choice of a disobedient sinner and an effeminate fool. As so often in the criticism we have encountered, the voice of authority can be heard loudly and clearly as it pronounces for obedience and against love. Milton criticism, which Will Stockton calls "a hell of ideological conservatives"[6] is a near perfect example: with a few important exceptions, the "Milton industry"[7] has lined up on the side of God, obedience, and submission where the question of Adam's choice is concerned, many even suggesting that Adam should have been written differently, so as to make the choice the critic confidently declares the only possible "correct" decision.[8]

As Milton writes the scene, Adam is suddenly confronted with an Eve who has disobeyed the primary injunction given to the first human pair, not to eat of the fruit from the tree of the knowledge of good and evil. His reaction, at first, is to silently bemoan her decision to disobey God:

> Speechless he stood and pale, till thus at length
> First to himself he inward silence broke.
> O fairest of Creation, last and best
> Of all God's Works, Creature in whom excell'd
> Whatever can to sight or thought be form'd,

---

6   Will Stockton. "An Introduction Justifying Queer Ways". *Early Modern Culture: An Electronic Seminar*. Issue 10. *Queer Milton*, ed. by Will Stockton and David L. Orvis, http://emc.eserver.org/1-10/stockton.html
7   Hill, 3.
8   Peter Herman notes that the trend of critics rewriting Milton goes all the way back to the seventeenth-and eighteenth-century Cambridge professor and classical scholar Richard Bentley. "Bentley decided that Milton could not possibly have meant what got published as *Paradise Lost*, and so he offered (in the notes) suggestions for what Milton really *meant* to write" (*Destabilizing Milton: "Paradise Lost" and the Poetics of Incertitude* [New York: Palgrave MacMillan, 2005], 12). Herman further remarks that though "a distance of 300 years separates [...] Bentley from twentieth- and early-twenty-first-century Milton criticism, the fundamental assumptions governing the reading of *Paradise Lost* have remained largely the same" (14). For Empson, Bentley's now-infamous 1732 edition of *Paradise Lost* "makes one feel that Bentley is trying to write his own poetry" (*Some Versions of Pastoral* [London: Chatto & Windus, 1935], 150). And as Gilbert Highet notes, "This was not the last time that an arrogant professor was to spoil great poetry in the belief that, while the poet had been blind, he himself could see perfectly" (*The Classical Tradition: Greek and Roman Influences on Western Literature* [New York and Oxford: Oxford University Press, 1949], 285).

> Holy, divine, good, amiable, or sweet!
> How art thou lost, how on a sudden lost,
> Defac't, deflow'r'd, and now to Death devote?
> Rather how hast thou yielded to transgress
> The strict forbiddance, how to violate
> The sacred Fruit forbidd'n![9]

It should be noted that Adam thinks this *inwardly*, relating none of this to Eve herself. Until this point, he is with the critics whose orthodox frames of reference lead them to perceive disobedience as the great original sin that led, once upon a time, to the mixed human condition of joy and pain, life and loss, hope and despair that is the definition of "fallen".

William Blake, *The Temptation and Fall of Eve*.
Illustration to Milton's *Paradise Lost* (1808).[10]

Adam's love and admiration for Eve come through clearly in these lines, even as he decries her decision: she is the "fairest of Creation", the "last and best / Of all God's works", even though she is—so far as Adam can tell—"lost" and now "to Death devote". He believes this latter, of course, because as he twice relates, the poem's God has told him that the penalty for eating the forbidden fruit is death. He speaks of this early

---

9   *Paradise Lost* 9.894–904.
10 https://commons.wikimedia.org/wiki/File:William_Blake_-_The_Temptation_and_Fall_of_Eve_(Illustration_to_Milton's_"Paradise_Lost")_-_Google_Art_Project.jpg

on with Eve: "God hath pronounc't it death to taste that Tree",[11] and then later with the angel Raphael, where he tells the story of what God told him:

> [...] of the Tree whose operation brings
> Knowledge of good and ill, which I have set
> The Pledge of thy Obedience and thy Faith,
> Amid the Garden by the Tree of Life,
> Remember what I warn thee, shun to taste,
> And shun the bitter consequence: for know,
> The day thou eat'st thereof, my sole command
> Transgrest, inevitably thou shalt dye.[12]

Adam, in this crisis moment, has nothing more than these words to fall back on, and is thus certain that Eve will die. And as A. J. A. Waldock notes, "it seems hardly fair to blame [Adam] for taking God at his word".[13]

As Adam stands before Eve, still processing the gravity of her choice, and the consequences that have been threatened for doing precisely what Eve has now done, he decides, in the space of perhaps only the shortest of awkward pauses, to face with her whatever will ensue, up to and including death:

> [...] some cursed fraud
> Of Enemy hath beguil'd thee, yet unknown,
> And mee with thee hath ruin'd, for with thee
> Certain my resolution is to Die;
> How can I live without thee, how forgo
> Thy sweet Converse and Love so dearly join'd,
> To live again in these wild Woods forlorn?
> Should God create another Eve, and I
> Another Rib afford, yet loss of thee
> Would never from my heart; no no, I feel
> The Link of Nature draw me: Flesh of Flesh,
> Bone of my Bone thou art, and from thy State
> Mine never shall be parted, bliss or woe.[14]

---

11 *Paradise Lost* 4.427.
12 *Ibid.*, 8.323–30.
13 A. J. A Waldock. *Paradise Lost and its Critics* (Cambridge: Cambridge University Press, 1947), 56.
14 *Paradise Lost* 9.904–16.

Adam thinks all this in silence before he speaks to Eve. And though the narrative voice of the poem insists that Adam is "fondly overcome with Female charm",[15] this is the same narrative voice that throughout the poem demands that readers deny the evidence of what they have just read, or spin the words in favor of heaven (and thus obedience). This narrative voice is so eager to redirect readers (rather like some modern critics) that it sometimes simply gets its facts wrong in its rush to impose the desired spin. For example, at the beginning of Book 4, the archangel Uriel is able to see through Satan's disguise because of the latter's cloudy and tempestuous emotions: Satan's "borrow'd visage" was "marr'd" by "pale, ire, envy, and despair". The narrative voice then insists that readers understand that "heav'nly minds from such distempers foul / Are ever clear",[16] but this turns out to be not quite true: "ire" lurks in a variety of "heav'nly minds" throughout the poem. The "ire" of the Son is referred to by Raphael at 6.843. The "just avenging ire" of God is celebrated by the angels at 7.184. Michael speaks of how "willingly God doth remit his Ire" at 9.885. The "ire" of the Father is also spoken of repeatedly by Satan and his followers, and this, perhaps, is one time when they just might be trusted after all.

Against the insistence of the narrator, John Peter notes that there is an ambiguity in "fondly" that can be read positively: "Adam falls 'fondly'—foolishly, lovingly. And we fall with him, sharing his generous improvidence, trusting his love".[17] Waldock concurs, arguing that "[if] Adam's words are permitted to have the meanings that words usually have in English, these lines mean *love*".[18] But C. S. Lewis begs to differ. For the great orthodox critic, whose stated ambition about *Paradise Lost* is to "prevent the reader from ever raising certain questions",[19] love is not the correct term. In Lewis' description, "Adam fell by uxoriousness",[20] and failed the test of absolute value:

> If conjugal love were the highest value in Adam's world, then of course his resolve would have been the correct one. But if there are things that

---

15 *Ibid.*, 9.999.
16 *Ibid.*, 4.115–19.
17 John Peter. *A Critique of Paradise Lost* (New York: Columbia University Press, 1960), 133.
18 Waldock, 46.
19 C. S. Lewis. *A Preface to Paradise Lost* (London: Oxford University Press, 1942), 69.
20 *Ibid.*, 122.

have an even higher claim on a man, if the universe is imagined to be such that, when the pinch comes, a man ought to reject wife and mother and his own life also, then the case is altered, and then Adam can do no good to Eve (as, in fact, he does no good) by becoming her accomplice.[21]

What is interesting and ironic about Lewis' stance is how high a bar he sets for Adam. In dismissing Adam's love for Eve as "uxoriousness", Lewis is working the same mines in which Stephen Greenblatt will later dig when he characterizes Othello as being too much in love with his wife:

> *Omnis amator feruentior est adulter*, goes the Stoic epigram, and Saint Jerome does not hesitate to draw the inevitable inference: "An adulterer is he who is too ardent a lover of his wife". Jerome quotes Seneca: "All love of another's wife is shameful; so too, too much love of your own. A wise man ought to love his wife with judgment, not affection. Let him control his impulses and not be borne headlong into copulation. Nothing is fouler than to love a wife like an adulteress… Let them show themselves to their wives not as lovers, but as husbands".[22]

Jerome's Latin[23] becomes a commonplace of anti-erotic Christian polemic in the early modern era. This reflects a long-term attempt by the Church, which gained momentum among the Gregorian reformers of the eleventh and twelfth centuries, "to outlaw sexual pleasure for all Christians", insisting that sexual pleasure was sinful, and that even pleasureless sexual encounters in a marriage were enough to "permanently taint both soul and body".[24] It reappears, in slightly altered form, in the fifteenth-century Flemish monk Dionysius the Carthusian: "Therefore, a wise dictum is, that every too-fervent lover is an adulterer, such that, all things being equal, his [love of his wife] is no marriage, but like an adulterous passion in its continual approaches, and the same is the case if the wife is a too-fervent lover of her husband".[25] Calvin

---

21 Ibid., 123.
22 Greenblatt, *Renaissance Self-Fashioning*, 247–48.
23 Adulter est inquit in sua uxore amator ardentior. In aliena quippe uxore ois amor turpis est, in sua nimius. Sapies uir iudicio debet amare coiugem, no affectu. Reget impetus uoluptatis, nec praeceps feretur in coitu, nihil est foedius q uxore amare quasi adulteram… nec amatores uxoribus se exhibeat, sed maritos.

Jerome. *Contra Jovinianum* (Vienna: Joannes Singrenius, 1516), 43, https://books.google.com/books?id=SUZRAAAAcAAJ&dq=Contra Jovinianum&pg=PA43

24 Reddy, 3–4.
25 "Vnde a sapientib dictum est, q, omnis amator feruentior est adulter, videlicet cp no maritali, sed adulterino affectu cōiugē suā accedit, & idē est si coniunx sit

expresses the same idea in the sixteenth century: "a marriage contracted in the Lord, should not overflow into extremes of wantonness. Ambrose gravely, but not unworthily noted his opinion, that when a man has no modesty or dignity in conjugal relations, he is an adulterer with his wife".[26]

One might wonder at the continual repetition of this idea by clerics whose sexuality is ostensibly sublimated into "spiritual" pursuits, and wonder again at the attractiveness of this idea for presumably "secular" academic critics, but that would be a book in itself. In the present case, this seems an unfair standard to apply to Adam's love for Eve, especially since in his conversations with Raphael, his mentions of passion are few, while his mentions of his admiration for Eve's wisdom and intelligence are many, indicating a relative standard of values that hardly qualifies as uxorious. What relation Lewis' own attraction to what he calls "the sensuality of cruelty" (expressed in the form of whipping)[27] plays in his enthusiasm for condemning Adam's relatively milder passions is unclear, though perhaps Adorno's observation is illuminating: "[t]he individual who has been forced to give up basic pleasures and to live under a system of rigid restraints, [...] is likely not only to seek an object upon which he can 'take it out' but also to be particularly annoyed at the idea that another person is 'getting away with something'".[28]

Empson disagrees with Lewis' entire line of thought, arguing, as John Leonard notes, that "Adam makes the right moral choice when he chooses to die for love".[29] John Peter agrees, claiming that "the highest

---

viri sui amatrix feruetior" (Dionysius the Carthusian. *Epistolarum ac Euangeliorum* [Cologne: Petrus Quentell, 1537], fol. LVII, https://books.google.com/books?id=CqP4kICSulwC&dq=Epistolarum ac Euangeliorum&pg=PT114).

26 "coniugium in Domino contractum, non in extremam quanque lasciuiam exundare. Ambrosius graui quidem, sed non indigna sententia notauit, quum vxoris adulterum vocauit qui in coniugali nullam verecundiae vel honestatis curam habet" (Jean Calvin. *Institutio Christianae Religionis* [Geneva: Oliua Roberti Stephani, 1559], 2.8.44, 139, https://books.google.com/books?id=6ysy-UX89f4C&pg=PA139).

27 Alister McGrath. *C. S. Lewis A Life: Eccentric Genius, Reluctant Prophet* (Carol Stream, IL: Tyndale House Publishers, 2013), 61–62.

28 Adorno, Theodore. "Studies in the Authoritarian Personality". In T. W. Adorno, Else Frenkel-Brunswik, Daniel J. Levinson, and R. Nevitt Sanford, *The Authoritarian Personality*, Vol. I of *Studies in Prejudice*, ed. by Max Horkheimer and Samuel H. Flowerman (Social Studies Series: Publication No. III) (New York: Harper & Brothers, 1950), 199, https://www.scribd.com/doc/35738019/Adorno-Theodor-W-Studies-in-the-Authoritarian-Personality).

29 John Leonard. *Faithful Labourers: A Reception History of Paradise Lost, 1667–1970, Vol. 2. Interpretive Issues* (Oxford: Oxford University Press, 2013), 633.

degree of human love as we know it, is now the focus of attention, and Adam and Eve's speeches emphasize its power. [...] Adam's devotion to his wife can fairly be called magnificent, and we should be less than human if we did not admire and honor him for it".[30] And yet, many critics not only do not "admire and honor him for it", they actively condemn Adam for the choice he makes (the choice his poetic creator, following scripture and existing literary tradition, has him make). As Leonard has demonstrated, the attitude among modern critics has often been one of condemnation of Adam's action along with speculation about what he *should* have done, which implicitly is a criticism of Milton for writing the scene as he did. For these critics, "[t]he question inevitably arises: 'What else could Adam have done?' Lewis is the first critic to raise this question, but he declines to engage with it".[31] In Lewis' treatment, the matter is uncertain, but he takes Adam to task for what Waldock describes as "taking God at his word":

> For all Adam knew, God might have had other cards in His hand; but Adam never raised the question, and now nobody will ever know. [...] Perhaps God would have killed Eve and left Adam "in those wilde Woods forlorn" [...]. But then again, perhaps not. You can find out only by trying it. The only thing Adam knows is that he must hold the fort, and he does not hold it.[32]

Later critics like Irene Samuel, Dennis Burden, and Stanley Fish will, as Leonard observes, "speculate about missed opportunities and possible remedies".[33] Samuel argues that Adam should "have risked himself to redeem Eve",[34] going on to argue that he should have maintained "faith that the benevolence he had always known would remain benevolent",[35] a pious observation that Empson wryly counters with his own remark that *Paradise Lost*'s "God is [...] peculiarly unfitted to inspire trust".[36] Burden asserts that Adam should have divorced Eve, an astounding rewriting of a poem in which such a concept does not even exist: "the

---

30 Peter, 132.
31 Leonard, 617.
32 Lewis, *A Preface to Paradise Lost*, 123.
33 Leonard, 624.
34 Irene Samuel. "The Dialogue in Heaven: A Reconsideration of Paradise Lost, III. 1–417". *PMLA*, 72: 4 (Sep., 1957), 611.
35 *Ibid.*
36 Empson, *Milton's God*, 189.

important thing is that Adam has a remedy and Milton of all people must know it,[37] and "[w]hat he should do is leave her. He would have good grounds for divorce".[38] *Yes, by all means, divorce her and leave her to die.* A better summation of the "less than human" responses of all too many critics to this scene is quite nearly impossible to find.

At this point, it is necessary to ask on what basis critics ground their contentions about what Adam *should* have done, rather than what he does. For example, consider Samuel's insistence—as Leonard describes it—that "Adam could have (and should have) saved Eve by dying in her place".[39] What indication do readers have that God would have accepted such an arrangement, and what is more, kept his word about it? His rhetoric is absolute—"Die hee or Justice must"[40]—and the Son even has difficulty in corralling God into an agreement to show mankind "Mercy"[41] in exchange for his own torture and execution. This does not sound like the kind of character likely to show anything like understanding or lenience for Eve, despite the arguments of what must finally be called the Obedience Chorus in Milton studies. Rather than a ruler that would offer mercy, *Paradise Lost*'s God seems rather more like Angelo from Shakespeare's *Measure for Measure*, a character who would accept Adam's sacrifice, then kill Eve anyway.

But not to be outdone in his enthusiasm for obedience, Stanley Fish takes the argument for what Adam *should* have done even further than Samuel or Burden. Fish "takes it as axiomatic that a freely chosen Fall cannot be understood",[42] and then spends hundreds of pages explaining it:

> If the Fall is explained or "understood" it is no longer free, but the result of some analysable "process" which attracts to itself a part of the guilt. Thus freedom of will is denied, the obloquy of the action returns to God

---

37 This is a reference to Milton's own writings (*Doctrine and Discipline of Divorce*, among other works) in an England where Burden's "remedy" was all but impossible for most people to obtain.
38 Dennis Burden. *The Logical Epic: A Study of the Argument of "Paradise Lost'* (Cambridge, MA: Harvard University Press, 1967), 169–170; also quoted in Leonard, 643.
39 Leonard, 637.
40 *Paradise Lost* 3.210.
41 *Ibid.*, 3.134.
42 Leonard, 637.

(who set the process in motion), and again reason—the reader's reason—has given law to God.[43]

According to Fish, we can't have readers giving law to God, even though that "God" is merely a literary character.[44] For Fish, Adam's choice of Eve is selfish—he makes her, in fact, a victim: "for by choosing her he implicates her in his idolatry, absorbing her into a love that is self-love".[45] Here, once again, is the what-seems-to-be-X-is-actually-Y move, as Fish claims that Adam's romantic outburst is really love of self.

Asking "What, then, ought Adam to have done?" Fish acknowledges that anything other than what *Paradise Lost* actually gives us "would seem forced and 'unnatural' in comparison to what he does do".[46] Not to be daunted by a little thing like that, however, Fish goes on to develop further Samuel's suggestion that Adam should have interceded with God on Eve's behalf:

> He might have said to Eve, "what you say is persuasive (impregn'd with reason to my seeming), but I would rather not make such a momentous decision without further reflection'. Or, as Lewis suggested, he might have 'chastised Eve and then interceded with God on her behalf. [Or as Irene Samuel suggests,] he 'might, like the Son, have risked himself to redeem Eve".[47]

Fish's first suggestion demonstrates the wide gap that too often exists between poet and critic. There is no music in Fish's would-be emendation, and one almost gets the sense that Fish is ridiculing his own suggestion by the time the word "impregn'd" lumbers along. His second and third suggestions follow other critics with whom Fish shares a desire to rewrite the scene, and thus the suggestions are simply pointless, unless the object is to raise the critic above the poetry and to tell readers more about the critic's desires, commitments, and complexes than about the ideas and structures of the poem.

More recent criticism has continued along the lines of Lewis, Samuel, Burden, and Fish. As Leonard points out, "The question of what Adam

---

43 Stanley Fish. *Surprised by Sin: The Reader in "Paradise Lost"*. 2nd ed. (Cambridge, MA: Harvard University Press, 1998, 256–57.
44 As John Peter rather dryly notes: "this is a character in a poem" (9).
45 Fish, *Surprised by Sin*, 263.
46 Ibid., 269.
47 Ibid., 269–70.

should have done is still an issue in Milton criticism",[48] which, if anything, indicates the tenuous connection much literary criticism has to reality. Waldock's observation that Lewis "declines to acknowledge the facts of the poem",[49] could be applied much more broadly now than in 1947. Dennis Danielson pursues the question in this way:

> Given Eve's fall, does Adam face a dilemma: either to disobey God or else to break the bond of human love, whose goodness we perceive as fundamental? And if Adam has no choice but to reject the sinner with the sin, or else to accept the sin with the sinner, then will most of us applaud Adam's choosing the latter?[50]

Danielson answers his own questions by saying that Adam "could have [offered] to take the punishment of fallen humanity on himself, to fulfill exactly "The law of God", as Michael puts it in Book 12".[51] And here, at last, we have a key to understanding the mentality of those who would rewrite Milton's scene: obedience and "love" go hand-in-hand in a way that for Danielson is illustrated by "the analogy between Adam-and-Eve and Christ-and-the-church", which according to a Christianizing critic like Danielson "breaks down precisely at the point where Adam chooses to sin with Eve rather than sinlessly face death for her".[52] Danielson manages to turn a scene of intense human emotion, of love and Adam's all-too-human realization of how utterly bereft he would be in a world without Eve, into a scene advertising the obedient virtues of human sacrifice, dying in supplication rather than defiance. Danielson claims, with all seriousness, that Adam's love for Eve should be given its highest form of expression through the same mechanism by which human beings in the pre-scientific ages of our species have tried to propitiate the implacable gods for millennia.

As Ludwig Feuerbach, the great nineteenth-century critic of Christianity, puts it, human sacrifice is at the heart of the religious worldview:

> Bloody human sacrifices are, in fact, the most rawly sensual expressions of the mysteries of religion. Where bloody human sacrifices are offered

---

48 Leonard, 624.
49 Waldock, 30.
50 Dennis Danielson. "Through the Telescope of Typology: What Adam Should Have Done". *Milton Quarterly*, 23: 3 (1989), 121.
51 Ibid., 124.
52 Ibid.

to God, they are offered as the highest form of life for the highest good. That's why one sacrifices life to God, in exceptional circumstances. It is believed therefore to give him the greatest honor.[53]

In Feuerbach's analysis, "only human blood makes God merciful, and stills his wrath".[54] Such a god, as Empson argues, is not worthy of worship:

> Men always try to imitate their gods, so that to worship a wicked one is sure to make them behave badly. But no god before had ever known before how to be so eerily and profoundly wicked. [...] The Christian God, the Father, the God of Tertullian, Augustine and Aquinas, is the wickedest thing yet invented by the black heart of man.[55]

Nor is a literary representation of such a God—the Father of *Paradise Lost*—worthy of the sacrifice of one of the poem's human characters, or the strangely submissive admiration of literary critics. In Empson's closing phrase, "If you praise it as the neo-Christians do, what you are getting from it is evil".[56]

More recent critics have persisted in arguing that the poem should be other than it is, and that Adam should choose differently than he does. Gerald Richman argues that Adam should have remonstrated with Eve in the way that Abdiel does with Satan in Book 5 of *Paradise Lost*. Richman claims that "if Eve had repented and Adam had refused to join her in sin, Eve would have found pardon".[57] Gordon Teskey argues that "Adam should trust God to find a better solution than his own. He forgot to trust, and might have remembered to if he had taken more time",[58] as if Milton's Adam is standing there with Eve muttering, "wait, I'm forgetting something…Eve, can you give me a minute?…I've

---

53 Das blutiger Menschenopfer sind in der Tat nur roh-sinnliche Ausdrücke von dem Geheimnissen der Religion. Wo blutige Menschenopfer Gott dargebracht werden, da gelten diese Opfer für die höchsten, das sinnliche Leben für das höchste Gut. Deswegen opfert man das Leben Gott auf, und zwar in außerordentlichen Fällen; man glaubt, damit ihm die größte Ehre zu erweisen.

Ludwig Feuerbach. *Das Wesen des Christentums*, ed. by Werner Schuffenhauer (Berlin: De Gruyter, 2006), 446.

54 "nur sein menschliches Blut macht Gott barmherzig, stillt seinen Zorn" (*ibid.*, 101).
55 Empson, *Milton's God*, 247, 251.
56 *Ibid.*, 277.
57 Gerald Richman. "A Third Choice: Adam, Eve, and Abdiel". *Early Modern Literary Studies*, 9: 2 (September 2003), 6.1–5, https://extra.shu.ac.uk/emls/09-2/richthir.html
58 Gordon Teskey. *The Poetry of John Milton* (Cambridge: Harvard University Press, 2015), 462. The Milton Society of America recently gave Teskey its highest award for the book containing this argument.

got it! *I should trust God!*" The continuing insistence that the literary character called God in *Paradise Lost* is in what Richard of Gloucester might call the "[for]giving vein"[59] is astounding, and while Teskey claims that he finds himself "a little bored by [...] discussions of the frigidity, or the wickedness, or the goodness of Milton's God",[60] here he lays his cards on the table: Adam should have remembered to trust what Teskey (following along with Lewis, Samuel, Burden, Fish, and Danielson) simply assumes is a good and merciful "God".[61] And so the Hippias of Thasos-styled rewriting of the poem in the image of its more pious critics[62] goes on and on (Teskey even refers back to C. S. Lewis as he delivers his judgment).

David Quint argues a more humane case, writing that Adam's is "an act that combines marital love, human solidarity, and Adam's fear of repeating his earlier loneliness before Eve's creation",[63] thus taking at least a brief break from the decades-long trend of moralizing over, and rewriting, Milton's scene. Quint emphasizes that it is "the force of his love [that] causes Adam to stay by [Eve's] side", and describes the narrative voice that accuses Adam of being "fondly overcome" as "censorious".[64] But despite Quint's more sympathetic reading, the Obedience Chorus has not left the stage, and perhaps never will; for as long as there are those among us who are more comfortable when subordinate to another—or who benefit from such subordination — there will be those who argue for necessary and natural subordination. Such ideas go back as far as Aristotle, thus it is no surprise to see Stanley

---

59 *Richard III*, 4.2.114.
60 Teskey, xiii.
61 Teskey seems to try having it both ways, however. Not long after arguing that Adam "forgot to trust", he goes on to claim that "Adam's decision to remain with Eve is moving, and surely right". He then maintains that "[t]he place of criticism is not to take sides at such moments" (464), a high-minded and disingenuous statement coming from someone who just took sides two pages earlier by arguing (very much in the tradition of Lewis, Samuels, Fish, and Danielson) that Adam should have chosen otherwise than he did. That's exactly what "tak[ing] sides at such moments" looks like.
62 The (probably misnamed) critic described by Aristotle (*Poetics*, 1461a, 22–23) as trying to save Zeus' honesty by suggesting that "δίδομεν" should be changed to "διδόμεν" in the speech in which Zeus sends a dream to Agammenon in Book 2 of the *Illiad*.
63 David Quint. *Inside Paradise Lost: Reading the Designs of Milton's Epic* (Princeton: Princeton University Press, 2014), 153.
64 *Ibid.*, 178.

Fish, as recently as in 2001's *How Milton Works*, arguing that obedience is Milton's single overarching idea:

> In Milton's world, however, there are no moral ambiguities, because there are no equally compelling values. There is only one value—the value of obedience—and not only is it a mistake to grant independence to values other than the value of obedience, it is a temptation. Indeed, it is *the* temptation—the temptation to seek a separate, self-sustaining existence—that Milton obsessively explores.[65]

A poet who sees the world as a simple matter of obedience and disobedience has done something rather odd in writing an epic poem in which he does nearly everything possible to convince readers that such things are not so simple as moralists like Fish claim (Fish will say, of course, that the idea that things are not simple is "a temptation"). A poet for whom "there are no equally compelling values" (at least when compared to the delights of obedience and submission) has done an even odder thing by writing a long work in which compelling values are put into nearly constant conflict and competition.

But those who see the poetry of Donne as "sick" will go on doing so, just as those who see the poetry of a revolutionary as a nearly endless hymn singing the praises and glories of obedience will go on doing so. In fact, the entire trend of critics insisting that Milton's Adam should have chosen otherwise than he does, resembles nothing so much as fundamentalist Christian thinking. Consider this passage on the same subject from *The Watchtower*, the publication arm of the Jehovah's Witnesses:

> Adam decided to accede to the wishes of his wife, who had already chosen to eat from the forbidden tree. His desire to please her was greater than his desire to obey his Creator. Surely, upon being presented with the forbidden fruit, Adam should have paused to reflect on the effect that disobedience would have on his relationship with God. Without a deep, unbreakable love of God, Adam was vulnerable to pressure, including that from his wife.[66]

---

65 Stanley Fish. *How Milton Works* (Cambridge, MA: Belknap Press of Harvard University Press, 2001), 53.
66 "If Adam was Perfect, How Was It Possible for Him to Sin?" *The Watchtower*, 129: 19 (1 October 2008), 27, https://wol.jw.org/en/wol/d/r1/lp-e/2008733

Given the difficulty of telling the difference between evangelists and academics on this topic, it is tempting to conclude that there has been little or no progress in the treatment of poetry over the last two millennia. Critics who make an interpretive principle out of faith in an authoritarian deity are not to be reasoned with, any more than they aim to reason about the faith they seek to impose on poetry. As David Hawkes argues, "the habits of thought developed by slavery are easily formed and hard to break".[67]

That we seem to have forgotten, or deliberately elided, Milton's status as a revolutionary—not a stiff-collared Puritan or a humorless William Prynne-style ideologue who never met a human joy he did not condemn—is an ironic testament to the increasingly authoritarian political character of our own time. It was not always so, as Hawkes reminds us:

> The Romantic poets worshipped him; Byron, Keats and Shelley were restrained from making him a god only by his own stern injunctions against idolotry. Wordsworth called for a Miltonic response to the industrial age [...]. The founding fathers of America saw themselves as completing the Miltonic reforms that had been thwarted in England. Karl Marx cited him as the ultimate exemplar of unalienated human activity.[68]

And yet somehow, today, Milton has been transformed into a prophet of obedience, a preacher of original sin, and a poet whose work inspires the crushing authoritarianism reflected in numerous critics' assertions that Adam should choose obedience over love. In Hawkes's view, this transformation began with "a critical campaign waged in the early twentieth century by T. S. Eliot and F. R. Leavis", who were "nostalgic for the world [Milton] helped to destroy".[69] Eliot, a poet and critic whose "solution", is "an extreme right-wing authoritarianism" in which "men and women must sacrifice their petty 'personalities' and opinions to an impersonal order",[70] provides a template for the history of Milton criticism in the twentieth century and until very recently in the twenty-first. This history has been dominated (with notable exceptions like

---

67 David Hawkes. *John Milton, A Hero of Our Time* (Berkeley: Counterpoint Press, 2009), 10.
68 Hawkes, 12.
69 *Ibid.*, 12, 13.
70 Terry Eagleton. *Literary Theory: An Introduction* (Oxford: Blackwell, 1983), 34.

Empson, Waldock, and a small number of other outliers) by a sustained effort to put the revolutionary back into the box of conformity. Is it any wonder that "Milton is now read mostly by reluctant undergraduates", and "retains a precarious position on university curriculums", while "the popular audience he enjoyed for centuries has largely evaporated"?[71]

Such critics argue in a style Bob Altermeyer describes as High Right-Wing Authoritarianism, which demonstrates a "tendency to disengage critical thinking when considering religion", and rewards "placing faith over reason".[72] Fish's argument that "affirming God is not something you do on the basis of evidence", but is instead "something you do against the evidence",[73] is a perfect example. It is an argument for the suspension of reason in favor of *un*reason. According to this line of unreason, God—for whom there is no evidence that is not always already trapped within a circular argument—must be taken as the foundational principle of a world for which there is evidence. At best, this is merely begging the question, taking the desired conclusion as part of the evidence for the desired conclusion, a maneuver that would not pass muster in an undergraduate essay, much less the magnum opus of a half-century-long career of critical writing about literature and culture. But at worst, it is classic authoritarian thinking, an insistence that evidence does not matter because the truth has already been provided by authority.[74] A style of thinking more different from Milton's own is inconceivable: "A man may be a heretick in the truth; and if he beleeve things only because his Pastor says so, or the Assembly so determins, without knowing other reason, though his belief be true, yet the very truth he holds, becomes his heresie".[75] Insisting that the man who stood up for reason must be understood as advocating for unreason, and that the revolutionary argues for submission at any price (even to God) simply makes no sense.

---

71 Hawkes, 12.
72 Altermeyer, 104.
73 Fish, *How Milton Works*, 10.
74 Authoritarians do not spend a great deal of effort "examining evidence, thinking critically, reaching independent conclusions […]. Instead, they have largely accepted what they were told by the authorities in their lives" (Altermeyer 93).
75 John Milton. *Areopagitica*. London, 1644, Sig.D2v, 26, https://books.google.com/books?id=tvhAAQAAMAAJ&pg=PA26

But, as we have now seen again and again, the argument does not need to make sense; it merely needs to be asserted with enough eloquent force that the poetry can be bent to the critic's will. Obedience is the principle through which Fish and numerous other critics will work to tame Milton's poetry, taking the scene in which Adam chooses Eve over God, and turning it into something that celebrates the virtues of obedience *through the absence of obedience in the scene*. Such manifest illogic dovetails nicely with Altermeyer's findings that authoritarian thinkers "contradict themselves more often than [others], and apparently do not notice it".[76] As an example, he relates an experience with his psychology students at the University of Manitoba:

> I asked students what they thought of Jesus' admonition [...], "Do not judge, that you may not be judged. For with what judgment you judge, you shall be judged" (Matthew 7:1). I also asked about Jesus' resolution [...]: "Let he who is without sin among you be the first to cast a stone at her". Twenty [...] said we should take the teachings literally. Twenty-seven [others] said we *should* judge and punish others, but none of them explained how they reconciled this view with Jesus' teachings. Apparently, they "believed" both (contradictory) things. But the kicker came when I looked at various measures of authoritarian aggression I had gathered from these students. No matter what they *said* they believed, both these groups [...] were quick with the stones on the Attitudes towards Homosexuals Scale, [and] the Ethnocentrism Scale.[77]

What Altermeyer's anecdote illustrates is the attractiveness, for authoritarian thinkers, of judgment and punishment of perceived offenders, a tendency that "extends beyond religion and has deeper roots, namely, authoritarian submission".[78] The deeply authoritarian strain in Milton criticism comes nowhere more sharply into focus than in the long-sustained argument that Adam should have submitted, and chosen Authority (God) over Love (Eve). Why has the rhetorical window of Milton criticism shifted so far, and for so long, to the right, into authoritarian reverence for submission and power? Why has the work of a regicide and revolutionary been so thoroughly co-opted by a reactionary insistence that Milton is not "a man who embraces the Hierarchical principle with reluctance, but rather [is] a man enchanted

---

76   Altermeyer, 99.
77   Ibid., 96.
78   Ibid., 104.

by it"?⁷⁹ The lovers of authority, it seems, see that love in others wherever and whenever possible.

It is by such principles, and in such hands, that poems about love between human beings become poems of love for God. It is by such principles, and in such hands that *Romeo and Juliet* comes to be described as part of a system of hegemony and oppression. And it is by such principles, and in such hands, that an epic poem defining disobedience as its hero's most noteworthy trait⁸⁰ comes to be twisted into an ornate tract that genuflects to the glories of obedience. But as Oscar Wilde remarks, it is "[d]isobedience" that "in the eyes of anyone who has read history, is man's original virtue". Not only that, but "[i]t is through disobedience that progress has been made, through disobedience and through rebellion".⁸¹ And so it is with Milton's Adam. The attentive reader of the poem who has not yet been overmuch addled by criticism is by no means surprised by Adam's choice. In writing this scene, Milton is more Ovid than Virgil, despite the critics for whom obedience, sovereignty, and the glory of a heavenly Augustus are the prime virtues of life and poetry. In fact, the poem has prepared the reader for this choice, not just by following the bare outlines of the story as presented in Genesis 3, but through the characterization of Adam and his tempestuous emotions—feelings he seeks advice about from precisely the wrong person, but also the only available person: the angel Raphael.

In Book 8, Adam tries to explain to the alien creature (who hasn't the slightest clue what it is like to be human) what and how he feels about Eve, and admits that he does not always know how to handle those feelings, while at the same time telling the angel that the lessons God has taught him do not always seem to match the facts of his experience. With Eve:

> [...] passion first I felt,
> Commotion strange, in all enjoyments else
> Superior and unmov'd, here only weak
> Against the charm of Beauty's powerful glance.⁸²

---

79 Lewis, *A Preface to Paradise Lost*, 78.
80 See Bryson, *The Atheist Milton*, 75–76.
81 Oscar Wilde. *The Soul of Man under Socialism* (Portland: Thomas B. Mosher, 1905), 11.
82 *Paradise Lost* 8.530–33.

This sensation of weakness—which any human being who has lived through adolescence will recognize as among the signs of passionate love and desire—is one Adam has insufficient experience to handle. He is a boy who often pretends to a knowledge and confidence he does not possess, in the mold of Shakespeare's Valentine or Romeo, despite Lewis' claim that both he and Eve "were never young, never immature or undeveloped", but were "created full-grown and perfect".[83] This bright but unseasoned boy admits that he is not at all sure that what he has been taught by God—another wholly alien life form—makes sense when compared to the experience of being a human male. And as, in the logic of the poem, Adam is the only one of these creatures who has ever existed, he is the only one who can speak with anything other than the hollow insistences of the ideologue about what is as opposed to what should be. As Adam explains it, he has been told one thing by God:

> For well I understand in the prime end
> Of Nature her th' inferior, in the mind
> And inward Faculties, which most excel,
> In outward also her resembling less
> His Image who made both, and less expressing
> The character of that Dominion giv'n
> O'er other Creatures;[84]

But his own experience tells him quite another thing, throwing the accuracy of his school-lesson in doubt:

> yet when I approach
> Her loveliness, so absolute she seems
> And in herself complete, so well to know
> Her own, that what she wills to do or say,
> Seems wisest, virtuousest, discreetest, best;
> All higher knowledge in her presence falls
> Degraded, Wisdom in discourse with her
> Looses discount'nanc't, and like folly shewes;
> Authority and Reason on her waite,
> As one intended first, not after made

---

83 Lewis, *A Preface to Paradise Lost*, 112.
84 *Paradise Lost* 8.540–46.

> Occasionally; and to consummate all,
> Greatness of mind and nobleness thir seat
> Build in her loveliest, and create an awe
> About her, as a guard Angelic plac't.[85]

What Adam is asking for, begging for, is some practical help with how to deal with his feelings and what to make of the fact that his experience of Eve does not match the lessons he has been given.[86] The theory is not matching the practice, and there is nothing in the textbook, so to speak, to help him deal with his confusion. What Adam desperately needs at this point is a *human* father—not a self-aggrandizing alien a being calling itself "the Father" who insists on being obeyed and worshipped without demonstrating either the slightest understanding of, or concern with, the actual experiences of its creations. In the absence of that, at least Adam could use a big brother—again, a human figure who has been through what Adam is going through. But Adam gets nothing besides lectures delivered by bloodless aliens who have experienced none of his confusions, and regard his questions as disturbing deviations from the approved curriculum. Certainly, Raphael demonstrates neither understanding nor sympathy:

> Accuse not Nature, she hath done her part;
> Do thou but thine, and be not diffident
> Of Wisdom, she deserts thee not, if thou

---

85 Ibid., 8.546–59.
86 At this point, Milton is giving his Adam a set of observations about Eve's possible *superiority* to him that has long been part of Renaissance thought by the time of *Paradise Lost*. Juan Rodríguez de la Cámara expresses similar ideas in 1438, in *Triumph of Women* (*Triunfo de las Donas*). Speaking of the creation story of Genesis 2, in which woman is created after man, Rodríguez writes that "The less noble creatures were created first and foremost in the world, and the most noble later, so that the more noble could be served by the hordes of the less noble" ("las criaturas menos nobles ayan seydo primeramente en el mundo criadas, e las mas nobles vltimamente, por que las menos nobles pudiesen por horden alas mas nobles seruir") (Juan Rodríguez de la Cámara. *Triunfo de las Donas*. In *Obras de Juan Rodríguez de la Cámara: (ó del Padrón)*, ed. by Antonio Paz y Meliá [Madrid: La Sociodad de Bibliofilos Españoles, 1884], 88, https://archive.org/stream/ObrasJuanRodriguezCamara/Obras_de_Juan_Rodriguez_de_la_Camara#page/n133). Cornelius Agrippa argued that "Woman is the ultimate end of creation, the most perfect accomplishment of all God's works" ("mulier sit ultima creaturarŭ, ac finis, & cŏplementŭoĭm operŭ Dei perfectisimŭ") (*De Nobilitate et Praecellentia Foeminei Sexus*. Antwerp: Michael Hillenius, 1529, Sig. A6r, https://books.google.com/books?id=ZoQNUzFZ5UEC&pg=PT12).

> Dismiss not her, when most thou needst her nigh,
> By attributing overmuch to things
> Less excellent, as thou thy self perceiv'st.
> For what admir'st thou, what transports thee so,
> An outside?...
> [...]
> But if the sense of touch whereby mankind
> Is propagated seem such dear delight
> Beyond all other, think the same voutsaf't
> To Cattle and each Beast; which would not be
> To them made common and divulg'd, if aught
> Therein enjoy'd were worthy to subdue
> The Soule of Man, or passion in him move.[87]

Raphael simply ignores "everything in what Adam has said that is at all inconvenient";[88] in fact, Raphael appears neither to understand, nor care to understand, Adam's point. Adam is saying that Eve seems better and wiser than he has constantly been told she is, and that "what she wills" generally seems to be the right, best, and smartest thing to do. He says nothing about sex in his conversation with Raphael, and yet that is immediately what the alien leaps to: not just sex, but cow sex. Raphael's response to Adam's urgent emotional confusion is to compare him to a cow (or a bull, though it is by no means certain the alien really knows the difference). Raphael's rhetoric is outlandish, and he "willfully misses the point".[89] The shame is that all too many critics are akin to Raphael; perhaps if they were not, Milton's failure to have written the scene of Adam's choice in the way that meets with their approval would not be so continually disappointing to them.

But a reader who is not a determined rewriter of the poem knows what to expect from Adam at the critical juncture. Adam will make the choice he was designed to make—the decision he was intended to make by his poet. Adam will choose Eve over God, love over obedience. After his shock at Eve's action, his pause for thought, and his silent decision for humanity over alien demands for obedience,

---

87 *Paradise Lost*, 8.561–68, 579–85.
88 Waldock, 44.
89 *Ibid.*

Adam delivers a speech that none of Milton's impassively virtuous critics could have written, or even conceived. He confirms that he will not be parted from her, despite God, despite Death, because he values his love for her above all other considerations:

> I with thee have fixt my Lot,
> Certain to undergo like doom, if Death
> Consort with thee, Death is to mee as Life;
> So forcible within my heart I feel
> The Bond of Nature draw me to my owne,
> My own in thee, for what thou art is mine;
> Our State cannot be sever'd, we are one,
> One Flesh; to lose thee were to lose myself.[90]

And so the choice is made, and human life as we know it is begun. What humankind has joined together, no God will put asunder. Adam will have his weak and petulant moments after making this choice; most of Book 10 is dedicated to Adam's doubts and recriminations. But the fact remains that Adam made the truly human choice; not just the only one the source story allows for, but the only one that shows humanity—in all its weaknesses and shortcomings—as a noble enterprise worth rooting for.

No reader should be surprised by this choice. It is the choice that much of the literature we have dealt with here illustrates, and it is the choice made in other treatments of the Edenic scene written before Milton's poem. The path of Christian in John Bunyan's *Pilgrim's Progress*, running away from his wife and children, sticking his fingers in his ears so as not to able to hear their cries, while crying out Life! Life! Eternal Life! is not Milton's way, though it seems to be the way of many of his critics. Milton's choices are more akin to those of Hugo Grotius, who in his Latin drama *Adamus Exul* (*Adam in Exile*) of 1601, portrays the scene of Adam's choice in terms similar to those that will later feature prominently in *Paradise Lost*. After a long debate with Eve, and with his own doubts, Grotius' Adam chooses Eve over God:

---

90 *Paradise Lost* 9.952–59.

> Quid est agendum? lubricas agitant duo
> Curas amores: hinc Dei, atque hinc conjugis:
> [...]
> Quid huîc negandum? vilis unius tibi
> Iactura pomi est. Ut ne contemnam boni
> Legem parentis? Fallor? an voluit Deus
> Conjugis amores anteserri caeteris
> Etiam parentum? Voluit: huc Pommum mihi.[91]
>
> What should I do? A dangerous provocation in two
> Cares and loves: for God and for my wife:
> [...]
> Which shall I deny? Worthless to you is the loss
> Of one apple. Should I condemn the good
> Parental law? Am I mistaken? Is it not God's will
> That marital love shall be preferred over all others,
> Even of parents? It is his will: give me the apple.

Later, Adam, amidst his doubts about whether or not he has done the right thing, decides that he will continue to choose Eve no matter the consequences: "What can I deny to you, my wife? / At your bidding, I will condemn the justice of God; / At your bidding, I will go on living".[92]

The consequences follow immediately, of course, so those who not only insist on, but seem to revel in the punishments inflicted on humanity for daring to chart its own course needn't worry overmuch.[93] But the point has been the choice—far more elaborate than the one found in Genesis 3.6:

וַתֵּרֶא הָאִשָּׁה כִּי טוֹב הָעֵץ לְמַאֲכָל וְכִי תַאֲוָה־הוּא לָעֵינַיִם וְנֶחְמָד הָעֵץ לְהַשְׂכִּיל וַתִּקַּח מִפִּרְיוֹ וַתֹּאכַל וַתִּתֵּן גַּם־לְאִישָׁהּ עִמָּהּ וַיֹּאכַל׃

> And when the woman saw that the tree was good for food, and that it was pleasant to the eyes, a tree desirable to look at and gain insight from,

---

91 Hugo Grotius. *Hugonis Groth Sacra in quibus Adamus exul tragoedia* (Hague: Alberti Henrici, 1601), Act IV, 54–55, https://books.google.com/books?id=pRY_AAAAcAAJ&pg=PP72

92 "...quid tibi, cunjux, negen? / Iubente te vel jussa contemnam Dei, / Iubente te vel sustinebo vivere" (*ibid.* Act V, 68, https://books.google.com/books?id=pRY_AAAAcAAJ&pg=PP86).

93 Authoritarians "want a God to exist as the absolute authority to which they can bow, [and the] concept of God underlying this way of thinking is that of the absolute essence of punitiveness" (T. Adorno. "Studies in the Authoritarian Personality", 444, https://www.scribd.com/doc/35738019/Adorno-Theodor-W-Studies-in-the-Authoritarian-Personality).

she took from its fruit and ate, and gave it also to the man who was with her, and he ate.

Genesis makes little of Adam's choice, and makes comparatively little of Eve's. There is no tortured questioning, deep soul-searching, or weighing of comparative values. There is desire for the fruit, for the wisdom the fruit was thought to offer, and a quick decision to eat. Eve eats, then gives the fruit to Adam, "who was with her", and he eats as well. But for Grotius, the scene is one of agonizing choices. Similarly, in *L'Adamo*, an Italian play of 1613, Adam's decision to eat the fruit is passionate, agonizing, and lengthy:

> Ahi, mi si spezza il core;
> Che far deggia non so; s'io miro il Cielo
> Sento vagarmi un gelo
> Per l'ossa che mi strugge,
> Vago sol d' osservar precetti eterni;
> Se la compagna miro.
> Piango al suo pianto, a' suoi sospir sospiro,
> E mi struggo, e m' accoro,
> S' ubbidirla rifiuto; il cor amante
> Fa eh' al Pomo veloce apra la mano,
> L' alma nel sen dubbiante
> La respinge, e la chiude;
> Misero Adamo, o quanti
> Accampano il tuo i or vari desire!
> Qui per r un tu sospiri,
> Per r altro godi, né saper t' è dato
> Se tu sarà' piegato
> Da sospiri o da gioia,
> Da la Donna o da Dio.
> [...]
> Dammi il frutto rapito,
> Rapitrice cortese,
> Dammi ill frutto gradito;
> S'ubidisca a chi tanto,
> Per farmi un Dio.[94]

---

[94] Giambattisti Andreini. *L'Adamo*, ed. by Ettore Allodoli (Lanciano: Carabba, 1913), 3.1.1839–57, 1907–11, https://archive.org/stream/ladamoand00andruoft#page/78, https://archive.org/stream/ladamoand00andruoft#page/80

> Alas, it breaks my heart;
> I do not know what to do; if I think of Heaven
> Then I feel a cold tremor
> Oppressing me even in my bones,
> And I want only to obey the eternal precepts;
> If I think of my companion,
> I share her tears and sigh with her sighs;
> I am tortured and distracted,
> To refuse her would wound her, and my loving heart
> Would teach me to sieze the apple with open hands,
> But my breast is doubtful
> Rejects, and closes;
> Miserable Adam, how many
> And various are the desires that assail your heart!
> One makes you sigh,
> Another gives you joy, nor can you know
> Which will most win you,
> The sighs or the joy.
> The woman or God.
> [...]
> Give me the stolen fruit,
> Courteous thief,
> Give me the pleasing fruit;
> It is right to obey
> The one who works to make me a God.

Again, we have an Adam who agonizes over the choice of Eve or God, and whose passion and love for his wife leads him to choose love for another human being over love for a figure who is wholly other, a figure whose benevolence always seems to be insisted on by the very same people who take delight in recounting his punishments of disobedience. Here, as in Grotius, the pious reader need not wait long for the penalties to ensue—but again, the passionate, human choice has already been made, and will not be unmade, no matter the lethal intent of God. Even in the 1647 Italian play *Adamo Caduto*, Adam's choice is agonizing, but human. At first Adam resists, even remonstrating with Eve the way Gerald Richman would have Adam do in *Paradise Lost*:

> Noon si deue piu tosto, ch'una volta
> Offender Dio, morir ben volte mille?
> Saprò vestir di rigidezza il volto,
> Saprò armar il cor'anco di idegno,
> Donna, nel tuo mal fare.
> […]
> Iniquio è quel che pecca;
> Ma di gran lunga è biasimevol quello;
> Ch'à le viste ruine altrui conduce.[95]

> Should you not, rather, but once avoid
> Offending God, than die a thousand times?
> I'll know how to clothe myself severely,
> I'll know how to arm my heart with shame,
> Lady, against your evil machinations.
> […]
> Wicked is the sinner;
> But far more blameworthy are those
> That with clear sight lead others to their ruin.

But eventually, Adam begins to realize that he cannot resist his wife: "She weighs on me, in part, making my heart tender; / But the love of Heaven still prevails".[96] Finally, here, as in the other versions of the Edenic story, Adam chooses Eve over God:

> Dolce ben mio,
> Cessa dal pianto, non stracciar più l'crine,
> Che ti prometto di mangiar' il Pomo.
> […]
> Ecco delitía mia, che'l mangio anch'io.[97]

> My sweetest,
> Stop your tears, no more tearing your hair,

---

[95] Serafino della Salandra. *Adamo Caduto* (Cosenza: Giovanni Battista Moio and Francesco Rodella, 1647), 2.10., 92, https://archive.org/stream/bub_gb_fbI8kobTkMQC#page/n110

[96] "M'hàmasso in parte, il cor m'hà in tenerito; / Ma pìu di quel l'amor del Ciel prevale" (*ibid.*, 93, https://archive.org/stream/bub_gb_fbI8kobTkMQC#page/n111).

[97] *Ibid.*, 95, https://archive.org/stream/bub_gb_fbI8kobTkMQC#page/n113

> I promise to eat the apple.
> [...]
> Behold, my delight, as I eat it too.

An astute reader will have noticed a difference, however, between the three versions just dealt with and Milton's rendering in *Paradise Lost*. Where the other seventeenth-century Adams agonize over their choices, Milton's Adam knows quietly, inwardly, immediately what he is going to do. For him the choice is obvious: he will love Eve, and he will choose Eve, despite the God who threatens him with pain and death, despite the willful misbearers and misconstruers like Raphael, and despite the long line of literary critics who would rewrite him into the image of their dry and pious imaginations.

Many of Milton's modern critics appear to read his treatment of Adam's choice, not in light of the seventeenth-century context outlined above, but as if Milton were following the much harsher example of Alcimus Ecdicius Avitus, the sixth-century Bishop of Vienne. Avitus' treatment of the scene, far from being sympathetic to the human emotions involved, is an exercise in condemnation:

> Accipit infelix malesuadi verba susurri,
> Inflexosque retro deiecit ad ultima sensus.
> Non illum trepidi concussit cura pavoris,
> Nec quantum gustu cunctata est femina primo;
> Sed sequitur velox, miseraeque ex coniugis ore
> Constanter rapit inconstans dotale venenum.
> Faucibus et patulis inimicas porrigit escas.[98]

> Unhappily, he accepts the seductive, whispered words,
> Bent back, hurled down finally from his proper senses.
> Nor does fear strike him with pain and trembling,
> Not so much as when the woman first hesitated to taste;
> But he follows quickly, from his wretched wife's mouth
> Firmly the unsteady man seizes the poisonous dowry,
> Stretches wide his mouth, and fills it with the hostile dish.

---

98 *De Mosaice Historiae Gestis.* 2.254–60. In *S. Aviti, Archiepiscopi Viennensis Opera* (Paris, 1643), 233, https://babel.hathitrust.org/cgi/pt?id=dul1.ark:/13960/t1hh95n3b; view=1up;seq=253

However, that is not the way Milton treats the scene. His Adam chooses Eve, not because he has been seduced by "whispered words", and not because he is *inconstans* (weak, unsteady, infirm of purpose), but because he is faced with the choice between human love and nonhuman (or inhuman) power, and he—like any truly decent man would—chooses the former.

To choose the ruler over one's own wife—that is the kind of choice that authoritarian regimes try to convince their subjects is good, right, and honorable. A primary feature of such regimes is that they have "forced individuals to renounce their private life, and especially to sacrifice their family life".[99] This phenomenon can be seen through an analysis of the literature of one such regime—North Korea:

> Love in North Korean literature is always achieved via the lovers' devotion for the *suryeong* [the Leader]. They recognize each other's human worth by measuring and examining the depth, breadth, and, above all, authenticity of the loyalty shown to the sovereign Leader. Without this quality, no one in North Korea is worthy of love or even deserves to live. […] They love each other because the other loves the *suryeong*.[100]

A love filtered through adoration of the ruler, what Sonia Ryang calls "sovereign love",[101] is the opposite of human love between two lovers who choose each other *for* each other—the love treated by the Song of Songs, Ovid, the troubadours, and Shakespeare. Such "sovereign love" is designed, in fact, to prevent the possibility of the human love so many of our literary critics seem curiously determined to dismiss or explain away: "romance should only develop if it is between two individuals, both of whom are equally loyal toward the Leader. No private feelings must be prioritized over […] endless reverence, adoration, and longing for, and loyalty toward, the Leader",[102] who is portrayed as "all-sagacious and all-loving" while great emphasis is laid on his "kindness, holiness

---

99   Gabriel A. Barhaim. *Public-Private Relations in Totalitarian States* (London: Transaction Publishers, 2012), 15.
100 Sonia Ryang. "Biopolitics or the Logic of Sovereign Love—Love's Wherabouts in North Korea". In Sonia Ryang, ed. *North Korea: Toward a Better Understanding* (Lanham: Lexington Books, 2009), 61, 62.
101 *Ibid.*, 74.
102 *Ibid.*, 65.

[and] wisdom".¹⁰³ Even one's worth as an individual is related solely to the extent of one's loyalty to the sovereign: "[t]he worth of another individual is recognized only when the other person is shown to be as loyal toward the Leader as oneself".¹⁰⁴ By this latter criterion, a North Korean literary critic (in an environment in which Kim Jong-il is reputed to have said, "I rule through music and literature"¹⁰⁵) would argue that a man whose wife has been disloyal to the Leader must abandon her to demonstrate his loyalty: "judgment is made as to whether the self is good or evil based on this criterion: how deeply and how truthfully one loves the Leader".¹⁰⁶

Such is the way so many Milton critics would have Adam choose. The obvious objection (often resorted to in Milton scholarship) is that it is one thing for a human sovereign to demand one's total love and loyalty, and quite another for a "divine" sovereign to do the same. In this line of thought, what is left implicit is the assumption that the same techniques that are evil and oppressive when used by a human being are good and just (even loving) when used by a god. Such arguments regard not principle but degree, and those who accept them provide fertile soil in which, with only a minimum of careful tending, tyranny will rarely fail to thrive.

Milton writes his Adam otherwise. Milton's Adam—despite his later doubts and accusations—makes the choice (in what Lewis calls "the pinch [in which] a man ought to reject his wife"¹⁰⁷) not to

---

103 *Ibid.*, 70.
104 *Ibid.*, 65.
105 Jang Jin-sung. *Dear Leader: My Escape from North Korea*. Trans. by Shirley Lee (New York: Simon & Schuster, 2014), 3.
106 Ryang, 74.
107 Lewis, *A Preface to Paradise Lost*, 123. Hannah Arendt notes that such "pinches" were a feature of Nazi purges that even affected privileged party organizations like the SS: "a Fuehrer decree dated May 19, 1943, ordered that all men who were bound to foreigners by family ties, marriage or friendship were to be eliminated from state, party, Wehrmacht and economy; this affected 1,200 SS leaders" (*The Origins of Totalitarianism* [San Diego: Harcourt, 1968], 391, n. 7). Here, the decree of Ezra 10:3 also comes to mind:

וְעַתָּה נִכְרָת־בְּרִית לֵאלֹהֵינוּ לְהוֹצִיא כָל־נָשִׁים וְהַנּוֹלָד מֵהֶם

Now, let us carve out an agreement with our God, to send away our foreign wives, and such children as they have borne.

When the "pinch" Lewis refers to comes, are we after all to believe that the moral thing, the humane thing is to abandon anyone our gods and dictators demand we

reject his wife; he makes the choice to face death with Eve, rather than abandon her, rather than lose her, and rather than indulge any hopes about the mercy of a God who is not going to forgive an Eve whom he has already condemned in advance of her choice to eat the fruit. In the eyes of the God so many critics would have Adam approach, it is always already too late:

> Man disobeying,
> Disloyal breaks his fealty, and sins
> Against the high Supremacy of Heav'n,
> Affecting God-head, and so losing all,
> To expiate his Treason hath naught left,
> But to destruction sacred and devote,
> He with his whole posteritie must dye,
> Dye hee or Justice must;[108]

This is a serious and deadly speech. There is no mercy to be found therein, nor is there any indication that the speaker is inclined to listen to Adam's (wholly imaginary) intercession. In fact, the speaker has already decided that the only remedy for a crime that has not yet been committed is a human sacrifice:

> unless for him
> Som other able, and as willing, pay
> The rigid satisfaction, death for death.
> Say Heav'nly Powers, where shall we find such love,
> Which of ye will be mortal to redeem
> Man's mortal crime, and just th' unjust to save,
> Dwells in all Heaven charity so deare?[109]

All of this sets the stage for the drama of the incarnation and crucifixion of the Son, a death by torture and slow exposure to the elements, a

---

abandon? What kind of ruler, what kind of god, would demand such a thing, and what kind of coward would submit to it? What Lewis, *et al.*, have been advocating for the last several decades is precisely the kind of submission and loyalty to the powerful leader that characterizes the worst tyrannies of human history.

108 *Paradise Lost* 3.203–10.
109 *Ibid.*, 3.210–16.

practice that Martin Hengel describes as an expression of obscene cruelty and sadism toward its victim:

> for the men of antiquity, Greeks, Romans, and Jews, the cross was not an indifferent or arbitrary matter, but an absolutely offensive thing, even "obscene" in the original sense of the word. [...] Even in the Roman empire, where the process of executions might be seen as having a standard or "normal" form—it included an initial flogging, and the criminal often carried the crossbar to the place of execution, where his arms were outstretched as he was nailed to the bar—the form of execution was quite variable: *crucifixion was a punishment in which the capriciousness and sadism of the executioner could run wild.*[110]

And here, we come to the darkest truth, and the greatest heroism of the choice Milton creates his Adam to make: it is in the face of a God who demands grotesque torture and death for the crime of disobedience (and the disobedience of relative children, at that), that Milton's Adam makes his decision for Eve, and for love. Critics like Lewis, Samuel, Fish, Danielson, Teskey, and those who follow them, will never, as Waldock observes, "acknowledge the facts of the poem", because for them, the power and passion of Adam's choice pales next to the "should" and "should not" of a prescriptive and obedience-driven rewriting of the poem. The facts are there, however, easily perceived as long as one does not make, as Raphael does, a willful attempt to misunderstand by letting one of the greatest *Liebestod*[111] scenes in all of world literature fall "on ears which have been deliberately deafened".[112]

---

110 für die antiken Menschen, Griechen, Römer und Juden, keine gleichgültige, beliebige, sondern eine durchaus anstößige, ja im ursprünglichen Sinne des Worte "obzöne" Sache bedeute. [...] Selbst in römischen Machtbereich, wo der Ablauf der Exekution in gewisser Weise als "genormt" erscheinen konnte—er schloß die vorausgehende Geißelung und häufig auch das Tragen des Balkens zur Richtstätte ein, wo der Delinquent emporgehoben und mit ausgestreckten Händen angenagelt wurde—, blieb die Form der Hinrichtung recht variabel: Die Kreuzigung are eine Strafe, bei der sich die Willkür und der Sadismus der Henker austoben konnten.

Martin Hengel. "Mors Turpissima Crucis: Die Kreuzigung in der Antiken Welt und die 'Toheit' des Wortes vom Kreuz". In Johannes Friederich, Wolfgang Pöhlmann, and Peter Stuhlmacher, eds. *Rechtfertigung: Festschrift für Ernst Käsemann zum 70 Geburtstag* (Tübingen: J. C. B. Mohr, 1976), 137, 139).

111 The term translates literally as Love-Death, but what it refers to in the realm of art is a duet between lovers—whether in song, poetry, dramatic performance, or some combination—in which they affirm their love in the face of death.

112 Waldock, 44.

For Samuel Taylor Coleridge, the poet and critic whose ears were definitely not deliberately deafened, the mutual love between Adam and Eve was perhaps the noblest part of *Paradise Lost*:

> The love of Adam and Eve in Paradise is of the highest merit—not phantomatic, and yet removed from everything degrading. It is the sentiment of a rational being towards another made tender by a specific difference in that which is essentially the same in both; it is a union of opposites, a giving and receiving mutually of the permanent in either, a completion of each in the other.[113]

In choosing death with Eve, Adam chooses a human life, a life of love rather than an existence of obedience, a mortal life faced with a courage Heidegger describes as "authentic being-toward-death";[114] thus Adam makes the only possible *human* choice, which the poet knows, even if his critics do not. In a sense, Adam makes the same choice that Odysseus makes, who when offered immortality by Calypso, can think only of return to Penelope, whom the goddess describes as "your wife, she that you ever long for daily, in every way".[115] Perhaps, in the spirit of Lewis, Samuel, Fish, Danielson, Teskey, and countless others, Odysseus should have chosen otherwise. But think how much poetry we would have lost if he had.

Somehow, all too many modern critics of Milton can no longer see or hear, so deliberately blind and deaf have they become to the love the poet tried to portray. Such critics, in Maurice Kelley's terms, are "proof-proof",[116] and will forever insist on their "homemade brand of orthodoxy"[117] in rewriting Milton's epic. But we needn't follow them into "wand'ring mazes lost",[118] wondering what might have been if only Milton had written his poem to conform to the expectations of his more obedience-focused readers. Despite the critics, in *Paradise Lost*, love

---

113 Samuel Taylor Coleridge. *The Literary Remains of Samuel Taylor Coleridge*, Vol. 1, ed. by Henry Nelson Coleridge (London: William Pickering, 1836), 177, https://archive.org/stream/literaryremainso01coleuoft#page/177

114 "eigentlichen Seins zum Tode" (*Sein und Zeit*. 266).

115 "σὴν ἄλοχον, τῆς τ᾽ αἰὲν ἐέλδεαι ἤματα πάντα" (Homer. *Odyssey*, 5.210. Vol. I, Books 1–12, ed. by A. T. Murray [Loeb Classical Library, Cambridge, MA: Harvard University Press, 1919]).

116 Maurice Kelley. "The Provenance of John Milton's Christian Doctrine: A Reply to William B. Hunter". *SEL*, 34 (1994), 159, https://doi.org/10.2307/450791

117 *Ibid*.

118 *Paradise Lost*, 2.561.

becomes most fully human. Mortal, and therefore even more precious in the face of death, love is the defining feature of a truly human life, chosen, as it seems it must ever be, in disobedience.

Epilogue
Belonging to Poetry: A Reparative Reading

Over fifty years ago, Susan Sontag described "the project of interpretation" as "largely reactionary, stifling", and placed it in the context of "a culture whose [...] dilemma is the hypertrophy of the intellect at the expense of energy and sensual capacity", before concluding that "interpretation is the revenge of the intellect upon art".[1] The situation does not seem to have improved in the intervening half-century. As Martin Paul Eve has very recently observed, "traditional literary criticism *always coerces* texts into new narrative forms", as "its practitioners [read] to seek case studies suited for exegetic purpose".[2] To come back to the observation with which this book began, one of the great shocks caused by reading love poetry alongside the work of its critics, is just how often the critics seem hostile to poetry, while aligning themselves with the very systems of power and authority poetry has tried to resist. Literary critics immersed in what Rita Felski calls the "institutionally mandated attitude" of an "institutionalized suspicion" are part of a system of authoritative and authoritarian cultural practices that are "diffused throughout society via the legal and executive branches of the modern state".[3] Inspiring "surveillance, investigation, interrogation, and prosecution",[4] such criticism is the

---
1 Sontag, 7.
2 Martin Paul Eve. *Literature Against Criticism* (Cambridge: Open Book Publishers, 2016), 26, https://doi.org/10.11647/OBP.0102. Emphasis added.
3 Felski, *The Limits of Critique*, 47.
4 Ibid., 47.

ethos of a prestige-driven elite claiming it "terrorizes received ideas",[5] while too often identifying with (or at least cooperating with) the systems of privilege and power it pretends to expose.

At a time when we are facing "the near-death of the university as a democratic public sphere", while caught in a situation in which "cynicism, accommodation, and a retreat into a sterile form of professionalism"[6] have become the coins of the realm, our poetry cannot be left to what Empson once called the "habitual mean-mindedness of modern academic criticism".[7] As Felski maintains, "[l]iterary studies sorely needs alternatives" to a style of criticism that traces "textual meaning back to an opaque and all-determining power, while presuming the critic's immunity from the weight of this ubiquitous domination".[8] We need a criticism that practices what Eve Sedgwick refers to as reparative reading, which teaches "the many ways in which selves and communities succeed in extracting sustenance from the objects of a culture—even a culture whose avowed desire has often been not to sustain them".[9] This is especially true now, in a Western world where so much of modern life is structured around obedience, a world in which, as Edward Herman and Noam Chomsky argue, the governing model is to "manufacture consent" in the various populations whose compliance is being demanded. In describing the "propaganda model" of the mass media, Herman and Chomsky outline "the rewards that

---

5 Robert Con Davis and Ronald Schleifer. *Criticism and Culture: The Role of Critique in Modern Literary Theory* (New York: Longman, 1991), 2.
6 Henry Giroux. *Neoliberalism's War on Higher Education* (Chicago: Haymarket Books, 2014), 16–17.
7 Empson. "Rescuing Donne", 159.
8 *Ibid.*, 152.
9 Sedgewick, *Touching Feeling: Affect, Pedagogy, Performativity*, 150–51. Sedgwick's discussion has elicited a great deal of commentary, an interesting amount of which seems dedicated to using a suspicion-based style of reading to claim that her argument means something other than it might otherwise appear. Heather Love's article, "Truth and Consequences: On Paranoid Reading and Reparative Reading" (*Criticism*, 52: 2 [Spring 2010], 235–41) is an excellent recent example of that trend. Love describes Sedgwick's article as "an act of aggression [...] that endlessly produces its own bad objects", readers who feel "personally" accused of being the type of critic "who picks up paranoid habits of mind as critical tools or weapons but is detached from the living contexts in which these frameworks were articulated" (236). Love deftly manages both to praise and bury Caesar all at once, arguing for the utility of a non-reparative reading of Sedgwick's call for a reparative reading practice. The long tradition of suspicion-based criticism will not, it seems, go down without a fight.

accrue to conformity and the costs of honest dissidence" as well as the "considerations that tend to induce obedience"[10] at all levels of our society.[11] This includes academia,[12] where what Chomsky refers to as "the self-selection for obedience that is [...] part of elite education"[13] influences the discourse and defines its possibilities and limits, "strictly limit[ing] the spectrum of acceptable opinion, but allow[ing] very lively debate within that spectrum".[14]

The reparative reading Sedgwick called for might, if put into practice, be able to give us a new relation to poetry, provide us a chance to hear the voices of the poets again, bring their music to the fore, and unearth it from beneath a century-long avalanche of modern criticism, much of which has insisted on its primacy over poetry. Those of us who teach, study, and write about poetry are enmeshed within a more than

---

10 Edward S. Herman and Noam Chomsky. *Manufacturing Consent: The Political Economy of the Mass Media* (New York: Knopf Doubleday, 2011), 305.

11 The findings of the infamous Milgram and Zimbardo experiments of the 1960s and 1970s have been updated by Halsam and Reicher in 2012. Where Milgram and Zimbardo portray their subjects as cooperating passively with authority, even when given instructions that seem malevolent in nature, Halsam and Reicher conclude that subjects will obey eagerly and actively, no matter the instruction, as long as they "actively identify with those who promote vicious acts as virtuous" (S. A. Haslam and S. D. Reicher (2012) "Contesting the 'Nature' Of Conformity: What Milgram and Zimbardo's Studies Really Show", *PLoS Biol* 10[11]: e1001426, https://doi.org/10.1371/journal.pbio.1001426).

12 Eric Anthony Grollman recently addressed this problem from the perspective of gender norms in the American academy, arguing that "academic training is about beating graduate students into submission and conformity", especially over the issue of self-presentation: "professional (re)socialization of graduate school is centrally a task of eliminating passion, love, creativity and originality from would-be scholars' lives—or at least presenting ourselves as detached, subdued, conforming" (Eric Anthony Grollman. "Gender Policing in Academe". *Inside Higher Education*, https://www.insidehighered.com/advice/2016/07/29/academy-polices-gender-presentation-scholars-essay). Joseph Katz noted some forty years ago that the academy "give[s] lip service to the value of originality, while in fact expecting products that conform rather strictly to specific canons of inquiry, schools of thought, and the personalities of the people on examining committees" ("Development of Mind". In *Scholars in the Making: The Development of Graduate and Professional Students* [Cambridge, MA, Ballinger, 1976], 124). And as A. W. Strouse poignantly notes, "[t]he profession is a closet that shuts up doctoral students and makes [them] write in prose rather than in poetry" ("Getting Medieval on Graduate Education: Queering Academic Professionalism". *Pedagogy: Critical Approaches to Teaching Literature, Language, Composition, and Culture*, 15: 1 [2014], 124, https://doi.org/10.1215/15314200-2799260).

13 Chomsky, 13 Nov 1995.

14 Noam Chomsky. *The Common Good* (Berkeley: Odonian Press, 1998), 43.

two-thousand-year-old tradition of suspicion-based stances toward literature, and since the rise of theories that posit the non-referentiality of language, the irrelevance of the artist, and the primacy of the critic, that tradition has been contributing to poetry's demise in a world that may need poetry now more than it ever has. But in an age in which criticism has long been enamoured of the idea that texts are deceptive, what potential for resistance does poetry have? What power *can* it have when so many of its critics seem dedicated to the idea that poetry must be approached through what Fish calls "the pleasures of diagnosis"[15] and what Kiernan Ryan decries as "the diagnostic attitude"[16] that has swept through literary studies? In such an environment, what is left of passion and desire, not only in poetry, but in its interpretation?

We might begin to address that question by taking our cue from a writer of both poetry *and* criticism. In an August 16, 1890 letter to the editor of *The Scots Observer*, Oscar Wilde noted that while "the critic has to educate the public", the responsibility of the artist is different, for "the artist has to educate the critic".[17] In that observation there is something crucial that contemporary academic criticism sometimes seems to have forgotten: artists respond to art differently than do critics (especially of the university-trained and theoretically-inclined variety). Wilde, who made a point in his work of exploring both sides of that dynamic (especially in such essays as *The Decay of Lying* and *The Critic as Artist*), is not favoring one over the other, but recommending a synthesis of approaches to experiencing, understanding, and commenting upon art. The ideas this approach leads to in his writing are not often of the sort likely to be welcome in modern criticism, as for example, his connection between life and art and his emphasis on the individual artist behind the work: "[t]he longer one studies life and literature, the more strongly one feels that behind everything that is wonderful stands the individual".[18] Reparative reading might well give us an opportunity to reincorporate both aspects of Wilde's statement into our critical practices—the reconnection of literature to life (*not* regarding literature

---

15   Fish, "Masculine Persuasive Force: Donne and Verbal Power", 223.
16   Kiernan Ryan, "King Lear", 377.
17   *The Scots Observer*, 4: 91, 332, https://books.google.com/books?id=94oeAQ AAMAAJ&pg=PA332
18   Oscar Wilde. "The Critic as Artist". *The Complete Works of Oscar Wilde* (New York: Barnes & Noble, 1994), 1021.

as purely self-referential after the fashion of Blanchot and others), and the reconnection of that literature to the individual writer *and* reader. This reparative reading, as imagined here, does not advocate a prescriptive method of reading, or lay down rules for what one must or must not see, hear, and feel in poetry and other forms of literature. But in the twin spirit of Sontag and Wilde, it suggests a defense of poetry, and in Sontag's terms, a less revenge-driven relation between the intellect and art, less driven by the hermeneutics of suspicion which often seems to triumph over texts rather than explore them or explain them. Such a reading practice suggests that now and then critics might do well to be educated by the artist, rather than the theorist—and that works of criticism, this one included, might do well to recover a sense of the passions of poetry, and what Sontag refers to as the "energy and sensual capacity" of art and life.

That sensual energy is still with us, and is amply represented in a wide variety of modern literature, across multiple genres and languages. It appears in places like the poetry of Aleksandr Pushkin, who, though most famous for his long-form works such as *Evgeny Onegin* (*Евгений Онегин*) and *Boris Godunov* (*Борис Годунов*), also wrote a number of powerful shorter poems. "When in My Embrace" ("Когда в объятия мои"), from 1830, is filled with the frustrated *eros* often found in the troubadour *albas*, where the lovers are threatened with separation by a jealous husband and the coming of the dawn. But in Pushkin's poem, something even more forbidding separates the lovers: their own doubts. The poem shows us the painful regrets experienced by a lover who is abashed before his beloved, filled with a sense of his own guiltiness and unworthiness before a woman whom he imagines as recalling previous betrayals by men such as himself:

>Когда в объятия мои
>Твой стройный стан я заключаю
>И речи нежные любви
>Тебе с восторгом расточаю,
>Безмолвна, от стесненных рук
>Освобождая стан свой гибкой,
>Ты отвечаешь, милый друг,
>Мне недоверчивой улыбкой;
>Прилежно в памяти храня
>Измен печальные преданья,

> Ты без участья и вниманья
> Уныло слушаешь меня…
> Кляну коварные старанья
> Преступной юности моей
> И встреч условных ожиданья
> В садах, в безмолвии ночей.
> Кляну речей любовный шепот,
> Стихов таинственный напев,
> И ласки легковерных дев,
> И слезы их, и поздний ропот.[19]

> When in my embrace,
> I enclose your shapely form,
> And in a gentle voice of love
> I delightfully praise you,
> Silently, from my shy arms
> By skillfully disentangling your figure,
> You answer, sweet friend,
> Smiling at me distrustfully;
> Keenly kept in your memory,
> The betrayal of sad devotion,
> You, without sympathy and attention,
> Are sadly listening to me…
> I curse my subtle schemes,
> My youthful crimes,
> And my arranged meetings, waiting
> In gardens, in the silence of night.
> I curse the speech of love's whispers,
> Poems with mysterious melodies,
> And the caresses of credulous maidens,
> And their tears, and their murmurs.

Though there is a note here of the unachievable beloved found in Dante and Petrarch, the lady is all-too-human, unachievable not because of her demi-divine status, but because of her distrust, and the self-doubts of a lover keenly aware of his own past and potential dishonesty. No authority, divine or otherwise keeps the lovers apart, except for the

---

19 Aleksandr Sergeevich Pushkin. "Когда в объятия мои". In *Sobranie sochinenii*, Vol. 2, 294, http://rvb.ru/pushkin/01text/01versus/0423_36/1830/0532.htm

promptings and warnings of their own hearts. Pushkin's poem speaks to an older tradition of poetry, and is informed by it, while transforming and internalizing its themes of separation and loss. Here, we have an initial clue as to what at least one kind of reparative reading practice might look like: reading those older poets can help us understand Pushkin, and reading Pushkin can help us understand them in turn.

We can see a further indication of what such a reading practice might look like by turning to Pablo Neruda's "I Can Write the Saddest Verses Tonight" ("Puedo escribir los versos más tristes esta noche"), poem 20 from his 1924 collection *Twenty Poems of Love and a Song of Despair* (*Veinte Poemas de Amor y una Canción Desesperada*). Neruda's verse laments a loss of love so affecting and so powerful that it feels like the tearing away of one's own soul:

> Mi corazón la busca, y ella no está conmigo.
> La misma noche que hace blanquear los mismos árboles.
> Nosotros, los de entonces, ya no somos los mismos.
> [...]
> Es tan corto el amor, y es tan largo el olvido.
> Porque en noches como esta la tuve entre mis brazos,
> mi alma no se contenta con haberla perdido.
> Aunque éste sea el último dolor que ella me causa,
> y éstos sean los últimos versos que yo le escribo.[20]

> My heart looks for her, and she is not with me.
> The same night whitens the same trees,
> But we, who were then, are no longer the same.
> [...]
> Love is so short, and forgetting is so long.
> Because on nights like this I held her in my arms,
> My soul has no peace, having lost her.
> Although this be the last pain that she causes me,
> and these the last verses that I write.

---

20 Pablo Neruda. "Puedo escribir los versos más tristes esta noche". In *Veinte Poemas de Amor y una Canción Desesperada* (Bogotá and Barcelona: Editorial Norma, 2002), 45–6, ll. 20–22, 28–32.

The voice in Neruda's poem—a lover who cannot seem to let go of the memories and regrets that revolve around the loss of love, the loss of a woman, and the peace of soul that came with her presence—can help us understand the Adam that Milton's critics would have choose God over Eve. Despite the vast differences between the poems in terms of their language, their time of authorship, and their place of origin, these poems speak to each other, and each speaks to us about the other. But they are not poems that speak *only* of other poetry. The key is, that they are poems that speak *to us*. They speak to and about poetry, yes; but more importantly, they speak about life, about human beings and our loves, losses, passions, and desires. That such a point has to be made at all, is a testament to how long it has been since we have truly been able to hear poetry over the urgent clamor of a suspicion-based criticism.

In learning to hear the poets again, one of the most important things we might begin to recover now is a practice of reading poetry, not through academic criticism, but *through other poetry*. Reading Milton through Neruda gives us an entirely different perspective on Adam's choice. As Adam expresses it to Eve, "to lose thee were to lose myself",[21] and as Neruda writes "love is so short, and forgetting is so long"—such poetry teaches us to imagine the weight and sadness of what happens after choosing God over Eve, after losing the love one once held in one's arms, finding her impossible to forget, and living with the regrets and loneliness across the seemingly-endless years. That empathy, that creative sympathy, is where the "energy and sensual capacity" of poetry, and the courage to commit to a reparative reading practice, might yet be found.

It can also be found in serious tales of fantasy, as in Mikhail Bulgakov's novel *Master and Margarita (Мастер и Маргарита)*. A story of black magic, love, and the triumph of art, written between 1928 and 1940 as a gesture of defiance against the Stalinist norms of Soviet Socialist Realism (a form of literary criticism raised to the level of state power),[22] Bulgakov's novel stands up powerfully against the forces

---

21   *Paradise Lost* 9.959.
22   In Stalinist Russia, only one form of literature was allowed to be written and published: socialist realism. The Soviet government required complete acceptance of sanctioned forms of Marxist ideology [...]. Early Soviet policies regarding literature were shaped by the ideas of Andrei Zhdanov, who believed that literature had a powerful influence over readers, claiming at the first Soviet Writers' Congress that socialists were writing "a literature which has organized the

hostile to poetry. In a scene at once comic and profound, the value of life and all its passions is voiced by the Devil, as he speaks to the severed head of a disdainful literary critic named Berlioz who is about to find out that his options were not quite so narrow as he had believed:

> You have always been an ardent preacher of the theory that cutting off a man's head ends his life, and then he turns into ashes and goes into non-being. […] Each will be given according to his faith. Yes, it comes true! You will go into non-being, and happily, from the cup of your transformation, I will drink to being.[23]

And in a scene more wistful than comic, Bulgakov gives us the reflections of a man who once had the chance to choose love and passion, but chose as Milton's critics would have his Adam choose, and passed them by from fear of disobedience: "Oh, I am a fool! Why, why didn't I fly away with her? What was I afraid of, old ass! […] Suffer it now, old cretin!"[24] This twentieth-century Russian novel, and that seventeenth-century English epic poem also speak to one another, and to us, and the fire that burns in them both is the energy and sensuality of an art that is very much connected to life.

But the spirit of poetry as resistance, of literature as the medium through which love is expressed and received in defiance of the critical, theological, and political authorities who would (and still do) censor it, is even more memorably captured by Nizār Qābbanī, the twentieth-century Syrian poet whose entire body of work served as an act of defiance against those who would channel, reformulate, and control

---

toilers and oppressed for the struggle to abolish once and for all every kind of exploitation". As a consequence, Zhdanov was wary of literature that might encourage dissenting views.

Ilona Urquhart. "Diabolical Evasion of the Censor in Mikhail Bulgakov's *The Master and Margarita*". In Nicole Moore, ed. *Censorship and the Limits of the Literary: A Global View* (New York: Bloomsbury Academic, 2015), 133.

23 Вы всегда были горячим проповедником той теории, что по отрезании головы жизнь в человеке прекращается, он превращается в золу и уходит в небытие. […] каждому будет дано по его вере. Да сбудется же это! Вы уходите в небытие, а мне радостно будет из чаши, в которую вы превращаетесь, выпить за бытие.

Mikhail Bulgakov. *Мастер и Маргарита* [Master and Margarita] (Moscow: Olma Media Group, 2005), 352.

24 "Эх я, дурак! Зачем, зачем я не улетел с нею? Чего я испугался, старый осел! […] Эх, терпи теперь, старый кретин!" (*ibid.*, 507).

poetry, passion, and human desire,[25] from the governments that banned his work, to the academic and theological critics who still regard his poetry with disdain and disapproval.[26] For Qābbanī, poetry and love were the only laws of life:

يوم تعثرينَ على رَجُل

يقدر أن يحوّل كلَّ ذرَةٍ من ذرّاتكِ

..إلى شِعرْ

ويجعل كلَّ شَعْرة من شَعَراتكِ .. قصيدة

..يوم تعثرين على رَجُل

ـ يقدر ـ كما فعلتُ أنا

..أن يجعلك تغتسلينَ بالشِعرْ

..وتتكحَلين بالشِعرْ

..وتتمشّطين بالشِعرْ

..فسوف أتوسّلُ إليكِ

..أن تتبعيه بلا ترَدُد

..فليس المهمّ أن تكوني لي

وليس المهمّ .. أن تكوني له

المُهمُّ .. أن تكُوني للشِعرْ[27]

---

25   As Amila Buturovic notes, Qābbanī's poetry was immediately regarded as blasphemous by the clerical powers-that-be in Syria, while revered by younger readers:

> His pointed criticism of the social milieu was directed at the relationship between the sexes in particular. His […] rejection of the blunt misogynist attitudes which left the Arab woman under the constant scrutiny of patriarchal canons [informed his call] to liberate the body from sexual repression and more specifically, to allow the Arab woman to cherish her erotic ecstasy openly and freely. Controversy erupted instantly: Sheikh al-Tantāwī characterized the poems as "blasphemous and stupid", while young Syrian readers treated the collection as a kind of manifesto of their culturally suppressed sexuality.

"'Only Women and Writing Can Save Us From Death': Erotic Empowering in the Poetry of Nizār Qābbanī". In *Tradition, Modernity, and Postmodernity in Arabic Literature: Essays in Honor of Professor Issa J. Boullata*, ed. by Kamal Abdel-Malek and Wael Hallaq (Leiden: Brill, 2000), 141. And in a a trenchant observation that might remind us that the theoretical stances of the West are not necessarily those of the rest of the world, Buturovic argues that "while much of the postmodern world speaks of the 'death of the author', we are reminded, quite lucidly, of Qābbanī's engaged presence every time we revisit his poetic corpus". (142).

26   For a fascinating example of this stance toward Qābbanī's work, see Bacem A. Essam. "Nizarre Qabbani's Original Versus Translated Pornographic Ideology: A Corpus-Based Study". *Sexuality and Culture*, 20 (2016), 965–86, https://doi.org/10.1007/s12119-016-9369-7

27   Nizār Qābbanī. "Love Letter 71". Arabic text published in Bassam K. Frangieh and Clementia R. Brown, eds. *Arabian Love Poems* (London: Lynne Rienner Publishers, 1999), 134.

> The day you find a man
> Who can transform your every atom
> Into Poetry,
> And who turns each strand of your hair into a poem,
> The day you find a man
> Who can — as I did —
> Make you bathe in Poetry,
> Line your eyes with Poetry,
> Comb your hair with Poetry,
> Then I will beg you
> To follow him without hesitation.
> It doesn't matter that you belong to me,
> And it doesn't matter that you belong to him.
> What matters… is that you belong to Poetry.[28]

The poet's final words are the key: belonging to poetry is feeling it inside oneself, feeling its music flowing through and over and around oneself. It is knowing *eros* as desire and joy. It is seeing life through art, and art through life. It is the passion in the Song of Songs, the troubadours, and Donne, the humor in Chaucer, the *carpe diem* ethos in Herrick, the empathy in Shakespeare, Milton, and Pushkin, the sadness in Neruda, and the irreverent joy in Ovid and Bulgakov. Those feelings are the very core of the human spirit that we might still hope poetry, and all forms of literature, can help us recover and defend. But whether that spirit of belonging to poetry will survive, in this era of renewed and intensified demands for obedience to the dictates of political and cultural authority, is up to all of us, not our theologians, philosophers, politicians, or literary critics. It is up to ordinary readers, everyday men and women who will act in the spirit hoped for by Benjamin Franklin. After the Constitutional Convention of 1787, "an anxious lady named Mrs. Powel" asked, "What type of government […] have you delegates given us?" Franklin replied, "A republic, madam, if you can keep it".[29] What the poets have given us is Love.

If only we can keep it.

---

28 Translated by Modje Taavon.
29 Walter Isaacson. *Benjamin Franklin: An American Life* (New York: Simon & Schuster, 2003), 459.

Bibliography

Abelard, Peter, and Heloise d'Argenteuil. *Magistri Petri Abaelardi epistola quae est Historia calamitatum: Heloissae et Abaelardi epistolae*, ed. by Johann Caspar von Orelli. Turici: Officina Ulrichiana, 1841, https://archive.org/details/magistripetriaba00abel

Abels, Richards and Ellen Harrison. "The Participation of Women in Languedocian Catharism". *Mediaeval Studies*, 41 (1979), 215–51, https://doi.org/10.1484/J.MS.2.306245

Adorno, Theodore. "Studies in the Authoritarian Personality". In T. W. Adorno, Else Frenkel-Brunswik, Daniel J. Levinson, and R. Nevitt Sanford, *The Authoritarian Personality*, Vol. I of *Studies in Prejudice*, ed. by Max Horkheimer and Samuel H. Flowerman (Social Studies Series: Publication No. III). New York: Harper & Brothers, 1950, 145–509, https://www.scribd.com/doc/35738019/Adorno-Theodor-W-Studies-in-the-Authoritarian-Personality

Agrippa, Cornelius. *De Nobilitate et Praecellentia Foeminei Sexus*. Antwerp: Michael Hillenius, 1529, https://books.google.it/books?id=ZoQNUzFZ5UEC&pg=PT2&redir_esc=y

Aist, Dietmar von. "Slâfest du, friedel ziere?" In *Des minnesangs frühling*, ed. by Friedrich Vogt. Leipzig: Verlag von S. Hirzel, 1920, https://books.google.com/books?id=DcQPAAAAMAAJ&pg=PR1

Alcuin. "Epistola CCVI, Ad Disciplum". In *Patrologiae Cursus Completus*, Vol. 100, ed. by Jacques Paul Migne. Paris: Apud Garnier Fratres, 1863, cols. 481–82, https://books.google.com/books?id=-JqsZH3ajIgC&pg=PA12

—. "Interrogationes et Responsiones in Genesin". In *Patrologiae Cursus Completus*, Vol. 100, ed. by Jacques Paul Migne. Paris: Apud Garnier Fratres, 1863, cols. 551–70, https://books.google.com/books?id=-JqsZH3ajIgC&pg=PA12

—. "Pectus amor nostrum penetravit flamma". *Monumenta Germaniae historica inde ab anno Christi quingentesimo usque ad annum millesimum et quingentesimum*, Vol. 1. Berlin: Apud Weidmannos, 1881, https://books.google.com/books?id=U6woAAAAMAAJ&pg=PP10

Allen, Peter L. *The Art of Love: Amatory Fiction from Ovid to the Romance of the Rose*. Philadelphia: University of Pennsylvania Press, 1992.

Allestree, Richard. *The Practice of Christian Graces, Or, The Whole Duty of Man Laid down in a Plaine and Familiar Way for the Use of All, but Especially the Meanest Reader: Divided into XVII Chapters*. London: Printed by D. Maxwell for T. Garthwait, 1658, https://quod.lib.umich.edu/e/eebo/A23760.0001.001/1:4?rgn=div1;vid=96830;view=fulltext

Alter, Robert. "Paul de Man Was a Total Fraud". *New Republic*. April 5, 2014, https://newrepublic.com/article/117020/paul-de-man-was-total-fraud-evelyn-barish-reviewed

Altermeyer, Bob. *The Authoritarian Specter*. Cambridge, MA: Havard University Press, 1996.

Althusser, Louis. "Idéologie et Appareils Idéologiques d'État" (1970). *Les Classiques des Sciences Sociales*. Quebec: Université du Québec à Chicoutimi, 1–60, http://classiques.uqac.ca/contemporains/althusser_louis/ideologie_et_AIE/ideologie_et_AIE.pdf

—. *Lire le Capital*. Paris: Presses Universitaires de France, 1996.

Ames, Christine Caldwell. *Medieval Heresies: Christianity, Judaism, and Islam*. Cambridge: Cambridge University Press, 2015.

Anderson, W. S. "The Heroides". In *Ovid*, ed. by James Wallace Binns. London: Routledge, 1973, 49–83.

Andreasen, Nancy Jo Coover. *John Donne: Conservative Revolutionary*. Princeton: Princeton University Press, 1967.

Andreini, Giambattisti. *L'Adamo*, ed. by Ettore Allodoli. Lanciano: Carabba, 1913, https://archive.org/details/ladamoand00andruoft

Arden of Faversham. In *A Woman Killed with Kindness and Other Domestic Plays*, ed. by Martin Wiggins. Oxford: Oxford University Press, 2008.

Aucassin et Nicolette, ed. by Francis William Bourdillon. London: Kegan Paul, Trench & Co., 1887, https://archive.org/details/AucassinEtNicoletteALoveStory

Aquinas, Thomas. *Summa Theologiae: Vol. 41, Virtues of Justice in the Human Community*, ed. by T. C. O'Brien. Cambridge: Cambridge University Press, 2006.

Arden, Heather. *The Romance of the Rose*. Boston: Twayne Publishers, 1987.

Arendt, Hannah. *The Origins of Totalitarianism*. San Diego: Harcourt, 1968.

Aries, Philippe. "The Family, Sex and Marriage in England, 1500–1800". *The American Historical Review*, 83: 5 (1978), 1221–24, https://doi.org/10.2307/1854694

Aristotle. *Nichomachean Ethics I*, ed. by H. Rackham. Loeb Classical Library, Cambridge, MA: Harvard University Press, 1926.

—. *Physics, Vol. II, Books 5–8*. Ed. and trans. by P. H. Wicksteed and F. M. Cornford. Loeb Classical Library, Cambridge, MA: Harvard University Press, 1934.

—. *Poetics*. Ed. and trans. by Stephen Halliwell. In *Aristotle: Poetics. Longinus: On the Sublime. Demetrius: On Style*. Loeb Classical Library, Cambridge, MA: Harvard University Press, 1995, https://doi.org/10.4159/dlcl.aristotle-poetics.1995

—. *Poetics*. Trans. by Richard Janko. Indiannapolis: Hackett, 1987.

—. *Politics*. Ed. and trans. by Harris Rackham. Loeb Classical Library, Cambridge, MA: Harvard University Press, 1932.

Armstrong, Rebecca. *Ovid and His Love Poetry*. London: Bloomsbury Academic, 2005, https://doi.org/10.5040/9781472539977

Astell, Ann W. *The Song of Songs in the Middle Ages*. Ithaca: Cornell University Press, 1990.

Aubrey, John. *Wiltshire. The Topographical Collections of John Aubrey, 1659–70*, ed. by John Edward Jackson. London: Longman, 1862, https://archive.org/details/wiltshiretopogra00aubr

Auerbach, Erich. *Mimesis: Dargestellte Wirklichkeit in Der Abendländischen Literatur*. 2nd ed. Bern: A. Francke, 1959.

Augustine of Hippo. *De Civitate Dei*. Paris: 1586, https://books.google.com/books?id=pshhAAAAcAAJ&printsec=frontcover&source=gbs_ge_summary_r&cad=0

Ausonius. "Ad Uxorem", Epigram 20. In *Ausonius: Epigrams. Text with Introduction and Commentary*. Ed. and trans. by Nigel M. Kay. London: Duckworth, 2001, 45.

—. "Attusia Lucana Sabina Uxor", Parentalia IX. In *Ausonius. Vol. I: Books 1–17*. Ed. and trans. by Hugh G. Evelyn-White. Loeb Classical Library, Cambridge, MA: Harvard University Press, 1919, 70, 72.

Austin, R. G. *P. Vergili Maronis Aneidos Liber Quartos*. Oxford: Clarendon Press, 1955.

Auweele, Bart Vanden. "The Song of Songs as Normative Text". In *Religion and Normativity, Vol. 1: The Discursive Struggle over Religious Texts in Antiquity*, ed. by Anders-Christian Jacobson, Bart Vanden Auweele, and Carmen Cvetkovic. Aarhus: Aarhus University Press, 2009, 157–67.

Avitus of Vienne (Alcimus Ecdicius Avitus). *De Mosaice Historiae Gestis*. In *S. Aviti, Archiepiscopi Viennensis Opera*. Paris, 1643, https://babel.hathitrust.org/cgi/pt?id=dul1.ark:/13960/t1hh95n3b;view=1up;seq=5

Bagot, Richard. "Letter from Richard Bagot to Richard Broughton, 1587 June 3". In *Papers of the Bagot Family of Blithfield, Staffordshire, 1428–1671 (bulk 1557–1671)*. Folger MS L.a.68, Folger Shakespeare Library, Washington, http://luna.folger.edu/luna/servlet/workspace/handleMediaPlayer?lunaMediaId=FOLGERCM1~6~6~361296~130605

Baker, Richard. *A Chronicle of the Kings of England* (London: Printed by George Sawbridge at the Bible on Ludgate-hill, 1670, https://books.google.com/books?id=BnIVsU0RtzUC&pg=PP12

Barazzetti, Donatella, Franca Garreffa, and Rosaria Marsico. *National Report*: *Italia. Daphne Project*: *Proposing New Indicators*: *Measuring Violence's Effects*. University of Calabria, Rende: Italy, 2007, http://www.surt.org/gvei/docs/national_report_italy.pdf

Barhaim, Gabriel A. *Public-Private Relations in Totalitarian States*. London: Transaction Publishers, 2012.

Barthes, Roland. "La mort de l'auteur". In *Le Bruissement de la Langue. Essais Critiques IV*. Paris: Seuil, 1984, 61–69.

Bell, Ilona. "Gender Matters: The Women in Donne's Poems". In *The Cambridge Companion to John Donne*, ed. by Achsah Guibbory Cambridge: Cambridge University Press, 2006, 201–16, https://doi.org/10.1017/ccol0521832373.013

Bell, Kimberly K., and Julie Nelson Couch. *The Texts and Contexts of Oxford, Bodleian Library, Ms Laud Misc. 108*: *The Shaping of English Vernacular Narrative*. Boston: Brill, 2011, https://doi.org/10.1163/ej.9789004192065.i-342

Belsey, Catherine. *Desire*: *Love Stories in Western Culture*. Oxford: Oxford University Press, 1994.

Ben-Ze'ev, Aharon and Ruhama Goussinsky. *In the Name of Love*: *Romantic Ideology and Its Victims*. Oxford: Oxford University Press, 2008, https://doi.org/10.1093/acprof:oso/9780198566496.001.0001

Bernays, Edward. *Propaganda*. New York: Horace Liveright, 1928, https://archive.org/details/EdwardL.BernaysPropaganda

Berry, Ralph. *The Shakespearean Metaphor*: *Studies in Language and Form*. New York: Macmillan, 1978, https://doi.org/10.1007/978-1-349-03563-2

Best, Stephen and Sharon Marcus. "Surface Reading: An Introduction". *Representations*, 108: 1 (Fall 2009), 1–21, https://doi.org/10.1525/rep.2009.108.1.1

Biblia Hebraica Stuttgartensia, ed. by Karl Elliger and Willhelm Rudolph. Stuttgart: Deutsche Bibelgesellschaft, 1983.

Blackwood, Adam. *Martyre de la Royne d'Escosse*. Edinburgh, 1587, https://books.google.com/books?id=_mZUAAAAcAAJ&printsec=frontcover&source=gbs_ge_summary_r&cad=0

Blair, Peter Hunter. *Ango-Saxon England*. New York: Cambridge University Press, 1959.

Blake, William. *The Complete Poetry and Prose of William Blake*, ed. by David V. Erdman. Berkeley and Los Angeles: University of California Press, 2008.

—. *The Works of William Blake*, ed. by Edwin John Ellis and William Butler Yeats, Vols. 1–3. London: Benard Quartich, 1893, https://archive.org/details/worksofwilliambl02blakrich

Blanc, Pierre. "Sonnet des origines, origine du sonnet: Giacomo da Lentini". In *Le sonnet a la Renaissance: des origenes au XVIIe siècle*, ed. by Yvonne Bellenger. Paris: Aux Amateurs de Livres, 1998, 9–18.

Blanchot, Maurice. "La Littérature et le droit à la mort". In *La Part de Feu*. Paris: Gallimard, 1949, 291–331.

—. "La Solitude Essentielle". In *L'Espace Littéraire*. Paris: Gallimard, 1955, 9–25.

Blank, Hanne. *Virgin: The Untouched History*. New York: Bloomsbury, 2007.

Blasia, Damián E., Søren Wichmannd, Harald Hammarströmb, Peter F. Stadlerc, and Morten H. Christiansen. "Sound-meaning association biases evidenced across thousands of languages". *Proceedings of the National Academy of Sciences* (27 September 2016), 113: 39, http://www.pnas.org/content/113/39/10818.full, https://doi.org/10.1073/pnas.1605782113

Blevins, Jacob. *Catullan Consciousness and the Early Modern Lyric in England: From Wyatt to Donne*. Aldershot: Ashgate, 2004.

Bloch, Ariel and Chana. *The Song of Songs: A New Translation and Commentary*. New York: Random House, 1995.

Bloch, R. Howard, and Stephen G. Nichols. "Introduction". In *Medievalism and the Modern Temper*, ed. by R. Howard Bloch and Stephen G. Nichols. Baltimore: Johns Hopkins University Press, 1996, 1–22.

Bloom, Harold. *Shakespeare: The Invention of the Human*. New York: Penguin, 1998.

—. *The Western Canon: The Books and School of the Ages*. New York: Harcourt Brace, 1994.

Blumenfeld-Kosinski, Renate. "Jean Gerson and the Debate on the Romance of the Rose". *A Companion to Jean Gerson*, ed. by Brian Patrick McGuire. Leiden: Brill, 2006, 317–56.

Boase, Roger. *The Origin and Meaning of Courtly Love: A Critical Study of European Scholarship*. Manchester: Manchester University Press, 1977.

Boccalini, Traiano. *I ragguagli di Parnasso: Or, Advertisements from Parnassus*. Trans. by Henry, Earl of Monmouth. London, 1674.

Bogin, Magda, ed. *The Women Troubadours*. New York: Paddington Press, 1976.

Bolduc, Michelle. "The Breviari D'Amor: Rhetoric and Preaching in Thirteenth-Century Languedoc". *Rhetorica*, 24: 4 (2006), 403–25, https://doi.org/10.1525/rh.2006.24.4.403

Born, Bertan de. *The Poems of the Troubadour Bertran De Born*, ed. by William D. Paden, Tilde Sankovitch, and Patricia H. Stablein. Berkeley: University of California Press, 1986.

Boswell, John. *Christianity, Social Tolerance, and Homosexuality: Gay People in Western Europe from the Beginning of the Christian Era to the Fourteenth Century*. Chicago, University of Chicago Press, 1980.

Boyd, Barbara Weiden. "The *Amores*: The Invention of Ovid". In *Brill's Companion to Ovid*, ed. by Barbara Weiden Boyd. Leiden: Brill, 2002, 91–116, https://doi.org/10.1163/9789047400950_004

Boyle, David. *Troubadour's Song: The Capture, Imprisonment and Ransom of Richard the Lionheart*. New York: Walker & Co., 2005.

Brady, Bernard V. *Christian Love*. Washington: Georgetown University Press, 2003.

Briffault, Robert. *The Troubadours*, ed. by Lawrence F. Koons. Bloomington: Indiana University Press, 1965.

Brogan, Walter A. "The Original Difference". In *Derrida and Différance*, ed. by David Wood and Robert Bernasconi. Evanston: Northwestern University Press, 1985, 31–39.

Brown, Peter, ed. *A Companion to Medieval English Literature and Culture, c.1350-c.1500*. Malden: Blackwell, 2007, https://doi.org/10.1002/9780470996355

—. *Through the Eye of a Needle: Wealth, the Fall of Rome, and the Making of Christianity in the West, 350–550 AD*. Princeton: Princeton University Press, 2012, https://doi.org/10.1515/9781400844531

Bruckner, Matilda Tomaryn, Laurie Shepard, and Sarah White, eds. *Songs of the Women Troubadours*. New York: Garland Publishing, 2000.

Bruckner, Matilda Tomaryn. "'Redefining the Center' Verse and Prose Charrette". In *A Companion to the Lancelot-Grail Cycle*, ed. by Carol Dover. Cambridge, UK: Brewer, 2003, 95–106.

Bryson, Michael. *The Atheist Milton*. Farnham: Ashgate, 2012, https://doi.org/10.4324/9781315613796

—. *The Tyranny of Heaven: Milton's Rejection of God as King*. London: Associated University Presses, 2004.

Bulgakov, Mikhail. *Мастер и Маргарита* [*Master and Margarita*]. Moscow: Olma Media Group, 2005.

Burckhardt, Jacob. *Die Cultur der Renaissance in Italien: Ein Versuch*. Basel: Schweighauser, 1860, https://babel.hathitrust.org/cgi/pt?id=gri.ark:/13960/t7fr4fg3z;view=1up;seq=5

Burden, Dennis H. *The Logical Epic: A Study of the Argument of "Paradise Lost'*. Cambridge, MA: Harvard University Press, 1967.

Burgwinkle, William E. *Love for Sale: Materialist Readings of the Troubadour Razo Corpus*. New York: Garland, 1997.

—. "The Troubadours: The Occitan Model". In *The Cambridge History of French Literature*, ed. by William E. Burgwinkle, Nicholas Hammond, and Emma Wilson. Cambridge: Cambridge University Press, 2011, 20–27, https://doi.org/10.1017/chol9780521897860.004

Burns, E. Jane. *Courtly Love Undressed: Reading Through Clothes in Medieval French Culture*. Philadelphia: University of Pennsylvania Press, 2002, https://doi.org/10.9783/9780812291247

—. "Courtly Love: Who Needs It? Recent Feminist Work in The Medieval French Tradition". *Signs: Journal of Women in Culture and Society*, 27: 1 (2001), 23–57, https://doi.org/10.1086/495669

Buturovic, Amila. "'Only Women and Writing Can Save Us From Death': Erotic Empowering in the Poetry of Nizār Qābbanī". In *Tradition, Modernity, and Postmodernity in Arabic Literature: Essays in Honor of Professor Issa J. Boullata*, ed. by Kamal Abdel-Malek and Wael Hallaq. Leiden: Brill, 2000, 141–57.

Byrne, Sister Marie José. *Prolegomena to an Edition of the Works of Decimus Magnus Ausonius*. New York: Columbia University Press, 1916.

Callaghan, Dympna. "The Ideology of Romantic Love: The Case of Romeo and Juliet". In *The Weyward Sisters: Shakespeare and Feminist Politics*, ed. by Dympna Callaghan, Lorraine Rae Helms, and Jyotsna Singh, Cambridge, MA: Blackwell, 1994, 59–101.

—. *Shakespeare's Sonnets*. Malden: Blackwell, 2007, https://doi.org/10.1002/9780470774878

Calvin, Jean. *Institutio Christianae Religionis*. Geneva: Oliua Roberti Stephani, 1559, https://books.google.com/books?id=6ysy-UX89f4C&printsec=frontcover&source=gbs_ge_summary_r&cad=0

Cameron, Alan. *Claudian: Poetry and Propaganda at the Court of Honorius*. Oxford: Clarendon Press, 1970.

Campbell, Joseph. *The Masks of God: Creative Mythology*. New York: Viking Press, 1968.

—. *The Power of Myth*, ed. by Betty Sue Flowers. New York: Doubleday, 1988.

Camproux. Charles. *Le "joy d'amor" des troubadours. Jeu et joie d'amour*. Montpellier: Causse et Castelnau, 1965.

Camus, Albert. "L'été à Alger". In his *Noces suivi de L'été*. Paris: Gallimard, 1959, 33–52.

Capellanus, Andreas. *De Amore Libri Tres: Von Der Liebe. Drei Bücher*. Berlin and Boston: De Gruyter, 2006.

—. *The Art of Courtly Love*. Trans. by John Jay Perry. New York: W. W. Norton & Co., 1941.

Carmina Burana: Lateinische und Deutsche Lieder und Gedichte einer Handschrift des XIII Jahihunderts aus Benedictbeuern auf der K. Bibliothek gu München, ed. by Johann Andreas Schmeller. Stuttgart: Literarischen Vereins, 1847, https://books.google.com/books?id=0XN3YW-EqacC&pg=PP1

Carroll, Lewis. *Through the Looking Glass: and What Alice Found There*. Philadelphia: Henry Altemus Company, 1897.

Casali, Sergio. "The Art of Making Oneself Hated: Rethinking (Anti-) Augustanism in Ovid's *Ars Amatoria*". In *The Art of Love: Bimillennial Essays on Ovid's Ars Amatoria and Remedia Amoris*, ed. by Roy Gibson, Steven Green, and Alison Sharrock. Oxford: Oxford University Press, 2006, 216–34, https://doi.org/10.1093/acprof:oso/9780199277773.003.0011

—. "The *Bellum Civile* as an Anti-*Aeneid*". *Brill's Companion to Lucan*, ed. by Paolo Asso. Leiden: Brill, 2011, 81–109, https://doi.org/10.1163/9789004217096_006

Castiglione, Baldassarre. *Il Libro del Cortegiano*. Milano: Giovanni Silvestri, 1822, https://archive.org/details/illibrodelcorteg00cast

Castor, Helen. *She-Wolves: The Women Who Ruled England before Elizabeth*. London: Faber and Faber, 2010.

Catullus, Gaius Valerius. *Catullus. Tibullus. Pervigilium Veneris*. Ed. and trans. by F. W. Cornish. Loeb Classical Library, Cambridge, MA: Harvard University Press, 1913.

Cazelles, Brigitte. *The Lady as Saint: A Collection of French Hagiographic Romances of the Thirteenth Century*. University Park: University of Pensylvannia Press, 1991.

Chaucer, Geoffrey. *The Canterbury Tales: Complete*, ed. by Larry Dean Benson. Boston: Houghton Mifflin, 2000.

Cheyette, Fredric L. *Ermengard of Narbonne and the World of the Troubadours*. Ithaca: Cornell University Press, 2001.

Chomsky, Noam. "Beyond a Domesticating Education: A Dialogue". In Noam Chomsky, *Chomsky on Miseducation*. Lanham: Rowman & Littlefield, 2004, 15–37.

—. LBBS, Z-Magazine's Left On-Line Bulletin Board. Online discussion posted at rec.arts.books, 13 November 1995, 03:21:23, http://bactra.org/chomsky-on-postmodernism.html

—. "Noam Chomsky on French Intellectual Culture & Post-Modernism [3/8]". Interview conducted at Leiden University, in March 2011 (posted March 15, 2012), https://www.youtube.com/v/2cqTE_bPh7M&feature=youtu.be&start=409&end=451 [6:49–7:31].

—. *The Common Good* (Berkeley: Odonian Press, 1998).

Chrétien de Troyes. *Le Chevalier de la Charrette*, ed. by Alfred Foulet and Karl D. Uitti. Paris: Classiques Garnier, 1989.

Cicero. *De Finibus Bonorum et Malorum*. In Cicero, *On Ends*, ed. by H. Rackham. Loeb Classical Library, Cambridge, MA: Harvard University Press, 1914.

Cirlot, Victoria, ed. *Antología de textos románicos medievales: siglos XII–XIII*. Barcelona: Edicions Universitat Barcelona, 1984.

Clark, Alice V. "From Abbey to Cathedral and Court: Music Under the Merovingian, Carolingian and Capetian Kings in France until Louis IX". *The Cambridge Companion to French Music*. Cambridge: Cambridge University Press, 2015, 3–20, https://doi.org/10.1017/cco9780511843242.003

Clark, David. *Between Medieval Men: Male Friendship and Desire in Early Medieval English Literature*. Oxford: Oxford University Press, 2009, https://doi.org/10.1093/acprof:oso/9780199558155.001.0001

Claudian (Claudius Claudianus). *Claudian: Vol. II*. Ed. and trans. by Maurice Platnauer. Loeb Classical Library, Cambridge, MA: Harvard University Press, 1998.

Clements, Ronald. E. *Ezekiel*. Louisville: Westminster John Knox Press, 1996.

Cohen, Elizabeth S. and Thomas V. Cohen. *Daily Life in Renaissance Italy*. Westport: Greenwood Press, 2001.

Cohen, Gerson D. "The Song of Songs and the Jewish Religious Mentality". In *Studies in the Variety of Rabbinic Cultures*. Philadelphia: Jewish Publication Society, 1991, 3–17.

Cohen, Thomas V. *Love and Death in Renaissance Italy*. Chicago: University of Chicago Press, 2004, https://doi.org/10.7208/chicago/9780226112602.001.0001

Coleridge, Samuel Taylor. *The Literary Remains of Samuel Taylor Coleridge*, Vol. 1, ed. by Henry Nelson Coleridge. London: William Pickering, 1836, https://archive.org/details/literaryremainso01coleuoft

Coltman, Rod. "Hermeneutics: Literature and Being". *The Blackwell Companion to Hermeneutics*, ed. by Niall Keane and Chris Lawn. Chichester: John Wiley & Sons, 2016, 548–56, https://doi.org/10.1002/9781118529812.ch67

Constans, Léopold Eugène. "Séquence de Sainte Eulalie". In *Chrestomathie de l'ancien français (IXe-XVe siécles)*. Paris and Lepzig: H. Welter, 1906, https://archive.org/details/chrestomathiede00cons

Cox, Catherine S. *Gender and Language in Chaucer*. Gainesville: University Press of Florida, 1997.

Crane, Susan. *Gender and Romance in Chaucer's Canterbury Tales*. Princeton: Princeton University Press, 1994, https://doi.org/10.1515/9781400863754

Cudini, Piero, ed. *Poesia Italiana del Duecento*. Milan: Lampi Di Stampa, 1999.

Curtius, Ernst Robert. *Europäische Literatur und Lateinisches Mittelalter*. Berlin: A. Francke AG Verlag, 1948.

Daniel, Arnaut. *Les Poesies D'Arnaut Daniel*, ed. by René Lavaud. Toulouse: Edouard Privat, 1910, https://archive.org/details/lesposiesdarna00arna

Danielson, Dennis. "Through the Telescope of Typology: What Adam Should Have Done". *Milton Quarterly*, 23: 3 (1989), 121–27, https://doi.org/10.1111/j.1094-348x.1989.tb00770.x

Dante (Dante Alighieri). *The Canzoniere of Dante Alighieri*, ed. by Charles Lyell. London: James Bohn, 1840.

—. *La Divina Commedia. Inferno*, ed. by Ettore Zolesi. Rome: Armando, 2009.

—. *La Divina Commedia. Purgatorio*, ed. by Ettore Zolesi. Rome: Armando, 2003.

Davis, P. J. "Ovid's Amores: A Political Reading". *Classical Philology*, 94: 4 (1999), 431–49, https://doi.org/10.1086/449457

Davis, Robert Con and Ronald Schleifer. *Criticism and Culture: The Role of Critique in Modern Literary Theory*. New York: Longman, 1991.

Dawson, David. *Allegorical Readers and Cultural Revision in Ancient Alexandria* [Los Angeles: University of California Press, 1992.

Day, Linda. "Rhetoric and Domestic Violence In Ezekiel 16". *Biblical Interpretation: A Journal of Contemporary Approaches*, 8: 3 (2000), 205–30, https://doi.org/10.1163/156851500750096327

Debating the Roman de la Rose: A Critical Anthology, ed. by Christine McWebb. London: Routledge, 2007.

De Graef, Ortwin. "Silence to be Observed: A Trial for Paul de Man's Inexcusable Confessions". In *(Dis)continuities: Essays on Paul de Man*, ed. by Luc Herman, Kris Humbeeck, and Geert Lernout. Amsterdam: Rodopi, 1989, 51–73.

Deleuze, Gilles. "Un manifeste de moins". *Superpositions*. Paris: Éditions de Minuit, 1979, 87–131.

De Man, Paul. *Allegories of Reading: Figural Language in Rousseau, Nietzsche, Rilke, and Proust*. New Haven: Yale University Press, 1979.

—. *Blindness and Insight: Essays in the Rhetoric of Contemporary Criticism*. New York: Oxford University Press, 1971.

—. *The Paul de Man Notebooks*, ed. by Martin McQuillan. Edinburgh: Edinburgh University Press, 2014, https://doi.org/10.3366/edinburgh/9780748641048.001.0001

—. *The Rhetoric of Romanticism*. New York: Columbia University Press, 1984.

Derrida, Jacques. *De la Grammatologie*. Paris: Éditions de Minuit, 1967.

—. *L'Ecriture et la Différence*. Paris: Seuil, 1967.

De Sanctis, Francesco. *Storia della letteratura italiana*, Vol. 1. Neaples: Morano, 1870.

Desmond, Marilynn. *Reading Dido: Gender, Textuality, and Medieval Aeneid*. Minneapolis: University of Minnesota Press, 1994.

Dillon, Martin C. *Merleau-Ponty's Ontology*. Evanston: Northwestern University Press, 1997.

Dilthey, Wilhelm. *Der Aufbau der geschichtlichen Welt in den Geisteswissenschaften*. Frankfurt am Main: Suhrkamp, 1970.

Dinshaw, Carolyn. *Chaucer's Sexual Poetics*. Madison, WI: University of Wisconsin Press, 1989.

Dionysius the Carthusian. *Epistolarum ac Euangeliorum*. Cologne: Petrus Quentell, 1537, https://books.google.com/books?id=CqP4kICSulwC&pg=PP5

Dodd, William George. *Courtly Love in Chaucer and Gower*. Gloucester: Peter Smith, 1959.

Doggett, Frank. "Donne's Platonism". *The Sewanee Review*, 42: 3 (1934), 274–92.

Donne, John. *John Donne: The Complete English Poems*, ed. by A. J. Smith. London: Penguin, 1986.

—. L.b.526: Letter from John Donne, The Savoy, London, to Sir George More, 1601/1602 February 2. Early Modern Manuscripts Online, http://emmo.folger.edu/view/Lb526/semiDiplomatic

Doss-Quinby, Eglal, ed. *Songs of the Women Trouvères*. New Haven: Yale University Press, 2001.

Dostoevsky, Fyodor. Братья Карамазовы [*Brothers Karamazov*]. St. Petersburg: A. F. Marx, 1895.

—. Бесы [*Demons*]. St. Petersburg: Azbuka, 2008.

—. Идиот [*The Idiot*]. St. Petersburg: A. Suvorin, 1884.

Dratyon, Michael. *Idea*. In *Daniel's Delia and Drayton's Idea*, ed. by Arundell Esdaile. London: Chatto & Windus, 1908, 67–141, https://books.google.com/books?id=mOiobc0PmsgC&printsec=frontcover&source=gbs_ge_summary_r&cad=0

Dreher, Diane. *Domination and Defiance: Fathers and Daughters in Shakespeare*. Lexington: University Press of Kentucky, 1986.

Dronke, Peter. *The Medieval Poet and His World*. Rome: Edizioni di Storia e Letteratura, 1984.

Duffell, Martin J. *A New History of English Metre*. London: Modern Humanities Research Association and Maney Publishing, 2008.

Dümmler, Nicola Nina. "Musaeus, Hero and Leander: Between Epic and Novel". In *Brill's Companion to Greek and Latin 'epyllion' and Its Reception*, ed. by Manuel Baumbach and Silvio Bär. Leiden: Brill, 2012, 411–446, https://doi.org/10.1163/9789004233058_019

Dunstan, William E. *Ancient Rome*. Lanham: Rowman & Littlefield, 2011.

Eagleton, Terry. *Literary Theory: An Introduction*. Oxford: Blackwell, 1983.

East, W. G. "This Body of Death: Abelard, Heloise and the Religious Life". In *Medieval Theology and the Natural Body*, ed. by Peter Biller and Alastair J. Minnis. Woodbridge, Suffolk: Boydell & Brewer, 1997, 43–59.

Easthope, Antony. *Poetry and Phantasy*. Cambridge: Cambridge University Press, 1989.

Eckhart, Meister. "Qui audit me, non confundetur". *Deutsche Mystiker des Vierzehnten Jahrhunderts: Meister Eckhart. Erste Abtheilung,* ed. by Franz Pfeiffer. Leipzig: G. J. Göschen, 1857, 309–12, https://books.google.com/books?id=-78FAAAAQAAJ&printsec=frontcover&source=gbs_ge_summary_r&cad=0

Edmondson, Paul, and Stanley Wells. *Shakespeare's Sonnets.* Oxford: Oxford University Press, 2004.

Edwards, Catharine. *Death in Ancient Rome.* New Haven: Yale University Press, 2007.

Edwards, David L. *John Donne: Man of Flesh and Spirit.* New York: Continuum, 2001.

Egan, Gabriel. *Shakespeare and Marx.* Oxford: Oxford University Press, 2004.

Eliot, T. S. "Donne in Our Time". In *A Garland for John Donne, 1631–1931,* ed. by Theodore Spencer. Cambridge, MA: Harvard University Press, 1931, 3–19.

Ellis, F. S., trans. *The Romance of the Rose.* 3 Vols. London: J. M. Dent, 1900.

Empson, William. *Milton's God.* Norfolk, CT: New Directions, 1961.

—. "Rescuing Donne". In *Essays on Renaissance Literature,* ed. by John Charles Robert Haffenden. Cambridge: Cambridge University Press, 1993, 159–99, https://doi.org/10.1017/cbo9780511627477.006

—. *Some Versions of Pastoral.* London: Chatto & Windus, 1935.

Epstein, Isidore, ed. *Tractate Sanhedrin.* In *Hebrew English Edition of the Babylonian Talmud,* Vol. 19. London: Socino Press, 1969.

Epstein, Stephen. "The Education of Daphnis: Goats, Gods, the Birds and the Bees". *Phoenix,* 56: 1–2 (2002), 25–39, https://doi.org/10.2307/1192468

Ermengaud, Matfré. *Le Breviari D'Amor,* ed. by Gabriel Azaïs. Béziers: Secrétariat de la Société Archéologique, Scientifique et Littéraire de Béziers, 1862, https://archive.org/details/lebreviaridamor01ermeuoft, https://archive.org/details/lebreviaridamor02ermeuoft

Eschenbach, Wolfram von. *Werke,* ed. by Karl Lachmann. Berlin: G. Reimer, 1879, https://books.google.com/books?id=-rwFAAAAQAAJ&pg=PR1

Essam, Bacem A. "Nizarre Qabbani's Original Versus Translated Pornographic Ideology: A Corpus-Based Study". *Sexuality and Culture,* 20 (2016), 965–986, https://doi.org/10.1007/s12119-016-9369-7

Eusebius, Bishop of Caesarea. *Ecclesiastical History.* Ed. and trans. by J. E. L. Oulton. Loeb Classical Library, Cambridge, MA: Harvard University Press, 1932.

Eve, Martin Paul. *Literature Against Criticism.* Cambridge: Open Book Publishers, 2016, https://doi.org/10.11647/OBP.0102

Everson, Jane E. *The Italian Romance Epic in the Age of Humanism: The Matter of Italy and the World of Rome.* Oxford: Oxford University Press, 2001, https://doi.org/10.1093/acprof:oso/9780198160151.001.0001

Falck, Colin. *Myth, Truth, and Literature: Towards a True Post-modernism*. Cambridge: Cambridge University Press, 1989.

Falconer, Rachel. "A Reading of Wyatt's 'Who so List to Hunt'". In *A Companion to English Renaissance Literature and Culture*, ed. by Michael Hattaway. Oxford: Blackwell, 2003, 176–86, https://doi.org/10.1002/9780470998731.ch14

Fay, Elizabeth A. *Romantic Medievalism History and the Romantic Literary Ideal*. New York: Palgrave, 2002, https://doi.org/10.1057/9781403913616

Febvre, Lucien. *The Problem of Unbelief in the Sixteenth Century, the Religion of Rabelais*. Trans. by Beatrice Gottlieb. Cambridge, MA: Harvard University Press, 1985.

Felski, Rita. *The Limits of Critique*. Chicago: University of Chicago Press, 2015, https://doi.org/10.7208/chicago/9780226294179.001.0001

—. "Suspicious Minds". *Poetics Today*, 32: 2 (Summer 2011), 215–34, https://doi.org/10.1215/03335372-1261208

Fernie, Ewan. *The Demonic: Literature and Experience*. New York: Routledge, 2013.

Ferrari, G. R. F. "Plato and Poetry". In *The Cambridge History of Literary Criticism, Vol. 1: Classical Criticism*, ed. by George Alexander Kennedy. Cambridge: Cambridge University Press, 1989, 92–148.

Fessler, Ignatius Aurelius. *Abälard und Heloisa*, Vol. 2. Berlin, 1806.

Feuerbach, Ludwig. *Das Wesen des Christentums*, ed. by Werner Schuffenhauer. Berlin: De Gruyter, 2006, https://doi.org/10.1524/9783050085456

Fichte, Johann Gottlieb. *Johann Gottlieb Fichte: Fichtes Reden an die Deutsche Nation*, ed. by Samantha Nietz. Hamburg: Severus, 2013.

Fields, Weston. "Early and Medieval Interpretation of the Song of Songs". *Grace Theological Journal*, 1: 2 (1980), 222–33, https://biblicalstudies.org.uk/pdf/gtj/01-2_221.pdf

Findlay, John Niemeyer. *Plato: The Written and Unwritten Doctrines*. New York: Routledge, 1974.

Firenzuola, Agnolo. "Belleza delle Donne". In *Prose di M. Agnolo Firenzuola Fiorentino*. Florence: Bernardo Guinta, 1548, 55–109.

Fish, Stanley Eugene. *How Milton Works*. Cambridge, MA: Belknap Press of Harvard University Press, 2001.

—. "Masculine Persuasive Force: Donne and Verbal Power". In *Soliciting Interpretation: Literary Theory and Seventeenth-Century English Poetry*, ed. by Elizabeth D. Harvey and Katharine Eisaman Maus. Chicago: University of Chicago Press, 1990, 223–52.

—. *Surprised by Sin: The Reader in "Paradise Lost"*. 2nd ed. Cambridge, MA: Harvard University Press, 1998.

Fleming, Bruce. *What Literary Studies Could Be, And What It Is*. Lanham: University Press of America, 2008.

Fortunatus (Venantius Fortunatus). *Venanti Honori Clementiani Fortunati Presbyteri Italici Opera Poetica*, ed. by Frederick Leo. Berlin: Apud Weidmannos, 1881, https://archive.org/details/venantihonoricl00unkngoog

Foucault, Michel. *Histoire de la sexualité, Vol. 1: la volonté de savoir*. Paris: Gallimard, 1976.

—. *Les mots et les choses: Une archéologie sciences humaines*. Paris: Gallimard, 1966.

—. "Le retour de la morale". In his *Dits et écrits, 1954–1988*. Vol. IV: *1980–1988*. Paris: Gallimard, 1994, 696–707, https://doi.org/10.14375/np.9782070739899

—. "Le sujet e le pouvoir". In his *Dits et écrits*. Vol. IV: 222–43, https://doi.org/10.14375/np.9782070739899

—. "Qu'est-ce qu'un auteur?" In his *Dits et écrits*. Vol. I: *1954–1975*, 789–821, https://doi.org/10.14375/np.9782070738441

—. "Sur les façons d'écrire l'Histoire" [interview with Raymond Bellour]. *Les Lettres françaises*, 1187 (15–21 juin 1967), 6–9. Reprinted in his *Dits et Écrits*. Vol. I, 585–600, https://doi.org/10.14375/np.9782070738441

—. *Surveiller et Punir: Naissance de la Prison*. Paris: Gallimard, 1975.

Frantzen, Allen J. *Before the Closet: Same-Sex Love from "Beowulf" to "Angels in America"*. Chicago: University of Chicago Press, 1998, https://doi.org/10.4324/9781315587271

Freeburn, Ryan P. *Hugh of Amiens and the Twelfth-Century Renaissance*. Farnham: Ashgate, 2011.

Frelick, Nancy. "Lacan, Courtly Love and Anamorphosis". In *The Court Reconvenes: Courtly Literature Across the Disciplines: Selected Papers from the Ninth Triennial Congress of the International Courtly Literature Society*, University of British Columbia, 25–31 July, 1998. Cambridge, UK: Brewer, 2003, 107–14.

Fuchs, Stephen. *Against Essentialism: A Theory of Culture and Society*. Cambridge, MA: Harvard University Press, 2009.

Gábor, Katona. "The Lover's Education: Psychic Development in Sidney's 'Astrophil and Stella'". *Hungarian Journal of English and American Studies*, 1: 2 (1995), 3–17.

Gajowski, Evelyn. *The Art of Loving: Female Subjectivity and Male Discursive Traditions in Shakespeare's Tragedies*. Cranbury, NJ: Associated University Presses, 1992.

Gamel, Mary-Kay. "This Day We Read Further: Feminist Interpretation and the Study of Literature". *Pacific Coast Philology*, 22: 1–2 (1987), 7–14.

Ganze, Alison. "Na Maria, pretz e fina valors": A New Argument for Female Authorship". *Romance Notes*, 49: 1 (2009), 23–33, https://doi.org/10.1353/rmc.2009.0010

Gascoigne, George. *The Complete Works of George Gascoigne*: Vol. 1, *The Posies*, ed. by John W. Cunliffe. Cambridge: Cambridge University Press, 1907, https://archive.org/details/cu31924013121292

Gaunt, Simon. "Poetry of Exclusion: A Feminist Reading of Some Troubadour Lyrics". *The Modern Language Review*, 85: 2 (1990), 310–29, https://doi.org/10.2307/3731812

—. "The Châtelain De Couci". In *The Cambridge Companion to Medieval French Literature*, ed. by Simon Gaunt and Sarah Kay. Cambridge: Cambridge University Press, 2008, 95–108, https://doi.org/10.1017/ccol9780521861755.007

Gaunt, Simon, and Sarah Kay. "Introduction". In *The Troubadours: An Introduction*, ed. by Simon Gaunt and Sarah Kay. Cambridge: Cambridge University Press, 1999, 1–7.

Gide, André. *Les Nourritures terrestres*. Paris: Gallimard, 1921.

Gigot, Francis E., and Charles G. Herbermann. "Glosses, Scriptural-I. Etymology and Principal Meanings". In *The Catholic Encyclopedia: An International Work of Reference on the Constitution, Doctrine, Discipline, and History of the Catholic Church: Father to Gregory*, ed. by Charles G. Herbermann *et al*. New York: Robert Appleton Company, 1909, Vol. 6, 588, https://archive.org/details/07470918.6.emory.edu

Gilead, Sarah. "Ungathering 'Gather Ye Rosebuds': Herrick's Misreading of Carpe Diem". *Criticism*, 27: 2 (1985), 133–53.

Giles of Rome. *Librum Solomonis qui Cantica Canticorum Inscribitur Commentaria D. Aegidii Romani*. Rome: Antonium Bladum, 1555, https://books.google.com/books?id=ZcjIK13ZCXAC&pg=PP4

Gillis, John R. "Affective Individualism and the English Poor". *Journal of Interdisciplinary History*, 10: 1 (1979), 121–28.

Gingrich, Andre. "Conceptualising Identities: Anthropological Alternatives to Essentialising Difference and Moralizing about Othering". *Grammars of Identity/Alterity: A Structural Approach*, ed. by Gerd Baumann and Andre Gingrich. New York: Berghahn Books, 2004, 3–17.

Giroux, Henry. *Neoliberalism's War on Higher Education*. Chicago: Haymarket Books, 2014.

Glancy, Ruth F. *Thematic Guide to British Poetry*. Westport: Greenwood Press, 2002.

Goebbels, Joseph. "Rede vor der Presse über die Errichtung des Reichspropagandaministeriums". In Joseph Goebbels, *Revolution der Deutschen: 14 Jahre Nationalsozialismus*. Oldenburg: Gerhard Stalling, 1933, 135–50.

Goethe, Johann Wolfgang von. *Faust*, Part I, ed. by Walter Kaufmann. New York: Anchor Books, 1990.

Golb, Norman. *The Jews in Medieval Normandy: A Social and Intellectual History*. New York: Cambridge University Press, 1998.

Golden, Mark. "Demography and the Exposure of Girls at Athens". *Phoenix*, 35: 4 (1981), 316–31, https://doi.org/10.2307/1087926

Goldin, Frederick. *The Mirror of Narcissus and the Courtly Love Lyric*. Ithaca: Cornell University Press, 1967.

Goldstien, Neal L. "Love's Labour's Lost and the Renaissance Vision of Love". In *Shakespeare and the Literary Tradition*, ed. by Stephen Orgel and Sean Kellen, London: Routledge, 1999, 201–16.

Goold, C. P. "The Cause of Ovid's Exile". *Illinois Classical Studies*, 8: 1 (1983), 94–107, http://hdl.handle.net/2142/11861

Gramsci, Antonio. *Quarderi del carcere, Vol. I: Quaderni 1–5*, ed. by Valentino Gerratana. Turin: Einaudi, 1977.

Gratian. *Corpus Iuris Canonici, Vol. 1: Decretum Magistri Gratiani*. Leipzig: Bernhard Tauchnitz, 1879, http://www.columbia.edu/cu/lweb/digital/collections/cul/texts/ldpd_6029936_001/index.html

Greaves, Richard L. *Society and Religion in Elizabethan England*. Minneapolis: University of Minnesota Press, 1981.

Greek New Testament, ed. by Barbara Aland. Stuttgart: Deutsche Bibelgesellschaft, 2014.

Greenblatt, Stephen. *Renaissance Self-Fashioning: From More to Shakespeare*. Chicago: University of Chicago Press, 1980.

—. *Shakespearean Negotiations: The Circulation of Social Energy in Renaissance England*. Berkeley and Los Angeles: University of California Press, 1998.

—. *The Swerve: How the World Became Modern*. New York: W. W. Norton & Co., 2011.

Greenstein, Edward L. "Medieval Bible Commentaries". In *Back to the Sources: Reading the Classic Jewish Texts*, ed. by Barry W. Holtz. New York: Simon & Schuster, 2006, 213–59.

Grégoire, Henri. *Rapport sur la nécessité et les moyens d'anéantir le patois, et d'universaliser l'usage de la langue française*. Paris: Imprimerie Nationale, 1794, https://books.google.co.uk/books?id=8PB2RBNrLZYC&pg=PA1

Greville, Fulke. *The Tragedy of Mustapha*. London: Printed for Nathaniel Butler, 1609, https://archive.org/details/tragedyofmustaph00grev

Grollman, Eric Anthony. "Gender Policing in Academe". *Inside Higher Education*, https://www.insidehighered.com/advice/2016/07/29/academy-polices-gender-presentation-scholars-essay

Grotius, Hugo. *Hugonis Groth Sacra in quibus Adamus exul tragoedia*. Hague: Alberti Henrici, 1601, https://books.google.com/books?id=pRY_AAAAcAAJ&pg=PP11

Guibbory, Achsah. "Erotic Poetry". In *The Cambridge Companion to John Donne*, ed. by Achsah Guibbory. Cambridge: Cambridge University Press, 2006, 133–48, https://doi.org/10.1017/ccol0521832373.009

—. "'Oh, Let Mee Not Serve So': The Politics of Love in Donne's *Elegies*". *English Literary History*, 57: 4 (1990), 811–33, https://doi.org/10.2307/2873086

—. *Returning to John Donne*. Farnham: Ashgate, 2015, https://doi.org/10.4324/9781315606170

Guilhem de Tudela and Anonymous. *Historie de la Croisade contre les Hérétiques Alibgeois*, ed. by M. C. Fauriel. Paris: Imprimerie Royale, 1837, https://archive.org/details/histoiredelacroi00guil

Guilhem IX (Guillaume IX, Duc D'Aquitaine). *Les Chansons De Guillaume IX, Duc d'Aquitaine (1071–1127)*, ed. by Alfred Jeanroy. Paris: Honoré Champion, 1913, https://archive.org/details/leschansonsdegui00willuoft

Guinizelli, Guido. *The Poetry of Guido Guinizelli*, ed. by Robert Edwards. New York: Garland Publishing, 1987.

Guynn, Noah D. *Allegory and Sexual Ethics in the High Middle Ages*. New York: Palgrave Macmillan, 2007, https://doi.org/10.1057/9780230603660

Hagstrum, Jean H. *Esteem Enlivened by Desire*: *The Couple from Homer to Shakespeare*. Chicago: University of Chicago Press, 1992.

Hallissy, Margaret. *A Companion to Chaucer's Canterbury Tales*. Westport: Greenwood Press, 1995.

Hara, Diana. *Courtship and Constraint*: *Rethinking the Making of Marriage in Tudor England*. Manchester: Manchester University Press, 2000.

Hardin, Richard F. *Love in a Green Shade*: *Idyllic Romances Ancient to Modern*. Lincoln: University of Nebraska Press, 2000.

Hartman, Geoffrey H. *Criticism in the Wilderness*: *The Study of Literature Today*. New Haven: Yale University Press, 1980.

Haskins, Charles Homer. *The Renaissance of the Twelfth Century*. Cambridge, MA: Harvard University Press, 1927.

Haslam, Alexander S., and Stephen. D. Reicher. "Contesting the 'Nature' of Conformity: What Milgram and Zimbardo's Studies Really Show". *PLoS Biology*, 10: 11 (2012), https://doi.org/10.1371/journal.pbio.1001426

Hawkes, David. *John Milton, A Hero of Our Time*. Berkeley: Counterpoint Press, 2009.

Hayyim, Yaakov Ben, ed. *Mikraot Gedolot* (תולודג תוארקמ), Vol. 4. Printed by Daniel Bomberg: Venice, 1524, https://archive.org/stream/The_Second_Rabbinic_Bible_Vol_4/4#page/n262

Hegel, Georg Wilhelm Friedrich. *Vorlesungen über die Aesthetik*, Vol. 1. Berlin: Dunder und Humblot, 1835.

Heidegger, Martin. "Der Ursprung des Kunstwerkes". *Holzwege*: *Gesamtusgabe*, Vol. V. Frankfurt am Main: Vittorio Klostermann, 1977, 1–74.

—. *Grundfragen der Philosophie. Ausgewählte "Probleme" der "Logik"*. *Gesamtausgabe*. II. *Abteilung*: *Vorlesungen 1923–1944*. Band 45. Frankfurt am Main: Vittorio Klostermann, 1984.

—. *Sein und Zeit*. Tübingen: Max Niemeyer, 1967.

Heisterbacences, Caesarii. *Dialogus Miraculorum*, ed. by Josephus Strange, Vol. 1. Cologne: H. Lempertz, 1851, https://archive.org/details/caesariiheister00stragoog

Heller-Roazen, Daniel. *Fortune's Faces*: *The Roman de la Rose and the Poetics of Contingency*. Baltimore: Johns Hopkins University Press, 2003.

Hengel, Martin. "Mors Turpissima Crucis: Die Kreuzigung in der Antiken Welt und die 'Toheit' des Wortes vom Kreuz". In *Rechtfertigung*: *Festschrift für Ernst Käsemann zum 70 Geburtstag, ed. by* Johannes Friederich, Wolfgang Pöhlmann, and Peter Stuhlmacher. Tübingen: J. C. B. Mohr, 1976, 125–184.

Herman, Edward S., and Noam Chomsky. *Manufacturing Consent*: *The Political Economy of the Mass Media*. New York: Knopf Doubleday, 2011.

Herman, Peter C. *Destabilizing Milton*: *"Paradise Lost" and the Poetics of Incertitude*. New York: Palgrave MacMillan, 2005.

Herrick, Robert. *The Complete Poems of Robert Herrick, 3 Volumes*, ed. by Alexander Balloch Grosart. London: Chatto & Windus, 1876.

Vol. 1: https://books.google.com/books?id=n14JAAAAQAAJ

Vol. 2: https://books.google.com/books?id=l_c7AQAAMAAJ

Vol. 3: https://books.google.com/books?id=wM0qAQAAIAAJ

Herzman, Ronald B., Graham Drake, and Eve Salisbury, eds. *Four Romances of England*: *King Horn, Havelok the Dane, Bevis of Hampton, Athelston*. Kalamazoo, MI: Medieval Institute Publications, Western Michigan University, 1999.

Highet, Gilbert. *The Classical Tradition*: *Greek and Roman Influences on Western Literature*. New York and Oxford: Oxford University Press, 1949.

Hilarius (Hilary the Englishman). *Versus et Ludi Epistolae*. Mittellateinische Studien und Texte, Vol. 16, ed. by Walther Bulst und M. L. Bulst-Thiele. Leiden and New York: Brill, 1989.

Hill, Christopher. *Milton and the English Revolution*. London: Faber and Faber, 1977.

Hjelmslev, Louis. *Omkring Sprogteoriens Grundlæggelse*. Copenhagen: Bianco Lunos Bogtrykkeri, 1943.

Hobbes, Thomas. Leviathan: Or, The Matter, Forme & Power of a Commonwealth, Ecclesiasticall and Civill (London: Andrew Crooke, 1651), https://books.google.com/books?id=L3FgBpvIWRkC&pg=PP19

Holmes, Nigel. "Nero and Caesar: Lucan 1.33–66". *Classical Philology*, 1999, 75–81, https://doi.org/10.1086/449419

Holmes, Olivia. *Assembling the Lyric Self Authorship from Troubadour Song to Italian Poetry Book*. Minneapolis: University of Minnesota Press, 2000.

Hölkeskam, Karl-J. *Reconstructing the Roman Republic: An Ancient Political Culture and Modern Research*. Princeton: Princeton University Press, 2010, https://doi.org/10.1515/9781400834907

Homer. *Odyssey*, Vol. I: Books 1–12. Ed. and trans. by A. T. Murray. Loeb Classical Library, Cambridge, MA: Harvard University Press, 1919.

—. *Odyssey*, Vol. I: Books 13–24. Ed. and trans. by A. T. Murray.

Horace. *Horace: Epodes and Odes*, ed. by Daniel H. Garrison. Norman: University of Oklahoma Press, 1998.

Horstmann, Carl, ed. *The Early South English Legendary or Lives of Saints*. London: N. Trubner, 1887, https://archive.org/details/earlysouthenglis00hors

Horváth, I. K. "Impius Aeneas". *Acta Antiqua Academiae Scientiarum Hungaricae*, 3–4 (1958), 385–93, http://real-j.mtak.hu/441/1/ACTAANTIQUA_06.pdf

Houlbrooke, Ralph A., ed. *English Family Life: 1576–1716: An Anthology from Diaries*. Oxford: Blackwell, 1988.

Hughes, Merritt Y. "The Lineage of 'The Extasie'". *The Modern Language Review*, 27: 1 (1932), 1–5.

Hult, David F. "Gaston Paris and the Invention of Courtly Love". In *Medievalism and the Modernist Temper*, ed. by R. Howard Bloch and Stephen G. Nichols. Baltimore: Johns Hopkins University Press, 1996, 192–224.

—. "Jean de Meun's Continuation of Le Roman de la Rose". In *A New History of French Literaure*, ed. by Denis Hollier. Cambridge, MA: Harvard University Press, 1989, 97–103.

—. "The Roman de la Rose, Christine de Pizan, and the querelle des femmes". In *The Cambridge Companion to Medieval Women's Writing*, ed. by Carolyn Dinshaw and David Wallace, 184–194. Cambridge: Cambridge University Press, 2003, https://doi.org/10.1017/ccol052179188x.013

Hume, David. "Of the First Principles of Government". In *Essays, Literary, Moral, and Political*. London: Ward, Lock & Co., 1870, 23–25, https://catalog.hathitrust.org/Record/007662825

Huppé, Bernard F. *A Reading of the Canterbury Tales*. Albany: State University of New York Press, 1964.

"If Adam was Perfect, How Was It Possible for Him to Sin?" *The Watchtower*, 129: 19 (October 1, 2008), 27, https://wol.jw.org/en/wol/d/r1/lp-e/2008733

Isaacson, Walter. *Benjamin Franklin: An American Life*. New York: Simon & Schuster, 2003.

Jackson, W. T. H. "Faith Unfaithful—The German Reaction to Courtly Love". In *The Meaning of Courtly Love*, ed. by Francis X. Newman, 55–76. Albany: State University of New York Press, 1969.

Jacobson, Howard. *Ovid's Heroidos*. Princeton: Princeton University Press, 1974.

Jameson, Frederic. *The Political Unconscious: Narrative as a Socially Symbolic Act*. Ithaca: Cornell University Press, 1981.

Jang, Jin-sung. *Dear Leader: My Escape from North Korea*. Trans. by Shirley Lee. New York: Simon & Schuster, 2014.

Japhet, Sara. "Rashi's Commentary on the Song of Songs: The Revolution of the Peshat and Its Aftermath". In *Mein Haus Wird Ein Bethaus Für Alle Völker Genannt Werden. Festschrift Für Thomas Wille Sum 75. Gerburgstag*, ed. by J. Männchen and T. Reiprich. Neukirchen: Neukirchener Verlag, 2007, 199–219.

Jeanjean, Henri. "Flamenca: A Wake for a Dying Civilization?", *Parergon*, 16: 1 (July 1998), http://ro.uow.edu.au/cgi/viewcontent.cgi?article=2958&context=artspapers

Jerome. *Contra Jovinianum*. Vienna: Joannes Singrenius, 1516, https://books.google.com/books?id=SUZRAAAAcAAJ&pg=PP7

Jewell, Helen M. *Women in Medieval England*. Manchester: Manchester University Press, 1996.

Johnson, Samuel. *The Lives of the Most Eminent English Poets, with Critical Observations on Their Works*, Vol. 1. London: J. Fergusson, 1819, https://books.google.com/books?id=e_sTAAAAQAAJ&pg=PP9

Jones, Michael K., and Malcolm G. Underwood. *The King's Mother: Lady Margaret Beaufort, Countess of Richmond and Derby*. Cambridge: Cambridge University Press, 1993.

Justinus, Marcus Junianus. *Epitoma Historiarum Philippicarum Pompei Trogi*. Leipzig: B. G. Teubner, 1886, https://babel.hathitrust.org/cgi/pt?id=uiug.30112023680843;view=1up;seq=7

Kauffman, Linda S. *Discourses of Desire: Gender, Genre, and Epistolary Fictions*. Ithaca: Cornell University Press, 1986.

Kaplan, David M. *Ricoeur's Critical Theory*. Albany: State University of New York Press, 2003.

Kates, Joshua. "Literary Criticism". In *The Routledge Companion to Phenomenology*. Ed. by Sebastian Luft. New York: Routledge, 2012, 644–54.

Katz, Joseph. "Development of Mind". In *Scholars in the Making: The Development of Graduate and Professional Students*, ed. by Joseph Katz and Rodney T. Hartnett. Cambridge, MA, Ballinger, 1976, 107–26.

Kay, Sarah. "Courts, Clerks, and Courtly Love". In *The Cambridge Companion to Medieval Romance*, ed. by Roberta L. Krueger. Cambridge: Cambridge University Press, 2000, 81–97, https://doi.org/10.1017/ccol0521553423.006

—. *Parrots and Nightingales: Troubadour Quotations and the Development of European Poetry*. Philadelphia: University of Pennsylvania Press, 2013, https://doi.org/10.9783/9780812208382

—. *Subjectivity in Troubadour Poetry*. Cambridge: Cambridge University Press, 1990, https://doi.org/10.1017/cbo9780511519550

—. *The Place of Thought: The Complexity of One in Late Medieval French Didactic Poetry*. Philadelphia: University of Pennsylvania Press, 2007.

Kelley, Maurice. "The Provenance of John Milton's Christian Doctrine: A Reply to William B. Hunter". *Studies in English Literature, 1500-1900*, 34 (1994), 153–63, https://doi.org/10.2307/450791

Kemp, Theresa D. *Women in the Age of Shakespeare*. Santa Barbara: Greenwood Press, 2010.

Kennedy, Elspeth. "The Rewriting and Re-reading of a Text: The Evolution of the Prose Lancelot". In *The Changing Face of Arthurian Romance: Essays on Arthurian Prose Romances in Memory of Cedric E. Pickford: A Tribute by the Members of the British Branch of the International Arthurian Society*, ed. by Alison Adams, Armel H. Diverres, and Karen Stern. Cambridge, UK: Brewer, 1986, 1–9.

Kennedy, William J. "European Beginnings and Transmissions: Dante Petrarch, and the Sonnet Sequence". In *The Cambridge Companion to the Sonnet*, ed. by A. D. Cousins and Peter Horwarth, 84–104. Cambridge: Cambridge University Press, 2011, https://doi.org/10.1017/ccol9780521514675.006

Kerrigan, William. "Kiss Fancies in Robert Herrick". *George Herbert Journal*, 14: 1–2 (1990), 155–71, https://doi.org/10.1353/ghj.1990.0014

King, Margaret L. "Children in Judaism and Christianity". In *The Routledge History of Childhood in the Western World*, ed. by Paula S. Fass. London: Routledge, 2013, 39–60.

Klein. Richard. "The Future of Literary Criticism". *PMLA*, 125: 4 (October 2010), 920–23, https://doi.org/10.1632/pmla.2010.125.4.920

Kleinman, Scott. "Animal Imagery and Oral Discourse in Havelok's First Fight", *Viator: Medieval and Renaissance Studies*, 35 (2004), 311–27, https://doi.org/10.1484/j.viator.2.300201

Knox, Peter E. "The Heroides: Elegaic Voices". In *Brill's Companion to Ovid*, ed. by Barbara Weiden Boyd. Leiden: Brill, 2002, 117–40, https://doi.org/10.1163/9789047400950_005

Köhler, Erich. "Zum 'Trobar Clus' Der Trobadors". *Romanische Forschungen*, 64: 1–2 (1952), 71–101.

—. "Observations historiques et sociologiques sur la poésie des troubadours". *Cahiers de civilisation médiévale*, 7: 25 [1964], pp. 27–51, http://www.persee.fr/doc/ccmed_0007-9731_1964_num_7_25_1296

Krass, Andreas. "Saying It with Flowers: Post-Foucauldian Literary History and the Poetics of Taboo in a Premodern German Love Song". In *After the History of Sexuality: German Genealogies with and Beyond Foucault*, ed. by Scott Spector, Helmut Puff, and Dagmar Herzog. New York: Berghahn Books, 2012, 63–75.

Kristeva, Julia. *Histoires d'amour*. Paris: Denoël, 1983.

Krueger, Paul, Theodor Mommsen, Rudolf Schoell, and Whilhelm Kroll, eds. *Corpus Iuris Civilis*, Vol. 2. Berlin: Apud Weidmannos, 1892, https://books.google.com/books?id=2hvTAAAAMAAJ&printsec=frontcover&source=gbs_ge_summary_r&cad=0

Labé, Louise. *Oeuvres De Louise Labé*, ed. by Prosper Blancheman. Paris: Librarie des Bibliophiles, 1875, https://books.google.com/books?id=w_fl8BM3_SUC&printsec=frontcover&source=gbs_ge_summary_r&cad=0

La Boétie, Étienne de. *Discours de la Servitude Volontaire* [1576]. Paris: Editions Bossard, 1922, https://fr.wikisource.org/wiki/Livre:La_Boétie_-_Discours_de_la_servitude_volontaire.djvu

Lacan, Jacques. "Discours de Jacques Lacan". *La Psychanalyse*, 1 (1956), 202–11, 242–55.

—. *Écrits*. Paris: Seuil, 1966.

—. *Le Séminaire de Jacques Lacan, Livre III: Les Psychoses: 1955–1956*, ed. by Jacques Alain Miller. Paris: Seuil, 1981.

—. *Le Seminaire de Jacques Lacan. Livre VII. L'Éthique de la Psychanalyse: 1959–1960*, ed. by Jacques Alain Miller. Paris: Seuil, 1986.

—. *Le Séminaire de Jacques Lacan, Livre XVII: L'envers de la Psychanalyse: 1969–1970*, ed. by Jacques Alain Miller. Paris: Seuil, 1991.

Lagerlund, Henrik. "The Assimilation of Aristotelian and Arabic Logic up to the Later Thirteenth Century". In *Mediaeval and Renaissance Logic*, ed. by Dov M. Gabbay and John Woods. Amsterdam: Elsevier, 2008, 281–346, https://doi.org/10.1016/s1874-5857(08)80026-x

Landrum, David. "Robert Herrick and the Ambiguities of Gender". *Texas Studies in Literature and Language*, 49: 2 (2007), 181–207, https://doi.org/10.1353/tsl.2007.0012

Lane, Joan. *Apprenticeship in England: 1600–1914*. London: UCL Press, 1996.

Lanham, Richard A. *The Motives of Eloquence: Literary Rhetoric in the Renaissance*. New Haven: Yale University Press, 1976.

Larson, Deborah Aldrich. *John Donne and Twentieth-century Criticism*. London: Associated University Presses, 1989.

Layton, Richard A. "Hearing Love's Language: The Letter of the Text in Origen's Commentary on the Song of Songs". In *The Reception and Interpretation of the Bible in Late Antiquity: Proceedings of the Montréal Colloquium in Honour of Charles Kannengiesser, 11–13 October 2006*, ed. by Lorenzo DiTommaso and Lucian Turcescu. Leiden: Brill, 2008, 287–315, https://doi.org/10.1163/ej.9789004167155.i-608.75

Lazar, Moshe. "Cupid, the Lady, and the Poet: Modes of Love at Eleanor of Aquitaine's Court". In *Eleanor of Aquitaine: Patron and Politician*, ed. by William W. Kibler. Austin: University of Texas Press, 1976, 35–60.

—. "Fin'amor". In *A Handbook of the Troubadours*, ed. by F. R. P. Akehurst and Judith M. Davis. Berkeley: University of California Press, 1995, 61–100.

Lazda-Cazers, Rasma. "Oral Sex in the Songs of Oswald von Wolkenstein: Did it Really Happen?" In *Sexuality in the Middle Ages and Early Modern Times: New Approaches to a Fundamental Cultural-Historical and Literary-Anthropological Theme*, ed. by Albrecht Classen. Berlin: De Gruyter, 2008, 579–98, https://doi.org/10.1515/9783110209402.579

Lea, Henry Charles. *A History of the Inquisition of the Middle Ages*, Vol. 1. New York: Macmillan, 1906.

Leggatt, Alexander. *Shakespeare's Political Drama: The History Plays and the Roman Plays*. New York: Routledge, 2003.

Léglu, Catherine, Rebecca Rist, and Claire Taylor. *The Cathars and Albigensian Crusade: A Sourcebook*. New York: Routledge, 2014.

Le Goff, Jacques, ed. *The Medieval World*. Trans. by Lydia G. Cochrane. London: Collins & Brown, 1990.

Leishman, J. B. *Themes and Variations in Shakespeare's Sonnets*. London: Routledge, 1961.

Lentini, Giacomo da. *A Critical Edition of the Poetry of Giacomo da Lentini*, ed. by Stephen Popolizio. Ph.D. dissertation, Indiana University, 1975; Ann Arbor: University Microfilms, 1980.

Leonard, John. *Faithful Labourers: A Reception History of Paradise Lost, 1667–1970, Vol. 2. Interpretive Issues*. Oxford: Oxford University Press, 2013.

Levi-Strauss, Claude. "Introduction à l'œuvre de Marcel Mauss". In Marcel Mauss, *Sociologie et Anthropologie*. Paris: Presses Universitaires de France, 1950, xxiv–xl.

—. *Les Structures Élémentaires de la Parenté*. Berlin: De Gruyter, 2002.

Lewis, C. S. *A Preface to Paradise Lost*. London: Oxford University Press, 1942.

—. *The Allegory of Love: A Study in Medieval Tradition*. London: Oxford University Press, 1936.

Lille, Alain de. *Alani de Insulis doctoris universalis opera omnia*. In *Patrologiae Cursus Completus*, Vol. 210, ed. by Jacques Paul Migne. Paris: Apud Garnier Fratres, 1855, https://books.google.com/books?id=c10k8WCYMBoC&pg=PA7

Livy (Titus Livius Patavinus). *Titi Livi Ab vrbe condita libri praefatio, liber primvs*, Vol. 1, ed. by H. J. Edwards. Cambridge: Cambridge University Press, 1912, https://books.google.com/books?id=gsNEAAAAIAAJ&printsec=frontcover&source=gbs_ge_summary_r&cad=0

Locke, John. *Concerning Civil Government, Second Essay*, ed. by Robert Maynard Hutchins. Great Books of the Western World, Vol. 35. Chicago: Encyclopedia Britannica, 1952.

Longus. *Daphnis and Chloe*. Ed. and trans. by Jeffrey Henderson. Loeb Classical Library, Cambridge, MA: Harvard University Press, 2009, https://doi.org/10.4159/dlcl.longus-story_daphnis_chloe.2009

Longxi, Zhang. "The Letter or the Spirit: The Song of Songs, Allegoresis, and the Book of Poetry". *Comparative Literature*: 193–217, https://doi.org/10.2307/1770241

Lorris, Guillaume de, and Jean de Meun. *Le Roman de la Rose*. 3 vols, ed. by Felix Lecoy. Paris: Honoré Champion, 1965.

—. *The Romance of the Rose*. Ed. and trans. by Charles Dahlberg. Princeton: Princeton University Press, 1971.

Love, Heather. "Truth and Consequences: On Paranoid Reading and Reparative Reading". *Criticism*, 52: 2 (Spring 2010), 235–241, https://doi.org/10.1353/crt.2010.0022

Lucan (Marcus Annaeus Lucanus). *The Civil War* (*Pharsalia*). Ed. and trans. by J. D. Duff. Loeb Classical Library, Cambridge, MA: Harvard University Press, 1962.

Luft, Joanna. "The Play of Repetition and Resemblance in The Romance of the Rose". *The Romanic Review*, 102: 1–2 (2011), 49–63.

Luther, Martin. Martin Luther. *Von Weltlicher Obrigkeit*. Berlin: Tredition Classics, 2012, 10.

—. *B. Patris Martini Lutheri Liber de Servo Arbitrio*, ed. by Sebastian Schmid. Strasburg: J. R. Dulsseckeri, 1707.

Macdonald, Aileen Ann. "A Refusal to Be Silenced or to Rejoice in Any Joy That Love May Bring: The Anonymous Old Occitan Canso, 'Per Ioi Que D'amor M'avegna'". *Dalhousie French Studies*, 36 (1996), 3–13.

MacFarlane, Alan. "Review of the Family, Sex and Marriage in England: 1500–1800, by Lawrence Stone". *History and Theory*, 18 (1979), 103–26, https://doi.org/10.2307/2504675

Macfie, Pamela Royston. "Lucan, Marlowe, and the Poetics of Violence". In *Renaissance Papers 2008*, ed. by Christopher Cobb and M. Thomas Hester. Rochester, NY: Camden House, 2009, 47–64, https://doi.org/10.1017/upo9781571137494.005

Macrobius. *Saturnalia*. Ed. and trans. by Robert A. Kaster. Loeb Classical Library, Cambridge, MA: Harvard University Press, 2011.

Mallarmé, Stéphane. "Crise de Vers". In *Divagations*. Paris: Bibliothèque-Charpentier, 1897, 235–49, https://fr.wikisource.org/wiki/Divagations/Texte_entier

Mann, Jill. *Life in Words: Essays on Chaucer, the Gawain-Poet, and Malory*. Toronto: University of Toronto Press, 2014.

Marcabru. *Poésies Complètes du Troubadour Marcabru*, ed. by Jean Dejeanne. Toulouse: Édouard Privat, 1909, http://gallica.bnf.fr/ark:/12148/bpt6k4240c/f3.item

Marenbon, John. *Medieval Philosophy: An Historical and Philosophical Introduction*. London: Routledge, 2007.

—. *The Philosophy of Peter Abelard*. Cambridge: Cambridge University Press, 1997.

Mariaselvam, Abraham. *The Song of Songs and Ancient Tamil Love Poems: Poetry and Symbolism*. Roma: Editrice Pontificio Istituto Biblico, 1988.

Marlowe, Christopher. "Hero and Leander". In *Christopher Marlowe: The Complete Poems and Translations*, ed. by Stephen Orgel. London: Penguin, 2007.

Martin, Catherine Gimelli. "The Erotology of Donne's 'Extasie'; And The Secret History Of Voluptuous Rationalism". *Studies in English Literature, 1500-1900*, 44: 1 (2004), 121–47, https://doi.org/10.1353/sel.2004.0008

Martinez, Ronald. "Italy". In *A Handbook of the Troubadours*, ed. by F. R. P. Akehurst and Judith M. Davis. Berkeley: University of California Press, 1995, 279–94.

Marvin, Laurence W. *The Occitan War: A Military and Political History of the Albigensian Crusade, 1209–1218*. Cambridge: Cambridge University Press, 2008, https://doi.org/10.1017/cbo9780511496561

Masten, Jeffrey. "The Two Gentlemen of Verona". In *A Companion to Shakespeare's Works*, Vol. III, ed. by Richard Dutton. Malden: Blackwell, 2003, 266–85, https://doi.org/10.1002/9780470996553.ch14

May, Simon. *Love: A History*. New Haven: Yale University Press, 2011.

McCloskey, Patrick, and Edward Phinney, Jr. "Ptolemaeus Tyrannus: The Typification of Nero in the Pharsalia". *Hermes*, 96 (1968), 80–87.

McGlynn, Sean. *Kill Them All*: *Cathars and Carnage in the Albigensian Crusade*. Stroud, UK: History Press, 2015.

McGowan, Kate. *Key Issues in Critical and Cultural Theory*. Buckingham: Open University Press, 2007.

McGrath, Alister. *C. S. Lewis A Life*: *Eccentric Genius, Reluctant Prophet*. Carol Stream, IL: Tyndale House Publishers, 2013.

McGuckin, John Anthony. "The Scholarly Works of Origen". *The Westminster Handbook to Origen*, ed. by John Anthony McGuckin. Louisville: Westminster John Knox Press, 2004, 25–41.

McWebb, Christine. "Hermeneutics of Irony: Lady Reason and the Romance of the Rose". *Dalhousie French Studies*, 69 (2004), 3–13.

Meaney, Audrey L. "The Ides of the Cotton Gnomic Poem". *Medium Ævum*, 48: 1 (1979), 23–39, https://doi.org/10.2307/43628412

Meschini, Marco. "'Smoking Sword': Le Meurtre Du Legat Pierre De Castelnau Et La Premiere Croisade Albigeoise". In *La Papauté et les Croisades*, ed. by Michel Balard. Farnham: Ashgate, 2011, 67–75.

Mews, Constant J. *Abelard and Heloise*. Oxford: Oxford University Press, 2005, https://doi.org/10.1093/0195156889.001.0001

—. "Abelard, Heloise, and Discussion of Love in the Twelfth-Century Schools". In *Rethinking Abelard*: *A Collection of Critical Essays*, ed. by Babette S. Hellemans. Leiden: Brill, 2014, 11–36.

—. "Accusations of Heresy and Error in the Twelfth Century Schools: The Witness of Gerhoh of Reichersberg and Otto of Freising". In *Heresy in Transition*: *Transforming Ideas of Heresy in Medieval and Early Modern Europe*. London: Routledge, 2016, 43–58.

—. *The Lost Love Letters of Heloise and Abelard*. New York: Palgrave MacMillan, 1999.

Miller, J. Hillis. "The Critic as Host". *Critical Inquiry*, 3: 3 (Spring 1977), 439–447, https://doi.org/10.1086/447899

—. "Walter Pater: A Partial Portrait". *Daedalus, In Praise of Books*, 105: 1 (Winter 1976), 97–113.

Miller, Patrick D. "A Fairy Tale Wedding?" In *A God so Near*: *Essays on Old Testament Theology in Honor of Patrick D. Miller*, ed. by Brent A. Strawn and Nancy R. Bowen, 53–71. Winona Lake, IN: Eisenbrauns, 2003.

Milton, John. *Areopagitica*. London, 1644, https://books.google.com/books?id=tvhAAQAAMAAJ&pg=PA26

—. *A Treatise of Civil Power*. London, 1659, http://quod.lib.umich.edu/e/eebo/A50959.0001.001/1:3?rgn=div1;view=fulltext

—. *Complete Poems and Major Prose*, ed. by Merritt Hughes. New York: Odyssey Press, 1957.

—. *Eikonoklestes*. London, 1650, http://quod.lib.umich.edu/e/eebo/A50898.0001.0 01/1:2?rgn=div1;view=fulltext

—. *Of Education*. London, 1644, https://books.google.com/books?id=7rJDAA AAcAAJ&pg=PP3

—. *The Doctrine & Discipline of Divorce*. London, 1644, https://books.google. com/books?id=6oI-AQAAMAAJ&printsec=frontcover&source=gbs_ge_ summary_r&cad=0

—. *The Tenure of Kings and Magistrates*. London, 1649, http://quod.lib. umich.edu/e/eebo/A50955.0001.001/1:2?rgn=div1;view=fulltext, https://books.google.com/books?id=EIg-AQAAMAAJ&pg=PA1 (1650 edition).

Minh-ha, Trink T. *Woman, Native, Other*. Bloomington, IN: Indiana University Press, 1989.

Minnis, Alastair. *Fallible Authors: Chaucer's Pardoner and Wife of Bath*. Philadelphia: University of Pennsylvania Press, 2008, https://doi. org/10.9783/9780812205718

—. *Medieval Theory of Authorship: Scholastic Literary Attitudes in the Later Middle Ages*. 2nd ed. Philadelphia: University of Pennsylvania Press, 1988.

Mitchell, Charles. "Donne's "The Extasie": Love's Sublime Knot". *Studies in English Literature, 1500–1900*, 8: 1 (1968), 91–101, https://doi. org/10.2307/449412

Monfasani, John. "The Swerve: How the Renaissance Began". *Reviews in History*, 1283, http://www.history.ac.uk/reviews/review/1283

Montahagol, Guilhem. *Le Troubadour Guilhem Montanhagol. Par Jules Coulet* (*Poésies De Guilhem Montanhagol*), ed. by Jules Coulet. Toulouse: Imprimerie et Librairie Édouard Privat, 1898, https://archive.org/details/ letroubadourguil00guil

Montaigne, Michel de. "Apologie de Raimond de Sebonde". In *Les Essais de Michel de Montaigne*, Vol. 2, ed. by Fortunat Strowski. Bordeaux: Pech, 1906, 140–370, https://archive.org/details/essaispublisda02montuoft

Montmorency, James Edward Geoffrey. *The Progress of Education in England. A Sketch of the Development of English Educational Organization from Early times to the Year 1904*. London: Knight & Co., 1904.

Morris, Colin. *The Discovery of the Individual, 1050–1200*. New York: Harper & Row, 1972.

Morrissey, Lee and Will Stockton. "What Swirls around The Swerve". *Exemplaria* 25.4 [Winter 2013], 332–36, https://doi.org/10.1179/1041257313Z.00000000036

Musaeus (Musaeus Grammaticus). *Hero and Leander,* ed. by Thomas Gelzer. Loeb Classical Library, Cambridge, MA: Harvard University Press, 1973, https://doi.org/10.4159/dlcl.musaeus-hero_leander.1973

Musgrove, S. "Is The Devil An Ass?" *Review of English Studies,* 21 (1945), 302–15.

Musil, Robert. *Der Mann Ohne Eigenschaften.* Berlin: Rowohlt Verlag, 1957.

Nelson, Lowry. *Poetic Configurations*: *Essays in Literary History and Criticism.* University Park: Pennsylvania State University Press, 1992.

Neruda, Pablo. "Puedo escribir los versos más tristes esta noche". In *Veinte Poemas de Amor y una Canción Desesperada.* Bogotá and Barcelona: Editorial Norma, 2002, 45–46.

Nevo, Yehoshafaṭ. פרשנות המקרא הצרפתית: עיונים בדרכי פרשנותם של מפרשי המקרא בצפון צרפת בימי הביניים [French Biblical Interpretation: Studies in the Interpretive Methods of the Bible Commentators in Northern France in the Middle Ages]. Reḥovot: Moreshet Yaʻaḳov, 2004.

Newman, Barbara. *From Virile Woman to WomanChrist*: *Studies in Medieval Religion and Literature.* Philadelphia: University of Pennsylvania Press, 1995, https://doi.org/10.9783/9780812200263

—. *Gods and the Goddesses*: *Vision, Poetry, and Belief in the Middle Ages.* Philadelphia: University of Pennsylvania Press, 2003, https://doi.org/10.9783/9780812202915

Niel, Ferdinand. *Albigeois et Cathares.* Paris: Presses Universitaires de France, 1974.

Nietzsche, Friedrich Wilhelm. *Jenseits Von Gut und Böse*: *Vorspiel einer Philosophie der Zukunft.* Leipzig: C. G. Naumann, 1886.

—. *Die Geburt der Tragödie aus dem Geiste der Musik.* Leipzig: C. G. Naumann, 1894, https://books.google.com/books?id=lSk2AQAAMAAJ&pg=PP17

—. *Zur Genealogie der Moral*: *Eine Streitschrift.* Leipzig: C. G. Naumann, 1887.

—. *Zur Genealogie der Moral (1887)*; *Götzen-Dämmerung (1889),* ed. by Claus Scheier. Hamburg: F. Meiner Verlag, 2013.

O'Sullivan, Daniel E. "Na Maria: Courtliness and Marian Devotion in Old Occitan Lyric". In *Shaping Courtliness in Medieval France*: *Essays in Honor of Matilda Tomaryn Bruckner,* ed. by Daniel E. O'Sullivan and Laurie Shepard, Cambridge, UK: Brewer, 2013, 183–200.

—. "The Man Backing Down from the Lady in Trobairitz Tensos". In *Founding Feminisms in Medieval Studies*: *Essays in Honor of E. Jane Burns,* ed. by Laine E. Doggett and Daniel E. O'Sullivan. Cambridge: Boydell & Brewer, 2016, 45–60.

Okamura, David Scott. *Virgil in the Renaissance.* Cambridge, UK: Cambridge University Press, 2010, https://doi.org/10.1017/CBO9780511762581

Olmert, Michael. *Milton's Teeth & Ovid's Umbrella*: *Curiouser and Curiouser Adventures in History.* New York: Touchstone, 1996.

Olson, Roger E. *The Story of Christian Theology: Twenty Centuries of Tradition & Reform*. Downers Grove: InterVarsity Press, 1999.

Oppenheimer, Paul. *The Birth of the Modern Mind: Self, Consciousness, and the Invention of the Sonnet*. Oxford: Oxford University Press, 1989.

—. "The Origin of the Sonnet". *Comparative Literature*, 34: 4 (1982), 289–304, https://doi.org/10.2307/1771151

Origen. *Origene: Commentaire sur le Cantique des Cantiques, Vol. 1. Texte de la Version Latine de Rufin*, ed. by Luc Bresard, Henri Crouzel, and Marcel Borret. Paris: Éditions du Cerf, 1991.

Outhwaite, R. B. *Clandestine Marriage in England, 1500–1850*. London: Hambledon Press, 1995.

Ovid. *Amores*. In *Ovid: Heroides and Amores*. Ed. and trans. by Grant Showerman. Loeb Classical Library, Cambridge, MA: Harvard University Press, 1958.

—. *Ars Amatoria*. In *Ovid: The Art of Love and other Poems*. Ed. and trans. by J. H. Mozley. Loeb Classical Library, Cambridge, MA: Harvard University Press, 1962.

—. *Metamorphoses*. Berlin: De Gruyter, 1998.

—. *The Art of Love*. Trans. by James Michie. Introduction by David Malouf. New York: Modern Library, 2002.

Paden William D. "Introduction". In *Medieval Lyric: Genres in Historical Context*, ed. by William D. Paden. Urbana and Chicago: University of Illinois Press, 2000, 1–17.

Paden, William D., and Frances Freeman Paden, eds. and trans. *Troubadour Poems from the South of France*. Cambridge, UK: Brewer, 2007.

Palmer, Nigel F. "The High and Later Middle Ages (1100–1450)". In *The Cambridge History of German Literature*, ed. by Hellen Watanabe-O'Kelly. Cambridge: Cambridge University Press, 1997, 40–90, https://doi.org/10.1017/chol9780521434171.003

Paris, Gaston. "Études sur les romans de la table ronde. Lancelot du lac, I. Le Lanzelet d'Ulrich de Zatzikhoven; Lancelot du Lac, II. Le Conte de la Charrette". *Romania*, 12 (1883), 459–534, http://www.persee.fr/doc/roma_0035-8029_1883_num_12_48_6277

—. *La Poesie du Moyen Age*. Paris: Librarie Hachette, 1895, https://books.google.com/books?id=LdHs-jMItRQC&pg=PR3

Parker, John. "The Epicurean Middle Ages". *Exemplaria* 25.4 [Winter 2013], 324–29, https://doi.org/10.1179/1041257313Z.00000000036

Parmenides. *Die Fragmente der Vorsokratiker*, ed. by Hermann Diels. Berlin: Weidmannsche Buchhandlung, 1903, 108–29.

Paterson, Linda M. *The World of the Troubadours: Medieval Occitan Society, C. 1100-c. 1300*. Cambridge: Cambridge University Press, 1993.

Patri, Gabriel Díaz. "Poetry in the Latin Liturgy". In *The Genius of the Roman Rite: Historical, Theological, and Pastoral Perspectives on Catholic Liturgy*, ed. by Uwe Michael Lang: Hillenbrand Books, 2010.

Patterson, Lee. "On the Margin: Postmodernism, Ironic History, and Medieval Studies". *Speculum*, 65: 1 (1990), 87–108, https://doi.org/10.2307/2864473

Pearsall, Derek. *The Canterbury Tales*. New York: Routledge, 2002.

Pecora, Vincent P. "The Limits of Local Knowledge". In *The New Historicism*, ed. by Harold Aram Veeser. New York: Routledge, 1989, 243–76.

Pegg, Simon. *A Most Holy War: The Albigensian Crusade and the Battle for Christian Freedom*. Oxford: Oxford University Press, 2008.

Pelagius. *Pelagius: Life and Letters*, ed. by B. R. Rees. Woodbridge: Boydell Press, 1998.

—. *Pelagii Sancti et eruditi monachi Epistola ad Demetriadem*, ed. by Johann Salomo Semler. Halae Magdeburgicae: Carol Herman Hemmerde, 1775, https://books.google.com/books?id=uw5qbOfGtgoC&pg=PP7

Peter, John Desmond. *A Critique of Paradise Lost*. New York: Columbia University Press, 1960.

Petrarca, Francesco. *Il Canzoniere*, ed. by Paola Vecchi Galli. Milan: Rizzoli, 1954.

—. *Triunfi*, ed. by Cristoforo Pasqualigo. Venezia: Giuseppe Bresciani, 1874, https://books.google.com/books?id=5_0FAAAAQAAJ&printsec=frontcover&source=gbs_ge_summary_r&cad=0

Pinker, Steven. *The Better Angels of Our Nature: Why Violence Has Declined*. New York: Viking, 2011.

Pizan, Christine de. *Le Débat sur le Roman de la Rose*, ed. by Eric Hicks. Paris: Honoré Champion, 1977.

Plato. *Cratylus. Parmenides. Greater Hippias. Lesser Hippias*. Ed. and trans. by Harold North Fowler. Loeb Classical Library, Cambridge, MA: Harvard University Press, 1926.

—. *Republic*. Books 6–10. Ed. and trans. by Christopher Emlyn-Jones and William Preddy. Loeb Classical Library, Cambridge, MA: Harvard University Press, 2013.

—. *Symposium*. Ed. and trans. by W. R. M. Lamb. Loeb Classical Library, Cambridge, MA: Harvard University Press, 1925.

Plotinus. *Ennead, Vol. V*. Ed. and trans. by A. H. Armstrong. Loeb Classical Library, Cambridge, MA: Harvard University Press, 1984.

Pollock, Linda A. *Forgotten Children: Parent-child Relations from 1500 to 1900*. Cambridge: Cambridge University Press, 1983.

Popper, Karl. *Conjectures and Refutations: The Growth of Scientific Knowledge*. New York: Basic Books, 1963.

Prudentius. "Hymnus Ante Somnum". In *Patrologiae Cursus Completus*, Vol. 59, ed. by Jacques Paul Migne. Paris: Apud Garnier Fratres, 1855, 831–41, https://books.google.com/books?id=jnzYAAAAMAAJ&pg=PA18

Prynne, William. *Histriomastix*. London: Printed by E. A. and W. I. for Michael Sparke, 1633, https://archive.org/details/maspla00pryn

Pushkin, Aleksandr Sergeevich. Собрание сочинений (Sobranie sochinenii). Collected Works, 10 Vols, ed. by D. D. Blagoi, S. M. Bondi, V. V. Vinogradov and Yu. G. Oksman. Moscow: Khudozhestvennaia literatura, 1959, Vols. 2, 4, http://rvb.ru/pushkin/toc.htm

Qābbanī, Nizār. "Love Letter 71". Trans. by Modje Taavon from the Arabic text published in *Arabian Love Poems*, ed. by Bassam K. Frangieh and Clementia R. Brown. London: Lynne Rienner Publishers, 1999, 134.

Quaglio, Antonio Enzo. *Al di là di Francesca e Laura*. Padova: Liviana Editrice, 1973.

Quchak, Nahapet. *Haryur u mek hayren*, ed. by Arshak Madoyan and Irina Karumyan. Yerevan: Sovetakan Grokh, 1976.

Quinones, Richard J. "Dante Aligheiri". In *Medieval Italy: An Encyclopedia*, ed. by Christopher Kleinhenz. New York: Routledge, 2004, 278–286.

Quint, David. *Inside Paradise Lost: Reading the Designs of Milton's Epic*. Princeton: Princeton University Press, 2014, https://doi.org/10.1515/9781400850488

Rabelais, Francois. *Gargantua et Pantagruel*. In *Œuvres de Rabelais*, Vol. 1. Paris: Dalibon, 1823, https://books.google.com/books?id=4EKEULv3EMkC&printsec=frontcover&source=gbs_ge_summary_r&cad=0

Raby, F. J. E. *A History of Secular Latin Poetry in the Middle Ages*. Oxford: Clarendon Press, 1934.

—. *A History of Christian-Latin Poetry: From the Beginnings to the Close of the Middle Ages*. Oxford: Clarendon Press, 1927.

Radice, Betty, ed. *The Letters of Abelard and Heloise*. London: Penguin, 1974.

Ram, Widow and Brothers, eds. *Mikraot Gedolot: Torah with Forty-Two Commentaries* (מיקראות גדולות: חומש ישימח מע הרות שיינם םיעבראו םיעבראו פירושים), Vol. 3. The Widow and Brothers Ram: Truskavets/Glukhov, Ukraine, 1907, https://books.google.com/books?id=fEUpAAAAYAAJ&pg=PA418

Ray, Chris. *Song of Solomon for Teenagers: And Anyone Else Who Wonders Why They Are Here*. Bloomington, IN: AuthorHouse, 2010.

Reddy, William M. *The Making of Romantic Love: Longing and Sexuality in Europe, South Asia, and Japan, 900–1200 CE*. Chicago: University of Chicago Press, 2012, https://doi.org/10.7208/chicago/9780226706283.001.0001

Reid, Charles J. *Power Over the Body, Equality in the Family: Rights and Domestic Relations in Medieval Canon Law*. Grand Rapids: William B. Eerdmans, 2004.

Reynolds, Barbara. *Dante: The Poet, the Political Thinker, the Man*. London: I. B. Tauris, 2006.

Richard of St. Victor. *Exposition in Cantica Canticorum*. In *Patrologiae Cursus Completus: Series Latina*, Vol. 196, ed. by Jacques-Paul Migne. Paris, 1855, https://archive.org/stream/patrologiaecurs104unkngoog#page/n271

Richman, Gerald. "A Third Choice: Adam, Eve, and Abdiel". *Early Modern Literary Studies*, 9: 2 (2003), https://extra.shu.ac.uk/emls/09-2/richthir.html

Richtmeyer, Eric. "Maurice Blanchot: Saboteur of the Writers' War". *Proceedings of the Western Society for French History*, 35 (2007), 247–62.

Ricoeur, Paul. *De l'interprétation. Essai sur Freud*. Paris: Seuil, 1965.

—. *Le Conflit des Interprétations: Essais D'Herméneutique*. Paris: Seuil, 1969.

—. *Temps et Récit*, Vol. 3: *Le Temps Raconté*. Paris: Seuil, 1985.

Rieger, Angelica. "Was Bieiris De Romans Lesbian? Women's Relations with Each Other in the World of the Troubadours". In *The Voice of the Trobairitz: Perspectives on the Women Troubadours*, ed. by William D. Paden. Philadelphia: University of Pennsylvania Press, 1989, 73–94, https://doi.org/10.9783/9781512805444-005

Rivarol, Antoine de. *Discours de l'Universalité de la langue Française*. Berlin, 1784.

Roberts, John. "John Donne's Poetry: An Assessment of Modern Criticism". *John Donne Journal*, 1 (1982), 55–67.

Robertson, D. W. "The Concept of Courtly Love". In *The Meaning of Courtly Love*, ed. by Francis X. Newman. Albany: State University of New York Press, 1968, 1–18, https://doi.org/10.1086/388953

—. "The Subject of the 'De Amore' of Andreas Capellanus". *Modern Philology*, 1953, 145–61, https://doi.org/10.1086/388953

Rodríguez de la Cámara, Juan. *Triunfo de las Donas*. In *Obras de Juan Rodríguez de la Cámara: (ó del Padrón)*, ed. by Antonio Paz y Meliá. Madrid: La Sociodad de Bibliofilos Españoles, 1884, https://archive.org/details/ObrasJuanRodriguezCamara

Romans, Bietris de. "Na Maria, prètz e fina valors". In *The Women Troubadours*, ed. by Meg Bogin. New York: Norton & Co., 1980, 132.

Rorty, Richard. *The Consequences of Pragmatism*. Minneapolis: University of Minnesota Press, 1982.

Roscelin of Compiègne. "Epistola XV: Quae est Roscelini ad P. Abaelardum". *Patrologiae Cursus Completus*, Vol. 178, ed. by Jacques Paul Migne. Paris: Apud Garnier Fratres, 1885, 358–72, https://archive.org/details/patrologiaecurs53unkngoog

Rougemont, Denis de. *L'Amour et l'Occident*. Paris: Plon, 1939.

Rousseau, Jean Jacques. *Contrat Social*. In *The Political Writings of Jean-Jacques Rosseau*, Vol. 2, ed. by C. E. Vaughan. Cambridge: Cambridge University Press, 1915, 21–134, https://books.google.com/books?id=IqhBAAAAYAAJ&printsec=frontcover&source=gbs_ge_summary_r&cad=0

—. *Discours sur l'Origine et les Fondements de l'Inégalité Parmi les Hommes* (1754), 1–99. *Les Classiques des Sciences Sociales*. Quebec: Université du Québec à Chicoutimi, http://classiques.uqac.ca/classiques/Rousseau_jj/discours_origine_inegalite/discours_inegalite.pdf

Rutherford, John, ed. *The Troubadours: Their Loves and Their Lyrics*. London: Smith, Elder, & Co., 1873, https://archive.org/details/troubadoursthei01ruthgoog

Ryan, Kiernan. "King Lear". In *A Companion to Shakespeare's Works*, ed. by Richard Dutton and Jean E. Howard. Malden: Blackwell Publishing, 2003, 375–92, https://doi.org/10.1002/9780470996539.ch20

Ryang, Sonia. "Biopolitics or the Logic of Sovereign Love—Love's Wherabouts in North Korea". In *North Korea: Toward a Better Understanding*, ed. by Sonia Ryang. Lanham: Lexington Books, 2009.

Saint Circ, Uc de. *Poesies de Uc de Saint-Circ*, ed. by Alfred Jeanroy. Toulouse: Édouard Privat, 1913.

Salandra, Serafino della. *Adamo Caduto*. Cosenza: Gio. Battista Moio and Francesco Rodella, 1647, https://archive.org/details/bub_gb_fbI8kobTkMQC

Salter, Elizabeth. "Courts and Courtly Love". In *The Medieval World*, ed. by David Daiches and Anthony Thorlby. London: Aldus Books, 407–444.

Samuel, Irene. "The Dialogue in Heaven: A Reconsideration of Paradise Lost, III. 1–417". *PMLA*, 72: 4 (1957), 601–11.

Sandys, John Edwyn. *A History of Classical Scholarship*, Vol. I: *From the Sixth Century B.C. to the End of the Middle Ages*. Cambridge: Cambridge University Press, 1903, https://archive.org/details/historyofclassic00sanduoft

—. *A History of Classical Scholarship*, Vol. II: *From the Revival of Learning to the End of the Eighteenth Century in Italy, France, England and the Netherlands*. Cambridge: Cambridge University Press, 1908, https://archive.org/details/historyofclassic02sandiala

Sanguineti, Edoardo. *Il Realismo di Dante*. Florence: Sansoni, 1966.

Sankovitch, Tilde. "Lombarda's Reluctant Mirror: Speculum of Another Poet". In *The Voice of the Trobairitz: Perspectives on the Women Troubadours*, ed. by William Paden. Philadelphia: University of Philadelphia Press, 1989, 183–93.

—. "The Trobairitz". In *The Troubadours: An Introduction*, ed. by Simon Gaunt and Sarah Kay, 113–26, https://doi.org/10.1017/cbo9780511620508.010

Sappho. *Greek Lyric*, Vol. I: *Sappho and Alcaeus*. Ed. and trans. by David A. Campbell. Loeb Classical Library, Cambridge, MA: Harvard University Press, 1982, https://doi.org/10.4159/dlcl.sappho_alcaeus_lyric_poet-fragments.1982

Sartre, Jean-Paul. *Qu'est-ce que la littérature?* Paris: Gallimard, 1948.

Saussure, Ferdinand de. *Cours de Linguistique Générale*, ed. by Tullio de Mauro. Paris: Payot & Rivages, 1967.

Saville, Jonathan. *The Medieval Erotic Alba: Structure as Meaning*. New York: Columbia University Press, 1972.

Sayce, Olive. *Exemplary Comparison from Homer to Petrarch*. Cambridge, UK: Brewer, 2008, https://doi.org/10.1515/9783110940237.3

Schulman, Nicole M. *Where Troubadours Were Bishops*. London: Routledge, 2001, https://doi.org/10.4324/9780203412213

Schultz-Gora, Oscar. *Die Provenzalischen Dichterinnen*. Leipzig: Gustav Fock, 1888.

Schwartz, Regina. *Loving Justice, Living Shakespeare*. Oxford: Oxford University Press, 2016, https://doi.org/10.1093/acprof:oso/9780198795216.001.0001

Schwoerer, Lois G. "Seventeenth-Century English Women Engraved in Stone?" *Albion: A Quarterly Journal Concerned with British Studies*, 16: 4 (1984), 389–403, https://doi.org/10.2307/4049387

Scolnic, Benjamin Edidin. "Why Do We Sing the Song of Songs on Passover?" *Conservative Judaism*, 1996, 53–72, https://www.rabbinicalassembly.org/sites/default/files/public/jewish-law/holidays/pesah/why-do-we-sing-the-song-of-songs-on-passover.pdf

Scève, Maurice. *The Délie of Maurice Scève*, ed. by I. D. McFarlane. Cambridge: Cambridge University Press, 1966.

Sedgwick, Eve Kosofsky. *Between Men: English Literature and Male Homosocial Desire*. New York: Columbia University Press, 1985.

—. *Touching Feeling: Affect, Pedagogy, Performativity*. Durham and London: Duke University Press, 2003.

Segal, M. H. "The Song of Songs". *Vetus Testamentum*, 12: 4 (October 1962), 470–90, https://doi.org/10.2307/1516936

Sextus Empiricus. *Against Logicians*. Ed. and trans. by R. G. Bury. Loeb Classical Library, Cambridge, MA: Harvard University Press, 1935.

Shakespeare, William. *Shakespeare's Sonnets*, ed. by Stephen Booth. New Haven: Yale University Press, 1977.

—. *The Complete Works*, ed. by Stephen Orgel and A. R. Braunmuller. New York: Pelican, 2002.

—. *The Sonnets; And, A Lover's Complaint*, ed. by John Kerrigan. New York: Penguin, 1986.

Shapiro, Marianne. *Woman Earthly and Divine in the Comedy of Dante*. Lexington: University Press of Kentucky, 2015.

Sharrock, Alison. *Seduction and Repetition in Ovid's Ars Amatoria, 2*. Oxford: Clarendon Press, 1994.

Shaw, George Bernard. "Caesar and Cleopatra". In *Three Plays for Puritans*. New York: Brentano's, 1906, , 87–208, https://babel.hathitrust.org/cgi/pt?id=hvd.32044014213078;view=1up;seq=9

Shelley, Percy Bysshe. "A Defence of Poetry". In *Essays, Letters from Abroad*, ed. by Mary Wollstonecraft Shelley, Vol. 1. London: Moxon, 1852, 1–49, https://babel.hathitrust.org/cgi/pt?id=wu.89000649913;view=1up;seq=7

Shotter, David. *Rome and Her Empire*. New York: Routledge, 2014, https://doi.org/10.4324/9781315798394

Sichel-Bazin, Rafèu, Carolin Buthke, and Trudel Meisenburg. "Prosody in Language Contact: Occitan and French". In *Prosody and Language in Contact: L2 Acquisition, Attrition and Languages in Multilingual Situations;* [*Session Speech Prosody, Shanghai, 2012*], ed. by Elisabeth Roussarie, Mathieu Avanzi, and Sophie Herment. Berlin: Springer, 2015, 71–100, https://doi.org/10.1007/978-3-662-45168-7_5

Sidney, Philip. *The Defence of Poesie*. In *The Complete Works of Sir Philip Sidney*, Vol. III, ed. by Albert Feuillerat. Cambridge: Cambridge University Press, 1923, 3–46, https://archive.org/details/completeworks03sidnuoft

—. *The Poems of Sir Philip Sidney*, ed. by William A. Ringler. Oxford: Clarendon Press, 1962.

Sidonius (Gaius Sollius Apollinaris). *Sidonius Poems and Letters: In Two Volumes*. Ed. and trans. by William B. Anderson, Vol. 1. Loeb Classical Library, Cambridge, MA: Harvard University Press, 1963.

Silvestris, Bernardi. *De Mundi Universitate*, ed. by Carl Sigmund Barach and Johann Wrobel. Innsbruck: Verlag der Wagnerschen Universitaets-Buchandlung, 1876, https://archive.org/details/bernardisilvest00silvgoog

Sinfield, Alan. *Shakespeare, Authority, Sexuality: Unfinished Business in Cultural Materialism*. London: Routledge, 2006, https://doi.org/10.4324/9780203965023

Sklenár, Robert J. "Ausonius" Elegiac Wife: Epigram 20 and the Traditions of Latin Love Poetry". *The Classical Journal*, 101: 1 (October-November 2005), 51–62.

Smythe, Barbara. *Trobador Poets: Selections from the Poems of Eight Trobadors*. New York: Cooper Square Publishers, 1966.

Sontag, Susan. *Against Interpretation: And Other Essays*. New York: Farrar, Straus and Giroux, 2013.

Spence, Sarah. *Texts and the Self in the Twelfth Century*. Cambridge: Cambridge University Press, 1996.

Spiller, Michael R. G. *The Development of the Sonnet an Introduction*. London: Routledge, 1992, https://doi.org/10.4324/9780203401507

Spivak, Gayatri Chakravorty. "Righting Wrongs". *The South Atlantic Quarterly*, 103: 2–3 (Spring/Summer 2004), 523–81, https://muse.jhu.edu/article/169150, https://doi.org/10.1215/00382876-103-2-3-523

Stehling, Thomas. "To Love a Medieval Boy". In *Literary Versions of Homosexuality*, ed. by Stuart Kellogg. New York: Haworth Press, 1983, 151–70.

Steinsaltz, Adin, ed. *Tractate Sanhedrin*. In *The Talmud: The Steinsaltz Edition*, vols. New York: Random House, 1996–1999, 15–21.

Sternberg, Robert. *Cognitive Psychology*. Belmont: Wadsworth Cengage, 2009.

Stilling, Roger. *Love and Death in Renaissance Tragedy*. Baton Rouge: Louisiana State University Press, 1976.

Stockton, Will. "An Introduction Justifying Queer Ways". Ed. by Will Stockton and David L. Orvis. *Early Modern Culture*: *An Electronic Seminar*, 10: *Queer Milton*, http://emc.eserver.org/1-10/stockton.html

Stone, Gregory B. *The Death of the Troubadour: The Late Medieval Resistance to the Renaissance*. Philadelphia: University of Pennsylvania Press, 1994, https://doi.org/10.9783/9781512807332

Stone, Lawrence. *The Family, Sex and Marriage in England, 1500–1800*. New York: Harper & Row, 1977.

Stopka, Krzysztof. *Armenia Christiana: Armenian Religious Identity and the Churches of Constantinople and Rome*. Krakow: Jagiellonian University Press, 2016.

Strabo. *Geography. Vol. I: Books 1–2*, ed. by Horace Leonard Jones. Loeb Classical Library, Cambridge, MA: Harvard University Press, 1917.

Strayer, Joseph R. *Western Europe in the Middle Ages: A Short History*. New York: Appleton-Century-Crofts, 1955.

Strouse, A. W. "Getting Medieval on Graduate Education: Queering Academic Professionalism". *Pedagogy: Critical Approaches to Teaching Literature, Language, Composition, and Culture*, 15: 1 (2015), 119–38, https://doi.org/10.1215/15314200-2799260

Strowick, Elisabeth. "Comparative Epistemology of Suspicion: Psychoanalysis, Literature, and the Human Sciences" *Science in Context*, 18.4 (2005), 649–69, https://doi.org/10.1017/S0269889705000700

Stubbs, John. *John Donne: The Reformed Soul*. New York: W. W. Norton & Co., 2007.

Sullivan, Ceri. "The Carpe Diem Topos and the 'geriatric Gaze' in Early Modern Verse". *Early Modern Literary Studies*, 14: 3, http://purl.oclc.org.libproxy.csun.edu/emls/14-3/Sullcarp.html

Surrey, Henry Howard, Earl of. *The Poetical Works of Henry Howard, Earl of Surrey*, ed. by Robert Bell. Boston: Little, Brown & Co., 1854, https://archive.org/details/poeticalworkshe00vauxgoog

Swabey, Ffiona. *Eleanor of Aquitaine, Courtly Love, and the Troubadours*. Westport: Greenwood Press, 2004.

Symonds, John Addington. *Renaissance in Italy*, Vol. 4, Part 1. New York: Mith, Elder & Co., 1881, https://books.google.com/books?id=K4sTAQAAIAAJ&pg=PP1

"Tagelied". In *Princeton Encyclopedia of Poetry and Poetics*, ed. by Alex Preminger, Frank J. Warnke, and O. B. Hardison Jr. Princeton: Princeton University Press, 1972, 841–42.

Tanner, J. Paul. "The History of Interpretation of the Song of Songs". *Bibliotheca Sacra*, 154: 513 (1997), 23–46, https://biblicalstudies.org.uk/article_song1_tanner.html or http://paultanner.org/English HTML/Publ Articles/Hist Song of Songs-P Tanner.pdf

Targoff, Ramie. *Posthumous Love: Eros and the Afterlife in Renaissance England*. Chicago: University of Chicago Press, 2014, https://doi.org/10.7208/chicago/9780226110462.001.0001

Tarrant, Richard. "Ovid and Ancient Literary History". In *The Cambridge Companion to Ovid*, ed. by Philip R. Hardie. Cambridge, UK: Cambridge University Press, 2002, 13–33, https://doi.org/10.1017/ccol0521772818.002

Teskey, Gordon. *The Poetry of John Milton*. Cambridge, MA: Harvard University Press, 2015, https://doi.org/10.4159/9780674286740

Thibault, John C. *The Mystery of Ovid's Exile*. Berkeley: University of California Press, 1964.

Thomason, T. Katharine. "Plotinian Metaphysics and Donne's 'Extasie'". *Studies in English Literature, 1500–1900*, 22: 1 (1982), 91–105, https://doi.org/10.2307/450219

Thomsett, Michael C. *Heresy in the Roman Catholic Church: A History*. Jefferson, NC: McFarland, 2011.

Toews, John E. *The Story of Original Sin*. Eugene: Wipf and Stock Publishers, 2013.

Topsfield, L. T. *Troubadours and Love*. Cambridge: Cambridge University Press, 1975.

Traub, Valerie. *The Renaissance of Lesbianism in Early Modern England*. Cambridge: Cambridge University Press, 2002.

Tullia d'Aragona. *Dialogo della infinità d'amore* [1547]. In *Della infinita d'amore dialogo di Tullia D'Aragona*. Milan: G. Daelli & Co., 1864, https://archive.org/details/bub_gb_1FOekK6PUbsC

Tyerman, Christopher. *God's War: A New History of the Crusades*. Cambridge, MA: Belknap Press of Harvard University Press, 2006.

Tyutchev, Fyodor. "Silentium". *European Romanticism: A Reader*, ed. by Stephen Prickett. London: Bloomsbury, 2010, 638–39.

Urquhart, Ilona. "Diabolical Evasion of the Censor in Mikhail Bulgakov's *The Master and Margarita*". In *Censorship and the Limits of the Literary: A Global View*, ed. by Nicole Moore. New York: Bloomsbury Academic, 2015, 133–46.

Vaux-de-Cernay, Pierre. *Historia Albigensium et sacri belli in eos anno MCCIX*. Trecis: Venundantur Parisiis, Apud N. Rousset, 1617.

Veeser, Harold Aram. "Introduction". In *The New Historicism*, ed. by Harold Aram Veeser. New York: Routledge, 1989, ix–xvi.

Vendler, Helen. *The Art of Shakespeare's Sonnets*. Cambridge, MA: Belknap Press of Harvard University Press, 1997.

Ventadorn, Bernart de. *Bernart Von Ventadorn: Seine Lieder, Mit Einleitung und Glossar*, ed. by Carl Appel. Halle: Max Niemeyer, 1915, https://archive.org/details/bernartvonventad00bern

Villaverde. Marcelino Agís. *Knowledge and Practical Reason: Paul Ricoeur's Way of Thinking*. Berlin: LIT Verlag Münster, 2012.

Virgil. *The Aeneid*. In *Virgil*, 2 vols. Ed. and trans. by H. Rushton Fairclough. Loeb Classical Library, Cambridge, MA: Harvard University Press, 1960.

—. "Eclogue X". In *Virgil*, 2 vols. Ed. and trans. by H. Rushton Fairclough. Loeb Classical Library, Cambridge, MA: Harvard University Press, 1960.

Vleeschouwers-Van Melkebeek, Monique. "Separation and Marital Property". In *Regional Variations in Matrimonial Law and Custom in Europe, 1150–1600*, ed. by Mia Korpiola. Leiden: Brill, 2011, 78–97, https://doi.org/10.1163/9789004211438_005

Vogelweide, Walther von der. *Die Gedichte Walthers von der Vogelweide*, ed. by Karl Lachmann. Berlin: George Reimer, 1891, https://archive.org/details/diegedichtewalt00lachgoog

Von Strassburg, Gottfried. *Tristan*, ed. by Karl Marold. Leipzig, E. Avenarius, 1906, https://archive.org/details/gottfriedvonstr00unkngoog

Vyvyan, John. *Shakespeare and the Rose of Love*. London: Shepheard-Walwyn, 1960.

Waldock, A. J. A. *Paradise Lost and its Critics*. Cambridge: Cambridge University Press, 1947.

Walters, Lori J. "'The Foot on Which He Limps': Jean Gerson and the Rehabilitation of Jean de Meun in Arsenal 3339". *Digital Philology*, 1: 1 (Spring 2012), 110–38, https://doi.org/10.1353/dph.2012.0006

Watkins, John. *The Specter of Dido: Spenser and Virgilian Epic*. New Haven: Yale University Press, 1995.

Watson, Lynette. "Representing the Past, Redefining the Future: Sidonius Appolinaris' Panegyrics of Avitus and Anthemius". In *The Propaganda of Power: The Role of Panegyric in Late Antiquity*, ed. by Mary Whitby. Boston: Brill, 1998.

Warnicke, Retha M. "The Eternal Triangle and Court Politics: Henry VIII, Anne Boleyn, and Sir Thomas Wyatt". *Albion: A Quarterly Journal Concerned with British Studies*, 18: 4 (Winter 1986), 565–579, https://doi.org/10.2307/4050130

—. *The Rise and Fall of Anne Boleyn: Family Politics at the Court of Henry VIII*. Cambridge: Cambridge University Press, 1991.

Weinrich, Lorenz. "'Dolorum solatium': Text und Musik von Abaelards Planctus". *Mittellateinisches Jahrbuch*, 5 (1968), 59–78.

Wetherbee, Winthrop. *Geoffrey Chaucer: The Canterbury Tales*. Cambridge: Cambridge University Press, 1989.

White, Peter. "Ovid and the Augustan Mileau". In *Brill's Companion to Ovid*, ed. by Barbara Weiden Boyd. Leiden: Brill, 2002, 1–27.

Wilde, Oscar. "The Critic as Artist". In *The Complete Works of Oscar Wilde*. New York: Barnes & Noble, 1994, 1009–59.

—. *The Soul of Man under Socialism*. Portland: Thomas B. Mosher, 1905.

—. "To the Editor of the Scots Observer". *The Scots Observer*, 4: 91, 332–33, https://books.google.com/books?id=94oeAQAAMAAJ&pg=PA332

Wilhelm, James J. *Seven Troubadours: The Creators of Modern Verse*. University Park: Pennsylvania State University Press, 1970.

Wilkins, Ernest Hatch. *The Invention of the Sonnet, and Other Studies in Italian Literature*. Rome: Edizioni De Storia e Letteratura, 1959.

Wilkinson, L. P. *Ovid Recalled*. Cambridge, UK: Cambridge University Press, 1955.

Wimsatt Jr., W. K. and M. C. Beardsley. "The Intentional Fallacy". *The Sewanee Review*, 54: 3 (July-September 1946), 468–488, http://www.jstor.org/stable/27537676

Winkler, John J. *The Constraints of Desire: The Anthropology of Sex and Gender in Ancient Greece*. New York: Routledge, 1990.

Woodbridge, Linda. *Vagrancy, Homelessness, and English Renaissance Literature*. Urbana: University of Illinois Press, 2001.

Wollock, Jennifer G. *Rethinking Chivalry and Courtly Love*. Santa Barbara: Praeger, 2011.

Woods, Marjorie Curry. "Where's the Manuscript". *Exemplaria*, 25.4 [Winter 2013], 321–24, https://doi.org/10.1179/1041257313Z.00000000036

Wrathall Mark A. *Heidegger and Unconcealment: Truth, Language, and History*. Cambridge: Cambridge University Press, 2010, https://doi.org/10.1017/cbo9780511777974

Wyatt, Thomas. *Sir Thomas Wyatt: The Complete Poems*, ed. by R. A. Rebholz. New Haven: Yale University Press, 1978.

—. *The Poetry of Sir Thomas Wyatt*, ed. by E. M. W. Tillyard. London: Scholartis Press, 1929.

Yeats, William Butler. *Yeats's Poetry, Drama, and Prose: Authoritative Texts, Contexts, Criticism*, ed. by James Pethica. New York: W. W. Norton & Co., 2000.

Young, R. V. *Doctrine and Devotion in Seventeenth-century Poetry: Studies in Donne, Herbert, Crashaw, and Vaughan*. Cambridge: Boydell & Brewer, 2000.

Ziolowski, Jan M. *Letters of Peter Abelard, Beyond the Personal*. Washington: The Catholic University Press of America, 2008.

Zumthor, Paul. *Essai de Poétique Médiévale*. Paris: Seuil, 1972.

Index

Abelard, Peter 10, 195, 196, 197, 198, 199, 200, 201, 202, 203, 204, 205, 206, 207, 208, 209, 210, 211, 212, 213, 270
Abels, Richard and Ellen Harrison 221
Adorno, Theodore 474, 490
Agrippa, Cornelius
 De Nobilitate et Praecellentia Foeminei Sexus 487
Aist, Dietmar von
 "Slâfest du, friedel ziere" 183, 184
Akiba (Rabbi Akiba ben Joseph) 47, 51, 53, 63, 106, 120, 158, 172, 453, 463
Alcuin 108, 109, 110
Al-Ghāzalī 407
Allen, Peter 62, 63, 64
Allestree, Richard 373, 381, 384
Altermeyer, Bob 483, 484
Althusser, Louis 11, 12, 455
Amaury, Arnaud 224, 226, 227
Ames, Christine Caldwell 197
Anderson, W.S. 95
Andreasen, Nancy Jo Coover 433, 435
Andreini, Giambattisti 491
 L'Adamo 491
Anonymous
 Arden of Faversham 369, 370
Anonymous
 Aucassin et Nicolette 215, 303
Anonymous
 "Coindeta sui" 136, 180

Anonymous
 Concilium Romarici Montis 126
Anonymous
 "En un vergier sotz fuella d'albespi" 185, 190
Anonymous
 Flamenca 221
Anonymous
 "Havelok the Dane" 275, 277, 278, 279
Anonymous
 King Horn 275, 278, 279
Anonymous
 "Soufrés maris, et si ne vous anuit" 191
Anonymous
 St. Austyn 276
Anthemius 101, 102, 103
Aquinas, Thomas 4, 130, 479
Arabi, Ibn
 "Gentle Now, Doves of the Thornberry and Moringa Thicket" 166, 167, 177
Arden, Heather M. 240, 243
Arendt, Hannah 496
Ariès, Philippe 372
Aristotle 3, 17, 38, 165, 372, 407, 412, 454, 480
Astell, Ann W. 42
Aubrey, John 375
Auerbach, Erich 121
Augustine of Hippo 3, 4, 9, 149, 150, 151, 279, 372, 479

Augustus Caesar 65, 84, 89, 102
  Lex Papia Poppaea (law penalizing married couples with no children) 70
Ausonius 106, 107, 108
Austin, R.G. 89
Auweele, Bart Vanden 56
Avitus, Alcimus Ecdicius
  De Mosaice Historiae Gestis 494

Babylonian Talmud, Tractate Sanhedrin 51, 52
Bagot, Richard 413
Baker, Richard 425
Barthes, Roland 19, 28, 29, 30, 32
Bell, Ilona 423, 429, 430, 431
Belsey, Catherine 424, 425
Bembo, Pietro 106, 330, 331, 332, 333, 334, 349, 351, 355, 356, 359, 426, 440, 441
Bene, Carmelo 408
Benton, John 210, 211
Ben-Ze'ev, Aharon, and Ruhama Goussinsky 1
Bernays, Edward 8
Berry, Ralph 403, 405
Best, Stephen, and Sharon Marcus 34
Blair, Peter Hunter 278
Blake, William 161, 167, 442
Blanchot, Maurice 23, 24, 26, 27
Blanc, Pierre 302
Blank, Hanne 395
Bloch, Ariel and Chana 41
Bloch, R. Howard, and Stephen G. Nichols 154
Bloom, Harold 372, 449
Blumenfeld-Kosinski, Renate 267
Boase, Roger 135
Boétie, Étienne de La 5, 6, 7, 8, 10
Bogin, Meg 140, 146
Boleyn, Anne 343, 344
Booth, Stephen 362
Born, Bertran de 137, 138, 139, 189, 190, 191, 261
  "Be·m platz lo gais temps de pascor" 137, 189

Borneilh, Giraut de 378, 401
Boswell, John 108, 109, 143
Boyd, Barbara Weiden 65, 71, 90
Boyle, David 220, 222, 227, 231
Brady, Bernard V. 248
Branagh, Kenneth 403
Briffault, Robert S. 165, 215, 217, 222, 231, 232, 237, 342, 353
Brogan, Walter A. 18
Brown, Peter 102, 276
Bruckner, Matilda Tomaryn 129, 141, 180, 187, 190
Brundage, James A. 191
Bryson, Michael 153, 429, 458, 485, 518
Bulgakov, Mikhail 508, 509
  Мастер и Маргарита (*Master and Margarita*) 508, 509, 511
Bunyan, John
  Pilgrim's Progress 489
Burckhardt, Jacob 159, 160
Burden, Dennis 475, 476, 477, 480
Burgwinkle, William 146, 147, 193
Burns, E. Jane 156, 157
Buturovic, Amila 510
Byrne, Marie José 108

Cabestanh, Guilhem de 178, 179
Callaghan, Dympna 360, 362, 363, 365, 407, 408, 419
Calvin, John 4, 5, 9, 473, 474
Cameron, Alan 103
Campbell, Joseph 141, 147, 148, 152
Camproux, Charles 173, 221
Camus, Albert 462
Capellanus, Andreas 123, 124, 126, 133, 134, 135
Cary, Elizabeth 375
Casali, Sergio 71, 76, 97
Castiglione, Baldassarre 330, 331, 334, 351, 440
  Il Libro del Cortegiano (*The Book of the Courtier*) 330
Castor, Helen 168
Catherine of Aragon 395
Cato the Younger 87, 97, 98

Catullus 64, 93, 108, 338, 339, 411, 424
Cavalcanti, Guido 106, 192
Charles II 434
Chaucer, Geoffrey 135, 176, 271, 280, 281, 282, 283, 284, 285, 286, 288, 289, 290, 291, 292, 293, 294, 295, 523
  The Canterbury Tales 176, 240, 280, 281, 282, 283, 285, 286, 290
  "The Knight's Tale" 280, 281, 282, 283, 284, 285
  "The Miller's Tale" 280, 282, 283, 284, 285
Cheyettee, Frederic L. 220, 221
Chomsky, Noam 11, 22, 33, 502, 503
Chrétien de Troyes 123, 125, 126, 127, 128, 129, 131, 132, 219, 240, 241
  Le Chevalier de la Charrette 127
Cicero 239, 257
Clark, David 109
Claudian 97, 100, 101, 102, 103, 108
Clements, Ronald E. 44
Cohen, Gerson 38, 42, 46, 47
Coleridge, Samuel Taylor 499
Colonne, Guido delle 313, 314, 317, 319, 326
  "Amor, che lungiamente m'hai menato" 313, 314
Coltman, Rod 27
Coulet, Jules 233
courtly love
  as an artificial construct 121, 122, 123, 124, 125, 129, 130, 131, 133, 136, 162, 212, 235, 240, 247, 248, 249, 252, 256, 262, 263, 269, 274, 282, 283, 284, 285, 286, 289, 293
Cox, Catherine S. 289
Crane, Susan 281, 290
Crawford, Charles 369
Culler, Jonathan 162
Cusset, François 20

Daniel, Arnaut 248, 322, 323
  "Lo ferm voler qu'el cor m'intra" 248
Danielson, Dennis 478, 480, 498, 499

Dante Alighieri 2, 3, 55, 106, 138, 158, 161, 164, 192, 293, 300, 306, 307, 309, 311, 315, 316, 317, 318, 319, 320, 321, 322, 323, 326, 330, 345, 350, 359, 367, 372, 422, 426, 458, 506
  "Di donne io vidi una gentile schiera" 317
  Inferno 138, 320, 322
  "Io mi sentii svegliar dentro a lo core" 316
  "Negli occhi porta la mia donna Amore" 315
  Purgatorio 323
d'Aurenga, Raimbaut 186, 188
  "Non chant per auzel ni per flor" 186
Davis, P.J. 69
Day, Linda 46
de Graef, Ortwin 33
Deleuze, Gilles 408
de Man, Paul 18, 21, 31, 33, 163, 446, 447, 452, 454
de Meun, Jean 254, 291, 293, 531
Derrida, Jacques 18, 24, 26, 447, 454
Dia, Comtessa de 129, 186, 188, 235
  "Estat ai en greu cossirier" 186
Dillon, Martin C. 447
Dilthey, Wilhelm 153, 154
Dinshaw, Carolyn 266, 291
Dionysius the Carthusian 473, 474
Dodd, William George 280
Doggett, Frank A. 157, 441
dolce stil novo
  Italian poetry, love as worship 3, 55, 121, 192, 302, 306, 307, 323, 342
Donne, John 3, 31, 32, 108, 110, 174, 197, 335, 338, 371, 375, 421, 422, 423, 425, 426, 427, 428, 429, 430, 431, 432, 433, 434, 435, 436, 437, 438, 439, 440, 441, 442, 443, 444, 445, 453, 459, 481, 502, 504
  "On His Mistress Going to Bed" 425, 426, 427, 428, 429
  "The Canonization" 433, 435, 436
  "The Extasie" 437, 440, 441, 442, 444

"The Sun Rising" 443, 444
Doss-Quinby, Elgal 137
Dostoevsky, Fyodor 411, 415, 456
    Бесы (*Demons*, aka *The Possessed*, or *The Devils*) 411
    Идиот (*The Idiot*) 415, 456
Drayton, Michael 348
Dreher, Diane 368, 374, 375
Dronke, Peter 111, 169
Duffell, Martin J. 302
Dümmler, Nicola Nina 117
Dunstan, William E. 101
Dutton, Richard 406

Eagleton, Terry 482
Easthope, Anthony 424
Eckhart, Meister 300
Edwards, Catherine 87
Edwards, David 432
Egan, Gabriel 371
Eleanor of Aquitaine 123, 158, 176, 220, 301, 343
Eliot, T.S. 32, 449, 482
Elizabeth I 427
Ellis, Frederick Startridge 262
Empson, William 424, 468, 469, 474, 475, 479, 483, 502
Eratosthenes 12
Ermengard of Narbonne 220
Ermengaud, Matfré 248
    Le Breviari d'Amor 233, 234, 235, 236, 237
Eschenbach, Wolfram von 181, 182, 183, 184
    "Den morgenblic bî wahtaeres sange erkôs" 181, 185
Essam, Bacem A. 510
Eusebius of Caesarea 39, 40
Eve, Martin Paul 501
Everson, Jane E. 314

Falck, Colin 415
Fay, Elizabeth 152
Febvre, Lucien 153
Felski, Rita 14, 15, 19, 20, 21, 142, 154, 267, 268, 454, 501, 502

Fernie, Ewan 411
Ferrari, G.R.F. 33
Fessler, Ignas 210
Feuerbach, Ludwig 478, 479
Fichte, Johann Gottlieb 33, 34
Fields, Weston 51
fin'amor 3, 34, 62, 113, 116, 122, 130, 135, 136, 164, 169, 172, 174, 175, 195, 203, 207, 212, 217, 226, 232, 233, 234, 235, 238, 239, 240, 242, 243, 247, 248, 249, 250, 256, 260, 274, 279, 280, 281, 282, 283, 286, 290, 292, 300, 322, 330, 336, 371, 381, 390, 401, 420, 436
    definition of 2, 173
Findlay, John Niemeyer 17
Firenzuola, Agnolo 335
Fish, Stanley Eugene 423, 475, 476, 477, 480, 481, 483, 484, 498, 499, 504
Fleming, Bruce 14, 21
Fortunatus, Venantius 104, 105, 106
Foucault, Michel 9, 18, 20, 26, 28, 29, 30, 154, 219, 373, 374, 428
Francesca da Rimini (Paulo and Francesca) 319, 321, 322
Franklin, Benjamin 511
Frantzen, Allen 109, 110
Frederick I (Barbarossa) 10
Frederick II 132, 300, 301, 302
Freeburn, Ryan P. 198
Frelick, Nancy 131
Freud, Sigmund 13

Gábor, Katona 350
Gajowski, Evelyn 416
Gamel, Mary-Kay 321, 322
Ganze, Alison 146
Gascoigne, George 151
Gaunt, Simon 2, 154, 155, 156, 163, 376, 410
George Chapman 116
Gerson, Jean 266
Gide, André
    Les Nourritures Terrestres 467
Gigot, Francis E. 288

Gilead, Sarah 22, 446, 447, 448, 449, 450, 452, 453, 455, 462
Giles of Rome 55
Gillis, John 372
Giroux, Henry 37, 502
Glancy, Ruth F. 421
Goebbels, Joseph 8
Goethe, Johann Wolfgang von 35, 356
Golb, Norman 221
Golden, Mark 43
Goldin, Frederick 157
Goldstien, Neal L. 324
Goold, G.P. 57
Gramsci Antonio 419
Gratian
  Decretum Magistri Gratiani 185
Greaves, Richard L. 461
Greenblatt, Stephen 18, 160, 370, 406, 442, 473
Greenstein, Edward L. 53
Grégoire, Henri 193
Greville, Fulke 149
Grollman, Eric Anthony 503
Grotius, Hugo
  Adamus Exul 489, 490, 491, 492
Guibbory, Achsah 424, 425, 427, 428, 436
Guilhem IX 129, 130, 158, 167, 168, 169, 170, 171, 172, 174, 233, 235, 237, 250, 261, 286, 306, 340
  "Ab la dolchor del temps novel" 168, 170
  author of the first *fabliau* 282
  "Companho faray un vers... convinen" 169
  "Farai chansoneta nueva" 168
  "Mout jauzens me prenc en amar" 170
  "Pus vezem de novel florir" 171
Guinizelli, Guido 192, 306, 307, 308, 309, 310, 311, 312, 313, 314, 317, 319, 323, 326
  "Al cor gentil" 307
  "Chi vedesse a Lucia un var cappuzzo" 306
  "Io vogl' del ver la mia donna laudare" 310
  "Tegno di folle 'mpres', a lo ver dire" 311
Guynn, Noah 254, 267

Hagstrum, Jean H. 79, 116, 195, 205, 292, 317, 330, 373, 413
Hallissy, Margaret 281, 282, 285, 290
Hardin, Richard F. 113, 115
Hartman, Geoffrey 31
Haskins, Charles Homer 175
Hawkes, David 482, 483
Hegel, Georg Wilhelm Friedrich 26, 27
Heidegger, Martin 7, 16, 17, 18, 447, 499
Heisterbacences, Caesarii 224
Heller, Joseph 162
Heller-Roazen, Daniel 159, 160, 405
Heloise d'Argenteuil 195, 196, 197, 199, 201, 202, 203, 204, 205, 206, 208, 209, 210, 211, 212, 213, 270
Hengel, Martin 498
Henry VII 394, 395
Henry VIII 343, 344
Heraclitus 16, 295, 453
Herman, Edward S. 502, 503
Herman, Peter C. 469
hermeneutics of suspicion
  style of interpretation 10, 12, 13, 14, 20, 22, 33, 34, 40, 42, 49, 146, 296, 320, 440, 447, 450, 451, 455, 463, 501
Herrick, Robert 3, 11, 421, 445, 446, 447, 448, 449, 450, 452, 453, 455, 456, 457, 458, 459, 460, 462, 463, 464
  "Corinna's going a Maying" 460, 461, 462
  "To Daffadills" 456
  "To the Virgins to Make Much of Time" 11, 445, 449, 450, 452, 453, 455

Hesiod 12, 13
Highet, Gilbert 469
Hilarius (Hilary the Englishman) 144
Hill, Christopher 468
Hippias of Thasos 38, 480
Hjelmslev, Louis 28
Hobbes, Thomas 150
Holbach, Paul Henri Thiry 9
Holmes, Nigel 98
Holmes, Olivia 155
Homer 12, 13, 79, 80, 93, 175, 301, 372, 499
Honorius 100, 101, 103
Honor killing 398
   relation to *Romeo and Juliet* 398
Horace 8, 13, 358, 421
Horváth, I.K. 96
Houlbrooke, Ralph A. 376
Howard, Henry, Earl of Surrey 346, 347, 348
   "Each beast can choose his fere according to his mind" 346
   "I never saw my lady lay apart" 347
Hughes, Merritt Y. 390, 440
Hult, David F. 131, 136, 266, 268
Hume, David 7, 8
Huppé, Bernard F. 283

Innocent III 197, 221, 223, 227, 228, 246, 259, 260, 336
Isaacson, Walter 511

Jackson, MacDonald P. 370
Jacobson, Howard 56, 94, 96
Jameson, Frederic 11
Jang Jin-sung 496
Janko, Richard 38
Japhet, Sara 52, 54
Jeanjean, Henri 221
Jerome (Eusebius Sophronius Hieronymus) 291, 473
Jewell, Helen M. 286
Jones, Michael K., and Malcolm G. Underwood 394
Julius Caesar 97, 98, 422

Kafka, Franz 162
Kahn, Coppélia 370
Kates, Joshua 18
Katz, Joseph 503
Kauffman, Linda 95
Kay, Sarah 2, 107, 129, 154, 155, 156, 163, 234, 321
Kelley, Maurice 499
Kemp, Theresa D. 279
Kennedy, Elspeth 321
Kennedy, William J. 309
Kerrigan, John 361
Kerrigan, William 464
Kim Jong-il 496
King, Margaret L. 43
Kleinman, Scott 278
Klein, Richard 27
Knox, Peter E. 90
Köhler, Erich 155, 156
Krass, Andreas 219
Kristeva, Julia 408

Labé, Louise 336, 337, 338, 340
   Sonnet 16 337
   Sonnet 19 338
Lacan, Jacques 24, 25, 26, 28, 130, 131, 452
Lagerlund, Henrik 407
Landrum, David 459
Lane, Joan 460
Lanham, Richard A. 75
Larson, Deborah 31, 32, 433
Layton, Richard A. 40
Lazar, Moshe 123, 135, 164, 192
Lazda-Cazers, Rasma 179
Leggatt, Alexander 453
Léglu, Catherine, Rebecca Rist, and Claire Taylor 224
Le Goff, Jacques 198
Leishman, J.B. 358
Lentini, Giacomo da 302, 303, 304, 305, 306, 364
   "Diamante, né smeraldo, né zaffino" 303
   "Dolce cominciamento" 304

"Io m'aggio posto in core a Dio servire" 302
Leonard, John 475, 476, 477
Lévi-Strauss, Claude 28, 377
Lewis, C.S. 125, 126, 129, 130, 135, 162, 288, 472, 473, 474, 475, 477, 478, 480, 485, 486, 496, 497, 498, 499
Lille, Alain de 143
  De Planctu Naturae 143
Lipmen-Blumen, Jean 377
Livy 73, 74
Longus 113, 114, 115
  Daphnis and Chloe 113, 116
Longxi, Zhang 39, 47, 48, 51, 56, 57, 156, 158, 209, 210, 212, 265
Lorris, Guillaume and Jean de Meun 291
Lorris, Guillaume de 210, 238, 239, 240, 241, 246, 250, 252, 254
Lorris, Guillaume de, and Jean de Meun 192, 210, 238, 239, 266, 268, 275, 328
  Roman de la Rose 106, 135, 192, 226, 239, 240, 241, 242, 243, 244, 245, 247, 249, 250, 252, 253, 254, 259, 260, 261, 262, 263, 264, 265, 268, 274, 275, 453
Lucan 97, 98, 99, 120
  Pharsalia 97, 98, 99
Lucretius 453
Luft, Joanna 263, 265
Luther, Martin 4, 9

Macdonald, Aileen Ann 412
MacFarlane, Alan 372
Macfie, Pamela Royston 120
Macrobius 85, 86, 239
Mallarmé, Stephan 28, 30
Mann, Jill 289
Marcabru 172, 173, 174, 291, 293, 307, 442
Marcus Junianus Justinus 87
Marenbon, John 198, 210
Mariaselvam, Abraham 39
Marlowe, Christopher 116, 120, 371

Marselha, Folquet de 229
Martin, Catherine Gimelli 441, 442
Martinez, Ronald 138
Martin, Philip 363
Marvell, Andrew 421
Marvin, Laurence W. 226
Marx, Karl 13, 371, 482
Masten, Jeffrey 382
May, Simon 9
McCloskey, Patrick, and Edward Phinney, Jr. 97
McGlynn, Sean 222, 223, 226
McGowan, Kate 21
McGrath, Alister 474
McWebb, Christine 239, 252
Menocal, Maria Rosa 166, 167
Meschini, Marco 228
Meun, Jean de 149, 210, 238, 239, 241, 252, 253, 254, 259, 262, 263, 265, 267, 268, 271
Mews, Constant J. 198, 199, 202, 204
Miksch, Walter 369
Miller, J. Hillis 20, 21
Milton, John 2, 3, 7, 8, 9, 89, 115, 151, 153, 240, 241, 362, 364, 389, 390, 397, 429, 443, 468, 469, 475, 476, 478, 479, 480, 481, 482, 483, 484, 485, 488, 489, 494, 495, 496, 498, 499, 508, 509
  Doctrine and Discipline of Divorce 7, 9
  Eikonoklastes 7
  Of Education 151
  Paradise Lost (or its characters) 2, 9, 22, 89, 148, 150, 288, 344, 362, 390, 397, 467, 468, 469, 470, 471, 472, 473, 474, 475, 476, 477, 478, 479, 480, 481, 482, 484, 485, 486, 487, 488, 489, 490, 491, 492, 493, 494, 495, 496, 497, 498, 499, 502, 508, 509
  Tenure of Kings and Magistrates 7
Minnis, Alastair 208, 289
Mitchell, Charles 441
Monfasani, John 160
Montaigne, Michel 5, 453, 454
Montanhagol, Guilhem 232, 233, 305, 306

Montfort, Simon de 223, 227, 228, 260
Montmorency, James Edward Geoffrey De 287
Morris, Colin 174, 175
Morrissey, Lee and Will Stockton 160
Musaeus 116, 117, 118, 120
   Hero and Leander 116, 117, 118, 431
Musil, Robert
   Der Mann Ohne Eigenschaften (*The Man Without Qualities*) 150, 404

Negotium pacis et fidei (*The business of peace and faith*) 228, 246
Nelson, Lowry 309
Nero 97, 98, 99, 100
Neruda, Pablo
   "Puedo escribir los versos más tristes esta noche" 507
Nevo, Yehoshafat 53
Newman, Barbara 134, 143, 202, 206, 209, 210, 212, 213
Nietzsche, Friedrich 13, 403, 404

obedience
   demands for, opposition to love 3, 4, 5, 6, 8, 9, 10, 33, 63, 77, 89, 94, 126, 129, 135, 186, 189, 197, 213, 219, 220, 229, 261, 265, 272, 368, 369, 374, 375, 376, 378, 380, 381, 383, 384, 385, 386, 390, 393, 395, 397, 398, 401, 408, 410, 420, 443, 444, 456, 467, 468, 469, 472, 476, 478, 481, 482, 484, 485, 488, 498, 499, 502, 503, 511
Obedience Chorus, The 476, 480
O'Hara, Diana 374, 376
Olmert, Michael 364
Olson, Roger E. 196
Oppenheimer, Paul 302, 306
Orff, Carl 112
Orgel, Stephen 49, 324, 354
Origen of Alexandria 39, 40, 41, 42, 47, 48, 50, 52, 53, 63, 106, 120, 158, 172, 453, 463, 464
O'Sullivan, Daniel E. 141, 145, 157
Outhwaite, R. B. 413

Ovid 9, 57, 58, 59, 61, 62, 63, 64, 65, 66, 67, 69, 70, 71, 72, 74, 75, 76, 77, 87, 89, 90, 91, 92, 93, 94, 95, 96, 97, 100, 101, 104, 106, 113, 126, 160, 192, 364, 367, 460, 485, 495
   Amores 57, 58, 60, 61, 63, 64, 65, 67, 69, 70, 76, 89, 90, 91, 460
   Ars Amatoria 57, 61, 62, 64, 71, 72, 74
   Heroides 9, 58, 90, 91, 93, 94, 95, 96
   Metamorphoses 89, 90, 92
   Tristia 61

Paden, William D. 137, 142, 157, 176, 179, 184
Paris, Gaston 122, 124, 128, 130, 131, 132, 133, 135, 136, 235, 240
Parker, John 160
Parmenides 16, 27
Parry, John Jay 124
Paterson, Linda 149
Pater, Walter 21
Patri, Gabriel Díaz 106
Patterson, Lee 160, 161, 406
Pearsall, Derek 282, 283
Pecora, Vincent P. 20
Pegg, Simon 223, 232
Pelagius 148, 149, 150, 151, 198
Peter, John 472, 474, 477
Petrarch, Francesco 3, 121, 137, 164, 300, 301, 309, 312, 313, 323, 324, 325, 326, 327, 328, 329, 330, 336, 338, 342, 343, 344, 345, 346, 347, 348, 349, 350, 359, 364, 367, 391, 422, 426, 458, 506
   Sonnet 11 324
   Sonnet 12 325
   Sonnet 36 325
   Sonnet 90 326
   Sonnet 106 327
   Sonnet 121 327
   Sonnet 133 328
   Sonnet 183 328
   Sonnet 364 329
Pinker, Stephen 226
Pizan, Christine de 265, 266

Plato 1, 12, 13, 17, 27, 32, 33, 38, 105, 163, 165, 222, 295, 296, 298, 299, 300, 306, 336, 372, 418, 440, 454
  Cratylus 27
  Symposium 296, 298, 300, 332, 356, 418, 440
Plotinus 298, 299, 300
Pollock, Linda A. 372
Pompey the Great 97, 99
Popper, Karl 16, 429
Princess Bride, The 114
Prudentius 104, 106
Prynne, William 1, 455, 461, 464, 482
Pushkin, Alexander Sergeyevich 9, 505, 506
  "Когда в объятия мои" ("Kogda v ob"yatiya moi") 505
  Евгений Онегин (*Evgeny Onegin*) 9, 505
  Борис Годунов (*Boris Godunov*) 505

Qābbanī, Nizār 509–510
Quaglio, Antonio Enzo 321
Quchak, Nahaphet 340, 341
  "Hayren 20" 340
  "Hayren 65" 341
  "Hayren 81" 342
Quinones, Richard J. 106
Quint, David 480

Rabelais, Francois 12
Raby, F.J.E. 101, 105
Radice, Betty 196, 206, 212
Raphael (Raffaello Sanzio da Urbino) 165
Rashi (Rabbi Solomon the Izakhite) 52, 53, 54, 456, 463
Ray, Chris 48
Raymond VI of Toulouse 221, 223, 230
Raymond V of Toulouse 222
Reddy, William M. 122, 144, 171, 235, 282
Rees, Brinley Roderick 150
Reid, Charles J. 208
Reynolds, Barbara 321

Richard I 220
Richard II
  rejection of 1391 petition to restrict education to the nobility 287
Richard of St. Victor 55
Richman, Gerald 479, 492
Richtmeyer, Eric 24
Ricoeur, Paul 13, 14, 18, 42, 56
Rieger, Angelica 142, 143, 144, 145, 146
Roberts, John 423
Robertson, D.W. 133, 134, 135, 209, 212
Rodríguez de la Cámara, Juan
  Triunfo de las Donas 487
Romans, Bietris de
  "Na Maria" 139, 141, 142, 144, 145, 146
Rorty, Richard 19, 20
Roscelin of Compiègne 200, 201
Rosenberg, Harold
  "The Herd of Independent Minds" 147
Rougemont, Denis de 199, 407, 410
Rousseau, Jean-Jacques 6, 33, 151
Rubin, Gayle 377
Ryang, Sonia 495, 496
Ryan, Kiernan 405, 406, 409, 504

Saint Circ, Uc de 146, 176, 308
Salandra, Serafino della 493
  Adamo Caduto 492
Salter, Elizabeth 165
Samuel, Irene 475, 477, 480, 498, 499
Sandys, John Edwin 12, 106
Sankovitch, Tilde 137, 155, 157
Santana, Carlos 404
Sappho 140, 141
Sartre, Jean-Paul 23
Saussure, Ferdinand de 25, 26, 28
  arbitrary nature of the sign challenged 27
Sayce, Olive 301, 302
Scève, Maurice 336
  "Délie 439" 336

Schulman, Nicole M. 229
Schwartz, Regina 404
Schwoerer, Lois G. 372
Sedgwick, Eve 22, 377, 386, 502
Segal, M.H. 39
Seneca 293, 473
Sextus Empiricus 25
Shakespeare, William 2, 9, 49, 68, 79, 108, 115, 121, 137, 174, 192, 195, 240, 241, 253, 270, 271, 279, 313, 324, 342, 353, 354, 356, 357, 358, 359, 360, 361, 362, 363, 364, 365, 367, 368, 369, 370, 371, 372, 376, 377, 378, 379, 380, 382, 385, 394, 403, 406, 408, 409, 413, 414, 415, 416, 420, 422, 426, 443, 445, 446, 453, 458, 476, 486, 495
  A Midsummer Night's Dream 377, 384, 385, 386, 387, 388, 389, 390, 391, 392, 393, 395, 397, 398
  As You Like It 178
  Hamlet 80, 359, 372, 376, 443, 458
  Henry V 370
  King Lear 405, 406, 409, 458, 504
  Macbeth 49, 446
  Measure for Measure 399, 476
  Much Ado About Nothing 403
  Othello 369, 377, 416, 473
  Richard III 480
  Romeo and Juliet 253, 368, 369, 377, 378, 393, 394, 395, 396, 397, 398, 399, 400, 401, 402, 403, 404, 405, 406, 407, 408, 409, 410, 412, 413, 414, 415, 416, 417, 418, 419, 420, 422, 485, 486
  Sonnet 1 353, 354, 355
  Sonnet 3 355, 356
  Sonnet 15 356, 357, 358
  Sonnet 18 358, 359
  Sonnet 116 359, 360, 361, 362
  Sonnet 130 363, 364, 365
  Sonnet 138 365, 366, 367
  The Tempest 463

  Two Gentlemen of Verona 369, 377, 379, 380, 381, 382, 383, 390, 416, 486
Shapiro, Marianne 311
Sharrock, Alison 64, 71, 75, 90
Shaw, George Bernard 377, 459
Shelley, Percy 20, 76, 482
Shotter, David 77
Sichel-Bazin, Rafèu, Carolin Buthke, and Trudel Meisenburg 193
Sidney, Philip 3, 13, 312, 342, 348, 349, 350, 353, 356, 364, 391
  Astrophil and Stella 348, 349, 350, 351, 356, 367, 391
  The Countess of Pembroke's Arcadia 348
  The Defence of Poesie 13, 348
Sidonius 97, 101, 102, 103, 104, 108
Silvestre, Hubert 210
Silvestris, Bernardi 133, 134
  De Mundi Universitate 134
Sklenár, Robert 108
Smythe, Barbara 179
Song of Songs 1, 11, 34, 37, 38, 39, 40, 41, 42, 47, 48, 50, 51, 52, 54, 56, 57, 63, 77, 109, 111, 113, 141, 160, 164, 264, 285, 286, 367, 453, 464, 495
Sontag, Susan 37, 501
Spence, Sarah 170
Spiller, Michael R.G. 301
Spivak, Gayatri 34
Stehling, Thomas 143, 144
Sternberg, Robert 429, 548
Stilling, Roger 371
Stockton, Will 469
Stone, Gregory B. 158, 161, 190, 405
Stone, Lawrence 368, 369, 371, 372, 373, 374, 375, 380, 384, 398, 416
Strabo 13
Strayer, Joseph R. 197, 198, 282, 283
Strouse, A.W. 503
Stubbs, John 432, 435
Sullivan, Ceri 460

Swabey, Ffiona 301
Symonds, John Addington 302, 306, 319

Taavon, Modje 398, 511
Tanner, J. Paul 56
Targoff, Ramie 345, 422, 457
Tarrant, Richard 90
Tchaikovsky, Pyotr Ilyich 404
Teskey, Gordon 479, 480, 498, 499
Thibault, John C. 61
Thomason, T. Katharine 441
Thomsett, Michael C. 226
Tillyard, E.M.W. 342
Timaeus of Tauromenium 86
Toews, John 150
Topsfield, L.T. 164, 170, 171, 172, 173, 192
Traub, Valerie 400
trobairitz 137, 139, 142, 160, 164, 186, 190, 242, 279, 402, 420, 426
troubadours 2, 9, 52, 54, 122, 125, 129, 131, 132, 133, 138, 139, 142, 143, 146, 147, 148, 149, 152, 155, 156, 157, 158, 161, 163, 165, 167, 169, 170, 174, 178, 179, 183, 184, 186, 189, 190, 192, 194, 217, 220, 229, 232, 233, 235, 240, 242, 246, 247, 248, 264, 280, 281, 282, 300, 302, 305, 306, 308, 310, 311, 314, 315, 322, 330, 336, 339, 340, 342, 350, 353, 355, 365, 371, 402, 410, 412, 420, 422, 426, 429, 442, 505
Tudela, Guilhem de 224, 225, 228, 230
Tullia d'Aragona
  Dialogo della Infinità d'Amore 334
Tyerman, Christopher 227

Vaux-Cernay, Pierre de 225
Vendler, Helen 354, 362, 363, 364
Ventadorn, Bernart de 129, 169, 174, 175, 176, 177, 178, 192, 203, 208, 235, 237, 261, 286, 291, 293, 307, 343
  "Can l'erba fresch'e·lh folha par" 175, 177, 178

  "Chantars no pot gaire valer" 174
  "Non es meravelha s'eu chan" 174
Vickers, Brian 370
Vidal, Peire 179
Virgil 70, 77, 78, 80, 84, 85, 87, 89, 90, 91, 92, 93, 94, 95, 97, 101, 319, 485
  The Aeneid 3, 77, 78, 81, 85, 86, 88, 89, 90, 97
Vleeschouwers-Van Melkebeek, Monique 393
Vogelweide, Walther von der 217, 218, 402
  "Under der linden" 217, 218, 219
Vyvyan, John 420

Waldock, A.J.A. 471, 472, 475, 478, 483, 488, 498
Walsingham, Francis 369
Walters, Lori J. 276
Watchtower, The 481
  "If Adam was Perfect, How Was It Possible for Him to Sin?" 481
Watson, Lynette 102
Watson, Robert 442
Weinrich, Lorenz 207
Wetherbee, Winthrop 285
White, Peter 71
Whitgift, John 369
Wilde, Oscar 485, 504
Wilhelm, James J. 192
Wilkinson, Lancelot Patrick 75, 76, 93, 94
Wilmott, John, Earl of Rochester 434
Wilson-Okamura, David Scott 95
Wimsatt, W.K., and M.C. Beardsley 29
Winkler, John J. 114
Wollock, Jennifer 135, 136
Woodbridge, Linda 380
Woods, Marjorie Curry 160
Wrathall, Mark A. 16
Wyatt, Thomas 343, 344, 345, 346, 348
  "Because I have thee still kept from lies and blame" 346

"Behold, Love, thy power how she despiseth" 345
"Such vain thought as wonted to mislead me" 344
"Whoso list to hunt" 343
Wycliffe, John 10, 287

Yeats, William Butler 161, 411, 412, 424

Zeno of Elea 17, 103
Ziolowski, Jan 199
Zumthor, Paul 152, 154, 155, 158, 159, 160, 161, 176, 190, 405

This book need not end here...

At Open Book Publishers, we are changing the nature of the traditional academic book. The title you have just read will not be left on a library shelf, but will be accessed online by hundreds of readers each month across the globe. OBP publishes only the best academic work: each title passes through a rigorous peer-review process. We make all our books free to read online so that students, researchers and members of the public who can't afford a printed edition will have access to the same ideas.
This book and additional content is available at:
https://www.openbookpublishers.com/product/591

Customize

Personalize your copy of this book or design new books using OBP and third-party material. Take chapters or whole books from our published list and make a special edition, a new anthology or an illuminating coursepack. Each customized edition will be produced as a paperback and a downloadable PDF. Find out more at:
https://www.openbookpublishers.com/section/59/1

Donate

If you enjoyed this book, and feel that research like this should be available to all readers, regardless of their income, please think about donating to us. We do not operate for profit and all donations, as with all other revenue we generate, will be used to finance new Open Access publications.
https://www.openbookpublishers.com/section/13/1/support-us

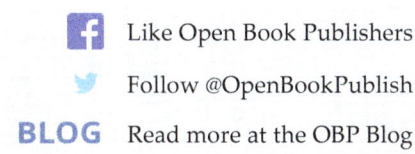

Like Open Book Publishers

Follow @OpenBookPublish

BLOG Read more at the OBP Blog

You may also be interested in:

The Classic Short Story, 1870-1925
Theory of a Genre

By Florence Goyet

https://www.openbookpublishers.com/product/199

Vertical Readings in Dante's 'Comedy'
Volume 1

Edited by George Corbett and Heather Webb

http://www.openbookpublishers.com/product/367

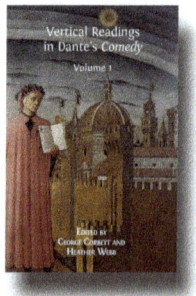

Vertical Readings in Dante's 'Comedy'
Volume 2

Edited by George Corbett and Heather Webb

http://www.openbookpublishers.com/product/499

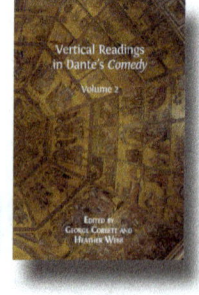

www.ingramcontent.com/pod-product-compliance
Lightning Source LLC
Chambersburg PA
CBHW052010040526
R18239700001BA/R182397PG44108CBX00014BA/1